ASIA

IN THE MAKING OF EUROPE

ASIA

IN THE MAKING OF EUROPE

DONALD F. LACH and EDWIN J. VAN KLEY

VOLUME

III

A Century of Advance

BOOK THREE: SOUTHEAST ASIA

THE UNIVERSITY OF CHICAGO PRESS

CHICAGO AND LONDON

DONALD F. LACH is the Bernadotte E. Schmitt Professor of Modern History, Emeritus, at the University of Chicago.

EDWIN J. VAN KLEY is Professor of History at Calvin College.

THE UNIVERSITY OF CHICAGO PRESS, CHICAGO 60637
The University of Chicago Press, Ltd., London

Library of Congress Cataloging-in-Publication Data
(Revised for volume 3)

Lach, Donald F. (Donald Frederick), 1917–
Asia in the making of Europe.

Vol. 3–   by Donald F. Lach and Edwin J. Van Kley.
Includes bibliographies and indexes.
Contents: v. 1. The century of discovery.   2 v.—
v. 2. A century of wonder.   Book 1. The visual arts.
Book 2. The literary arts.   Book 3. The scholarly dis-
ciplines.   3 v. — v. 3. A century of advance. Book 1.
Trade, missions, literature. Book 2. South Asia.
Book 3. Southeast Asia. Book 4. East Asia. 4 v.
    1. Europe—Civilization—Oriental influences.
2. Asia—History.   3. Asia—Discovery and exploration.
I. Van Kley, Edwin J.   II. Title.
CB203.L32   303.48′2405′0903   64-19848
ISBN 0-226-46753-8 (v. 3. bk. 1)
ISBN 0-226-46754-6 (v. 3. bk. 2)
ISBN 0-226-46755-4 (v. 3. bk. 3)
ISBN 0-226-46756-2 (v. 3. bk. 4)
ISBN 0-226-46757-0 (v. 3 : set)

This publication has been supported by a grant
from the National Endowment for the Humanities,
an independent federal agency.

This book is printed on acid-free paper.

Endpaper: Javanese dancers. From Willem Lodewyckszoon,
Premier livre de l'histoire de la navigation aux Indes orientales . . .
(Amsterdam, 1609).

Contents

[v]

Contents

Contents

(Contents of other books in Volume III)

BOOK ONE

PART I

The Continuing Expansion in the East

PART II

The Printed Word

[vii]

Contents

BOOK TWO

PART III

The European Images of Asia

Contents

Contents

Abbreviations

AHSI   *Archivum Historicum Societatis Iesu*

Annales.   *Annales: Economies, sociétés, civilisations; revue trimestrielle*
E.S.C.

Asia   Earlier volumes of this work: D. Lach, *Asia in the Making of Europe,* Vols. I and II (Chicago, 1965–77)

BR   Blair, Emma H., and Robertson, James A. (eds.), *The Philippine Islands, 1493–1898* (55 vols., Cleveland, 1903–9)

BTLV   *Bijdragen tot de taal-, land- en volkenkunde van Nederlandsch-Indië*

BV   [Commelin, Isaac (ed.)], *Begin ende voortgangh van de Vereenighde Nederlantsche Geoctroyeerde Oost-Indische Compagnie* . . . ([Amsterdam], 1646). (First edition published 1645. Facsimile edition published in Amsterdam, 1969. The facsimile edition has volumes numbered I, II, III, and IV, corresponding to vols. Ia, Ib, IIa, and IIb of the 1646 edition.)

CV   [Churchill, Awnsham and John (eds.)], *A Collection of Voyages and Travels, Some Now First Printed from Original Manuscripts* . . . (4 vols.; London, 1704)

"HS"   "Works Issued by the Hakluyt Society"

JRAS   *Journal of the Royal Asiatic Society*

Abbreviations

NR L'Honoré Naber, Samuel Pierre (ed.), *Reisebeschreibungen von deutschen Beamten und Kriegsleuten im Dienst der Niederländischen West- und Ost-Indischen Kompagnien, 1602–1797* (The Hague, 1930–32)

NZM *Neue Zeitschrift für Missionswissenschaft*

PP Purchas, Samuel, *Hakluytus Posthumus, or Purchas His Pilgrimes: . . .* (20 vols.; Glasgow, 1905–7. Originally published 1625.)

SCPFMR *Sacrae Congregationis de Propaganda Fide Memoria Rerum* (Freiburg, 1971)

Streit R. Streit, *Bibliotheca Missionum* (30 vols.; Münster and Aachen, 1916–75)

Ternaux-Compans H. Ternaux-Compans, *Bibliothèque asiatique et africaine* (Amsterdam, 1968; reprint of Paris, 1841–42 ed.)

TR Thévenot, Melchisédech, *Relations de divers voyages curieux qui n'ont point esté publiées, ou qui ont esté traduites d'Hacluyt, de Purchas & d'autres voyageurs anglois, hollandois, portugais, allemands, espagnols; et de quelques Persans, Arabes, et autres auteurs orientaux* (4 vols.; Paris, 1663–96)

"WLV" "Werken uitgegeven door de Linschoten Vereeniging"

ZMR *Zeitschrift für Missionswissenschaft und Religionswissenschaft*

A Note to the Illustrations

Study of the illustrations of Asia published in seventeenth-century Europe shows that the artists and illustrators tried in most cases to depict reality when they had the sources, such as sketches from the men in the field or the portable objects brought to Europe—plants, animals, costumes, paintings, porcelains, and so on. Many of the engravings based on sketches and paintings are convincing in their reality, such as the depiction of the Potala palace in Lhasa (pl. 384), the portrait of the "Old Viceroy" of Kwangtung (pl. 323), and the drawings of Siamese and Chinese boats. A number of Asian objects—Chinese scroll paintings, a Buddhist prayer wheel, and small animals—appeared in European engravings and paintings for the first time. Asians, like the Siamese emissaries to France, were sketched from life in Europe and their portraits engraved.

When sources were lacking, the illustrators and artists filled in the gaps in their knowledge by following literary texts, or by producing imaginary depictions, including maps. The illustrations of Japan, for example, are far more fantastic than those depicting other places, perhaps because Japan so stringently limited intercourse over much of the century. Printing-house engravers frequently "borrowed" illustrations from earlier editions and often "improved" upon them by adding their own touches which had the effect of Europeanizing them.

Illustrations were "translated" along with texts in various ways. If the publisher of a translation had close relations with the original publisher or printer he might borrow the original copperplate engravings or have the original publisher pull prints from the original plates to be bound with the translated pages. Engraved captions could be rubbed out of the plate and redone in the new language, although many printers did not bother to do so. Lacking the cooperation of the original printers, new engravings could still be made from a print. The simplest method was to place the print face down on the varnished and waxed copper plate to be engraved and then to rub the back of the print causing the ink from the print to adhere to the waxed surface of the plate. The resulting image was then used to engrave, or etch with nitric acid, the new plate, and being reversed it would print exactly as the original version printed. If the engraver wanted to avoid damaging the print, however, which he might well need to finish the engraving, he would use a thin sheet of paper dusted with black lead or black chalk to transfer the image from the print to the new copper plate. He might further protect the print by putting oiled paper on top of it while he traced the picture. This procedure worked whether the print was face down or face up against the plate. In fact it was easier to trace the picture if the print were face up, in which case the new plate would be etched in reverse of the original plate. For a seventeenth-century description of the ways in which new plates could be etched from prints see William Faithorne, *The Art of Graveing and Etching* (New York, 1970), pp. 41–44 (first edition, London, 1662). See also Coolie Verner, "Copperplate Printing," in David Woodward (ed.), *Five Centuries of Map Printing* (Chicago, 1975), p. 53. We have included a number of illustrations that were "borrowed" by one printer from another: see, for example, plates 113 and 114; 117, 118, 121; 174; 312 and 313; 412 and 413; 419–21.

Most of the following illustrations were taken from seventeenth-century books held in the Department of Special Collections in the Regenstein Library at the University of Chicago. Others have been obtained from libraries and archives in Europe and the United States, which have kindly granted us permission to reproduce them. Wherever possible, efforts are made in the captions to analyze the illustrations and to provide relevant collateral information whenever such was available.

Almost all of the four hundred or so illustrations were reproduced from the photographs taken (or retaken) by Alma Lach, an inveterate photographer and cookbook author. We were also aided and abetted by the personnel of the Special Collections department—especially the late Robert Rosenthal, Daniel Meyer, and Kim Coventry—in locating the illustrations and in preparing them for photography. Father Harrie A. Vanderstappen, professor emeritus of Far Eastern art at the University of Chicago and a man endowed with marvelous sight and insight, helped us to analyze the illustrations relating to East Asia. C. M. Naim of the Department of South Asian Languages at the University of Chicago likewise contributed generously of his skills, particularly with reference to the Mughul seals (pls. 117, 118, and 121) here depicted. The China illustrations have benefited from the contributions of Ma Tai-loi and Tai Wen-pai of the East Asian Collection of the Regenstein Library and of Zhijia Shen who generously gave freely of her time and knowledge. The captions for the Japan illustrations have been improved by the gracious efforts of Yoko Kuki of the East Asian Collection of the Regenstein Library. Tetsuo Najita of Chicago's History Department lent a hand in the preparation of the caption for pl. 432. Ann Adams and Francis Dowley of Chicago's Art Department helped us to analyze some of the engravings, especially those prepared by Dutch illustrators.

To all of these generous scholars we express our sincere gratitude for their contributions to the illustration program.

Illustrations

BOOK ONE

FOLLOWING PAGE 338

Illustrations

[xx]

BOOK THREE

FOLLOWING PAGE 1380

BOOK FOUR

FOLLOWING PAGE 1730

Maps

CHAPTER XIV

Continental Southeast Asia: Malaya, Pegu, Arakan, Cambodia, and Laos

The early history of continental Southeast Asia, like that of its insular counterparts, essentially records the rise and fall of chiefs and chiefdoms and is replete with accounts of intrusions from abroad.[1] This thinly populated land of mountains, valleys, and peninsulas is drained by four major south-flowing rivers—Irrawaddy, Salween, Menam, and Mekong—around whose deltas and in whose highlands small chiefdoms then competed with one another. Overshadowed traditionally by the neighboring high cultures of China and India, mainland Southeast Asia was a congeries of peasant societies ruled from time to time from ceremonial centers, inland cities, or coastal ports. The present-day nation-states of Malaysia, Burma, Siam, Laos, Vietnam, and Cambodia emerged only slowly and painfully as viable political entities in response to the challenges posed by Islamic and Christian-European intrusions. While the Hinduism earlier imported disappeared before Islam in the south, Therevada Buddhism survived as the dominant faith in Burma, Thailand, and Cambodia. Vietnam, ruled as a Chinese province until the tenth century, remained culturally and religiously a part of the Sinic world when the Europeans first appeared off its shores. Over time this intermediate group of states between India and China continued in various ways to be similar to both, but different from each, of its great continental neighbors.

The Portuguese and Spanish had revealed in their European publications of the sixteenth century the general dimensions and configurations of conti-

[1] On the intricacies of political and cultural change in urban generation and formation in continental Southeast Asia see P. Wheatley, *Nagara and Commandery. Origins of the Southeast Asia Urban Traditions* (Chicago, 1983), chap. ii.

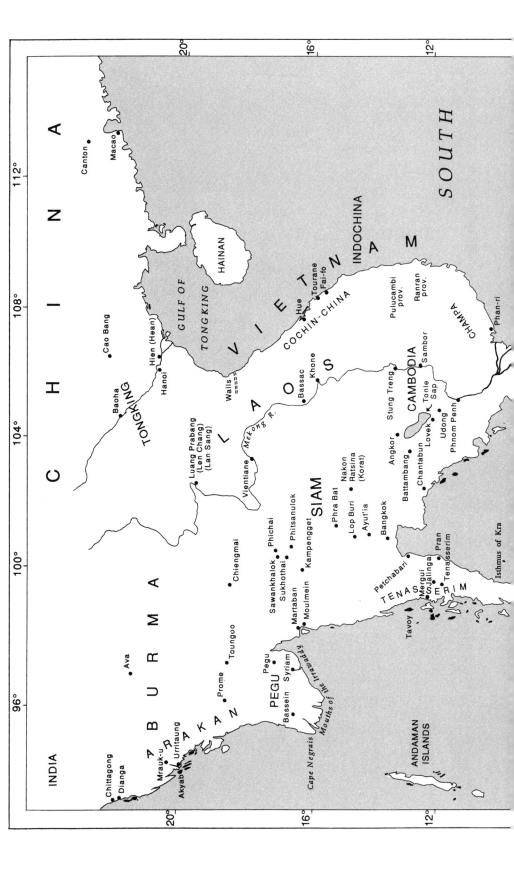

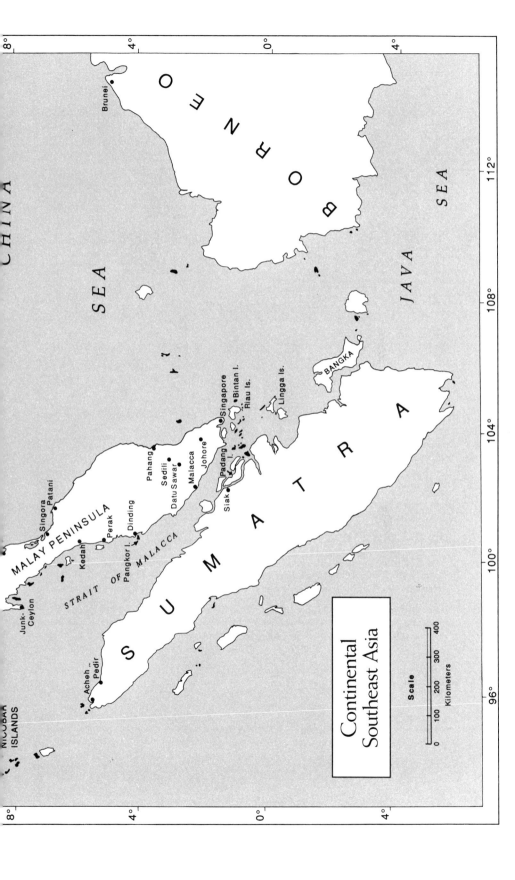

Continental
Southeast Asia

Scale

0 100 200 300 400

Kilometers

nental Southeast Asia. The earliest observations were circularized in the 1550's through Ramusio's *Navigationi*. During the latter half of that century more detailed accounts were published by the Iberians, the Jesuits, and the north European merchant-travelers. Most of these documents and descriptions related to the outer fringes of the region, or to Malacca, Pegu, Siam, and Cambodia. A few discrete expositions by the more intrepid travelers included glimpses of inland places in the Malay peninsula, Laos, and Siam. From these publications it can be clearly seen that the Europeans had less direct contact with the continental fringe states and knew correspondingly less about them than about the places and peoples of the archipelago. This condition would continue to prevail in European writings until the second half of the seventeenth century.[2]

At the dawn of the seventeenth century the Portuguese had commercial and religious outposts at Malacca, Pegu, Ayut'ia, and Macao, from which they participated in local, regional, and inter-Asian trade. The Spanish, whose dreams of invading Cambodia and Siam from the Philippines had evaporated in the 1599 massacre at Phnom Penh, still hoped through the quieter activities of missionaries from Malacca and Manila to extend their influence into Indochina.[3] The appearance of Dutch ships in the Malay world during the 1590's presaged a new and destabilizing element in the fortunes of the entrepôt cities and the Portuguese positions in western Indonesia and Siam. To prepare themselves against the Dutch threat, the Portuguese sent large-scale reinforcements to Malacca in 1601 and 1605.[4] The newly reinvigorated empire of Siam enjoyed good trading relations with the Portuguese, the Spanish Philippines, China, and Japan; its king also welcomed the appearance of the Dutch as a new trading partner and in 1608 optimistically dispatched an embassy to Prince Maurice at The Hague.[5] The English, who were just a step behind the Dutch, likewise began to investigate the possibility of establishing commercial relations with kingdoms like Siam and entrepôt states like Acheh on Sumatra, which remained indepen-

[2] On the European printed sources see *Asia*, I, pp. 493–505. Also see W. G. Maxwell, "Barretto de Resende's Account of Malacca," *JRAS, Straits Branch*, LX (1911), 1–24.
[3] Missionaries from Manila and Malacca carried on work in Cambodia until Siamese forces occupied the Mekong valley in 1603. The Dominican fathers Gabriel de San Antonio and Diego Aduarte were meanwhile en route to Spain in search of help. See L. P. Briggs, "Les missionaires portugais et espagnols au Cambodge, 1555–1603," *Bulletin de la société des études indochinoises*, n.s., XXV (1950), 28–29; and Manuel Teixeira, "Diogo Veloso e a Gesta Lusiada em Camboja," in Congresso Internacional de Historia dos Descobrimentos, *Actas* (Lisbon, 1961), Vol. V, Pt. 1, pp. 359–61. On San Antonio's report see below, pp. 1147–51.
[4] See I. A. Macgregor, "Notes on the Portuguese in Malaya," *JRAS, Malayan Branch*, Vol. XXVIII, Pt. 2 (1955), p. 27, n. 93.
[5] See J. J. L. Duyvendak, "The First Siamese Embassy to Holland," *T'oung Pao*, XXXII (1936), 255–92. On their arrival see P. Pelliot, "Les relations du Siam et de la Hollande en 1608," *ibid.*, pp. 223–29. An eleven-page brochure was published at the time, describing the embassy's official reception, entitled, in incorrect French: *Ambassades du Roy de Siam envoyé à l'Excellence du Prince Maurice, arrivé à la Haye le 10. Septem. 1608.*

dent of the Iberian powers. The sultanate of Acheh, the Malay center for Muslim merchants after the Portuguese occupation of Malacca, was almost constantly waging war against Portuguese shipping.[6] In their early ventures to break into the trade of the Straits region, the Dutch and English naturally sought the cooperation of Acheh and other enemies of the Portuguese.

I

MALAYA

In Catholic Europe, the early reports of the missionaries about the Malay world focused on Malacca. Ribadeneira, the Franciscan, writes in 1601 of Malacca as "a melting pot of races, customs, and cultures." Here the Italian Friar Juan Bautista and two others had founded in 1580 a Franciscan convent of the Discalced order from which their Portuguese brothers continued to minister to the faithful and to educate the young.[7] The Jesuits, who had established a college at Malacca in 1549, generally used this crossroads city for stopovers on their way to and from the mission fields further to the east.[8] In their letters of the century's first few years, the Jesuits report that eight of their number are generally kept at Malacca to minister to the Portuguese Christian minority living in that city.[9] The two chief enemies of the Portuguese in Malaya are Acheh and Johore.[10]

The Jesuits soon begin reporting on the depredations and machinations of the Dutch in the vicinity of Malacca. The heretical Dutch make treaties with local Muslim rulers to form a confederation in preparation for an attack on Malacca. Finally, combined European and native fleets attack the city on April 29, 1606. André Furtado de Mendoça (1558–1610), the captain of Malacca, has only 180 soldiers and Japanese auxiliaries to defend the city against the 14,000 which encircle it on land and sea. Despite these overwhelming odds, Malacca holds out for just short of four months until relieved by an armada which arrives from India under the command of Viceroy Dom Martim Afonso de Castro. In October the Portuguese fleet is annihilated, and one month later the viceroy dies. While the siege is lifted,

[6] For a description of Acheh around 1600 see Denys Lombard, *Le Sultanat d'Atjéh au temps d'Iskandar Muda, 1607–1636* (Paris, 1967), chap. i.
[7] See P. G. Fernandez (trans.), *History of the Philippines and Other Kingdoms by Marcelo de Ribadeneira, O.F.M.* (2 vols.; Manila, 1970), I, 421–22.
[8] On Malaya in the sixteenth-century European accounts see *Asia*, I, 505–19.
[9] At the beginning of the century the Diocese of Malacca was in a parlous state. Under D. Frei Cristóvão de Sá e Lisboa, bishop from 1603 to 1610, religious conditions improved. See Manuel Teixeira, *The Portuguese Missions in Malacca and Singapore (1511–1598)* (3 vols.; Lisbon, 1961–63), I, 188–96.
[10] See A. Viegas (ed.), *Relação anual . . . nos anos de 1600 à 1609 . . . pelo Fernão Guerreiro* (3 vols.; Coimbra, 1930, 1931, 1942), I, 49.

the city continues to be in grave danger from the marauding Dutch and Achenese fleets.[11] Johann Verken, a German in the employ of the VOC, vividly describes the continuing activities of the Dutch during 1608–9 in the waters and islands near Malacca and at the court of Johore. He notes that in 1604 "old Johor" was abandoned under the attack of the Portuguese and that its king built a new city upriver. While preying on Portuguese and Muslim shipping in the straits, the Dutch carry on trade at Johore and seek its king's help in planning how to capture Malacca.[12] After the siege of 1606, Furtado left for Goa, where he became governor in 1609. Diogo do Couto, the venerable guardian of the Goa archives, published in 1610 at Lisbon a discourse praising Furtado's elevation to high office as a harbinger of better days to come. Ironically Furtado died in this same year.[13]

Resolutely determined to break into the Eastern trade, the Dutch and English quickly began to compile and disseminate materials relevant to it. Cornelis and Frederick de Houtman, joint commanders of two Dutch trading vessels, tried in 1599 to inaugurate commercial relations with the sultan of Acheh. While successful negotiations at first seemed possible, the sultan suddenly struck out against the Christian Europeans. Cornelis was killed and Frederick taken prisoner. After resisting all attempts to convert him to Islam, Frederick was released in August, 1601, after more than two years of confinement.[14] While in prison he compiled Malay conversations and word lists which were published in 1603 at Amsterdam as *Spraeck ende woordboeck, maleysche ende madagaskarsche talen.* . . . This work provided an introduction to and a method for studying spoken Malay, a leading commercial language of the Indonesian region. It was quickly reprinted, translated into

---

[11] *Ibid.*, II, 312–16. This was but one of a series of attacks launched by the Dutch against Iberian strongholds in the colonial world. For a similar account of the Malacca siege of 1606 see F. C. Danvers, *The Portuguese in India* (2 vols.; London, 1894), II, 135–37.

[12] Verken's diary was first published in 1612 at Frankfurt as *Pars IX Indiae Orientalis . . . auctore Gotardo Artusio* by the printer De Bry. Hulsius reprinted it shortly thereafter. A modern edition may be found in S. P. L'Honoré Naber (ed.), *Johann Verken, Molukken-Reise 1607–1612,* NR, Vol. II. The materials on Malacca and Johore are found on pp. 50–63. For modern commentary on his references to Johore see E. W. Kratz, "The Journey to the Far East. Seventeenth- and Eighteenth-Century German Travel Books as a Source Study," *JRAS, Malaysian Branch,* Vol. LIV, Pt. 1 (1981), p. 70. Also *cf.* the materials on Malaya as reported by the Englishman John Smith in his journals and papers that were not published until the twentieth century. Smith was employed at Patani by the VOC. See A. Hale, *The Adventures of John Smith in Malaya, 1600–1605* (Leyden, 1909).

[13] The best account of the siege of Malacca and of Furtado's role is found in C. R. Boxer and Frazão de Vasconcelos, *André Furtado de Mendoça (1558–1610)* (Lisbon, 1955), chap. iv. Appended to this book is a facsimile of a rare publication by Couto which is entitled *Fala que fez Diogo de Couto Guarda Mor da Torre do Tombo da India, em nome da Camara de Goa, a Andre Furtado de Mendoça, entrando por Governador da India, em successão do Conde da Feyra Dom Ioão Pereyra.*

[14] On the efforts made to convert him to Islam see Lombard, *op. cit.* (n. 6), pp. 235–39. His captor was 'Ala ad-din Ri'ayat Syah (r. 1589–1604).

Latin and English, and used by later compilers as a basis for their works.[15] De Houtman also included in this book his catalog of the southern stars, a work designed to be an aid to navigators to the East Indies and the first such work to be issued in Europe.[16] The English pilot John Davis, who sailed aboard Cornelis' ship, wrote a memoir of the Dutch voyage which Purchas published in 1625. This report, addressed to Earl Robert of Essex, let the English know in some detail about the market of Acheh, its ruler and his aides, and its longstanding war with Johore.[17] The English, acting on Davis' information, dispatched embassies of their own to Acheh in 1602, 1613, and 1615. Reports on Acheh by Sir James Lancaster and Thomas Best, the leaders of the first two of these embassies, were likewise printed in Purchas' collection.[18]

Iskandar Muda, sultan of Acheh from 1607 to 1636, extended his control along the west coast of Sumatra as far south as Padang and on the east coast down to Siak. On the Malay Peninsula he invaded Johore in 1613, 1618, and 1623 and made forays against Patani about halfway up the east coast. All of these activities were but preliminaries to his major objective: the defeat and expulsion of the Portuguese at Malacca. By the spring of 1629 he was ready to attack. Acheh's huge armada arrived at Malacca in July to besiege the city and to capture its fortress. The beleaguered Portuguese held out against overwhelming odds until a Portuguese fleet arrived in October. This armada, aided by vessels sent from Johore and Patani, shortly lifted the siege and captured some and dispersed others of the Achenese ships.[19] Iskandar's disastrous defeat was first related to the public of Portugal in two pamphlets printed at Lisbon in 1630. Three years later the Jesuit Manoel Xavier published his *Vitorias* at Lisbon, a compilation of the various letters and reports of the 1629 campaign sent from Malacca. Later commentators, such as Faria y Sousa, based their briefer accounts of this victory upon Xavier's collection.[20] In 1634 Francisco de Sá de Meneses jubilantly published his heroic epic called *Malacca Conquista* (Lisbon), a work esteemed by some to be a literary product second only to the *Lusiads* of Camoens. It celebrates Albu-

---

[15] Strangely, no Portuguese vocabularies of Malay seem to be extant. De Houtman's work has been reissued in a scholarly edition by Denys Lombard *et al.*, *Le "Spraeck ende Woord-Boek" de Frederick de Houtman. Première méthode de malais parlé (fin du XVIe)* (Paris, 1970). For its seventeenth-century reprints and adaptations see W. Linehan, "The Earliest Word-Lists and Dictionaries of the Malay Language," *JRAS, Malay Branch*, Vol. XXII, Pt. 1 (1949), pp. 183–87.

[16] Lombard *et al, op. cit.* (n. 15), p. 4.

[17] Davis' account of Acheh may be found in *PP*, II, 305–24.

[18] Lancaster's report is in *ibid.*, pp. 406–28; Best's is in *ibid.*, IV, 137–42.

[19] See Lombard, *op. cit.* (n. 6), pp. 96–97; and Leonard Y. Andaya, *The Kingdom of Johor, 1641–1728* (Kuala Lumpur, 1975), pp. 22–23.

[20] *Vitorias do governador da India Nuno Alvarez Botelho.* For discussion of this work and the pamphlets of 1630 see C. R. Boxer, "The Achinese Attack on Malacca in 1629 as Described in Contemporary Portuguese Sources," in J. Bastin and R. Roolvink (eds.), *Malayan and Indonesian Studies* (Oxford, 1964), pp. 105–21.

querque's victory at Malacca as Camoens does Vasco de Gama's triumphs in India. In its final line and elsewhere, Sá de Meneses betrays a general and growing fear that Albuquerque's glorious conquest is being endangered by the Dutch and by Acheh and Johore.[21]

The defeat of Acheh was a victory for Johore as well as Malacca. Relieved of the threat of invasions from across the straits, Johore hereafter concentrated on reestablishing its commercial and political position in the Malay world. Its friendship with the Dutch, dating back to 1602, now served Johore well in its continuing struggle to free itself from the Portuguese threat. Johore and the Dutch in 1639 signed an agreement to work together for the capture of Malacca. The Dutch blockade of Malacca inaugurated on August 2, 1640, culminated in the city's conquest on January 14, 1641. While the Johorese did not actually participate in the fighting, they aided by transporting materials, building fortifications, and cutting off the Portuguese escape routes by land. In return for Johore's assistance, the VOC agreed to protect the Malay state from its local rivals, to mediate a peace treaty between it and Acheh, and to grant its merchants extraordinary trading privileges in Malacca. As the VOC hereafter concentrated its economic activities in Batavia, Malacca became merely another port on the peninsula. The port of Johore gradually replaced both Acheh and Malacca as the major entrepôt on the straits.[22]

Information on Malaya was relayed to Europe during the latter half of the seventeenth century by a series of missionaries, merchants, and adventurers who stopped over at Malacca. Father Alexandre de Rhodes, who had been at Malacca for nine months in 1622–23 and again for forty days early in 1646, published his experiences there in his *Divers voyages* (Paris, 1653).[23] Johann Nieuhof, the Dutch merchant, visited Malacca at the end of 1660; his journal record was published posthumously by his brother in 1682.[24] The Spanish Dominican missionary, Friar Domingo Navarrete, visited Malacca early in 1670 on his way from Macao to Rome. His journal entries were published as part of his *Tratatos historicos* (Madrid, 1676).[25] The German gar-

[21] For an English translation of this poem's third edition (1779) see E. C. Knowlton, Jr. (trans.), *The Conquest of Malacca. Francisco de Sa de Meneses* (Kuala Lumpur, 1970). The editions of 1658 and 1779, published after the fall of Malacca to the Dutch in 1641, naturally had to be revised substantially.

[22] Based on Andaya, *op. cit.* (n. 19), pp. 25–27, 37–38. Also see J. E. Hoffman, "Early Policies in the Malacca Jurisdiction of the United East India Company: The Malay Peninsula and Netherlands East Indies Attachment," *Journal of Southeast Asian Studies*, III (1972), pp. 3–38; and B. W. Andaya, "Melaka under the Dutch, 1641–1795," in K. Singh Sandhu and P. Wheatley (eds.), *Melaka . . .* (2 vols.; Kuala Lumpur, 1983), I, 195–200.

[23] For additional bibliographical detail see above, p. 408. Translated into English by Solange Hertz as *Rhodes of Vietnam* (Westminster, Md., 1966).

[24] *Gedenkwaerdige zee- en lant-reize door de voornaemste landschappen von West en Oostindien* (Amsterdam). An English version is in *CV*, 1744–46 ed., II, 138–305. The portion of this English version dealing with Malaya has been reprinted in J. J. Sheehan, "Seventeenth Century Visitors to the Malay Peninsula," *JRAS, Malay Branch,* Vol. XII, Pt. 2 (1934), pp. 72–88.

[25] Edited English translation in J. S. Cummins (trans. and ed.), *The Travels and Controversies*

dener George Meister in 1692 published *Der orientalisch-indianische Kunst-und Lust-Gärtner* (Dresden). While traveling between Java and Japan for the VOC, he had made a three months' stopover at Malacca in 1686.[26] Three years later Captain William Dampier stayed for one month in Malacca, which he describes in his *Voyages* (London, 1699).[27] Finally, the Neapolitan lawyer and world traveler Francesco Gemelli Careri visited Malacca in 1695. His account was published in his *Giro del mondo* (Naples, 1700).[28] These six accounts of Malacca and Malaya appeared originally in six different western European languages, and several of them were translated into others before century's end.

Rhodes, the French Jesuit, is the only one of these observers who had himself visited Malacca under both the Portuguese and the Dutch. In January, 1646, after a twenty-three years' absence, he admits that "tears came to my eyes" upon entering the city. To make matters worse, the Dutch are celebrating the sixth anniversary of their capture of Malacca. Now he walks through a city from which "every mark of the true faith [is] completely obliterated." Its churches and the Jesuit residence have either been torn down or desecrated by the Dutch Protestants. While "idolaters" are permitted to have a temple at the city's gate, its native Catholics are not even permitted a small chapel. Along with an Italian and a Portuguese Jesuit, Rhodes ministers to these native Catholics. He is also well received by Malacca's Dutch governor, who allows him to say mass in public and to hold religious processions outside the city. This friendly governor was thereafter accused by the Dutch of being overly partial to the Catholics and was eventually transferred to the Moluccas "where they thought he wouldn't see priests so often."[29]

According to Nieuhof, Malacca's harbor is open to traffic throughout the year, "a conveniency belonging scarce to any other in the Indies." The town itself is built on the side of a hill on the west bank of the Malacca River. On the opposite bank stands its fortress. A stone bridge with several arches links the fortress to the town. The town itself is large and populous, and before 1660 the Dutch had built around it a wall of square stones topped by

---

of *Friar Domingo Navarette* (2 vols.; "HS," 2d ser., CXVIII, CXVIX; Cambridge, 1962), pp. 279–86.

[26] For bibliographical details see above, pp. 542–43. On his work and his study of the Malay language see Kratz, *loc. cit.* (n. 12), pp. 69, 79.

[27] For further bibliographical detail see above, pp. 582–85. His voyage to and his description of Malacca may be found in John Masefield (ed.), *Dampier's Voyages* (2 vols.; London, 1906), II, 80–90.

[28] Reprinted from Churchill's English version (1745) in Sheehan, *loc. cit.* (n. 24), pp. 94–107.

[29] Hertz (trans.), *op. cit.* (n. 23), pp. 187–91. *Cf.* Justus Schouten's report on conditions in Malacca prepared in 1640–41 and translated in *JRAS, Malay Branch,* Vol. XIV, Pt. 1 (1936), especially pp. 112–13. Arnold de Vlaming van Oudshoorn was the acting governor of Malacca while Rhodes was there. Early in 1647 he was appointed governor of Amboina. See W. Wijnaendts van Resandt, *De gezaghebbers der Oost-Indische Compagnie . . .* (Amsterdam, 1944), p. 202.

bastions. While its streets are mainly narrow, there are a few broader ave-
nues lined on both sides with trees. Most of its houses are built of bamboo
canes "which are very durable in dry weather." Its few stone houses are
small, low structures divided into little apartments. On a hill in the center of
the town stands a fine church dedicated to St. Paul "where divine service is
performed in Dutch." Formerly the Portuguese charged a 10 percent duty
on all ships passing through the Strait of Malacca but this fee has been abolished by the Dutch. Malacca produces little itself and lives from trade and
on imports. But since the Dutch have taken the city, the traders have become fewer. Previously the only medium of exchange was a heavy tin coinage, but under the Dutch they mint both gold and silver.

Malacca is inhabited mainly by Luso-Asians, Chinese, Hindus, and Jews,
as well as many Dutch. The native "Malayars" (Malays) are "tawny with
long black hair, great eyes and flat noses." Their clothing is limited to a
breech clout, and their only ornaments are gold bracelets and earrings. Most
Malays are Muslims or Christians. Another, rather peculiar, group of people
live in Malacca who are called "Kakerlakken" (*kakkerlaken,* cockroaches) by
the Dutch because they sleep all day and work at night and look like Europeans. The coastal country near Malacca is flat and marshy. In the interior
there are high mountains that can readily be seen from the sea. While they
grow only small quantities of rice, nature produces many edible fruits. Durians are better and larger here than those which grow elswhere in the Indies. Wild and ferocious beasts which formerly forced people to sleep in
trees are seldom heard of since the Dutch occupation of Malacca.

Near Malacca is a very large mountain that is called "Madian" (Malay,
mĕsin, saltpeter) because of the saltpeter found "within its bowels."[30] In
1646 this mountain erupted with "such a terrible noise and earthquakes, as if
the day of judgement was at hand."[31] Near Singapore, "the most southern
point of all Asia," another large mountain yields "excellent diamonds."[32]
East of Singapore cape the Johore River flows into the sea. At its entrance[33]
are two islands "shaped like sugar loaves"; one is four times the size of the
other. Close to Malacca's harbor are several small islands, one of which supplies the ships with fresh water. In the sea some distance north of Malacca is
the uninhabited island called "Dingding" (an island off Dinding on the
mainland; now also called Pangkor), which abounds in wood for fuel and
excellent water.

The Malay Peninsula includes, besides Malacca and Singapore, several
other city-states: "Patany" (Patani), "Pahan" (Pahang), "Pera" (Perak),

[30] Saltpeter is used in Malaya in making gunpowder, in poultices for skin diseases, and in
goldsmith's work. See I. H. Burkill *et al., A Dictionary of the Economic Products of the Malay Peninsula* (2 vols.; London, 1935), II, 1944.
[31] While volcanic ash and rock are found in Malaya, no volcanoes, active or extinct, are now
known. See E. H. G. Dobby, *Southeast Asia* (New York, 1951), p. 90.
[32] Possibly quartz crystals. See Burkill *et al., op. cit.* (n. 30), I, 801.
[33] For a map of the Johore River region see Andaya, *op. cit.* (n. 19), fig. 5.

"Queda" (Kedah), Johore, "Ligor" (Ligor or Lakon), and Tenasserim. Johore, together with its insular possessions, is named for the capital city "called by some Goer or Goera, and Joar or Goar or Gohor." This kingdom is bounded by the straits, Malacca, and Pahang. Its old and magnificent capital was destroyed in 1603 by the Portuguese. With financial help from the Dutch, its ruler in 1609 built a new city farther upriver that is called "Batusabar" (*Batu Sawar,* Sewar) and is located a half-day's journey from "Sedalli" (Sedili) on the sea. Johore is a fertile land which produces an abundance of fruit and lesser amounts of pepper and cinnamon. In its forests there are buffaloes, cows, deer, wild boars, and all sorts of monkeys and birds. Its inhabitants, equally divided between Muslims and pagans, are "naturally brave, but very lascivious, great dissemblers, and proud beyond measure." Johore also rules the island of Lingga, whose three thousand inhabitants (as of 1606) produce an abundance of sago.

The kingdom of Pahang is north of Johore and borders on Patani. Its capital, a small city, is populated only by nobility, while all the commoners live in the suburbs. It is surrounded by a palisade of closely joined tree trunks. The streets are enclosed on both sides by reed hedges and by coconut and other trees. Its houses are made of reed and straw, though the royal palace is constructed of wood. While the Pahang River is very broad, it is navigable by galleys only at floodtide. In its valley grow small amounts of pepper as well as calambac, eaglewood, and camphor trees. In the interior, wild elephants and "coarse gold" are found. Pahang makes great quantities of baskets and a few huge cannons weighing three thousand pounds.[34] Most of Pahang's inhabitants are pagan or Muslim in religion and its king is a vassal of Siam.

Patani is situated north of Pahang on the peninsula's east coast. To its north is "Lugor" or "Ligor," a dependency of Siam. Its capital, located not far from the sea, is "surrounded to the land side by bogs." The harbor and royal court buildings are enclosed by palisades. In the city the Muslims have a stately brick mosque with pillars, whose interior is richly gilded. There are also a number of pagan temples "among which three excel the rest." When the Dutch first settled at Patani in 1602, they saw large gilded statues in the temples "belonging to the subjects of the king of Siam."[35] The country around Patani abounds in rice and tropical fruits. Its farmers cultivate pepper, a commodity that is more expensive here than in most places in the Indies. Wild hogs "do incredible mischief" to the rice fields, and the farmers kill them. The carcasses are buried, because the powerful local Muslims will not eat, or permit others to eat, pork. Patani is much more important as a foreign trade mart than either Johore or Pahang. It is also more populous than the other Malay states and is able to put 180,000 armed men into the

[34] On gold and iron in Pahang see Dobby, *op. cit.* (n. 31), pp. 126–27.
[35] *I.e.,* Buddhist temples and idols.

field. Malay, Siamese, "Patne," and Chinese are the languages used in Patani. Its king sends annual tribute to Siam "consisting of a flower wrought with gold, some fine cloths, velvets, and scarlets." His chief ministers are called "Mentary" (*menteri*).[36]

Navarrete, the Spanish Dominican, was in Malacca for twelve days in 1670. Although Spain was then at peace with the Dutch, Governor Baltasar Bort was not particularly hospitable to the fiery Navarrete.[37] He was eventually permitted to visit and minister to the two thousand Catholics who lived upriver outside the Dutch zone of control.[38] The place where the Catholics live is a garden spot. The Dutch are generous in almsgiving to the Catholic poor, "but almost oblige'd them to be present at their Service." Heretic preachers also baptize and marry the Catholics. The old Church of St. Paul now serves as part of Malacca's wall and the Jesuit residence is used as a storehouse. Some Filipinos of Manila enjoy living in Malacca, where they escape the heavy taxes and duties exacted by the Spanish in the Philippines. On leaving Malacca, the Spanish priest touched on the uninhabited island of "Pulo Pinang" (Pulau Pinang), and his ship threaded between two of the Nicobar Islands, whose warlike people reputedly "devour alive the Europeans they catch."[39]

Unlike Navarrete, the English adventurer William Dampier in an opium-laden ship received a cordial welcome at Malacca when he arrived there in mid-October, 1689. He stayed there for one month while his ship was being repaired. At this time the city is inhabited by two to three hundred Dutch and Portuguese families, "many of which are a mixt Breed." The Malays live in small cottages on the edges of the town and the Dutch boast houses of stone. While the streets are wide and straight, they are not paved. In the town's northwestern section there is a gate in the wall and a small, constantly guarded fort. About one hundred paces from the sea a drawbridge spans the river between the town and its strong fort on the east side of the river. This chief bastion is built close to the sea on a bit of low-level land at the foot of a "little steep Hill." Semicircular in shape, the fort faces the sea, from which it is protected by a high, thick wall. Behind the hill a waterway is cut from the sea to the river "which makes the whole an Island." The back of the hill itself "is stockaded round with great Trees set up on end." On a

---

[36] Based on Nieuhof's account in Churchill, *op. cit.* (n. 24), II, 167–74. From the historical references in this account it is clear that the compiler or publisher, or both, added materials to the journal drawn possibly from unpublished Dutch reports then available in Amsterdam.

[37] By a proclamation of January 15, 1666, Bort had decreed that Portuguese priests might not come ashore in Malacca. See Teixeira, *op. cit.* (n. 9), I, 313–14.

[38] On the fate of the Catholics of Malacca see W. H. C. Smith, "The Portuguese in Malacca during the Dutch Period," *Studia* (Lisbon), VII (1961), 87–106. At this time the Catholics seem to have been confined to Bunga-raya.

[39] Navarrete in Cummins (trans. and ed.), *op. cit.* (n. 25), pp. 281–87. For an account of conditions in Malacca in the 1660's see W. Ph. Coolhaas, "Malacca under Jan van Riesbeeck," *JRAS, Malaysian Branch*, Vol. XXXVIII, Pt. 2 (1965), pp. 173–82.

hill within the fort stands a small church which is large enough to accommodate all the townspeople who come there on Sundays to worship. The fort appears old, and the part facing the sea still has marks on it made by the shots fired during the Dutch siege. It was only the general mismanagement and poor planning of the Portuguese that enabled the Dutch to conquer "a Place so naturally strong."

Malacca is no longer a great international center of trade, but some foreigners still live and do business there. Several Muslim merchants run shops in which they sell the products of India. Some industrious Chinese import tea and operate teahouses; others are pork butchers, tradesmen, and gamblers. Fish are sold in a special marketplace. Soldiers carry off the best of the catch for the officers in the fort before others are allowed to buy. Individual catches are then sold by auction, usually to fishwives who are the retailers. Rice and all other provisions except fruits and poultry are imported.[40] The surrounding countryside is one great forest from which come "most of our Walking-Canes [Malacca canes] used in England." The governor lives in the fort; the "Shabandar," now a Dutchman, lives in town, is second in command, and is in charge of trade and customs. Guard-ships owned by the town patrol the straits. It is said that the Dutch now charge a duty to all ships except those of the English.

Most ships stop over at Malacca for wood, water, and "Refreshments." When a Danish ship anchored there on its way to Johore, the Dutch informed its captain that the trade at Johore was their monopoly. The Danish ship nevertheless went on to Johore, "found all this a Sham," and proceeded to do a brisk business. Johore retains its independence because, were the Dutch to take it, the people of Johore would flee. Too few in number to settle it themselves, the Dutch ordinarily keep a guard-ship there and remain content periodically to enforce a monopoly of Johore's trade. They follow the same practice at Kedah and "Pulo Dinding" (or Pulau Pangkor), two places also too unimportant to warrant the establishment of a factory. This policy of quiet intimidation outrages the Malays, and it is probably responsible for the piracies and robberies so frequent on this coast. The Dutch prohibit the importation of opium, a drug "much used by the Malayans in most Places." While the Malays may not compete against the Dutch in foreign commerce, their merchants manage to earn a good livelihood in local trading.[41]

On leaving Malacca, Dampier's ship was forced after losing a mast to make for "Pulo Dinding." The Dutch, the only inhabitants of this small island, have a fort on its east side with a governor and twenty to thirty soldiers. It faces the peninsular lowland and a bay into which flows a river that

---

[40] Meister, who was in Malacca just three years before Dampier, claims that the city enjoyed a surplus of fruit and produce and had little need of imports (*op. cit.* [n. 26], p. 202).
[41] Dampier in Masefield (ed.), *op. cit.* (n. 27), II, 83–91.

is navigable by small craft.[42] At the mouth of the river the Dutch usually keep a guard-ship or two to prevent others from participating in the region's valuable tin trade. The Dutch also try, but with less success, to monopolize the tin trade at Kedah. The Malays of Dinding bitterly resent the Dutch for excluding others from this trade. As a consequence, the Dutch live in continual fear and never dare go to the mainland or even far from the fort.[43]

Careri estimates that in 1695 Malacca has a population of five thousand, the majority being good Portuguese Catholics. Its population is so diverse that the governor's proclamations are issued in Dutch and four other languages. Portuguese Catholics must practice their religion in the woods outside the city and are forced to pay special taxes that are higher than those required of Jews and Muslims. The present governor commands a garrison of 180 soldiers. All ships passing through the straits pay duties to Malacca except those of the English. Spanish and Portuguese vessels pay more than any of the others. The Dutch zone of control extends only for three miles around the city. Its hinterland is dominated by wild people called "Menancavos" (Minangkabau), who are Muslim thieves and mortal enemies of the Dutch. Their king called "Pagarivyon" (Pagar Ruyong, now a placename) has his residence at "Nani" (Naning, in modern Negeri Sembilan), a village set in the thickest part of the woods.[44] The Muslim Malays called "Salittes" (Cellates, or Orang Selat) live along the Singapore strait in "portable and floating houses." They are ingenious fishermen who spear the fish with bamboo spikes. Because they are subjects of Johore, its king maintains in the channel a "custom-house for fish." The "Salittes" and the people of Johore both wear a garment from the waist down. The men shave their heads and faces and tie a small rag around their foreheads instead of a turban.[45]

2

PEGU AND ARAKAN

While Portuguese Malacca was busily defending itself, Lusitanian missionaries and adventurers sought to establish footholds in the nearby Burmese

---

[42] For a map showing the Dutch fort and the course of the Dinding River see B. W. Andaya, *Perak, the Abode of Grace. A Study of an Eighteenth-Century Malay State* (Kuala Lumpur, 1979), p. xiv. The ruins of the fort may still be seen on Pangkor Island.

[43] On the tin trade in general see G. W. Irwin, "The Dutch and the Tin Trade of Malaya in the Seventeenth Century," in J. Ch'en and N. Tarling (eds.), *Studies in the Social History of China and South-east Asia, Essays in Memory of Victor Purcell* (Cambridge, 1970), pp. 267–87.

[44] This is possibly a vague and confused reference to the monarchy of Pagar Ruyong, the Minangkabau center on the peninsula between the Muar and Pahang rivers. Naning is about eight miles north and inland from Malacca. See Andaya, *op. cit.* (n. 19), pp. 110–12.

[45] Careri in Sheehan, *loc. cit.* (n. 24), pp. 94–107. For earlier references to the Cellates see *Asia*, I, 507–8.

coastal states of Arakan and Pegu. Independent since 1404, Arakan in the sixteenth and seventeenth centuries was involved with the Mughuls of India in a struggle for control of the upper reaches of the Bay of Bengal. The Indian port city of Chittagong, acquired by Arakan in 1459, was the center from which the Arakanese attacked ships going to the Ganges delta. Hundreds of Portuguese freebooters had advanced their own interests in the sixteenth century by working in Arakan, by fighting on its side in the wars against Pegu, and by making piratical forays against Bengal's commerce. Dominican and Franciscan missionaries had worked in Pegu since 1557; around 1560 the Portuguese were permitted to build a fortress at Syriam, then the most important of Pegu's port cities. In 1599–1600 King Minyazagyi (r. 1592–1612) of Arakan with the aid of Portuguese mercenaries defeated the Toungoos and burned and depopulated the capital city of Pegu.[46] Thereafter the missionaries generally went to Bengal or Arakan.[47] The Jesuits, who had never been numerous in either Bengal or Pegu, began around 1600 to work with the Portuguese freebooters to establish a Christian colony in Burma.

Nicolas Pimenta, Jesuit Visitor to India, sent from Goa to Rome at the end of 1600 a batch of letters relayed to his headquarters from the Jesuits of his province working in the Bay of Bengal region. Three of these letters were from two priests of a party of four who had left Goa for Bengal in 1598. Francisco Fernandez (*ca.* 1547–1602) dispatched reports to Pimenta from Dianga just south of Chittagong in 1599 and from Martaban about one year later. The other report was from Andréa Boves (1569–1634), a native of Messina, who wrote from Syriam in Pegu on March 28, 1600. These missives were first published at Rome in 1602 in the letterbook called *Copia d'una del P. Nicolo Pimenta . . .* , a volume which was quickly reissued both in Italian and in Latin translation.[48] Excerpts from the last two of these letters were later translated into English and published in *Purchas His Pilgrimes* (1625).[49] In the letter from Dianga, Fernandez informs his superiors that the ruler of Arakan has sent a letter requesting the dispatch of missionaries to his kingdom. In his other letter the Jesuit notes that Martaban had been a large kingdom but is "now desolate by the Siamites warre no lesse then Pegu." Its king holds sway over no more than two or three fortified cities, and two hundred thousand of its "Inhabitants lurke in Woodes and Mountaines." In addition to producing three rice crops annually, these rich lands can yield enough "Pitch and Timber to lade yeerly twenty of the

---

[46] On the Europeans in the Burmese wars of the sixteenth century see *Asia*, I, 539–60.

[47] On the downfall of Pegu according to the Jesuits see Pierre du Jarric, *Histoire des choses plus memorables . . .* (3 vols.; Bordeaux, 1608, 1610, 1614), I, 612–29. This description has been translated into English in A. Saulière, S.J. (trans.), "The Jesuits in Pegu at the End of the Sixteenth Century," in *Bengal Past and Present*, XIX (1919), 64–80.

[48] In the first edition the letters in question appear on pp. 63–71, 75–80, 80–83.

[49] *PP*, X, 215–17.

greatest ships." Syriam, the best port of Pegu, is a "lamentable spectacle" of ruined temples and buildings, whose fields are covered with the dead and whose river is choked with corpses.

In other letters to Europe, the Jesuits claim that Arakan, or "the kingdoms of the Mogos [Mughs]," is the most powerful of all the states of "Bengala."[50] At Chittagong, where there is a governor and a fortress, the Portuguese enjoy great favor for services rendered and virtually control the port. After ruining Pegu, King Minyazagyi returns in triumph to his capital city, also called Arakan (or Mrauk-u), with immense loot and the precious white elephant of Pegu. To this capital, more populous than Lisbon, two Jesuits and a Portuguese gentleman hurry to greet the victorious ruler. The Europeans, accompanied by the "Coramgarino" (*karangri,* or chief of the bodyguard), are taken to the royal barge anchored in the Lemro River. After questioning the Jesuits about their beliefs, the king ends the interview by assuring them that he will gladly receive Jesuits at Chittagong and Arakan and that he will provide them with maintenance and a stipend. Shortly after this the Arakan king, accompanied by his Portuguese mercenaries and a Jesuit, decides to return to Pegu to collect whatever loot was earlier missed. Andréa Boves, the Jesuit of this company, concludes after inspecting the devastation of Lower Burma that it is now "a kingdom of jungles" and not able to sustain a mission. Victimized by tyranny, civil war, and foreign invasion "the countless inhabitants of Pegu [were] destroyed, as well as those of Ava, Prum [Prome], Martaban, Murmulam [Moulmein], and other adjacent kingdoms, so that there are now no people left in all this region."[51]

The Portuguese mercenary then most favored by King Minyazagyi is "Felippe de Brito Nicote, a rich and honorable man and the Captain of many Portuguese, whom he had brought with him to Pegu."[52] As a reward for his services De Brito is made "Governor and lord of the kingdom of Pegu, such as it was" with permission to build a fort at Syriam, the port on

[50] By "Bengala" the Portuguese meant the coastal territories and islands at the head of the Bay of Bengal and in the Ganges delta. The inhabitants of Arakan were called "Mughs" (from Bengali, *magh*) by others.

[51] Guerreiro in Viegas (ed.), *op. cit.* (n. 10), I, 44–49. For an English translation see C. H. Payne (trans. and ed.), *Jahangir and the Jesuits* (New York, 1930), pp. 185–93.

[52] Payne, *op. cit.* (n. 51), p. 194. Once Portugal had been taken over by the Habsburg rulers of Spain, the mentality of the *conquistadores* spread into the Iberian empire of the East—into the Philippines, Cambodia, and the Bay of Bengal. Other self-styled Portuguese "kings" set themselves up in the Bay of Bengal on Sandwip Island and at Dianga. De Brito was born in Lisbon, the son of Julio Nicot, brother of Jean Nicot, the French ambassador to Lisbon from 1559 to 1561 and the reputed introducer of tobacco to France. His mother was a Portuguese noblewoman. In India he was a salt merchant and controlled the industry on Sandwip Island thanks to a concession from Arakan. He was highly regarded by the Jesuits, who hoped to find in him a benefactor. See Provincial Pimenta's Annual Letter translated into English and edited by H. Hosten, S.J., "Fr. N. Pimenta's Annual of Margão, Dec. 1, 1601," *JRAS, Bengal Branch,* XXIII (1927), 95–97. Other writers, beginning with Faria y Souza, no admirer of De Brito, usually claim that he came from a poor background. See Faria y Sousa, trans. by M. V. G. S. Ferreira, *Asia portuguesa* (6 vols.; Porto, 1945–47), V, 246. This myth persists. See M. Htin Aung, *A History of Burma* (New York, 1967), p. 135.

the Gulf of Martaban, into which the rivers of Pegu empty.[53] Between 1599 and 1602 he constructs a stone fortress "well equipped with guns and munitions, and very favorably situated for defensive purposes." At the same time he begins to build a town for the displaced of Lower Burma who gravitate to Syriam "to live in peace and security under his rule." By the autumn of 1603 the town has "from fourteen to fifteen thousand inhabitants all engaged in cultivating the land." With the rapid recovery of the city, King Minyazagyi begins to be alarmed by the independent power De Brito is acquiring. Certain Muslims at Minyazagyi's court and the emissaries of the "King of Massulapatam" (probably the sultan of Golconda) urge him to expel the Portuguese from Pegu and to open it to their people. When De Brito visits the court and learns of these machinations, he advises the king to remember that the Portuguese are lords of the sea, loyal to one another, and allies needed by Arakan in its wars against Akbar. While the king thereafter turns his back on the Muslims and maintains friendly relations with the Portuguese, he also orders De Brito to tear down his fortress, "otherwise he would send his armies to do it." He also commands the Portuguese to respect the "Banha" (*bayin*) or duke whom he had left behind in Pegu to keep a check on De Brito. Despite these admonitions De Brito and his followers attack the "Banha's" troops and force that official to flee for his life.[54]

In the following period of peace, the cultivators of Syriam make the region self-sufficient in rice and expect soon to be exporting it to India. In these prosperous times "all are disposed to receive baptism." For his part De Brito sends emissaries to "Tangu" (Toungoo), "Prum" (Prome), "Iangoma" (Chiengmai, then in Laos, now in Siam), "Syam" (Siam), and other nearby states, to make treaties of friendship "and to dissuade them from alliances with the King of Arracam [Arakan], the common enemy of all." All send favorable replies, except for the king of Siam, who is told by Martin de Torres, a Portuguese at Ayut'ia, that De Brito is the slave of Arakan and not recognized by Goa. Accompanied by ambassadors from the other Burmese states, De Brito goes to Goa "to make over the fortress and the kingdom of Pegu to the [Portuguese] state." He returns from Goa in December, 1602 (probably a mistake for 1603), with a fleet of sixteen "rowing vessels manned by three hundred Portuguese." With this fleet and the other Portuguese vessels already in the Bay of Bengal, the Portuguese, "God willing," will be made "undisputed masters of all the ports of Bengala and Pegu."[55]

While in Goa in 1603, De Brito dispatched a report to the Portuguese

---

[53] Payne, *op. cit.* (n. 51), p. 194. Syriam was located on the left bank of the Pegu River about three miles from its junction with what is now called the Rangoon River on the eastern side of the Irrawaddy delta.

[54] On the office of *bayin* (exalted governor) see V. B. Lieberman, *Burmese Administrative Cycles: Anarchy and Conquest, c. 1580–1760* (Princeton, 1984), pp. 33–38.

[55] Guerreiro in Viegas (ed.), *op. cit.* (n. 10), I, 290–93; English translation in Payne (trans. and ed.), *op. cit.* (n. 51), pp. 194–200.

king along with a petition asking for official appointment as commander of Syriam for life, for a portion of the port's revenues, and for succession rights for his son.[56] His report was summarized by the Lisbon Jesuits and included in Guerreiro's *Relação anual* as ten good reasons for holding the states around the Bay of Bengal.[57] First, the crown will be able to reclaim to its service the twenty-five hundred Portuguese and Luso-Asians who, as outlaws or refugees, now work for the gentile and Moorish kings of the region; second, the collection of customs will provide additional revenues for the Estado da India; third, in Pegu and elsewhere, timber for shipbuilding is cheap and abundant; fourth, from these ports supplies and munitions can be sent at all seasons, and more easily than from Goa, to Malacca and other Portuguese outposts further east; fifth, from Pegu it would be simple for the Portuguese fleets to wrest away from Siam those places occupied in the course of the wars in Lower Burma: Martaban, "Reitavai" (kingdom of Tavoy), Tenasserim, "Junsalão" (Junk-Ceylon), and Kedah; sixth, the occupation and development of Pegu as a Portuguese base will put an end to Siam's ambitions and pretensions in this area; seventh, from Pegu the Portuguese can command the nearby seas "just as they patrol the coast of Malabar in India"; eighth, from Syriam the Portuguese could subdue Toungoo "in two years time," confiscate the vast treasure kept there, and extend their authority along the whole coast of the Gulf of Martaban;[58] ninth, "by means of this conquest" the Portuguese will be able to check the spread of Dutch power in the region; and tenth, "of far more account than temporal gains" are the "countless souls" that can be won among these people who "are by nature docile and easy to convert."

On his way back from Goa, De Brito stops at Cochin in 1603 to request the provincial of the Jesuits to dispatch priests to Syriam. Two Jesuits are thereafter sent from "Bengala," where matters were going badly for the Christians in 1602–3 as the Arakanese take control over Sandwip Island and other places in the Ganges delta. The Jesuits arrive in Syriam during February, 1604, "to the great contentment and consolation of the Portuguese who were in the fortress." Urged on by Muslims at the court, King Minyazagyi decides at the end of 1604 to expel the Portuguese from Syriam and to extend his authority southward to the ports and cities of Martaban, Tavoy, and Tenasserim. To this end he outfits a fleet of "nearly five hundred and fifty ships, carrying a force of fifteen thousand men" under the command of his eldest son and "all the chief captains of his kingdom." To meet this armada the Portuguese have but eight well-equipped ships manned by one hundred and eighty Portuguese. The two fleets meet off "a point of the land which is

---

[56] See Payne (trans. and ed.), *op. cit.* (n. 51), p. 262, n. 1.
[57] Viegas (ed.), *op. cit.* (n. 10), I, 293–95.
[58] At this point there is a summary of De Brito's personal observations of the city and fortress of Toungoo and of its king's available troops and munitions.

called Negrais."[59] The two fleets continue the sea fight across the entire Irra-waddy delta from west to east. In January, 1605, a fourth and final engagement takes place in the river leading to the Syriam fortress. Here the Arakan fleet is bottled up in a narrow channel and forced to surrender. Abandoning their vessels, the prince and great lords of Arakan seek to escape overland. On being intercepted by De Brito and his forces, the prince and his aides are held prisoners to be ransomed by the king of Arakan. As a result of this great victory, the foundations are laid by 1605 for a prosperous Portuguese "estate" and a flourishing mission in the Irrawaddy delta.[60]

On the basis of De Brito's reports and those of the Society's priests in the field, the Jesuits in Lisbon foresee a great future for both church and state in Burma. This country, so rich in agricultural products as well as precious metals and stones, is ripe and ready for the picking. A thousand men could easily proceed up the river from Syriam and take the rich "kingdoms" of Toungoo, Prome, and Ava. Naval vessels, based at Syriam, could readily capture the southern coastal cities of Tavoy, Tenasserim, Martaban, and Junk-Ceylon, which are now points of entry to "Jancoma" (Chiengmai), Siam, and "Langam" (Luang Prabang). Even all of "Bengala" could be conquered by fleets sent to the Ganges delta from Syriam. This extended empire, as well as Malacca and other Portuguese outposts to the south and east, could be supplied from Syriam. The fertile soil of Pegu, "if it is well irrigated," will "yield . . . good crops . . . of anything that is sown in it." The poor subjects of the Portuguese king can be rewarded in Burma with grants of rich land whereas in India "not a span" is available for distribution. Ships can sail directly from Lisbon to Syriam and be assured of a return cargo of pepper from Kedah and Acheh as well as Burmese and Bengali products that can be loaded in the splendid harbor of Negrais. Cotton textiles from Coromandel, now being imported into mainland Southeast Asia through other ports, can be funneled through Syriam, as they were in previous times, to produce new customs revenues for the crown and better trading conditions for Portuguese merchants. A new empire centered on the Gulf of Martaban would render Syriam secure, establish Portuguese superiority on the surrounding seas, and overawe the neighboring kings "so that none of them would dare to raise a hand against us."

While these visionary bubbles are being blown, De Brito extorts a peace treaty from Arakan while holding its prince for ransom. Negotiated by the Sicilian Jesuit Father Natale Salerno (d. 1607), this treaty returns custody of "Sundiva" (Sandwip Island) to De Brito. When De Brito sends his son Marcos with a party of Portuguese to take possession of the island, they are in-

---

[59] Cape Negrais or Pagoda Point is at the southern limit of Arakan. East of the point is the estuary of the Bassein River on the west side of the Irrawaddy delta.

[60] Guerreiro in Viegas (ed.), *op. cit.* (n. 10), II, 137–41; and Payne (trans. and ed.), *op. cit.* (n. 51), pp. 207–15.

tercepted treacherously by the Arakanese and ruthlessly slain. The outraged Minyazagyi, who apparently had no intention of observing the treaty, also embarks upon a crusade against the more than five thousand Christians living in his territories and the Portuguese traders in his ports. He prepares a fleet for a new attack upon Syriam even though his "talapojos" (*talapois*, or Buddhist monks) advise against it. Learning of these preparations, De Brito sends Father Salerno to beleaguered Malacca to ask for reinforcements. The Jesuit returns with two galleys and six sailing vessels as De Brito musters whatever ships he can to confront the armada of twelve hundred being sent against him. While these steps are being taken the two Jesuits continue to minister to the faithful at Syriam, one in the fort and the other in the ships at sea.

De Brito is kept informed of Arakan's preparations by intelligence relayed to him through the king of Prome. This time the armada of Arakan, mostly small oared vessels of shallow draft supported by five heavily armed galley-type vessels, comes prepared to lay siege to Syriam. It carries about thirty thousand soldiers, many from India and Persia, who are led by Minyazagyi himself. A small Portuguese fleet of twelve vessels commanded by Paulo do Rego, a longtime associate of De Brito, again meets the Arakanese armada at Negrais. A first bloody battle begins on March 31, 1607, that ends indecisively. In the second battle of April 4, the Portuguese flagship is lost and along with it Captain Do Rego and Father Salerno. The rest of the fleet, on learning of this grave loss, retreats in good order to the fortress of Syriam. The Arakanese fleet blockades Syriam while a large allied force from Toungoo moves overland against the fort. It is surrounded on one side by the Toungoos and on the other by soldiers landed from the blockading fleet. For thirty days the little Portuguese garrison withstands the repeated attacks of its besiegers. Discouraged by this vigorous resistance and their heavy losses, the Arakanese withdraw on May 10 and set sail for their homeland. On January 12 of the following year, the hastily repaired Portuguese fortress burns to the ground, a conflagration in which De Brito and his wife almost lose their lives. Fearing the return of Arakan's forces, De Brito commences the construction of a new fortress on higher ground and in a more defensible position. In 1608–9 Arakan is prevented from taking advantage of De Brito's plight by the attacks being launched against Dianga by Portuguese freebooters from India led by Sebastião Gonçalves Tibão, the leader of the "sea-wolves" who terrorize the towns on the Bay of Bengal.[61]

While Arakan sought to maintain its supremacy in Lower Burma, a kingdom was arising in Upper Burma under Nyaungyan Min (r. 1597–1605, a usurper of the Toungoo dynasty) which would overwhelm the South and

[61] Guerreiro in Viegas (ed.), *op. cit.* (n. 10), II, 317–20; III, 77–84. Payne (trans. and ed.), *op. cit.* (n. 51), pp. 216–40. On Sebastião Gonçalves Tibão's activities at Dianga and its environs see D. G. E. Hall, *Europe and Burma . . . to . . . 1886* (London, 1945), pp. 36–37.

lead by 1635 to the restoration of the dynasty. It was under Anaukpetlun (r. 1605–28) that Prome was subdued and a pincer attack prepared in 1609–10 against the Toungoo state and the city of Pegu. Two-thirds of Toungoo's population being thereafter carried off to Upper Burma a vacuum was created in De Brito's hinterland that he sought to fill. In 1612 the Portuguese and their auxiliaries, in alliance with land troops from Martaban, were able to sack Toungoo. In revenge Anaukpetlun in 1613 sent a massive army to besiege Syriam. The town fell after three months and De Brito was executed by impalement, the punishment prescribed by Burmese law for ravagers of Buddhist temples. His Christian followers, persons skilled in making and using firearms and cannons, were transported north and settled in special villages, northwest of Ava, as hereditary military units. While Anaukpetlun thus reunited the Irrawaddy basin to its agricultural hinterland, the Arakanese king in 1615–17 with the help of the Dutch destroyed the island empire created by Sebastião Gonçalves Tibão at the head of the Bay of Bengal.[62]

In Portugal itself very little was published about these defeats. In 1614, the year following De Brito's death, a small relation in Spanish appeared, evidently celebrating De Brito's romantic career and the sack of Pegu in 1612.[63] Three years later there appeared at Lisbon the *Breve discurso* written in Castilian by Father Manuel de Abreu Mousinho, a native of Evora who had worked for a time in the Chancellery of Goa.[64] From internal evidence it appears that he had returned to Europe before writing his account of the Portuguese at Syriam between 1600 and 1603. He derived at least part of his geographical descriptions of Pegu from Barros' work. Evidently it was while he worked in Goa—for he makes no reference to a personal visit to Pegu—that he learned about the efforts of the Portuguese to establish themselves at Syriam and of the exploits there of Salvador Ribeyro de Souza, a native of the Guimares district in Portugal's province of Douro-Minho. Abreu Mousinho was clearly determined to make certain that Ribeyro de Souza receive the credit due him for defending the Portuguese outpost at Syriam against all comers during the earliest days of its existence. He argues that the bishop of Cochin and the viceroy Ayres de Saldanha, uncle of De

---

[62] Based on Htin Aung, *op. cit.* (n. 52), pp. 139–41; Lieberman, *op. cit.* (n. 54), pp. 48–54; and V. B. Lieberman, "Europeans, Trade, and the Unification of Burma, *ca.* 1540–1620," *Oriens Extremus,* XXVII (1980), 217–20. These modern works correlate most of the obvious European sources with the Burmese sources on the Portuguese efforts to establish military enclaves in Burma. Generally, however, they do not refer in any detail to the secular Portuguese or to the Jesuit sources.

[63] We have not seen Juan Pérez' *Relacion muy verdadera de un caso nuevamente encedido en la India de Portugal, en que se cuento como un cavallero Portugues llamado Felipe Brito, que es governador, y Capitan general en aquellas partes por su Magestad vencio a un Rey gentil del Pegú* (Cuenca) or its Italian translation, *Relatione breve del tesoro grandissimo nuovamente acquistato nell' Indie Orientali di Portugallo . . .* (Milan and Bologna, 1614).

[64] For bibliographical details see above, p. 329.

Brito's wife, were misinformed about De Brito's role in the first establishment of the Syriam fort. While Ribeyro de Souza stood off hostile Burmese forces, De Brito, the "Changa," or steward, of the king of Arakan, was in Bengal working for this "Moorish" ruler. In the meantime Ribeyro de Souza saved the fort, brought peace to the land, won great local support, and was acclaimed "Quiay Massinga or god of the country" by the grateful people of Pegu. Replaced by De Brito in 1602, Ribeyro de Souza left Syriam with the monsoon of 1603. While the partisan Abreu Mousinho is probably guilty of exaggeration in recounting the exploits of his hero, this small book is informative on the wars in Lower Burma from 1600 to 1602. It includes references to the names and offices of participating Burmese and Portuguese. But it is especially valuable for the splendid detail it gives on the construction of fortresses, siege tactics, military movements on land and sea, and the armaments used by both Portuguese and Burmese.[65]

In the journal (1611–15) of Pieter Floris, excerpts from which were published by Purchas (1625), notice is taken of the activities of De Brito, once called "Xenga, that is Honest by the king of Arakan."[66] While at Masulipatam in February, 1614, Floris learns from a native of Pegu about De Brito's defeat and execution by "the King of Awa [Ava]" in the previous March. While urging his subjects to rebuild Syriam, the victorious king goes south to attack Tenasserim with the support of fifty thousand Burmese previously in the service of Siam. These events are cheered by the Muslims of Masulipatam who "hope to get the trade of Pegu into their hands again."[67]

William Methwold, who was in Masulipatam from 1618 to 1622, reveals that the "king of Arakan" (Minhkamaung, r. 1612–22) continues to fight a defensive war against the Mughuls in eastern Bengal, is friendly to the many Muslims living in his land, and regularly invites the Dutch and English "to resort unto his country." Fearing the conditions in Arakan, the English and the merchants of other nations prefer to establish commercial relations with Pegu, a land "yet hardly recovered from the desolation wherewith warre, plague, and famine in former years infested it." Its new ruler, the king of Ava, while initially responsive to the English in 1617–18, is thought to treat

---

[65] For the Portuguese text see M. Lopes d'Almeida (ed.), *Breve discurso em que se conta a conquista do reino de Pegu* (Barcelos, 1936); the English quoted here is from A. Macgregor's translation from the Portuguese version, "A Brief Account of the Kingdoms of Pegu," *Journal of the Burma Research Society*, Vol. XVI, Pt. 2 (1926), pp. 99–138.

[66] "Xenga" is not a Burmese title, but seems to be a nickname current in the patois of the seaports meaning "good man." See G. E. Harvey, *History of Burma . . . to . . . 1824* (London, 1925), p. 189. Anthony Schorer in his relation of 1614 about Coromandel refers to the "execution of Schengan." See W. H. Moreland (ed.), *Relations of Golconda in the Early Seventeenth Century* (London, 1931), p. 69.

[67] Floris in *PP*, III, 326–27, 335–36. Also see W. H. Moreland (ed.), *Peter Floris, His Voyage to the East Indies in the Globe, 1611–15* (London, 1934), pp. 53–55, 188–89. While Anaukpetlun regained Martaban readily, as well as some of the southern territories held by Siam, Tenasserim itself was successfully defended in 1614 by Portuguese mercenaries employed by Siam. Thereafter Anaukpetlun consolidated his hold on Burma and sought to revive its international trade. See Htin Aung, *op. cit.* (n. 52), pp. 141–43; and Lieberman, *op. cit.* (n. 54), p. 54.

all foreigners "as his slaves" and is a tyrant to his own subjects and all others.[68] Although the English merchants find conditions unsatisfactory for trade in Pegu, its king sends another letter with them to the English in India "signifying his desire to give free trade and entertainment to the English nation." The rulers of Arakan, Pegu, Tenasserim, and Siam are all "gentiles" who hold "all meates and drinkes indifferent."[69] In Arakan the king "marrieth constantly his owne sister," a custom that is justified by the fact that "Adams sons married Adams daughters."[70] The rudiments of their religion were received from the Chinese "who without question sometimes commanded those countries."[71]

Friar Sebastião Manrique (d. 1669), a Portuguese Augustinian, worked in the Bengal mission of his own order from 1629 to 1636. After a sojourn of almost forty years in the East, he reached Rome in 1643. While a missionary in foreign parts, he had kept a detailed journal of his travels. In writing up his recollections he also borrowed without acknowledgement from De Laet, Mendez Pinto, and probably others. But his descriptions of "Bengala" and Arakan are based largely on his personal experiences and notes. He wrote in Spanish rather than in his native Portuguese, Spanish being more widely read in Europe. His *Itinerario de las missiones del India Oriental* (Rome, 1649), although penned in an atrocious Spanish, is a memoir "of exceptional interest and value" for reconstructing the history of "Bengala" and Arakan, for which there exist few other sources. Although he does not appear to have learned a Burmese language, he was able to converse with the rulers and merchants of Arakan in Portuguese or in Urdu, then a major vernacular of the Mughul Empire widely used, like Portuguese, in the commerce of the Bay of Bengal.[72]

Manrique's ship from Cochin, carrying a large cargo of chanks, founders

[68] The English merchants referred to here were Henry Forrest and John Stavely. On their activities in Lower Burma see D. G. E. Hall, *Early English Intercourse with Burma, 1587–1743* (2d ed.; New York, 1968), pp. 35–43.

[69] They were Buddhist in religion and indifferent to the taboos of the Muslims, much to the relief of Methwold and his Christian contemporaries.

[70] He married a half-sister to keep the royal bloodline pure. This rule remained in effect among the Burman kings until 1885. Also see below, pp. 1144, 1165, 1227, n. 207.

[71] Certainly these regions were peopled in part by successive migratory waves of Tibeto-Burmese tribes from the north; also certain of the several states of modern Burma were occasionally vassals of China. Buddhism was no longer widely practiced in India but was widespread in China at Methwold's time, hence his erroneous assumption of its Chinese origin. Many of the early Europeans believed that the Chinese at one time controlled everything on the continent to the east of India and from the Philippines to Madagascar in the insular world. Methwold's report was first published by Purchas in 1626. For a twentieth-century edited version see Moreland (ed.), *op. cit.* (n. 66), pp. 42–49 (this is the edition quoted in the text above).

[72] His *Itinerario* was reprinted at Rome in 1653. The modern critical edition (in *"HS"*, 2d ser., LIX) was translated and edited by C. E. Luard and H. Hosten, S.J., *Travels of Fray Sebastien Manrique, 1629–43* (2 vols.; Oxford, 1927); Vol. I is on Arakan. Also see M. Collis, *The Land of the Great Image, Being Experiences of Friar Manrique in Arakan* (New York, 1943). For the appraisal of Manrique's work quoted above, see D. G. E. Hall, *A History of South-East Asia* (2d ed.; London, 1964), p. 373.

early in 1629 on the shoals of Chandekhan to the east of the Hugli River in
the Ganges delta. After a series of misadventures with the local authorities,
the friar and his companions are taken to the Augustinian residence at Hugli,
the Ganges port founded by Portuguese traders in the time of Akbar.[73] On
September 11, 1629, he is sent by his superiors to the port of Dianga, the
Portuguese-dominated military and naval outpost in Arakan where the Augustinians maintain a church and a residence. Left alone for nineteen months
in this remote town, Manrique quickly becomes involved in the local troubles
revolving about a new governor of Chittagong who was hostile to the Portuguese employed in Arakan as royal soldiers and slave-hunters. In letters of
1630 to King Thirithudhamma at Mrauk-u, the governor accuses the Portuguese at Dianga of conspiring to throw Chittagong province open to the
Mughul viceroy of Dacca. To prevent this, the king prepares a huge armada
to attack the Portuguese at Dianga. Through native Christians the Portuguese learn of these preparations and decide to send emissaries to the court
at Mrauk-u to convince the king that the governor is lying and that the Portuguese remain loyal to Arakan.[74]

Accompanied by Captain Sebastião Gonçalves Tibão, son of the notorious pirate king, Manrique embarks early in 1630 on a galley despite the
heavy monsoonal rains and winds. Three days later he arrives at Ramu, a
town whose governor advises the Portuguese to abandon sea travel in favor
of a dangerous land route over the mountains to Peroem on the Mayu
River. From here, inland waterways may then be followed into Mrauk-u.
While living in constant fear of tigers and wild elephants, they desperately
traverse a series of lofty and rock-strewn ranges. On the final summit of
"the Range of the Pora" they see a shrine cut in the rock, in which a stone
image sits "with the legs crossed, in the manner in which Orientals usually
sit."[75] Manrique and the Muslims of the company watch disapprovingly
while the Arakanese prostrate themselves and offer thanks to this idol for
"their safe passage across the mountains." These rituals having been observed, Manrique and his companions descend the mountains on their elephants and ride through the lowland rice fields into Peroem.[76]

On the next day the governor of Peroem sends two "Ceriones" (Talaing
[Mon], *saren,* or palanquins) to carry the emissaries to him. Following local

---

[73] See above, pp. 678–84 for Manrique on Bengal and Hugli.
[74] Luard and Hosten (trans. and eds.), *op. cit.* (n. 72), Vol. I, chaps. i–xi.
[75] "Pora" is Arakanese *Hpura,* a term of respect used to address persons and things of special
sanctity or dignity. The images of Buddha are usually so designated. See H. Yule and A. C.
Burnell, *Hobson-Jobson* (rev. ed.; London, 1968), pp. 728–29.
[76] Luard and Hosten (trans. and eds.), *op. cit.* (n. 72), Vol. I, chaps. xii–xiii. Manrique, always impatient with pagan practices, was evidently unaware that the "Pora" was an image of
the Buddha and that he was entering a Buddhist kingdom. *Cf.* the journey of Father A.
Farinha, S.J., from Dianga to Mrauk-u in 1639–40. Included in a Jesuit Annual Letter of 1640
from Cochin, it was published in English translation by H. Hosten in *ibid.,* pp. 172–75.

custom the Portuguese send ahead exotic gifts of "four fair-sized gilt Chinese trays filled with cloves, cinnamon, pepper and cardamoms." Once in his presence they are courteously offered betel "as is usual in most parts of India" when receiving "persons of position." After informing him of their mission, the governor orders his "Coram" (*koran*), a police official, to find a galley to carry them across the "gulf of Maum," as the mouth of the Mayu River was then known. Haste becomes imperative to the Portuguese when they learn in Peroem that an Arakanese fleet is being readied at the port of "Orietan" (Urritaung, now Ponnagyun) to sail against Dianga at the first favorable moment. After a terrible crossing of the broad mouth of the Mayu River, they make it to Urritaung and the camp of the admiral. In an interview with this officer they assure him that the Portuguese of Dianga have not betrayed Arakan and that they have sent their vicar as a hostage to the king as proof of their innocence. The admiral informs them that the king is not at Mrauk-u but on pilgrimage at the shrine of Mahamuni, "the home of the most important of their false gods."[77]

On boats provided by the admiral they wind their way inland on the waterways running through the rice plain of Arakan. Monkeys cavort in the trees lining the waterways and in the brush an occasional rhinoceros or a bevy of peacocks is glimpsed. Progress is slowed by the houseboats and numerous smaller craft crowding the waterways and landing places. During two months of the summer, the king of Arakan usually travels these lowlands in a "floating palace" of bamboo in which he carries on his business of governing "as he would have on dry land." Divided into living rooms, bedrooms, dressing rooms, and reception rooms, this "floating pleasure house [is] a thing of wonder." Still more astonishing is "the sight of Cities moving along the river" which is produced by the boats of the courtiers and officials who accompany the king on his rounds.[78] Unable to proceed further by water, Manrique sends one of his guides overland with a communication to the king. While awaiting a response, he is visited by Japanese Christians who serve in the royal guard. Not having seen a priest for seven years, the Japanese receive the missionary with great awe and reverence. While discoursing with the Japanese, a "Puchique" (*Bo-sikke*, or comptroller-general) appears with a warm message of welcome from the king and with assurances that Manrique will be granted an audience. He and his companion are then taken in the official's barge to the precincts of Mahamuni, where they are feted at a banquet. This feast "in the Magh style" is served in "some hundreds of small dishes" containing "ordinary rational articles of food [as well as] others of a disgusting nature" such as rats, snakes, and rotten fish. To all

---

[77] *Ibid.*, chap. xiv. For a detailed description of the Mahamuni shrine and a ground plan see Collis, *op. cit.* (n. 72), chap. xv.

[78] These floating cities made their stately progress by the tidal movements in the rivers and creeks. See Collis, *op. cit.* (n. 72), p. 119.

their dishes they add a garnish called "Sidol" (Arakanese, *sahtol*), a dry and malodorous kind of paste made of decomposed fish and shrimp laced with condiments.[79] The following day the emissaries prepare their gifts for presentation to the king: a crown of cloves, a box of bottled Persian scents, fourteen packets of "Catayan" (Tibetan) musk,[80] and four yards of green Spanish woolen cloth. While awaiting a call to the royal audience, Manrique outfits a chapel, celebrates mass, and inquires about the number and condition of the Christians in Arakan. The audience is delayed until King Thirithudhamma completes a ritual fast and consults his "Raulins" (Burmese, *rahan,* or priests) about an auspicious day and time to meet the foreigners. On July 31 he is advised to wait until the next day, when food is ordinarily sent to "the Idol." Once this is done, he must release nine birds to "go ahead and offer his fast to Pora."[81] The king then makes a pilgrimage to "the Idol" accompanied by his courtiers and priests. On his return he orders the "Puchique" to usher the Portuguese into his presence after dinner.[82]

On August 1, 1630, the Portuguese are carried to the royal palace in palanquins in the company of the "Puchique." They pass through three halls before arriving at the audience chamber. Here the "Puchique" knocks three times on its door to announce their arrival. After they have knelt before the door "for over half an hour in complete silence," a beautiful young maiden appears in the wicket above the door to welcome them. The door is then opened by "matronly women" who conduct them into the young king's presence. Immediately the "Puchique" prostrates himself three times and the others follow suit.[83] Then the Portuguese are permitted to approach the king, who is seated at a window. At this moment, their gifts are brought in "by some eunuchs"; the king accepts the presents without comment. Through a Portuguese interpreter the king inquires about their mission. Following court etiquette punctiliously, Manrique reminds the king of the good and mutually beneficial relations which the Portuguese have long enjoyed with his predecessors and himself. He discourses on the loyalty of the Portuguese and of their contributions to the defense of Arakan "against the

---

[79] The equivalent of the Burmese *nga-pi,* this fish sauce is still added to rice and vegetable dishes throughout Southeast Asia. For the preparation and use of *nga-pi* see J. George Scott, *Burma: A Handbook of Practical Information* (London, 1911), p. 211; and S. Yoe, *The Burman, His Life and Notions* (London, 1910), pp. 280–85. On its use in Vietnam see below, p. 1259. See A. Reid, *Southeast Asia in the Age of Commerce, 1450–1680,* Vol. I, *The Lands below the Winds* (New Haven, 1988), p. 29.

[80] "Cathay" was often used as a name for Tibet in the travel accounts. On the confusion over the location of "Cathay" see below, pp. 1575–78.

[81] The release of captive birds and other animals is a common Theravadin method used to win merit.

[82] Luard and Hosten (trans. and eds.), *op. cit.* (n. 72), I, 124–42. King Thirithudhamma climbed to the shrine at the top of Mount Sirigutta to offer his devotions. See Collis, *op. cit.* (n. 72), p. 126.

[83] This is the ceremonial *shi-ko.* It requires kneeling with the hands clasped above the head and falling forward to touch the forehead to the ground.

mighty power of the Mogol" and refers to the repopulation of its territories with captives taken in the Bay of Bengal. Throughout many troubled years the Portuguese have turned aside the blandishments of the Mughuls and have remained unswerving in their fidelity to Arakan. This being true, "as you know that it is," how is it possible for you to believe the allegations of the governor of Chittagong against the Portuguese? The king, who probably had the matter investigated before the audience, acknowledges the truth of Manrique's statements and agrees to order his fleet's recall.

After sending a special messenger off to Dianga with this good news, Manrique pays ceremonial visits and expresses his gratitude to the court council and to "Prince Longaraja" (*Loka-raja*, or Ruler of the World), the person next in importance to the members of the royal family. He is again received in audience by the king, to whom he presents a letter from the Augustinian provincial in India. The missionary reassures the ruler that the Portuguese in India have been expressly commanded by Lisbon to support kingdoms fighting the Mughuls, "the common enemy of all." At Manrique's request the king promises to cashier the governor of Chittagong, who had falsely accused the Portuguese of disloyalty, to liberate the Christians held captive in "Cuami" (Khemi village on the Kaladan River), and to permit the erection of a church in the Christian quarter of his capital city. Once *farmans* are issued to effect these orders, the Christian captives are entrusted to Manrique. He then departs for Mrauk-u, accompanied by his European, Indian, and Japanese followers. As they approach the capital, they are festively greeted by the Portuguese and other European residents of the city. Arriving in he city itself, they are received "by the rest of the Christian community with every sign of goodwill."[84]

Once established in a house in the Christian quarter, Manrique begins to minister to the local Christians. Within five days' time, he hears the confessions of 89 persons and baptizes 227, including 160 adults. At this juncture he falls deathly ill of fever and is forced to remain in bed for the next three months (August to November, 1630). In the meantime the Christians begin to erect a church of bamboo and wood, which is dedicated on the third Sunday in October, an event attended by many important pagans. Even the king admits to Manrique of hearing about "the great tamaxa [Arabian, *tamasha*, or celebration] . . . held in the varela [temple] of your Quiay [Javanese, *kiaï*, a term of respect]."[85] The missionary takes this opportunity to proclaim the Christian God as universal and to revile the brazen images worshipped by the king. Two Buddhist priests indignantly inquire as to why the Christians refuse to respect their images and have the audacity to proclaim their faith as the only true one. One seeks to explain the place of paradise or salvation in the Burmese cosmology and the other discourses on

---

[84]Luard and Hosten (trans. and eds.), *op. cit.* (n. 72), I, 142–63.
[85]For the derivation of "Quiay" as "god" see S. R. Dalgado, *Glossário Luso-Asiático* (2 vols.; Coimbra, 1919, 1921), I, 236.

transmigration—neither makes much of an impression on the religious ideas of the Augustinian friar! At a later audience Manrique is successful in having the former Christian captives taken into royal service and put on salary.

Since no Christian priests had worked in Arakan for seven years, Manrique undertakes a visitation of the Christians settled there. He is appalled to find some of them practicing concubinage, a condition submissively accepted both by the married women and the concubines. By threatening excommunication, he is able to force the termination of some of these illicit unions. Other earlier converts and neophytes continue to practice idolatry and to "mingle certain pagan ceremonies with Catholic rites in their public observances." To minimize their contacts with pagan pollution, he seeks to bring all Christians into their own communities despite the growing opposition of the Portuguese and the king to his high-handedness. He learns a new and more subtle tactic from the queen herself, a native of Pegu who had flirted with Christianity in her youth. She suggests that he ask the king to permit him to engage some servants for his new church, a grant which would parallel the practice of assigning pagoda slaves to a newly completed Buddhist temple.[86] After making a ceremonial visit of gratitude to the queen, Manrique quickly contrives a way of presenting to the king a petition of the sort she advised. He attends a festival at which the king appears with his two sons to celebrate the arrival of two baby elephants. Armed with mechanical toys for the children, Manrique grasps this occasion as an opportunity to present his petition. The king, surrounded by domestic joy and bliss, quickly agrees to permit the Augustinian to select as many temple servants as are needed. After due deliberation he chooses eighteen Christians to come with their families to live near the church on land and in houses purchased by a subscription raised from the faithful Christians of Arakan.[87]

Mrauk-u, the capital of the Mughs, is estimated as of 1630 to have a population of 160,000, not counting foreign merchants and soldiers.[88] It stands in a lovely valley wholly enclosed "by high rocky mountains which serve as natural fortifications." Forts provided with artillery command the passes into the mountains and the roads which lead into the valley. A swift river (the Lemro) flows through the city, whose numerous branches form a network of deep waterways and are "the principal means of traffic, both public and private."[89] At the two mouths of this river stand settlements of foreign

[86] The "queen" was Lady Htwe Naung, the Grand Dowager since 1622. See Collis, *op. cit.* (n. 72), p. 175. On religious slaves see V. B. Lieberman, "The Political Significance of Religious Wealth in Burmese History: Some Further Thoughts," *Journal of Asian Studies*, XXXIX (1980), 761.

[87] Luard and Hosten (trans. and eds.), *op. cit.* (n. 72), I, 163–204.

[88] M. S. Collis, who surveyed the ruins of this old city early in the twentieth century, considers this estimate to be "quite possible." See his article on "The City of Golden Mrauk-U," in *Journal of the Burma Research Society*, XIII (1923), 245.

[89] Although it was sixty miles from the sea, the largest oceangoing vessels of the time could go upstream to dock at Mrauk-u (*ibid.*, p. 244).

merchants, most of whom are Muslims. Movements in this river basin are governed by the tides, which rush into and retreat from the city with great force. Most houses in the city are thatched bamboo and wood structures held together by "Bengal canes, as we call them in Portugal [*cana da Bengala*]." The size and ornamentation of these houses vary with the station and means of the builder. Bamboo houses with wooden supports will last for twelve to fifteen years. In the interiors they hang mat walls "of the finest texture and of many colors." The better houses and palaces have rooms of wood "ornamented with carving, gilt mouldings, and enamel work in various tints."

Even the royal palaces "are made of these reedy materials," although they include great wooden pillars which are often gilded. Some palaces boast rooms of sandal or other aromatic woods. One rich palace includes a "House of Gold," a pavilion decorated from floor to ceiling in that precious metal. Within this chamber stand seven golden idols ornamented with precious stones as well as eight golden vessels and nine dishes. Here they also keep the famous "Chanequas" (earrings) of Toungoo in a golden casket. These ruby jewels, over which so much blood has been spilled in Burma, are worn only at coronations or at "some especially solemn feast." In one of the inner courtyards is the bronze statue of Tabinshwehti, founder of the Toungoo dynasty (r. 1531–50), which was also carried away to Mrauk-u after the defeat of Toungoo.[90] Held in great reverence, this statue reputedly has the power to cure dysentery. Close to the royal palace there is an artificial lake dotted with islands on which the native priests and monks live. In addition to the Portuguese, there are many Asian Christians in the city "of Japanese, Bengali, and of other nationalities."[91]

The four nations of Burma—Mughs (Arakanese), Peguans, Burmese, and the people of Ava—as well as many of their neighbors, are pagans who belong to various sects. While not in agreement on the number of such sects, they all believe "that salvation can be attained through any of them." The priests and monks of all sects are usually called "Raulins" (Burmese, *Rahan*). They are of three types: "Pungrins" (Arakanese, *Pongyi,* a fully ordained monk), "Panjans" (*Pazin,* fully ordained monks without a monastery), and the clerical are the "Mozans" (*Maung-shin* or novices).[92] All wear yellow robes and shave their heads; the "Pungrins" also wear a yellow tiara. They take a vow of chastity; violators are disgraced, defrocked, become subject to secular law, and are required to pay taxes.[93] All orders of monks in

[90] These were all a part of the Siamese loot acquired when Arakan defeated Toungoo in 1599–1600.

[91] Luard and Hosten (trans. and eds.), *op. cit.* (n. 72), I, 205–20. Also see the accompanying plans of Mrauk-u reproduced from those published by Collis in connection with his article cited above (n. 88).

[92] For the modern hierarchy of monks in Burma see M. E. Spiro, *Buddhism and Society. A Great Tradition and Its Burmese Vicissitudes* (New York, 1970), pp. 310–11.

[93] The *Vinaya* (Rule) stresses celibacy, and the modern Burmese see it as the basic feature

Arakan recognize a primate called the "Xoxom Pungri."[94] He is venerated by all, and even the emperor prostrates himself before this primate.

Many "Raulins" live in temples and monasteries. Some of these are as sumptuous as palaces and richly endowed by founders, who were important persons, even kings, seeking to gain merit. The sons of princes and other men of high station are educated by the "Raulins" in these monasteries and temples. Lesser men send their sons for instruction to monks who live outside such institutions. Education stresses the learning of "correct customs" and literature.[95] Arakanese have many good customs, the most conspicuous of which is charity. Their houses are always open to wayfarers of all classes; "indeed a Raulin's house is the same as a public hospice."[96] Besides the "Raulins" there are religious hermits who live in lonely and deserted places "like anchorites and cenobites."[97] All monks, and especially those who live as hermits, are venerated as saints by laymen.

Burmese keep idols in their homes to whom "they daily offer part of their own meals"; some also send out food to the idols in the temples.[98] Even the kings send food to the temple "Pora" (Buddha) each day before dining. The royal gift of food is carried on litters by men "specially deputed for this work." They are led to the temple by musicians playing instruments. Food is placed before the idol and prayers are recited by one of the temple "Raulins." Then the priests take up the food and "appropriate it to themselves." All "Raulins" except the primate go barefoot at all times. These priests and monks try to cure the sick with prayers or by propitiating the responsible gods and spirits by sacrificing domestic animals. Persons who recover perform ritual dances before the appeased god and anoint with oil the gods of the temple. In the cold season, idols "standing in the open country" are likewise anointed, and pieces of cloths are tied on them to secure the god's protection for the devotee.[99]

Deceased persons lie in state in "the center of their houses" until they are taken out on a bier for cremation. "Raulins" meanwhile sing death chants and the most important members of the family watch the body while "striking a gong all the time." Precautions are thus taken to prevent a black cat from crossing the corpse and forcing it back into life. Before removing the corpse from the house, it is customary to provide a banquet for the crows "on behalf of the dead man's soul." If the crows fail to eat the food set out,

---

of monastic morality. While few, violators are still expelled from their orders. See *ibid.,* pp. 366–69.

[94] "Xoxom" is possibly a corrupt form of Sitthaung. In Manrique's time the primate of Arakan was the head of the Sitthaung temple.

[95] For a vivid description of elementary education in a monastery see Scott, *op. cit.* (n. 79), pp. 366–67.

[96] On their hospitality and generosity see Spiro, *op. cit.* (n. 92), pp. 351–52.

[97] On the isolated monk in forest hermitages see *ibid.,* p. 54.

[98] On daily household rituals see *ibid.,* pp. 209–10.

[99] On protection rituals see *ibid.,* pp. 151–53.

the soul of the deceased is condemned to go to the "house of smoke, as they call hell." The corpse is placed in a big chest or on a funeral pyre, the size varying with the wealth of the deceased. Believing as they do in transmigration, they paint representations of the animal on the bier into which the deceased wishes for his soul to pass. The bier is then placed in an open spot and encircled with wood, odoriferous woods for those of high status and common woods for others. "Raulins" perfume the pyre while walking about it chanting hymns. After the corpse is reduced to ashes, the mourners, in white garb, pay visits to certain temples to anoint some of the idols. Because the idols are so numerous in the larger temples, it is not reasonably possible to anoint them all. Most of the temples are "pyramidal in shape," with a spire that "terminates in a gilt metal globe" on which small bells hang that tinkle in the wind. Temples are usually constructed of sun-dried bricks and their interiors decorated with "frescoes done in gold and colors." [100]

Like most foreign visitors to Southeast Asia, Manrique was intrigued by the importance attached to the white elephant. He was so fascinated by the stories about this beast that he studied its legendary past in "the ancient histories of the monarchy of the Bramas [Burmese]." After telling a rambling story about the white elephant as the moon's son and hence a deity, Manrique sees it as the symbol which gives a ruler his legitimacy and his right to rule the diverse peoples of Burma. Possession of the white elephant, whether it be god or devil, thus becomes the main object of those contending for power. Arakan invaded and conquered Pegu, and King Minyazagyi returned in 1600 with its treasures, the most precious of which in local estimation was the white elephant. Manrique himself observes "the adornment and service used towards the elephant." [101] Wherever it goes, even though only to a tank to bathe, the elephant is attended by servants and musicians in procession. On feast days it wears "a coat of the finest crimson velvet, edged with gold and embroidered with fair-sized pearls," as well as golden ornaments. [102]

The Muslim Mughuls, like the rulers of Southeast Asia, hoped to capture

[100] Luard and Hosten (trans. and eds.), *op. cit.* (n. 72), I, 220–31. In this section Manrique appears to have borrowed without acknowledgment from the descriptions of Mendes Pinto. On Pinto see *Asia*, I, 554–56. For Buddhist funeral rites in modern Burma *cf.* Spiro, *op. cit.* (n. 92), pp. 248–54. Manrique follows this description of popular Buddhism with an account of a festival commemorating the dead which he calls "Sansaporace" (full-moon feast?). This festival, a puzzling combination of Buddhist and Hindu practices, seems to derive entirely from Pinto's portrayal of a festival he had earlier observed in Toungoo.

[101] Collis, *op. cit.* (n. 72), p. 157, believes that this white elephant was one of four taken by the Burmese from Siam in 1563.

[102] Very little is known about the origin of the cult of the white elephant. It appears to derive from Hinduism; at least Brahmans were usually in charge of the white elephant in Buddhist courts. That the elephant was regarded as a symbol of royalty and universal sovereignty is beyond dispute. For example, when Minyazagyi returned to Arakan he triumphantly had medals struck proclaiming himself "Lord of the White Elephant." See *ibid.*, pp. 157–60. For Manrique's lengthy and confusing summary of the Burmese legends about the white elephant see Luard and Hosten (trans. and eds.), *op. cit.* (n. 72), I, 238–75.

the white elephant, as part of a sustained effort to extend their dominion eastward. Understanding these plans, the "idolatrous Magh" has contrived to seal off the land and sea entries to Arakan by retaining Portuguese in his service. He grants more than seven hundred of them revenue-producing lands with the understanding that they will always maintain ships and men in the Ganges delta to deter aggression by the Mughuls. The Augustinians began to work in the Portuguese settlements of Arakan and Pegu in 1621. In the process they made converts among the natives, especially the Bengalis. In January, 1631, Manrique returns from Mrauk-u to Dianga, the Christian center in the Ganges delta, with a royal order permitting him to bring together all its Christians from the vicinity of Chittagong at a fishing village close to Dianga called Angaracale. These are mostly Christianized Indian refugees employed by the Portuguese in their settlements. Many are married to non-Christian women who are reluctant to leave their homes and friends to live in a Christian sanctuary. Faced by this resistance, Manrique sends a woman convert and her husband "to convert these women and impress on them all they would gain by abandoning their false religion." While he builds a church at Angaracale, his female convert returns with "two hundred and twenty-three persons" whom she has saved from the "bonds of hell." In the thirteen years of Augustinian activity in the delta, Manrique claims that over sixteen thousand Indians were baptized, as well as more than five thousand others. Among others, they baptized and brought up as Christians two of the grandsons of Minyazagyi, the sons of the king's second son.[103]

In the autumn of 1633, after almost two years in Dianga, Manrique receives two letters which oblige him to return to Mrauk-u. One of the letters is from a Portuguese emissary sent from Goa to negotiate a treaty with Arakan; the other is from the Augustinian provincial of India asking Manrique to go to Mrauk-u to assist the legate in the negotiations. Despite Manrique's aid, the negotiations go on for five months and end inconclusively. The king, Thirithudhamma, possibly because he blamed Manrique for the failure of the negotiations, refuses to permit the Augustinian to leave his capital. Over the next fourteen months he is required to remain there without the company of other Catholic priests. He passes the time by ministering to the city's seven hundred Christians and by converting a few heathens; he also brings over to Catholicism two Europeans, a German Lutheran and a Belgian Anabaptist. His quiet life is interrupted one day by the arrival of a Buddhist priest who brings him a palm-leaf letter written in Latin. Its author is a Portuguese who had been shipwrecked off Arakan in 1608. He and

---

[103] Luard and Hosten (trans. and eds.), *op. cit.* (n. 72), I, 276–321 *passim*. The elder of the two princes was baptized in 1619 as Dom Martin. He served in the Portuguese navy based in Goa, and some time after 1640 was received at court in Lisbon by King John IV. Also see M. S. Collis and S. S. Ba, "Dom Martin, 1605–1643, the First Burman to Visit Europe," *Journal of the Burma Research Society*, Vol. XVI, Pt. 1 (1926), pp. 11–23.

a dozen companions were then taken prisoner and banished to the "mountains of Maum" (probably the Maumowe range near Arakan) west of the capital. The writer begs Manrique to visit him, and to baptize his wife, children, and the families of seven other Christians who live nearby. Since no one except the "Raulins" are permitted to visit this mountain prison, Manrique decides to don the yellow robe and to pretend to be the companion of the authentic monk who had brought him the letter. After a dangerous trip, he ministers to the imprisoned Christians and within six weeks is safely back in Mrauk-u by May, 1634.[104]

In the capital, shocking events were meanwhile unfolding. Thirithudhamma, king since 1622, had ruled for twelve years without coronation because of an old prophecy which claimed that he would die a year or so after being formally crowned. While Manrique was in the mountains, a Muslim physician had wormed his way into the king's confidence. This evil adviser had convinced the king that he might escape the prophecy by taking a secret elixir which would render him invisible and invincible. This magical elixir had to be made from "six thousand hearts of his own subjects, four thousand hearts of white cows, and two thousand from white doves." According to Manrique, cruelty of the sort here advocated is not unknown or uncommon to "Barbarian Monarchs." On the advice of their priests, they would often have fires secretly set in the cities to propitiate their idols. Those caught setting fires, even while following orders to do so, would usually be impaled as a public example of royal justice being done. After a brief hesitation, Thirithudhamma orders the execution of six thousand of his own subjects. For several months terror reigns in the city and its environs, the people being "driven to the point of revolt." The holocaust finally ends with the discharge of cannon from the palace walls and a declaration that the coronation will take place six months from that date.[105]

In the ensuing half year the inhabitants of the capital seem to forget the "sad past" as they festively prepare for the coronation ceremonies by putting on "preliminary displays." Sacred water is fetched from the Ganges to be used ceremonially to purify the king before he receives "the Imperial Crown." Meanwhile the great nobles and governors congregate in Mrauk-u to attend the coronations of twelve minor "kings" who must be crowned before the imperial investment can take place.[106] Each of these lesser coronations lasts for eight days. On the first day of the first ceremony the notables of the realm, including Manrique and the Portuguese, assemble in a "vast

---

[104] Luard and Hosten (trans. and eds.), *op. cit.* (n. 72), I, 322–50.

[105] *Ibid.*, pp. 351–61. For an elaboration on this horror story see Collis, *op. cit.* (n. 72), pp. 210–16. On its possible historicity see Harvey, *op. cit.* (n. 66), p. 144, n. 317.

[106] Arakan was then divided into twelve provinces each ruled by a governor. Each governor had to be elevated to the level of kingship if Thirithudhamma were to realize his plan of becoming an emperor with vassal rulers. See Collis, *op. cit.* (n. 72), pp. 219–20. *Cf.* R. Heine-Geldern, "Concepts of State and Kingship in Southeast Asia," *The Far Eastern Quarterly,* II (1942–43), 15–30.

hall" of the royal court to witness the investing of Prince Toon-htan, governor of Urritaung. Thirithudhamma himself presides over the ceremony on
an elevated throne. He is assisted by thirty priests who encircle the throne.[107]
The proceedings commence with a concert by three groups of instrumentalists who accompany singers chanting in the Mugh, Burman, and Pegu
dialects. After an hour of this music, twenty-four female dancers, some
playing instruments, perform with "the greatest skill and dexterity." They
are followed by twelve young girls, each of whom carries a crown in her
hand which she lays at the king's feet. Twelve others then enter to deposit
golden scepters at the ruler's feet. Prince Toon-htan, "a gallant youth," appears and is preceded by forty handsome attendants. Prostrate before his
king, the young prince is raised up by four priests who lead him to the first
step of the throne. While he again prostrates himself, three new priests enter, one holding a golden idol. Thirithudhamma respectfully arises and
stands to one side to allow the chief priest to take his seat. The prince is then
brought up to the throne by the two acolytes where he makes seven prostra-
tions. Then he takes the idol in his hands, places it on his head, and while
kneeling down repeats an oath of loyalty "to his true Emperor and Lord."
The king then regains his throne while a priest celebrates his coming grandeur as "the most brilliant ornament among all the Kings of the earth." The
prince kneels before the king to receive his crown and scepter. With the
crown on his head and the scepter in his left hand, he kisses the king's feet
five times in recognition of "his true Sovereign."

At the coronation's end, the king retires and the celebration begins. Manrique, worn out by the long ceremony, reluctantly agrees to participate in
the riotous procession to the new "king's" palace. After traversing the chief
streets of the city, the parade, dominated by the elephants, arrives at the palace at dusk to be greeted by a "tremendous salute" and by torch-bearing
courtiers. The banquet hall is decorated with silk hangings and rich rugs and
lighted by lamps hanging from the ceiling in which burn "precious, sweet-
smelling oils." The new "king" sits at the end of the hall under a canopy
flanked by two eminent officials. All the banqueters sit on the floor, each
with a little table before him on which "five or six porcelain dishes are
placed." The food brought on silver trays includes every kind of meat imaginable as well as sweets "made after their own fashion," which are quite palatable. After many hours of eating, women dancers clad in diaphanous
garments entertain until just before sunrise. Then all go home "very weary
and peevish."

Over the next week the celebrations for the first "king" continue. Similar
ceremonies and festivities are then held in turn for each of the other eleven
"kings," thus crowding more than three months with pomp and gaiety. In

---

[107] Probably the court Brahmans who were in charge of all state ceremonies. Collis, *op. cit.*
(n. 72), p. 220.

the meantime merchants from the surrounding countries and commercial centers flock to Mrauk-u, where they may sell during these coronations all their goods free of duty. They "form streets of shops" in which to sell "every kind of merchandise" at low prices. While guards keep the crowd of shoppers orderly, entertainments preserve a festive air in the market during the day while the evenings are brightened by illuminations and fireworks. Preparations meanwhile go ahead for the imperial coronation, the streets being decked in gold and silver cloths. In the center of each street gilded triumphal arches are erected in whose niches stand wooden and metal idols wearing crowns which symbolize the religious character of the coronation. Finally, the royal palace is festooned with colored banners, pennant, and flags.

The imperial coronation is held on January 23, 1635, a bright summery day. All the princes and nobles, as well as the Portuguese resident in the capital, assemble early in the morning in the great ceremonial hall of the royal palace. Its golden roof, "ornamented with flowers in various colors," is supported by thirty gilded pillars.[108] The hall is open on three sides; the fourth side is shut off from view by a rich tapestry. In the center of the hall stands a silver-plated and embossed arch which is "closed by a curtain of green satin" covered with golden embroideries and encrusted with precious stones. Once all are seated on rich carpets, the festivities commence with five drumrolls, five strokes of a bell, and a cannonade that lasts for fully one-half hour. When silence again reigns, three drumbeats sound, all prostrate themselves, and the curtain flies open to reveal a silver throne resting on the backs of four silver elephants. On their upraised trunks the elephants support a green velvet canopy that is embroidered with "pearl sprays" and fringed with gold and bunches of pearls. Seated on the throne, the king wears a long coat of blue velvet covered with pearls and in his ears the two precious rubies of Toungoo. Below his sandal-covered feet, the twelve lesser "kings" kneel on the throne's steps with their crowns on their heads and their scepters in their hands. Behind the king stand two ladies-in-waiting dressed in white satin who alternately fan him. At this juncture the Master of Ceremonies asks the Portuguese captain, who wears an artificial silver hand, to withdraw from the hall so the coronation rites can proceed.[109]

A priest inaugurates the ceremony by performing certain rituals. Then he exhorts the assemblage for over an hour to pray for the sanctification of the king as an emperor whose rule will be "just, pious, and equitable." Describing how the king listens impassively to the praises lavished on him, Manrique piously prophesies that a ruler who listens to flatterers may end up as badly as this king who "a few years after his coronation died a violent

---

[108] All traces of these palace buildings have since disappeared. See *ibid.*, p. 229.
[109] Persons with physical defects were often considered to be omens of evil on ritual occasions in the East.

death."[110] Once the coronation sermon ends, a grand procession is formed to escort the king to the temple of the "Xoxom Pungri" (Sitthaung head priest, or pontiff of Arakan).[111] The king's palanquin, borne by eight youths in green velvet, proceeds through the silent crowd along a path carpeted and partially enclosed by cotton sheets of various colors.[112] At the temple's entrance he is met by the head priest and two thousand yellow-robed priests and monks. After the king enters the door, only believers are permitted to follow him into the temple. The Muslims and the Portuguese, including Manrique, are courteously told that they must remain outside the temple's sacred precincts. The coronation ceremony lasts for two hours, until several strokes of a bell signal its end. Following a loud and lengthy artillery salute, the Portuguese are free to enter the temple's courtyard to watch the imperial exit. Wearing his new jewel-studded crown, the emperor mounts a tall elephant on which he sits under a white umbrella of state. Umbrellas or parasols are "one of the insignia of Imperial rank" and "no one else can own one." A man's rank in this hierarchy may be discerned by the color of the shaft on his umbrella.[113] Preceded by an honor guard of two hundred armed elephants, the ruler and the twelve lesser "kings" ride in style while the princes and nobles walk behind in two lengthy files. When passing under the triumphal arches the procession is showered with flowers from the "clouds" mounted on them, is serenaded with songs in praise of the ruler, and is presented with insignia symbolizing various virtues. Most striking are the bejeweled royal ladies and princesses who, "although of dusky hue," are quite as beautiful as "our own European ladies with their fair skins and delicate complexions." Back in the royal palace, the new emperor is greeted by the new empress, who is both his wife and eldest sister. To conclude the day the imperial couple stand in a window and throw to the people silver money "especially coined for this purpose."[114]

While Arakan celebrated the coronation in peace, the rest of Burma retreated into isolation. The rulers of the restored Toungoo dynasty, after securing their frontiers with Siam, had retired after 1635 to Ava and Upper Burma. Trade and diplomatic relations with the Western nations thereafter virtually ceased in Lower Burma; the government at Ava concentrated on internal problems as power slipped gradually from the king's hands into those of his ministers. What trade existed was carried on intermittently by Dutch and English merchants at Syriam and Ava. Representatives of both

---

[110] For details behind the plot which ended in the murder of Thirithudhamma in 1638 see Collis, *op. cit.* (n. 72), chap. xxx.

[111] Sitthaung pagoda remains today structurally intact. See *ibid.*, p. 229. For photographs of its exterior and a sculptured wall of the interior see *Report of the Superintendent, Archaeological Survey, Burma* (Rangoon, 1921), Pl. I, figs. 1–2.

[112] A so-called Spirit Road.

[113] On the varieties of official umbrellas see S. Yoe, *op. cit.* (n. 79), pp. 409–10. Actually a man's class or rank was distinguished by the patterns on the handle.

[114] Luard and Hosten (trans. and eds.), *op. cit.* (n. 72), I, 362–92.

East India companies stayed on in hopes of establishing trade with western China by way of the "old Burma road." The Dutch had begun to trade at Arakan in 1623, their vessels from Batavia going there irregularly to buy rice and Bengali slaves taken by the marauding *feringhi* of the Bay. A trade treaty between Arakan and Batavia was concluded in 1653 by which the Dutch were to enjoy duty-free trade under royal license. This trade continued successfully until 1665 when the Mughuls took Dianga and Chittagong and exterminated the Arakanese fleet. After this defeat, Arakan, having lost its profits from piracy and trade, declined rapidly.[115]

Wouter Schouten (1638–1704), a Dutch sailor-merchant of some renown, was in Arakan for four months at the end of 1660 and the beginning of 1661. He returned to Amsterdam in 1665, and eleven years later the journal of his Eastern experiences from 1658 to 1665 was published at Amsterdam as *Oost-Indische voyagie. . . .*[116] In late 1660, he reports, the little Dutch fleet of three vessels with which he is traveling rides out a dreadful storm, known to the natives as the "Elephant of the Bay of Bengal." On the way into port, Schouten passes "Orijenton" (Urritaung), a city famous for its pagodas and as a place of pilgrimage. At Akyab Gerard van Voorburg, the chief Dutch factor in Arakan, meets the fleet at the "Bandel" (Portuguese corruption of *bandar,* meaning the "harbor" or "wharf") in his "Lakno" (a small galley). At the Dutch factory the newcomers are formally greeted by the "Sikkan" (?), or royal councillors, who accept the letter of introduction addressed to the king and depart for Mrauk-u in their "ijeliasen" (galleasses) or light, fast boats.

After several days pass, the Dutch are permitted to go in formal procession to the royal palace, led by an Arakanese governor on a great elephant and accompanied by musicians.[117] There they present gifts to the king of lacquerworks, mirrors, and fine spices and receive Arakan cloths in return. The king is about twenty-eight years old, heavy-set, and almost white in color. He is dressed in scarlet with a bejeweled turban on his head, great golden rings on his arms, and costly jewelry in his ears and around his neck.[118] Every five years, generally on November 15, the king emerges from the palace, tours the city, and publicly accepts an oath of fealty from his subjects. Once the formal reception is over, Schouten and his friends have time to go sightseeing while awaiting their cargo of rice.

---

[115] Based on Hall, *op. cit.* (n. 72), pp. 357–62, 375–79.

[116] For bibliographical detail see above, pp. 496–97. What follows is based on a reissue of Schouten's work entitled *Reistogt naar en door Ostindien* (two parts, 4th ed.; Amsterdam, 1780). A summary of Schouten's account of Arakan is in A. F. Prevost (comp.), *Histoire générale des voyages* (16 vols.; Paris, 1764–91), XI, 277–85.

[117] For a detailed description of this procession translated from the *Daghregister* see D. G. E. Hall, "Studies in Dutch Relations with Arakan," *Journal of the Burma Research Society,* Vol. XXVI, Pt. 1 (1936), p. 21.

[118] This was the king known as Sandathudamma (r. 1652–84), one of the most famous rulers of Arakan and an ally of the Dutch. For a brief biography see J. M. Maring and E. G. Maring, *Historical and Cultural Dictionary of Burma* (Metuchen, N.J., 1973), p. 212.

Arakan's cities, towns, and villages are heavily populated. Mrauk-u, the royal capital, is of about the same area as Amsterdam, but more populous. It is also one of the richest cities of Asia. Arakan is crowded because of its favorable climate, punishments for leaving the country, and lack of interest in seafaring. Foreigners come in large numbers for trade and employment. Many Muslims live permanently as artisans at the "Bandel," and others come annually to buy elephants for India and Persia. Three miles from the capital live the Portuguese who are employed by the king as soldiers and sailors.[119] Some are married to Portuguese women and others to Arakanese who have become converts to Catholicism. Arakan's fort, where many of the Portuguese work, looks out on a vast plain by the river.[120] The natives are heathens called "Mogen" (Mughs), who highly respect monks and monasteries. The king's harem is replenished annually with twelve beautiful girls who are quite white.

Much of Schouten's account is concerned with the "Bengal Prince" and his entourage who appeared in Mrauk-u on August 26, 1660, or several months before the Dutch author arrived there.[121] The exiled prince immediately becomes a political liability to Arakan. He and his suite are lodged outside the city and kept in isolation. His followers come from India to join him and run riot in the capital upon being told to leave. Further confrontations occur, but Schouten leaves Arakan before the problem is resolved. Eventually the war between Arakan and the Mughuls led to the withdrawal of the Dutch in 1665.[122]

3

CAMBODIA AND LAOS

Thai attacks on Lovek, the capital of Cambodia, in the later years of the sixteenth century had induced its king to appeal for help to Manila. After the fall of Lovek to the Thais in 1594, certain of the Spanish had boldly taken over positions of power in Cambodia and had begun to call upon Manila and Madrid to undertake conquests in continental Southeast Asia. In Manila hotbloods of church and state envisaged the establishment of a protectorate over Cambodia as a first step to the conversion and conquest of Indochina

---

[119] See the plan of Mrauk-u in Collis, *op. cit.* (n. 72), p. 145. See also our pl. 243.
[120] Located on the east side of the city, the fort was designed to thwart an invasion from Burma. See *ibid.*, p. 144.
[121] This prince was Shah Shujah, the second son of the deposed Shah Jahan. Shujah, governor of Bengal since 1637, resisted his brother Aurangzib's usurpation and was defeated in 1660 by Mir Jumla. For these events see above, pp. 704–5.
[122] Schouten, *op. cit.* (n. 116), Pt. I, pp. 103–56. The discussion of the problem posed by Shujah is found on pp. 122–45.

and China. While Madrid debated these proposals, the Spanish in the field continued their political and military machinations. Aroused by these activities, the Cambodians and their Malay-Muslim mercenaries massacred the handful of Spanish at Phnom Penh in July, 1599. Thereafter the Thais gradually established a protectorate over Cambodia and set up Barom Reachea IV (r. 1603–18) as its new king. Over the course of the seventeenth century, Cambodia retained a degree of independence by playing off the Vietnamese against the Thai. As for the Europeans, they had to limit their activities to intermittent trading and missionary activity.[123]

Because of the Iberian involvements in the affairs of Cambodia, the European sources published in the first half of the century are Spanish and Portuguese accounts which relate largely to the possibilities of conquest. The earliest seventeenth-century references to Cambodia are contained in the Franciscan Ribadeneira's *Historia* (Barcelona, 1601). From his informants he learned about the ruins of Angkor and is the first European, to our knowledge, who published notices of them.[124] But the most influential of these Spanish writings was the *Breve y verdadera relacion de los sucesos del Reyno de Camboxa* (Valladolid, 1604) by the Dominican father Gabriel Quiroga de San Antonio (d. 1608).[125] While he had spent nine years (1595–1603) working in the East, San Antonio apparently did not visit Cambodia during that time. Most of what he knew he learned from informants in Manila, Malacca, Goa, and Spain. In Valladolid he associated himself with the interventionists led by Pedro Sevil, a veteran of the first Cambodian campaign who had published a memorial in 1603 advocating new military action in Cambodia.[126] In 1609 two additional books relating to this subject were published in Mexico and Madrid, the first by an official based in the Philippines, Antonio de Morga, and the second by a royal propagandist, Bartolomé

---

[123] On the Iberians in Cambodia in the sixteenth century see *Asia*, I, 309–12, 565–70. Also see C. R. Boxer, "The Spaniards in Cambodia," *History Today*, XXI (1971), 280–87; and D. P. Chandler, *A History of Cambodia* (Boulder, Colorado, 1983), pp. 80–87.

[124] See the Spanish text as reprinted in P. G. Fernandez (trans.), *op. cit.* (n. 7), I, 169, 181–82. Do Couto had written, possibly earlier than Ribadeneira, a description of Angkor. It was first published in the twentieth century by B. P. Groslier and C. R. Boxer in *Angkor et le Cambodge au XVIᵉ siècle d'après les sources portugaises et espagnoles* (Paris, 1958), pp. 68–74.

[125] The original has been reproduced and translated into French in A. Cabaton (trans. and ed.), *Brève et véridique relation des événéments du Cambodge par Gabriel Quiroga de San Antonio . . .* (Paris, 1914). For a critique of Cabaton's edition see Groslier and Boxer, *op. cit.* (n. 124), pp. 84–86.

[126] His *Conquista de Champan, Camboja, Siam, Cochinchina y otros paises de Oriente* is translated into French in A. Cabaton (ed.), "Le mémorial de Pedro Sevil [de Guarga] à Philippe III . . . *Bulletin de la commission archéologique de l'Indochine* (Paris, 1914–16), pp. 1–102. San Antonio seems also to be heavily in debt to Christobal de Jacque, another of the Cambodian veterans active in Valladolid. His memorial (1606) remained unpublished until it was printed in H. Ternaux-Compans, *Archives des voyages* (Paris, 1840–41), pp. 241–350. Groslier and Boxer, *op. cit.* (n. 124), pp. 84–87, concluded that its text is practically identical to that of San Antonio and argue, contrary to Cabaton, that San Antonio probably borrowed extensively from Jacque's work. Groslier and Boxer also attribute the errors in San Antonio's text to additions made by the Dominican which he possibly derived from Ribadeneira's *Historia*.

Leonardo de Argensola (1562–1631), who wrote from the reports of others. Scattered throughout Morga's *Sucesos de las islas Filipinas* are references to the projects for conquering Cambodia and his opposition to them.[127] San Antonio saw the manuscript of Morga's book before he left Manila early in 1598 but was evidently left unimpressed by Morga's contrary position. The *Conquista de las islas Malucas* of Argensola, while glorifying Spain's conquest of the Moluccas, includes a general description of Cambodia as a target for Spanish expansion in the future. Like San Antonio, Argensola may have profited from reading Morga's work in manuscript. On the other hand, it may have been that Morga, once having learned of Argensola's activities, finally decided to publish what for a long while was his semi-private manuscript.[128] Care must be exercised in using Argensola, for he sometimes confused Cambay in Gujarat with Cambodia while putting together his otherwise excellent compilation. Hereafter, a large gap appears in the European sources. In 1640 Bishop Diego Aduarte's *Historia de la provincia del Santo Rosario* was published at Manila; it details Dominican activities in the East, including Cambodia, from 1587 to 1636.[129] The Jesuits in Cambodia were under the jurisdiction of the Province of Japan.[130] Some notices of their activities in Cambodia are included in António Francesco Cardim's *Relatione* (Rome, 1645) for the period to 1644.[131] In general, the European sources are of two kinds: those like the work of San Antonio, which describe the country as well as Spanish activities there, and those like Morga's, which deal mainly with the European political and missionary contacts.

For more than a century the Portuguese had known the coasts of Indochina, in particular those of Cambodia.[132] This kingdom is bounded on the west by Siam, on the north by Laos, on the east by Champa, and on the south by the sea.[133] Its principal river is the Mekong, which, like the Nile, seasonally floods and inundates the surrounding plain. Six months each year the winds pile up the sands at its mouth, causing a reversal of flow in the river, which creates great lakes in the interior.[134] Cambodia's main cities are

---

[127] On Morga and his book see above, pp. 326–28.

[128] See J. S. Cummins (trans. and ed.), *Sucesos de las islas Filipinas by Antonio de Morga* ("HS," 2d ser., CXL; Cambridge, 1971), pp. 18, 27. For bibliographic details on Argensola's *Conquista* see above, pp. 311–12.

[129] For bibliographical data see above, pp. 342–43.

[130] For a listing of the Portuguese Jesuits in Cambodia during the entire seventeenth century see Teixeira, *op. cit.* (n. 9), I, 436.

[131] See above, pp. 378–79. A brief description of Cambodia is on pp. 179–80 of the French translation, Cardim's *Relation* (Paris, 1645–46).

[132] San Antonio in Cabaton (trans. and ed.), *op. cit.* (n. 125), p. 94. Commencement of regular Portuguese trade in Indochina should probably be dated around 1525–30. See P. Y. Manguin, *Les Portugais sur les côtes du Viêt-Nam et du Campā: étude sur les routes maritimes et les relations commerciales, d'après les sources portugaises (XVIe, XVIIe, XVIIIe siècles)* (Paris, 1972), p. 184.

[133] Cardim, *op. cit.* (n. 131), p. 179. Earlier authors are not as precise on these boundaries.

[134] In the flood season from June to October the Mekong sediments its distributaries and its waters then flow upstream into the lake known as the Tonle Sap. See Dobby, *op. cit.* (n. 31),

"Anchor" (Angkor), "Churdumuco" (Chaturmukha or Phnom Penh), and "Sistor" (Srei Santhor) which means "great village." This last is so named because it is very important, possesses more than fifty thousand inhabitants, and is the royal capital.[135] Local products include cotton, silk, incense, benzoin, and a great abundance of rice and lac. Cambodia has silver, gold, lead, copper, tin, and alum. Precious stones are found there in large quantities. Rhinoceroses and elephants, especially the white ones, are the most striking of its wild animals. Fish are plentiful in the Mekong and the lakes, especially a kind of "thon blanc" which swims upriver with the tide.[136]

The ruins of Angkor are remarked upon by Ribadeneira, San Antonio, and Argensola.[137] Informed by their contemporaries of this fantastic ancient city, these authors produce a picture of Angkor which is remarkably consistent, though not free of errors.[138] Located in an inaccessible wilderness near Siam and Laos, Angkor's ruins were first discovered in 1570 by hunters.[139] It is a marvel of construction, with streets of marble slabs and artistic monuments which are as well preserved as if they were modern works. Reputedly it was constructed by foreigners, perhaps by Alexander the Great or the Romans. Angkor is also called "the city of the five points," because of its five pyramids topped by decorated copper balls. On the inside of the stone battlement wall there are representations of elephants, ounces (a kind of panther), tigers, lions, eagles, and dogs.[140] Its beautiful stone houses are placed on the streets in an orderly fashion, and the workmanship both inside and out appears to be Roman. There are many stone cisterns and canals, for the living quarters are at a long distance from the temples and marketplaces.

---

p. 301. San Antonio (Cabaton's edition, cited in n. 125), p. 94, and B. Leonardo y Argensola, *Conquista de las islas Malucas* (Zaraqoza, 1891), p. 213, possibly derive their explanations of this phenomenon from Gaspar da Cruz. See *Asia,* I, 566.

[135] San Antonio in Cabaton (trans. and ed.), *op. cit.* (n. 125), p. 95. Srei Santhor does not mean "great village" according to Groslier and Boxer, *op. cit.* (n. 124), p. 100. It may be that San Antonio is confusedly referring to one or another of the several names which mean "great city." Cardim, *op. cit.* (n. 131), p. 179, asserts that Cambodia's principal city is called "Rauecca" (*râcâthânî* [?], or royal city).

[136] San Antonio in Cabaton (trans. and ed.), *op. cit.* (n. 125), p. 95, and Argensola, *op. cit.* (n. 134), pp. 213–14. This fish is probably the *Scumber thunina.* For an evaluation of these assertions about Cambodia's natural wealth see Groslier and Boxer, *op. cit.* (n. 124), pp. 152–54.

[137] Fernandez (trans.), *op. cit.* (n. 7), pp. 169, 181–82; Cabaton (trans. and ed.), *op. cit.* (n. 125), pp. 96–97; Argensola, *op. cit.* (n. 134), pp. 214–15. A description also is included in João dos Santos, *Ethiopia Oriental . . .* (Evora, 1609), Pt. II, Bk. 2, chap. vii, fols. 39v–40r. For French translations of these Portuguese and Spanish texts see Groslier and Boxer, *op. cit.* (n. 124), pp. 75–80. Cardim, *op. cit.* (n. 131), p. 179, mentions the ruins of a great city which tradition avers was built by the Romans of old.

[138] For their sources and their relationships to one another see Groslier and Boxer, *op. cit.* (n. 124), pp. 81–89. San Antonio is guilty of making more errors than the others.

[139] Angkor was abandond around 1432 and rediscovered around 1550. After 1570 King Satha (r. 1576–96) established his court near the ruins. By 1593 the court had been moved to Lovek. See *ibid.,* p. 23.

[140] That there were such representations is possibly an error. See *ibid.,* pp. 91–92.

Ships may even sail on its great moats. A stone bridge is superb in all its details and its arches are supported on the heads and hands of stone giants.[141] One of the ruins is near the edge of a lake (the Tonle Sap). On these ruins there are epitaphs, inscriptions, and characters which no one has so far been able to decipher. When Angkor was rediscovered, no living creatures were found there. Only trees and plants continued to live on in the crevasses of its ruins. Today the town is again inhabited and the Augustinians and Dominicans have gone there to preach the gospel. Were the histories of the Chinese known to us they would tell why this city was abandoned and would explain the writings on the monuments which cannot even be read by the natives. The Jews of India say that the Chinese Jews built Angkor and then abandoned it when they emigrated to China.[142]

Cambodia is densely populated by a dark people of medium height, who are sweet and simple. They recognize just one king and their society is divided simply into noble and common classes. Their titles of nobility are "Mambary" (*montrei?*, minister), "Chunadechu" (*chau decho*), "Ocuña" (*oknea*), and "Chapina" (*chau ponhea*).[143] All nobles have several wives, the number depending on how rich they happen to be. Wives of high rank are white and beautiful; those of the commoners are brown. Common women cultivate the land and their husbands are soldiers. The various wives of one husband are typically jealous and disagreeable. Nobles dress in silk and extremely fine cottons; commoners wear coarse cottons and fustian. Nobles travel in palanquins called "crey" (*krê*), which men carry on their shoulders;[144] commoners travel by cart, on buffaloes, or on horseback. Farmers pay to the principal mandarins, and to the king, one-tenth of all produce taken from the sea and the land.

Their language (Khmer) differs from all others, but it is easy to learn and to speak. They have a special script which they draw on "papier de Chine" with a pencil.[145] They write from right to left and not in the reverse direction as others do in these kingdoms. They play a game with mallets, not on foot as in Castile, but on horseback.[146] They fly kites made of paper and reeds

---

[141] On the waterways of Angkor Thom, the site of the royal palace near the Buddhist monastery Angkor Wat, see *ibid.*, p. 101. San Antonio asserts that it is located on the Mekong, a mistake for the river of Siemreap.

[142] On these connections to China see *ibid.*, pp. 84, 88.

[143] These titles and variations on them are given by Morga in Cummins (trans. and ed.), *op. cit.* (n. 128), pp. 125–30, and by San Antonio in Cabaton (trans. and ed.), *op. cit.* (n. 125) p. 98. For their Khmer equivalents see Groslier and Boxer, *op. cit.* (n. 124), p. 156.

[144] On these somewhat extraordinary palanquins see Groslier and Boxer, *op. cit.* (n. 124), pp. 156–57.

[145] For details on their traditional manners of writing see E. Aymonier, *Le Cambodge* (3 vols.; Paris, 1900–1904), I, 42. Chinese paper was in use in Cambodia by 1600. See Reid, *op. cit.* (n. 79), p. 228.

[146] That they played polo in old Cambodia is attested by a celebrated *bas relief* of the terrace of the royal elephants at Angkor Thom. See Groslier and Boxer, *op. cit.* (n. 124), p. 161. Compare this to *ti-khi*, a ritualistic form of hockey played in Laos.

tied together by a cord which sings in the wind like a vibraphone.[147] Like the Tagalogs they enjoy fights between cocks whose feet are spurred. They treat their maladies with herbs and simples and burn the remains of those persons who die a natural death. Those who are condemned to death are impaled, skinned, or exposed to the mosquitoes. Cambodia has its own gold and silver coins imprinted with a cock, a serpent, and a heart with a flower in the middle.[148]

Although the Cambodians are pagans, they recognize a supreme cause and a single and most powerful god whom they call "Amida" (Japanese for Buddha). They also adore the sun and moon and have distinct gods of war, peace, health, illness, and sowing.[149] The images of their principal gods are made of gold and silver with ruby and diamond eyes; the lesser gods are of copper and cast iron. In their numerous pagodas the monks and priests live, whom they call "chucus" (*chao ku* or "my master"). Those who wish to follow a life of religion begin their training in childhood. On reaching adulthood these religious take four vows: not to lie, not to kill, not to steal, and not to fornicate with women.[150] They enter the choir seven times daily and confess to one another before beginning their prayers. Their chants are sung by antiphonal choirs and in a special language (Pali).[151] Both the religious and the laity believe in the immortality of the soul. They also hold that the animals have immortal souls and that is why they never kill them for food. This precept is followed indifferently by the laity but faithfully by the clerics. At the entry of a road, where Christians would place a cross, the Cambodians erect a high pole on the top of which hangs a decorated serpent which they worship. When they have personal differences or quarrel, they restore friendship by a special ceremony. They mix samples of their blood in a vase which each in turn drinks. By this act they take a vow to be always of the same blood, heart, and will.[152]

In the European sources, the history of Cambodia is reported mainly with respect to contacts with the Portuguese and Spanish. Ribadeneira and his Franciscans even take note of the ruins of Angkor in the hope that it might be "rehabilitated to become an outpost of Christian missions outside the Philippines."[153] In 1598 Morga in Manila receives a letter in Spanish written in red ink from "Prauncar" (probably Barom Reachea II, r. 1596–99), the puppet king of Cambodia, in which he details his obligations to the Span-

---

[147] Kites with one or three bamboo cords are still flown in Cambodia. See *ibid.*, p. 161, n. 4.
[148] The museum at Phnom Penh possesses (possessed?) a number of coins which fit these descriptions exactly. See *ibid.*, p. 163.
[149] A correct but not a complete list. See *ibid.*, p. 159, n. 2.
[150] The hostile Dominican San Antonio believes that this last vow is easy for them to follow, because they are passive sodomists as children who become active after reaching maturity.
[151] On this chanting see Groslier and Boxer, *op. cit.* (n. 124), p. 160.
[152] On these customs of the Cambodians see San Antonio in Cabaton (trans. and ed.), *op. cit.* (n. 125), pp. 98–100.
[153] Fernandez (trans.), *op. cit.* (n. 7), I, 441.

ish, asks for missionaries, and announces that he has given the adventurers Diego Veloso and Blas Ruiz de Hernan Gonçales respectively the provinces of "Trân" (Treang) and "Bapano" (Baphnom).[154] Both Morga and Aduarte report on the dispatch of the Dominican mission of 1603 to the court of the new king Barom Reachea IV. The delegation, well received at Phnom Penh by the court, soon runs into trouble with the Malay Muslims, the Chinese, and the Cochin-Chinese of the capital. After making a few conversions, the Dominicans quickly give up in their efforts to work in Cambodia.[155] In 1628 a new Dominican mission is dispatched to Cambodia. While it is graciously received, the king refuses to give permission for the baptism of his subjects, allowing only the Chinese and Japanese to be converted.[156] In the meantime the Jesuits of Macao infiltrate Cambodia to minister to its Japanese refugees. Two Japanese Christian priests aid them in this endeavor. In 1629 several European priests go to Cambodia to obtain permission to travel up the Mekong into Laos, a kingdom without a seaport of its own. It requires eight months to travel into Laos because of the difficulty of fighting the rapid current of the river and because it is necessary at one place to go a long distance overland to avoid a waterfall and to find another navigable part of the river.[157] From these and many other indications it can be seen that Cambodia and Laos were in process of being isolated from intercourse with the Europeans in the years following the establishment of Thai hegemony. The Christians, for their part, are exasperated by the tolerance and the indifference of the Cambodian Buddhists to the Christian message. What is to be gained in a country which offers the possibility neither of conversion nor of martyrdom?

Over the latter half of the century Cambodia quickly fades in importance within the European sources. The tug-of-war between the Annamese and Siamese for control of Cambodia produced intense factionalism within its royal family, as contenders for power in the capital region sought support from one or the other of these two outside powers. The VOC had tried irregularly, beginning in 1620, to open a permanent office in Cambodia. The halting of Japan's trade with Cambodia after 1635 led the government at Batavia to direct serious attention to Cambodia and Laos. Japanese merchants, now prohibited from traveling abroad, were quickly succeeded by

---

[154]Cummins (trans. and ed.), *op. cit.* (n. 128), pp. 119–20. This letter was accompanied by another to Morga from Ruiz detailing the activities of the Iberian adventurers during the wars in Cambodia and reproduced as part of Morga's history in *ibid.*, pp. 120–35.

[155]*Ibid.*, pp. 211–12; and Aduarte in *BR*, XXXI, 175–80.

[156]Aduarte in *BR*, XXXII, 172. The king was Ponhea To (r. 1628–30); he ruled at a time when Cambodia began to be isolated from the sea by the southward expansion of the Vietnamese of Cochin-China.

[157]Cardim, *op. cit.* (n. 131), pp. 180–82. The Jesuits had converted a Laotian emissary in Tongking who, on returning home, convinced his master to write the Jesuits inviting them to Laos. Cardim wrote while Giovanni Maria Leria was on his way to Laos, the first Jesuit to serve there. His mission of six years' duration (1642–47) is reported on in Marini's summary (1663) of the activities in the Jesuit Province of Japan. See below, pp. 1157, 1159–64.

the VOC in Cambodia. These Dutch merchants purchased rice for Batavia and deerskins and stick-lac for sale in Japan at a substantial profit. From 1636 to 1670 the Dutch merchants lived at Udong on a semi-permanent basis. Political instability, and the advent of many Portuguese after the fall of Malacca in 1641, imperiled the VOC's position in Cambodia and led to extended hostilities and repeated cessations of trade. Finally, around 1670, troubles within Cambodia itself forced the VOC to cease its efforts to trade on a regular basis in Udong.[158] The English East India Company maintained a factory in Cambodia from 1651 to 1656 as part of its effort to break into the Japan trade. Once the Company declared this enterprise unsuccessful, English private traders went to Cambodia for their own ends and profits.[159]

Dutch affairs in Cambodia from the establishment of the VOC's factory in 1636 to the assassination in 1643 of the VOC's legate and his staff, an act of official violence that ended regular trade for more than ten years, are detailed in the account published by Pieter Casteleyn in 1669. This Dutch report is one of the very few sources to throw light on events in Cambodia during one of its darkest hours.[160] From their vantage point in the capital, the Dutch watched closely and reported on the anarchy, intrigues, and murders which preceded the rise to power of Barom Reachea VII (r. 1659–72). In 1635 three kings try to rule the divided country, each hoping to outlive the other. One of these, the "old king," has more authority and support than the other two.[161] Each has a party of officials at court and a bodyguard. In Cambodia three official titles exist; in order they are "Oknea" (*okna*), "Tevinia" (a minor courtier), and "Nappra" (*nak prah*). The foreign merchants generally work through the *shahbandar,* who is often a Chinese. Contending factions at court vie to win the support of the Western merchants and their armed vessels. Along with the Portuguese many Muslim-Malays came to Cambodia after the Dutch capture of Malacca in 1641. These newcomers, to the consternation of the Dutch, support the brother of the regent. On January 5, 1642, the "old king" and his family are murdered and his brother takes over the throne with the aid of the Malays. Somewhat later he accepts Islam and assumes the name of Ibrahim, much to the dismay of the Buddhist Cambodians, who refer to him as "Rama the Apostate" (Rama Thupdey Chan, or Barom Reachea VI, r. 1642–59). Supported by the Malays, Portuguese, and Javans, he turns against the Dutch and does whatever

---

[158] For a full discussion of the VOC in Cambodia see W. J. M. Buch, "La Compagnie des Indes Néerlandaises et l'Indochine," *Bulletin de l'école française d'Extrême-Orient,* Vol. XXXVII, Pt. 1 (1937), pp. 195–237. See our pl. 239.

[159] See D. K. Bassett, "The Trade of the English East India Company in Cambodia, 1651–1656," *JRAS* (1962), pp. 35–61.

[160] See above, pp. 489–90. Entire report in Hendrik P. N. Muller (ed.), *De Oost-Indische Compagnie in Cambodja en Laos* ("WLV," XIII; The Hague, 1917). Also see Aymonier, *op. cit.* (n. 145), III, 772–73.

[161] The "old king" was probably "Preah Outei" (Prah Udaya) who acted as regent for the young princes and kings contending for power. See Aymonier, *op. cit.* (n. 145), III, 770.

he can to limit and tax their trade. One dispute leads to another, until finally the Dutch ambassador is murdered in 1643 and all further peaceful intercourse halted.[162]

The European Catholics likewise had a hard time of it in turbulent Cambodia. Around 1630, following an influx of Japanese Christian expellees from Siam, Dominicans from the Philippines and Jesuits from Macao made short-lived efforts to evangelize in Cambodia. Portuguese priests and prelates from Malacca were followed into Cambodia after 1641 by Jesuits from Macao, including Giovanni Maria Leria, who was destined to penetrate Laos.[163] In the 1650's Nguyễn Phúc-Tân or Hiền-Vòung (r. 1648–87) of Cochin-China undertook military expeditions against Champa and Cambodia. His invasion of Cambodia was abetted by a Nguyễn princess of Cochin-China, the widowed sister-in-law of Ibrahim, who profited from the king's unpopularity to organize an internal resistance which culminated in military intervention by her relatives. Udong was sacked in 1658 and Ibrahim and his family imprisoned. As a war indemnity, the Bien-hoa region just north of Saigon was ceded to Cochin-China and its army occupied Cambodia to maintain order. After being liberated, Ibrahim died in 1659 and was succeeded the following year by his nephew, the son of Chei Chetta II, who reigned as Barom Reachea VII.[164] In the meantime the Savoyard Jesuit Carlo della Rocca (1613–70) was sent to Udong in 1659, probably to minister to the Cochin-Chinese Christians in the occupying forces. It was from Della Rocca's letters that Giovanni Filippo de Marini (1608–82) obtained the information on Cambodia published in his *Delle missioni* (1663).[165]

Cambodia, Marini reports, is a large but sparsely populated kingdom ruled by a tyrannical and dissolute king called "Nac Cian" (Rama Thupdey Chan). He is dominated by Malay Muslims who hold all the important offices and titles. Tension has long prevailed between the Muslim ruler and his Buddhist subjects, particularly over the issue of succession. The Nguyễn princess conspires with her relatives to bring about the conquest of Champa and the invasion of Cambodia. From the sack of Udong, the Annamese carried off enormous booty. Twenty-seven large ships and seventy smaller ones were needed to transport the royal treasury. Eight hundred elephants, and even more horses, as well as sixteen hundred pieces of artillery were captured by the invaders. The Dutch lost all their merchandise, and the English a fully loaded ship, in the fire that swept Udong after the sack. On June 15, 1659, Della Rocca temporarily leaves Cambodia for Macao in the company of Leria and Antonio Lopez. In the course of their stay in Cambodia, they

---

[162] Based on Castelyn in Muller (ed.), *op. cit.* (n. 160), pp. 11–27. Also see Buch, *loc. cit.* (n. 158), pp. 213–19.

[163] See above, p. 1152, n. 157.

[164] See H. Chappoulie, *Aux origines d'une église. Rome et les missions d'Indochine au XVIIᵉ siècle* (Paris, 1943), I, 167–68.

[165] *Delle missioni*, pp. 389–406; see n. 175 below. A letter from Della Rocca of 1664 about Cambodia was separately published in a pamphlet in 1670. See Streit, V, 620–21.

learned that the Buddhists there were no more receptive to the Christian message than their co-religionists in Japan.

Louis Chevreuil, a priest of the Paris Society, was sent to Cambodia in 1665 to help out Paulo d'Acosta, the old and ill governor of the bishopric of Malacca.[166] Dropped by a Siamese ship at one of the mouths of the Mekong, Chevreuil is fortunate enough to find a Cochin-Chinese Christian family to take him upriver in their barge. After threading through the heavy river traffic, he arrives on November 21, 1665, at "Colompe" (Phnom Penh). Here the governor ministers to a Portuguese colony made up almost exclusively of refugees from Makassar, which had been taken by the Dutch in 1663. In addition to aiding the governor, Chevreuil ministers to the Christians among the occupying forces. A lone Jesuit at Udong performs similar services for those Cochin-Chinese at the royal capital.[167]

At Phnom Penh, Chevreuil was well located to survey the river traffic. He saw Portuguese vessels from Macao bringing rich China wares to Cambodia to sell on behalf of the Jesuits. Because he was open in his denunciation of this unchristian commerce, he soon had difficulties with the Portuguese. Early in 1670 he was kidnapped and taken off to Macao, charged with heresy, and after four months in prison sent to Goa for trial. Finally he was released and in 1671 arrived in Surat. Two years later he was back in Siam.[168]

Chevreuil's reminiscences of his five years in Cambodia were published at Rome by the Propaganda in the *Relatione* of 1677.[169] Eight days' journey overland from Phnom Penh is a very ancient temple and place of pilgrimage called "Onco" (Angon, an old name for Angkor). It is revered by gentiles throughout Southeast Asia as St. Peter's in Rome is by the Catholics of Europe.[170] Chevreuil hopes one day to visit this shrine, where the principal teachers reside whose decisions are as much respected in this part of the world as are the decrees of the Holy See in Europe. Pilgrims from Siam, Pegu, Laos, and Tenasserim continue to come here even when at war with Cambodia. The king of Siam, at odds with Cambodia since its revolt, still sends religious emissaries annually to this holy site. Whether or not Chevreuil actually visited Angkor is not indicated in the contemporary sources. The *Relatione* makes perfectly plain, however, that the Cambodians, a hos-

---

[166] The Portuguese in Asia appointed a governor to act as suffragan when a bishopric was vacant.

[167] Presumably Della Rocca returned to Udong after 1660, witness his letter of 1664 cited above, n. 165. Chevreuil reports that this learned man would have preferred the college at Macao to the forests of Cambodia. See Chappoulie, *op. cit.* (n. 164), pp. 187–88.

[168] *Ibid.*, pp. 188–89, 303.

[169] Pp. 93–110. Put together in Rome, this account also includes background material extracted from Marini's book. For bibliographical history see above, p. 383.

[170] Is this a reference to the Preah Khan of Angkor, a most holy Buddhist site? See Ly Kim Long, *An Outline of Cambodian Architecture* (Varanasi, 1967), pp. 36–37. In a Dutch letter of 1657 it is remarked likewise that Angkor is eight to ten days' journey overland from Phnom Penh. See Muller (ed.), *op. cit.* (n. 160), p. 360. For a discussion of Chevreuil's reference see Groslier and Boxer, *op. cit.* (n. 124), pp. 131–32.

pitable and tractable people, are firm in their native faith. Chevreuil admits that he has not made a single convert after working in their midst for over three years. During these years Chevreuil had to remain content to minister to the four hundred Christians at Phnom Penh. Like Della Rocca at Udong, he is handicapped in working with the Cochin-Chinese Christians because he does not understand their language and cannot find interpreters skilled enough to translate correctly Christian terms and ideas. While the Cambodian king is generally kind to all comers, the Cochin-Chinese occupation forces are bitterly resented by him and by the populace at large. In 1666 many of them were massacred and all trade and relations cut off between Cochin-China and Cambodia. Shortly before leaving in 1670, Chevreuil converts two Cambodian ladies who promise to carry on the Christian work after his departure. Still he concludes that Cambodia is one of the most difficult places in Asia in which to preach the Christian message.

Dampier learned about disorders in Cambodia during 1687 from a "Captain Howel," who served the king of Siam by undertaking expeditions against pirates to keep the sea-lanes open for Ayut'ia.[171] The estuary of the Mekong with its many islands was a favorite lair for pirates who preyed on the sea trade between Siam and the Far East. Many of these pirates were Chinese who had fled their homeland in their own ships "rather to live free any where, than to submit to the Tartars [Manchus]." Entering the "river of Cambodia," they built enclosed villages on previously uninhabited and desolate islands. While they might easily have lived from agriculture in this fertile land, they preferred to pillage their neighbors and to attack shipping. The king of Siam first sent forces overland to rout them from their fortified villages. After the failure of this expedition, he sent two frigates up the river, commanded by English captains and manned by Luso-Asians born in Siam. They bombarded and set fire to the villages and took as prisoners many of the inhabitants. To ingratiate themselves with the Manchus, the English delivered the Chinese refugees to the authorities at Macao.[172] From this brief episode it can readily be seen that Cambodia was beset on all sides by foreigners and could do little on its own at the end of the seventeenth century to defend itself from long-term or brief incursions by land or sea.

Landlocked between Siam and Cambodia, the peoples and products of Laos were known to sixteenth-century Europe through the Portuguese reports of João de Barros and the Dominican Father Gaspar da Cruz.[173] Substantial accounts next appeared in Dutch and Italian in the 1660's, but with reference to Laos in the 1640's. Geeraerd van Wusthof, a junior merchant of the VOC, led a commercial mission from Cambodia into Laos in 1641–42.

[171] Howell was the anglicized name taken by Ralph Lambton Verstecken. See J. Anderson, *English Intercourse with Siam in the Seventeenth Century* (London, 1890), p. 322.
[172] Dampier in Masefield (ed.), *op. cit.* (n. 27), II, 36–38.
[173] See *Asia*, I, 523, 565.

Parts of the diary he kept were published by Pieter Casteleyn, a printer of Haarlem, in 1669.[174] Shortly after Van Wusthof left Luang Prabang (previously called Lan Sang), the Jesuit Giovanni Maria Leria (1597–1665) and his companions arrived in Laos. Leria remained there from 1642 to 1647, mostly at Vientiane. At Rome in 1663 there appeared a systematic description of Laos prepared by Marini as Book V of his report on the activities of the Jesuits in the Province of Japan.[175] Most of this material was apparently obtained from Leria's reports to his superiors.

Van Wusthof leaves Lovek on July 20, 1641, in the company of two assistants, two servants, and a barber, all of them Dutch. Their guide is a Laotian merchant and their intrepreter is called "Intsie Lannangh" (a Malay title, *Enche lanang*). They proceed up the Mekong, usually called the "river of Laos" in the Dutch sources, passing by Phnom Penh, then a small market town, to "Sombaboer" (Sambor) where they change vessels. On August 17 they spend the night in a ruined old temple at "Baetjong" (Bakkong) near Stung Treng, a place famed for its Khmer temple-mountain.[176] At the impassable and roaring waterfalls of Khone they are forced to unload their boats and to carry their wares across the marked border between Cambodia and Laos.[177] Bypassing the waterfalls takes them twelve days. After a total of two months on the way, they finally arrive at Bassac, the first important town in Laos. For a fortnight they progress slowly and painfully over the next eighty miles or so through the Khemmerat rapids. In the middle Mekong, navigation becomes simpler and swifter as they approach That Phanom. The following day they reach Lakhon, a crossroads and a market center held in "great repute" by the Laotians. Here they witness an autumn festival similar to those they had seen in Cambodia.[178] On their way upriver they are met in mid-November near Vientiane by royal barges which had

---

[174] It is entitled *Vremde geschiedenissen in de konninckrijcken van Cambodia en Louwen-Lant, in Oost-Indien.* . . . Casteleyn's compilation is reprinted in Muller (ed.), *op. cit.* (n. 160), along with the entire Van Wusthof journal and other contemporary documents. Excerpts from the diary not published by Casteleyn, as well as a summary of Van Wusthof's experiences, are to be found in Paul Lévy, "Two Accounts of Travels in Laos in the Seventeenth Century," in René de Berval (ed.), *Kingdom of Laos. The Land of the Million Elephants and of the White Parasol* (Saigon, 1959), pp. 50–59. Van Wusthof's account was closely examined by Francis Garnier before he and his group explored the Mekong region from 1866 to 1873. See his "Voyage lointain aux royaumes de Cambodge et Laowen par les Néerlandais et ce qui s'y est passé jusqu'en 1644," *Bulletin de la société de géographie de Paris*, 6th ser., Vol. II (1871), pp. 249–89.

[175] *Delle missioni de' padri della Compagnia di Giesu nella provincia del Giappone.* . . . This book was quickly reissued in Italian and translated into French. For further bibliographical detail see above, pp. 382–83.

[176] See G. Coedès, *The Making of South-East Asia*, trans. H. M. Wright (Berkeley, 1967), pp. 104–5.

[177] This is still the frontier.

[178] Probably the *Boun Ok Vassa*, or the end of Lent festival, a time of general rejoicing. See Frank LeBar and A. Suddard (eds.), *Laos, Its People, Its Society, Its Culture* (New Haven, 1963), p. 58.

come to examine the letter to the king of Laos. When Van Wusthof refuses to turn over the letter or to divulge its contents, the letter and the Dutch mission are transported into the city in a huge boat and under a gilded dome. The king of Laos was then Souligna Vongsa (r. 1637– *ca.* 1694), one of its greatest and most popular rulers. Early on the morning of November 16, the royal elephants arrive to take the Van Wusthof mission to an audience. The letter from Governor-General Van Diemen in Batavia is placed in a golden box on the back of the first elephant.[179] The emissaries follow, each mounted on an elephant and holding his gift. This procession passes through lines of soldiers and in front of the royal palace. Near the audience site they dismount and are ushered into tents to await the royal call. One hour later, the king arrives on a white elephant, and the Dutch imitate the Laotians in kneeling as he passes their tents. A young man of about twenty-three, the king is preceded by about three hundred armed foot soldiers and followed by a few war elephants and their armed riders as well as a troupe of musicians.[180] Following the king and his bodyguard comes a contingent of another two hundred soldiers and sixteen elephants carrying the king's five wives and their attendants. After this procession passes by, the emissaries return to their tents to dine. Sent for at around four o'clock in the afternoon they are taken to a large square enclosed by a stone wall pierced by apertures. In the center of the square stands a huge pyramid with gilded designs at the top. When entering this square all the Laotians customarily walk and carry lighted candles. The Dutch gift is carried through a door into another square and placed on a mat sixteen paces in front of the king. Each of the Dutchmen is then presented with a candle as if he were a "Tevinia."[181] With candles in hand they are led before the king, who is standing in a great temple near a large idol and in the midst of his nobles. Following instructions they sit down on their knees behind the gift and knock their heads on the ground three times. The letter is then read and the Dutchmen relieved of their candles. The king invites them to sit down on mats near him under the dome of the temple. The ensuing conversation is carried on through a "Tevinia." The king expresses his pleasure at their visit and at the letter they have brought. He wonders if he should send an emissary back with them to ask the governor-general to send him a letter annually as well as more traders and other visitors.[182] After being dismissed, the Dutchmen are each given a present and invited to attend plays as well as wrestling, boxing, and fencing matches. After nightfall they witness dances, one by a wife of the king, and a fireworks display.[183]

[179] *Cf.* the Siamese practice of paying more respect to the letter than to the bearer, below, pp. 1191–92.
[180] According to the Laotian annals the king was twenty-eight years old at this time. See Lévy, *loc. cit.* (n. 174), p. 57.
[181] An old title for a minor courtier which corresponds to the present title of *Panga*.
[182] In short, the king is suggesting annual tribute missions.
[183] Based on Van Wusthof in Muller (ed.), *op. cit.* (n. 160), pp. 28–39. The account of the

As part of his reconnaissance, Van Wusthof learns about the caravan routes which connect Laos with Siam and its other neighbors. Laos is at peace, but not on particularly good terms, with the bordering states. Because of tension with Cambodia, the king decides not to send an emissary of his own along with Van Wusthof.

Laos is governed by three chief dignitaries. One controls the armed forces, governs Vientiane and its vicinity, and acts as regent in an interregnum. Another serves as viceroy of the southern part of the kingdom. The third rules on matters of foreign relations.[184] These chiefs are not necessarily of the same blood as the king. While they are his councillors, they attend a royal audience only once every two or three months or when the king expressly calls them together. Royal revenues are derived from the export of stick-lac, benzoin, and gold.[185] Much of this wealth goes to the priests and temples of the idols.

His wares sold, Van Wusthof returns to Cambodia on December 24, 1641; his two assistants are left behind and do not return until almost one year later.[186]

For the Jesuits, Laos was virgin territory in the center of continental Southeast Asia and a natural extension of their Indochinese missions that could possibly be penetrated by missionaries from Ayut'ia, Cambodia, or Tongking. The Jesuits in Tongking had converted a Laotian emissary who, on returning home, convinced his royal master to invite the missionaries to Laos. The Portuguese Jesuit Cardim, the first to try, was in Ayut'ia from 1621 to 1629 with the intention of entering Laos via Siam. His effort failed because of hostilities between Laos and Ayut'ia. Several Jesuits were sent to Cambodia in 1629 in hopes of traveling upriver to Laos; again local conditions thwarted their enterprise. Giovanni Battista Bonelli (1589–1638), a Jesuit Visitor from Macao, was actually enroute from Tongking to Vientiane when he died in 1638. In 1642, Leria entered Laos, as Van Wusthof had, by following the Mekong northward; in 1647 he departed over the Tongking route.[187]

Marini makes a studied effort to provide a geographical description of Laos, a kingdom "scarcely heard of in Europe," based on Leria's reports. It is a long, narrow country situated inland three hundred miles from the sea. Surrounded by high mountains, it has an "expanse of only one hundred fifty miles of flat and level country" suitable for agriculture. The encircling

---

audience is translated almost verbatim into English in Lévy, *loc. cit.* (n. 174), pp. 54–56. The translation is flawed, however, and should be used with care.

[184] On this tripartite division of traditional government *cf.* LeBar and Suddard (eds.), *op. cit.* (n. 178), pp. 116–17.

[185] Gold was mined on the Boloven plateau until the ore played out in the mid-nineteenth century. Elsewhere alluvial gold was panned. See *ibid.*, p. 211.

[186] Van Wusthof in Muller (ed.), *op. cit.* (n. 160), pp. 42–52.

[187] For the Jesuit efforts to enter Laos and Leria's voyage there see Marini, *op. cit.* (n. 175), pp. 492–503.

mountains protect the lowlands from Laos' more powerful neighbors and abundantly provide the kingdom with wood for export. Between Vientiane and the Tongking frontier there is a desert region surrounded by high mountains. Mount "Rumai" (?) stands on the border. The forests at the bases of the high mountains seem to have been planted for the express purpose of protecting the lowlands and of moderating the effects of the seasonal and violent storms which fall upon them. The waters from the mountains flow into the lowlands "by given routes" where they form waterways that run into "the great river they call the mother of waters." The Mekong, "incorrectly located by geographers ancient and modern," actually has its source in a deep marsh in the high mountains of "Iunnam" (Yunnan) on the border of China.[188] From there it rushes noisily downward through narrow valleys to the level land near Laos, where it quietly widens out as it receives large infusions of water from its tributaries. West of Laos it splits into two great rivers, the one to the west flowing through Pegu into the Bay of Bengal. The Mekong proper works its way through the mountains surrounding Laos into the level country, where it divides into a number of branches. Then it flows southward to divide the region into two great provinces.[189] The rivers of Laos begin to rise in May because of the thaws in the mountains of Tibet, visible from Laos, and because this is when the stormy season begins. The swelling of the river continues, especially from September to January, but at no time does the Mekong overflow its high banks. Navigation is not interrupted by the rising waters, and trade and transport continue on the rivers and canals. But the difficulty of rowing upstream is increased and it becomes very dangerous to abandon one's craft to the swift flow of the river. At all seasons it is necessary, when passing by river from Laos into Cambodia, to spend ten days getting by the precipices and falls at Khone. A plan for building several locks to facilitate the transit of goods proposed to the king of Laos by a missionary (Leria presumably) was rejected out of hand because it would provide a key to the enemies of his landlocked kingdom.[190]

The history of Laos begins around A.D. 600 when the Lao emigrated from China to drive out the earlier "Lai" (probably Thai).[191] In the mountains to-

---

[188] It actually rises near the borders of Tibet. Many questions regarding the river's origin and course still remain unanswered, "for no man, as far as is known, has ever set eyes on its source or followed it through all the fantastic ravines of its upper course." Quoted from an official publication of the Mekong Project in M. Osborne, *River Road to China. The Mekong River Expedition, 1866–1873* (New York, 1975), p. 240.

[189] Today the Mekong forms the boundary between Laos and Thailand. In the seventeenth century the west bank of the river, or large stretches of what is now northeastern Thailand, was under the control of Laos.

[190] Marini, *op. cit.* (n. 175), pp. 444–47, 536–40.

[191] *Ibid.*, p. 456. On Laotian traditions and legends about origins see LeBar and Suddard (eds.), *op. cit.* (n. 178), pp. 7–9. Recorded history begins in the mid-fourteenth century.

wards Ava there still live a savage and primitive people called "Gnai" (?).[192] Because the land is so fertile, the Lao flourished and steadily multiplied. On a certain narrow strip of land in the middle of the country an excellent type of rice is grown that is not equaled in taste or aroma by any other Oriental rice.[193] The rivers and other waterways produce fish in quantity, some prodigious in size. Small fish caught at certain times of the year are salted down or made into a sauce that poor people use as seasoning for their rice.[194] Because of the abundance of life's necessities, the population continually grows. A census taken "not long ago" revealed that there were five hundred thousand men capable of bearing arms. If necessary, another whole army could be formed of those who have reached one hundred years of age.[195] The "Langians" (or people of Lansang, the "land of a million elephants") are a peaceful and docile people who live quietly and simply in their naturally fortified country. Justice is so severe that thievery and adultery are almost unknown. They are most hospitable to foreigners and eager to learn about alien customs, laws, and religions. Generally speaking, they are affable, courteous, trustworthy, sincere, and open to reason.[196]

Their chief town and royal capital is called "Langione" (Vientiane) and it is situated in the midle of the kingdom.[197] It is surrounded by high walls and protected on one side by the great river and on the other by fine moats. The royal palace, visible from a long way off, covers such a vast expanse and houses so many people that it could easily be mistaken for a town. The king's quarters in this symmetrical structure are adorned with a splendid gateway through which he enters into a great hall flanked by a number of fine rooms. The palace is built of incorruptible wood and decorated both within and without by gilded sculptures. In the surrounding courtyards stand great rows of wooden houses for the royal officials, which are likewise admirably constructed and ornamented. In general, the houses of the noble and rich are "vey high and very fine" wooden dwellings that are ornamented according to the amount of money each is able to spend. Commoners and the poor are badly housed in tiny huts. Only the priests are permitted to build their monasteries and houses of brick and stone.[198]

---

[192] Marini, *op. cit.* (n. 175), p. 445. On the tribal groups in modern Laos see Peter Kunstadter (ed.), *Southeast Asian Tribes, Minorities, and Nations* (2 vols.; Princeton, 1967), I, 241–42.

[193] Marini, *op. cit.* (n. 175), p. 447. Probably refers to the narrow flood plain of Samneva province and its wet-rice lands. See LeBar and Suddard (eds.), *op. cit.* (n. 178), p. 26.

[194] Marini, *op. cit.* (n. 175), p. 449; *i.e.,* Laotian, *padek,* the fermented fish sauce, whatever its local name, used all over Southeast Asia.

[195] *Ibid.,* p. 454. *Cf.* the census of 1376 discussed in LeBar and Suddard, *op. cit.* (n. 178), p. 11. The census referred to here was probably taken shortly after 1637, the date of Souligna-Vongsa's accession to the throne.

[196] Marini, *op. cit.* (n. 175), pp. 451–52, 454.

[197] It had become the royal capital in the mid-sixteenth century. Lan Sang, the old capital, was then renamed Luang Prabang in honor of Pra Bang, its revered golden Buddha.

[198] Marini, *op. cit.* (n. 175), pp. 449–50.

Like many other Asians, the Laotians believe in "Xaca" (*Shaka*, Japanese for Buddha). His doctrine spread from India eastward, so their sacred books are written in "Indian characters" (Pali). Its priests are called "Phe" (*pho?* or father) in Lao or "Talapoi," a foreign word imported from Pegu.[199] Most live in monasteries and many are mendicants. The novitiate begins in early adolescence and lasts to the age of twenty-three. Many of the monasteries of the towns are rich establishments in which the monks follow a strict routine. Other monks live in solitude as recluses of the woods. All monks remain forever chaste or leave the order. They are held in high esteem by the laity because of their magical powers and because of the pious example set by the king. The king appoints their Grand Master (*phra sangkharaja*), protects them, and endows them with land, entire towns, and slaves and servants. He accords them preferences and even intercedes on their behalf when they are guilty, because he fears their disapproval. The "Talapois" reap their greatest harvest in the month of April, when lavish offerings are made to "Xaca."[200] Every day in this month the laity flocks to the temples with offerings. At the end of the month a famous "Talapoi" preaches a sermon. Standing like a statue and without making gestures he exhorts the congregation to bring their sons to the monasteries for education. Their other teachings are but prohibitions against killing, adultery, lying, stealing, and drinking. In their services they give no thanks and their sacrifices are not sacraments. On special occasions, they obtain merit by releasing imprisoned birds.[201]

From the outset the Buddhists inveighed against Leria and his teachings. Like a good Jesuit, Leria directed his efforts to the conversion of the king—*cuius regio, eius religio* in Laos! He composed a book in the Lao language recounting the story of creation, the life of Christ, and basic Christian beliefs. When he gave this book as a gift to the king, he was accused by the priests and courtiers of trying to destroy the national religion. In March, 1645, he was hailed before a tribunal for investigation and trial. After the king interceded on his behalf, Leria circulated his book to others and propounded a list of the eight fundamental errors in Lao beliefs. While controversy raged, the king instructed him to write a life of "Xaca" to compare to the life of Christ! More religious heat was generated but few conversions made. On December 2, 1647, the disappointed Jesuit left Laos for a fifteen-day trip to the frontier of Tongking.[202]

---

[199] Its origin is obscure but some linguists derive it from Peguan *tala*, "lord," and *poin*, "wealth." See Yule and Burnell, *op. cit.* (n. 75), p. 891.

[200] This is the New Year Celebration. *Cf.* the description in LeBar and Suddard (eds.), *op. cit.* (n. 178), pp. 56–57.

[201] Marini, *op. cit.* (n. 175), pp. 465–92.

[202] *Ibid.*, pp. 492–540. He stayed in Tongking for about one year before going on to Macao in 1649. He died at Macao in 1665.

According to the Jesuits, the king, originally a military chieftain, is an absolute and independent ruler and supreme lord in civil and religious affairs.
All land is his private property, as are the possessions of his subjects. Nothing whatever may be passed down in a family by inheritance. Titles of nobility are not acquired by birth, purchase, or meritorious service; indeed,
there is really no noble class. Offices, pensions, and honors are conferred
only by the king. At his pleasure, honors and pensions may be withdrawn in
the holder's lifetime and always are at death. Orphans may inherit small bequests or chattels but never lands, houses, precious metals, or arms. No individual owns an inch of land, but the priests may dispose of that on which
they dwell. The king assigns all other lands to the great Mandarins who rent
it to the cultivators. Farm leases run for three years only and require payment to the crown of one-half of the third year's harvest.

Eight chief officials aid the king in governing. A viceroy-general relieves
him of general administrative burdens and acts as regent on the death of the
king; at such times all the Mandarins owe him obedience until a new king is
crowned.[203] The royal council includes the governors of the seven provinces
(*moung*) into which the kingdom is divided.[204] The provincial governors are
equal in power and ordinarily reside at the court, leaving the everyday administration of the provinces and subdivisions to lieutenants sent there.
From the court, the governors run the financial and military affairs of the
provinces. Each province maintains a militia with revenues earmarked for
its support. The splendor of the royal court is enhanced by the governors'
presence and by the numerous pages or office- and gift-seekers who daily
dance attendance on the king. In addition to these officials the palace staff
includes an infinity of others who are employed in a wide range of occupations. The rank of an official can be distinguished by the size and shape of
the ceremonial box his page carries in public gatherings. The "Grand Viceroy" is the only person besides the king who may ride an elephant in their
processions. The governors are carried in small litters and are accompanied
by armed pages in elegant livery; all other courtiers walk.

The king of Laos considers himself to be superior to all other rulers and
even claims equality with the emperor of China. He rarely appears in public
so that, as time passes, his subjects come to think of him as a hidden deity.
All business, no matter how important, is handled through an intermediary
or spokesman. He portrays the extent of his power by acting as a sovereign,
that is, by accepting gifts from vassal kings who come to pay him homage.
He receives such tribute-bearers while seated on a high throne in a great
hall and speaks to them only through others. Particularly proud of his lib-

---

[203] The *maha oupahat* or "second king" as this official is called in Western literature. See LeBar
and Suddard (eds.), *op. cit.* (n. 178), p. 11.

[204] These were probably princes of the blood royal who acted as governors. The "second
king" was not necessarily of royal blood. See *ibid.*

erty and independence, the king enjoys the fact that the far richer kings of Siam and Tongking pay tribute to China while he does not.[205]

Changing conditions in Malacca and the Malay Peninsula emerge clearly from the European sources. Acheh, after its defeat by the Portuguese in 1629, was no longer able to interfere actively in the affairs of the peninsula. Under Dutch occupation after 1641 Malacca's importance as an entrepôt declined as Johore and Patani became more independent and prominent in regional trade and war. The area of Dutch control at Malacca was limited to the city and its immediate vicinity. Dampier described its forts in considerable detail. Careri estimated that in 1695 Malacca had a diverse population of around five thousand Europeans, Asians, and mixed breeds. Its Catholics were forced to live in isolation outside the city, while the Dutch tolerated heathens and even Muslims and Jews within Malacca. Guard-ships of Malacca patrolled the straits and collected tolls from all ships except those of the English. The Dutch merchants and officials studied the Malay language and collaborated with the Muslim rulers of the peninsula's ports and states. North of Malacca was the homeland of the hostile Minangkabau Muslims. The Dutch tried by quiet intimidation rather than by war or occupation to monopolize the foreign commerce of Johore and Kedah, especially the latter's tin trade. In 1689 the Dutch maintained a small fort off Dinding from which they sought to control the maritime traffic in tin. In the straits the Cellate fishers lived under the jurisdiction of Johore. Patani on the east side of the peninsula was one of the most populous trading centers and it sent annual tribute to Siam.

Of the various states of Burma only Pegu and Arakan received detailed treatment in the published sources. Arakan, after its conquest of Pegu in 1599–1600, dominated the scene until the Mughuls defeated its armada in 1665 and drove its officials and their Portuguese auxiliaries out of "Bengala." The Portuguese freebooters of the Bay of Bengal, joined around 1600 by Jesuits from India, had sought in the early years of the century to fill the vacuum in Lower Burma created by Arakan's devastation of Pegu. De Brito and his cohorts had built a fortress at Syriam which they had successfully defended against the avenging armadas of Arakan while appealing to Goa and Lisbon for support and involvement in their Pegu enterprise. In recounting these sea battles the Portuguese sources provided rich, dated detail on armaments, the number of ships and men involved, and the construction of forts. In their letters forwarded to Europe, the Jesuits sketched a plan for the creation of a new Portuguese trading empire in the Gulf of Martaban, based on Syriam. Such an enterprise, if undertaken with the support and cooperation of the Portuguese in "Bengala," might lead eventually, they

[205] Marini, *op. cit.* (n. 175), pp. 456–60. This claim of independence is supported by the Laotian annals. See Lévy, *loc. cit.* (n. 174), p. 67, no. 13.

suggested, to control of most of the ports of the eastern side of the Bay of Bengal and even of some of the rich Burman cities in the interior to the north of Syriam. These reveries were dissipated by Ava's conquest of Syriam in 1613 and by Arakan's descent two years later upon the Portuguese-controlled Islands in "Bengala."

The description of Arakan in the 1630's by Manrique and that of Wouter Schouten for 1660 are of exceptional interest and value for the reconstruction of its seventeenth-century history. In addition to giving vivid descriptions of the overland routes and waterways leading into Mrauk-u, both European authors remarked on the presence in Arakan of numerous Muslim traders and artisans and Japanese Christians and mercenaries. They also observed that Arakanese were not allowed to go abroad. Both described royal audiences, ceremonies, and processions, and the physical appearance of the king then on the throne. Mrauk-u, Arakan's capital, was seen to cover about the same area as Amsterdam but with a denser population estimated at around 160,000. Manrique, who was in Arakan much longer than Schouten, gave the names and titles of the royal officials and noted the presence at court of Brahmans and eunuchs. He described royal palaces, shrines, and temples of which no trace now remains; he also referred, though not in great detail, to the still extant shrine of Mahamuni and its temple. As an Augustinian priest and missionary, Manrique showed a particular interest in the externals of Buddhism and a great disdain for the few of its teachings which he learned about. He gave details on its hierarchy, monastic vows and practices, household observances, and burial customs. Temples, idols, and religious rites also attracted his attention. He was most impressed by the charity and tolerance of both the Buddhist priests and laity.

But he was even more discursive on matters of state. Entranced by the white elephant and the legends told about it, Manrique concluded, probably correctly, that it symbolized the legitimacy and sovereignty of the ruler who possessed it. He reported on the futile efforts of Goa in 1633 to work out a treaty with Arakan. In horror he described the holocaust of 1634 visited upon the populace by its ruler as part of the preparation for his long-delayed coronation. He participated in the coronation ceremonies of 1634–35 in which Thirithudhamma crowned twelve vassal kings and had himself elevated to the imperial dignity. As an eyewitness he was able to describe the rites and to note that the ranks of officials were indicated by the shafts of the umbrellas they were given permission to carry. He participated in royal banquets and observed eating habits and foods served. He learned, as earlier Europeans also had, that the kings of Arakan married their sisters to keep the bloodline pure. These kings reputedly also received one maiden annually from each of Arakan's twelve provinces for the harem. While conversions in Arakan proper were difficult and rare, the Augustinians of the delta converted two Arakan royal princes. One of them, whose name in religion was Dom Martin, worked in the Portuguese navy in Goa and after 1640 was received at court in Lisbon. From Schouten it was learned that an oath of loyalty to the king was sworn every five years, usually on November 15. And it was also the Dutchman who discussed the problem posed for Arakan when Shah Shujah fled to Mrauk-u in 1660 to seek refuge from the wrath of Aurangzib. Five years later, the Dutch and other foreigners left Arakan to avoid involvement in the hostilities with the Mughuls.

In the seventeenth century much less was published on Cambodia than in the previous century, probably because of the foreign and civil wars in the Mekong delta. The Europeans who wrote about Cambodia were the occasional merchants and missionaries who entered the country during intervals when relative peace and order reigned. They noted the names of Cambodia's chief cities, and began to ask questions about the ruins of Angkor. Their curiosity about this ancient city's builders was piqued, in particular, by the revelation that its inscriptions could not be read by the local literati. At the court and in the market towns along the Mekong they saw Malay Muslims, Chinese, Japanese, and Annamese, and even an army of occupation from Cochin-China. They gave the names for three polygamous noble classes and observed that a tax of 10 precent was levied by the crown on all produce. The missionaries reported on the rising influence of Malay Muslims at the court and the conversion to Islam of Barom Reachea VI. They described the sack and burning of Udong in 1658 by the Cochin-Chinese and their occupation of Cambodia. In 1666 the remnants of this occupying force were massacred and all relations severed with Cochin-China. Khmer writing and coins, as well as local sports such as cock-fighting, kite-flying, and polo, were remarked upon. The missionaries in particular commented on Buddhism and the various nature gods revered in Cambodia. Exasperated by the indifference of the Cambodians to Christianity, the Jesuits mainly saw Cambodia as an entryway to Laos.

Two European sources—Van Wusthof and Marini—gave rich detail on Laos in the 1640's during the celebrated reign of Souligna Vongsa. Both provided itineraries for the journey up the Mekong from Lovek to Lan Sang, the old royal capital of Laos. In particular they described the Khone falls, the Khemmerat rapids, the stopover towns, and the bisecting caravan routes. The Jesuits, who had long planned to enter Laos from Siam and Tongking, sought information on internal routes; Leria on his exit explored the way to Tongking. Surrounded on all sides by high mountains, the flat heartland of Laos was watered by the Mekong and its distributaries. The river itself was thought to have its source in Yunnan and to be fed by waters from the snow-capped mountains of Tibet visible from the plateau of Laos. The history of Laos, according to native informants, could be traced back to A.D. 600. A census revealed that five hundred thousand soldiers could be raised if needed. Throughout the kingdom Buddhism was dominant and justice was so severe that thievery and adultery were practically unknown.

A cheerful and spirited people, the Laotians reveled in games, sports, fireworks, dramas, and dances at their festivals.

But most attention was focused on the court, the king, and the government. The capital city and its royal palace buildings were described in some detail along with audiences and processions. Descended from military chieftains, the king was an absolute ruler and the sole proprietor of the land. No class of landed nobility existed, and all officials owed everything to royal favor. Mandarins were assigned lands which they rented to cultivators on three-year leases. One-half of the third year's harvest went as payment to the crown. Lands and towns assigned to Buddhist priests and monasteries were held in perpetuity and could be disposed of by the holder. In addition to gifts and land rents, the king received revenues from the royal monopolies on stick-lac, benzoin, and gold. The king ruled through a council of eight ministers comprised of "a second king" or viceroy and the governors of the seven provinces. The governors lived at court and each ran his province and its militia through appointed lieutenants. The central administration was divided into three chief bureaus. The viceroy controlled the armed forces, governed the capital, and acted as regent in an interregnum. Another official served as viceroy in the south and a third was charged with the administration of foreign affairs. The pontiff of the Buddhist hierarchy was appointed by the king. The king himself lived like a hidden deity with his five wives, rarely appeared in public, and conducted his business through intermediaries. He claimed to be the equal of the emperor of China, since he paid no tribute to Peking and did receive tribute himself from vassals.

Therevada Buddhism was the element common to all the coastal states here reviewed except Malaya. Muslims, mostly from Malaya, were employed in all the Buddhist courts as soldiers, and many others worked as merchants throughout the region. Japanese, many of whom were Christian refugees, were hired as soldiers and often lived in separate communities. Brahmans were in charge of astrology and ceremonies in Arakan and Cambodia, and merchants from the Coromandel Coast were prominent in most port cities, especially in Malaya and Arakan. Chinese merchants and artisans sometimes sought refuge in the ports of Southeast Asia to escape the Manchus. Annual gifts were sent by the king of Siam to a famous Buddhist shrine in Cambodia. Even in times of war pilgrims regularly visited this shrine from all the other Buddhist countries of Southeast Asia. The Buddhists, unlike the Muslim princes and the Dutch Christians of Malacca, were generally tolerant of foreigners and their beliefs. When the Jesuit Leria wrote a book in Laotian on Christian beliefs, he was instructed by Souligna Vongsa to write a life of the Buddha, too!

CHAPTER XV

Siam

While the Portuguese were on the defensive in Malacca and while Lower Burma lay in disarray, the empire of Ayut'ia (Siam) was recovering from the sixteenth-century ravages inflicted by its hostile and aggressive neighbors.[1] As a center of international trade, Ayut'ia had long functioned as a vital cog in the Asian state system and the international junk trade, both dominated by China. It had attracted traders and shipping from as far away as Japan and Europe, particularly those who were eager to buy Chinese goods in its marts. For its own part, Ayut'ia had acquired firearms from the Portuguese and had imported other weaponry from Japan. Its own trading vessels had ranged widely from India to the Philippines. The rebuilding of an independent Siam had begun around 1580 under the direction of the "Black Prince," Naresuan, who shortly became Phra Naret (r. 1590–1605). He had first sent off a diplomatic mission to China in an effort to obtain Peking's support of his nascent independence movement. Strengthened Siamese forces had meanwhile made more costly the periodic raids of the Khmers of Cambodia. Naresuan had defied his Burmese suzerain and in 1590 proclaimed himself king of Ayut'ia. After successfully defending his state against a final Burmese offensive of 1593, Naresuan undertook successful campaigns in Cambodia and in the Burmese provinces of Tenasserim and Tavoy on the Bay of Bengal. While securing his inland frontiers, Naresuan continued to maintain and expand relations with his European and Asian trading partners and had even concluded a treaty with Spanish Manila in 1598.[2]

[1] See *Asia*, I, 519–38, for Siam in the sixteenth century. In what follows in this chapter we have tried to follow the general system of phonetic transcription of Thai characters into roman devised by the Royal Institute of Bangkok (1954), except for place-names and most proper names.

[2] See David K. Wyatt, *Thailand: A Short History* (New Haven, 1984), pp. 100–105. On

The Portuguese, who had begun to trade in Siam in 1512, dominated the European trade with China and Japan until the last generation of the sixteenth century. It was with the rise of Manila after 1565 and the development of a regularized trans-Pacific trade that this Portuguese monopoly was broken. The Philippines, long involved in the junk trade of the Eastern seas, now became a launching pad for Spanish commercial, military, and missionary activities. In Manila and Spain a debate went on, particularly after the union of the Spanish and Portuguese crowns in 1580, over whether or not to take advantage of the Thai-Cambodian wars to send a military expedition into Indochina. When Portuguese Dominicans and Spanish Franciscans were periodically sent to work in Siam, they were caught up in the whirlwinds of the continental wars and were fortunate when they escaped with their lives. Once Siam had reestablished its independence by defeating Pegu in 1593, a new delegation of Franciscans was dispatched to Ayut'ia in an effort to put relations between Manila and Siam on a firmer footing.

I

IBERIAN AND DUTCH ACCOUNTS

On the basis of communications from a few of his brother Franciscans, Marcelo de Ribadeneira put together a brief account of Siam which he included in his *Historia* (1601). There is very little here which goes beyond or modifies significantly what was found in the Portuguese descriptions of the Thai monarchy published in the sixteenth century. He reports on state ceremonies and the reception of a Cambodian envoy, but he discourses best on the capital city of Ayut'ia in the end years of the sixteenth century.[3] It is a large "lake-island . . . accessible by the navigable streams surrounding it."[4] The shoreline is fortified by a high wall of cemented bricks that is topped by watchtowers and protected by "about eight hundred pieces of artillery" on its ramparts. It is further defended by the river which floods the whole city

---

Siam's place in the Chinese tributary system and in the international junk trade of maritime Asia see S. Viraphol, *Tribute and Profit: Sino-Siamese Trade, 1652–1853* (Cambridge, Mass., 1977), pp. 1, 7–8.

[3] After the defeat of 1569 the walls of Ayut'ia were probably dismantled and then gradually rebuilt as defiance of Burma grew. While scholars disagree on the dismantling, it is beyond dispute that a renovation of the city's fortifications was being undertaken by 1580. Although Ribadeneira's is one of the earliest Western descriptions of Ayut'ia's rebuilding, it is not cited in Larry Sternstein's otherwise excellent article on "Krung Kao, the Old Capital of Ayutthaya," *Journal of the Siam Society,* Vol. LIII, Pt. 1 (1965), pp. 83–132. See also the description in J. Gatty, *Voiage de Siam du Père Bouvet* (Leyden, 1963), p. 107.

[4] P. G. Fernandez (trans.), *History of the Philippines and Other Kingdoms by Marcelo de Ribadeneira, O.F.M.* (2 vols.; Manila, 1970), I, 427. Ayut'ia was actually built on an island in the Menam River at the center of the Chao Praya water system. On the canals at the southern extremity of the floodplain in the Ayut'ia period see Yoneo Ishii, "History and Rice-Growing," in Y. Ishii (ed.), *Thailand: A Rice-Growing Society* (Honolulu, 1978), pp. 27–29 and fig. 4.

"for at least one-half of the year" and renders it safe from siege or conquest during that period. From a distance the city presents a panorama "of towers and gilded pagodas carved with diverse figures in silver." While its temples and palaces are "grand edifices," the common people live in simple straw houses. In the surrounding streams can be seen ships from China, Macao, Malacca, Patani, Java, and Borneo. Most of the city's residents "own at least one vessel and the majority own large vessels" which engage in trade. The official in charge of foreign visitors is a naturalized Chinese who himself owns a great number of trading vessels. Siam exports cotton thread, brazil-wood, silver, lead, and deerskins. Although it is sinful to kill deer, they are nonetheless hunted in the dry season when they come down from the mountains to graze in the plain. Their meat is preserved and the skins sold. The Siamese likewise kill and capture other wild animals—elephants, tigers, rhinoceroses, and goats—when these beasts descend to the plain.[5]

The learned men of Siam recount a legend of how one of their earliest kings came from a vast desert in Cambodia and brought to them their religious beliefs and practices. After enjoying the blessings of marriage, this king forsook the world to live a solitary life of prayer and penance in the mountains. After a time he returned to the city and gave to the priests the following six commandments: honor and worship the idols, never kill any creature, never steal, never lie, never cohabit with a foreign woman, and do not drink or engage in debauchery. In China and Japan the name of this great king is Amida (Buddha) but in Siam he is called "Perdeneab" and various other names.[6] All his teachings and revelations are the "secret possessions of the educated and the priests." Three kinds of religious orders prevail: hermits; monks who live within a community, follow a rule, and beg for food; and contemplative groups which observe a vow of silence. The duties of these monks are limited to tending and comforting the sick, the performance of funeral ceremonies, and chanting in choirs. All who live within temple compounds follow daily routines under the watchful eyes of a superior and other members of the hierarchy. They exhibit fraternal concern for one another and give deference to age and rank. Ordinarily one brother shaves the other's head, the young being particularly honored to be shaved by elders.

Siam's "only worthwhile science" is the art of reading and writing. There is simple handwriting and easy reading for the masses in books of religious and secular history and culture; the reading of the laws is a subject "reserved only for the scholarly few."[7] Young boys and men, both commoners and

---

[5]Fernandez (trans.), *op. cit.* (n. 4), I, 427–28. On hunting and trapping *cf.* W. A. Graham, *Siam* (3d ed.; 2 vols.; London, 1924), II, 52–58.

[6]Fernandez (trans.), *op. cit.* (n. 4), I, 429–30. For the Siamese names of the Buddha see *ibid.*, pp. 214–15, and H. Alabaster, *The Wheel of the Law. Buddhism Illustrated from the Siamese Sources* (Varanasi, 1972), pp. 163–64.

[7]Fernandez (trans.), *op. cit.* (n. 4), I, 431–32. On the vast number of legal books see Graham, *op. cit.* (n. 5), I, 281–82.

nobles, study at the first two levels; the law is taught at an exclusive school "where only the select few may enter." A wide range of materials on religion are written in an elaborate script on wide palm leaves and framed by varnished and gilt edges. In their temple schools, foreign students are also trained who come from Pegu, Patani, Cambodia, China, Cochin-China, and Japan. Educated youths, even commoners, have the right to choose whether or not to remain in the temple as novices destined for the priesthood. Much reverence and deference for the priesthood exists in all social classes, even to the point of tolerating those who have entered the religious life to escape the law or to have a secure existence. The support of temples and priests is "the bounden duty of each citizen." When entering their temples the Siamese to show reverence "place their hands on their shoulders and sway their heads from side to side." While the Franciscans were told that the Siamese had no need for a new law or religion, the Christian friars were well treated by both the laity and the Buddhist priests. The Christians were permitted to practice their religion just as the Muslims were allowed to teach the Koran and the Jews the law of Moses. Many of the Jews had married Siamese women and had built their own synagogues.[8]

Phra Naret, who had built up trade relations with the Europeans, was succeeded by his brother Ekathotsarot (r. 1605–11) who had virtually ruled jointly with him. The new king, who had inherited a secure and vigorous state, quickly sent an ambassador to Goa in hopes of establishing closer relations with the Portuguese. The Jesuits, who had long been concerned about their Japanese converts in Ayut'ia, sent Father Baltasar Sequeira (1551–1609) in 1606 from San Thomé in India to Siam. He arrived at Ayut'ia in March, 1607, and remained there for slightly more than two and one-half years.[9] News of this initial Jesuit endeavor was first relayed to Europe by letters published in the collection of Guerreiro. Sequeira was to reconnoiter the ground to determine whether a mission could be fruitfully set up in Ayut'ia. He interviewed the "talapaios" (Buddhist priests) about their beliefs, watched their religious processions and burials, and studied the temples with their "singular architecture." On two occasions he was received graciously by the king and reassured that the Portuguese traders and the Jesuits would continue to be welcome at Ayut'ia. On the basis of these experiences, Sequeira concluded that this land appeared to be a large and populous "seedbed" for the planting of the evangel. Despite this favorable report, the Jesuits did not quickly move to establish a permanent mission in Siam.[10]

Jesuit hesitancy to move into Siam can probably be accounted for by ref-

---

[8]Fernandez (trans.), *op. cit.* (n. 4), I, 434–35. Other references to Manila's relations with Siam in this period may be found in Antonio de Morga's *Sucesos de las islas Filipinas* (1609), as translated and edited by J. S. Cummins ("HS," 2d ser., CXL; Cambridge, 1971), especially pp. 80–83, 151, 189–91.

[9]See J. Burnay, "Notes chronologiques sur les missions Jésuites de Siam au XVII° siècle," *AHSI*, XXII (1953), 170–76.

[10]On the Jesuit residence finally set up at Ayut'ia see below, p. 1188.

erence to a general deterioration in Portuguese relations with Ayut'ia. Most Jesuits traveled there in Portuguese ships and were there by permission of the Portuguese king. The growing threat of the Portuguese in the Bay of Bengal, and especially the activities of De Brito in Lower Burma, evoked concern in Ayut'ia about the security of Tenasserim, Siam's main port since 1593 for trade with India. The Dutch, who had established commercial relations in 1602 with Patani, were meanwhile becoming increasingly active in the Gulf of Siam. Always anxious to obtain China goods, the Dutch sent an embassy in 1604 to establish relations with Siam, the most important of China's vassals in the region. The Thais welcomed this overture in the hope of finding an ally in their fight to check Portuguese expansion. In 1607 King Ekathotsarot signaled a shift in policy by sending diplomatic missions to both Goa and the Netherlands. While the embassy to Goa complained about Portuguese activities in Lower Burma, the authorities in Goa and Madrid reacted angrily to the establishment of Thai-Dutch relations. The Dutch, being both rebels and heretics in the eyes of Philip III, would certainly use their new relations with Siam to form a league against Malacca and to acquire a port and fortress on the Gulf of Martaban to halt the spread of Syriam's authority southward. While the Siamese embassy was returning from the Netherlands, King Ekathotsarot in 1610 offered the VOC the opportunity to build a fort at Mergui, a port adjacent to Tenasserim, located about midway between the Portuguese bases at Syriam and Malacca. Although the Dutch were eager to participate in the trade of Ayut'ia, they were not prepared to commit themselves at this time to a political alliance which would involve a possible war against the Iberians.[11] The emissaries returned to Ayut'ia in 1611 when a succession struggle was in progress following the death of Ekathotsarot. His successor Song Tham (r. 1611–28) continued to favor the Dutch even though the VOC refused to become openly involved in the struggle between Siam and Burma for the Tenasserim coast following the death of De Brito in 1613. Finally, in late 1617, Burma and Siam arrived at a peace settlement by which Chiengmai was ceded to Ayut'ia and Martaban to Burma.[12]

The English East India Company ship, the "Globe," reconnoitered the Gulf of Siam in 1612. Its merchants set up a factory at Patani and went on to Ayut'ia to deliver to its ruler a letter from King James I. The English were received cordially by Song Tham and obtained permission to set up a factory. Despite the obvious discontent of the Dutch, the English began to compete in the general inter-Asian trade and to infringe upon Thai-Japanese commerce. Pieter Floris, one of the merchants aboard the "Globe," spent

---

[11] In 1609, while the Siamese emissaries were still in the Low Countries, the Dutch had concluded a twelve-year truce with Spain.

[12] Based on George V. Smith, *The Dutch in Seventeenth-Century Thailand,* Special Report No. 16 of the Northern Illinois University Center for Southeast Asian Studies (De Kalb, 1977), pp. 10–17.

more than one year in Siamese waters before returning to England in 1615. Excerpts from his journal were published by Purchas in 1625. From this disjointed account it is possible to learn a few facts about economic, social, and political conditions in the Gulf of Siam. Details about the succession crisis of 1610–11 in Ayut'ia emerge, and there are references to the continental wars of 1612 between Lan Sang and Ayut'ia which produce "bad times so unfitting for Trade." In Patani, where the English spent the winter of 1612–13, a queen rules who is "a comely old woman . . . tall and full of Majestie." This queen's younger sister was married to the king of Pahang twenty-eight years ago, a union that led to strife rather than alliance between the two Malay states.[13] On July 12, 1613, the king of Pahang is finally forced by war and famine to seek refuge with his wife and two sons in Patani. He brings news of Acheh's seizure of "Raja Boungson" (Bongsu) of Johore and his children, and the flight of this ruler to the island of Bintan. While the Pahang ruler enjoys Patani's hospitality, he encourages the English to seek trade at his port. On October 4 the English and Dutch help to suppress an uprising of Javan slaves. This is the third rebellion, the first two being by Japanese, in which "Patania hath been burned."[14] From these few references it can be vaguely seen that Patani, the vassal of Ayut'ia, enjoyed a high degree of independence and was deeply involved in the affairs of the Malay Peninsula.[15]

The English at Patani and Ayut'ia soon found that they were unable to compete profitably and by 1623 closed their factories in Siam.[16] The Dutch, who were also disappointed by the returns from trade in Siam, nonetheless continued to maintain their factory and to negotiate with Ayut'ia. While they closed their office briefly in 1623–24, it quickly became apparent that Batavia needed Siam's rice and other provisions for survival. On the death of Song Tham in 1628, another succession crisis occurred in Ayut'ia which hampered trade. The accession of Prasat Thong (r. 1630–56) inaugurated political and commercial changes which produced an alliance between the Portuguese and Patani directed against the Dutch and Ayut'ia. When Japan temporarily reopened its doors to international trade in 1633, the VOC without further hesitation became actively involved in the wars between Siam and its rebellious vassals on the Malay Peninsula. The Portuguese, who supported Patani, were banned from trading in Ayut'ia; the Spanish in Manila were likewise in disrepute with the Thais. As a consequence the

[13] The first two queens of Patani, Raja Ijan and Raja Biru, ruled from 1584 to 1624. Raja Ijan was married after 1584 to Sultan Abdul-Ghafur Mohaidin Syah (r. 1590–1614) of Pahang. During the period of the queens they were known by the Thai term *phrao-cao,* one indication among others that they recognized the overlordship of Ayut'ia. See A. Teeuw and D. K. Wyatt, *Hikayat Patani. The Story of Patani* (2 pts.; The Hague, 1970), Pt. I, pp. 13–14. *Cf.* pl. 244.

[14] *PP,* III, 322–33. For Floris' full account of these events and many others see W. H. Moreland (ed.), *Peter Floris and His Voyage to the Indies in the Globe, 1611–15* ("HS," 2d ser., LXXIV; London, 1934), chaps. iv–viii.

[15] *Cf.* B. W. Andaya and L. Y. Andaya, *A History of Malaysia* (London, 1982), p. 67.

[16] This was related, of course, to the general decision of the English East India Company to concentrate on India rather than on the further East. *Cf.* above, pp. 77–78.

Dutch by 1633 were the only Europeans on good terms with Ayut'ia. Joost Schouten (d. 1644) of Rotterdam, who had been an assistant in the VOC's skeleton staff in Ayut'ia from 1624 to 1629, was appointed its director in 1633. He remained in this post over the following three years, during which time the VOC tightened its relations with Ayut'ia while becoming a much more active military force in continental Southeast Asia.[17]

In the last year of his residence in Ayut'ia, Schouten wrote his *Beschrij-vinghe van . . . Siam,* a work which first appeared in print during 1638. Over the course of the seventeenth century it was several times reissued in Dutch and translated into German, French, English, Latin, and Swedish.[18] This was the first general account of Siam published in the seventeenth century; as such it was widely distributed and generally consulted as a source by later writers.[19] Designed as a report to the VOC, Schouten's *Description* is that of a capable and devoted servant of the Company. It is nonetheless an incisive discourse in which the author truthfully records and sympathetically comments on what he observed during eight years of service in Siam.[20]

"A famous and potent Kingdom," Siam borders on the north with Pegu and Ava, extends westward to the Bay of Bengal, stretches southward to the Gulf of Siam, and runs eastward into the "Desart of Cambodia" and to Luang Prabang. Shaped like a half moon, this country has many ports and bays, and off its coasts lie numerous islands. While mostly level in its interior, the lands along the sea are mountainous, woody, and marshy. Its chief river, called the Menam, or the Mother of Waters, is wide, long, and "the most frequented Haven of the whole Kingdom." While it swiftly runs from north to south through Ava and Pegu into Siam, its source is unknown; it discharges itself into the Gulf of Siam through three mouths.[21] Like the Nile and Ganges, the Menam floods annually and inundates the surrounding country for four or five months. Its great eastern mouth is traversed at its entry by a sand flat that can be safely crossed by seagoing vessels only at high tide or in the flood season.[22] Ships can easily go up river as far as Bangkok. Those that proceed to Ayut'ia are sometimes forced to remain there until the autumn floods come to provide the river with more water.

[17] See Smith, *op. cit.* (n. 12), pp. 17–27.
[18] For further bibliographical detail see above, pp. 456–57.
[19] Van Vliet's description of Siam, first published in 1692, is heavily dependent on Schouten's work. See above, p. 501.
[20] What follows is based on the English translation of 1663 as introduced and edited by C. R. Boxer, *A True Description of the Mighty Kingdoms of Japan and Siam by François Caron and Joost Schouten* (London, 1935).
[21] In fact there is not a single river "Menam," the general Thai word for river. Originating from four main streams of the Thai Northern Mountains, a short river is formed that quickly divides into distributaries. It is the main distributary to the east, the Menam Chao Praya, which is traditionally referred to as the Menam, or the chief river of Siam. See E.H.G. Dobby, *Southeast Asia* (9th ed.; London, 1966), pp. 263–64.
[22] This obstructing bar of sand or mud was about ten miles wide. At low water it was covered by three feet of water or less. See John Crawfurd, *A Descriptive Dictionary of the Indian Islands and Adjacent Countries* (1856 ed., reprinted Varanasi, 1974), p. 380.

The southern portion of Siam is replete with towns, villages, and people. Its twenty principal towns are governmental centers. Ayut'ia, the royal capital, is built on a little round island in the Menam and encircled by a thick stone wall. Its suburbs lie across the river in "a flat and fruitful country." Within the walled town the streets are "large, straight, and with channels running through them" which come up "to their very doors." More than three hundred "faire Temples and Cloysters" adorned with gilded towers, pyramids, and innumerable images add to the city's beauty. The magnificent royal quarters stand on the river like "a little town apart" with many gilded buildings and towers. Well situated for trade and defense, Ayut'ia is frequented by people of "all Nations."

Siam's government is in the hands of an absolute monarch of venerable lineage. He legislates, judges, and negotiates alliances "without any advice or consent of his Council, or Lords." Only on occasion does he ask his council to deliberate upon matters of state. Whatever advice it may offer is presented in the form of a supplication "which he confirms, changes, or rejects, as he thinks good." He alone makes appointments to offices and awards all honors. In general he favors the members of the oldest and greatest families as well as all those, noble or non-noble, who serve him well and loyally. He is equally arbitrary in meting out punishments and dismisses officials even "for small faults." His subjects proudly recognize that they are royal slaves or vassals by the titles they take. While he acts absolutely, the king as sovereign does "nothing without some appearance of reason" or without consideration for Thai custom and law. He does, however, exercise his prerogative to bend or reinterpret ancient traditions "to his Arbitrary will and pleasure." He appears in public rarely and meets with his officials only "at certain appointed times and daies." At a royal audience he sits richly clad on a golden throne with a crown on his head and attended by a bodyguard of three hundred armed soldiers. His subjects as well as foreigners kneel throughout an audience with hands folded and head bowed down. When addressing him they remain prostrate and their remarks bestow upon him high titles and flattering phrases. His responses are "esteemed Oracles, and his commands unchangeable." [23]

This absolute king "lives happy in all imaginable worldly pleasures" in many magnificent palaces and pavilions scattered throughout the kingdom. In addition to his queen, he possesses a great number of concubines chosen from "the most honourable and beautiful Maidens" of the realm. While he eats well, his drinks are restricted to water and coconut milk, since all "strong drinks" are prohibited by religion and law. The king and his court ordinarily are rowed from place to place in a fleet of barges; on the royal barge the king sits on a throne covered by a pavilion. In a royal progress by

---

[23] *Cf.* the description of a state audience at the time of the coronation of King Prajadhipok in 1926 in H. G. Quaritch Wales, *Siamese State Ceremonies, Their History and Function* (London, 1931), pp. 177–80.

land, the king and his courtiers are silently carried in palanquins while the observers quietly do him reverence by prostrating themselves as his entourage passes by. Each year around October the king shows himself in state to the public when he goes in procession to sacrifice at the main temple. In a march overland on this occasion, the king either sits on an elephant or is carried on a gilded throne; he is accompanied by fifteen to sixteen thousand attendants and six hundred armed men. His passage by water to the temple is followed by a similar vast train which winds its way through the spectator boats lining the river.[24]

As one of "the richest Princes of India," the king receives revenues amounting annually to "many Millions." Profits are derived for the crown from the sale to foreigners of Siam's rice, sappanwood, tin, lead, saltpeter, and "Sand and Mountain Gold."[25] Royal ships trading to India and China also bring in great returns. Maritime customs, tribute from vassals and governors, and presents for favors swell the royal purse. Local merchandise is sold by royal factors, since foreign trade is a crown monopoly.[26] Several appointed officers collect and account annually for the royal revenues. Most of this income is spent on the construction and rehabilitation of temples, merit payments, and running expenses. The surplus, which is thought to be considerable, remains in the royal treasury.

While the laws and customs of Siam are strange, they are not without order. On the death of a king he is legally succeeded by his brother rather than by his son. When there is no brother, the succession reverts to the eldest son and his brothers successively. Once this line ends, the royal succession falls to the sons of the eldest brother. Daughters have no right of succession or any role in government. This order is not always observed, as in the succession of Prasat Thong, the present king. Of a powerful family and popular with the people, he eliminated the legitimate heirs and usurped the throne.[27]

Civil and criminal justice are administered by appointed judges who enforce traditional customs and laws. In Ayut'ia, besides the ordinary courts, there sits a college of twelve, headed by a president, which acts as a final court of appeal in both civil and criminal cases. Appeals to the crown are permitted but they are costly and likely to be useless, for the king and the royal council ordinarily reaffirm the decisions of the court of appeals and order the execution of its sentences. Civil disputes are brought into the ordinary courts by lawyers who examine the witnesses and plead their client's case before the justices. These proceedings are summarized in writing by a

[24] Schouten in Boxer (ed.), *op. cit.* (n. 20), pp. 95–99. This is the royal *Kathina,* a Buddhist observance of great splendor. See Wales, *op. cit.* (n. 23), ch. xvi.

[25] On gold in Siam see Graham, *op. cit.* (n. 5), II, 71–72.

[26] On Prasat Thong as a developer of royal trade monopolies see Viraphol, *op. cit.* (n. 2), p. 19.

[27] On succession and usurpation at Ayut'ia see Wales, *op. cit.* (n. 23), p. 67, and Wyatt, *op. cit.* (n. 2), pp. 105–8.

secretary, entered into a record book, and signed by the litigants or their deputies. The book is sealed until the next sessions, when it is opened in the presence of both parties. Further debates ensue, which are entered in the book before it is sealed again. These legal wrangles often drag on for many years before the case is "finally adjudged and ended by a full Colledge." In criminal cases—robbery, personal injury, murder, and treason—the suspect is imprisoned and then examined. If he denies the accusations leveled against him, he is "forced by torture to confession." The confession is entered into a book which is presented to the judges who sentence the accused. Capital punishments are reserved to the king, who decides whether to pardon, banish, or execute the condemned individual. Punishments are designed to fit the crime and range from dismissals from office to exile, slavery, confiscation of property, mutilation, and execution. Whenever guilt cannot be clearly established, litigants are subject to trial by ordeal.

The royal naval and land forces, recruited mainly from the Thais and their vassals, include a few foreign mercenaries: Muslims, Malays, and some five hundred highly regarded Japanese.[28] The native levies serve without pay and must always be in readiness for the king's command. Depending upon the crown's needs, one man in every hundred, or fifty, or twenty, or ten, or five may be called into service. The retainers of nobles, ordinarily some hundreds for each lord, accompany their masters to the field. When it is required, the king can raise "some hundred thousand men" and two to three hundred war elephants along with the necessary supplies and arms. As a rule, however, his armies rarely exceed one hundred thousand and usually number only forty or fifty thousand. The infantry is fairly well organized but armed only with bows and arrows, shields, swords, pikes, and a few muskets; the cavalry is armed only with swords, shields, bows, and lances. Several hundred trained elephants, each mounted by three armed men, constitute the main striking force. While they have a fair number of cannons, they "do not well know how to use them."[29] At sea their galleys and frigates are well armed with great guns although their sailors "are but pitiful." Their innumerable *prāos* are poorly armed and their sailors badly trained. Even so, the Thais manage them well enough to deal with their "neighboring enemies." Given inspired leadership, these unwarlike people can be trained to be good soldiers, as is proved by the conquests they have made in the surrounding kingdoms and provinces. Siam continues to war against Pegu and the rebellious Cambodians while protecting its battle-scarred frontiers "with small flying armies of twenty or thirty thousand men."[30]

[28] On the Japanese in Siam see E. M. Satow, "Notes on the Intercourse between Japan and Siam in the Seventeenth Century," *Transactions of the Asiatic Society of Japan*, Vol. XIII, Pt. 2 (1885), pp. 139–210, and Y. Ishii, "Seventeenth-Century Japanese Documents about Siam," *Journal of the Siam Society*, Vol. LIX, Pt. 2, (1971), pp. 161–74.

[29] The Europeans report by way of contrast that the Annamese are excellent in their use of European weaponry. See below, p. 1252.

[30] Schouten in Boxer (ed.), *op. cit.* (n. 20), pp. 99–102.

The Thais, like their neighbors, are idolaters and heathens who erect temples and cloisters everywhere "for the service of their Gods and the dwellings of their Priests." These sumptuous edifices of wood or stone house an incredible number of richly adorned idols of all sizes, one of these figures being one hundred twenty feet high. Siam's many men of religion are well disciplined, obedient to superiors, and subject to the final authority of the high priest of Ayut'ia. His spiritual power, while "vastly great," is still subordinate to that of the king.[31] Ayut'ia alone boasts at least thirty thousand yellow-clothed and celibate priests and monks. Those religious unwilling to observe their vows are free to doff their robes and take up another way of life, and many do. The most learned of these religious "are professed Priests, out of which the Regents of their Temples are chosen." Priests teach, preach, and make offerings on feast days and holy days. All religious celebrate the gods daily in their cloisters by songs, readings, and other services. They live on the charity of the king and the "great ones," and on the returns from the lands they hold. But mainly they are sustained by the people at large, who daily fill their "begging bags." Old shorn nuns live "in Chappels near the greatest Temples" and assist in religious services; they follow no rule but freely volunteer their help.[32]

The Siamese believe generally in one chief god "who created all things"; he lives in heaven with many lesser deities. The souls of all men are immortal and are rewarded or punished "according to their merits and actions."[33] These tenets of their faith "have been delivered to them in writing many hundred years since" and have been reaffirmed by the examples set by many holy men. They worship the memory of holy men in their images, "which they have set up like so many lesser Deities." Since they believe that the souls of the deceased are reborn in animals and fish, they kill no living creatures; to gain merit they release captured birds and fish on the feast days celebrated in their temples. All other evils "which Nature teaches us to be sin" their priests likewise preach against. They propitiate their gods by placing offerings before the idols. They solemnly celebrate at the "new, full, and quarters of the Moon." Once a year they fast for three months and pray for the sick and the deceased.[34] The dead are prepared for the funeral pyre by being "shaven, anointed, charmed, and with much ceremony" and praying by the priests. The ashes of the deceased are collected, anointed, and buried

[31] On the "divine" attributes of kingship see Wales, *op. cit.* (n. 23), pp. 29–41. On the relation of church and state in early Buddhism see M. E. Spiro, *Buddhism and Society: A Great Tradition and Its Burmese Vicissitudes* (New York, 1970), p. 379.

[32] On the role of women in Thai Buddhism see B. J. Terwiel, *Monks and Magic* (Bangkok, 1975), pp. 257–60.

[33] Thai Buddhist laymen never talk of nirvana for themselves, for they believe that virtue will be rewarded first in heaven (*sawan*) or the realm of the dead, a happy state on the way to transmigration. See Spiro, *op. cit.* (n. 31), p. 77.

[34] This is *Vassa*, often called the Buddhist Lenten season. It is usually observed from the full moon of July to the full moon of October, with fasting from sunup to sundown.

near a temple. At much expense to the survivors they erect a rich pyramid on the grave.[35]

Marriage customs vary according to social and financial circumstances. Persons of substance who marry need to obtain the consent of parents or friends, the "Priests not intermeddling at all." Divorce and remarriage are not frowned upon. A married man may have as many concubines as he chooses. They live in subordination to the wife "whose children onely inherit." The wealth and possessions of "great men" are divided on death into three parts: one each for the king, the priests and the funeral, and the children. Among the common people it is customary for the man to purchase a bride from her father or friends. Like the upper classes they may divorce or remarry at will. Children of commoners inherit equally, except for "some little advantages for the eldest Son."

The Thais are tawny, well-proportioned, "modest enough in civil conversation," deceitful, timid, and "very lying." Males are "lazy and slow," and force their women and slaves to cultivate the fields and perform other labors which elsewhere belong to men. Both men and women wear "painted petticoats" and little else. Gentry and nobles are attended by many slaves and even ordinary citizens are followed by a slave or two when they "go abroad." Their houses, built "according to the fashion in India," are elevated by three or four feet to be above the floods. Townsmen work as officials, merchants, artisans, or fishermen "each one containing [confining] himself in [to] his vocation." Rural people grow rice and fruits and raise "swarms" of domesticated animals and fowls. Provisions are abundant and cheap, even though large quantities of rice are exported. Bricks, lime, wood, and other building materials are readily available for the construction of temples, forts, houses, and ships.

Trade in the market towns, especially Ayut'ia, is "very good and free in its course." The principal commodities for sale are textiles from Coromandel and Surat, China wares, jewels, gold, benzoin, gum-lac, wax, sappanwood, eaglewood, tin, lead, and deer hides for the Japan trade.[36] The king himself is a merchant who annually sends his ships, factors, and capital to Coromandel and China; in the trade with China he has for long been more favored and privileged than other monarchs.[37] The incredible profits he derives from foreign and domestic commerce occasion "no small disturbance to private Merchants." Thai currency is a round of fine silver "impressed with the King's picture" in denominations called "Ticlas" (ticals, or *băt* in Thai), "Mase" (*maas,* or Thai, *sa-luⁿg*), and "Fong" (the silver *fuang* or Thai *bia* is equal to six hundred cowrie shells). Ordinarily they reckon in

---

[35] Schouten in Boxer (ed.), *op. cit.* (n. 20), pp. 104–6. *Cf.* the description of modern funeral ceremonies in Terwiel, *op. cit.* (n. 32), pp. 260–68.

[36] In Japan deer hides were used to make shields and moccasins.

[37] Maritime trade between China and Siam goes back to the thirteenth century. On the court-managed trade see Viraphol, *op. cit.* (n. 2), chap. ii.

terms of "Cattys" (Thai, *chăng*), each equalling twenty "Tayls" (1 tael = 4 ticals). These are the only coins accepted in transactions, except for the cowrie shells used by the poor for petty purchases.[38]

In their relations with Europeans the Thais had given great preference to the Portuguese during the sixteenth century. Not only did they receive the Portuguese envoys and merchants, the king also awarded offices and "preferments" to the Portuguese residing in his country. They enjoyed the freedom to practice their own religion and their chief priest received a monthly stipend from the crown "for his more splendid subsistence." While the Catholic priests, like the Muslims, enjoyed freedom, the Thais showed no interest in becoming their converts. The Buddhists condemn no faith "but believe that all, though of different tenets, living virtuously, may be saved." The Portuguese began to lose favor as the Dutch interrupted the commerce between Siam and the Coromandel Coast and started to trade on their own at Ayut'ia. In 1624 the Thais barred the Spanish from Manila because of their attacks upon shipping in the waters of Siam. Thereafter the Portuguese totally lost their credit at court, and by 1631 their nationals in Siam were imprisoned, in part because of the machinations of the Dutch. While the Dutch "hath not profited much" from trading at Ayut'ia, it is in the best interests of the VOC to foster good relations with Siam in order to feed Batavia and to keep the other European merchants, especially the Spanish, from returning to Ayut'ia.[39]

All Spanish efforts at reconciliation failed to allay the hostility of the Siamese. In 1626 the Jesuit fathers Pedro Morejon and Antonio Cardim, accompanied by a Japanese brother, arrived in Ayut'ia from the Philippines. Morejon obtained the release of some Castilian prisoners and returned to Manila with the Castilians, a letter from the king of Siam, and a part of the booty confiscated in 1624 from the Spanish offenders. Cardim, who was delegated to set up a mission in Laos, was joined at Ayut'ia in 1627 by Giulio Cesare Margico (d. 1630), an Italian Jesuit. Prospects for the mission appeared to be promising, until new maritime hostilities broke out in 1628 between the Siamese and the Iberians. Refused permission by the Siamese to proceed to Laos, Cardim returned to Manila in 1629 with a Spanish mission sent to iron out relations with Ayut'ia. In the following year another mission from Manila brought a declaration of war. Margico and the Japanese brother were at once imprisoned. The Italian died in prison but the Japanese was rescued by his compatriots and left Ayut'ia in 1632. With his departure the Jesuits vanished from Siam until another residence was established there in 1655.[40]

---

[38] Schouten in Boxer (ed.), *op. cit.* (n. 20), pp. 107–9. On Thai weights and currencies see Smith, *op. cit.* (n. 12), pp. 134–35. Also see pl. 35.
[39] Schouten in Boxer (ed.), *op. cit.* (n. 20), pp. 106, 109–10.
[40] See Burnay, *loc. cit.* (n. 9), pp. 180–83.

Antonio Cardim (*ca.* 1596–1659), a Portuguese Jesuit, reports on these events in his *Relatione* of the Japan Province of the Society first published at Rome in 1645. In this work he summarizes what had occurred to 1644 in Siam, Tongking, Cochin-China, Cambodia, and the projected mission to Laos, all then within the jurisdiction of the Japan Province headquartered at Macao.[41] Cardim studied the Thai language and claims to have read Buddhist texts in order to write refutations of their teachings. The country known as Siam to the Chinese, Japanese, Portuguese, and some of its own natives is commonly known to its inhabitants as "Muahthai" (Maha-Thai, or Great Thai), "Crug" or "Crug Cia" (Krung or Krung Kao, meaning the "old city," or Ayut'ia),[42] "Pramachanacara" (?), "Sri" (an honorific expletive), and "Ajothia" (Ayut'ia). "Crug Cia," a name that they also give to China, is an honorific indicating that Siam is superior to all other kingdoms and inferior only to China. "Pramachanacara" means a "conqueror kingdom" which has never been vanquished. "Sri" is a title so revered that they give it to their temples. "Ajothia" is the proper name of the principal city which often appears on world maps as "Odin." Siam's vassals are the "kingdoms" of "Pan" (Pran), "Patani" (Patani), "Singora" (Singora), and "Ligor" (Ligor or Lakon).[43]

The royal palace is a great brick building on the bank of the Menam, a river three times as wide as the Tiber. Several entryways lead into a spacious court, inside of which stand several brick towers housing the royal treasures. The hall where the king receives foreign embassies has three portals. The central portal is reserved to the king; all others enter and exit by the other two.[44] The king himself resides in a high chamber that has a large opening overlooking the reception hall, through which glitter the golden statues standing on all sides. On this window there is a large grille of gilded iron and a very precious curtain. When the king shows himself, the curtain is immediately pulled aside, the trumpets, fifes, and drums resound, and the courtiers prostrate themselves. Behind the king stand two court Brahmans who offer him betel from time to time while singing his praises. When the king indicates that he wants to speak with a certain person, that individual immediately joins his hands, kisses the tips of his fingers, returns to his pre-

[41] For full bibliographical data see above, pp. 378–79. What follows on Siam by Cardim is from the French translation *Relation de ce qui s'est passé depuis quelques années, iusques à l'an 1644. au Iapon, à la Cochinchine, au Malabar, et en plusieurs autres isles et royaumes de l'orient compris sous le nom des Provinces du Iapon et du Malabar, de la Compagnie de Iesus* (2 pts.; Paris, 1645–46), Pt. I, pp. 153–78. Only Pt. I is by Cardim, whose original report to Rome was written in Portuguese. Only the Italian and French translations were published.

[42] *Krung* is used only as a designation of a capital city. See C. H. Philips (ed.), *Handbook of Oriental History* (London, 1951), p. 110.

[43] For their locations see the map in E. W. Hutchinson, *Adventurers in Siam in the Seventeenth Century* (London, 1940), frontispiece.

[44] Cardim, *op. cit.* (n. 41), p. 156, claims to have entered this reception chamber in "1619," probably a misprint for 1629.

vious posture, and listens to what the king has to say; in replying, the supplicant must follow the same ceremony. Twice each year at the equinox the
king receives an oath of fidelity from his "Mandarins."[45] For these occasions
courtiers clothe themselves in the white garb of mourning and penitence.
The "Viceroys" (probably court Brahmans) wear a small crown of gold on
their turbans. Once they are assembled in the royal hall, a golden vase full of
water arrives, into which they plunge various weapons. Thereafter each
member of the assemblage takes a drink of this water. It is said that if a person is meditating disloyalty he will be killed by these arms.[46]

The government of Siam is divided into tribunals, each with a president. These officials and the president of the "Mandarins" report directly
to the king. There are five orders of "Mandarins": "Ocun" (*ǫk-khun*),
"Ocmun" (*ǫk mu'n*), "Ocluang" (*ǫk-luang*), "Ocpra" (*ǫk-phra*), and Oýa"
(*Phă-ya*).[47] Members of the last two groups sit in the king's council. On in-
stallation these "Mandarins" receive as an insignia a small betel box, those
given to the "Ocpra" being silver and those of the "Oýa" of fine gold. For
their maintenance they are endowed with elephants, boats, villages, and retainers. Half of their retainers ordinarily work and live in the village while
the other half attend the master at court or elsewhere.[48]

The floods of the Menam are more extensive than those of Tongking and
Cochin-China.[49] As the flood approaches the people send their beasts to the
mountains and put their small domestic animals on especially prepared
floors. Once the water begins to retreat, the king leads a procession on the
river.[50] Twenty days upriver from Ayut'ia stand the cities of "Passaloco"
(Phitsanulok), "Socotay" (Sukhothai), and "Capeng" (Kampengget), all of
which are surrounded by villages.[51]

The Siamese observe the law of "Xaca" (Japanese for Buddha). Their
"Bonzes" (Japanese for Buddhist clerics) preach and teach while sitting in a
chair. Their letters are not hieroglyphs like those of China but are completely different. Their funeral rites are likewise diverse. After death the

---

[45] Cardim and others apply several terms to the Siamese scene which are usually used by Europeans with respect to China and Japan. Perhaps the word "Mandarin" is used to indicate that
the Thai nobility, like the Chinese, was not hereditary.

[46] Cardim, *op. cit.* (n. 41), pp. 156–57. This is a brief but essentially correct account of the
ceremony of the Drinking of the Water of Allegiance. *Cf.* Wales, *op. cit.* (n. 23), chap. xv.

[47] These are the *Yasa*, a series of honorific titles here written in an old form. See H. G.
Quaritch Wales, *Ancient Siamese Government and Administration* (London, 1934), p. 35.

[48] In 1454 the whole population of Siam, including the officials, was divided into civil and
military administrations. Officials were entirely dependent for their livelihood on the persons
committed to their charge and received no direct remuneration from the crown. See *ibid.*,
pp. 34, 41.

[49] During floods, lower Thailand is covered with water from one inch to ten feet deep. Elsewhere in Southeast Asia the floods are more controllable. See Dobby, *op. cit.* (n. 21), pp.
274–75.

[50] This is the ceremony of the "Speeding of the Outflow." See Wales, *op. cit.* (n. 23), pp.
225–26.

[51] Cardim, *op. cit.* (n. 41), pp. 157–59.

corpse is retained for about one month in the home. Its limbs and members are stretched out flat and tied down with cords. Salt water is introduced into the eyes and mouth to have it penetrate the body. Once prepared, the body is then taken outside the town to a burning ground. "Mandarins" are taken there in a boat procession. Mourners, including the wives, walk nine times around the pyre before it is lighted. If the deceased is a chief "Mandarin," the king in person lights the pyre; priests light it for lesser persons. Three days after the cremation they gather up the remains and ashes and take them in a silver vase to the temple. They take the deceased's jewelry home as a remembrance. The bodies of children are not burned but are exposed to be eaten by birds of prey.[52]

Thai absolutism and its succession crises, especially the intrigues and re-volts attending usurpations, caught the interest of the European observers of the seventeenth century. In Europe the popular revolts of the middle years of the century had made it emphatically clear that absolutists had to take a united stand against the spread of the infection of insurrection. With the successes of the "barbarian" Manchus against the mighty emperors of China, civilization and legitimate rule seemed everywhere to be in danger. Even in remote Siam the absolutist rulers faced periodic revolts that were aided and abetted by outsiders. The history of the kingship and the wars of Siam in the first half of the century were summarized for Europe by Jeremias van Vliet, a leading Dutch merchant who was situated in Ayut'ia from 1633 to 1641. Written in 1640, Van Vliet's *Historiael verhael* was first published in Europe in the French translation of Abraham de Wicquefort and included as a supplement (beginning p. 569) to the *Relation du voyage de Perse et des Indes orientales. Traduite de l'Anglois de Thomas Herbert* (Paris, 1663).[53] Based on Siamese annals no longer extant, Van Vliet's chronicle is one of the oldest remaining records of the dynasty of Ayut'ia and of the reign dates of its kings. It stresses that the fundamental law of Siam provides that the legitimate heir to the kingdom is the brother rather than the son of the deceased monarch.[54] To some extent a biography of King Prasat Thong (r. 1630–56), this work centers on his usurpation of the throne and of the part played in Siam's succession coups by the court nobility. It also records the difficulties experienced by Ayut'ia in maintaining control over its vassal

[52] *Ibid.*, pp. 168–71.
[53] This French version was translated into English in 1904 by W. H. Mundie. It is reprinted in *Selected Articles from the Siam Society Journal*, VII (1959), 31–90. It is followed in this collection by Frances H. Giles, "A Critical Analysis of Van Vliet's Historical Account of Siam in the Sev-enteenth Century," *ibid.*, pp. 91–158. The original Flemish text is published in parallel with the French translation of 1663 in S. Iwao (ed.), *Historiael verhael der sieckte ende doot van Pra Interra-Tsia 22ᵐ coninck in Siam, ende den regherenden coninck Pra Ongh Srij door Jeremias van Vliet, 1640* . . . (Tokyo, 1958). The Flemish text was then analyzed in Thai (1967) by Kaehorn Sukhabanij. See Smith, *op. cit.* (n. 12), pp. 127–28.
[54] On the ideal monarch in the Siamese tradition see Prince Dhani, "The Old Siamese Conception of Monarchy," *The Siam Society Fiftieth Anniversary Commemorative Publication* (Bangkok, 1954), II, 160–75.

states during and after succession crises. It brings out clearly the important role taken by the Japanese mercenaries in a Siam internally torn by the rise of Prasat Thong from 1629 to 1633.[55] The maze of intricate political detail accumulated by Van Vliet for the decade of the 1630's throws light on a period about which other sources are silent. Married to a Thai woman who was influential at court, Van Vliet was in a position to observe and to learn from both Siamese and Dutch informants about the beginning years of Prasat Thong's reign.

Prasat Thong's rise had been marked by a growing Dutch involvement in the political and military affairs of Siam. The VOC supported Prasat Thong economically and militarily in 1634 in his anti-Iberian policies and in his wars against Patani. In return for its support, the VOC demanded and received important commercial concessions. To counterbalance the growing Dutch influence, Prasat Thong in 1636 made new overtures to the Portuguese at Malacca and to the Spanish at Manila. While playing this balancing game, Prasat Thong had eliminated his internal enemies, had pacified all his vassals except for Cambodia, and had established a stable and secure government. In 1641 the Portuguese lost Malacca to the Dutch as well as much of their influence in the Malay Peninsula. Siam's relations with the Dutch again became closer in the late 1640's when Siam began to experience new resistance from its southern vassals. In the last few years of Prasat Thong's reign the position of the VOC at Ayut'ia once again deteriorated. Batavia, involved elsewhere in wars with the Iberians, the English, and their collaborators of the insular world, was no longer in a position to render naval aid to Siam for its wars of pacification in the peninsula.[56]

With the decline of Dutch influence at Ayut'ia, the Jesuits returned to Siam in 1656, the year of Prasat Thong's death.[57] After a new but brief succession crisis, Narai gained the throne and began the consolidation of his power with the aid of a loose confederation of Japanese-Thais, Patani-Malays, and Iranian Muslims.[58] The new king, who faced very little internal opposition during the remainder of his lengthy reign (1656–88), tended at first to maintain an "open-door" for the European traders and missionaries. At the same time he and his factors managed and monopolized foreign trade at Ayut'ia and increased Siam's own direct trade with Japan, China, and Taiwan. The VOC, engaged in war with Koxinga over its expulsion from Taiwan, was forced by economic considerations to close its factory in Ayut'ia during 1663–64. Outstanding grievances between Siam and Batavia were

---

[55] Many of the Japanese residents were eliminated in this period.
[56] Based on Smith, *op. cit.* (n. 12), pp. 21–35.
[57] See Burnay, *loc. cit.* (n. 9), p. 185.
[58] The role of the Iranians in the commerce of Southeast Asia is obscured in the European sources by the Christian writers who in their hostility refer to most Muslims as "Moors" and rarely make distinctions by using words such as "Turks" or "Persians." For the participation of the Iranians in the rise of Narai see John O'Kane (trans.), *The Ship of Sulaiman* (New York, 1972), pp. 94–97.

worked out in a treaty of 1664 which reconfirmed and regularized the commercial rights and obligations of the Dutch Company, granted it a virtual monopoly on the export of hides, gave it reasonable assurance that debts could be collected from local traders, and conceded it extraterritorial rights over its European employees.[59] To the early 1680's good trading relations prevailed under the terms of the treaty and the Dutch managed in 1671 to obtain a monopoly of the tin exports from Ligor in the peninsula. Narai himself was supplied by the Dutch with luxury goods from Europe, military wares, and European artisans and soldiers. For the Dutch this happy situation was beclouded by the arrival in Ayut'ia of French missionaries and English merchants. The English East India Company maintained a factory there from 1674 to 1684, an enterprise that failed because of local gross mismanagement, peculation by the Company's servants, and the mounting influence of France.[60]

2

NARAI (R. 1656–88) AND THE FRENCH

The French, who had long been watching jealously the commercial successes of the Dutch and English in the East, first gained entrance to Asia through the Congregation of the Propaganda. The French clergy, like the French merchants, were eager to participate in the winning of Asia. The Propaganda, which had tried to free the missions from the control of the secular states, reluctantly agreed in 1658 to appoint three Frenchmen to act as its titular vicars apostolic in the Far East. During the organizing of the Paris Society of Foreign Missions as a national adjunct of the Propaganda, money was raised in France to finance the dispatch of the vicars to their posts in Asia. The first to leave was Lambert de La Motte, titular bishop of Berytus (Beirut) with ecclesiastical jurisdiction over Cochin-China, four provinces of southeastern China, and the island of Hainan. He and two companions left quietly from Marseilles in 1660 for the overland trip to Surat. After a forty-one-day trek across India to Masulipatam, they took a Moorish ship to Tenasserim. From this eastern port of Siam, they proceeded to Ayut'ia, where they arrived in 1662.[61] Unable to proceed to any of his jursidictions because of hostility to the Christians, Lambert and his associates were forced to remain in Ayut'ia, a tolerant city that then included an estimated two thousand Christians.

---

[59] For the complete text of this treaty in English see Smith, *op. cit.* (n. 12), Appendix 6.
[60] See *ibid.*, pp. 35–42; and D. K. Bassett, "English Relations with Siam in the Seventeenth Century," *JRAS, Malaysian Branch*, Vol. XXXIV, Pt. 2 (1961), pp. 90–105.
[61] For the Propaganda and its relations with the French clergy see above, pp. 222–69.

Jacques de Bourges (*ca.* 1630–1714), a companion of Lambert and a secular priest, was sent back to France after a stay of one year in Siam. On his return to Paris he published a *Relation* (1666) of his trip based on the diary he had kept.[62] After a twenty-day sojourn at Masulipatam, the priests leave on March 26, 1662, on a Moorish vessel piloted by a Portuguese. They arrive at Mergui after a voyage of thirty-three days across the Bay of Bengal. On the way they are almost wrecked in the Andamans, islands renowned for the cruelty of their inhabitants, who massacre without pity all strangers who come to their shores.[63] At Mergui they are examined by the Siamese customs officials before being allowed to proceed to Tenasserim.[64] Arrived there on May 19, they are picked up by the small boat of João Cardozo (1619–76), the Portuguese Jesuit with whom they are to stay. On the next day they claim their luggage and learn that duties are levied at 8 percent *ad valorem*.[65] The baggage inspection being perfunctory, it is easy to hide the small European curiosities which are needed for presents. While waiting in Tenasserim for passports, they learn that most of its inhabitants are pagan and under the religious jurisdiction of priests called "Talapoins." They converse through an interpreter with a native priest about his beliefs and are appalled that he answers all their questions by quoting from sacred books. He also reassures them that as Christians they will be tolerated and permitted to teach their beliefs freely. The French also notice that the Muslims are increasing in number at Tenasserim and that they are likewise free to follow their faith.[66]

On June 30 they leave Tenasserim with an interpreter on three river boats, each with a crew of three. Each craft is hollowed out from the trunk of a tall tree and is thus all one piece. Such boats are well adapted to swift streams so full of rapids and waterfalls. Progress upstream is slow, and living is difficult because it is too dangerous to go ashore into the dense jungle where there are tigers, elephants, and other carnivorous beasts. Although the boatmen are adept at pulling the boats through rapids or lifting them over waterfalls, an accident occurs in which the Frenchmen lose their passports. Father

---

[62] The second edition (Paris, 1668) of Bourges' *Relation du voyage de monseigneur l'évêque du Beryte, vicaire apostolique du royaume de la Cochinchine par la Turquie, la Perse, les Indes . . . jusqu'au royaume de Siam, et autres lieux . . .* is cited in what follows. Extracts from Bourges' manuscript diary (Archives des Missions Etrangères [Paris], DCCCLXVII, 117; and CXXI, 626) were translated by E. Hutchinson, "Journal of Mgr. Lambert, Bishop of Beritus, from Tenasserim to Siam in 1662," in *Selected Articles from the Siam Society Journal*, VIII (1959), 91–94; and also by L. A. C. Chorin, "From Paris to Ayuthia Three Hundred Years Ago, June 18th 1660 to August 22nd 1662," *The Journal of the Siam Society*, L (1962), 23–33.

[63] On the sea nomads of the west coast of the Malay Peninsula see D. E. Sopher, *The Sea Nomads* (Singapore, 1965), pp. 57–58.

[64] The French were here following the route to Ayut'ia usually used by Indian and Persian traders. They were doing so to avoid conflict with the Portuguese and the Dutch.

[65] This is the *changkob sinka,* a tax levied on both import and export merchandise. See Viraphol, *op. cit.* (n. 2), p. 25.

[66] Bourges, *op. cit.* (n. 62), pp. 121–30.

François Deydier (1634–93) is forced to return to Tenasserim for new passports while Bourges and Lambert await his return in a thatch-roofed hut which they rent in the village of Jalinga. Finally they leave Jalinga on July 27 for a tortuous three-day journey overland in carts and on foot to the village of Menam, where they are required to show their passports before being permitted to proceed. From here they descend a steep mountain to a pleasant, cultivated valley. Proceeding northward they pass by "Couir" (Koui), "a town of two hundred houses" before reaching "Pram" (Pran), a riverine town close to the sea. On August 13 they arrive in "Pipili" (Petchaburi), a "big city with brick walls." The following day they charter a boat and proceed upriver to Ayut'ia where they arrive on August 22 almost two months after their departure from Tenasserim.[67]

The placement of Siam is advantageous because it lies between the two seas, which offer passages to all the neighboring countries. From its many coastal cities ships sail regularly to India, Japan, China, Champa, Cambodia, Java, and the Philippines. Siam is divided into eleven provinces: Siam, Martaban, Tenasserim, Junk-Ceylon, Kedah, "Pera" (Perak), Johore, Pran, Patani, "Ligor" (Lakon), and "Siara" (Singora). Previously independent kingdoms, these provinces and their governors are now under the domination of Siam. Each province, including Ayut'ia, bears the same name as its principal city. The last four of these provinces on the east coast of the peninsula are more independent than the rest but still pay tribute to Siam. Densely peopled, the coastal cities are surrounded by fertile and well-cultivated lands. Although the whole of Siam is fertile, many lands lie fallow because of a shortage of labor produced by earlier wars. Although they are skilled fishers, and fishing is a great industry, the Siamese are not adept as overseas navigators. As a consequence, so many foreign merchants come to Ayut'ia that twenty different languages may be heard in its streets.[68]

There is probably no country in the world where all religions enjoy the freedom they have in Siam. Ayut'ia's two thousand Christians, most of them Portuguese refugees from other Eastern places, are as free to practice their faith as if they were in Goa. While this tolerance is economically motivated to a degree, it is also consonant with Thai beliefs that all religions are good. It is this pernicious indifference which stands as the greatest obstacle to their conversion to Christianity. Since they have so many idols, great temples, and innumerable monks and priests, their devotions are to the externals of their pagan faith. It is not possible to determine whether or not they believe in a future life or in the immortality of the soul. Their precepts can be reduced to two which include all the others: avoid evil and do good. Their priests, who survive on public charity, live as hermits or in communities under the jurisdiction of a "Sancrat" (*sang-khă-rat,* or Prince of

[67] *Ibid.,* pp. 130–40.
[68] *Ibid.,* pp. 140–45.

the Church) who presides over the royal temple located in the outskirts of Ayut'ia.[69]

Bourges arrived at Rome in 1664 to report on conditions for missionizing in Siam and to complain about the hostile response of the Portuguese and the Jesuits to the advent of Bishop Lambert. In Paris, at about the same time, both the French East India Company and the *Société des Missions étrangères* were officially established. François Pallu, the titular Bishop of Heliopolis (Baalbek) with jurisdiction over Tongking, Laos, and five provinces of southwestern China, arrived in Ayut'ia in this same year with four more priests and a secretary. Lambert, who had been estranged from the Portuguese by orders from Goa calling for his arrest, had taken up residence in the Annamese settlement at Ban Plahet on the south bank of the river facing the city.[70] Once Pallu learned about the adverse conditions prevailing in Annam and other parts of Vietnam, he and Lambert decided that centrally located and tolerant Ayut'ia should become their center for religious propaganda in Southeast Asia. While Pallu started off for Rome in January, 1665, to explain this decision, the Frenchmen in the field began to construct a headquarters in Ayut'ia. In 1668 a two-story brick seminary and a large church were erected at Ban Plahet on land granted the mission by Narai.[71] Schools were started for the training of boys as part of the program for recruiting native clerics. Christian Annamese were sent to Ayut'ia for training and ordination. A ship of the French East India Company in 1669 conveyed Lambert to Hanoi to ordain native priests. French priests from Siam established a small permanent mission in Pegu, and others began to minister to the sick.

In Europe from 1667 to 1670, Pallu was received by Louis XIV and got royal assurances of increased support for the mission. He also published a brief *Relation* (Paris, 1668) reporting on the voyages and the mission activities of the French bishops.[72] In 1670 Pallu left France for the long trek to Siam with letters and gifts for Narai from the French king and the pope. While in India he began to write the king for naval support against the Portuguese enemies of the mission. The king, who was more interested in defeating the powerful Dutch, sent a fleet in 1672 to attack their installations on the Coromandel Coast. Pallu, who returned to Ayut'ia in 1673, was heartily received by Narai, who was certainly aware of the appearance of the French warships in the Bay of Bengal. The bishop obtained a grant of land at Lop Buri in 1673, and here the French built a seminary in which they soon

[69] *Ibid.*, pp. 157–85. The *sang-khă-rat* is chosen by the king from the executive council of the *sang-kha* (priesthood). See W. Blanchard *et al.*, *Thailand, Its People, Its Society, Its Culture* (New Haven, 1958), p. 99.
[70] Hutchinson, *op. cit.* (n. 43), p. 46.
[71] The outlines of their foundations can still be seen in Ayut'ia. *Ibid.*, p. 48.
[72] Pallu's *Relation abregée des missions et voyages des evesques françois, envoyez aux royaumes de la Chine, Cochinchine, Tonquin, et Siam* was translated into Italian for publication at Rome in 1669. A second French edition was published in 1682.

had one hundred students in attendance. In Rome meanwhile Pallu won another victory when the papacy erected Siam in 1673 as an Apostolic See under the jurisdiction of Louis Laneau, a newly appointed vicar apostolic. The same papal decree also declared that the French bishops were exempt from Goa's jurisdiction and commanded the members of the religious orders to obey the vicars in all territories not directly under Portugal's control. Narai, who was obviously pleased to receive a letter from the leading monarch of Europe and by the other attentions he was receiving, quickly expressed his desire to send a mission to France to establish closer relations.[73] In Europe a new *Relation* (Paris, 1674) was published to bring fresh information on the condition of Christianity in Siam (1666–71) and of the missionizing of the French and native priests in Cochin-China, Cambodia, and Tongking.[74] Rumors also began to circulate that Narai was interested in Christianity and himself a prospect for conversion.

Brimming over with optimism for the future of French Christianity in Siam, Pallu in 1674 again left Ayut'ia. These high hopes were dashed temporarily when the French fleet of warships in the East was defeated in 1674 by the combined forces of Golconda and the Dutch. Pallu himself was captured by the Spaniards and did not reach Rome until 1677, and then only after papal intervention at Madrid. The embassy proposed by Narai could not be dispatched to France because of the tight control the Dutch held over the sea-lanes. Nonetheless the French mission in Ayut'ia continued to prosper as a training center of Annamese clergy. The Jesuits in Siam in 1677, after much debate and foot-dragging, finally accepted the authority of the French vicars. Once the Dutch war ended in 1678–79, the French East India Company in 1680 established a factory in Ayut'ia to inaugurate a French economic presence in Siam. In the following year a French vessel carrying Narai's long-delayed embassy to France disappeared after taking on water at Mauritius. Reports of this disaster did not reach Ayut'ia until 1683. Narai immediately sought to verify these reports. Once he was satisfied about their accuracy he sent two new envoys to France in 1684 to find out whatever they could about the ill-fated first mission and to request advice from the French as to the most appropriate method for strengthening relations.[75] The Siamese emissaries arrived in France in the autumn of 1684 to inaugurate a few years of close Franco-Siamese relations which produced in France a brief vogue for things Siamese.

The Siamese legates, two minor officials, were accompanied by six other Siamese and one interpreter. This mission of inquiry was placed in the

---

[73] On the question of whether or not Narai at this time saw the French as a counterpoise to the Dutch see Smith, *op. cit.* (n. 12), p. 42.

[74] The *Relation des missions des evesques françois aux royaumes de Siam, de la Cochinchine, de Camboye, et du Tonkin* was probably written by Luc Fermanel de Favery. See Streit, V, 630. An Italian translation was published in 1677 and another French edition in 1684.

[75] See L. Sitsayamkan, *The Greek Favourite of the King of Siam* (Singapore, 1967), p. 55.

charge of Father Benigne Vachet (1641–1720), a French missionary priest who had spent most of his Asian career in Cochin-China. On learning of the dispatch of the first Siamese embassy, the French had quickly jumped to the conclusion that Narai "wanted to make an alliance with a prince [Louis XIV] who . . . had been able to humiliate the Dutch, a nation considered in the Indies to be the most powerful of Europe because of the great number of its ships."[76] The king of Siam had chosen as his original chief ambassador a very important mandarin who had acted on three occasions as ambassador to China. This experienced envoy was expressly chosen by the king, who hoped to learn from his reports the differences between "the Empire of China and the Kingdom of France, countries at the two extremities of the universe, from his viewpoint." Because the French public demanded more information, the *Mercure galant* and the *Gazette de France* in 1684 began publishing articles and news about Siam.[77] The letters from Bishop Laneau to the Paris Mission Society had stressed Narai's favorable disposition to the French and his ardent desire to see the operations of their East India Company enlarged. By this time the French missionaries in Siam had given up trying to convert the king himself.[78] It was evidently Vachet who suggested to the French court that an embassy should be sent to Ayut'ia with the object of concluding commercial agreements, of securing and regularizing the position of the French missionaries, and of converting Narai to Christianity. All this was to be effected with the aid of Constantine Phaulkon (1647–88), the Greek favorite of Narai who had been recently converted himself by the Flemish Jesuit Antoine Thomas (1644–1709). The Jesuits in France, led by Father François de La Chaise (1624–1709), Louis XIV's Jesuit confessor since 1675, were quick to support Vachet's suggestion that a plenipotentiary be sent to Siam to invite Narai to become a Christian. Such a conversion fitted snugly into the Jesuit program of concentrating on rulers, a policy that was being followed contemporaneously in Peking.[79]

Louis XIV's ambassador was the Chevalier Alexandre de Chaumont (b. *ca.* 1640), scion of one of the oldest French families, a naval officer who had won distinction in the Levant, and a recent convert from Calvinism to

---

[76] From the preface to the geographer Claude de L'Isle's *Relation historique du royaume de Siam* (Paris, 1684). This is a compendium based on the printed eyewitness materials then available. This book was published in the autumn of 1684, perhaps to coincide with the arrival of the envoys.
[77] On the growing interest of the French public with respect to Siam see also Gatty (ed.), *op. cit.* (n. 3), pp. xi–xix.
[78] De L'Isle remarks in 1684 that because of the good impression made by the French missionaries "we will perhaps succeed in bringing about the conversion of this people." See *op. cit.* (n. 76), p. 266.
[79] On Vachet's role see Hutchinson, *op. cit.* (n. 43), pp. 98–99; Sitsayamkan, *op. cit.* (n. 75), pp. 56–57; and L. Lanier, *Etude historique sur les relations de la France et du royaume de Siam de 1662 à 1703* (Versailles, 1883), pp. 40–44. On the contemporary activities of the Jesuits in France and China see above, pp. 193–200.

Catholicism.[80] Chaumont's coadjutor was François Timoleon de Choisy (1644–1724), a highly literate *bon vivant* known as the Abbé de Choisy. He had titillated and scandalized Paris society in his earlier years by his mania for masquerading as a woman. After a serious illness he gave up his riotous living and attached himself to the *Missions étrangères*. When he learned that the king was looking for an ambassador to Siam, he volunteered his services as chief of mission. Instead he was appointed second-in-command to replace Chaumont in case of need or to remain in Siam as instructor to Narai should the king decide to embrace the Christian faith. Six Jesuit scientists destined for China were sent along with the Chaumont mission. Guy Tachard (1648–1712), one of their number, later went back to France with Chaumont to recruit Jesuit scientists for Siam. On their return, Chaumont, Choisy, and Tachard all published accounts of this first French mission based on their diaries. These three works complement and supplement one another to provide a splendid documentation on the embassy to Narai's Siam in 1685–86.[81] But each is also unique in certain ways. Chaumont's *Relation* is dry, official, and apologetic, for in essence his mission had failed to win Narai over to Christianity, its major objective. Choisy's *Journal* is an intimate, facile, and lively book, cast in the form of familiar letters to a friend which were allegedly not intended for publication. Tachard's *Voyage,* a report he was ordered to write by Louis XIV, was designed to keep alive the belief that Siam and its king were ripe for conversion, especially by the Jesuits, and that France should do its utmost to develop closer economic, political, and intellectual ties with Ayut'ia. Choisy, despite an initial rebuff from Versailles, was used as an escort and interpreter for the Siamese emissaries. In 1687 the reformed Abbé was elected to the French Academy and he spent the rest of his long life writing popular histories of the French kings as well as books of piety.

Each of these accounts tells essentially the same story about the reception of the embassy in Siam and the great deference shown by Narai and his court to the French in the autumn of 1685.[82] The French are somewhat bewildered by the Siamese practice of giving greater deference and precedent to the royal letter than to the ambassador who carries it. All are pleased, especially Chaumont, by the great respect accorded the French emissaries

---

[80] Louis XIV in 1684–85 had launched his anti-Huguenot program. Many Calvinists converted to Catholicism; others fled from France. In taking this action the king was very much under the influence of the French Jesuits, especially Father de La Chaise.

[81] A. de Chaumont, *Relation de l'ambassade de Mr. . . . de Chaumont à la cour de roy de Siam* (Paris, 1686); Abbé de Choisy, *Journal du voyage de Siam fait en 1685 et 1686* (Paris, 1687); Choisy's work was reprinted with illustrations added by Maurice Garçon (Paris, 1930); G. Tachard, *Voyage de Siam des Pères Jesuites . . .* (Paris, 1686). For further bibliographical details see above, pp. 420–21.

[82] For summaries based on these and other sources see Hutchinson, *op. cit.* (n. 43), pp. 101–15; and Sitsayamkan, *op. cit.* (n. 75), chaps. vii–viii.

and note that honors given them exceed even those bestowed upon Chinese ambassadors. The French, unlike the English and Dutch envoys, are not even required to prostrate themselves when in the king's presence. While the French writers cherish this special concession, they all hold Narai in high regard as a builder and as an open-minded king eager for new knowledge.

From Phaulkon with whom he was particularly intimate, Choisy learned the king's daily schedule. The monarch rises at 5:00 A.M. and gives alms from his own hand to the first Buddhist priest who comes to the door of the palace. At 7:00 A.M. he holds an audience for the women, eunuchs, and others living in the palace. Thereafter he instructs the captains of the guard and listens to them if they have anything to report. Then appear the mandarins and the officials in charge of foreigners who live in the palace. The civil judge reports on trials and judgments of consequence, which the king approves or revises according to his pleasure. Around 11:00 A.M. he receives all the great mandarins. At noon he dines with the princess, his sisters, and his aunts; his brothers see him only twice annually. While dining, he hears reports on criminal trials and decides on punishments or clemency. Then he retires to his chamber, lies down on the floor, and is lulled to sleep by having read aloud to him the annals of his ancestors. From 6:00 to 9:00 P.M. a general audience is held with the highest officials of the realm at which they present their petitions. At 10:00 P.M. the secret council assembles, which includes the royal tutor, an eighty-year-old man who is deaf but who still has a good head on his shoulders. It also includes the chief criminal judge, who is also in charge of physicians; the Grand Chamberlain; a young favorite of the king; and Phaulkon, the dominant official of the crown and the soul of the council. Ordinarily this council meets until 2:00 A.M. The royal physician is the only one permitted to interrupt the session, which he sometimes does when he thinks it time for the king to go to bed. This physician remains all night at the king's door and inspects all the food he eats. The king is at "Louvo" (Lop Buri) for eight months of the year, a time when there are fewer councils and more hunting.[83] During the thirty years of his reign Narai has spent more than eight hours daily in taking care of affairs of state. About fifty-five years of age, he is quite thin, with great black eyes. He is active, full of life, and speaks fast and with a stutter. He has the look of a good man who will certainly not be damned for knowing only half the truth.[84]

Foreign trade at Ayut'ia has been curtailed by a variety of factors. Difficulties in their homelands have limited the activities of the Chinese and Japanese merchants. Constant war with Cambodia, Laos, and Pegu has pre-

---

[83] Choisy in Garçon (ed.), *op. cit.* (n. 81), pp. 180–81. On the king's daily timetable first set up in 1458 see Wales, *op. cit.* (n. 47), pp. 71–73. Phaulkon, the "Barcalon" of the Europeans, was then the *Chao Phya Wijayendra* or prime minister. Choisy spoke Italian to him and he replied in Portuguese.

[84] Choisy in Garçon (ed.), *op. cit.* (n. 81), p. 189.

occupied the Siamese. In Cambodia the war is not going well; two kings vie for power, one the vassal of Siam and the other of Cochin-China. Many "Moors," by which term is understood the Muslims of Makassar, Java, Malaya, Turkey, Persia, the Mughul Empire, and Golconda, have left Ayut'ia and taken refuge in Golconda, which is in a naval war with Siam. In November, 1685, a Persian embassy arrives in Tenasserim much to Narai's displeasure. Fearing further Muslim incursions he continues to fortify Mergui and other east coast ports.[85] He is also apprehensive that the Dutch and English will take advantage of his many military involvements to make new demands. It is for all these international reasons that Narai is more concerned about a political alliance with France than about becoming a convert to Christianity.[86]

Wars in Southeast Asia are fought to capture slaves rather than to kill off enemies. Entire villages are moved, for example, from Pegu into Siam, where the captives are given land to cultivate. Almost one-half of Siam's population are slaves taken in Pegu who work the soil. They are beginning to sow wheat in the highlands where it does quite well. Grapes flourish at first but the vineyards die out because of white ants which attack the roots. The Siamese themselves are mainly artisans, especially masons and carpenters. They are able to copy perfectly the best European works of sculpture and gilt but have not yet learned how to imitate paintings.[87] At their festivals they put on Chinese plays, Siamese operas, high-wire acts, and dances by Peguans.[88] One of Choisy's most important assignments was to help Phaulkon select the gifts for dispatch to France, a generous collection which included all the Chinese porcelains in the king's possession.[89]

In France the embassy of 1686 inspired hope for the establishment of viable Asian outposts in Siam. By the beginning of 1687 the French had decided to send a contingent of troops to establish bases in Siam; others were to continue working for the conversion of Narai and his kingdom. To achieve these ends a new embassy was sent out led by Claude Ceberet Du Boullay, a director of the French East India Company, and Simon de La Loubère (1642–1729), a man of letters and an experienced diplomat. The six warships of this embassy, its military contingent, and fifteen Jesuits reached Siam in September, 1687. Despite growing hostility at court to Phaulkon and his French friends, Narai signed a commercial agreement with the French on December 11, 1687. Early in 1688 the French diplomats left for Europe, leaving behind the troops, the merchants, and all the Jesuits except

---

[85] *Ibid.*, p. 199. Persian materials on this embassy of Shah Sulaiman (r. 1666–94) and on contemporary Siam in O'Kane (trans.), *op. cit.* (n. 58), *passim.*

[86] Chaumont, *op. cit.* (n. 81), pp. 80–99.

[87] Choisy in Garçon (ed.), *op. cit.* (n. 81), pp. 241–43. On warfare in Southeast Asia see A. Reid, *Southeast Asia in the Age of Commerce, 1450–1680,* Vol. I, *The Lands below the Winds* (New Haven and London, 1988), pp. 121–29.

[88] Choisy in Garçon (ed.), *op. cit.* (n. 81), pp. 172–73.

[89] *Ibid.*, pp. 173–74, 177. For a list of the gifts sent see Chaumont, *op. cit.* (n. 81), pp. 152–68.

Tachard. Tachard was dispatched to Europe, it is said, as the representative of Siam, charged with working out a political alliance with France.[90]

The excitement provoked in France by these events led Nicolas Gervaise (*ca.* 1662–1729), a young secular priest and missionary in Siam from 1681 to 1685, to publish his *Histoire naturelle et politique du royaume de Siam* (Paris, 1688).[91] According to his own testimony the author traveled widely in Siam and was competent in the language. He had evidently kept memoirs which he prepared for publication only at the urging of friends. According to the publisher's foreword, Gervaise was befriended by the Siamese emissaries in 1686–87 and held frequent conversations with them while preparing his history. He is an eyewitness with a substantial acquaintance with everyday life, and he studiously seeks, although not always successfully, to avoid repeating what was already well known in Europe about Siam. Like others among his contemporaries, Gervaise in his dedication flatters Louis XIV by asserting that Narai bases "his conduct on the incomparable life of Your Majesty, which he takes as a model." This being true, the Siamese king must become a convert and show "as much zeal in abolishing idolatry from his states as you have in ridding your lands of the monster of heresy [the Huguenots]." Gervaise evidently prepared his book as background reading for the Frenchmen who would hereafter go to Siam to implement Louis' program. The young priest had also brought back two boys, sons of the deposed king of Makassar. He presented them at court on his return to France and provided them as far as possible with a French education. In 1688, the year of his history of Siam, Gervaise also published his *Description historique du royaume de Macaçar* (Paris).[92]

Simon de La Loubère, Louis XIV's envoy-extraordinary to the court of Siam, returned to Europe on July 27, 1688, more than one month after the execution of Phaulkon and slightly more than two weeks after Narai's death. News did not reach Europe of the "Revolution of 1688" before the end of the following year. After receiving that news, Father Tachard and others nonetheless continued to believe that the French position in Siam could be salvaged, even though Phra Phetracha (r. 1688–1703), Narai's successor, had concluded a treaty of amity with the Dutch and had forced the retirement of the French garrison in November, 1688. La Loubère, who knew of Narai's death, continued to work on the book to which he owes his reputation: *Du royaume de Siam* (2 vols.; Paris, 1691).[93]

[90] See L. R. Martignan, *La monarchie absolue Siamoise de 1350 à 1926* (n.d., n.p.), p. 133.

[91] In what follows, we cite H. S. O'Neill (trans.), *Nicolas Gervaise. The Natural and Political History of the Kingdom of Siam, A.D. 1688* (Bangkok, 1928).

[92] See above, p. 422 and below, pp. 1448–55.

[93] The English translation (London) of 1693 has been reprinted twice in recent years: in an undated microphoto copy by Bell and Howell Co. in Cleveland and in 1969 by the Oxford University Press at Kuala Lumpur with an introduction by David K. Wyatt as *A New Historical Relation of the Kingdom of Siam*. To date no critical edition of this comprehensive study has yet appeared. Added to the beginning of Volume I of the first edition (Paris, 1691) is an *Avertisse-*

This book is dedicated to Jean-Baptiste Colbert (1665–1746), the young Marquis of Torcy who was appointed secretary of state in charge of foreign affairs in 1689. A native of Toulouse, La Loubère had gone to Paris at an early age, where he frequented the salons and cultivated friendships in the right places. After receiving appointment as Louis' envoy, he began avidly to read everything about Siam and the East that he could lay his hands on. In the course of his book he refers to twenty-three European authors from Pinto to Gervaise. He quotes conversations with Siamese and European informants, especially the missionaries of the Paris Society. Although he himself was in Siam for only three months, he diligently and systematically asked questions and recorded the answers, as well as his own observations, in a memoir. He was probably stimulated by the Jesuit scientists who accompanied the mission to take more than a passing interest in Siamese cosmology, astronomy, and mathematics. Nor was he content to study Siam alone. Aware of the importance of India and China to Siam's past, he read Abraham Roger and Roberto de Nobili on Hinduism, Bernier on the Mughul Empire, and the works of Navarrete, Martini, and Semedo on China. He perused the published letters of the Jesuits and the French missionaries of the Paris Society as well as the work of Alexandre de Rhodes on Indochina. For his Volume II he collected French translations of native works.

While his book reflects the depth of his research and his reliance on the observations of others, Volume I is a well-organized, comprehensive, and mostly accurate survey of Ayut'ia in his day. It has been praised unreservedly by modern commentators, who have too often not appreciated the extent of his borrowings from earlier writers or his tendency to combine others' observations with his own without regard to the fact that some of them were speaking of Siam at a much earlier date. Mostly, however, he seeks to make clear that his borrowings refer to Siam of a previous period. Some recent scholars have stressed his objectivity by comparing him favorably to Tachard and other writers with strong European and Christian biases; others have complacently remarked that his observations have been confirmed repeatedly by later travelers and scholars and by what still can be seen in the less modernized parts of Thailand. While his book is "universally regarded as the finest work on seventeenth-century Thailand,"[94] this judgment should be tempered by the realization that it is a history as well as a primary source. He himself remarks that "this preparation has supplied the defect of a longer residence, and has made me to remark and understand in

---

ment necessaire in which La Loubère remarks on the death of the king of Siam and of the accession of Phra Phetracha. Occasionally the translator of the English edition omits words or summarizes a few sentences into one. Otherwise the English translation seems to be true to the original and to include all its illustrations. In what follows we will cite the Oxford edition introduced by Wyatt.

[94] Wyatt in his introduction, *op. cit.* (n. 93).

the three months I was at Siam, what I could not have perhaps understood or remarked in three years, without the assistance and perusal of those Discourses."[95]

Contemporaneous with the publication of La Loubère's magisterial description, a spate of books appeared in French dealing with the "Revolution of 1688" in Siam and the career of Constantine Phaulkon. Pierre Joseph d'Orleans (1641–98), a Jesuit, published in 1690 such a work based on the published writings and unpublished letters of Father Tachard.[96] The French Jesuits, who then had a heavy commitment to the Siamese and Chinese missions, hoped by such publications to encourage the king and the pope to continue supporting their enterprise in Siam despite the debacle suffered by the French. D'Orleans makes a martyr of Phaulkon, the minister who had worked so closely with the French, and, following Tachard, writes optimistically about a return to Siam. The Jesuit Marcel Le Blanc (1653–93), who, like Tachard, had been driven out of Siam, returned to Europe in 1690 with some French military officers to bring firsthand news of the disaster. In 1692 Le Blanc's book appeared, a memoir whose publication was delayed by the censor because of certain references to Jesuit machinations in Siam during the revolution.[97] The situation for the Jesuits in France was then particularly sensitive, for they were under attack over their policy of accommodation in the Chinese and Indian missions and needed no more divisive issues.[98] Certain French officers from Siam were captured by the Dutch at the Cape of Good Hope and taken as prisoners back to Holland. Soon they began to publish their versions of the French retirement from Siam under General Desfarges.[99] In 1690–91 Abraham Duquesne-Guiton of Dieppe made a voyage of reconnaissance to the remaining French footholds in the East, but not to Siam.[100] In Siam seventy French hostages, including Bishop Laneau, were kept in prison until the spring of 1691. While Tachard and others continued to work to obtain a new French foothold at Mergui, the Dutch were the only Europeans to continue doing regular business in Ayut'ia at the dawn of the eighteenth century.

[95] From "The Occasion and Design of this Work," *ibid.*, p. 2.
[96] *Histoire de M. Constance . . . et de la dernière révolution . . .* (Paris, 1690; reprinted in 1962). This work was dedicated to Pope Alexander VIII.
[97] *Histoire de la révolution du royaume de Siam. Arrivée en l'année 1688 . . .* (Lyon, 1692). For a discussion of the role of the censor and of the relation of Le Blanc's memoir to that of his colleague Father de Bèze see E. W. Hutchinson (trans. and ed.), *1688 Revolution in Siam. The Memoir of Father de Bèze, S.J.* (Hongkong, 1968), pp. xi–xv. These two memoirs were meant originally only for the eyes of the Jesuits' superiors.
[98] See above, pp. 134–35.
[99] For the accounts of Desfarges' critical subordinates—De St. Vandrille (1690) and Vollant des Verquains (1691)—see above, pp. 425–26, and Hutchinson (trans. and ed.), *op. cit.* (n. 97), pp. 125–26.
[100] An account of it was published at Brussels in 1692 as *Journal du voyage de Duquesne aux Indes Orientales, par un garde-marine servant sur son escadre.*

3

THE PHYSICAL ENVIRONMENT

In his *Natural History* (Pt. I) Gervaise notes that the rains of March to October, so much commented upon by his predecessors, vary in intensity and
are repeatedly interrupted. Ordinarily the rivers overflow in August and
flood the fields to a depth of eight to thirteen feet. Only drought or an in-
sufficiency of rain are feared, while the flood is welcomed. It brings fish so
numerous that "without leaving his threshold a man may fish and catch in
an hour more than he can eat in several days." The Siamese, in their boats
called "rua" (*rua*), play games and hold races "amid public rejoicings" during the rains. The south winds which prevail at this season make it easy for
ships to enter ports on the Gulf of Siam. On the principal of Siam's three
rivers, ships of three to four hundred tons can proceed from its mouth upriver as far as Ayut'ia; larger vessels are forced to anchor in the roads because they might become stuck on the sandbank at the river's mouth. Since
the water off the bar's edges is deep, the merchants "make a bridge of their
vessels in order to discharge their merchandise on the quays."

The word "Menam" in Siamese means simply river. Since these people
believe that "rivers are the sources of the waters," they call all of them by
this word which literally means "mother of waters." One river is differentiated from the other by naming them after the towns through which they
pass. The source of Ayut'ia's river is still unknown, but the Siamese think it
originates in a great lake discovered a few years ago in Laos. While potable
in the dry season, the water of this river becomes contaminated in the rains
and "causes dysentery if care is not taken to preserve it in great water vessels" in which it purifies.[101] The commonest river fish is called "caboche"
(Portuguese, *cabóz*, frosh-fish or frog-fish) by the Europeans; it is dried in
the sun and exported to the Dutch in Batavia. In isolated places along the
river, great crocodiles "make war on man and fish alike" (see pl. 212). Traveling on the river from sunset to dawn is made miserable "by a small army
of mosquitos which follow you everywhere." The second river is that
which flows by Tenasserim and originates in the mountains of Ava. The
third is that of "Chantaboon" (Chantabun or Chantaburi) which empties
into the Gulf of Siam on its eastern side and accommodates larger vessels
than the river of Ayut'ia. Siam's most important ports are on its eastern side
at Mergui and Junk-Ceylon (now Phuket). Mergui is one of the safest ports
in the Indies; its harbor is open all year round, and it is an excellent place to
repair ships because wood is so cheap there. Junk-Ceylon's only drawback is
that its harbor is not deep enough for large vessels.[102]

---

[101] Water is kept in martaban jars until it clarifies.
[102] Gervaise in O'Neill (trans.), *op. cit.* (n. 91), pp. 1–6.

Rice ordinarily flourishes in the water no matter what its depth. The "ears" of rice grow above its surface unless the flood comes too swiftly. When this happens the rice cannot grow quickly enough and so is submerged, rots, and dies.[103] Rice is sown only in May and is generally reaped as soon as the flood recedes. Sometimes it must be reaped before recession of the floodwaters because it has grown too high to support itself. This special harvest is gathered by boats, while the normal crop is collected in oxcarts. Ordinary rice is of three kinds. Wild rice, which does not require marshy soil, is "cheap and not very good"; of the two cultivated varieties, "ponlo" (?) is whiter and more expensive than the other type. Harvesting of rice is carried out by groups working and eating together. By daylight they carry the sheaves indoors and by night bullocks trample out the grain.

While most of their rice is grown in the flood plain, the Siamese also cultivate another sort in dry fields which keeps longer and is relished more. They sow it in one place and transplant its seedlings to another. Before transplanting they flood the field with water from reservoirs. Rain and irrigation water are both contained in the field "within little Banks made all around." After leveling the field, they transplant the seedlings one by one by pushing them into the soil with the thumb.[104] Wheat grown in the highlands is watered by hand or flooded with rainwater stored in reservoirs above the fields. Wheat or "Kaou Possali" (*khao sali*) is made into a dry bread that is reserved to the use of the king.[105] For farm work they use both oxen and buffaloes to pull the plow. They guide them with a rope that runs through the cartilage separating the nostrils; it is attached by running it through a hole at the end of the "draught Tree of their Plough." The plow itself has no wheels and is made of four pieces of wood held together by leather thongs.

Everything planted in Siam's fertile soil grows well "without any great care in cultivation." Roses, carnations, and tuberoses flower in all seasons. Two of their chief flowers, "mungery" (*mali*, or jasmine) and "Poursone" (*phut-san*, or gardenia), are not known in Europe. Maize was first planted in the highlands twelve or fifteen years ago (*ca.* 1670) and it grows there so well that it might soon become a common product.[106] Millet, beans, and pepper vines are also cultivated; "peas is the only crop not found in the country." Nothing is more profitable than the brown sugar they produce. Except for lemons and oranges, the fruits of Siam are different, sweeter, and

---

[103] Gervaise is here (*ibid.*, p. 7) describing the floating rice "which grows at the internodes as the water level rises." It is still cultivated around Ayut'ia. See H. Fukui in Y. Ishii (ed.), *op. cit.* (n. 4), p. 248. Also *cf.* a Japanese description of *ca.* 1690 cited in *ibid.*, p. 27.

[104] La Loubère in Wyatt (intro.), *op. cit.* (n. 93), p. 19. Rain-fed rice culture was practiced on the elevations. See S. Tanabe in Ishii (ed.), *op. cit.* (n. 4), p. 42.

[105] La Loubère in Wyatt (intro.), *op. cit.* (n. 93), p. 17.

[106] As indeed it has, particularly since World War II. It now ranks second after rice. Introduced from Mexico, maize was grown in Southeast Asia as early as the mid-sixteenth century. See Reid, *op. cit.* (n. 87), p. 19.

tastier than those of Europe. They include pomelos, bananas of seven or eight kinds, mangosteens, custard apples, mangoes, jackfruits, papayas, and pineapples. Siam's forests are spread over more than half the kingdom. Dense with bamboo, the forests make the land frontiers almost impenetrable. The Siamese also plant hedges of bamboos around their cities and personal properties. Their forests produce two types of ironwood that are almost indestructible; these are cut into planks for building. Eaglewood and calambac, both rare woods, are found in the forests near Cambodia.[107] Although no gold mines exist in Siam, many signs indicate that gold is there. Nuggets found in the rivers have often led the king to employ men to search for gold deposits.[108] The failure of these efforts has recently been balanced by the discovery of iron, tin, *calin* (a mixture of copper and tin), and saltpeter. From these mines come hot and cold springs which are thought by the Europeans to be as efficacious as the waters of Bourbon and Vichy. The Siamese, "as their temperament is different from ours, do not credit these springs with healing powers."[109]

The forests are populated by wild elephants, cruel rhinoceroses, and ferocious tigers. Birds of many kinds exist which are not seen in Europe. In the southerly forests hares and deer are common, and "it is a great pleasure to see a troop of monkeys, young and old, playing by the water's edge." This tropical climate produces many venomous animals and insects. Some snakes are twenty feet long and a foot and one-half in diameter, with a multi-colored skin of surprising beauty. Because they can be seen from afar, they are not the most dangerous of the snakes and they usually feed on poultry. Small snakes are the more to be feared, for they get into houses and beds. The common scorpions found in brushwood are black and their sting is fatal. Centipedes are black and one foot long, with venom at least as virulent as that of the scorpion. But worst of all is the "tokay" (*tok-ke,* a gecko), which gets its name from its cry. It is a lizard-like animal which hunts rats in the thatched roofs, and its bite is fatal. Strangely, the Siamese, who are so exposed to poisonous creatures, have not developed remedies for snakebite.[110] The annual inundation drowns many of the lowland's pesky insects. White ants ravage the books of the missionaries. To preserve them, the Europeans varnish the covers and edges with a little colorless lac. Gnats called "marin-gouins" (*mă-lang?*) sting the legs of the Europeans through their "shamois stockings." Thousand-leggers about six inches long pinch the unsuspecting with head and tail. Fireflies with four wings give off light from their two lower wings when flying.[111]

While Siam includes many hamlets and villages, only nine of its habita-

---

[107] *Cf.* below, pp. 1205, 1259.
[108] *Cf.* Graham, *op. cit.* (n. 5), II, 70–72.
[109] Gervaise in O'Neill (trans.), *op. cit.* (n. 91), pp. 6–12.
[110] *Ibid.,* pp. 12–14. For the gecko see our pl. 269.
[111] La Loubère in Wyatt (intro.), *op. cit.* (n. 93), pp. 15–17.

tions can reasonably be rated as towns. The capital called "Muang Syouthed" by the Siamese is referred to as "Juthia" or "Odia" (Ayut'ia) by Europeans, a name given it by the Chinese.[112] Others call it "Siam" after the name used by foreigners for the country.[113] The Siamese themselves always call their nation "Nuang Thai" or "Muang Thep Mahanakorn," the latter meaning "a kingdom of great strength." Ayut'ia was founded a little more than two hundred years ago by "Chao Thong" (Chao U Thong, who became Rama Tibodi I) or "the King of Gold."[114] The oval capital is now surrounded on three sides by a ruined brick wall that is in process of being replaced by "a better one." Canals entering the city from the great river are "very long, very straight, and fairly deep, in order to carry the biggest ships." The city is divided into quarters called "Bhans" (*bans*), the most attractive of these being the royal section located in its southernmost part. In the first two courtyards of the palace live the officers of the royal household; in the others "are to be seen the old apartments of former kings which are respected as sacred places." In the last courtyard stands the new royal palace in the form of a cross, from the center of which arises a high pyramid, the symbol of royalty. The apartments of the Queen Princess, the king's daughter, and of his wives look out upon "large, well laid-out gardens." On the nearby riverbanks, the king's more than five hundred boats are housed in large sheds. In another quarter of the city live the foreign merchants. All the trading ships moor there in a wide basin. While trade is being carried on in this teeming district, the shipyards on the river are busily repairing and building vessels. The third quarter, the largest of all, is peopled by the natives, many of whom are artisans. In its square, markets are held daily in the morning and evening. Because of its numerous waterways, Ayut'ia has five or six attractive brick bridges and many more insubstantial ones of bamboo. The populace is so numerous that the king can muster one hundred twenty thousand men of military age from Ayut'ia's streets and suburbs.[115] Ayut'ia's beauty and magnificence depend mainly upon its more than five hundred pagodas with their innumerable golden idols.

Siam's second town, known as "Porseluc" or "Pit-se-lou-louc" (Phitsanulok), is located north of Ayut'ia on the great river. Its founder was "Chao Muang Hang" (Phra Muong?) who ruled about two hundred fifty years before the foundation of Ayut'ia. This ruler, who fought a long-

---

[112] Probably derives from Ayodhya, the city of Rama in India. See Sternstein, *loc. cit.* (n. 3), p. 85, n. 2.

[113] The word "Siam" is probably derived from the Cambodian term for "prisoners of war." See G. Coedès, *The Making of South-East Asia* (Berkeley, 1967), pp. 101–2.

[114] He actually founded the Ayut'ia dynasty in 1350, or more than three hundred years before Gervaise wrote. U *Thong* means "the origin of gold." *Chao* means chief or king. See Prince Damrong, "The Foundation of Ayuthia," in *Selected Articles from the Siam Society Journal*, III (1959), 200–201. On the birth of Ayut'ia see C. Kasetsiri, *The Rise of Ayudhya* (Kuala Lumpur, 1976), chap. iv.

[115] On Ayut'ia's population around 1685 see Sternstein, *loc. cit.* (n. 3), p. 98, n. 60. It certainly numbered several hundred thousand.

drawn-out war against Laos, established this town as the capital and one of the early palaces may still be seen there. In size and population it approximates Ayut'ia and is the best-fortified town in Siam.[116]

Between Phitsanulok and Ayut'ia lies "Louveau" (Lop Buri), which is the Versailles of Siam.[117] Earlier kings had a pleasure house here that was abandoned more than a century ago. Narai has constructed a canal linking it directly to Ayut'ia and has built a new and charming palace on the tributary of the great river which runs by it. Three distinctly different courtyards face towards the town proper. In the first there are two small prisons and a room for judging those accused of high treason. Nearby is a great reservoir which was built by a Frenchman and an Italian learned in hydraulics, who completed it after others had tried vainly for ten years to build it.[118] It provides water for the royal palace and pagoda and for the fountains in the gardens. The second courtyard is entered through a grove of trees and a gateway, on each side of which are stables for "four elephants of the Second Order." A square enclosure with white ornamented walls, this courtyard is divided into small compartments which are decorated for ceremonies with Chinese porcelains. Facing the entrance is a large stable where the elephants of the First Order live in luxury. To the side stands a magnificent structure with a large window in the middle, where the king makes an appearance to greet foreign dignitaries. The audience chamber has three doors, and its walls are covered with mirrors brought back from France by the two Siamese emissaries. Its ceiling is divided into four equal squares and decorated with floral designs and Chinese crystals. At the back of the chamber stands a "rather magnificent throne," which the king ascends from the rear. The third courtyard is lower than the other two, and in it are a group of buildings used as the royal living quarters. These rich, gilded apartments are surrounded by a parapet at whose four corners stand awning-covered pools in which the royalty bathe. Nearby is an artificial grotto, covered with evergreens and flowers, whose fountain supplies water to the pools. Around the parapet stand the guardhouses close to a garden of "very rare flowers" which the king sometimes cultivates with his own hands. Facing the royal apartments is a large garden of native trees with walks lined by walls in whose niches lanterns are lighted at night when the king is in residence. Behind the apartments of the king and the princess is a gallery housing the ladies of the court. Only the eunuchs are permitted access to these quarters.[119]

[116] Phitsanulok was a viceregal capital and later a Province of the First Class. See Coedès, *op. cit.* (n. 113), pp. 124–25. Located on the banks of the Nan River, it is today a gateway to the ruins of the ancient capital at Sukhotai. See J. Basche, *Thailand: Land of the Free* (New York, 1971), pp. 171–74.

[117] "Louveau" and "Lawo" are French transcriptions of Luvo or Lo-hu, the town's original name. It is forty miles north of Ayut'ia. See Hutchinson, *op. cit.* (n. 43), p. 15.

[118] The reservoir or artificial lake was known to the Siamese as *ta-le-chup-son.*

[119] Based on Gervaise in O'Neill (trans.), *op. cit.* (n. 91), pp. 17–21. The author provides a rough sketch of the royal quarters at Lop Buri in the French edition. This is the fullest available

Bangkok is without doubt the "most important place in the kingdom," because it is the only coastal town prepared to defend Siam against its enemies to the south. Small forts on either side of the river are manned by one hundred Luso-Asiatic, Christian soldiers, commanded by captains "who drill them every day." The French engineer left behind by Chaumont is about to build new and more substantial fortifications at this site. In the extreme northern reaches of Siam there are only two towns of any importance: "Locontaje" (Sawankhalok)[120] on the frontier with Laos, and Tenasserim on the coast. Tenasserim previously belonged to Ava.[121] Burmese is still used there and Thai is not generally understood. Although its foreign trade has declined over the last five or six years, it is still one of Siam's best dependencies and it is ruled by a viceroy or governor appointed by Ayut'ia. While it takes around six weeks to travel overland from Tenasserim to Ayut'ia by the usual routes, the king knows of a shorter road "hidden in the depths of the great forests."[122] The towns of the southern portion of the country are not so important. Chantabun (or Chantaburi), a fortified and pretty town on the Cambodian frontier, was founded at a site one day's journey from the sea by the ruler who created Phitsanulok. Across the gulf from Chantabun is "Piply" (Petchaburi), a very old town previously used as a royal residence. To its south is Ligor (Lakon or Nakon Sithammarat), where the VOC maintains a factory. The only other town on this coast which belongs to Siam is called "Soncourat" or "Singor" (Singora, or modern Songkhla).[123] This town, spurred on by Patani, rebelled "not more than twelve years ago" against Siam. A Thai expedition snuffed out the rebellion and brought the instigators to the court for punishment.[124]

While Siam's river valleys are heavily populated, the country has "dreadful deserts and vast wildernesses" dotted only with small huts at great distances from one another. Over one-third of the inhabitants are foreigners, many of whom are war prisoners from Pegu and Laos who are "scattered up and down the country in all habitable places." They were dispersed to prevent rebellion and are now so "intermixed with the Siamese that it is difficult to distinguish them," even though they do retain their own languages.

---

verbal account of the palaces and grounds of Lop Buri. See the collection of descriptions in R. W. Giblin, "Lopburi Past and Present," in *Selected Articles from the Siam Society Journal*, VIII (1959), 119–23.

[120] It is shown as "Lacontai" on the map in La Loubère's work. See below, p. 1204.

[121] The city of Tenasserim is a river port in the upper Malay Peninsula.

[122] *Cf.* Bourges' account of his trip from Tenasserim to Ayut'ia, above, pp. 1186–87.

[123] In 1685 Narai hoped to negotiate arrangements in France for the establishment of French troops at Singora. The French wanted their soldiers to be based at Mergui and Bangkok. With the aid of Phaulkon the French got their way. D. G. E. Hall, *A History of South-East Asia* (London, 1964), pp. 345–46.

[124] Gervaise in O'Neill, *op. cit.* (n. 91), pp. 21–23. Included in the original French edition is a map of Siam corrected by the Jesuits and designed in 1687 by M. V. Coronelli, the distinguished cosmographer of the Venetian Republic.

Other foreigners have come to Siam as refugees, and some of these have been given offices of great importance by the king. Seven or eight Portuguese families live in great poverty. Colonies of Japanese, Tonkinese, Cochin-Chinese, and Cambodians live under their own chiefs and according to their own laws. Fierce Malay Muslims are to be found in great numbers and to them "are imputed all the crimes committed." Despite all their bad qualities, these Muslims render the king good service as soldiers. Of the foreign traders who come to Siam for business, the French, though few in number, are preferred to all others. The English abandoned Siam three or four years ago, except for a few who remain in the king's service. The Dutch, who have traded in Siam for the last forty years, are the most important of the Europeans. Their factory building near Ayut'ia stands on a bank of the river and "is assuredly one of the finest and most spacious in the kingdom." At the mouth of the river (at Paknam) they have a warehouse to which their vessels come in May to obtain goods for the Japan trade and in October with wares for the Siamese market. While their trade continues to be profitable, the king distrusts the Dutch and is looking "for a favorable opportunity to drive them out of his dominions." The Moors, like the Dutch, are feared and are tolerated only because of the great amount of business they bring. The Chinese, almost as numerous as the Moors, have "the best of the trade" and annually send fifteen to twenty junks loaded with the best wares of China and Japan.[125]

The Siamese themselves have prepared no maps; or if they have, it is a well-kept secret.[126] To remedy this deficiency, La Loubère obtained a map prepared by a European who traveled all the way up the river to the country's northern frontier. Dissatisfied by this amateur chart, La Loubère asked Jean-Dominique Cassini (1625–1712), the celebrated director of the Paris Astronomical Observatory, to correct it by "some memorials" acquired in Siam. While recognizing that this revised map is still defective, La Loubère includes it in his book, claiming it provides data previously "never heard of" and records more exactly everything that is known.[127] One of the fundamental ideas he questions is the well-established European cartographic convention which shows the great rivers of continental Southeast Asia originating in a great lake near "Chiamai" (Chieng-mai). He learned from the Siamese who had participated in the Thai conquest of that city about thirty

[125] Gervaise in *ibid.*, pp. 24–29.
[126] For a compilation of the European cartography of Siam from the sixteenth through the eighteenth centuries see Lucien Fournereau, "Le Siam ancien . . . ," *Annales du Musée Guimet*, XXVII (1895), 3–43. In the mid-1930's a set of five historical maps were issued in Thai by the Royal Survey Department. For a discussion of these maps see Larry Sternstein, "An Historical Atlas of Thailand," *Journal of the Siam Society*, Vol. LII, Pt. 1 (1964), pp. 7–20.
[127] Strangely, this general map is not reproduced in the collection of Fournereau, *loc. cit.* (n. 126), even though he does know La Loubère's book and the map of the tortuous course followed by the river from Ayut'ia to the sea.

years before that they had not seen a great lake. So he deduces that it is either more remote than previously conceived or "that their is no such lake."[128] Such a conclusion is reinforced for him once he learns that the Menam is "small in its entrance" into Siam.

Essentially Siam is a great valley bounded on its interiors by high mountains which divide it from Laos, Pegu, and Ava. Most of its population is concentrated along the southern waterways, which are navigable by sea-going vessels. To illustrate this point La Loubère includes a detailed map of the Menam valley from Ayut'ia to the gulf prepared by a group of French engineers. Far to the north is the town of "Menang fang," a place famous for its sappanwood and its "tooth of Buddha." The word *fang,* he correctly asserts, is the name for the dyewood called "sappan" by the Portuguese; pilgrims, however, call it "Meuang fan" or "the city of the tooth." East and north of Lop Buri is a place named "Pra bat" (Phra Bat), an honorific word followed by the Buddhist word for "foot." Here there is a footprint of Buddha which they worship as the Sinhalese revere Adam's footprint in Ceylon. Annually the king himself goes to adore it, even though the old men say that the tradition goes back less than ninety years.[129] On the Pegu frontier is the city of "Cambory"[130] and on the border of Laos the town of "Corazema."[131]

The valley of Siam is intersected with waterways called "Cloum" (*klong*). Ayut'ia, an island which stands in the middle of several other islands, is joined to the mainland by a causeway on the east. While the walled city is spacious, only the southeast, or less than one-sixth of it, is inhabited. The rest is uninhabited, though dotted with temples.[132] To make Ayut'ia's organization clearer, La Loubère includes a map of the city which shows its streets, waterways, suburbs, and quarters for foreigners. The Siamese of this region call themselves "Tai Noe" (*thai-nọi*), or "little Thai," and those of the mountains "Tai yai" (*thai-yai*), or "great Thai," whom they call savages. The mountains of the north flatten out as they go southward to the peninsula, which terminates at Singapore. The rivers, which fall from these

[128] Tradition dies hard and slowly. The nonexistence of the lake was not conclusively established until the Lagrée-Garnier mission of 1868. For an interesting study of the origins of this idea see K. Unno, "The Asian Lake Chiamay in the Early European Cartography," in C. C. Marzoli *et al., Imago et mensura mundi. Atti del IX Congresso internazionale di Storia della Cartografia* (Turin, 1985), pp. 287–96.

[129] Pilgrimages are still made in January and February to the *Phra Phutta Bat,* or "Holy Buddha's Foot" east of Lop Buri. This footprint was discovered around 1626. See Graham, *op. cit.* (n. 5), II, 248–50.

[130] Shown on La Loubère's map in upper Siam to the south of "Laconte" (Sawankhalok).

[131] Wyatt (intro.), *op. cit.* (n. 93), pp. 3–6. "Corazema" is probably a reference to the two northeastern frontier towns of Khorat and Sima which were combined in the latter half of the seventeenth century and transfered to a new site at Nakhon Ratsima. See C. Kasetsiri, *op. cit.* (n. 114), p. 115, n. 17.

[132] With Narai spending the dry season in Lop Buri, Ayut'ia's population was considerably diminished during the eight or nine months of the court's absence. See above, p. 1200.

mountains into the Bay of Bengal and the Gulf of Siam render the east coast habitable and make the frontier between Siam and Cambodia less formidable. The numerous islands of Siam's east coast have very excellent ports, fresh water, and cheap wood. They are "an invitation for new colonies," because the king of Siam has only a loose hold on them.[133]

Much of Siam's land is covered with trees not known in Europe. While bamboos called "Mai pai" (*mai-pai*) in Siamese grow thickly in forests, there are very few of the banyans so common in India. Very useful are the numerous "cotton trees" from which they collect the kapok which they use instead of down.[134] From other trees they extract certain oils which they use to whiten plasters and cements. Others yield the gums which become bases in the lacquers of the Chinese and Japanese; the Siamese craftsmen themselves are not skilled in their use. They make an inferior paper of cotton rags or of the bark of a tree called "Ton coi" (*ton-khoi*). Ordinarily they blacken these sheets to give them greater body and a smoother surface. They write on the blackened cardboard-like sheets with "a kind of Crayon" made of dried clay.[135] Their unbound books are made of a single long sheet folded backwards and forwards into fan-like pleats. The Siamese also write on unblackened sheets with Chinese ink, and with a stylus on palm-like leaves called "Bailan" (*ton lam*, book palm). They cut these leaves into long, narrow rectangles and write on them the prayers which their priests chant in the temples. Wood for shipbuilding is abundant; the type called "Wood-Mary" by Europeans "is better than any to make the Ribs of Ships." While cotton grows easily, flax is unknown. The Siamese prefer cotton to linen cloths because they are more absorbent. Cinnamon is produced, but it does not rival that of Ceylon. While their eaglewood is inferior to the "Calamba" of Cochin-China, it is better than that of any other country.[136] Formerly the precious calambac was very expensive in Paris, "but is at present to be had at a reasonable rate."[137]

Siam has an unparalleled reputation for mineral wealth, perhaps because of the great number of its idols, molded metalworks, and gilded temples. It appears that its mines were more productive formerly than now, from the remains of the old pits and furnaces daily discovered; it is thought that they were abandoned during the wars with Pegu. The present king vainly persists, with the aid of Europeans, to search for worthwhile deposits of gold and silver. In the process they have located a few inconsequential mines of copper in which bits of gold are found. Not knowing how to separate the metals, the Siamese add more gold and market it as "Tambac" (Malay, *tam-*

[133] Wyatt (intro.), *op. cit.* (n. 93), pp. 6–8.
[134] On kapok and the *Ceiba indica* see E. A. Menninger, *Fantastic Trees* (New York, 1967), pp. 109–10.
[135] This is the soft pencil called *toa rong*. See Graham, *op. cit.* (n. 5), I, 285.
[136] On the calambac of Cochin-China see below p. 1259.
[137] Wyatt (intro.), *op. cit.* (n. 93), pp. 8–13.

baga, gold and copper alloy; *nak* in Siamese).[138] From their productions of tin and lead the Siamese regularly obtain good revenues. According to the Portuguese a form of soft tin called "Calin" (Hindi, *kala'i*) is sold throughout the East, examples of which can be seen in the tea canisters of Siam. To render the "Calin" harder and whiter they melt it and add powder of "Cadinia" (cadmium or zinc and copper). This mixture produces a yellowish and brittle metal called "Tontinague" (*tutenag*) or white tin.[139] Lodestone is found in a mountain near Lop Buri and at Junk-Ceylon. "Campeng-pet" (Kamphaengphet, or Kampengget) is famous for its iron mines. Its inhabitants make sabers, poniards, and knives of general utility called "pen" (?). They have no pins, needles, nails, chisels, or saws. Their houses are held together by bamboo pegs. From Japan they import iron and copper locks. They sell great amounts of saltpeter and make locally "very bad Gunpowder."[140]

The Siamese divide the year into just three seasons: winter is called "Nanaou" (*na-nao*), or "the beginning of cold;" the "Little Summer" is "Naron" (*na-rǫn*), or "the beginning of heat;" and the "Great Summer" is "Naron-yai" (*na-rǫn-yai*) or "the beginning of great heat." While they have no word for "week," their days "correspond to ours" but begin "about six hours sooner." Like ours their seven days are named for the planets.[141] "Mercury" (our Wednesday) is called "Pout" (*wan-put*) from a Persian word meaning "idol." From this is derived "Pout Gheda" (*put-chedi*) or "temple of idols," the original of the word "Pagoda."[142] The year in Siam begins on the first day of the full moon in November or December. Each year is more often called by a special name rather than by a number. Like other Eastern peoples, the Siamese group the years into a sexagenary cycle. They divide the cycle of sixty years into five subcycles, in each of which they repeat the twelve animal names given to the years.[143] For two years running the year is divided into twelve months, the third year in the series has thirteen months. It is commonly assumed that their month consists of thirty days, but some are longer and others shorter. They give no names to the months and refer to them simply by their number in the order.[144] Their seasons are uneven in

---

[138] Supposedly rarer and more expensive than pure gold. See H. Yule and A. C. Burnell, *Hobson-Jobson* (rev. ed., London, 1968), p. 929.

[139] Tutenag is a whitish alloy of copper, zinc, and nickel. On the confusion in sixteenth-century Europe over these alloys see *Asia,* Vol. II, Bk. 3, pp. 426–27.

[140] La Loubère in Wyatt (intro.), *op. cit.* (n. 93), pp. 13–15.

[141] *Cf.* Philips (ed.), *op. cit.* (n. 42), p. 129; and see the listing given by La Loubère in Wyatt (intro.), *op. cit.* (n. 93), p. 168.

[142] On this as a possible etymology for this mysterious word see Yule and Burnell, *op. cit.* (n. 138), p. 653.

[143] La Loubère gives the names of the years in Siamese in Wyatt (intro.), *op. cit.* (n. 93), p. 169.

[144] The year in old Siam "is a lunar one of 354 days. It is divided into twelve months of alternately 29 and 30 days. To bring them into line with solar time a thirteenth month is added in approximately every third year" (Philips [ed.], *op. cit.* [n. 42], p. 129).

length, the first two months being winter, the next three "Little Summer," and the remaining seven the "Great Summer."

In La Loubère's estimation the ancient Siamese were primitives who lived on fish and fruit. They were probably taught agriculture by the Chinese. Evidence for this assumption is to be found in the ceremony by which the rulers of China, Tongking, Cochin-China, and Siam formerly inaugurated the plowing season. Originally the king performed this ceremony in person on a certain day of the year. He now leaves the conduct of it to "an imaginary King" who is chosen annually to be "Oc-ya-Kaow" (*ǫk-ya-khao*) or "lord of the rice." On the day selected, this temporary king rides on an ox to the plowing field, accompanied "by a great train of Officers." Since this office is thought to be ominous and unlucky for the one who performs it, the temporary king is paid enough for this one-day masquerade "to live on the whole year." This ceremony was possibly "invented only to gain credit to Husbandry, by the Example of Kings themselves." But it now involves a religious sacrifice to supplicate the good and propitiate the evil spirits in order to assure a plentiful harvest. To this end the temporary king offers the spirits a sacrifice by setting ablaze with his own hand a pile of rice sheaves.[145]

Siamese gardens are fertilized with manure. Of their root crops, the potato deserves special mention. Similar to a parsnip in size and shape, its interior is usually white but may also be red or purple. Roasted under ashes, it "eats like the chestnut." While they grow "chibbols" (green onions), they seem not to have onions, truffles, garlic, turnips, "gittruls" (pumpkins), watermelons, artichokes, celery, beets, cauliflower, parsnips, leeks, kale, carrots, lettuce, or other salad greens. Since the Dutch grow most of these fruits and vegetables in Batavia, it would seem that they might also be grown in Siam. The Siamese have an abundance of asparagus, which they do not eat, and a few kinds of large but tasteless mushrooms. Like other Eastern peoples, they eat raw cucumbers, green onions, garlic, and radishes which are sweeter than those of France. The grapes grown in the royal garden of rare plants at Lop Buri are small and bitter.[146]

Near Lop Buri the king has a small house or hunting lodge at "Tlee Poussone" (*ta-le-chup-sǫn*), or "Rich Sea," where rain- and groundwater are caught in a great reservoir for his consumption. City-dwellers "for pleasure and conversation" prefer to drink tea, which they, like the Chinese, call

---

[145] La Loubère in Wyatt (intro.), *op. cit.* (n. 93), pp. 19–20. Modern scholars debate as to whether the Siamese form of the plowing ceremony originates in India or China. For a lengthy recent description and discussion of the ceremony see Wales, *op. cit.* (n. 23), chap. xxi. For an illustration of the modern ceremony see S. Nimit Co. (pub.), *Thailand in Colour* (Bangkok, n.d.).

[146] La Loubère in Wyatt (intro.), *op. cit.* (n. 93), pp. 20–21. This account seems to be contradictory in part and certainly does not square with those of earlier observers. For example, it seems likely that the Siamese did grow garlic.

"Tcha" (*cha*). Tea comes in three varieties, all of which are also used as medicines. Water for tea is boiled in "copper pots tinn'd on the inside" made in Japan, or in earthenware bowls.[147] They drink the tea from "China dishes" while chewing candy. From rice they make beer, aquavit, and vinegar. The Moors in Siam drink coffee and the Portuguese, chocolate. The Siamese relish fruit and eat it all day long when they have it. Oranges, lemons, and pomegranates are those of their fruits known in Europe. Their lemons are very small and sour, while their oranges and pomegranates are sweet. The best of the oranges are called "soum-keou" (*som-kaeo*), or crystal oranges, and they are very expensive. Oranges of some kind and bananas called "clouei" (*kluai*) are available throughout the year. All their other fruits are seasonal. They blacken their teeth with sour lemon juice and certain oils. To redden the nails of their little fingers they apply "rice bruised in Citron Juice with some leaves of a tree."[148]

The small elevated houses of the Siamese are surrounded by "pretty large Grounds." The cattle walk up a ramp to enter their stable in the bottom of the house. Fires for cooking are built outside, where they are laid on a basketful of earth supported by three sticks. While thatch and bamboo dwellings burn often and easily, they are quickly and simply rebuilt. Inns for travelers do not exist in Siam. Between Ayut'ia and Lop Buri there is a caravanserai at which the king sometimes stops to dine. But since most travel is by water, the boats serve as inns. Hospitality by individuals is unknown, possibly because of the care the Siamese take to conceal their wives. Priests and monks who have no wives are more hospitable. For La Loubère and his embassy the Siamese built houses "after their Country fashion," which were richly furnished with mats, carpets, and hangings. Europeans, Chinese, and Moors have brick houses, but the Siamese seem to have trouble building such structures. The courtiers live in timber houses which stand within a bamboo enclosure along with the separate houses of their attendants and their families. All houses have but a single story, reportedly because no person may be higher than the king when he passes by. To make certain that no one looks down upon him, the people leave their houses and prostrate themselves before the royal entourage. Since the royal buildings are also all of just one story, it is more probable that this is merely a traditional way of showing respect and has no relation to their custom of building single-storied structures.

The palaces and several pagodas at Ayut'ia and Lop Buri are low brick constructions. The pagodas are shaped like "our Chappels," and their interiors are darker "than our Churches." It is probable that brick construction was introduced to Siam by European factors, for the natives call their oldest

[147] On their earthenware teapots see Graham, *op. cit.* (n. 5), II, 87.
[148] La Loubère in Wyatt (intro.), *op. cit.* (n. 93), pp. 20–24. For a listing of the principal local fruits with their Siamese names see *ibid.*, pp. 171–72.

brick temples "the Pagoda of the Factory."[149] The exterior ornamentation of their palaces and temples is limited to covering the roofs with "calin" or tiles. Their stairs are narrow and without railings. That which gives the single-story buildings distinction is the different interior levels joined by steps. Their gabled roofs are likewise of various levels, the lower ones seeming to emerge from higher roofs to give the building a certain grandeur. In the temples the highest roof is the one that covers the place where the idol stands. The principal ornaments of the temples are their accompanying "pyramids" (pagodas) of brick and mortar, which are round at the bottom and then become narrower to terminate "like a dome." Those of lesser height are topped with sharp tin pinnacles.[150]

Everyone knows how to use a saw and plane, for all build their own houses or supervise the slaves who do so. Their simple furnishings are likewise homemade. Bedsteads, where they exist, are simple wooden frames without head or posts, which are designed to hold a mat. Tables are like drums with turned-up edges and legs. The people sit on mats and may not have carpets unless they receive them from the king. The rich have cushions stuffed with cotton, which they lean against while sitting on the floor. Their vessels are of earthenware, porcelain, copper, and wood. The royal furnishings are similar to, but richer than, the others. La Loubère includes a list in Siamese of common portable possessions, including arms, which was prepared for him by two mandarins.[151]

Fish and rice are the staples of the Siamese diet. From the sea they obtain a variety of fish as well as turtles, small oysters, and lobsters of all sizes. From the rivers they get very good eels and freshwater fish of many kinds. Two sorts of small river fish, "Pla out" (?) and "Pla cadi" (*pla-kra-di*) are salted down and left in the brine until they become part of "a very liquid paste." They prefer dried, salted, or "stinking fish" to fresh fish; they also eat rotten eggs, locusts, rats, lizards, and most insects. Their sauces are simple and consist of water flavored with spices, garlic, green onions, or sweet herbs. Their *kapi,* a liquid sauce like mustard, is nothing but "Cray Fish corrupted." Although their milk has heavy cream, they make no cheese and very little butter. They cut dried fish into thin slices which they eat like spaghetti. When the Siamese eat meat, which they rarely do, they prefer the intestines and what is in them over other parts of the animal. In their markets they sell broiled or roasted insects. The Siamese feed no poultry. Of those which forage for themselves there are two sorts of chickens and plenty of ducks. While game birds are numerous and sometimes eaten, the Siamese

[149] Apparently the upper classes learned from the Europeans a barrack-like style of architecture in brick and mortar which persisted into the nineteenth century. See Graham, *op. cit.* (n. 5), II, 193.

[150] On the two main types of pagodas see J. B. Pratt, *The Pilgrimage of Buddhism* (New York, 1928), pp. 153–54.

[151] In Wyatt (intro.), *op. cit.* (n. 93), pp. 29–34, 165–68.

neither hunt nor capture them. Almost all birds have beautiful plumage but unpleasant and grating calls. While some imitate human speech, other birds are noisy but never sing. Sparrows boldly enter the houses to eat the numerous insects found therein. Crows and vultures are very bold and unafraid because the Siamese feed them. Young children who die before the age of four are usually exposed to these birds of prey. Small goats and sheep are raised and sold by the Moors. Pigs are very small and overly fat. Siamese suffer from numerous diseases but generally live as long as Europeans. Canker sores and abcesses are common, but there is no scurvy or dropsy. Periodic outbreaks of smallpox occur in which many die. To halt the contagion they bury its victims for three years or longer "without burning them." [152]

The only domesticated animals for riding are the ox, the buffalo, and the elephant. Female elephants perform ordinary daily functions, since the males are trained for war. While horses are not bred in Siam, the king maintains two thousand imported from abroad. The king himself prefers to ride on an elephant rather than on a horse. In the palace a guard elephant is constantly on duty and is kept ready for the king to mount. The king is never seen on foot except by the ladies, eunuchs, and officials in the palace. Their sedan chairs are squares with flat, raised seats which are carried by four to eight men. The better litters have chairs with backs and arms. On both types of seats, the Siamese sit cross-legged. Palanquins are a "kind of bed that hangs almost to the ground" from a bar carried on men's shoulders. As a rule, they are reserved for the use of the sick, but sometimes Europeans are permitted to ride in them. Wherever the king goes, he is accompanied by a bearer who carries the royal umbrella called the "Pat-boouk" (*pat-bok*). Since most travel is by water, La Loubère gives a lengthy and detailed description, as well as illustrations, of the different types of "balons" (Portuguese, *balāo*, English, *baloon*, meaning a rowing craft or barge). [153] The use of umbrellas ("Roum" [*rom*] in Siamese) is another of the privileges granted by the king only to his favorites and to Europeans. Most officials are permitted to have a single-tiered umbrella or parasol. Multi-tiered umbrellas are reserved to the king alone. "Sancrats" (*sang-khă-rat*s) carry a one-tiered umbrella called a "clot" (*klot*), from which hang several painted cloths. Ordinary priests and monks carry a sunshade made of a folded palm-leaf called *ta-la-pat* in Siamese; it is probably from this word that the Europeans derive "talapoin," the name they give to those priests who are known in Thai as "Tchaou-cou" (*ăhao-khun*). [154]

---

[152] La Loubère in Wyatt (intro.), *op. cit.* (n. 93), pp. 35–39.
[153] The Portuguese applied this term to all East Indian canoe-like vessels. It was possibly derived from the Mahratti word *balyanw*, a type of barge. See Yule and Burnell, *op. cit.* (n. 138), p. 53. See our pls. 214, 215.
[154] On the general use in Asia of the talipot (Hindi, *talpat,* or leaf of the *tala* tree) see *ibid.,* pp. 892–93. On its use in Ceylon see above, p. 963. Also pl. 195.

4

STATE SERVICE AND ADMINISTRATION

Siamese freemen constitute a militia in which every person is registered. Even though women and priests are not required to do state service, they are still listed in the roll of the people. All males are "Taban" (*tha-han-boks*, or soldiers), who serve the king six months annually. Their arms and animals are provided by the crown, but they must clothe and feed themselves. In the register of the population, the men are divided into those of the right and the left "to the end that everyone may know on what side he ought to range himself in his Functions." [155] These two divisions are subdivided into "bands" under the leadership of a "Nai" (*nay*, or chief). The numbers in these "bands" vary and it is the "Nai's" function to furnish for either military or civil service as many men from his "band" as are required. [156] Children belong to the same "band" as their parents.

Should the parents be of different "bands," the odd-numbered children are members of the mother's "band" and the even-numbered, the father's, providing only that their union had been sanctioned by the mother's "Nai." A "Nai" has the right to be the first to lend money to a soldier of his "band" and to place him in bondage for debt. The king provides every "Nai" with a "Balon" which is paddled by oarsmen from his "band" called *baos* (young men). They are branded on the outside of the wrist with a hot iron to show that their duties include rowing as well as other services.

"Nais" are not all of equal importance. Their status is reckoned by the numbers in the "band." There are "seven degrees of these Nai," though only six are now in use. Beginning with the highest, their titles are "Pa-ya, Oc-Pra, Oc-Louang, Oc-Counne, Oc-Meung, and Oc-Pan." [157] The word "Oc" (*ǫk*), although it is not Siamese, seems to mean chief. "Pan" (*phan*) means one thousand and "Meung" (*muᶜn*) ten thousand: hence "Oc-Meung" means "chief of ten thousand." It is possible that the other titles likewise refer to numbers, or that they are from the Pali language. Another "Title without Function" is "Oc-Meuang" (*ǫk-muᶜang*) which seems to mean "chief of a city," a dignity which must be acquired before effectually becoming "Tchaou-Meuang" (*c̆hao-muᶜang*) or "Lord of a city." The true Siamese word for "chief" is "Houa" (*hua*), which is used in titles such as "Houa Sip" (*hua-sip*), or "chief of ten," borne by the official who "mounts the royal elephant at the Crupper [rump]," and in "Houapan" (*hua-phan*), or "chief of one thousand," borne by the official who holds the royal standard

---

[155] That is, into military and civil divisions.
[156] On these lesser divisions see Wales, *op. cit.* (n. 47), pp. 138–39.
[157] These are the *Yasa*, a series of honorific titles. See Wales, *op. cit.* (n. 47), pp. 29, 35–36; and above p. 1182.

in the king's "balon." The honorific word "Oc" (*ọk*) is omitted from the title when a superior addresses an inferior. The Portuguese have translated "Pa-ya" (*pha-ya*), the highest title, as "Prince," a designation which is inexact, since the king bestows it on officials as well as on princes. In Laos the titles of "Pa-ya" and "Meuang" were still in use in La Loubère's time.[158]

Just as there are six titles, so there are six classes of cities in Siam, whose status was "anciently determined according to the Rolls of the Inhabitants." The most populous were governed by a "Pa-ya" and those of fewer numbers by an "Oc-ya" or a lesser dignitary. The old cities of "Me-Tac" (Mae-tak) and "Parselric" (Phitsanulok) had "Pa-yas" as governors. Tenasserim, Ligor (Lakon), and "Corazema" (Nakhon Ratsima) still have "Oc-yas"; lesser places like Bangkok have the "Oc-pra" or governors with less distinguished titles. All officials have titles, but the "same Title is not always joyned to the same Office." Men often have more than a single office and may therefore have more than one title. It is not rare that the same man occupies nominal as well as effectual posts. For example, "Oc-ya Pra Sedat" is the governor of Ayut'ia by title, but actually functions now as "Oc-ya Barcalon," or minister in charge of foreign trade. This multiplicity of titles, offices, and names causes great confusion to Europeans who try to understand Siam.[159]

Higher civil and military officials and their children are called "Mandarins" by the Europeans. When the king creates a mandarin, the appointee receives a new name as an *elogium*. Often ancient and venerable names are given as marks of great favor. For Europeans and other foreigners the Siamese invent appropriate names. Dignitaries of differing levels in the hierarchy will often be given the same name and are thereafter addressed only by their honorific titles. According to Siamese law, all offices should be hereditary. In practice, however, offices are taken away by the king without question or compensation, especially from court families. Mandarins receive no salaries but are maintained by the king, who provides for all their needs and gives them gifts, even of arable land. When an official leaves the royal service, the king takes back the office and all his bequests. Officials most often fatten their personal purses by extortions, pillaging, and gifts. All royal officials, even foreigners, must swallow the water of loyalty.[160] The public law of Siam is compiled in three volumes. The first, called "Pra Tam Ra," contains the names, functions, and prerogatives of the various offices. The second, entitled "Pra Tam Non," is a collection of the "Constitutions of the Ancient Kings." The final one is the "Pra Rayja Cammanot," a work in which are recorded the laws compiled by Narai's father.[161]

---

[158] On titles in contemporary Laos see above, p. 1163.
[159] La Loubère in Wyatt (intro.), *op. cit.* (n. 93), pp. 78–80.
[160] For this ceremony see above, p. 1182.
[161] La Loubère in Wyatt (intro.), *op. cit.* (n. 93), pp. 80–82. The ancient laws of Siam were derived from the Hindu code of Manu. Many of these quasi-religious and quasi-legal texts

Northern, or upper, Siam is divided into seven provinces, which are named for their chief cities: Phitsanulok with ten jurisdictions, Sukhothai with seven, "Lacontai" (Sawankhalok) with eight, "Campeng pet" (Kampengget) with ten, "Coconrepina" (Kambenbejira) with five, "Pechebonne" (Phetchabun) with two, and "Pitchai" (Phichai) with seven.[162] There are also twenty-one other jurisdictions in upper Siam which are independent of the major provinces and "do resort to the Court, and are as so many little provinces." In the south there are the provinces of Johore with seven jurisdictions, Patani with eight, "Ligor" (Lakon) with twenty, Tenasserim with twelve, "Chantebonne" (Chantabun) with seven, "Petelong" (Phat tă lung) with eight, and "Tchiai" (Chaiya) with two.[163] There are thirteen small jurisdictions in lower Siam which "are as so many particular Provinces." Ayut'ia or "the City of Siam has its Province apart" in the heart of the country.

The office of provincial governor is hereditary and includes the administration of justice and the command of whatever provincial armed forces are maintained. Powerful governors and those in places remote from the court seek to be partially or completely independent of Ayut'ia. Johore, for example, no longer pays tribute or "renders Obedience." Patani continues to pay a formal tribute every three years of gold and silver trees, just as the king of Siam sends triennial gifts to China for the continuation of commerce. Elsewhere the king has sought to eliminate the most powerful of the hereditary governors, or "Tchaou-Meuang" (*c̆hao-mu⁽ang*, or lord of the country), and to replace them by governors called "Pouran" (*phŭ-ran*), appointed for three-year terms. In addition to the customary gifts from the king, the hereditary governors are legally entitled to share with the king the rents paid for arable land, to pocket all confiscations, and to take 10 percent of all fines. From the king the hereditary governor receives "men to execute his orders," to paddle his boats, and to accompany him wherever he goes. These men are called "Painted Arms" or *ken-lai*, because they tattoo their arms a faded blue color.[164] Governors of the maritime provinces collect customs from merchant shipping; at Tenasserim it is assessed at 8 percent.[165] Some governors arrogate rights of sovereignty to themselves by demanding extraordinary taxes from frontier peoples. Others engage in commerce

---

were collected at the beginning of the Ayut'ia period and put into book form. Most were destroyed in 1767 in the sack of Ayut'ia, probably including the collections mentioned here. Modern students of Thai law are unable to identify the texts mentioned by La Loubère. See Wales, *op. cit.* (n. 47), p. 175.

[162] These "jurisdictions" were fourth-class provinces dependent on each of the major provinces. See Wales, *op. cit.* (n. 47), pp. 109–10, n. 2.

[163] Johore and Patani were not provinces but tributary states. For the provinces omitted by La Loubère see *ibid.*

[164] This is a reference to the *prai*, an hereditary service class. See Graham, *op. cit.* (n. 5), I, 235–37.

[165] *Cf.* above, p. 1186.

through agents or demand the best fish for themselves when ponds are emptied. Appointed governors have the same authority and entitlements as the hereditary governors, but they profit less from them. They are appointed to fill a vacancy or to replace a hereditary governor during an absence. In the first instance, the appointee receives only what has been allocated to him, and in the second, he shares equally with the absent governor.[166]

Judicial tribunals are headed by the governor, who is aided by a number of officials with lesser titles. The deputy who helps him in the performance of his duties may not preside in the governor's absence, since he is a consulting officer only. Another official is a kind of "attorney general," who is appointed by the king to check on the governor and to report independently to the king. The commander of the provincial garrison, "if there is any," reports to the governor and has no direct authority over the soldiers when they are not in the field. Another official and his staff are in charge of calling up levies and provisioning them. He also checks on "the Rolls of the People" and on the offices that prepare and control them. These departments are subject to great corruption; bribes are taken to keep the names of particular individuals off the registers. Police powers are in the hands of the department in charge of the watch. Another official maintains the governor's palace and commands the bodyguard. The legal books are kept by an official who determines what laws have been contravened; and he also pronounces sentences. Goods subject to the royal monopoly are sold by the official in charge of the king's warehouse. Foreigners are subject to an inspector who protects and polices them. In every superior tribunal there are officers designated to fill vacancies when they occur among the lesser justices. Other officials act as provosts, jailers, and guardians of the royal elephants kept in the provinces. In every department there is an archive and an archivist who reads the royal commands and preserves them. These are all officers "from within" the province. Others of inferior status are called "from without" to serve the province. Every officer "within" has an aide and secretary and in his house a hall given him by the crown for his hearings.[167]

One form of legal procedure is followed in both civil and criminal cases. All accusations must be made in writing and surety given. The ordinary plaintiff first goes to his "Nai," who draws up a petition on his behalf, which is presented to the governor. The governor examines it to determine whether or not it merits trial. If he decides that it is not a legitimate case, the plaintiff is supposed to be chastised to prevent others from making unfounded accusations. If the governor admits the petition to trial, it is read aloud to an assembly of councillors for their consideration and advice.

---

[166] For an amplification of La Loubère's description of the governors see Wales, *op. cit.* (n. 47), pp. 118–19.

[167] La Loubère in Wyatt (intro.) *op. cit.* (n. 93), pp. 82–85. He lists the titles and names of the provincial officials. For more accurate detail on some of these officials and their functions see Wales, *op. cit.* (n. 47), chap. v.

Reconciliation failing, witnesses give depositions to a clerk, who writes them down. Witnesses never appear in court or confront the litigants. After hearing the depositions read, the members of the assembly write down their opinions. The assembly then meets in the presence of the governor, who has not attended their previous meetings. After listening to a reading of the relevant documents, the governor interrogates "those whose Opinions seem to him not just." Then he declares "in general terms, that such of the Parties shall be condemned according to the Law." The appropriate section of the law with respect to the case being considered is then read aloud. Arguments about equity are resolved by the governor; he pronounces the sentence, which is put down in writing.[168] Three or four appeals to superior tribunals are permitted in all cases, but court charges and travel expenses discourage repeated appeals. When ordinary proofs are not sufficient, they resort to torture and trial by ordeal before the judges and the public. The death sentence is "reserved to the King alone," unless he expressly grants this power to an agent or a commission. Justice is a slow and expensive process, and its costs are borne by both parties. La Loubère gives a list of the monetary charges, translated from the Siamese, which are levied by officials of every level and for each separate act performed, from hearing the case to copying the petitions.[169]

In Ayut'ia "where there is no other Tchaou-Meuang than the King," judicial and administrative functions are divided between two offices. The president of this tribunal called "Yumrat" (*yama-rat-chă*) heads the court to which "all the Appeals of the Kingdom do go." When the king is resident in the city, this court is held in the royal palace. In the king's absence it is held outside the palace in a tower of the city. This official alone has a "determinative Voice" and through him it is possible to appeal to the king, though at a heavy price. Appeals to the king are reviewed by a royal council which has advisory powers. The king is present only when it is time to render a verdict. In discussing the council's recommendations and in arriving at a decision "the present King acquits himself herein with a great deal of Ingenuity and Judgement." The civil governor of Ayut'ia is called "Prasedet" (*Phra-sa-det*), the "sedet" being a Pali word which according to some means "the King is gone."[170] From the mouth of the Menam to Ayut'ia, the surrounding country is divided into five small jurisdictions: "Pipile" (Petchaburi), "Prepadem" (Nakhon Phatom?), "Bangkok," "Talacaan" (Tavoy?), and "Siam" (Ayut'ia).[171]

Civil administration throughout the country is supervised by the "Tchary" (*kă-kri*). All governors "report to him in his capacity as president of the Council of state." The "Calla-hom" (*kă-la-hom*) commands the military di-

---

[168] Cf. the discussion of judicial procedure in Wales, *op. cit.* (n. 47), pp. 185–87.
[169] La Loubère in Wyatt (intro.), *op. cit.* (n. 93), pp. 85–88, 163.
[170] Gervaise calls him "Pesedet." See O'Neill (trans.), *op. cit.* (n. 91), p. 35.
[171] On the the capital province, see Wales, *op. cit.* (n. 47), p. 85.

vision of government throughout the kingdom and is the royal generalis-
simo. But elephants and horses, "Siam's Principal Forces," are under the
command of another officer called "Petratcha" (*beda-rat-chǎ*);[172] this is now
"one of the greatest Employments of the Kingdom." His family has managed to hold high offices for a long time by allying themselves with the
crown. It is rumored that he or his son might succeed Narai if they survive him.[173]

The art of war is barely cultivated in Siam. Like most Asians, the Siamese
lack courage and the "sight of a naked [European] sword is sufficient to put
an hundred" to flight. Their "lack of the Spirit of War" may be attributed to
the excessive heat, "the flegmatick Ailments, and the Despotick Government." Abhorring blood, they fight and invade their neighbors only to take
slaves. When their armies meet, they are under orders not to kill or to shoot
directly at the enemy. Their soldiers, like other freemen, are unpaid workers
who are called up for six months annually, at the end of which time they
are replaced by others. About four hundred soldiers man the garrison at
Bangkok and about double that number are stationed at Lop Buri. The
natural defenses of the kingdom—woods, mountains, canals, and inundations—make unnecessary the construction of forts. The Siamese also disdain to fortify strong places "for fear of losing them, and not being able to
retake them." They have few artillery pieces and their armies consist mainly
of elephants and naked, poorly armed infantrymen.

In battle they "range themselves in three lines, each of which is composed
of three great square Battalions," or nine battalions in all. The general
stands in the middle battalion, which is made up of the best troops. Like the
other commanders he stands at the center of the square "for the security of
his person." Each battalion has sixteen war elephants behind it who bear
standards; each male elephant is accompanied by two females who help to
control it. Every elephant, except the baggage carriers, is mounted by three
armed men. The artillery is mostly carried on boats or in wagons, but a few
elephants also carry light pieces. Fighting commences with artillery fire followed by advances to bring the enemy within the range of small shot and
arrows. Close fighting is avoided. If the enemy does not flee, they themselves break for the woods to regroup. While they rely heavily on elephant
charges, this animal is not well suited for war. It is frightened by gunfire,
virtually uncontrollable, and frequently turns on its own masters when
wounded. Siamese are utterly incapable of siege warfare, for they will not
attack directly any even lightly fortified position or place. At sea warfare

[172] Van Vliet (see above, pp. 1183–84) reported that the Elephant Department was under the
Kǎ-la-hom. It was created as a separate department under the civil division in the reign of King
Prasat (r. 1629–56). Also see Wales, *op. cit.* (n. 47), pp. 143–44.

[173] La Loubère in Wyatt (intro.), *op. cit.* (n. 93), pp. 88–89. After the death of Narai in 1688,
the chief of the Elephant Department actually seized the throne and ruled as King Phra Phetracha (r. 1688–1703). On the importance of foreign families and their ability to monopolize
certain royal offices see Wyatt, *op. cit.* (n. 2), pp. 108–9.

they are even less able. The king possesses five or six very small merchant vessels which he arms as privateers in time of war. He must depend for officers and seamen on the Europeans he recruits. As on land, the Siamese are more interested in taking prizes than in killing people or sinking ships. Besides these seagoing vessels, the king has fifty or sixty galleys which protect the coasts of the Gulf of Siam.[174]

The "Pra Clang" (*phrakhlang*), or the "Barcalon" of the Portuguese, is in charge of both domestic and foreign trade, superintends the royal warehouses, and is effectively the foreign minister, since almost all of Siam's external relations relate to commerce. Royal revenues are derived from urban and rural taxes, the former being paid to the "Barcalon" and the latter to the "Oc yo Palateys" (?). Tax on cultivated land is determined by the area and is paid in cash. Revenues from it are divided with the governor and "it is never well paid to the King on the Frontiers." Traditionally uncultivated land paid no tax, but Narai "to force his subjects to work" has ordained that this tax should apply to the whole of the land and that it should be collected "from those that have possessed Lands for a certain time."[175] Boats, depending on their size, pay cash duties which are collected at certain stations along the river. In addition to customs, seagoing vessels pay fees calculated according to their carrying capacity. Taxes are also levied on arrack, a duty which "has been doubled under this Reign." The owners of fruit-bearing trees pay an annual tax in money for each tree in their gardens or orchards. In the capital, duties are paid both by the prostitutes and by their owners, called the "Oc ya Meen" (?). The royal domains produce food and fodder for the king's establishment, "and the rest he sells." He receives occasional revenues from presents, legacies of officials, extraordinary taxes, confiscations, and fines. He accepts payments in kind, or in money from the rich, in lieu of the six months' annual service obligation. The remainder of his income derives from monopolies. He sells cotton cloth to his own subjects and has forced individual merchants out of this commerce by flooding the market. Tin is a royal monopoly except for that produced in Junk-Ceylon. Ivory, saltpeter, lead, and sappanwood can be bought only at the royal warehouses by both natives and foreigners. The sale of arrack for export is also a royal monopoly. Arms and ammunition can be bought or sold only at the royal warehouses. By treaty with the Dutch the king is obliged to purchase hides which he sells only to them. The rest of Siam's commerce is open to all.[176]

The royal seal belongs to the king alone, is entrusted to no other person, and is used only on "whatever proceeds immediately from him." Every official with power to write orders has a seal with which to stamp the documents he issues. A secretary coats the seal with red ink and stamps the docu-

---

[174] La Loubère in Wyatt (intro.), *op. cit.* (n. 93), pp. 90–92. Wales agrees with La Loubère's analysis of the reasons for Siam's military weakness. See *op. cit.* (n. 47), pp. 163–64.
[175] These are the produce taxes known as *ākara*. See Wales, *op. cit.* (n. 47), pp. 201–2.
[176] La Loubère in Wyatt (intro.), *op. cit.* (n. 93), pp. 93–95. *Cf.* Wales, *op. cit.* (n. 47), chap. ix.

ments, but the official to whom it belongs is obliged "to pluck it with his own Hand from the Print." [177] At Ayut'ia there is no chancellor, but rather a "first Officer of the Kingdom" called the "Maha Obarat" (*mă-ha ŭ-pra-cha* or *wăng-na*). He is "a Viceroy" who performs the royal functions when the king is absent. He has the right to sit down in the king's presence and enjoys the title of "Pa-ya." [178] The royal palace has its officers "within" and "without," and those "within" are superior in rank. Those "within" perform their functions within the confines of the palace; those "without" work for the palace but outside its confines. The innermost of the palace's three enclosures is called the "Vang" (*wăng*) and the entire grand palace is known as the "Prassat" (*pră-sat*). The "Oc-ya Vang" (*ǫk-ya-wăng*) is the minister of the palace in charge of its maintenance, the expenditures for its residents, and royal ceremonies. [179]

The gates of the palace are always closed and behind each stands an armed porter. Permission for entrance and exit must be obtained from the captain of the guard. Armed or drunken persons are never admitted. Guards are changed every twenty-four hours. Between the first two enclosures stands a small group of "Painted Arms" who act as the royal executioners, bodyguard, and rowers. For ceremonial occasions the royal slaves are clothed in red muslin shirts and given arms. The royal horse guard is composed of men from Laos and another neighboring country. A son of the commander "of the right hand" has been in France for some years learning the craft of fountain-making. When the king leaves the palace he is accompanied by a horse guard of one hundred and thirty foreigners which includes Moors, Mughuls, "Chinese Tartars" (Manchus?), Hindus, and Rajputs. The horses and elephants kept within the palace grounds, like the officers "within," are given special names by the king. White horses as well as white elephants are venerated by the Siamese. The "Calla-hom" (*kă-la-hom*) is in charge of maintaining and guarding the royal barges and galleys. [180]

When holding court the king sits in a window about nine feet above the audience hall. In the two corners of the hall on either side of the window are doors at about the same height, each reached by narrow staircases. In front of the window stands a nine-tiered umbrella, flanked on either side by seven-tiered umbrellas. [181] Officials and ambassadors deliver everything into the king's hands in a golden cup with a very long golden handle. It is in this hall that the king gives his orders to his forty-four "inner" pages, who are called "Mahatleks" (*mă-hat-lěk*s). They are divided into four units of eleven

---

[177] On the seals of officials see Wales, *op. cit.* (n. 47), pp. 83–84.
[178] Commonly called "second king" by the Europeans. See Wales, *op. cit.* (n. 23), pp. 52–53.
[179] On this officer see Wales, *op. cit.* (n. 47), pp. 92–93.
[180] La Loubère in Wyatt (intro.), *op. cit.* (n. 93), pp. 95–99.
[181] The great white umbrella of state is nine-tiered only for kings who have attained full power. Before the coronation ceremony he is entitled only to seven-tiered umbrellas. See Wales, *op. cit.* (n. 23), p. 93. See our pl. 230.

each and given individual names and sabers by the king. Some perform personal services for the king and others are employed as messengers to carry his orders to the numerous pages who live outside the palace or to the officials in the provinces. The four officers who command the pages have great power "because they so nearly approach the Prince."[182] At royal audiences there is a master of ceremonies, the only person who does not prostrate himself before the king. The king himself possesses great intellectual curiosity and seriously tries to inform himself about Europe. He has a Siamese version of Quintus Curtius (a Roman historian who wrote a life of Alexander the Great) and has given orders for "several of our Histories to be translated."[183]

Women are the "true Officers" of the king's chamber, for they alone tend to his personal needs. They never leave the harem without express orders or unless in the company of the king or the eunuchs.[184] His deceased queen, "both his Wife and his Sister," was called "Nang Achamahisii" (*Phră-ra-chĭ-ni?*); the king's name is concealed during his lifetime or else he has no name until given one by his successor.[185] This queen was the mother of the king's only daughter, "who now has the Rank and House of a Queen." Other royal wives called "Tchaou Vang" (*ĉhao-wang*) respect the queen as their sovereign and are subject to her rule. The court recruits ladies continually, but the Siamese give up their daughters only reluctantly. Some even pay to keep them from being incarcerated in the harem for life. The king parsimoniously keeps only eight to ten concubines. While the women actually dress the king, there are official custodians of the royal wardrobe. The highest of these officers is the keeper of the royal hat, a post now occupied by a prince of the royal house of Cambodia. The queen has her own elephants, boats, and guardsmen. She is seen only by the eunuchs and the women of the harem. Outside the palace, when riding on an elephant or in a boat, she is concealed by curtains. She engages in trade and has her own ships and warehouses. Daughters may not, however, succeed to the throne. According to law the eldest son of the queen is the rightful successor.[186] In practice, however, the succession is achieved by other means, usually by force.[187]

While the people of Siam have no clocks, there is "a kind of water clock"

---

[182] These were young boys from prominent official families who were presented to the court by their fathers. For a more detailed description see Wales, *op. cit.* (n. 47), pp. 40–41.

[183] La Loubère in Wyatt (intro.), *op. cit.* (n. 93), pp. 99–100.

[184] La Loubère (*ibid.*, p. 101) learned by report that the king keeps "eight or ten Eunuchs only, as well white as black." Wales, usually a close student of La Loubère's work, declares that there were no eunuchs, his source being Pinto. See *op. cit.* (n. 23), pp. 47, 50. Gervaise (*op. cit.* [n. 91], p. 104) also refers to eunuchs.

[185] The king's personal name, when he had one, was taboo and considered to be too sacred for common use. After death a king was called "the Lord within the Urn" to distinguish him from his successor.

[186] The Palatine law of 1458.

[187] La Loubère in Wyatt (intro.), *op. cit.* (n. 93), pp. 100–102.

by which time is kept in the royal palace.[188] Court is held daily at ten in the morning and ten at night. Reports are read on affairs of state and advisory opinions are prepared for the king. When he enters the hall, he studies the opinion and issues a decision. If lengthier deliberations are required, he renders no decision, but reviews the problems involved and appoints a committee to examine the matter further and to prepare a new report. This is read by a committee member "in a full Council and before the King." Usually the king makes a decision quickly, but in rare cases he will consult the priests or will call in officials from the provinces for advice and counsel. In the final analysis he pronounces all his decisions when he pleases and without following "any other advice than his own."

Since he punishes bad and rewards what he considers good advice, his ministers "much more apply themselves to divine his sentiments, than to declare him theirs." He examines officials on their prescribed duties and punishes those "who answer not very exactly." To prevent cabals from forming, custom ordains that courtiers should meet with the king only on invitation and always in the presence of a third person. Every individual in Siam is required on pain of death to act as an informer and not to remain silent about matters important to the state. While the king employs professional spies, he is still easily deceived by false reports designed to please or to mislead him. The king punishes by death those who misinform him, if they are discovered. In other cases, punishments are more likely to fit the crime: extortion and robbery by swallowing molten gold or silver, lying by sewing up the mouth, forgetfulness or laxness in the execution of orders by cutting the head slightly "to punish the memory." Blood is never shed in punishing princes or others of the royal family. They are executed by starvation, suffocation, or burning. Criminals are often punished by being forced to wear in public places the cangue (*ka* in Siamese), irons, or manacles. Some are buried up to the shoulders and have their head touched or stroked by others. But ignominy lasts only as long as the punishment. Royal chastisements, even the bastinado, are viewed by the recipients as marks of affection. To be demoted is common and not shameful. Fathers are punished for the crimes of their children and superiors for the delinquencies of those subject to their orders. To be charged is tantamount to being judged guilty, particularly if the accused is a high state official.

The king displays his despotism by the arbitrary and cruel treatment he metes out to all; this includes his own brothers, whom he fears as contenders for power. Liberty and the enjoyment of life are experienced only by the people at large and by the officials in the provinces. Those closest to the king, especially his ministers, lead tempestuous lives as the servants of an unpredictable and constantly suspicious ruler. The people have no loyalty or devotion to a particular monarch or to a reigning family. To die for prince or

---

[188] *Cf.* the descriptions of the waterclocks used in Ceylon and India, above, pp. 811, 992.

country is not a great virtue. Since they have no property at home, the Siamese war prisoners live placidly in Pegu cultivating the lands assigned them. Because the ruler delegates no responsibility, there are few to support him when he is under attack. The people will obey unquestioningly any ruler who possesses the royal seal and controls the public treasury. While the people show great respect outwardly for their god-like ruler, subjects and kings are divided because they have no common interest in the state and its defences.[189]

Ambassadors throughout the East are regarded as mere messengers and not as representatives of their rulers. No distinction is recognized between an envoy and an ambassador. Permanent resident ambassadors do not exist. Siamese embassies always include three ambassadors, one of whom is the superior and is called "Rayja Tout" (*rat-chă-dut*), or royal messenger. Once the king accepts a letter he issues a receipt to the messenger. Replies are not entrusted to the visiting ambassador but are carried by Siamese messengers sent along with him. Foreign emissaries are stopped on entering Siam until the king has been told of their arrival. An ambassador may not enter Ayut'ia before his first audience. The king provides food and lodgings for foreign emissaries. After presenting their letters of credence and instructions, foreign envoys may engage in trade. On the evening before "the Audience of Leave" the king inquires whether the ambassador has anything more to propose. At the final audience the king asks "if he is contented." The ambassador departs at once from the metropolis "and negotiates nothing more." Public audiences are held exclusively in Ayut'ia; those conducted elsewhere are private audiences "and without ceremony." Audiences held in Lop Buri are less elaborate, but follow the same pattern as those of Ayut'ia. At all formal audiences the king speaks first, asks the ambassador a few standard questions, and then orders the envoy to negotiate with the "Barcalon." Then the ambassador is given arrack, betel, and a Siamese vestment that he immediately puts on. In their negotiations "the Siamese never depart from their Customs," and they write down as little as possible. Courtesy requires them to be demonstrative about the presents brought by foreign ambassadors. Presents are essential, for they are items of trade "under an honorable Title and from King to King." All Asian potentates are happy to receive embassies, for they see them as a form of homage. As a consequence they themselves send out as few as possible and detain foreign ambassadors overly long to enhance their own prestige. The Mughul Empire, China, and Japan never send out embassies, and the Persians send ambassadors only to Siam. Persia dispatched an ambassador to Siam to establish trading relations and to convert its king to Islam.[190]

[189] La Loubère in Wyatt (intro.), *op. cit.* (n. 93), pp. 102–8.
[190] La Loubère, *ibid.*, pp. 108–10. *Cf.* the reception of foreign embassies in Wales, *op. cit.* (n. 23), pp. 180–85. In 1668 Muslim missionaries arrived in Ayut'ia from Acheh. See Sitsayamkan, *op. cit.* (n. 75), p. 9.

Freedom of trade originally attracted many foreigners to Ayut'ia where they were permitted to follow their own customs and to practice their own religion. Each nation has its own quarter (*ban*) in the suburbs outside the metropolis. Here they live under a chief of their own choice. He manages their affairs in conjunction with a mandarin who is specially appointed to deal with him. But important negotiations are handled by the "Barcalon." The Moors are the best established of the several nations doing business in Siam. Previously the "Barcalon" was a Moor, as were many other principal royal officers. Narai, who was most interested in promoting foreign trade with nearby Muslim centers, erected mosques for them and paid for their great annual festival in memory of the death of Ali. Siamese who embraced Islam were exempted from the six months' personal service. Things changed rapidly, however, when the Muslim "Barcalon" fell into disfavor. The Muslims were dismissed from office and the Siamese Muslims were forced to pay in cash for their exemption from personal service. The wealthiest Muslim merchants have left Siam, but three or four thousand remain and continue to worship freely in their mosques.[191] Equal numbers of Luso-Asians, Chinese, and Malays likewise remain in Siam.

Many of the wealthiest foreign merchants, in addition to the Muslims, have left the country since the king "has reserved to himself alone all the foreign commerce." Merchant ships are required to sell their entire cargo to the king and to purchase from him alone all goods except for certain local products. Goods may not be directly exchanged "when there are several foreign ships together at Siam," or between foreign and private Siamese merchants. The king buys the best imports at his own price and resells them at his pleasure. When the season for departure of the ships arrives, the foreign merchants sell the remainder of their goods at a loss and are forced to pay high prices for export goods. Siam, lacking raw and manufactured products for export, is not a tempting market. Its people have no money to pay for imports. The king himself contributes to the problem by accumulating wealth and not returning it to the economy.[192]

5

SOCIETY, CULTURE, AND BUDDHISM

The Siamese, according to Gervaise, are a naturally timid and servile people who are so respectful of their king that they dare not look at him when he speaks. Anger and drunkenness are vices to them, but they have no com-

---

[191] On the Muslims in Siam during the time of Phaulkon see Sitsayamkan, *op. cit.* (n. 75), p. 26.
[192] La Loubère in Wyatt (intro.), *op. cit.* (n. 93), pp. 112–13.

punctions about dissembling. They make a sharp distinction between doing and wishing to do harm. Not dangerous as enemies, they are unreliable as friends. Being born to indolence, they prefer an easy and quiet life to all the pleasures won by work. While not inventive, they are capable of imitating the most complex creations of others. Every artisan has many trades and performs each perfectly. While despising other peoples, they expect respect for themselves and their supposed great knowledge. In daily life they are frugal, temperate, and charitable. While the rich practice polygamy, their wives are accomplished and faithful women of good sense.[193]

Physically the Siamese are well proportioned and relatively small. The breasts of women hang down to their navels but they are otherwise well proportioned. Faces of both sexes are broad with high cheek-bones. The nose is short and round on the end. Their eyes are large and they do whatever they can to make them look larger. The forehead terminates in a point like the chin. Their eyes are slanted upward, small, and "generally yellowish." Their jaws are hollow, their mouths large, and their lips thick. Their skin is reddish brown in color. Women use neither "Paint nor Patches," but the king and some great lords dye their legs a dull blue.[194] Their hair is "black, thick, and lank" and both sexes wear it close-cropped just to the top of the ears. Unmarried young people wear a topknot and let the rest of their hair grow down almost to the shoulders. Personally they are very neat and bathe three or four times daily. They perfume the body in several places and whiten their lips to contrast with their blackened teeth. They use oil and powder on their hair to make it glossy. While they pluck their beards, their nails are allowed to grow long. Professional dancers put on long copper fingernails which "make them appear like Harpies."[195]

Society is divided into classes of slaves and freemen. Masters have all powers except death over their slaves. Freedom is so limited and freemen so severely handled that slavery is preferred to life as a freeman–beggar. Private slaves are paid an annual pittance for cultivating the fields and gardens and for domestic service. Siamese may be born or become slaves. Freemen are enslaved for debt or infractions of the law and when taken as prisoners of war. Debt slaves may regain their freedom by satisfying the debt; children born even to a temporary slave remain permanently in servitude. The ownership of birth slaves follows the system of child division obtaining in divorce: odd-numbered children belong to the mother's master, while the even-numbered belong to the father if he is free or to his master if a slave. The master of the mother must agree beforehand to relations between his

---

[193] Gervaise in O'Neill (trans.), *op. cit.* (n. 91), pp. 24–25.

[194] Possibly a reference to members of one of the great Lao clans of northern Siam who tattoo their thighs and the lower parts of the body. See Graham, *op. cit.* (n. 5), I, 167.

[195] La Loubère in Wyatt (intro.), *op. cit.* (n. 93). pp. 27–29. For an illustration of the fingernail dance see Librairie Larousse (publ.), *La Thaïlande* (Paris, 1983), p. 89.

female slave and the father. If his consent is not obtained, he owns all the offspring. The king employs his slaves in personal labor the year around; the free subjects of the crown work for six months annually at their own expense. Private slaves owe no service to the crown, and the king expects no indemnity when the labor of a freeman is lost because he has become a slave. The only distinction between freemen is that some possess offices and the rest do not. It is rare that offices are held in the same families for a great length of time. The distinction between priests and others is blurred by the fact that men pass continually between the religious and the secular life.[196]

Siamese wear very few clothes except on ceremonial occasions. The king wears a vest of brocaded satin; others are forbidden to wear this kind of garment unless it is a royal bequest.[197] He sometimes gives his officers a scarlet vest which is worn only for war and hunting. A high and pointed white headdress is a "Coif of Ceremony" worn by the king and the royal officials. The royal hat is adorned with a circle of precious stones, while those of the officials are decorated with circles of gilt or with nothing, according to the rank of the wearer. Since they wear them for royal audiences and other court ceremonies, it was hats like these which the Siamese ambassadors wore at the court of France (see pls. 223–25). Officials also wear these hats when traveling. Fastened under their chins, they are never removed as a salutation. Ordinary people go bareheaded or cover the head with a cloth to protect themselves from the sun. While their costumes leave parts of the body exposed, the Siamese are extremely modest about showing off what custom obliges them to conceal. They object to the French soldiers bathing naked in the river, for Siamese men and women bathe and swim in clothes. To preserve the modesty of eyes and ears, the laws prohibit indecent paintings or bawdy songs. Lavish costumes are permitted only to those who receive them from the king. Most of their self-expression appears in the jewelry they wear. Fashion permits them to display any number of rings on the three last fingers of each hand. Women and chidren of both sexes wear in their ears pear-like pendants of gold, silver, or vermilion gilt. Youngsters of good families wear bracelets on their arms and legs until they put on clothes at six or seven years of age.[198]

When the king is in Ayut'ia he traditionally appears in public only five or six times annually. With great pomp and ceremony he performs his religious duties on these occasions. At the beginning of the sixth and twelfth months he goes to present gifts to the priests and monks of the city's principal temples and monasteries. On these days called "Van pra" (*wan-phra*),

[196] La Loubère in Wyatt (intro.), *op. cit.* (n. 93), pp. 77–78. For a more extended discussion of slavery see Wales, *op. cit.* (n. 47), pp. 58–63. On debt bondage in general see A. Reid (ed.), *Slavery, Bondage and Dependency in Southeast Asia* (New York, 1983), pp. 8–12.

[197] Possibly a reference to the Brahman girdle. See Wales, *op. cit.* (n. 23), p. 101.

[198] La Loubère in Wyatt (intro.), *op. cit.* (n. 93), pp. 25–27.

or holy days, the king first makes a pilgrimage on the back of an elephant to the temples within the city. He follows this by a trip downriver to a temple outside the city. He then sends alms to the smaller pagodas which he has not visited himself.[199] At Lop Buri, "where it is permitted him to lay aside his Kingship," he lives less ceremonially and hunts much more. Whenever he goes out, the Europeans are warned in advance to avoid him and his retinue. Footmen with staves and pea-shooters lead the retinue "to drive all the People out of his way."[200]

Like many other European visitors, La Loubère reports in detail on the various means used to capture wild elephants, one of the king's favorite diversions. To the Siamese, the elephants are as rational as humans and lack only the power of speech. The three young elephants "intended for the . . . Grandsons of [the king of] France" were embarked on a French ship while their keepers whispered words of solace and encouragement directly into their ears. When two war elephants fight for the entertainment of the court, the beasts are constrained by cables so that neither they nor their keepers will be hurt or killed. While the Siamese love cockfights, the king has outlawed them under pressure from the priests. La Loubère and his retinue were entertained by a "Chinese comedy" enacted on a stage with "a cloth on the bottom and nothing on the sides." The Siamese, like the Europeans, enjoy these comedies without understanding what is being said or depicted. They are able to guess at the roles of the actors by the costumes they wear and by the gestures they make. Mute puppet shows, especially those from Laos, are much appreciated in Siam. Excellent Siamese tumblers perform for the king when he arrives in Lop Buri. Some dancers called "Lot Bouang" (*rot-luang*) balance themselves on their heads in a hoop mounted on a high bamboo pole. Others dance on a copper wire and still others balance themselves and dance on the top of an unsupported bamboo ladder with sharp sabre steps. Snakes are trained to dance to music. Religion decrees that in thanksgiving they illuminate the waters and land with many lanterns for several nights while the flood recedes. The Chinese of Siam excel in the manufacture of fireworks. Paper kites called "Vao" (*wao*) are flown for the king by mandarins every night during the two months of winter. Sometimes they fasten fire on them to lighten the sky. Occasionally they attach a piece of gold, which goes to the finder of the kite if the string breaks or if it falls in a place from which "it cannot be drawn back again."[201]

The Siamese put on three kinds of dance dramas. The "Cone" (*khon*) is a figured dance accompanied by music, in which masked and armed actors

[199] The royal *Kathina*, a Buddhist festival. See also above, p. 1176.
[200] La Loubère in Wyatt (intro.), *op. cit.* (n. 93), pp. 39–44.
[201] *Cf.* Wales, *op. cit.* (n. 23), pp. 221–22 on kite-flying as the national pastime. Also see C. Hart, *Kites. An Historical Survey* (rev. ed.; New York, 1982), pp. 47–49, and Librairie Larousse (publ.), *op. cit.* (n. 195), p. 74.

engage in mock combat.²⁰² The traditional serious drama called "Lacone" (*lă-khon-nai*) is "a Poem intermixt with Epic and Dramatic." Several actors sing these histories in verse, performances which last for three days from eight in the morning to seven at night.²⁰³ The "Rabam" (*rambong*) is a stately and spirited dance by men and women who wear false copper fingernails. They sing a few words while dancing individually "with a great many slow Contorsions of the Body and Arms." While this dance proceeds "two men entertain the Spectators with several Fooleries." In all these dance dramas costume is unimportant, but the "Cone" and "Rabam" dancers are distinguished by the high pointed and gilded "Paper Bonnets" they wear while performing. These last two dramas are secular shows presented at funerals and at other occasions which priests are forbidden to attend. The "Lacone" is usually used as a dedicatory drama at the opening of a temple or at the presentation of a new image of the Buddha. At these festivals they also put on ox races, wrestling matches, and boxing exhibitions. Thai boxers protect their hands with several rounds of cord instead of the copper rings used by the Laotians.²⁰⁴ The Siamese bet on these contests as well as on boat races. Insatiable gambling is a vice whose addicts may end up as debt slaves. While they do not play cards, they enjoy "tick-tack" (backgammon), which they call "Saca" (*să-ka*), and chess, which they play in both the European and Chinese ways.²⁰⁵ One of their greatest pleasures is the smoking of tobacco, a habit to which Siamese women of all classes are addicted. Although they do not dip snuff, they smoke the strong tobacco grown in Manila, China, and Siam. The Chinese and Moors use water pipes "to diminish the strength" of the tobacco (see pl. 216). While they love their wives and children exceedingly, the greatest pleasure of the Siamese men is to pursue a life of leisure during the six months when they are not working for the king. Since their royal corvée is assigned to them, these men have no particular crafts or training for an independent occupation. While they lie around, their wives plow the land or act as merchants in the cities.²⁰⁶

Unmarried girls are watched closely and kept away from young men. They are married young, for they reach childbearing age at twelve or earlier and rarely give birth after forty. Some remain unmarried throughout life, but unlike the bachelors, they cannot dedicate themselves to religion until

---

²⁰² *Khon* is a masked pantomime ordinarily performed by men only. Episodes from the *Ramayana*, often battle scenes, are dramatized in this form of court theater. See J. R. Brandon, *Theatre in Southeast Asia* (Cambridge, Mass., 1967), pp. 64–66.

²⁰³ See Chua Sariman, "Traditional Dance Drama in Thailand," in M. T. Osman (ed.), *Traditional Drama and Music of Southeast Asia* (Kuala Lumpur, 1974), p. 169; and Brandon, *op. cit.* (n. 202), pp. 63–64. Actresses gradually replaced the all-male cast as *lă-khon-nai* became increasingly popular as a court performance.

²⁰⁴ On Thai-style boxing today see Basche, *op. cit.* (n. 116), pp. 115–16.

²⁰⁵ For a description of the Chinese chess game see La Loubère in Wyatt (intro.), *op. cit.* (n. 93), pp. 181–82.

²⁰⁶ *Ibid.*, pp. 44–50.

they are "advanc'd in years." Marriages are arranged on the initiative of the prospective groom's parents, who request respectable old ladies to approach the girl's parents. Before responding the parents consult their daughter and their astrologer. When the auguries are favorable, the young man three times takes tokens of his esteem to the prospective bride. On his third visit the relations on both sides are present to witness the payment of her dowry to him. Then they both receive presents from their uncles, and the couple is thereby married. There is no religious ceremony and priests are prohibited from attending the wedding; a few days after the marriage a priest appears at the house of the newlyweds to sprinkle holy water and recite prayers. The nuptial feast is held in the house of the bride's relations, where the bridegroom has built a separate room for the honeymoon. The newlyweds stay there for several months before moving to a house of their own.

Only the rich take more than one wife, and "that more out of Pomp and Grandeur, than out of Debachery." When lesser wives are purchased, they are treated as slaves and are entirely subject to "the great Wife." The children of lesser wives call their father "Po Tchaou" (*phǫ-čhao*), or "Father Lord," while those of the principal wife call him simply "Po" (*phǫ*) or "Father." Marriage is prohibited between those of "the first degrees of Kindred" but not between cousins-german. A man may be married to two sisters but not at the same time. These customs are not followed by the kings, for they marry their sisters. The present king, Narai, married both his sister and the daughter he had by her, who lives in a queenly house and is called "Princess Queen" by the Europeans.[207] In ordinary families the chief wife and her children are the only legal heirs. Her children receive equal portions from the estates of both parents. Since the Siamese make no wills, the father has to make provision before he dies for his lesser wives and their children if he is so inclined. Otherwise they may be sold by the heirs. Daughters of lesser wives are sold to the highest bidder to become lesser wives themselves. While land may legally be bequeathed and sold, nobody but the king may own it outright. The bulk of their estates is consequently in "moveables," such as diamonds, which are easy to hide and transport.

Families are generally happy in Siam, as is indicated by "the Fidelity of the Wives in nourishing their Husband, whilst he serves the King." Divorce is legal and husbands never refuse to consent to it. The husband returns the wife's dowry and they divide the children between them, the mother taking the first and all other odd-numbered offspring and the husband the rest. After the divorce both may legally remarry. Divorce is nonetheless thought of as a great evil, because the children are often badly treated in the second marriage, or sold. Although the Siamese "are fruitful" and frequently have

[207] Marriage of sisters, and even daughters, had the practical advantage of keeping the royal line pure. See Wales, *op. cit.* (n. 23), p. 117.

twins, their country is still not well populated.[208] Parents may not kill each other or their children, for all murder is prohibited. Sexual relations between the unmarried are not disgraceful in the eyes of the public at large.[209]

The father's power over his children is unquestioned. Still, parents are beloved and respected by their children. Parents are responsible to the king for the behavior of children, share their punishments, and must turn them over to the law when they have broken it. If an offender flees, he returns when his parents or other loved ones are held in his stead. Children are brought up to be quiet, modest, and civil, qualities necessary to succeed in trade or in the royal service. The Thai language "is much more capable than ours [of expressing] whatever denotes Respect and Distinction." Proper ceremonial behavior is almost as essential to the Siamese as it is to the Chinese. Salutations follow formulas which make rank distinctions clear. Superiors never ask inferiors about the king's health. A higher seat or place is more honorable than a lower one, just as standing is more dignified than sitting. The right side is more honorable than the left and the floor of the chamber facing the door more highly regarded than the sides. They know precisely when to sit or stand, when to bow or prostrate themselves, or when to join their hands or not. They are restrained by a reciprocity of respect in all they do or say, so that familiarity between superiors and inferiors is very rare. Trained from infancy to observe these customs, they find them neither troublesome nor complex. In some regards their habits lack civility in European eyes. They carry no handkerchiefs, belch publicly, wipe the sweat from their foreheads with the fingers, spit into pots carried in their hands, and greedily grab anything offered. They are most affronted by anyone who touches their heads, hair, or hats. On the other hand it is an act of extreme respect to place a gift or letter upon one's own head. It is impolite to use one hand only in shaking hands. A Siamese puts both his hands "underneath yours, as to put himself entirely into your power." Courtesy also prescribes that presents be taken in both hands.[210]

While they live a quiet and reserved life, the Siamese are a social people. They pay visits to one another at which they punctiliously observe traditional ceremonies. When a commoner visits a person of rank, he throws himself down on a mat when entering "and raises both hands to his forehead." The visitor knocks his head gently on the ground and requests per-

---

[208] In modern times Orientals bear fewer twins than Westerners. "Siamese twins" are so called because of the "double-boys" named Chang and Eng who were born in Siam in 1811 and exhibited as freaks in Europe and America. For the biography of the original "Siamese twins" see Irving and Amy Wallace, *The Two* (New York, 1978). For the extent to which Siamese sexual and marital customs resemble those of insular Southeast Asia see Reid, *op. cit.* (n. 87), pp. 146–72.

[209] La Loubère in Wyatt (intro.), *op. cit.* (n. 93), pp. 51–53.

[210] *Ibid.*, pp. 54–58. For the complexities of Thai social practices see Akin Rabibhadana, *The Organization of Thai Society in the Early Bangkok Period,* Data Paper No. 74, Cornell University Southeast Asia Program (Ithaca, N.Y., 1969).

mission to greet his superior. These ceremonies are less obsequious when men meet who are of nearly equal rank. Between men of equal rank it is enough for the visitor to bow slightly and to raise his hands to the level of his temples. The host responds in kind and exclaims "Maleou, Chaou, Maleou" (he has come, Master has come), a greeting which it is a grievous insult to omit. After being seated on mats or carpets, host and visitor inquire after each other's well-being and partake of betel offered in a small gold or silver vessel called a *talap*. Lunch is served on low tables whose tray-like tops are enclosed with a railing to prevent spilling. The visitor then asks his host's permission to leave, and upon receiving it repeats the ceremonies observed on entering the house.[211] Failure to observe proper ceremony constitutes an affront which can make the best of friends into bitter enemies. The greatest of insults is for one to call the other a "Tauaque" (*čhă-wăk*) or "Potspoon," and legal punishments are prescibed for such an affront. When walking in the streets, they go one behind the other and never side by side.[212] When meeting a friend or on seeing a priest or a pagoda, they raise a hand to the level of the forehead. They never cross a bridge when people are passing beneath in a boat, for it is an insult to have any thing or person over one's head. As a consequence their houses are all on one level.[213]

All classes live simply on cooked rice, several kinds of fruit, bits of dried fish, and plain water. Game, poultry (especially ducks), goats, pigs, eggs, and beef are all very cheap. Sheep are brought into Siam from Batavia and north India. Siamese cooks spoil all meats, no matter how good they are, by putting into all their stews a stinking fish paste called "capy" (*kă-pĭ*) or "balachan" (Malay, *bĕlachan*). It is made of fish roe, salt, pepper, fine spices, garlic, white onions, and "several strong herbs." At feasts meat is served, but in no particular sequence, along with fruit and rice in gold, silver, or porcelain dishes. Milk is sold by Moors, for the Siamese have no taste for it. Butter is rare and most foods are fried in coconut oil. Mealtimes are not social occasions for conversation and good cheer. In the family the husband eats alone, the mother is next, the children follow in turn, and the rest goes to the servants.[214]

The clothes of men called "Pa-nonc" (*pha-nung*) consist of two pieces of silk or cotton material. One piece is used as a scarf around the shoulders and the other is tied around the waist and pulled between the thighs to make breeches which fall just below the knees. A mandarin's dress includes underclothes and a "Pa-nonc" of richer and more ample materials than that worn by others. In the winter these gentlemen wear a close-fitting cloak of Chi-

---

[211] *Cf.* Phya Anuman Rajadhon, *Thai Traditional Salutations* ("Thai Culture, New Series," no. 14; Bangkok, 1963).
[212] Until very recently the walks were so narrow that no two people could walk side by side.
[213] Gervaise in O'Neill (trans.), *op. cit.* (n. 91), pp. 41–43.
[214] *Ibid.*, pp. 43–45. On the ubiquitous Southeast Asian fish sauce see Reid, *op. cit.* (n. 87), p. 29.

nese brocade or European cloth which buttons down the front and has wide sleeves. Everyone goes without shoes except for some mandarins who wear "slippers of a Moorish pattern." When going through the streets their slaves walk behind them carrying their hat, sword, and "bousette" (betel box). The "Pa-nonc" worn by the women seems to be larger. It hangs almost to the ankles, is generally black in color, and is often embroidered in gold and silver. They cover the bosom with a small piece of muslin, but the rest of the body is bare. While they go barefooted and bare-headed, these ladies are very clean and neat. Both men and women treat their hair with a sweet-smelling oil called "Namam hom" (*nam-man-hom*) which makes it glossy.

A newborn child is washed in the river and then placed naked in a little bed. It is weaned at six months of age. Many children die a few days or a few months after birth. They are all named at birth by their parents, who give them names which differ altogether from the family name; the king alone may change the original name by the bestowal of a title.[215] Only devils and beasts have white teeth, and at puberty the parents make the child's teeth black and shiny. Higher-class people redden the nail on the little finger of each hand. Their homes are sparsely furnished, though some boast Chinese cabinets and porcelains, Persian carpets, and silk-covered pillows. Straw mats serve as a bed on which they sleep with all their clothes on.[216]

Boys at seven or eight years of age are sent to a convent for training and education. These young novices called "Nen" (*nen*) are sent their food from outside, and the rich among them are served by one or more slaves. In addition to the "three R's," they are taught the rudiments of religion and the Pali language.[217] Most make little progress in Pali, a language used only in religion and law. It is preserved mainly by priests and officials who need it in their occupations. Siamese and Pali have letters which are combined to make syllables and words. One Thai alphabet consists of thirty-seven consonants, a second of a series of vowels, a third of a collection of diphthongs, and a fourth of a sequence of syllables.[218] This phonetic language is written from left to right like the European languages. The vocabulary is not copious, so

---

[215] Like most Europeans of his era, Gervaise simply assumes that all families have last names. Patronymics were first instituted in Siam by a royal decree of 1916. See Graham, *op. cit.* (n. 5), pp. 243–44.

[216] Gervaise in O'Neill (trans.), *op. cit.* (n. 91), pp. 45–48.

[217] For an excellent discussion of Thai education in the seventeenth century see D. K. Wyatt, *The Politics of Reform in Thailand: Education in the Reign of King Chulalongkorn* (New Haven, 1969), pp. 7–23.

[218] La Loubère in Wyatt (intro.), *op. cit.* (n. 93), pp. 170, 176. See our pl. 219. "The Thai alphabet consists of a series of consonants and another entirely separate series of vowels, which latter are again divided into simple and compound vowels. The compound vowels are made up of combinations of a simple vowel with certain consonants or two or more simple vowels used together as one. . . . Each series has to be learned separately in its own order" (Stuart Campbell and Chuan Shaweevongse, *The Fundamentals of the Thai Language* [4th ed.; Kent, 1957], p. 9). From this description it is easy to see how La Loubère or his informants arrived at "four alphabets."

variety in meaning depends on the turn of phrase and on tones. Most of its words, as in Chinese, are monosyllables which have various meanings depending on the tone in which they are pronounced. The Thai language also shares with Chinese an absence of declensions and conjugations. Noun cases rely on placement, while tenses, numbers, and moods are indicated by particles placed before or after the verb.[219] Pali has an alphabet of thirty-three consonants and others of vowels and diphthongs. Unlike the Thai language, Pali is inflected.

Their arithmetic, "like ours," is a decimal system based on zero. They are quick at figures but "have no use of Algebra." Calculations are made on paper with a pen and not on the abacus of the Chinese. They learn easily, think clearly and rationally, and react quickly and knowingly. But they suffer from an "invincible laziness" and a lack of application, so they consequently "invent nothing in the Sciences which they love best as Chymistry and Astronomy." Spirited and imaginative, "they are naturally poets." Their poetry is metrical and rhymed but next to impossible to translate, "so different is their way of thinking from ours." They have love poems as well as historical and moral songs.[220] While their genius is poetry, they are poor in oratory and narration. Their preachers expound on texts and eschew exhortation. Thai books contain simple and unstyled narrations or maxims "of a broken Style full of *Ideas.*" While they "know how to speak to a Business," their compliments follow pat formulas and are always the same. They ignore philosophy except for moral maxims and "have not any sort of Theology."[221] Law is not an academic subject and there are no professional lawyers. They learn the laws "only in their Employment" from manuscript books pertinent to their occupation.[222]

Siamese history contains many fables. Books about it are very few because they do not have "the use of printing." According to a brief Siamese annal their first king began to reign 934 years ago, or in A.D. 755. Over the course of this history they have had fifty-two kings "but not all of the same Blood." In recent years, according to Gervaise and Van Vliet, palace revolutions and usurpations continue to be common. It is not clear whether the Siamese are descended from the original inhabitants or from invading people who settled there over time. This question arises because of the use they make of two languages; the vulgar and simple Siamese tongue and the dead, inflected Pali language from which they derive their terms of religion, jus-

[219] Thai grammar is relatively simple. La Loubère in Wyatt (intro.), *op. cit.* (n. 93), pp. 173–80, provides a survey of Thai and Pali which is mainly an introduction to spoken Thai.
[220] See the discussion on poetry in Graham, *op. cit.* (n. 5), I, 282–86. For German translations of ten poems see K. Wenk, *Studien zur Literatur der Thai. Texte und Interpretationen* (Hamburg, 1982), Vol. I. The first of these is a *khlong* poem in praise of Narai.
[221] "The Siamese has no turn for metaphysics" (Graham, *op. cit.* [n. 5], II, 227).
[222] La Loubère in Wyatt (intro.), ·*op. cit.* (n. 93), pp. 58–62. "Of legal books the number is almost plethoric" (Graham, *op. cit.* [n. 5], I, 281).

tice, administration, and "all the Ornaments of the Vulgar Tongue." It seems that Pali in which "they compose their best Songs" was brought in by foreign invaders. The Siamese themselves assert that their laws and their kings were imported from Laos, a belief that may exist only because of similarities between the two legal and monarchical traditions. While the religion of these kingdoms is the same, it does not follow that one borrowed from the other; it is possible that they all derive from a common source. Some Siamese and certain European missionaries suspect that Pali is related to the languages of the Coromandel Coast and that it is still alive there. Tradition also holds that "Sommona-Codom" (*să-mă-nă-kho-dom,* or "the ascetic Gautama") was the son of a king of Ceylon. Monosyllabic Siamese, on the other hand, in its similarity to Chinese, seems to relate the Siamese to the Sinic world. The Siamese resemble both the Chinese and the Indians in physiognomy. After all these speculations La Loubère concludes that "it is certain that the Siamese blood is much mixed with foreign." Since they take an annual census, it can readily be seen that the population is small in relation to the size of the land. At the last reckoning they counted "but Nineteen Hundred Thousand [1,900,000] Souls." [223]

Medicine is not a science in Siam, for their doctors treat everything by traditional remedies which they refuse to alter. The king's personal physicians are Chinese, Siamese, Peguan, and lately the Frenchman named Paumart of the Paris Mission Society. Asiatic physicians know nothing about anatomy, surgery, or the circulation of the blood. They treat all afflictions by diet and by the administration of mineral and herbal medicines. From the Europeans they have learned how to use quinine. They do not understand chemistry, but continue, like European alchemists, to seek out secret processes for making the philosopher's stone, gold, and the elixir of life eternal. Mathematics is not well developed because they quickly weary of following a "long thread of Ratiocination, of which they do foresee neither the end nor the profit." As a result they know nothing of geometry or mechanics and are concerned with astronomy only for purposes of divination, charting horoscopes, and preparing their almanac and calendar. The Thai calendar has been reformed twice by able astronomers. To produce astronomical tables they established two epochs arbitrarily. The more recent of these begins in A.D. 638, a date chosen only for its convenience in making astronomical calculations. [224] The more ancient of their epochs begins in 545 B.C. and is said to date from the death of Buddha. But it appears to be as

---

[223] La Loubère in Wyatt (ed.), *op. cit.* (n. 93), pp. 8–11.
[224] This is the conclusion of Cassini of the Paris Observatory, to whom La Loubère sent a translated copy of this calendar. Cassini's analysis is included by La Loubère in Wyatt (intro.), *op. cit.* (n. 93), pp. 186–227. Cassini compares it in detail to the Indian and Chinese calendars. Actually this is the Burmese system of dating which was imposed on Siam in 1569 and remained officially in use until 1889. See Philips (ed.), *op. cit.* (n. 42), p. 128.

unhistorical and arbitrary as their other calendar.[225] In Siam dates are reckoned still in terms of both of these calendars.[226]

The Siamese "understand nothing of the true System of the World, because they know nothing [about it] by Reason." Like other Asians they believe an eclipse occurs when a dragon devours the sun or the moon. They envisage a square earth of vast extent, covered by an "Arch of Heaven" that stands on its extremities. Their earth is divided into four habitable zones separated by the seas. Standing in the middle of these four zones is a high, pyramid-like mountain with four equal sides called "Caou pra Soumene" (*khao-phra-su-men*). The world of man is located to the south of the great mountain. The sun, moon, and stars revolve around the great mountain to produce day and night. Atop this mountain is a heaven for persons and a heaven of angels.[227]

The Siamese are as superstitious as were the ancient Greeks and Romans. They believe that soothsayers can heal the sick and foresee the future. When the king's physicians or soothsayers fail to fulfill a promised curse or prophecy they are bastinadoed "as negligent persons." Neither prince nor subject undertakes a trip or an "Affair" without first consulting the diviners. The royal diviners are all Brahmans or Peguans. Annually a Brahman astrologer prepares an almanac which gives the most and the least propitious days for undertaking tasks performed regularly. The Siamese take as dreadful omens the howls and cries of wild beasts, a snake crossing the path, lightning striking a house, and "any thing that falls as it were of itself." To forestall fate they perform ceremonies or accept as an oracle the first words spoken. Sorcerers enjoy a great reputation for being able to drive away the evil spirits and attract the good. With talismens called "cata" (*kha-tha*) they claim to be able to kill or accomplish whatever else is asked of them. To drive off evil spirits they attach papers to vials of medicine and to the gear of ships. Pregnant women, who are thought to be impure, are kept in bed for one month lying before a smoky fire.[228]

Their understanding of music is no better than their knowledge of geometry and astronomy. They compose "Airs by Fancy, and know not how to prick [write] them by Notes."[229] Sometimes they sing without words and simply repeat "noi, noi." Their music has little harmony and few quavers or trills. Their choruses sing in unison; there are no parts. For instruments they have "very ugly" little three-stringed violins called "Tro" (*sǫ?*) and shrill

---

[225] In Siamese this era is called the *phra-phut-tǎ-sak-kǎ-rat,* and it is still used in rural areas. The date 543 B.C., rather than the 545 B.C. given here, is the year ascribed to Buddha's attainment of nirvana. Philips (ed.), *op. cit.* (n. 42), p. 128.

[226] La Loubère in Wyatt (intro.), *op. cit.* (n. 93), pp. 62–65.

[227] On the Siamese cosmogony *cf.* Graham, *op. cit.* (n. 5), II, 220–22.

[228] La Loubère in Wyatt (intro.), *op. cit.* (n. 93), pp. 65–67.

[229] Melodies, all by anonymous composers, were passed from generation to generation by wandering minstrels. See Blanchard *et al., op. cit.* (n. 69), p. 472. See our pl. 218.

oboes named "Pi" (*pi-nai*). In their ensembles these instruments are accompanied by copper "Basons" (*ching*) hung up on a string, and by two kinds of wooden drums called "Tlompoumpan" (*klǫng-that?*) and "Tapen" (*tǎ-phon*). They have another crescent-shaped instrument called "Pat-cong" (*khǫng-wong?*), which is hit with two sticks by a player seated cross-legged at its center.[230] Soloists sing accompanied by two short sticks which they strike one against the other or by a drum called "Tong" (*ton*) which is an earthenware cone with a skin drumhead that they carry and strike with the hand.[231] Their trumpets called "Tre" (*trae*) are small and sound harsh. Their "true drums, which they call 'Clong' [*khlǫng*]," most frequently accompany dances. The people as a whole get most of their physical exercise from rowing rather than from dancing.[232]

The arts and crafts do not flourish in Siam "by reason of the Government under which they live." Since most private wealth is hoarded, there is no demand for the fine arts. Artisans in the royal service do what they must to escape punishments, but they do not strive for distinction. They are fearful of being "forced to work gratis" for the remainder of their lives. Disinterested in innovation and efficiency, they employ five hundred for several months to accomplish what several well-paid Europeans could finish in a few days. While Europeans are readily employed by the king, they are too often paid in promises and rarely become wealthy in the royal service. Siamese carpenters are "reasonable good Joyners" and adept at fitting pieces together. Others make bricks and good cement, but their brick structures do not last, because they are built without foundations. Since they make no glass products, the king was so intrigued by the fossette-cut mirrors which reflect multiple images that he asked for "entire Windows with the same property." While they claim to be sculptors, they do not understand the carving of stone. The statues in their temples are poorly made masses of brick and mortar which they cover over with thin coatings of gold, silver, or copper. They are excellent gilters "and know very well how to beat the Gold." Royal letters to other kings are written with a blunt stylus on a paper-thin sheet of gold. They are bad smiths and tanners, so their horses have no shoes and only very poor saddles. While they weave coarse cottons, they make no silken or woolen materials. Their embroideries are well designed and pleasing. Neither the Chinese nor the Siamese paint with oil. In their paintings they eschew naturalism and extravagantly represent men, beasts, birds, and plants "which never were."[233]

Commerce is the occupation followed by all Siamese with capital, includ-

---

[230] On Thai band instruments see Thai Delegation, "Thai Traditional Music" in Osman (ed.), *op. cit.* (n. 203), pp. 234–45.

[231] Cf. Graham, *op. cit.* (n. 5), II, 198.

[232] La Loubère in Wyatt (intro.), *op. cit.* (n. 93), pp. 68–69.

[233] *Ibid.*, pp. 69–71. *Cf.* Graham, *op. cit.*, (n. 5), II, 154–74, for a twentieth-century impression of Siamese arts and crafts.

ing the king himself. Foreign trade is almost completely a royal monopoly and internal trade is so slight as to make impossible great profits from it alone. Personal loans are recorded in promissory notes written by a third person who acts as a witness if terms are disputed. Private transactions in writing are neither signed nor stamped with a seal. Instead of a signature, they make a single but personalized cross. Since they purchase land and other immovables only rarely, they have no use for deeds, other long-term commitments, or notaries. In ordinary bazaar transactions both the buyer and seller trust each other and do not bother to count the money or to measure the goods exchanged. They measure in fathoms (a unit of six feet in length) the canals and roads generally used by the king; for example, the road from Ayut'ia to Lop Buri is lined with milestones. They have many measures for grain and liquids but no single standard. Weights are likewise not exact or uniform. Their silver coins are all stamped and have the same shape, though some are smaller than others. They have no gold or copper coins. Gold is sold as a commodity and is valued at twelve times the price of silver. Chinese copper coins and Japanese gold coins also circulate in Siam. Petty purchases are made with the cowrie shells generally used in Asia.[234]

The Siamese are in general good people who detest vices and do not tolerate them "as conceit, or as sublimity of mind." Adultery is uncommon "because the Women are not corrupted by Idleness." Women do not gamble, receive visits from men, frequent the public theater, or waste their money on luxuries. While wives of tradesmen move about freely, those of the nobles are closeted and glory in their role. Wives guilty of infidelity may be killed or sold by the offended husband; palace women caught in disloyalty are thrown to the animals. Errant daughters and wives are sold to a titled whoremaster who operates under a royal license. Age is highly respected, even when the difference is but a few years. Lying is common, even though it is severely punished by superiors and the king. Families typically form a united front and do not suffer from divisions based on conflicting interests. Begging is shameful both to the individual and his family. Stealing is even more ignominious for both the thief and his relations. Nonetheless they seldom refuse to steal when an opportunity presents itself. Robbers who live in the woods outside the law steal from travelers but rarely kill them. While mutual trust is common in commercial dealings, usury knows no limits and avarice is their "essential vice." Naturally averse to bloodletting, the Siamese rarely resort to murder and their quarrels end "only in blows, or reciprocal defamations." Even when they take a vow of eternal friendship in blood, their loyalty cannot be counted on. In general they are calmer and more moderate than Europeans. They act only when necessary and see no virtue in activity for its own sake. Since they have no curiosity, they admire

---

[234]La Loubère in Wyatt (intro.), *op. cit.* (n. 93), pp. 71–73. See the illustrations of their coins in our pl. 35. Also *cf.* above, pp. 1179–80.

and invent nothing. Subtle and wavering, they react proudly to gentleness and become humble in the face of rigor.[235]

"Talapoins" (priests and monks) live in convents called "Vats" (*wăts*) and "use" temples called "Pihan" (*wĭ-hans*), the *pagode* of the Portuguese.[236] The convent and the temple stand in a square surrounded by a bamboo fence. The temple is in the center of the enclosure, and the cells or huts of the priests are lined up in rows inside the bamboo fence. The temple is enclosed by an interior wall and surrounded by "pyramids" or pagodas. Between the temple's wall and the living cells is an empty plot which is the court of the convent.[237] Women of advanced years live in some of the *wăts* along with the male religious but in cells of their own. The "Nens" (*nens*) are the children who are sent by their parents to live as novices with the priests and monks. They serve the temple and the priests and some spend their entire lives as "Nens." The school of the "Nens" is a bamboo hall that stands apart, and next to it is another building where alms are brought when the temple is shut.

Each convent is ruled by a superior called "Tchaou-Vat" (*t̆hao-wăt*). Superiors are not all of equal rank. The most elevated are those called "Sancrat" (*sang-khă-rat*) and the one of the palace is the most revered of all.[238] Yet no "Sancrat" possesses jurisdiction over other superiors. Like bishops, the "Sancrats" ordain priests. But they have jurisdiction only over the members of their own convent. The convents of the "Sancrats" are distinguished from the others by "some stones planted around the Temple and near its Walls."[239] From the king the "Sancrats" receive, as badges of office, a name, an umbrella, and a sedan chair with carriers. The religious objective of all priests and monks is to live sinless lives and to do penance for those sinners who give them alms. Individually they live off alms which they are forbidden to share with others. In cases of grave necessity they give charity to one another and are always hospitable to laymen. On each side of their convent doors, they have lodgings for wayfarers.

"Talapoins" are of two types, rural recluses and city dwellers; hermit ascetics are more highly regarded than those who live in convents. All are obliged to be celibate or to withdraw from the order. They are exempted

---

[235] La Loubère in Wyatt (intro.), *op. cit.* (n. 93), pp. 73–76. *Cf.* the section on "the temper of life" in Blanchard *et al., op. cit.* (n. 69), pp. 15–17, for some twentieth-century generalizations on Siamese character.

[236] The central hall of worship is known as the *bot;* the *wĭ-han* is a second large hall in which sacred images are stored. See Pratt, *op. cit.* (n. 150), pp. 151, 153. On "pagode" see above, pp. 1208–9.

[237] La Loubère reproduces an engraved plan of the *wăt.* See pl. 220.

[238] He is appointed by the king to be the "Prince of the Church" or its active head. The king is a believer and the principal support of the church, but he is not of the clergy. See Blanchard *et al., op. cit.* (n. 69), p. 99.

[239] These are the *sima,* or the eight boundary stones, which enclose the consecrated land on which a hall is built for ordination and other official rites. See K. E. Wells, *Thai Buddhism, Its Rites and Activities* (Bangkok, 1939), pp. 141–42.

from the six months' personal service obligation, a privilege that attracts many to the religious life. To keep down the numbers in religion the king has them examined to ascertain their competency in Pali and the sacred writings. Those failing are returned, though they be many thousands, "to the Secular condition."[240] The monks educate the youths and preach sitting cross-legged in "a high chair of State" on the day following every new and full moon.[241] The laymen come to the temple with great constancy, listen to the sermons, and give alms to the preacher. For a long period the "Talapoins" fast to celebrate their Lent.[242] After the rice harvest they retire at night to the fields for three weeks; in the day they return to the temple compounds to sleep in their cells. The "Talapoins" have chaplets of 108 beads "on which they recite certain Balie [Pali] words."[243] Their yellow "linen" costumes come in four pieces: a scarf called "Angca" (*ăng-să*) which is thrown over the left shoulder, a gown named "Pa Schiwon" (*pha-čhi-wǫn*) which covers the right shoulder and falls to the ground, a kind of hood called "Pa Pat" (*pha-phat*) over the left shoulder which is sometimes red, and around the middle a belt called "Rapparod" (*rắt-phrằ-dŏt*) which keeps the other pieces in place.[244] When begging, they carry an iron basin in a cloth bag which hangs on their left side from a rope over the right shoulder. With copper razors, they shave off their beards, the hair of their heads, and their eyebrows. Superiors must shave themselves, but older priests and monks may shave those who are younger. On the day of the new and the full moon they shave, and the laity out of devotion fast after noon, abstain from fishing, and take alms to the convents.[245] Cattle brought as alms are eaten if dead; if not, they graze about the temple until they die and can be eaten. On these days the almsgivers show off their new clothes and obtain merit by buying and releasing animals in captivity. Offerings are taken by the "Talapoins," who present them to the idol ceremonially and then take them for their own use. Lighted taper offerings are attached by the "Talapoins" to the knees of the idol. At the full moon of the fifth month they wash the entire idol, except the head, with scented water. This is followed by a general washing of one another, involving both the clerics and the laity. In Laos they bathe the king in the river.[246]

After washing at daybreak, the "Talapoins" go to the temple with their superior. For two hours they sit cross-legged and chant their prayers from

---

[240] On the examination system now in use see Blanchard *et. al., op. cit.* (n. 69), p. 101.
[241] *Wăn Phră* or the Buddhist sabbath.
[242] Buddhist Lent or *Vassa*. See above, n. 34.
[243] On the Buddhist rosary see Spiro, *op. cit.* (n. 31), p. 210. The 108 beads represent the markings on the Buddha's foot as well as the number of his reincarnations.
[244] These three robes and the girdle are the *trai-chi-wǫn* of the monks. See H. Alabaster, *op. cit.* (n. 6), p. 202.
[245] Fishing is held in contempt even though fish are not technically killed by the fishermen. See Spiro, *op. cit.* (n. 31), p. 45.
[246] Probably refers to the New Year celebration. *Ibid.,* pp. 220–21.

Pali books. They chant in unison while keeping time with their fans. In entering and leaving the temple both monks and laymen prostrate themselves three times in front of the idol. After prayers the monks go into the town to beg for an hour. They stand silently at the gate with their begging bowls. Rarely are they without alms, for their parents, at least, never fail them. At their return to the convent from begging, they prostrate themselves before the superior and take one of his feet and place it upon their head. Then they eat breakfast and study until noon, when they have dinner. After dining they read to the novices and sleep. In the waning hours of the day, they sweep the temple and chant for two more hours. In the evening they sometimes eat fruit or take a walk outside the convent.[247] In the convents they raise food on tax-free land which their slaves cultivate. Besides slaves each monk has one or two white-clothed servants who are laymen called "Tapacaou" (?).[248]

When a superior dies, the members of the convent elect another, usually the eldest or most learned priest of the house. If a layman wishes to build a new temple, he chooses an elderly "Talapoin" as its superior. A postulant begins by obtaining permission from the superior to join the convent. He is then ordained by a "Sancrat." Parents are happy when a son enters a convent, because he is taken care of and does not necessarily have to remain there for life. Indeed, it is a sin to oppose the application of anyone to the religious life. Once he is formally admitted, his parents, friends, and musicians accompany him in procession to the convent. The women, dancers, and musicians remain outside the convent while the postulant and the men of his retinue enter for the initiation ceremony by the "Sancrat." With all the hair shaved from his face and head, the postulant receives and dons the monkish habit while the "Sancrat" pronounces "several Balie words." When this ceremony is ended, the new monk is accompanied to his hut by his parents and friends. When his parents some days later give an entertainment before the temple, neither he nor his fellows may see the dances or listen to the music. Nuns, called "Nang Tchii" (*mae-chi*), dress in white "and are not esteemed altogether religious." Priests who break their vow of chastity are burned, but errant nuns are sent to their parents to be bastinadoed, because the monks themselves are not permitted to strike anyone.[249]

The "Talapoins" believe that all of nature is animated, including the earth,

---

[247] *Cf.* the daily routine of the modern Buddhist monks in *ibid.*, pp. 305–10.

[248] La Loubère in Wyatt (intro.), *op. cit.* (n. 93), pp. 113–18. These white-clothed servants are possibly those who have left the order of monks. See Wells, *op. cit.* (n. 239), pp. 139–41.

[249] La Loubère in Wyatt (intro.), *op. cit.* (n. 93), pp. 118–19. In this section La Loubère quotes Gervaise to the effect that there are "Talapoins" of three grades. La Loubère himself was not so informed and questions Gervaise's account. Actually Gervaise is more nearly correct, even though his names for the three grades seem to be incorrect. The three grades in effect were based on educational achievements as determined by the state-regulated ecclesiastical examinations described by La Loubère himself. See S. J. Tambiah, *World Conqueror and World Renouncer: A Study of Buddhism and Polity in Thailand* . . . (Cambridge, 1976), p. 203.

planets, heaven, and "the other Elements." Souls are not physically united to a single body and indifferently move from one to the other. The "supreme Felicity of the Soul" is to be bodyless and "to remain eternally in repose." The "true Hell of the Soul" is in passing perpetually from one body to the other "by continual Transmigrations." The universe is eternal, but the perceived world decays, dies, and revives. The Siamese have trouble grasping the idea of pure spirit entirely bereft of substance. They assume that the "Souls are of a matter subtile enough to be free from touch and sight." These material souls are imperishable and are punished or rewarded "at their departure out of this life" until they reenter another human body. Human souls are happy or miserable in relation to the amount of good and evil "they have committed in a former life." While human souls may pass to plants and animals, the Siamese also believe in "several places out of this World where the Souls are punished or rewarded." According to most of their books there are nine happy places above and nine unhappy places below. The souls are reborn in these places and live there a life concealed from us. Thousands of years may pass before souls are reborn into this world.[250]

In writing of burials La Loubère compares the Chinese with the Siamese customs, "because that the Customs of a Country do always better illustrate by the comparison of the Customs of the neighbouring Countries."[251] In Siam the corpse is placed in a gilded wooden coffin. Mercury is poured into the mouth to consume the intestines in hopes of killing the stench. The coffin stands on an elevated place and perfumed wood and tapers are burned around it. Each evening the "Talapoins" arrive to chant services for the deceased and to receive alms. The family meanwhile chooses a cremation ground, ordinarily near the temple. They enclose this spot with a bamboo fence, over which they build a bower that they adorn with "Papers Painted or Gilded" and cut into representations of houses and animals. Scented woods are carefully built into an intricate funeral pyre at the center of the enclosure. The corpse is carried to the pyre in the morning by the parents and friends. The coffin heads the procession, followed by the deceased's family and friends, all dressed in white and with white veiling over their heads. In magnificent funerals they carry "great Machines [contrivances] of Bamboo" covered with paper effigies of palaces, elephants, and hideous monsters.

At the cremation ground the body is removed from the coffin and placed on the pyre. The "Talapoins" chant for one-quarter of an hour and then withdraw from the ceremony as it begins to take on a festive air. To render

---

[250]La Loubère in Wyatt (intro.), *op. cit.* (n. 93), pp. 119–22. *Cf.* Blanchard *et al., op. cit.* (n. 69), pp. 94–97.

[251]However commendable as a general idea, La Loubère's excursion here into comparative religion and ethnology is more misleading than enlightening. While vaguely conscious of the Indian background of Therevada Buddhism, La Loubère's sources for China are mainly concerned with Confucian rather than Buddhist practices. On Chinese religion in the contemporary European sources see below, pp. 1648–61, 1731–41.

the funeral more spectacular they put on "Cone" (*khon*) plays and fireworks while the mourners "make great Lamentations."[252] Around noon the pyre is lighted by a "Tapacaou" (?), a secular servant of the "Talapoins." Although it burns for two hours, the body is never entirely consumed. If the deceased is of the royal family or a great lord, the king himself lights the pyre without leaving his palace. From a window in the palace he slides a lighted torch down a rope to the pyre. The family entertains the guests after the funeral and for three days successively bestows alms upon the "Talapoins," the whole convent, and the temple. After the body is cremated the remains are placed in the coffin, often along with gold or other valuables for the next life. The coffin is then placed within one of the temple pyramids called "Pra Tchau di" (*phră-čhe-di*), or place of "sacred repose." Those who do not have access to the pyramids keep at home the remains of their parents. But every Siamese of substance tries to build a temple as an inviolable sanctuary for the family's riches. Those who are not so rich have idols built which they give to the existing temples. The poor bury their parents without burning them or expose them on a scaffold to be devoured by the crows and vultures. They never cremate or otherwise give funeral honors to criminals, stillborn infants, women who die in childbirth, suicides by drowning, or those killed in natural disasters or accidents. These exceptions are justified "because they believe that such Misfortunes never happen to innocent Persons." No specified period of mourning is prescribed in Siam as it is in China. While the Siamese do not pray to the dead, they offer food at the tombs to keep from being tormented "with their Apparitions." The good souls are transformed into angels and the bad into devils who continually protect or torment humans. No deity judges good or evil, for all is governed by "a blind fatality."[253]

Five negative precepts constitute the Siamese moral code: do not kill, steal, commit "any impurity," lie, or drink intoxicants.[254] Orthodox believers will eat only fruits and even then not the kernel or the seeds. Fruits, unlike seeds, are only parts of a living thing and they may be taken without harm to the tree, bush, or plant. While careful not to kill what is living, they have no hesitation about eating dead things once the "Soul has been expelled out of a body." They abhor blood and will not make bodily incisions or cut certain plants with blood-colored juice. Murder may be praiseworthy if it delivers a soul from a miserable existence. Suicide is "a Sacrifice advantageous to the Soul." Believers sometimes hang themselves from the sacred tree called "Ton Po" (*ton-pho* or the Bo-tree [pipul]), which they plant in their temple compounds. Self-immolation brought on by despair is an act of

---

[252] For the *khon* dance-drama see above, pp. 1225–26. The performance of a play is sometimes part of a religious ceremony in Thailand even yet. See Brandon, *op. cit.* (n. 202), p. 195.
[253] La Loubère in Wyatt (intro.), *op. cit.* (n. 93), pp. 122–26. *Cf.* Blanchard *et al.*, *op. cit.* (n. 69), pp. 94–98. The "blind fatality" is the effect of each individual's *karma*.
[254] The gravest act of impurity is adultery.

personal sacrifice which elevates the individual to sainthood, or the status of "Pra tian tec" (?). Among the prohibited acts of impurity are adultery, fornication, and marriage itself. Celibacy is a state of perfection, so marriage is a sinful state. Virtue is not universally expected but is reserved to the "Talapoins." While the laity is expected to sin, the "Talapoins" live blamelessly and pray for those who sin. But they have no hesitation about forcing others to sin. The "Talapoins" themselves refuse to kill rice by boiling it, so they have others do it for them. Forced by circumstances to be sinners, the laymen expiate their sins by giving alms generously. The "Talapoins" observe a long list of moral maxims by which they alone achieve purity and become "Creeng" (?).[255]

When a soul has acquired so much merit that no world or place is worthy of it, "this Soul is then exempt from every Transmigration and every Animation." It neither revives nor dies any more but enjoys "an eternal Unactivity, and a real impassibility [or freedom from pain and emotion]." It has achieved "Nireupan" (*Nă-rŏe-phan* or nirvana), or a state of complete disappearance from all worlds. The Portuguese have translated this word as "it is annihilation" or "it is become God." But the Siamese object that it is "not a real Annihilation, nor an Acquisition of any divine Nature."[256] The true hell for the Siamese is to be condemned eternally to transmigrate from one body to the other, the body being "a Prison for the Soul." Before entering nirvana to disappear, the man approaching it "enjoys great Privileges from this life." He becomes an efficacious teacher and acquires prodigious knowledge, "invincible strength of Body," and the power to perform miracles. He dies a noble death and disappears "like a Spark, which is lost in the Air." The Siamese dedicate their temples to the memory of these holy men. While several have won this "supreme Felicity," they honor only one alone, whom they "esteem to have surpassed all the rest in Virtue." They call him "Sommona-Codom" (*Să-mă-nă-kho-dom*), or "Codom," the "Talapoin of the Woods" (Gautama, the ascetic). Within the doctrines of the Siamese, there exists no idea of a divine creator, for their religion "is reduced all intire to the worship of the dead."[257]

The "Talapoins" explain to the people the fabulous stories in their books. These fables, like their moral precepts and doctrines, are recounted similarly throughout the East. Everywhere they belive in metempsychosis, spirits, sacred animals, and trees. The life of "Sommona-Codom" is likewise told

---

[255] La Loubère in Wyatt (intro.), *op. cit.* (n. 93), pp. 126–29. On pp. 158–63 La Loubère provides a list of the principal maxims of the "Talapoins" translated from Siamese with a few of his own comments in italics.

[256] This is probably the first mention by name of the Buddhist nirvana in European literature and it is "an amazingly modern evaluation of the term." See G. R. Welbon, *The Buddhist Nirvana and Its Western Interpreters* (Chicago, 1967), p. 21.

[257] La Loubère in Wyatt (intro.), *op. cit.* (n. 93), pp. 129–30. On the ancestor cult and the divinity of the king see K. P. Landon, *Southeast Asia, Crossroads of Religions* (Chicago, 1949), pp. 120–22.

in the anonymous and undated Pali books used throughout the region. The Siamese expect the appearance of another "Sommona-Codom" whom they call "Phra Narotte" (*Phra Sri An*).[258] Great tales are told of "Sommona-Codom's" perfect life, physical strength, miraculous powers, and his sudden enlightenment. He had two main disciples, called "Pra Mogla" (*Phra Mok-khăl-la*) and "Pra Scaribout" (*Phra Saribut*), whose statues are placed respectively on his right and left sides in the temples. Before achieving "Nireupan," he ordered that statues and temples should be consecrated to his memory. Since he went into a "State of Repose," the Siamese pray to him and ask him for "whatever they want." He is not respected as the author of their doctrines or laws. He seems to have been invented as an ideal man of virtue, as his relative "Thevetat" (*The-wa-that*), his enemy, was conceived as an ideal man of vice.[259] The Siamese believe that the worship of "Sommona-Codom" is for them alone and that other nations revere other worthy men. They remain utterly devoted to their own traditions and beliefs and cannot comprehend why anyone brands them false. Since they believe in no creator or supreme lawgiver, their worship of idols is a commemoration of great men rather than reverence for deities. This being true, they should be called atheists as well as idolators.[260]

Deliberate and conscious efforts were undertaken, especially by Jesuit missionaries, Dutch merchants, and French diplomats and soldiers, to learn as much as possible about Siam. Schouten, Van Vliet, Gervaise, certain Jesuits, and many of La Loubère's missionary informants had spent substantial periods of time in Ayut'ia, where they learned the Thai language. Their reports, as a consequence, included for the first time many Thai words for places, official titles, administrative divisions, costumes, and everyday practices and items. Since no separate map of Siam existed, Gervaise and La Loubère had projections made of its placement and extent, its most obvious physical features (such as coasts, mountains, and river courses), and the situation of its most important cities. French military engineers, beginning with the Chaumont mission, began systematically to collect data and to draw maps and plans of strategically important places. La Loubère published a detailed map of the course of the Menam from Ayut'ia to the Gulf of Siam prepared by an engineer. He quite ingeniously deduced from what he learned that the great rivers of Southeast Asia possibly did not originate in the great lake of Chiengmai previously postulated by others. He also provided plans of Ayut'ia, its royal palace, and a Buddhist temple, as well as

[258] The Future Buddha, the fifth and last in this world cycle, is the Buddha Maitreya who is to appear five thousand years after the death of the Buddha Gautama.
[259] La Loubère includes in his documentation the life of "Thevetat" (Devadatta in India) translated from Pali in Wyatt (intro.), *op. cit.* (n. 93), pp. 149–57. On Devadatta see H. Kern, *Manual of Indian Buddhism* (Varanasi, 1968), pp. 38–40.
[260] La Loubère in Wyatt (intro.), *op. cit.* (n. 93), pp. 135–40.

engraved depictions of flora, fauna, boats, houses, alphabets, coins, the royal palace, a convent, musical scores and instruments, idols, and a Chinese chessboard.

The natural history of Siam was best delineated in the writings of Schouten, Gervaise, and La Loubère. Of particular interest is the emphasis they placed on the forests and their products, on Siam's reputed wealth in gold, and on its store of tin and other minerals. They described rice irrigation, planting, and harvesting, and noticed the different types produced. While rice outstripped all other crops in economic and social value, wheat was grown in the highlands, where maize was also introduced around 1670. In Siam grew many unknown flowers and fruits, but only a few vegetables unknown to Europe. Wild and ferocious beasts, snakes, poisonous insects, and pesky gnats and mosquitoes stood in sharp contrast to shy deer, playful monkeys, curious talking birds, plodding oxen, and trained elephants who were almost human in their behavior. Fish were plentiful in the rivers, ponds, and surrounding seas. The annual floods in the lowlands enriched the soil, furnished water for rice cultivation, and killed off many rats and insects. Domesticated animals, particularly poultry, were generally saved from the flood by the foresight and planning of their owners. Nature was universally bountiful, but much land was left idle because of labor shortages. The Thai diet was based on fish, rice, and fruit. Although they killed no animals for food, they would eat the flesh of animals that died naturally, including everything from elephants to lizards.

Houses were usually one-story bamboo and thatched huts raised on poles several feet above the ground. Only the houses of the foreigners were made of brick. Furnishings were generally simple and unnecessary trappings rare; luxury items were found exclusively in the dwellings of those who enjoyed the royal favor. Most travel and communication was by water in a myriad of boats and barges. Since roads were few, inns and hostels were unknown. In Ayut'ia the foreign merchants and soldiers lived in their assigned sections and under the immediate jurisdiction of their own leaders, who enforced their own laws and answered to the Siamese authorities for their nation. Prisoners of war from Pegu and other neighboring territories were held as slaves and required to work as farmers. The rebuilding of Ayut'ia was reported on regularly in the European writings which appeared throughout the century. Descriptions of its internal divisions, suburbs, and royal palace were given repeatedly with variations which suggested the changes occurring over time or the removal of the court to Lop Buri for the dry season. Gervaise depicted Lop Buri as the "Versailles of Siam"; others brought out the role of towns north of Ayut'ia and of the vassal cities on the gulfs of Bengal and Siam.

With a population of 1,900,000, Siam was a complex hierarchical society in which the position and role of each individual was carefully specified by law and tradition. State service of six months annually was required of all registered males between the ages of nineteen and sixty, except for priests, monks, slaves, and aliens. As a rule, officials were appointed on the basis of merit by the crown. The bureaucracy which they ran was divided by function into civil and military branches. These branches were subdivided into six "bands" led by chiefs of six different titles. The number of provinces varied from seven to eleven in the European materials. Each province had either a hereditary or an appointed governor. Those appointed for a term of three years were gradually replacing the hereditary governors earlier tolerated in certain of the outer provinces. Each province bore the name of its chief city, which was usually its administrative and judicial center. The provinces were subdivided into lesser political and judicial jurisdictions of districts and towns. Those at a distance from Ayut'ia were far more independent of royal control than the inner provinces. In all provinces it was the function of the bureaucracy to provide leadership and control, to raise troops, and to furnish and organize supplies.

The absolute king and his ministers headed both the bureaucracy and the legal system. While the king remained the final authority in all matters, he generally ruled in accordance with the written codes and the ancient traditions. Legal procedure was always written, lengthy, and tedious. Appeals to higher jurisdictions and the crown were possible. They were mostly too expensive and impracticable, for the courts and the king himself were likely to affirm the decisions of the lower jurisdictions. The law provided that the eldest brother should succeed to the throne but both Prasat Thong and Narai took the kingship by usurpation. The king, who showed himself in public only for traditional ceremonies, was surrounded by a complex palace officialdom of ministers, guardsmen, and pages. Those officials and servitors who worked within the palace were generally superior in prestige and influence to those who acted for the crown on the outside.

Narai, who was esteemed to be an intellectually curious and constructive king, followed a rigorous daily schedule of audiences and interviews. To maintain the purity of his line he married both his sister and their daughter, even though incest was condemned by both religion and law. He ruled with the aid of a "second king," an official whose role was not limited to ceremony. Like previous monarchs of Siam he required his officials to drink annually the water of loyalty. All officials, especially courtiers, were constantly under close surveillance and were quickly cashiered when suspected of disloyalty or malfeasance. Although the king employed professional spies, every subject was required by law to be an informer in matters relating to the welfare of the state. Punishments administered by the king, even those that were unjust and cruel, were regarded by the recipient as marks of royal affection. The king's subjects, other than officials, displayed no loyalty to the king, the dynasty, or the state, for they had no vested interest in its maintenance or defense. They were just as happy to work as slaves in Pegu as to live as freemen in Siam.

All the land was owned in perpetuity by the crown, except for certain properties assigned to monasteries and temples for their maintenance. Artisans of talent were required to work in the royal workhouses, and lands were parceled out to cultivators. Foreign trade had become virtually a crown monopoly much to the disgruntlement of private Siamese merchants and foreign traders. It was administered by an official appointed by the king to manage all foreign affairs. Taxes were levied by the crown on produce, boats, and internal trade. Duties of 8 percent were collected on both exports and imports. On stated occasions the crown expected to receive "gifts" from its subjects, especially from those to whom favors or concessions had been granted. The mercantilistic king hoarded gold and other precious metals and returned as little as possible of his wealth to the economy.

Foreign embassies were well received, for they were esteemed to be tribute missions which would enhance the prestige of the king. Greater respect was shown to the letter of a foreign ruler than to the emissary who carried it. Ambassadors were expected to bring gifts and in return were permitted to engage in trade for the duration of their stay. Malay Muslims, Indians, Iranians, Chinese, Japanese, and Europeans lived permanently in Siam and many served the crown as soldiers, sailors, and officials. Muslim mullahs and Catholic priests made only very few converts to their faiths. The Chinese dominated Siam's foreign trade. Malays, Japanese, and Portuguese fought in Siam's inland and maritime wars that were waged mainly to take slaves and booty. Because of its excellent natural defenses, Siam had no need for fortifications. Timid as warriors, the Thais avoided pitched battles and preferred to protect their borders with small and highly mobile contingents. While the Thais depended upon war elephants to charge in battle, the Europeans soon learned that the elephants could be frightened by gunfire and made to flee.

Thai society was divided into freemen and slaves, many of the latter being in bondage for debt. Ordinary Thais wore very few clothes, but were clean and neat in appearance and modest in behavior. In their daily transactions in the market they trusted one another to be honest, for they had no uniform system of weights and measures. Usury and avarice were their worst vices. Much attention was given to the ceremonial costume of the courtiers and the king and to the relation of dress to rank. At court an official dialect was used which differed from ordinary Thai speech. The Thai language, like Chinese, was monosyllabic, tonal, and almost bereft of grammar. Instead of characters, the Thai language was written in letters drawn from four alphabets. Many words and terms were borrowed from the languages of India, especially from Pali. Buddhist priests and certain officials and scholars continued to read Pali texts. Thai arithmetic was based on a decimal system and used the zero. Two calendars were in use, one of which began with the death of the Buddha in the sixth century B.C. The Siamese had manuscript annals and books of history and law; unlike the Chinese they did not command a knowledge of printing. Thais were thought to be natural poets and musicians. While they had no musical notation, they played a variety of strange instruments singly or assembled in concert. They put on dances in elaborate costumes and acted dance-dramas depicting traditional scenes and events. Because of the repressive absolutism, the arts and sciences did not flourish. Thai craftsmen were content to imitate European products and were not interested in learning European arts. The ordinary folk amused themselves with traditional sports and games. In everyday life great reliance was placed on omens, spirits, and astrological prognostications.

Marriage was a secular act arranged by families without the participation of the clergy. Brides of commoners were often bought; prostitution was legal and the owner and his women taxed. Women had no role in government at any level. Wives worked to support the family while the husbands were performing their annual corvée. When free of state service, the husbands, untrained for other jobs, lolled around while the wives continued to work at their occupations. The exchange of money was a pursuit followed exclusively by women. Polygamy was restricted to men of position and wealth, their proud wives usually being closely kept and watched. The king himself kept only a moderate number of concubines, and the queen had her own ships and engaged in trade. Adultery on a wife's part could be punished as a capital offense or she could be sold into prostitution. In polygamous families the children of the first wife had their own word for "father" and were the only legal heirs. Old women often chose to work as aids in the monasteries and temples.

Buddhism was a highly organized religion supported and controlled by the king. He appointed its primate from the council of the oldest and ablest priests. Its clergy was divided into monks and priests who lived in compounds on land granted by the king or in wastelands as hermit recluses. Its temples were often paid for by the donations of laymen seeking merit or bent upon erecting memorials. All youths received their early education from the monks. Those students who chose to remain in religion were trained for ordination. Monks always had the possibility of resigning and returning to the lay status. The clergy was periodically tested on their knowledge of the Pali texts by royal examiners. Those who failed, like those who violated their vows, were evicted from the order. Monks and priests wore yellow costumes, shaved their heads, and carried a rosary of 108 beads. They followed a regular routine of prayer and services, and daily begged for their sustenance. Priests presented the offerings of the laity to the idols and exhorted the laity to feed monks, to free captive animals, and to send their sons to the monastery for education. They presided at funerals and at cremation rites. They led pilgrimages to holy places, especially to the shrine at the footprint of the Buddha. And they shepherded the faithful through the festivals of Lent and the New Year.

Buddhists, especially the clerics, strictly followed five or six negative commandments; the laity was sinful and constantly in need of clerical guidance. They believed in no creator, supreme lawgiver, or deity; rather they worshipped great and holy men whom they consecrated in their idols. After death the soul, it was believed, goes to one of a number of heavens or hells. From these stations it eventually invades another material being and continually and mercilessly passes from one transmigration to the next. It was Gautama Buddha, their great teacher, who reached nirvana, a state of eternal repose and freedom from transmigration. While most Buddhists never dreamed of nirvana for themselves, the Siamese believed in a "Future Buddha." The Europeans very clearly understood that Buddhism was practiced throughout the East from Siam to Japan. Elsewhere in Asia, especially in Japan and Vietnam, the Buddhists persecuted the missionaries and their converts as dangers to the state and its religion. While benefiting from the tolerance of the Siamese, the Europeans deplored the indifference of the Buddhists to the Christian message.

CHAPTER XVI

Vietnam

Traders and missionaries from Macao and Japan arrived in Vietnam at a time when two great families—the Trịnh in the north and the Nguyễn in the south—were struggling for control of the Indo-Chinese peninsula. Their rivalry led to a series of indecisive wars which went on from 1620 to 1674. Gradually two separate states emerged in this period: Tongking to the north and Cochin-China to the south of the Gianh River of central Vietnam. Both sides wanted modern arms and expert gunners from the Europeans.[1] Trade and missions were therefore tolerated, especially by the Nguyễn in the south because of their greater need for arms. European activities were nonetheless abruptly halted from time to time when arms shipments ceased or were deemed insufficient. Ming China, which claimed to be sovereign over Vietnam, was unwilling or unable to control the peninsula to its south. The failing Ming dynasty itself began to be attacked by Manchu advances southward beginning in 1620. Japan's growing hostility towards the Christian missionaries and their converts led also to an outflow of Japanese refugees, many of whom were welcomed as reinforcements for the contending armies in Vietnam. Missionaries from Macao and Japan were quick to take advantage of the opportunity presented to minister to the Japanese Christians and to the Europeans working in these Vietnamese lands. And the Catholic missionaries were most eager to open a new mission field in virgin territories.

The Portuguese of Macao had established trading relations with both Tongking and Cochin-China before the end of the sixteenth century. At Tongking they had bought raw silk for sale in Japan. In Cochin-China they

[1] See C. R. Boxer, "Asian Potentates and European Artillery in the Sixteenth to Eighteenth Centuries: A Footnote to Gibson-Hill," *JRAS, Malaysian Branch*, Vol. XXXVIII, Pt. 2 (1966), pp. 166–67.

traded at Fai-fo (Hội An), the foreign commerce center and capital of Quảng-Nam province.[2] In Tongking and Fai-fo they competed with Chinese and Japanese traders, the overseas commerce of Vietnam being almost entirely in the hands of foreigners. In 1592 the Japanese had begun to send officially licensed "red-seal" ships to Vietnam; private voyages from Japan had certainly preceded this official commerce. Early in the seventeenth century the Dutch and English began to insinuate themselves into Vietnam's foreign trade. In 1614, just as the Christians began to leave Japan in large numbers, English and Dutch merchants in a Japanese junk and with a Japanese interpreter landed at Fai-fo with a cargo for sale. They were killed and their goods confiscated; two years later another Englishman actually began to work in Cochin-China.[3] Contemporaneously several Jesuits, stranded in Macao because of their exile from Japan, decided to carry their work to Fai-fo. Early in 1615 they arrived there under the leadership of Francesco Buzomi (1576–1639), the Neapolitan who headed the mission to Cochin-China until 1629.[4] Late in 1624 a new delegation of six Jesuits joined this mission. It was headed by Gabriel de Matos (1572–1633) and included Alexandre de Rhodes (1593–1660), who had arrived at Macao the year before.[5] Three years later, in 1627, Rhodes pioneered the first Jesuit mission to Tongking. In 1630 he was expelled and thereafter the Jesuits had to work secretly in Tongking.[6]

During the sixteenth century the Europeans had learned very little about the Vietnamese states.[7] Aside from a few vagrant references in Purchas' compilation (1625),[8] the firsthand materials on Vietnam published in Europe during the first half of the seventeenth century came from the pens of missionaries. In his *Historia* (1601) Ribadeneira reports on what he had learned about Cochin-China from his Franciscan colleagues, especially from a friar named Bartolome Ruiz, who managed to stay there for two years.[9] Giuliano Baldinotti (1591–1631), a Jesuit and a native of Pistoia in Italy, made a reconnaissance trip in 1626 to Tongking at the behest of his superiors. He remained there for more than five months (March 7 to August 18) before returning to Macao. On November 12 he wrote a report to the general in

---

[2] On international commerce at Fai-fo see Lê Thành Khôi, *Histoire du Viet Nam des origines à 1858* (Paris, 1981), pp. 278–83. The town itself was almost totally destroyed by the wars attending the Tây-Son rebellion of 1771 to 1778. Also see D. J. Whitfield, *Historical and Cultural Dictionary of Vietnam* (Metuchen, N.J., 1976), pp. 112–13.

[3] See the reports of Richard Cocks from Japan in Purchas: *PP*, III, 557–58, 561.

[4] Six Jesuits, four secular priests, and two lay brothers set up a mission at "Pulocambi" in Qui-Nhòn province. See Streit, V, 448.

[5] See H. Chappoulie, *Aux origines d'une église. Rome et les missions d'Indochine au XVIIe siècle* (2 vols.; Paris, 1943), I, 23.

[6] *Ibid.*, pp. 32–39; also see above, pp. 237–44.

[7] See *Asia*, I, 570.

[8] For example, see the rather bizarre description of Cochin-China by a M. de Monfart (Henri de Feynes) who traveled there for two months *ca.* 1604 in *PP*, XII, 494–95. On De Feynes see above, pp. 401, 554.

[9] For bibliographical detail see above, pp. 321–22.

Rome summarizing his experiences, the first substantial European account of Tongking. At Rome his letter was published in 1629 as an addition to the *Lettere dell'Etiopia*. In the same year it was translated into French and Polish along with the rest of the original Italian letterbook.[10] Two years after the publication of Baldinotti's report on Tongking, Cristoforo Borri's (1583–1632) *Relatione* (1631) on Cochin-China was issued at Rome. Borri had spent at least four years (1617–22) with the Jesuit mission in Cochin-China. From Vietnam he went on to Goa in 1623 where he met Pietro della Valle, the intrepid traveler.[11] A mathematician and astronomer by training, Borri was also an exceptionally talented observer and a serious student of the Annamese language. The first part of his *Relatione* deals exclusively with Cochin-China; its second part records the history of the mission and describes Tongking.[12] Finally there is the *Relatione* of Antonio Francesco Cardim (published at Rome in 1645) which discusses the Jesuit mission in both Tongking and Cochin-China to 1644.[13]

I

FIRST NOTICES

Baldinotti arrived in Tongking in 1626 when Trịnh Tráng (r. 1623–57) ruled the kingdom in the Red River delta. He was accompanied by a Japanese brother as he sought to determine if Tongking was ready for a Christian mission. The Portuguese merchant vessel on which he traveled was escorted upriver by four royal galleys to protect it from pirates. Arrived in Tongking city (latter-day Hanoi), he and the others are welcomed by the king, who promises to take care of all their needs. He provides them with native costumes and lodges them in one of the best houses in the city. He invites them to see elephant fights, horse races, a regatta on the river, and festivals. All this hospitality, Baldinotti believes, is closely related to the king's desire for more trade with the Portuguese. The king, on learning of Baldinotti's knowledge of mathematics and astronomy, invites the Jesuit to remain at the court to instruct him in these sciences. The invitation is declined, because Baldinotti is required by his superiors to return to Macao with the merchants to

[10] The Italian version and a French translation of Baldinotti's report are reproduced in the *Bulletin de l'Ecole Française d'Extrême-Orient* (Hanoi), III (1903), 71–78. For further bibliographical detail see above, p. 376.

[11] On Della Valle and his valuable work see above, p. 380.

[12] The first part of Borri's account in the English translation (1623) of Robert Ashley was reprinted in 1970 by the *Theatrum Orbis Terrarum* as No. 223 of its series on *The English Experience*. The entire work in English translation may be found in *CV*. This translation is reprinted in John Pinkerton, *A General Collection of . . . Voyages and Travels* (10 vols.; London, 1811), IX, 772–828. For complete bibliographic detail see above, p. 377.

[13] In the French *Relation* (Paris, 1645), pp. 51–113. For bibliographical details see above, pp. 378–79.

whom he ministers. He promises that once he is back in Macao, he will request permission to return to Tongking to serve its king. Satisfied by this
response, the king invites the Jesuit to a banquet. After answering the king's
questions about the mathematics of the sphere, Baldinotti is presented with
gifts by the queen mother and with letters patent by the king and similar
ones from the heir apparent permitting him to return and to live in Tongking at the crown's expense.

This serenity ends when a "Moor" charges that the Portuguese are in the
pay of the king of Cochin-China and have come to Tongking as spies. While
the king does not react strongly to these charges, he requires the Europeans
to take an oath not to go to Cochin-China, never to favor its ruler, and to
remain always his good and faithful friends. After a long wrangle as to
whether this oath should be taken following Buddhist or Christian practices, the king finally is satisfied when they make their promises aloud before an image of the Christ. Relieved of his suspicions, the king sends the
Christians presents and a license to embark. On August 18 they leave the
city with a favorable wind and accompanied by two royal galleys. Baldinotti
concludes his letter by urging the establishment of a mission in Tongking
from which both south China and Laos might be penetrated more readily.
The Laotians, according to Alexandre de Rhodes, are ready to receive the
Divine Law.

Following the instructions of his superiors, Baldinotti systematically
gathered information while in Tongking. The kingdom and the court city
(now Hanoi, or "On the River") are both called Tongking. On the north the
kingdom borders China, on the south Cochin-China, on the west the "Lai"
(Laotians), and on the east the sea of China. Great rivers run through this
flat land to help it produce an abundance of foods, such as rice, meat of domestic and wild animals, poultry and birds, and many fruits similar to those
of China. Still, food is not cheap, because of the huge population that must
be sustained. The people are idolaters. Some practice the magic of the Chal-
deans while others follow astrology. Some embrace the teachings of the
gymnosophists of India, but most worship a native idol called "Zinum." To
it they make their offerings out of fear. They say that the head of this image,
which has been cut off, has the power to parch the trees, spoil the gardens,
and kill the animals towards which its eyes are directed. Its head is kept in
the city where this man was born; situated at a distance of four days' journey
from the court, this city is inhabited by his nephew and their descendants.
Still others of his descendants belong to its pagoda.[14] Generally the An-

---

[14] Baldinotti (*loc. cit.* [n. 10], p. 77), vaguely appreciates the mixed character of Annamite
popular religion: magic, animism, astrology, Buddhism, and Hinduism. The story of "Zinum"
possibly refers to the cult of the thirteenth-century General Trần Hủng-Đạo. According to
legend he captured and decapitated a Chinese commander named O-ma-nhi. In popular lore
Hủng-Đạo and his descendants are regarded as good spirits while O-ma-nhi and his descendants are believed to be evil spirits working constantly against the beneficence of Hủng-Đạo.
See P. Giran, *Magie et religion annamites* (Paris, 1912), pp. 430–31.

namese are only slightly attached to the cult of the pagodas, because they are intelligent enough to recognize its falsity. The bonzes, who do not make a profession of letters and are unkempt, are not held in high regard or listened to seriously.

The Tonkinese are devoted to arms, particularly to the artillery and musketry of which they are skilled users. Soldiers sling their swords and scimitars over their shoulders. They have white skin, are tall in stature, and are jolly and courageous. They wear a long shirt-like gown which is open in the front and falls to mid-leg. Their long hair they cover with a cap (*cf.* pl. 267). As people they are sensitive, tractable, faithful, and cheerful; they do not have the vices of China and Japan (presumably sodomy). Commoners are inclined to steal. That is why thieves, like adulterers, receive the death penalty. The king (*vua*) in Tongking is lord of nine provinces; he is paid tribute by the rulers of Laos, Cochin-China, and "Bao."[15] He himself pays tribute to China and each year sends three gold and three silver statues to Peking. Tongking is able to put great armies into the field; six hundred high mandarins are obliged to furnish, at their own expense, one thousand to two thousand soldiers recruited from their fiefs. War is the sole occupation of these mandarins. In various places the king keeps four thousand galleys, each with twenty-six oars on a side. Almost all carry artillery when cruising. On one occasion five hundred of them assemble to celebrate the anniversary of the death of the present king's father, who some years before had been assassinated by his youngest son then overly eager to reign.[16] Thereafter this son was killed by the eldest son, the present king Trịnh Tráng (r. 1623–57), and the legitimate successor to the throne. The king of Tongking is very bellicose and continually practices shooting at a target while mounted on a horse or elephant. He also takes pleasure in making his galleys maneuver. The capital, which swelters until the monsoon begins to blow in June each year, has neither walls nor fortifications for protection. The royal palace is built of stout and well-worked blocks covered with tiles. Other houses are made of native bamboo covered with straw. In the city there are several large lakes whose waters are used to extinguish fires when they endanger the houses; huge fires have burned down five or six thousand houses within a period of four to five days. The town of Tongking is six leagues in circuit and possesses an innumerable population. It is on a great, navigable river which empties into the sea eighteen leagues away. Its water is muddy, but everyone drinks it, for there is in the entire town no spring, well, or cistern. The river generally floods at the beginning of June and again in November. It then inundates half the city, but the flood is not of long duration.

---

[15] "Bao," or Baoha, a small state on the Cầu River, was surrounded by China's Kwangsi province, Laos, and Tongking.
[16] The father was Trịnh Tùng (r. 1570–1623), the king who established the Trịnh court at Hanoi in 1593.

Borri, who knew Baldinotti's account of Tongking, provides one of his own, based on what he was able to learn in Cochin-China.[17] He was told in Macao to learn the Annamese language in Cochin-China as preparation for eventually carrying the mission to Tongking. As a consequence he also sought during his time in Cochin-China to learn about Tongking, "the language being the same, as formerly it was but one kingdom." From the natives he learned that Cochin-China is a vassal of Tongking, whose king also reigns over four other provinces "all extending equally in length and breadth." Tongking, four times as large as Cochin-China, is in shape a square in the exact center of which stands the royal capital "incompassed on all sides" by its four provinces.[18] Trade between China and Tongking is "so mutual and constant" that no gates or walls stand at the frontier. The Jesuits therefore hope to enter China by way of Tongking to avoid the impediments and controls of Canton. Laos, the great kingdom to the west of Tongking, must border on its east with Tibet since "it seems impossible that any other land should lie betwixt them."[19] Tongking is an hereditary monarchy ruled by "one they called Buna [*vua*, king]." He is sovereign in name only, for all powers reside in his favorite "whom they call Chiuua [*chúa*, lord]."[20] The "Buna" stays in his royal palace at Tongking and is satisfied to be treated "as a sort of sacred person, with the authority of making laws, and confirming all edicts."[21] The power of the "Chiuua" is so absolute in the management of public affairs both in peace and war that he has "come by degrees to own no superior." While the "Chiuuas" try to pass on the succession to their sons, the tutors of these sons generally conspire to eliminate the legal heir and usurp the crown. The "Chiuua" of the larger state of Tongking can put into battle three or four times the number of men raised by the ruler of Cochin-China; he can easily require his mandarins to furnish him with "three hundred thousand armed men or more." Although the "Buna's" guard (see pl. 266) numbers no more than forty thousand soldiers, he is always esteemed as sovereign by the three contending families (Mạc, Trịnh, and Nguyễn) and receives "a certain tribute" from Laos. Un-

---

[17] In Pinkerton, *op. cit.* (n. 12), IX, 825–27.
[18] Refers to the provinces north, south, east, and west of the capital. See below, p. 1277.
[19] Like many of the Jesuit commentators, Borri is impressed by the supposed size and importance of Laos. He is also aware of contemporary Jesuit activities in Tibet. See above, pp. 147, 338–39, and below, pp. 1773–75.
[20] For these identifications see C. B. M. Maybon, *Histoire moderne du pays d'Annam (1592–1820). Etude sur les premiers rapports des Européens et des Annamites . . .* (Paris, 1919), p. 15, n. 3. The name *chúa* was applied to the heads of both the Nguyễn and Trịnh families. The former was called "lord of the south" and the latter "lord of the north." The Nguyễn formally acknowledged the suzerainty of the Lê monarch (*vua*) while remaining entirely independent in their actions.
[21] The Lê dynasty was restored to power in 1533 by the powerful Nguyễn family. Thereafter the Mạc kings actually ruled Tongking until 1592–93, when they were replaced by the Trịnh. The puppet Lê sovereign was then moved from Tây-dô to Hanoi or Tongking city. The later Lê dynasts remained nominal rulers until 1804. See D. G. E. Hall, *A History of South-East Asia* (2d ed.; London, 1964), pp. 188–89, 892–93.

like the others, the "Buna" is always succeeded by his own children for sovereignty remains hereditary in his family.

Cardim, who repeats much of what his Jesuit predecessors had reported, was one of those who went to Tongking early in 1631, ten months after the expulsion of Rhodes. From his personal experiences he was able to add a few, new strokes to the sketches of Tongking previously published.[22] The Chinese call it "Tunquim" (Tongking), but the native name is "Anam" (Annam) which means "west country." It is so called because it lies west of China; the term "Tunquim" itself means "west court" just as "Peking" means "north court."[23] On the south it is bounded by "Chiampa" (Champa) and ends in the north with the kingdom of "Ciocanque" (Cao-bằng) which borders on China. Tongking's metropolitan city is called "Kecio" (*Ke-cho, the market*) by the natives.[24] Very high mountains on the west divide Annam from Laos. Waters from these mountains feed the rivers which regularly flood the low country and fertilize the land. Each grain of rice sown here produces more than one hundred. The numerous inhabitants of this kingdom are white like the Japanese and Chinese. Soldiers dress in knee-length drawers, over which they wear a "Cabaye" (Arabic, *kaba*, a vestment like a jacket). They cover the head with a long skullcap. While the king keeps many galleys for war, he also has lighter crafts for parades. On festival occasions the galleys perform a water ballet in response to the beating of a drum. In this country the sect of "Xaca" (Japanese for Buddha) is in fashion. A son of the king of India named "Iobon" (Do Dau ha), "Xaca" married a lady called "Maia" (Mara), by whom he had a son. After the birth of this son, the Buddha abandoned the world and went from place to place winning disciples. First he taught them philosophy and then how to do a thousand sorceries. He lived four hundred years before the coming of our Savior.[25]

After Baldinotti's favorable report on Tongking, the Jesuits of Macao sent Pedro Marquez and Alexandre de Rhodes as missionaries to Tongking. They arrived at the port of Tongking on March 19, 1627, the feast of Saint Joseph. Father Alexandre, already fluent in the Annamese language, at once begins to preach, instruct, and make converts in the port town. Soon a eunuch is sent from the court with orders to bring the ship's cargo and the fathers to Trịnh Trắng. After receiving them cordially, the king, who is about to leave the city, asks them to await his return at a place in the prov-

---

[22] See Cardim, *op. cit.* (n. 13), pp. 51–93. He left Macao with Gaspar d'Amaral and Antoine des Fontaines on February 18, and arrived at Tongking on March 15 (*ibid.*, p. 90).

[23] Incorrect. An-Nam is a Chinese name meaning "the pacified south." Tongking or Đông-Kinh means "eastern capital" and is likewise a Chinese designation; the royal capital was officially named Hà-Nội only in 1831. See Whitfield, *op. cit.* (n. 2), p. 95.

[24] In the twentieth century, Hanoi was still called "the market" in common parlance. See A. Schreiner, *Les institutions annamites en Basse-Cochinchine avant la conquête française* (3 vols.; Saigon, 1900–1902), I, 4n.

[25] Like the other Jesuits of the Japan Province, Cardim was exceptionally sensitive to the presence of Buddhism and to its temples, monks, and priests.

ince of "Sinusa" (Portuguese, Sinoa, is Vietnamese Thanh-Hóa) where the court had previously been.[26] Here they build a church and erect a cross before its door. These activities soon attract the attention of the priests at a nearby large Buddhist pagoda. The Jesuits convert "bonzes" who begin to preach, to help in the construction of a new church, and to make and encourage donations to the Christian enterprise. Cures and miracles help to convince the idolaters of the power of the Christian God. Nonetheless, rumors begin to circulate that the fathers convert people in this world to make them slaves of the Portuguese in the next and that they burn the books of the ancient sects of Tongking to introduce their own. In spite of this, the Jesuits convert two hundred at this place, including a kinswoman of the king.

With the return of the king, the Jesuits visit him and present him with a book of mathematics written in Chinese. They accompany him on his return to Tongking and on the way try to explain the mathematics in his book. When they lead the conversation to Christianity, the king loses interest. By the time they arrive at court they have won the ears of a number of courtiers. With the king's consent, they baptize his sister. By May, 1628, just over one year after their arrival, the Jesuits had baptized fifteen hundred persons, including a mandarin close to the king. On the sudden death of this mandarin shortly after his baptism, the king orders the Jesuits to baptize no more of his subjects, the Christian law being in his eyes the religion of death. When the queen is given a Christian book she promptly rejects it saying she wishes to know of no faith other than that of the pagodas.[27]

Despite royal opposition, the Jesuits baptized 5,727 persons in the year 1631. By the end of another decade they had baptized a total of 108,000 and had 235 churches scattered about the country. These figures, Cardim admits, would seem to be beyond belief, particularly because of the king's opposition and the small number of available priests. Such great successes must therefore be attributed to the enthusiasm of the neophytes and catechists in spreading the gospel, the charity displayed by formerly arrogant mandarins after their conversion (wolves become sheep), the honors shown to the dead in Christian funerals, the successful exorcising of the evil spirits which bedevil the souls and even the homes of the natives, and the equality which prevails among Christians of all classes. But the principal reason for these successes is to be found in the persecution of the Christians instituted by the royal edict of March, 1629, banishing the Jesuits for tearing down pagodas and teaching a doctrine of death. During their exile the Vietnamese Christians continue the baptisms and at court press the king for a change of heart. When the Jesuits, including Cardim, return to Tongking in March,

[26] The ancestral homeland of the Lê dynasty in central Vietnam. Lê-Lợi, the founder of the Lê dynasty, was born in this province.

[27] Rhodes' activities in Tongking are similarly, and more clearly, summarized in his *Divers voyages* (Paris, 1653). For an English version see S. Hertz (trans.), *Rhodes of Vietnam* (Westminster, Md., 1966), pp. 61–75.

1631, the king welcomes them and lodges them in the palace. He invites them to accompany the entourage which is proceeding on an assigned day to administer the state examinations to the literati. Finally he explains that the banishment of their predecessors was not based on ill will. He would be very happy for the Jesuits to live in his kingdom providing they not disturb the Buddhists or destroy the pagodas of the capital; the Buddhists belong there. He assigns the Jesuits a large residence in a place surrounded by many houses and officially permits them to instruct and baptize all those who wish to become Christians.

While the Jesuits got off to a shaky start in Tongking, they had a better initial experience in Cochin-China. The Portuguese and Spaniards who had traded at Fai-fo for three or four months annually had usually been accompanied by chaplains. These secular priests had ministered exclusively to the Christians, had not learned the language of the country, and had failed to promote Christianity with the natives. Still, one of these chaplains had the audacity to publish in *The Voyages of the World* the false claim that he had baptized the Infanta or Princess of Cochin-China and a great many of her female attendants. When the Jesuits began working in Cochin-China in 1615, they found no evidence of the Infanta being a Christian "or so much as knowing what a Christian is."[28] Buzomi began his mission at "Turon" (Tourane, the French name for Đà Nẵng), a town downriver from the place where the king resides.[29] When he first arrived, the Cochin-Chinese thought that to be a Christian meant to give up being an Annamese and to become a Portuguese. This misunderstanding being straightened out, converts were soon made and a church built at Tourane. Jesuit progress was set back when they were accused of bringing a severe drought to the country, an allegation made against them by one of the "omsaiis" (*ông sư*), or hermit monks. Relief was sent from Macao in 1617 in the persons of Fathers Pedro Marquez, a Luso-Japanese, and Cristoforo Borri, a Milanese; they arrived with the rains. Thereafter with the help of the Japanese Christian community of Fai-fo, the persecution of the Jesuits ceased. At this point they were visited at Tourane by the governor of the province of Pulucambi (Qui-Nhơn). He immediately favored the foreign priests and took three of the four of them off to his capital, the town of Pulucambi. This governor, who was as powerful in the neighboring province of "Quanghia" (Quảng-Nghiã) as in his own, entertained and lodged the Jesuits as if they were visiting royalty. He built them a church and a residence at Pulucambi. Then he suddenly took a fever

---

[28] Borri in Pinkerton, *op. cit.* (n. 12), IX, 797–98. This is a reference to the *Historia y viage del mundo* (Madrid, 1614) of Pedro Ordóñez de Cevallos who was allegedly in Cochin-China *ca.* 1590. This travel book should be compared to that of Pinto published in the same year; we suspect both are a mixture of fact and fiction. For a scholarly discussion see E. C. Knowlton, Jr., "South East Asia in the Travel Book by Pedro Ordóñez de Ceballos," *Proceedings of the Second International Symposium on Asian Studies* (Hong Kong, 1980), pp. 499–510.

[29] The Nguyễn court was located after 1600 in the Thanh-Hóa province at the confluence of the Mã and Chu rivers near the Tongking border.

and quickly died. Again the Jesuits faced problems and their mission languished over the next three years. Shortly after Borri's departure in 1622, their enterprise again began to prosper when they made a few important converts, bested the local astrologers at predicting eclipses in 1620 and 1621, and won over the commoners by converting heathen priests and exorcizing devils.[30]

In 1629 the royal edict had forced the Jesuits to abandon some fifteen thousand converts, eight churches, and the residences at Tourane, Fai-fo, "Caciane" (Chi-Ciam, the king's court town), and at "Nurcrnan" or Pulu-cambi (on the border of Champa). Two of the missionaries retired to Macao, three went to Champa, two hid themselves in the middle of Cochin-China, and the three others went to the southern edge of the kingdom in the province of Ranran, where they were badly treated by the natives. The Jesuits asked the Portuguese of Macao to send an embassy to the king to negotiate the return of the missionaries. The king agreed finally to permit the Jesuits to return, but only for the period during which the Portuguese vessels remained in port. With the consent of the old king, two or three remained in the country as exceptions to this rule. His son and heir had refused since coming to power to make any exceptions, and so the fathers came and left with the Portuguese merchants each year.[31] For example, around 1640 Alexandre de Rhodes and Father Bento de Matos (1600–*ca*. 1658) came from Macao in a Portuguese vessel. On arriving in Tourane, Matos went to the court and Rhodes toured the provinces of the south, being especially successful in Ranran where a hospital for the poor was built. And after about three months' stay they quietly returned to Macao.[32]

Borri's account of Cochin-China is a systematic survey based on personal experiences supplemented by the reports of others.[33] "Cochinchina" is the name given to this part of Annam by the Portuguese. It derives from the Japanese "Cochi," a word like "Annam" which means "west country." The Portuguese combined this word with China and applied it to this country "as if they called it Cochin of China, the better to distinguish it from Cochin the city in India."[34] Situated between Champa and the greater kingdom of Tongking, Cochin-China is a long, narrow strip of flat land between the mountains and the sea. The mountains are inhabited by the "Kemois"

[30] Based on Borri in Pinkerton, *op. cit.* (n. 12), IX, 798–820.
[31] Cardim, *op. cit.* (n. 13), pp. 96–98. Sãi Vương, or Chúa Sãi, died in 1635 and was succeeded by Chúa Thượng, or Nguyễn Phúc-Lân (r. 1635–48).
[32] *Ibid.*, pp. 105–13, includes Rhodes' letter of 1641 reporting on the state of Christianity in Cochin-China.
[33] After he left Cochin-China in 1622, he received letters from the Jesuits who stayed on there.
[34] Borri in Pinkerton, *op. cit.* (n. 12), IX, 773. For the various derivations of "Cochin" see *Asia*, I, 561n.; H. Yule and A. C. Burnell, *Hobson-Jobson* (rev. ed.; London, 1968), p. 226. In modern Japanese "cochi" or *cocchi* means "this side." For the derivation of "Cochin" from Malay *Kutchi* and Portuguese *Cauchi* see also A. Lamb (ed.), "British Missions to Cochin China, 1788–1822," *JRAS, Malaysian Branch,* Vol. XXXIV, Pt. 3 (1961), p. 1, n. 1.

(*mọi*) or "savage peoples" near the border with Laos, who in no way submit
to outside rule. Cochin-China itself is divided into five provinces: the royal
province of "Sinuva" (Thanh-Hóa) bordering on Tongking; "Cachiam"
(Chi-Chiam, or Quảng-Nam) governed by the king's son; "Quamguya"
(Quamghia, or Quảng-Nghiã); "Quignin" (Qui-Nhin, or Qui-Nhôn) called
"Pullucambi" by the Portuguese; and "Renran" (Ranran) bordering on
Champa.[35]

While much hotter than Europe in summer, Cochin-China enjoys four
distinct seasons and is much more temperate than India. Autumn brings the
rains, winter the cold northerly winds, and in spring "all things become
green and blossoming." The rains and floods of autumn are happily greeted
with celebrations and the joyful expression "daden lut, daden lut"[36] meaning "the inundation is come, it is here."[37] When the flood comes suddenly, it
often drowns domesticated animals. According to custom the carcasses belong to whoever recovers them. Rats flee to the trees to escape the flood and
little boys in their boats make a sport of shaking them off the branches to
drown in the water—a "pastime wonderfully beneficial to the country."
Floods are also advantageous in that the whole country becomes navigable
so people with their boats can more easily transport commodities from
place to place and even bring in wood from the mountains. It is during such
times that they hold their "greatest fairs and markets."[38]

The inundations leave the coastal plain so fertile that three crops of rice
may be harvested annually. Great quantities of fruit of several kinds are
available throughout the year. Oranges are bigger than those of Europe
with a skin so thin and tasty that it is eaten with the pulp and juice. Bananas
grow on trees with leaves which "are so long and wide that two of them
would cover a man from head to foot." The fruit called "can" (*mãng-cầu*,
custard apple, *Annona squamosa* L.) is unique to Cochin-China; its shape and
rind are like the pomegranate and its soft interior is taken out and eaten with
a spoon. Another called "gnoo" (*nhãn*, small litchi) grows like cherries but
tastes like raisins. Watermelons "are large and delicate" but the other melons
"are not so good as ours in Europe." Jackfruits are larger in Cochin-China
than those grown elsewhere in the East, one of them being as much as a man
can carry. Pineapples, also common in India and Brazil, grow on a stalk like
an artichoke. Pared with a knife and eaten raw, their taste is "sharp-sweet."
Areca nuts are never eaten by themselves but are cut into pieces for a betel
quid. In Cochin-China one person in each family, usually a woman, is
charged with preparing the quid for chewing. So much areca is used "that

[35] Later Jesuits mention six provinces. See Chappoulie, *op. cit.* (n. 5), I, 19, and below,
p. 1277.
[36] "*Lụt đã đen, lut đã đen*" probably makes more sense.
[37] Rainfall is more irregular and fluctuating in Vietnam than in other Southeast Asian territories. Rice farming is critically dependent on regular rain and sunshine. See E. H. G. Dobby,
Southeast Asia (9th rev. ed.; London, 1966), pp. 290–91.
[38] Borri in Pinkerton, *op. cit.* (n. 12), IX, 773–75.

the greatest revenues of that country comes from the fields of it." Tobacco is used "but not so much as betel." While the country produces sugarcane and all sorts of pumpkins and gourds, European fruits "are not yet come thither." European herbs, such as lettuce, go to leaf in Cochin-China and produce no seeds "so that they must still by supplied out of Europe." Meat is plentiful, and delicious fish abundant. Daily before sunrise, troops of people carry fish from the seaside fishing villages to the backlands and the mountains. From fish they make a sauce called "balachiam" (Malay, *bĕlachan*) which they always pour over their rice. They keep on hand vast stores of it in barrels and tubs. Peculiar to Cochin-China are the birds' (sea swallows') nests which the peasants gather from the high rocks beside the sea. After being softened in water, these gelatinous nests are used as a condiment in all sorts of dishes. The sale of these nests is a royal monopoly, the king's best customers being the Chinese who pay high prices for them. The Vietnamese eat no white meats or milk. It is considered sinful to take away milk which nature intended for the sustenance of the young.

"Cochinchina abounds in all other things necessary for the support of human life." Silk is so abundant and cheap that peasants and artisans generally dress in it. Mulberry trees are cultivated in vast fields to produce the leaves on which the silk worms feed. Local silk materials are "stronger and more substantial" than those of China but "not so fine and soft." Silk is exported to Japan and Laos "whence it afterwards spreads as far as Tibet." The wooden structures of Cochin-China are the equal of any, for they are built with the "best timber in the universe." While they have many varieties of wood, only two types are used for construction. One is black, the other red, and both are impervious to rot and so solid and heavy that they will not float. The mountains being full of these trees, every man is free to cut down as many as he pleases. The pillars, removable floors, and ornaments of their houses are made of wood from the trees called "tin" (*tin-bi*).[39] A wood called eagle or calambac is one of Cochin-China's prime exports. The mountains of the "Kemois" produce this tree, whose wood when cut young is called eagle and when old is known as calambac. Since eaglewood is abundant, everyone may cut as much as is needed. The calambac, an odoriferous wood, is found only at the tops of inaccessible mountains where the young trees escape destruction. This scarce aromatic wood is reserved as a royal export monopoly for sale to the Japanese who make fine wooden pillows from it and to the Indians for their funeral pyres.[40] Cochin-China is also rich in precious metals, especially gold.

Numerous beasts of all kinds roam the forests, especially elephants and

[39] Probably *Thunbergia grandiflora,* a common tree.
[40] According to modern botanists, *Aquilaria agallocha,* also known as aloewood, is native only to the countries around the Bay of Bengal and to Sumatra. But early botanists also associate it with Annam. See G. Watt, *A Dictionary of the Economic Products of India* (7 vols. in 10; Calcutta, 1885–96), I, 279–81.

"abadas" (rhinoceroses). Not knowing how to capture or train wild elephants, the Cochin-Chinese import tamed elephants from Cambodia. These elephants are twice as big as the Indian variety "usually exhibited in Europe." Trained elephants generally carry thirteen or fourteen persons on both land and water. On orders from its "nayre" (*nayar* or mahout) the elephant kneels and makes a ladder of its legs by which the passengers mount into the coach strapped to its back. In battles the roof is removed from the coach to make it into a tower for soldiers. Sometimes the mahout prods the elephant with a hook to demand its attention, but most instructions are given orally in any one of several languages. The only thing that disturbs this placid creature is getting a thorn stuck in the soft part of its foot. Elephants were formidable foes in war until the Portuguese learned how to use fireworks to scare and rout them. Trained elephants fight only against wild elephants and the rhinoceros. Elephants are used to hunt and kill the one-horned rhinoceros. The rhinoceros is roasted and eaten by the Cochin-Chinese. Its hoofs and horn are made into an antidote for poison.[41]

Because of their country's natural wealth, the Cochin-Chinese never go abroad to trade. They welcome foreign merchants who exchange silver for their products. Silver is traded as a commodity whose market price varies in terms of the local currency. Their money consists of rounds of brass with a hole in the middle, each stamped with the royal insignia. Every year a fair or market is held for about four months. To it the Chinese bring silver and the Japanese quantities of fine silks. The king and the country derive great profit from the trade, the customs, and the taxes. Since the Cochin-Chinese apply "themselves very little to arts," they willingly pay high prices and bid against one another for trinkets such as combs, needles, bracelets, and glass pendants. They also buy curiosities such as European garments. Coral is the imported product they value most highly. While they have more than sixty harbors and landing places along their coast, the most important port is that in the province of "Cacchian" (Quảng-Nam). Here there are two inlets from the sea on one of which is located Tourane and on the other "Pullu-chimpello."[42] At the place where these two inlets meet, the annual fair is held. Here the king assigned a plot of land to the resident Chinese and Japanese merchants. This city called Fai-fo (Hội-An) is really two cities in which the Chinese and Japanese live separately with their own governors and under their own laws. While the Portuguese and others are free to attend its fair, the Dutch, "as notorious pirates," are excluded. The Portuguese have been offered a site near Tourane on which to build a city of their own.[43]

The Cochin-Chinese resemble the Chinese in color, shape of face, flat nose, and small eyes. Not as tall as the Chinese or as short as the Japanese, they are stronger and more active than either. While braver than the Chi-

[41] Borri in Pinkerton, *op. cit.* (n. 12), IX, 775–84.
[42] On his map Rhodes shows an island called "Polociampeilo."
[43] Borri in Pinkerton, *op. cit.* (n. 12), IX, 795–97.

nese, they cannot match the Japanese in contempt for death. The Cochin-Chinese are the most courteous, affable, and hospitable of all Asian peoples. Of a loving disposition, they treat one another "as familiarly as if they were brothers or of the same family." They are charitable to the poor and never refuse to give alms. They are also prone to ask for anything they see that is new or curious to them. In breeding and civility they are like the Chinese in "always punctually observing all niceties." In every house they have three kinds of seats. Equals and family sit on a mat spread on the floor, persons of higher quality perch on a low stool covered with a finer mat, and high administrators and divines repose on a small couch. They are courteous to foreigners and respectful of alien customs, unlike the Chinese "who despise all but their own customs and doctrine."

Generally members of all classes wear silk garments. Women modestly cover their entire body and from the waist down wear five or six petticoats of various colors. Above the waist they don checkered bodices, over which they drape a thin and transparent veil. Their hair is worn loose and as long as it will grow. Over the head they wear a cap so broad that it covers the face; the caps of women of quality are "interwoven with silk and gold." In greeting another person, women lift up the brim of the hat to show the face.[44] Men wrap themselves with material over which they wear five or six colored silken gowns with wide sleeves. From the waist down, these gowns are slashed to reveal their various colors. Like the women, men wear their hair long and cover the head with the same sort of broad hat. They never cut their sparse beards, and men of substance let their fingernails grow long as a mark of distinction. Scholars and physicians cover their gowns with black damask, wear a stole about the neck, blue silk on the arms, and cover the head with a miter-like cap. Both sexes carry fans for ornament. For mourning they wear white. To uncover the head in public is deemed unmannerly. They wear neither shoes nor stockings but prefer leather sandals or bare feet. Before entering their houses they remove their sandals and wash their feet.

The basic, everyday food is boiled rice, with which they stuff themselves before tasting other dishes. They eat four times daily, sitting cross-legged on the ground before a small round table. Each person has his own table, as a rule. Since the food is cut into small pieces before being served, they have no need for knives or forks. They eat so neatly with two little sticks that they require no napkins. When entertaining guests, rice is not served, since "every man has enough of that at home." At feasts they serve each guest with at least one hundred dishes of all the varieties of food the country offers. When the masters have eaten their fill, their principal servants take their places. Since custom requires that all the dishes must be eaten, the lowliest servants finish off as much as they can and take home whatever re-

---

[44] This is a cone-shaped hat called *nón* that is unique to Vietnam, where it is worn by both sexes. See Whitfield, *op cit.* (n. 2), pp. 213–14.

mains. Instead of grape wine they drink a rice liquor which tastes like brandy. Between meals they drink "chia" (*chà,* tea), the root of an herb boiled in water, probably as medicine. The Chinese and Japanese boil the leaves of this same plant to make their own form of tea.

In Cochin-China there are many physicians, both Portuguese and native. From experience the local doctors are able to cure a number of diseases which the European physicians "know not how to treat." When first meeting a patient, the native physicians feel the pulse for a long while. Then they make a specific diagnosis or say frankly that the patient has an incurable ailment. If the disease is treatable, they indicate that they have an appropriate cure and will effect it within a specific period of time. Then a contract, either oral or written, is concluded, in which the amount of the physician's fee is agreed upon. The physician prepares his own medicines to keep secret his prescriptions. As a consequence there are no apothecaries in the country. If the patient is cured in the time agreed upon, "as generally happens," the patient pays the fee. If the cure fails, the physician receives nothing. Their medicines "do not alter the course of nature" but are palatable, nourishing, and assist nature "in its usual operations." Bleeding is used but not as often as in Europe. They open the vein with a saw-like tool fashioned from a goose quill by adding bits of fine porcelain to it. The wound made by this instrument is so slight as to be closed by the pressure of the physician's thumb.[45]

The governors of Cochin-China depend upon an amalgam of the learning esteemed by the Chinese and of the military prowess revered by the Japanese. They encourage learning and skill in war equally, sometimes giving precedence to one and sometimes to the other. As in China, they have several universities "in which there are professors, scholars, and degrees conferred by way of examination." They read the same books and authors, especially Confucius. Many years are spent studying language. But what they value most highly "is moral philosophy or ethics, economy and policy." When studying they read and repeat their lessons aloud. The spoken language is different from the written and "from what they read and teach in the schools." The Cochin-Chinese in general use only three thousand characters for letters, petitions, and memorials.[46] Books are printed in Chinese characters, for "printing was known" in China, and Cochin-China, long before it was in Europe.[47] Besides books of morals they have sacred books called "saye-kim" (?) to distinguish them from the secular works known as "saye-chin" (?). While the Cochin-Chinese language is monosyllabic and tonal like Chinese, its individual words include more vowels. Like

---

[45] Borri in Pinkerton, *op. cit.* (n. 12), IX, 784–90.

[46] This is *chữ nôm,* a written language devised by the Vietnamese. Its characters are generally simple ones chosen from the Chinese vocabulary. See E. J. Diguet, *Les Annamites: société, coutumes, religions* (Paris, 1906), pp. 50–51; and Whitfield, *op. cit.* (n. 2), p. 213. It is no longer in use.

[47] Xylographic printing was introduced from China in the fifteenth century. See Whitfield, *op. cit.* (n. 2), p. 235.

Chinese it does not conjugate verbs or decline nouns. Within six months it is possible to know enough of the spoken language to hear confessions, but four years are required to master it.

While the Cochin-Chinese reward the learned with "dignities, employments, and revenues," they also provide well for good soldiers. Instead of rewarding valor by benefices, the king assigns a certain number of persons to each commander. These vassals pay him all the taxes due the king and serve him with their weapons. As a consequence the commanders are known as the lords of a certain number of men. Civil government is conducted in a military manner by the viceroys and governors of the provinces. For four hours daily they hold court in their own palaces to hear complaints and hand down judgments. They question the litigants before an audience which applauds when agreeing with the plaintiff or defendant. The governor, taking notice of the public reactions, quickly pronounces his judgment and sees to the execution of the punishment, "every crime being punished as the law appoints." Most severe are the punishments meted out against "false witnesses, thieves, and adulterers." Those who give false testimony receive the punishment assigned to the crime for which they gave evidence. Major thefts are punished by beheading the offender. First offenders in minor thefts have a finger cut off; four-time repeaters are beheaded. Adulterers, both men and women, are killed by being thrown to the elephants. Every man may legally have but one wife, though the rich may have as many concubines as they can reasonably maintain; generally these are chosen by the wife. Divorce is legal, but only if reasons and proofs are provided by the plaintiff. Remarriage then may follow. Husbands provide the dowry and live in the house of the wife. She manages all household affairs and governs the family while he lives idly at home.

While Borri was in Cochin-China from 1617 to 1622, its king was constantly at war.[48] His ongoing rebellion against Tongking is encouraged and sustained by the many cannons he had salvaged from the wrecks of Portuguese and Dutch ships off his shores. About sixty of the largest of these cannons can be seen at the king's palace. The Cochin-Chinese are better and more skillful in gunnery than the Europeans. The king also has more than one hundred galleys to render him formidable at sea. And because of the constant trade with Japan, the Cochin-Chinese have acquired large numbers of excellent *katana* (scimitars) for war. Soldiers carry a light oval hollow shield that covers the entire body. The country itself abounds in small horses from the backs of which riders cast darts at the enemy. While the king can put eighty thousand men into the field, Tongking's available manpower is four times as great. The king of Cochin-China "for quietness sake" pays tribute to Tongking, particularly gold, silver, rice, and timber for galleys.

---

[48] This "king," Nguyễn Phúc-Nguyễn (r. 1613–35), was known to Europeans as "Sai Vuong." By 1599 the title "Vương" had become hereditary in the Nguyễn family. See Maybon, *op. cit.* (n. 20), p. 15, n. 1.

But he allies himself with the enemies of Tongking (the Mặc) who occupy its northernmost province on the China frontier. Due to the constant threat from Tongking, the king of Cochin-China maintains his headquarters in the province bordering on Tongking. Here he was also faced by an internal rebellion in these years, led by two of his brothers whom he defeated and now holds as prisoners. To the south and west he is almost constantly at war with Champa, a weak country held in check by the forces of the governor of Ranran. He has married his "bastard daughter" to the king of Cambodia and sends his galleys to support Cambodia in its wars against Siam. The royal galleys are rowed by men impressed into the king's service, who are well paid and whose families are provided for while the men are away from home. Because the cities of this kingdom are built of wood, their inhabitants when threatened by invasion burn their houses and flee into the mountains. This scorched-earth tactic leaves the enemy without food or fortifications. Once the disappointed invader retires, the city's inhabitants return and quickly rebuild their houses. Even a church can be built in a single day by having the pillars, beams, capitals, and planks pre-cut and put together by large troops of men under the direction of an architect.[49]

On the death of the friendly governor of Pulucambi, the Jesuits observed the rites and ceremonies followed in terminal illnesses and death. Armed men make thrusts and cuts in the air with their scimitars to frighten away the devils who might lodge themselves in the governor's soul as it leaves his body. After death the "omsaais" (hermit monks) convene to determine the cause of death. They unanimously decree that it was caused by a beam that fell in his new palace. Once this decision is made they burn down the entire palace. Necromancers then find someone bedeviled by an evil spirit—in this case, the governor's sister—to rave and rant while telling of the state and condition of the departed's soul. It is customary in the case of great men to canonize them and to give them eternal veneration by adding them to the number of the gods.[50] While preparing for the canonization they hold a wake for eight days. Then the body is carried in a silver coffin under a canopy to its place of birth accompanied by a multitude of rejoicers. On arrival at a plain near the city they set to work to build a palace more sumptuous than the one in which he died. To make a show of his wealth and strength they build galleys on wheels as well as wooden elephants and horses. In the middle of the new palace they erect a temple and an altar on which to place the coffin. Five or six hundred "omsaais" clad in white perform sacrifices and ceremonies for three days while public entertainments and feasts are put on "for above two thousand men of note." At the end of this three-day period they burn the new palace and temple. The coffin and the body are bur-

[49] Borri in Pinkerton, *op. cit.* (n. 12), IX, 793–95.
[50] A reference to the cult of the guardian spirit or Thành-Hoàng. Most villages had a patron saint sanctified by the emperor. In many places national heroes were also worshipped in the communal hall. See Whitfield, *op. cit.* (n. 2), pp. 275–76.

ied together in one of twelve graves so that the people will "always be in doubt where it had been left." This increases the honor of the new idol since they will adore it "in all those places where they thought the bones might be." These solemn ceremonies are repeated several times over the following three years, during which the governor's soul continues to administer the province aided by his son as deputy-governor in fact. Thus a new idol is made.[51]

Astrology, particularly the forecasting of eclipses, is highly regarded and occupies much time. It is taught in the universities, and special allowances and lands are assigned to the maintenance of astrologers. The king has his own astrologers, as has his son, who concentrate on the prediction of eclipses. When their predictions are exact, they are rewarded with a certain amount of land; when inexact the same amount of land is taken from them. The king is given the day and hour of an eclipse one month before it is to occur. He then sends out a notice for all to be in readiness for the celestial event. On the day of the eclipse, whether solar or lunar, the lords of every province foregather with the gentry, commanders, and governors. The greatest assembly is at the royal court where the king in mourning clothes leads the ceremony. They lift their eyes to the heavens and make obeisances and adorations while expressing sorrow for the pain endured by the planets on high when "the dragon swallows either the sun or moon." Starting at the king's palace and then throughout the city, they fire muskets, ring bells, and beat drums to frighten the dragon and make him vomit up what he has eaten.[52]

Temples and "omsaais" are everywhere, even in the smallest towns. Some among the priests resemble "abbots, bishops, and archbishops, and they use gilt staves not unlike our crosiers." Holy men wear special colored habits which indicate their various professions. Some live in communities, others survive on charity, and others tend the sick and do pious works. Some beg to raise money for public works such as bridges and temples. Others tend animals "without taking any reward, being satisfied with anything that is freely given them." The "omsaais" look after monasteries of women who "are all their wives." Still others teach the doctrines of their religion in public schools.

Some of these pagans believe in the soul's immortality, while others hold that "all ends when the body dies." All their sects derive from "Xaca" (Buddha), a metaphysician of Siam who was the equal of Aristotle in "the knowledge of natural things." After long reflection he wrote several books entitled *On Nothing,* in which he concluded that "moral as well as physical and natural things were nothing, came of nothing, and ended in nothing." Material substances, as well as humans, have no individuality but are com-

---

[51] Borri in Pinkerton, *op. cit.* (n. 12), IX, 806–9.
[52] *Ibid.,* pp. 815–17.

posites which change constantly.[53] The happiness of man resides not "in a positive concurrence of all that is good, but rather in being free from all that is evil" and from the suffering in this world. When these teachings were carried into China by his disciples, they were rejected. Disappointed in his followers, "Xaca" wrote several new books in which he taught of the "real origin of all things, a lord of heaven, hell, immortality, and transmigration of souls from one body to the other." This revised doctrine (Mahayana Buddhism) was taken up by the Chinese and Japanese. The Cochin-Chinese likewise rejected the doctrine of "nothing" and hold now to "the immortality of the soul" and eternal rewards for the just and punishments for the wicked. Their holy books, often used for astrology, claim that men have three souls and seven spirits while women have three souls and nine spirits.[54] They err by not distinguishing between the immortal soul and the demons, both of which they call "Maa" (*ma*), by believing that the better souls, even though common, may transmigrate into the body of the king, and by holding that the souls of the dead need corporeal sustenance. They also mistakenly adore and add to their idols the souls of men who were famous in this world. In their temples the sidewalls are replete with idols, arranged so that the least stand first, followed in order by those that are larger and more important. But with all this adoration of idols they reserve a special place for the invisible god, the creator of heaven and earth. Behind the altar a space is left dark and vacant as the proper place for an invisible creator who could not be represented by visible images. The idols are intercessors with the incomprehensible "that they may obtain favors and blessings of him."[55]

2

THE NGUYỄN AND THE CHRISTIANS

Six principal European works were published between 1650 and 1700 dealing with Cochin-China and Tongking. Alexandre de Rhodes, the Jesuit "Apostle of Vietnam," published at Rome in the Jubilee year of 1650 his retrospective *Relazione* of Tongking where he had evangelized from 1627 to 1630.[56] Three years later, as he worked to arouse French interest in Asian missions,[57] he published at Paris his *Divers voyages et missions,* a general sum-

[53]The Buddha preached first on the non-existence of beings. See Diguet, *op. cit.* (n. 46), p. 211.
[54]Cardim, *op. cit.* (n. 13), p. 102.
[55]Borri in Pinkerton, *op. cit.* (n. 12), IX, 820–23.
[56]Rhodes' *Relazione de' felici successi della santa fede predicata da' padri della Compagnia de Giesu nel regno di Tunchino* includes two books, the first on temporal conditions and the second on the mission to Tongking. Both are based on his own experiences and on what he learned from his cohorts after his personal expulsion in 1630.
[57]On his part in the founding of the Paris Society of Foreign Missions see above, pp. 229–31.

mary of his personal activities which center on his experiences from 1640 to
1645 in Cochin-China.[58] Another Jesuit publication, that of G. F. de Marini
(1608–82) appeared at Rome in 1663. In his *Delle missioni,* Marini concentrates on Tongking where he worked as a missionary for fourteen years before being recalled to Rome in 1661 to report on conditions in the Japan
Province.[59] At Rome in 1677 there appeared the *Relatione* of the missions
sponsored and undertaken by the vicars apostolic in Siam, Cochin-China,
Cambodia, and Tongking between 1667 and 1670. Much of the general
background in this book derives from the works of Rhodes and the remainder details the activities of individual missionaries.[60] In his *Voyages and
Descriptions* (1699) Dampier recounts his experiences and observations of
1688 in Tongking. Finally there is the summary account of the persecution
of the Jesuits in Cochin-China by Manoel Ferreira (1631–99), a Portuguese
priest based in Macao who had been superior in Tongking during 1674–75.
His *Noticias summarias das perseguições da missam de Cochinchina* (Lisbon, 1700)
is the last of his several reports on Jesuit activities in Tongking and Cochin-
China. Ferreira was also the compiler of an unpublished Portuguese-
Annamese dictionary.[61]

A book of dubious merit as a genuine source needs to be mentioned since
it circulated so widely in Europe during the last generation of the century.
In 1676 there appeared at Paris *Les six voyages* of Jean Baptiste Tavernier, the
French jewel merchant who was so well informed on Mughul India.[62] He
followed this popular record of his travels by publishing three years later a
diverse collection of materials on the East not included in *Les six voyages.*
Book IV of this melange purports to be a "new and singular relation" of
Tongking based on his brother Daniel's memoirs and maps and on interviews he himself had in Batavia and Bantam with Tonkinese merchants
doing business in those insular ports and with members of their families and
staffs.[63] Daniel had made eleven or twelve voyages during the 1640's to
Tongking from outposts in Indonesia, during which he purportedly collected pertinent materials and prepared the map published along with Jean

[58] Translated into English in Hertz (trans.), *op. cit.* (n. 27).
[59] Marini was expelled from Tongking in 1658 shortly after the accession of Trịnh Tạc
(r. 1657–82). While in Macao as provincial of the Japan Province, Marini reentered Tongking
in 1673 and was promptly forced to leave again as a *persona non grata.* See J. Dehergne, S.J.,
Répertoire des Jésuites de Chine de 1552 à 1800 (Rome and Paris, 1973), pp. 72–73. On pp. 1–2 of
Marini's *Delle missioni de' padri della Compagnia di Giesu nella provincia del Giappone, e particolar-
mente di quella di Tumkinó, libri cinque,* he lists the names of the Jesuits who worked in Tongking
from 1626 to 1660.
[60] This anonymous *Relatione delle missioni de' vescovi vicarii apostolici mandata dalla S. Sede
Apostolica alli regni de Siam, Cocinchina, Camboia, e Tunkino* was published by the Propaganda
Fide.
[61] See Streit, V, 632.
[62] See above, pp. 416–18, for bibliographical details.
[63] *Relation nouvelle et singuliere du royaume de Tunkin avec plusieurs figures et la carte du pay,* Book
IV of Tavernier's *Recueil de plusieurs relations et traitez . . . qui n'ont point esté mise dans ses six
premiers voyages* (Paris, 1679).

Baptiste's *Relation* (see pl. 240). In 1680 Tavernier's collection was issued in an English translation at a time when the East India Company was developing a great interest in trading at Tongking. On the request of the Company, Samuel Baron (b. *ca*. 1650), a native of Hanoi and an employee of the Company, prepared a critique at Madras in 1685–86 of Tavernier's *Relation*. While Tavernier claims that his is the first comprehensive and accurate description of Tongking, Baron at the beginning of his essay asserts that the accounts of Rhodes and Marini, "both Jesuits," are superior. He labels Tavernier's compilation "fabulous and full of gross absurdities."[64] A close examination of Tavernier's description also reveals that he probably obtained some of his less fantastic materials from the writings of the Jesuits, especially Father Joseph Tissanier (1634–88). Despite its obvious inaccuracies, Tavernier's account was probably widely read, and believed, because of the author's renown and popularity among some of his contemporaries. It will, however, not be included here as a source of the European image of Tongking, since many contemporaries besides Baron suspected Tavernier's veracity and had no hesitation in saying so.[65] It is also omitted because it adds no new dimensions of significance.

Alexandre de Rhodes, during the seven years (1627–30, 1640–45) that he worked in Cochin-China and Tongking, learned the language and obtained a deep understanding of the customs and character of the Annamese. On his return to Europe he published his history of Tongking (1650) and the general account (1653) of his experiences in Vietnam to arouse zeal for the mission. Independently of these works he had published at Rome a catechism in Latin and Annamese that is still currently in use by Christian Vietnamese.[66] And he also had published an Annamite-Portuguese-Latin dictionary which had gradually been assembled by Rhodes and his Jesuit predecessors in Vietnam.[67] These works, when combined with the report (1663) of Marini, encapsulated for Europe what the Jesuits had learned about Vietnam between 1627 and 1658, the date of Marini's expulsion from Tongking. Like many Jesuit works, these reports are collaborative in the sense that their authors incorporated materials forwarded to them in letters by their colleagues in the mission field.

[64] Baron's own description of the "Kingdom of Tonquun" was first published in Volume VI of *CV*. It was reprinted in Pinkerton, *op. cit.* (n. 12), IX, 656–707. Baron was one of the first to point out the importance of the Red River valley as a commercial route. See G. Taboulet, *La geste française en Indochine. Histoire par les textes de la France en Indochine des origines à 1914* (2 vols.; Paris, 1955–56), I, 88.

[65] *Cf.* above, pp. 416–18.

[66] The *Catechismus . . . in octo dies divisus . . .* was first published by the Propaganda press in 1651. See also Hertz (trans), *op. cit.* (n. 27), pp. xiii–iv.

[67] Published by the polyglot press of the Propaganda in 1651, its final thirty-one pages are devoted to a discussion of the Annamese language. These same missionaries, especially Rhodes, invented *quốc-ngữ*, or the "national script," the romanization of the Annamese language which is universally used today. For a discussion of the complex history of the invention of *quốc-ngữ* see Maybon, *op. cit.* (n. 20), pp. 36–37, n. 4. For a reproduction of the dictionary's title page see Taboulet, *op. cit.* (n. 64), I, facing p. 16.

In the latter half of the century the European sources are much fuller on Tongking than on Cochin-China. As a separate kingdom, Cochin-China is seen to be a smaller state with but a brief history of independence. Its name, a constant source of confusion to the Europeans, is indifferently applied either to the whole peninsula from China to Champa or to the territories controlled by the Nguyễn. The distinction between Tongking and Cochin-China is primarily political, since both states are Chinese in background and identical in religion, language, and customs.[68] The grandfather of the present king of Cochin-China was sent out as governor from Tongking. He revolted against his master and maintained his independence and control by superiority of arms.[69] Successful in resisting Tongking's attacks, the Nguyễn made "Kehue" (Hue) their royal capital.[70] The court is very grand and staffed with gorgeously dressed nobles. Its buildings of wood are comfortable and rather beautiful because of "the well-wrought columns that support them." The holdings of the Nguyễn are divided into six provinces, each with its own governor and legal system.[71] At all times the king maintains one hundred fifty galleys which are kept in three different harbors.

The Nguyễn lands are heavily populated by gentlefolk, who nonetheless make good soldiers. While their religion, laws, and customs derive from China, they are more modest, more tractable, and much better as soldiers than the Chinese. Because the soil is very fertile, they live well. The country is watered by twenty-four beautiful rivers which greatly facilitate both transport and trade. They flood annually in November and December. Cochin-China has gold mines and produces for export great quantities of pepper, silk, and sugar. Silk is so abundant that it is ordinarily used to make fish nets and the rigging for ships. It is only here that the famous tree grows which produces three kinds of calambac.[72] It is only here that little birds' nests are found which are used as garnishes in soups and in meat dishes.[73]

Great fruit is quickly gathered in preaching the gospel in this rich and fertile kingdom. The governor of "Quinhin" (Qui-Nhòn), a favorite of the

---

[68] Rhodes, *op. cit.* (n. 56), pp. 1–3.

[69] The grandfather was Nguyễn Phúc-Nguyễn (Sai Vương). The grandson was Nguyễn Phúc-Tần (r. 1648–87).

[70] Phú-xuan or Hue officially became the Nguyễn capital only in 1687. See Lê, *op. cit.* (n. 2), p. 262.

[71] The northern provinces were Quambin (Quảng-Bình) and Thanh-Hóa, and the central province was Cham or Ciam (Quảng or Quảng-Nam). The three southern provinces were Quamghia (Quảng-Ninh), Qui-Nhin (Qui-Nhòn), and Ranran (modern Phu-Yen). The royal city of "Kehue" (Hue or Sinoa, the Portuguese word) is in the province of Thanh-Hóa. Cham is the province best known to the Europeans for it included the trading cities of Kủa-Hản (Tourane) and Fai-fo (Han-San in Cochin-Chinese). Rhodes and others often mention "Katscham" as the capital of Cham province. This is probably the same city which is later called Quảng-Nam-Định, or the "main city" of Quảng-Nam province. See G. M. Pachtler, *Das Christenthum in Tonkin und Cochinchina* (Paderborn, 1861), pp. 8–9.

[72] *Cf.* above, pp. 1205, 1259.

[73] Rhodes in Hertz (trans.), *op. cit.* (n. 27), pp. 43–46. The edible nests of sea swallows (*yến-sào*) are also used as medicine.

Nguyễn, supported the first Jesuit missionaries and helped them to establish their initial firm foothold in his capital.[74] In 1624, the Jesuit Visitor to Cochin-China and five other priests, including Rhodes, were sent to the aid of the overworked pioneers. Rhodes, impressed by the language ability of Father Francisco de Peria, began to take daily lessons in Annamese. One of his teachers was a little boy who taught him the correct pronunciation and tones.

Within six months he was able to preach in the local language. By 1625 ten religious had preached in all the kingdom's major centers. At Hue they converted a court lady who was a close relative of the king. She built a chapel in her palace, took the Christian name of Mary Magdalen, and became a mainstay of the mission.[75] With success came new problems, particularly from the king. Angered by the failure of the Portuguese ships to appear in 1625, the king began to impose restrictions on the missionaries and their neophytes. After eighteen months in Cochin-China, Rhodes was ordered by his superiors in 1626 to leave for Macao and to go to the mission in Tongking.[76]

After serving in Tongking (1627–30), Macao, and Kwangtung (1630–40), Rhodes was sent to Cochin-China for the second time early in 1640. He went back alone to replace the deceased Buzomi (d. 1639), to win back the king who had expelled the Jesuits in 1639, and to minister to the twelve thousand neophytes. At first he discreetly stayed under cover in the Japanese quarter of Fai-fo. With the help of the Japanese governor, rich presents, and the intercession of Mary Magdalen, it came about that the king (Nguyễn Phúc-Lân) received him in audience and treated him civilly. Then Rhodes returned to Fai-fo and went back into hiding while the Portuguese ships prepared to leave. When Governor "Onghebo" (Ông Nghê Bộ) of Cham province realized that the Jesuit had not left with the Portuguese ships, he ordered Rhodes and his companion to depart immediately and by any means whatsoever. With the help of young Annamese Christians, they made the trip to Macao safely in a very small boat in September, 1640. By the following Christmas Eve he was back in Tourane to celebrate with the Christians who hurried there on hearing of his arrival. Alarmed by the renewed activity of the Christians, "Onghebo" plundered their homes and churches and seized their images and their persons. Rhodes secretly left Tourane early in 1641 for a leisurely tour of the towns and principal villages of Cham province to visit their Christians. Then he and his companion Father Bento de Matos parted company. Matos worked in the northern provinces and Rhodes spent the next six months in the three southern provinces, escorted by a local Christian. Aside from reporting that he has been hearing

---

[74] Modern Bình-Định province, the capital of which is Qui-Nhởn.
[75] "Madam Marie" is the matriarch of the South Vietnamese church. She was the Princess Minh-Đức, concubine in his old age to the founder of the Nguyễn dynasty. See Hertz, *op. cit.* (n. 27), p. 52n.
[76] *Ibid.*, pp. 46–55.

confessions and performing baptisms and exorcisms, Rhodes notes that many galleys are kept in the ports of Ranran "to prevent inroads from Champa." The Christian wife of its governor has founded a hospital for incurable Christians, especially lepers. Rhodes' activities were abruptly halted by an order from the king to leave his country with the next Portuguese ships.[77]

In July, 1641, Rhodes left on a vessel headed for the Philippines, islands which he sees as being "neither beautiful nor very fertile." After five weeks on Luzon, he left for Macao. At the end of January, 1642, he returned to Cochin-China with gifts for "Onghebo" and the king, in hopes of winning their favor. This stratagem worked, for the governor left him in peace for two years, and the king kept him at court while the Portuguese merchants carried on their trade. The king was particularly pleased to receive "some new clocks marked with Chinese characters," and to learn "certain mathematical secrets" from the Jesuit. Dismissed from court in time to return with the Portuguese, Rhodes instead went to Tourane to lay plans for a tour of the entire kingdom. Not daring to show himself in public, Rhodes traveled at night and was often carried in a hammock of the kind used to transport the sick and the dead. He first toured the south to visit and minister to its fervent Christians. As the only priest in the kingdom he was joined in the south by ten young men, "all from different provinces," who aided him in preaching the faith. God "reserved the glory of being martyrs" to three of these: Andrew, Ignatius, and Vincent.[78] Ignatius, a former magistrate, was a "man of high learning, because he knew Chinese letters perfectly." For two years this troop traveled far and wide, ministering to the faithful and making converts. Before leaving again in September, 1643, Rhodes bound his ten catechists by a solemn oath to serve the church, never to marry, and to obey the Fathers of the Society. Then the troop was divided into two squads; one to work in the north and the other in the south, under the general direction of Ignatius as their superior.[79]

The catechists acquitted themselves too well as preachers and missionaries, and so alarmed the pagans. A new governor of Ranran, hostile to the Christians, ordered that the catechists should be hunted down and punished. In the north the catechists were equally successful in making converts and in stimulating persecution. After five months in Macao, Rhodes returned early in 1644 and was met at Tourane by the ten catechists. They then accompanied the Jesuit on his trip to the court to offer new gifts to the king and to pay their respects. The king had by this time become suspicious that his aunt, Mary Magdalen, was conspiring with the Christians to have the succession fall to her descendants rather than to his own. Rhodes added to

---

[77] Rhodes in Hertz (trans.), *op. cit.* (n. 27), pp. 77–94.
[78] See below, pp. 1273–74.
[79] Rhodes in Hertz (trans.), *op. cit.* (n. 27), pp. 95–107.

the king's fears by using her palace in Hue as a base from which to make converts in the royal palace. From here he went to Quảng-Bình, the northernmost province bordering on Tongking, "where a strong wall separates the two kingdoms."[80] The king's suspicions were further aroused when a delegation of ten Tongking Christians came to see Rhodes and to request that he cross over the wall to visit them. Although he refused their invitation, he was bold enough to send Ignatius in his place. On his return to Hue Rhodes enlisted the services of several magistrates who were influential at the court "to speak seriously to the king about the Christian religion." In their presence, he and Ignatius debated with the Buddhist priests to the outrage of some of them. Despite the machinations of Rhodes' enemies, the king now seemed more favorably disposed towards the Christians. While reaping the benefits of the king's kindly feelings, Rhodes again stirred up trouble by trying to convert important military leaders. He tried to convince them to ignore "any of those profane ceremonies that pagans foolishly think are necessary for succeeding" at battle.[81]

Sickened by a violent fever in June, 1644, Rhodes had firsthand experience with Vietnamese physicians and medicine. Although their physicians are not trained in medical schools, "they are not inferior to our doctors and in some things they even surpass them." It is a family science taught by father to son from private books "containing the secrets of the art." When doctors call on a patient, they first take the pulse and spend time contemplating it. They feel it with three fingers and read it very well. For them the pulse is divided into three parts corresponding to the head, stomach, and belly (see pls. 356, 357). By taking the pulse the physician is supposed to identify the ailing part of the body and to describe for the patient the symptoms he has suffered. Should the doctor be wrong in his description, he is at once dismissed; if correct, "he is to be trusted." Physicians are always accompanied on their visits by a valet who carries a bag filled with the simples used in the preparation of medicines. Whatever they prescribe they make for the patient themselves or instruct him in how to do it. Their medicines are inexpensive and "never hard to take like ours." Intermittent fevers are cured by medication without all the purging, enemas, and bloodletting prescribed in Europe. Cupping glasses are frequently applied, even on the street. When the doctor is retained by the patient, a fee is agreed to, which is paid only after the patient is cured. Once cured of his own fever, Rhodes tried to cure the physician's soul by instructing him in Christianity. When the physician learned that he would be required not to worship graven images and to keep no altar dedicated to one, he lost interest in becoming a Christian. This Christian requirement ran directly counter to the tradition of his profession

---

[80] Actually two walls were built oblique to the coast. The more important one, built in 1631, ran from the mountains to the delta of the Nhụt Lệ River. See Maybon, *op. cit.* (n. 20), p. 18.

[81] Rhodes in Hertz (trans.), *op. cit.* (n. 27), pp. 107–25.

to keep in the household an altar dedicated to an ancient and revered doctor "who had first taught medicine." Should he destroy or remove this altar he would lose his credibility as a physician and might even be punished for his irreverence.[82]

One of the greatest triumphs of the new church was the martyrdom of the catechist Andrew in July, 1644. "Onghebo," acting on the orders of the queen, the sworn foe of the Christians and particularly of Ignatius, began at this time a systematic persecution.[83] His soldiers pillaged and burned the houses and churches of the Christians. They imprisoned the nineteen-year-old Andrew and indicted him for being a Christian, a preacher, and a disobedient subject of his ruler. He and a companion were put on trial by the governor, and Andrew was condemned to death without a hearing. On the next day he was led out of the city with a heavy cangue around his neck to the spot of execution. Kneeling on the ground he was encircled by soldiers. From behind, he was pierced by a lance and then his head was cut off by a scimitar. Rhodes and the native Christians carried off the corpse and sent it off to Macao as a holy relic. Rhodes kept the head for himself and took it back to Rome as a testimony to the "glory of this faithful friend of God."[84]

The martyr's companion, an older man and a magistrate also called Andrew, was not executed, because of his age and family responsibilities. Always staunch in the faith, he became a leader of the Christian resistance and a proud wearer of the cangue known to the faithful as the "cross of Cochinchina." After the martyrdom, Rhodes was again given express orders to leave with the Portuguese ships. Not wishing to desert the faithful, he again went underground as "Onghebo" stepped up his search for Christian images and other symbols of the faith. The rich and powerful among the Christians protected the others and paid their fines. Prisoners were taken and publicly beaten by the authorities as an example to the recalcitrant and unbending Christians. To escape the governor's fury, Ignatius went to the northern and Rhodes to the southern provinces in September, 1644. In Qui-Nhơn province the Jesuit hid out in the boats and houses of friends both in the town and in places "where many Christians worked making salt." He spent Christmas with Ignatius and the faithful in the towns around the salt-beds. Taking advantage of the distraction of the Christmas celebration, the authorities captured both Ignatius and Rhodes and charged them with propagating Christianity contrary to the interdiction of the king. Eventually

---

[82] *Ibid.*, pp. 125–28. The altar was to Tuê-Tĩnh, a mandarin of the tenth century and the patron saint of Thuốc Nam (southern Vietnamese medicine).

[83] The queen was Tông-thị-Toại, a lady maintained by Nguyễn Phúc-Tần as his wife. This union was illegal since she had formerly belonged to his brother. See *ibid.*, pp. 121–22.

[84] Andrew's head is today in the Jesuit Curia in Rome. His body was burned along with those of other martyrs when the church in Macao was accidentally destroyed by fire. See *ibid.*, p. 132n. As part of his propaganda effort, Rhodes published a martyrology called *Relatione della morte di Andrea catechista che primo de christiani nel regno di Cocincina . . .* (Rome, 1652), for the edification and inspiration of the faithful in Europe. A second edition was published at Paris in 1653.

they were both released and allowed to preach until the beginning of Lent, 1645, when Ignatius and two others were taken off to prison. Like other prisoners they wore the cangue and left their prison by day to go to the town square to "beg for a living." Once this new persecution began, four Christian ladies were fastened by a rope to a very heavy, thick bar, a punishment regularly meted out to the worst female criminals. They were also subjected to torture by being exposed to the sun at high noon.

Still at large and with the king's permission to travel freely, Rhodes left Qui-Nhòn province on February 15, 1645, under pressure from its governor. He went by sea to Fai-fo where two vessels had just arrived from Macao. In a nearby harbor a Spanish ship was anchored which had two Franciscans aboard on their way from Macao to Manila. Four Spanish nuns of the Order of St. Clare had also arrived on the Spanish vessel. The advent of the nuns stimulated local curiosity, especially at the court, about the restricted and pious life led by these religious women. They were summoned to court, entertained at a lavish reception, and asked to unveil themselves. They refused utterly to uncover their shaved heads, and permitted only the queen to see their faces. The general curiosity with respect to the nuns had the effect of checking temporarily the persecution of the Christians. Games, mock combats, and tournaments were put on in honor of the Spaniards over the ten days of their visit to Hue.[85] After the Spanish departed, Rhodes and his nine catechists were taken into custody and imprisoned. Rhodes was shortly condemned to death by decapitation. After intercession by an important pagan magistrate, the king commuted the death sentence to one of exile "as soon as possible." Rhodes was escorted by soldiers from the prison at Hue to another at Fai-fo where he was kept until he was put aboard a Portuguese vessel on July 3, 1645.[86]

Rhodes was succeeded in Cochin-China by Metello Saccano and Carlo della Rocca, who won over the king by gifts of exquisite pearls. On Nguyễn Phúc-Lan's death in 1648 he was succeeded by Nguyễn Phúc-Tần, who was known to the Europeans as "Hien Vuong" (r. 1648–87). An ambitious ruler, the new king extended his frontier southward at the expense of Champa and Cambodia and northward into the two southern provinces of Tongking. In principle, Christianity continued to be interdicted, but enforcement remained inconstant and unpredictable. The Jesuits remained at Fai-fo and ordinarily went out at nights for secret meetings that the catechists had arranged with the Christians. When preparing for or actually waging war

---

[85] As Rhodes suggests, the king was probably aware of the hostility between the Portuguese and Spanish which was then at a high point in the Far East. He probably hoped to obtain arms from Manila as well as Macao.

[86] Rhodes in Hertz (trans.), *op. cit.* (n. 27), pp. 128–78. After his departure the nine catechists were decapitated on July 26, 1645. While in Macao from July 23 to December 20, 1645, Rhodes instructed Fathers Metello Saccano (1612–62) and Carlo della Rocca in the Annamese language (*ibid.,* p. 185). Rhodes left Macao accompanied by a Chinese Christian called Tcheng Wei-Su Ma-no, whom he had himself baptized. See Dehergne, *op. cit.* (n. 59), p. 216.

against the north, the king would conciliate the Portuguese and relax his persecution of the Christians. Failure of the Portuguese to send annual shipments of arms usually resulted in increased pressure on the Jesuits and the Christians. Calm and relative peace prevailed from 1659 to 1661 until Hiền-Vồng suffered a severe defeat in the north. It was at this time of renewed persecution in Cochin-China that the French bishops arrived at Siam in hopes of extending their activities into Vietnam.[87]

In Europe, news of the French reconnaissance of Cochin-China between 1664 and 1671 was relayed to the public in the *Relatione* of 1677.[88] Louis Chevreuil, the French priest who was later stationed in Cambodia,[89] was sent to Fai-fo in 1664 as vicar-general representing Bishop Lambert de La Motte.[90] The French, despite the hardships experienced by the Jesuits of Macao, seemed to believe that the populace of Cochin-China would quickly submit to Christianity were it not for the stubborn opposition of the king. They were also informed by a French priest (presumably a Jesuit) that efforts should be made to convert the "Moi-Ro" (*moi rộ*, or savages), a black hill people with no organized religion, who were almost all under the control of Cochin-China. Chevreuil was accompanied by a Japanese interpreter who could speak Annamese and act as intermediary with the Japanese Christians of Fai-fo. Chevreuil quickly left Fai-fo to visit the Jesuits at Hue and Tourane, to show them his letters-patent as vicar-general, and to ask their submission to his authority. The Jesuits, while recognizing Chevreuil's position, refused to write a formal submission without the approval of their superiors in Macao. And thus began the jurisdictional struggle between the French clergy and the Jesuits of the *padroado* that would finally have to be settled in Rome.[91]

Persecution of the Christians became increasingly more intense in 1664–65. The three Macao Jesuits were expelled in February, 1665, and one month later Chevreuil was forced to depart. After a short respite in Ayut'ia, Chevreuil returned in August to Cochin-China accompanied by Antoine Hainques. They carried letters from Lambert de La Motte empowering them to rule the mission in his name. Arrived at Phan-ri in Champa, Chevreuil fell ill, and Hainques, dressed as a Japanese, went alone across the border into Cochin-China, where he took refuge with the Christians of Ranran province. After traveling four months in the interior, Hainques arrived at Fai-fo in the spring of 1666 to find two Jesuits already there. When they left shortly thereafter on a Portuguese ship, Hainques was the only missionary in Cochin-China over the next two years. The Jesuits made visits to their converts in Tongking and proclaimed that they owed no obedience

---

[87] Based on Chappoulie, *op. cit.* (n. 5), I, 164–75.

[88] *Op. cit.* (n. 60), pp. 51–92.

[89] See above, pp. 383, 1155–56.

[90] On his role in the Paris project see above, pp. 239–46. Chevreuil was probably chosen because he was not as anti-Jesuit as the others.

[91] See above, pp. 239–69.

to the French pro-vicar. In the spring of 1669 Hainques was joined by Pierre Brindeau, a French priest who was earlier arrested by the Portuguese and taken before the Inquisition of Goa. By 1670 the French estimated that there were thirty-four hundred Christians in Cochin-China. In an epidemic of late 1670 and early 1671 Hainques and Brindeau both died. The Christian converts then determined to send a delegation to Siam in May, 1671, to request replacements. Shortly thereafter Lambert de La Motte himself went to Cochin-China in the company of Guillaume Mahot and Benigne Vachet.[92]

In 1688 William Dampier's ships skirted the coast of Cochin-China from Pulau Condore (Côn Sôn) northward to Pulau Canton (Cù-Lão-Rẽ) and other offshore islands. Fishermen from southern Cochin-China frequent these islands, where they capture porpoises and turtles, from which they make oil. The uninhabited islands of "Champello de la Mar" (?) face the mouth of a large and navigable river on whose banks stand "Quinam" (Qui-Nhòn) the capital of Cochin-China. Among English seamen the rulers of Cochin-China have an evil reputation for mercilessly enslaving shipwrecked persons. The Cochin-Chinese wish to engage in trade and have a small commerce with China in pepper, rare woods, and betel. While they appear to have no fleet of their own for international commerce, they use small open boats for fishing and for carrying pitch and tar from Pulau Condore to the mainland.[93]

3

TONGKING UNDER THE TRỊNH

The two best Jesuit accounts of Tongking are the *Relazione* (1650) of Rhodes and the *Delle missioni* (1663) of Marini. While the Frenchman was there for three years and two months (1627–30), the Italian remained there for fourteen years before being expelled in 1658. Both were well acquainted with China and consequently highly sensitive to the historical relationships between the Chinese and the Annamese. They suggest that much of the confusion about the names of the Annamese states arises from their complicated past. The Chinese claim in their histories that their control over Annam extends back to 441 B.C. Over this long historical span the Chinese histories refer to these southern provinces by a variety of names.[94] The rise of these

---

[92] On Lambert de La Motte in his vicariate of Cochin-China see Chappoulie, *op. cit.* (n. 5), Vol. I, chap. xxii. The story of the French missionaries in the East from 1672 to 1677 is told in two works each entitled *Relation des missions* . . . published at Paris in 1680.

[93] Dampier in J. Masefield (ed.), *Dampier's Voyages* (2 vols.; London, 1906), I, 561–63.

[94] For a catalog of the Chinese names for Vietnam see G. Devéria (ed. and trans.), *Histoire des relations de la Chine avec l'Annam-Vietnam du XVIᵉ au XIXᵉ siècle; d'après des documents chinois traduits pour la première fois* (Paris, 1880), pp. 1–2, n. 2.

states as independent entities has produced new Annamese names not recognized by the Chinese, such as "Day Viet" *(Dại Việt,* or Greater Viet).[95] The Ming government refuses to recognize the independence of these states and will not accord them the status of vassals because that implies a diminution in China's traditional sovereignty. The Europeans, who know little about this history or about these official relations, adopt names for these states learned from Chinese, Japanese, and native informants which they in turn corrupt and apply indifferently to various parts. European cosmographers ignorantly give the name "Cochinchina" to the whole of the peninsula.[96]

For eight hundred years Annam was an integral part of China, a not unsubstantial province among that gigantic country's seventeen.[97] Independent Tongking is divided into six provinces, the most frequently named being "Guiaom" (Nghệ-An) and "Thign Hoa" (Thanh-Hóa) to the south of the capital. The other four surround "Ke Ci" (Tongking city or Hanoi) and are referred to as "Ke-Bak" (north province), "Ke-Nam" (south province), "Ke-Dom" (east province), and "Ke-Tay" (west province).[98] These provinces include 8,600 towns and an infinite number of villages called *thôn* *(thuyen).*[99] In fact, the whole country seems to be one immense city. Behind the coastal lowlands live the mountain savages called "Rumoi" who are black in color and speak a different language.[100]

The king administers justice with the aid of a supreme council composed of a great number of learned magistrates. The council acts as court of last resort for civil and criminal cases and as tribunal of final appeal from decisions handed down by the provincial governors and magistrates. The governor in each province is empowered to administer justice and may even pronounce the death penalty if speed is required and the province is at a long distance from the capital. But generally all death sentences are reviewed by the supreme council. Death sentences are given for murder, theft, and adultery. Day-to-day administration of justice is in the hands of two chief bu-

---

[95] Lý Thần-Tông (1054–72) gave this name to the Annamese country over which he ruled. See G. Coedès, *The Making of South East Asia* (Berkeley, 1967), p. 84. During the Lê dynasty (1428–1788) it became the name for the whole of Vietnam.

[96] Marini, *op. cit.* (n. 59), pp. 18–22. This Jesuit observer apparently learned about the content of the Chinese histories from António de Gouvea (1592–1677), a Portuguese Jesuit and a student of Chinese history. Gouvea was in China from 1636 to his death in Foochow. See Dehergne, *op. cit.* (n. 59), pp. 115–16.

[97] It was not until the first century A.D. that Chinese governors began to come into the Red River delta, or just about eight hundred years before Đihn Bộ-Lĩnh established the first native dynasty in A.D. 968. See Coedès, *op. cit.* (n. 95), pp. 43, 81.

[98] Marini, *op. cit.* (n. 59), p. 23. Other European contemporaries, including Rhodes, count seven provinces, for they identify "Ke Ci" as the capital province, and others include Bô-chinh, the southernmost province. Bô-chinh was the great bone of contention between Cochin-China and Tongking.

[99] In modern Vietnamese *thôn* means countryside or hamlet.

[100] Marini, *op. cit.* (n. 59), pp. 32–34; Rhodes, *op. cit.* (n. 56), p. 5, calls these hill people "Remoé."

reaus, the "Van" (*văn*) and the "Vû" (*võ*).[101] The "Van" is made up of learned doctors who interpret the law and who are always dressed in long black robes and bonnets. To the "Vû" belong titled persons chosen from the military nobility who pronounce judgments in certain cases and who never are without their arms. To this second group belong the provincial governors, who are princes of the blood, lords, or the principal military leaders of the kingdom. To each governor is assigned an assessor learned in the law who advises him on the judgments he renders.

Two tribunals function in the principal city of each province. The higher of these two courts, called "Gna-to" (?), takes the more important cases; the lower court, named "Gna-hien" (?), has jurisdiction in the lesser cases. Both exercise jurisdiction throughout the province and are staffed by learned men. In addition, there are three subordinate courts, the lowest of which is held in each town. A town court is composed of the noblest and oldest citizens, who hear the civil suits brought by their fellow townsmen. Decisions of a citizen's court may be appealed to the next higher one, called "Gna-huyên," which holds jurisdiction over the ten or twelve towns of a district or a "Huyen" (*huyên*).[102] Each district has a special governor named the "Cai-huyen" (*cai-huyên*) who judges appeals lodged with him. Further appeals may be carried to the tribunal of the "Cai Phu" (*cai-phù*) and from it to the two provincial courts already mentioned. Because of their vast extent, the provinces are divided for judicial purposes into "Phu" (*phù*), each of which is administered by a lord or captain comparable in rank to a French count or marquis.[103] Each "Phu" is again divided into "Huyen" which are administered by an official comparable in rank to a French baron. Finally, each "Huyen" is composed of a certain number of towns that they call "Xa" (*xã*), and each town has a governor comparable to a lord of the manor. These comparisons are admittedly misleading, because no offices or ranks are hereditary, and ordinarily even the governors of the provinces hold office for three years only. In the provinces there are no public prisons. Criminals are detained in the judge's house where they are sometimes subjected to torture. All prisoners are shackled and forced to wear the cangue. In the capital the prisons are subterranean cells without air vents or windows; no visitors are permitted as a rule. The ordinary form of capital punishment is decapitation. As in Cambodia, nobles of the blood are strangled rather than decapitated.[104]

---

[101] The mandarinate, as in China, was divided into civil (*quan văn*) and military (*quan võ*) classes. See P. Pasquier, *L'Annam d'autrefois* (Paris, 1929), p. 119.

[102] The *huyên* was an administrative unit—a subprefecture—within the province which first came into use in the fifteenth century. See Whitfield, *op. cit.* (n. 2), p. 118.

[103] Each province was divided into several *phù* or prefectures. *Ibid.*, p. 225.

[104] Rhodes, *op. cit.* (n. 56), pp. 37–42; and Marini, *op. cit.* (n. 59), pp. 77–86. On judicial procedure *cf.* Pasquier, *op. cit.* (n. 101), pp. 211–26. The Jesuits did not seem to know that all legal procedure was written.

All royal officials, according to Rhodes, are ordinarily doctors or licentiates of the law who take civil service examinations to obtain their degrees and posts. Every third year, public notices are posted advertising the day on which the first examination will be held. Those who consider themselves to be sufficiently prepared are invited to appear at the palace of the "Bua" (*vua* or king) commonly called the "Den" (*đình* or the court).[105] Each candidate is locked in a small room prepared for the occasion. He is allowed no books but only paper, ink, and a writing brush. To each a soldier is assigned to attend to his needs and to prevent anybody from coming to his aid. All day the candidates write on a theme given them by the doctors who preside over the examination. After finishing the essay they sign it, write on it their assigned number, and take it to the presidents of the examination. Those whose essays pass receive a bachelor's degree which they call "Sin do" (*sinh-do*).[106] Each bachelor receives a diploma signed by the king and an exemption from one-half the annual capitation tax. The second examination deals with the law and is open only to those in possession of the first degree for at least three years. Successful candidates are given licentiates of law that they call "Huan com" (*nhân-cu?*), signed by the king, and receive total exemption from paying head tax. They are then generally assigned to judgeships in the lower tribunals. The third examination is open only to those who have had the licentiate for at least three years. By law there may be only a fixed number of doctors or "Tensi" (*tiến-si*) in the kingdom; as a consequence, some candidates do not receive the degree even when they pass the examination. These unfortunates are registered for the next examination three years hence and meanwhile are given employment as judges either within or outside the royal court. It is said that there was formerly a fourth degree in letters, but it is no longer in use.[107] New doctors are rewarded by being given a tax-exempt status that passes on to their children whether or not they become literati. They are also assigned to the most important domestic and foreign posts. From their number are chosen the royal councillors, the envoys who carry the customary tribute to China, and the king's closest advisers. Twice monthly the "Tensi" appear at the palace to pay private homage to the king.[108]

Marini's discussion of education and the examination system differs in a number of details from that of Rhodes. Perhaps this merely reflects a difference in their understanding. Or it may also indicate a change in the system

[105] Triennial examinations called *Thi Đình* were held in the imperial palace; provincial, regional, and metropolitan examinations were also given. See Whitfield, *op. cit.* (n. 2), pp. 278–79.
[106] These were those students who had passed the first three parts of the provincial examinations. See Lê, *op. cit.* (n. 2), p. 260.
[107] In the Chinese system there were four degrees. *Cf.* R. Petit, *La monarchie annamite* (Paris, 1931), p. 58, who indicates that four degrees were also used in Annam.
[108] Rhodes in *op. cit.* (n. 56), pp. 13–18. It seems from later descriptions of the organization of the mandarinate that Rhodes did not understand that the Tongking system, following that of China, was divided into two orders of nine degrees, each of which was subdivided into two classes.

between 1630 and 1658, the dates respectively when Rhodes and Marini left Tongking. According to Marini, in each province Tongking has seven types of public schools and a university. Candidates for the first degree are examined in the provinces. Those who pass this first examination are called "Sinh-Do" (*sinh-do*), excused from military service, and pay only half the normal head tax and gabelles. Those who pass the second provincial examination are called "Ou Cou" (?) and enjoy higher exemptions and honors. Both grades of degree-holders work in the province of examination and the holders of the second degree are usually mayors of towns or villages. Every six years examinations are held at court for the degree of "Tan Sy" (*tiến-si*). There the candidates prepare a composition on a subject proposed by the king. Holders of the highest degree become royal councillors and neither they nor their descendants for several generations are required to pay taxes or imposts.[109]

The strength of Tongking, according to Rhodes, derives first and foremost from the size of its population. Some idea of its vast numbers may be obtained by estimating the population of "Che Ce" (*Ke-Chồ,* or Hanoi), its capital. This city is more than six thousand paces (almost thirty miles) in length and an equal number in width (an area of nine hundred square miles).[110] Its streets are wide and capacious enough to permit ten to twelve horses to walk abreast through them. Nonetheless, twice each month, at the new and full moon, when all the people cease work and gather for their feasts, the streets are choked. Judging from these crowds, it is commonly believed that on these occasions the population swells to one million persons.[111] Because of the vast numbers of his subjects the king (*chúa*) can easily raise one hundred thousand soldiers from the various provinces he controls. Early in the war against Cochin-China, he put 120,000 men into the field. He was unable to regain control over the revolting southern provinces with this great force because he lacked adequate arms and supplies.[112]

From this teeming population the king amasses huge revenues. All males from nineteen to sixty years of age, except for those exempted, are required to pay an annual tax.[113] Those who live in the four provinces which previ-

---

[109] Marini, *op. cit.* (n. 59), pp. 95–98. Rhodes makes no mention of provincial examinations. For a description of the fully developed system of literary examinations see Schreiner, *op. cit.* (n. 24), II, 77–87.

[110] Hanoi, like most East Asian cities, was an urban agglomeration of mostly single-story buildings divided into various sections based on function. It was an administrative capital, a densely populated market, and a collection of villages. See H. Bernard, S. J., *Pour la compréhension de l'Indochine et de l'Occident* (Paris, 1950), p. 131.

[111] Estimates of crowd size are notoriously inaccurate. Modern Hanoi proper has a population of around one million; its metropolitan area includes about two and one-half million persons.

[112] Rhodes, *op. cit.* (n. 56), pp. 28–30. Also *cf.* above, p. 1253.

[113] The head tax (*dung*) was assessed on three categories of registered males. The basic group consisted of men aged twenty to fifty. Youths from seventeen to nineteen years of age, men from fifty to sixty, and the *sinh-do* (students) paid just one-half as much as the regular registrants. Men over sixty, civil officials, and the whole population of the Thanh-Nghệ region (the Trịnh homeland) were exempted from paying the *dung* at all. See Lê, *op. cit.* (n. 2), p. 260.

ously rebelled are each required to pay additional taxes and four times as much tribute as those who have always remained loyal to the Trịnh. This head tax is levied equally, but perhaps unjustly, on rich and poor alike. There is a lesser tax which may be paid in kind and is ostensibly a civic voluntary present given three or four times each year. At the end or the beginning of the year it is a New Year's gift. The next occasion is the king's birthday. The third is the anniversary of the late king's death. And the final present is expected at the beginning of the harvest season. "Gifts" are often put together by members of a town or village to send to the king by an envoy who presents it in their name.

Most of Tongking's towns and villages pay their taxes without delay to the king or to those who collect for him. Some places are required to pay theirs to the nobles of the region, to the local captains and soldiers, or to those whom the king wishes to reward by personal tax grants. Tax farms are usually only for the life of the grantee and do not pass to his heirs. Sometimes the king even cancels the grant during the holder's lifetime. In distributing tax farms the king usually favors his relatives by blood or marriage, as well as military chieftains and heroes. Those so favored are expected to give "gifts" of gold or silver to the king three or four times annually in proportion to the value of the benefices they have received. Because almost one thousand captains enjoy tax assignments, the revenues extracted from the king's subjects are oppressive.[114]

Tongking and Cochin-China maintain at great expense large standing armies and naval forces. Because of the prolonged and stalemated civil war, the king of Tongking is known as the "lord of water" and the king of Cochin-China as the "lord of fire."[115] Both states rely mainly on natural defenses rather than on fortresses or walled cities. Towns and villages are surrounded only by bamboo fences and are easily ravaged by fire. Munitions and war materials are kept in primitive shelters rather than in protected arsenals. The movements of armies are hampered by floods, swampy lands, and forests. Coasts and river mouths enjoy the natural protection of reefs and sandbars. Invaders from the seaside are faced by rapids and currents which make it difficult to go upstream. The strength of their armies is in their numbers, discipline, and manner of recruitment. Captains in the provinces raise soldiers and provide them with arms and maintenance. In addition to the 40,000 troops kept at the court, 300,000 more can readily be raised. A count of the available forces in 1640 was included in the Tongking census for 1641. It claimed 335,000 infantry, 112,000 cavalry, and 2,000 elephants for war and transport. Sixty thousand men guard the frontier within Cochin-China, and the northern border is also heavily manned because of the southward progress of the Manchus in China. If a European ruler had the strength

[114] Rhodes, *op. cit.* (n. 56), pp. 28–32.
[115] Marini, *op. cit.* (n. 59), pp. 32–33. Cochin-China maintained its independence by its superior firepower. See above, p. 1269.

and wealth of Tongking, he would have long ago vanquished all these small and pesky internal enemies. Irresolute and inconstant, the Tongking kings prefer tribute to conquest.[116]

In addition to its massive ground forces, Tongking maintains a formidable fleet for war and transport. While Cochin-China keeps at least two hundred war galleys in its three main ports, Tongking has a minimum of five to six hundred. Ordinarily these long galleys are rowed by twenty-five to thirty men on each side, and sometimes by as many as thirty-five to forty. Their oars are light enough to be handled by one or two standing rowers who push their oars forward rather than pulling them back. The pilot stands on the poop deck and keeps the rowers in rhythm by the beat of a small stick. To them the occupation of rowing is not degrading or ignominious as it is with us; the crews in their war vessels are usually soldiers who consider it an honor to be selected for the job. They mount one medium-sized piece of artillery on the prow and two on the stern. The galleys of Cochin-China and Tongking are alike, except that the latter are wider and more commodious because they are used for carrying gold from China.[117]

For three main reasons the Tonkinese scarcely ever go abroad to trade.[118] Since they do not understand the art of oceanic navigation, they restrict themselves to coastal sailing. Further, their vessels would not weather the storms ordinarily encountered on a lengthy sea voyage, since the planks are held together only by cords which must be replaced every year. Finally, they are forbidden by the king to leave the country because of the revenues he would lose if they settled elsewhere. Annually the king does send some coastal trading vessels to Cambodia and Siam.[119] Foreign vessels and merchants come regularly to the fifty ports or so of Annam, much to the profit of the local merchants. Without risk to themselves or their goods, they reap great profit two or three times annually by these exchanges. Chinese and Japanese merchants have traditionally come to the ports of Annam to buy silk and aloe wood. The Japanese merchants, who formerly brought in much silver and arms, ceased to appear in Annam about twenty-five years ago.[120] Japanese are now forbidden on pain of death to travel abroad, because a large number of Japanese Christians posing as merchants left Japan between 1614 and 1624 to seek out their exiled priests. As in China, all the coins minted in Tongking are copper because gold and silver in bullion form

[116] *Ibid.*, pp. 61–69. In 1664 Trịnh Tạc placed the five military regions under a single commander.

[117] Rhodes, *op. cit.* (n. 56), pp. 20–28; Marini, *op. cit.* (n. 59), pp. 63–64, claims that Tongking could put two thousand galleys into the water as well as a multitude of other vessels.

[118] Both Tongking and Cochin-China maintained what might be called a closed economy. Limiting exports had the dubious advantage of keeping the prices of local products low and more constant. See Taboulet, *op. cit.* (n. 64), I, 78.

[119] He apparently also sent trading ships to Japan. See S. Viraphol, *Tribute and Profit: Sino-Siamese Trade, 1652–1853* (Cambridge, Mass., 1977), p. 68. And he certainly sent them to China.

[120] Certainly they no longer came regularly after 1636.

are more highly valued than coins. Their copper coins are of two types, large and small. The larger are accepted throughout the kingdom as the basic means of exchange; the smaller are circulated only in the royal city and the four surrounding provinces. All are polished rounds of copper with a hole in the middle and with four characters on one side. Six hundred are threaded on a cord with a divider between each sixty coins. Thus they are conveniently carried over the arm or the shoulders. The value of these coins is never certain or constant and entirely dependent on the supply available.[121]

Most of Tongking's imports are luxury items, arms, and precious metals. The country is self-sufficient in food, rich harvests being gained with relatively little labor. Rice is harvested in June and November. Where they do not sow rice, they plant orchards. Fruit is available throughout the year. Fish from ocean and river are abundant, though supplemented by fish cultivated in many private ponds. Wild boars run in troops, much to the detriment of the rice fields. They and the domesticated pigs provide the populace with plenty of pork. Surpluses of sugarcane, hemp, cotton, and silk are produced, which they sell to the Chinese and Dutch. Almost every kind of metal is mined or collected. From the forests comes an ironwood like ebony, from which they make forts and ships' anchors. Gold and pearls are royal monopolies, so in the king's treasury there reposes a vast hoard of gold.[122]

As a people the Tonkinese are robust in body and generous in spirit, much like the Italians; it is the royal tyranny which makes them meek and timid. Only slightly skilled in arts and crafts, they are uninterested in acquiring new techniques. They spend most of their time learning how to read and write. City-dwellers are lighter in color than the farmers. Both urban and rural women are modest and decent in their dress and behavior. Common men spend little for clothes, since they go about almost nude throughout the year. Around their simple habitations they have orchards, fish ponds, and all sorts of domesticated animals. Richer houses are flat, earthen edifices built around a courtyard. Temples are not as rude as the houses, for they are built partly of stone and are adorned with wooden columns. Commoners invoke various spirits and demons, especially one of the earth.[123]

"Ke Cio" (Hanoi) is a splendid city with a vast assemblage of houses and a world of people. Its urban sprawl is not enclosed by walls, moats, or palisades. The houses are small and low, each with its own pond, whose water is used for drinking, laundering, bathing, and fish cultivation. The city is divided into seventy-two sections, each with its own main street, which together compose the court and the market.[124] The royal court is not just a

---

[121] Rhodes, *op. cit.* (n. 56), pp. 51–53, 58–59.
[122] Marini, *op. cit.* (n. 59), pp. 37–46, 70.
[123] *Ibid.*, pp. 46–57. On the earth spirit in popular lore see L. Cadière, *Croyances et pratiques religieuses des Vietnamiens* (Saigon, 1958), pp. 50–53.
[124] Hanoi was divided into thirty-six sections, each of which was subdivided into two. See Bernard, *op. cit.* (n. 110), p. 137.

structure planned by an architect; it is rather a grand city populated by officials, soldiers, and servants. Its wooden buildings are decorated with gold
intaglie. The palace of the "Bua" (*vua*) is surrounded by a stone wall that is
entered through great arches. It was probably built originally by the Chinese when they were overlords. It has many rooms, covered galleries, and
spacious courtyards. Within one of these courtyards is the harem, the prison
of the many women shut in there. Each woman has a little house and garden
and a eunuch at her beck and call. Although their number is not known,
there must be many hundreds of women and an equal number of eunuchs in
the harem. One is the first wife and is always so respected unless she is barren. No men may enter the harem, not even the very young pages assigned
to the courtiers. In the contiguous merchant city, a fair is held twice monthly
as well as the daily market. Its unpaved streets become bogs in the rainy
season. All foreign merchants come legally to Hanoi through only one port
and by no other way. Here all taxes and duties are collected by the royal
officials. At the royal palace, tribute-bearers are received from Laos, Cochin-
China, "Cincanghe" (Civa Canh or Cao-bằng), and Baoha. Emissaries of
China are welcomed at a spectacular reception at which the *vua* and *chúa*
dress *à la Chine*. As in Siam, they show more respect for the imperial letters
than for the bearer and his entourage.[125]

Court and temple etiquette are strictly prescribed and closely observed.
Formulas of salutation, modes of entry, and proper behavior are customarily observed when addressing members of each rank from the king down.
They even have ceremonies for making and drinking tea. Officials studiously practice modesty and moderation, but many are Pharisees. The laws
are so well ordered that Plato would recognize in them the realization of his
ideal of a just and wise government. The laws balance the public good with
individual interests and champion moderation, loyalty, and reverence, to assure the peace and tranquility of the kingdom.[126] But what they legislate differs sharply from their practices. Their formal manners contrast sharply to
the crudity of their taste in foods; they eat bees, beetles, and the trunks of
elephants. Ignoring their wise and good laws, the king rules like a tyrant.
He takes everything for himself and will not permit others to retain their
inheritances unless he himself makes an exception. While high officials are
recruited through an admirable system of education and examination, the
eunuchs called "Quan trao" (*quan-trai*) wield more influence at court than
the civil mandarins.[127]

[125] Marini, *op. cit.* (n. 59), pp. 67–74.
[126] The first Annamese legal code was promulgated in A.D. 1042 and was followed by many
additions and revisions. For a French translation of the nineteenth-century code of the Lê dynasty see R. Deloustal, "La justice dans l'ancien Annam," *Bulletin de l'Ecole Française d'Extrême-
Orient* (Hanoi), VIII (1908), 117–20; IX (1909), 91–122, 471–91, 765–96; X (1910), 1–60,
349–92, 461–505; XI (1911), 25–66, 313–37; XII (1912), no. 6, 1–33; XIII (1913), no. 5, 1–59;
XXII (1922), 1–40.
[127] Marini, *op. cit.* (n. 59), pp. 57–61, 74–77.

Tonkinese are not much interested in speculation or metaphysics. They are learned in agriculture, military affairs, history, medicine, and moral philosophy. Plato and Aristotle are united for them in Confucius, a Chinese rational philosopher who taught the proper relations of vassal to lord and of children to parents. They study both poetry and prose. Of the sixty thousand characters, they must learn at least four thousand to read the classics. They study astrology and astronomy and produce almanacs and lunar charts. Their moral and civil teachings derive from the books of Confucius who is called "Khou Tu" (Khồng-Tử) in Tongking. His Four Books and his parables are used in the schools to teach good civil and moral behavior. Like Confucius they adulate the past for its justice. He is so highly regarded that a quotation from his writings is enough to end all debate.[128]

Three religions are practiced, the Annamese word for religion being "Tam Iau" (*tôn-qiáo*).[129] The first is the sect of Confucius or "Dau ni hu" (*Đạo Nho*). Solemn ceremonies and worship services are performed in his memory. The second sect, called "Dau thic" (*Đạo Thích*) or "Thic Ca" (*Thích Ca,* the Buddha's family name), was introduced into China from India and then into Tongking. Its southern and northern forms meet in Tongking. Priests called "Sai" (*tu si,* monk) make offerings to idols and study texts. Their doctrines are contained in five thousand books which elucidate the teachings of "Thicca" (Buddha), the same teacher the Japanese call "Xaca." He taught the doctrine of transmigration of souls, known in Annamese as "Lo An Hoy" (*Lộ An Hồn*) and postulated six hells and four heavens.[130] God is in everything as a vital spirit; the principle of the non-existence of beings and their impermanency is the first law of the Buddha's teachings. Fortunately, because of the rational influence of Confucianism, this sect, which plays on the credulity of the common folk, is not universally respected. Another false sect worships an ancient magician named "Lauta" (Lao-tu or Lao-tse). Many followers of Lao-tu (Taoists) are physicians given to superstition and wizardry. Aside from the established cults, the Annamites believe in a host of demons as well as household gods. Physicians and soldiers even have gods of their professions.[131]

Irrespective of a deceased's religion, three things are common to all funerals: coffins, participation by mourners other than close relatives and friends, and burial in a grave at a site determined by a geomancer called the "Dialy" (*địa lý*).[132] Ceremonies and processions are typically led by the eldest son. Lavish banquets are put on for the mourners at the funeral and every month

---

[128] *Ibid.,* pp. 98–105.

[129] This single term for religion reflects the fact that the Vietnamese think of their three religions as one and the same faith expressed in different ways.

[130] The Annamese netherworld is divided into ten kingdoms ruled by ten judges. After leaving a human body, the soul is judged and it then transmigrates to a superior or lesser being.

[131] Marini, *op. cit.* (n. 59), pp. 105–30; Rhodes, *op. cit.* (n. 56), pp. 59–81, 108–14.

[132] On the selection of a burial site see Giran, *op. cit.* (n. 14), pp. 374–75; and Diguet, *op. cit.* (n. 46), p. 165.

thereafter during the three-year mourning period. When in mourning, close relatives wear only white cotton garments, never silk, and no foot coverings. A square piece of cloth is sewn to the back of the garment and part of the head is shaved as signs of respect for the deceased. During the mourning period they refrain from attending festivals, dances, or dramas. Marriages are not then permitted for brothers and sisters, and the parents of the deceased live together in continence.[133] All of these mourning requirements are upheld by law, and infractions warrant fines. While graves are often just simple mounds, tablets and sepulchers are erected whenever possible to honor the dead. Worship of the ancestors is practiced by the king and almost everyone else. A principal eunuch prostrates himself each day before the tablets of the king's father and makes burnt offerings while reciting the king's name. The funeral honors given "Thay Thuong" (*Trịnh Tráng*), the king who died on May 26, 1657, at the age of eighty-two, were lavish and lengthy.[134]

Weddings are neither civil nor religious ceremonies; they are arrangements concluded between two families following long established practices codified in the law. The parents of the future groom go to the house of the intended bride to offer gifts. If the gifts are accepted, the contract is made. A dowry, hardly more than a token, is given to the bride on a propitious day agreed upon by the two families.[135] Then a day is set for the public celebration, a banquet given by the groom for relatives and friends of the two families; it is a crime to be married secretly. After the banquet, the bride goes to the groom's house accompanied by singing relatives and friends. Upon arrival they first pay their respects to the kitchen god. Then she prostrates herself before her new husband and promises obedience. For the next forty days she appeals to her new household god for protection.[136] Weddings are celebrated only for first wives; polygamy is generally limited to the noble and the rich. Descendants of two brothers are forbidden to marry, but the descendants of two sisters may marry beginning in the fifth generation.[137]

Tongking, like other Asian countries, follows a lunar calendar. The year is divided into twelve months and 360 days. Every third year a thirteenth month is added to reconcile the lunar with the more accurate solar calendar. The year begins and ends at midnight on the first day of the moon closest to February 5. Days are divided into twelve units rather than twenty-four, each being named for one of the animals in their zodiac: rat, buffalo, tiger, cat, dragon, snake, horse, goat, monkey, chicken (cock), dog, and pig. They also use these celestial signs as the names for the years in a twelve-year

[133] On more recent mourning practices see Diguet, *op. cit.* (n. 46), pp. 168–71.
[134] Rhodes, *op. cit.* (n. 56), pp. 82–98; Marini, *op. cit.* (n. 59), pp. 152–55. Father Francesco Rangel (1614–60), superior of the Jesuit mission in 1657, prepared an eyewitness description of Trịnh Tráng's funeral which is included in Marini, pp. 155–67.
[135] This is the engagement ceremony known as the *Ăn Hỏi*.
[136] Cf. the description of a modern wedding ceremony (Lễ Hôn-Nhân) in Whitfield, *op. cit.* (n. 2), pp. 144–45.
[137] Rhodes, *op. cit.* (n. 56), pp. 103–8; Marini, *op. cit.* (n. 59), pp. 86–95.

cycle. The Annamese group their years into periods of sixty. Children are one year old at birth.

Festival dates are set by the Brahman astrologers, who draw up the almanacs of auspicious and inauspicious days.[138] The New Year's celebration (*Tết*) is the most important of the year for all classes and ages. At this time the king (*chúa*) disposes of his old clothes, bathes, and gets into new rich vestments. Then he holds a formal audience for his family and his mandarins. The *vua* and the *chúa* both offer sacrifices to heaven, after which they ceremonially wash their hands. Then they receive gifts from their mandarins. Throughout the kingdom, superiors give gifts to their inferiors: lord to vassal, teacher to students, and father to children. Efforts are made to terminate matters left over from the old year: debts are paid and prisoners released. On the last day of the old lunar year they erect a bamboo pole in front of the house to which they attach a small basket and decorated red streamers. It remains there throughout the celebration and like a scarecrow drives off the old demons and evil spirits.[139] Instead of a pole the Christians raise a cross and inscribe their streamers with religious messages. The Buddhist priests do not participate in this festival. They do hold religious festivals in which they perform sacrifices to national heroes who are respected like saints. Even the king worships the great historical figures and defenders of the kingdom. In the fifth moon the farmers sacrifice to the idol "Than Nao" (Thần Nông), the god of agriculture and good harvests.[140] In the seventh month everyone participates in a solemn festival in which prayers are offered to win pardon for dead souls. Rich gifts are given to the Buddhist priests, and the king presents gold and silver to his servants and to children.[141] Other festivals are held in memory of the dead on the king's birthday, and when the royal guard takes its oath of loyalty.[142]

In 1677 there appeared at Rome a *Relatione* dealing with the activities of the missionaries of the Paris Society in Tongking from 1667 to 1670. This was precisely the period when Trịnh Tạc undertook an expedition against the Mạc ruler of Cao-bằng. Beginning in 1660 Mạc-Kinh-Vũ (r. 1638–77) had refused to pay tribute to Tongking. The missionaries report that in 1667 Trịnh Tạc mustered a great army of 150,000 men, including about 100 Christians, for a surprise attack on Cao-bằng. Within five months, on March 29, 1668, he returned victoriously to Tongking. Overwhelmed by Tongking's vast numbers Mạc-Kinh-Vũ had fled into China with his best troops. The Tonkinese burnt his villages and confiscated his treasure and many animals. Before retiring from Cao-bằng, Trịnh Tạc appointed magis-

---

[138] But many festivals are still celebrated on fixed dates.
[139] This is the *Cay Nên*, or New Year's Tree. The basket contains areca nuts and betel as offerings to attract the good spirits.
[140] For details see Diguet, *op. cit.* (n. 46), pp. 249–50.
[141] This is *Trung Nguyên* or "Wandering Souls' Day," the second most important festival of the year. *Ibid.*, pp. 234–35.
[142] Rhodes, *op. cit.* (n. 56), pp. 99–103; Marini, *op. cit.* (n. 59), pp. 141–45.

trates and officials loyal to him. He also left behind an army and one of his generals to guard the frontier. In this campaign he lost 10,000 men, who died not in battle but from the bad waters of the region.[143] The conquest of Cao-bằng became at once a matter for negotiation between Tongking and the new Manchu government of China.[144] In 1668 emissaries are sent to China and Japan.[145] An ambassador from China has his first audience with Trịnh Tạc on March 1, 1669. In the imperial rescript the king is ordered to restore Cao-bằng to Mạc-Kinh-Vũ. Over the next three to four months bitter negotiations proceed. In a show of bravado Trịnh Tạc puts on a military display which concludes with a volley of artillery. In the end, however, he is forced to acquiesce. Possibly out of frustration, Trịnh Tạc issues new edicts against the Christians and resumes systematic persecution.[146]

The English merchant-sailor Dampier was in Tongking for five or six months in 1688–89. He chronicles in minute detail his own observations and the information he gathered from the European merchants and missionaries then residing or visiting there. Since he knew only his own language and a smattering of Spanish and Portuguese, what he picked up through oral inquiries was far more limited than what he was able to learn through his own acute, equable, and delighted vision. His word picture of the approach to the land from the Gulf of Tongking brings to life what most perceptive Europeans probably saw and felt as they worked their way through the maze of islands off the mouths of the Red River (Sông Côi). The landmark for this river is a high, ridged mountain called "the Elephant." Through one of the river's mouths the Chinese and Siamese junks enter, while the larger European vessels make for another channel which is deeper and over one mile wide. Because of shoals, sandbars, and the tides, pilots are taken aboard who reside at the mouth of the river and make their regular living by fishing. The first riverine habitation of note is "Domea," a village of about one hundred houses where the Dutch anchor their ships.[147] Three miles further upriver, and about twenty miles from the sea, the English have an an-

---

[143] *Relatione* (see n. 60), pp. 135, 140, 149–50. As a testimonial to this source's reliability see on pp. 144–45 a report of a comet which was visible to the west of Hanoi from March 8–16, 1668. In Goa this same comet was being studied daily between March 9 and 17 by Gottignies. See G. W. Kronk, *Comets. A Descriptive Catalog* (Hillside, N.J., 1984), p. 11.

[144] In 1667 the Lê had been formally recognized as the only legitimate rulers of Annam and invested as a vassal of China. This recognition finally came from the Ch'ing dynasty after it had reduced its internal enemies to submission. See Maybon, *op. cit.* (n. 20), p. 103.

[145] "On Gia Phu Do An" was sent to China; a eunuch was sent to Japan, probably to inquire about trade and the handling of the Europeans.

[146] *Relatione* (see n. 60), pp. 164, 173, 176–78. Tongking seized Cao-bằng again in 1672 and kept it. The Ch'ing were then preoccupied with putting down the revolt of Wu San-kuei in Yunnan. Thereafter Annam paid tribute to Peking only every six years, instead of every three years as previously. See Devéria, *op. cit.* (n. 94), p. 10. For an Italian translation of the text of the third edict (June 29, 1669) against the Christians see *Relatione* (n. 60), pp. 179–80.

[147] The Dutch maintained trade relations with Tongking almost without interruption from 1640 to 1700.

chorage.[148] After an official inspection of the ships and their cargoes, the English officers proceed upriver with their wares in hired boats manned by natives. As they sail or row through the flatlands of the delta, lepers come from their colonies to beg from them. In four days' time they arrive at "Hean" (Hien, or Phô-hien, today Nhơn-đúc), a town of about two thousand houses eighty miles inland from the sea. One of its streets is occupied by Chinese merchants expelled from Hanoi, where they had become too numerous to suit the Tonkinese. The French, who are also not allowed to reside permanently in the capital, have a factory and a "Bishop's Palace" in Hien.[149] The governor of the southern province (Ke-nam) resides here and maintains a garrison. All vessels traveling up or down the river must obtain the governor's "Chop or Pass" before being allowed to proceed. In the middle of the river, ships of the royal fleet as well as Siamese and Chinese trading junks lie at anchor.[150] "Cachao" (Hanoi) is reached finally by a further two days' voyage upriver of about twenty miles.[151]

According to Dampier, Tongking includes eight large provinces in 1688.[152] Lac, silk, and rice abound in these provinces "tho in different proportions." While these peoples eat rice mainly, they have also yams and potatoes for variety. Greens grow everywhere, although the dry lands are overrun with wild purslane which chokes out many other plants.[153] They weed it out of their fields and gardens although it would make a good salad green in this hot country. They eat another herb which grows in stagnant ponds and floats on the surface of the water.[154] In their gardens they grow many other herbs and an abundance of onions. Their fruits include pumpkins, melons, pineapples, mangoes, oranges, limes, coconuts, guavas, mulberries, and lichees. Oranges are of two main kinds called "Cam-chain" (*cam-sành*) and "Cam-quit" (*cam-quât*, or kumquat); in Annamese the word "Cam" means orange.[155] The first is a large, delicious orange, the second a very small fruit of a deep, red color. The lowlands are, in general, rice fields and pastures, with groves of trees growing only around the villages. There is a fir-like tree called "Pone"(?) that produces a soft wood used for making cabinets and other things which will be lacquered.[156] Mulberry trees rarely grow fruit

---

[148] Beginning in 1672 and in connection with new efforts to trade in Japan, the English began buying silks at Tongking for the European market. They abandoned these efforts in 1697.

[149] The French merchants followed the missionaries of the Paris Society into Tongking, their factory being founded in 1680.

[150] The admiralty was located here. European seagoing vessels could not proceed to Hien at this period.

[151] Dampier in Masefield (ed.), *op. cit.* (n. 93), I, 563–70.

[152] Hanoi province, the four surrounding provinces, and the border provinces of "Tenan" (a former name for Cao-bảng?), "Teneboa" (Thiñ-Hoa), and "Ngeam" (Nghê-hiên). *Ibid.,* p. 573. Also *cf.* above, p. 1277.

[153] *Portulacca oleracea,* a yellow-flowered weed.

[154] Bindweed, a vine-like vegetable that grows on ponds and in marshes. See Whitfield, *op. cit.* (n. 2), p. 245.

[155] "Cam-chain" is the *Citrus nobilis;* the kumquat is the fruit of the *Citrus japonica.*

[156] Possibly *Calophyllum inophyllium.*

fit to eat because they are replaced every year so that the silk worms will have the tender young leaves they prefer. While they raise poultry of several sorts, ducks are accorded special treatment. They are kept at night in little houses where they lay their eggs.[157] Wild birds are caught in square nets which are stretched out at nightfall near the ponds where they nest. Swarms of locusts emerge from the earth in January and February, which the natives skim off the waters where they fall with little nets; they eat them fresh or broiled and "pickle them to keep." They also relish frogs, turtle eggs, and all sorts of shellfish. In their ponds they stir up the muddy bottom with their feet until the fish rise to the surface to be easily taken in small nets "fastened to a Hoop, at the end of a Pole." From small and ungutted shrimp and fish they make the paste called "Balachaun" (Malay, *bĕlachan*) whose liquor when poured off is named "Nuke-mum" (*nửớc-mắm*). They eat raw pork rolled in leaves, pickled raw beef, horseflesh, and elephant meat.[158]

In Tongking the dry months from November to March are the most pleasant. If the wet season is drier than ordinary, the rice crop suffers. When shortages occur they import rice by sea and it becomes expensive. But famine never rages in Tongking as it does in Malabar or Coromandel, for its mighty rivers never dry up completely. Water from the rivers is channeled into the fields to keep them wet. When too much rain falls, as it rarely does, they have dikes to hold in the rivers and ditches to drain the land. Those who suffer most from scarcities are the urban poor and especially the small merchants and silk workers. Many sell their children or die in such a time of scarcity.[159]

The lowland people are tawny with a complexion so fair and clear that you can see them blush. Both boys and girls have their teeth dyed black at puberty, a treatment which requires three or four days. Generally active and adroit, they are "ingenious in any Mechanik Science they profess." While industrious and diligent, many remain unemployed in this populous country. Little work is available in the silk and lacquer industries until the foreign ships arrive with money and exchange goods. The ordinary craftsmen who are without capital do not work until they receive orders for products from the English and Dutch merchants. The foreign merchants must advance them money of at least one-third to one-half of the cost of goods on order. Since no stocks are on hand, the foreign ships must remain five or six months until the orders can be filled.[160] The poor and the soldiers ordinarily wear simple cotton clothes dyed a dark color, while rich men and officials go about in silk or in red or green English broadcloth garments. For light,

---

[157] Like the Filipinos, the Vietnamese eat partially hatched duck eggs.
[158] Dampier in Masefield (ed.), *op. cit.* (n. 93), I, 573–82.
[159] *Ibid.,* pp. 585–89.
[160] The best craftsmen worked in the state shops on royal orders, and the public lacked the buying power to support the development of private industry and crafts. See Lê, *op. cit.* (n. 2), p. 285.

their humble, low houses have small square holes in the wall, which are covered over with a board at night. Outer rooms are furnished with stools and a table, to the side of which stands the household shrine. Villages usually include from twenty to forty houses of peasants who work on farms owned by great men. In the flatlands the villages and their groves of trees are surrounded by dikes to keep out the flood. Deep ditches then fill with water that is conserved for use in the dry season. Individual gardens are watered from little ditches attached to the village reservoir which run on either side of the garden plot and divide it from the one next door. Each house stands separately in the middle of a hedge-enclosed garden that is entered through a small gate. Pleasant in the dry season, these villages in the wet season are isolated and "like so many Duckhouses all wet and dirt." The forest settlements in the higher country are cleaner and more comfortable, since they are never surrounded by water.[161]

"Cachao" (Hanoi), the capital city, is located in the higher country on the west bank of the river about one hundred miles from the sea. It may include as many as twenty thousand low, thatched houses. Most have a yard in which stands "a small arched Building made somewhat like an Oven." It is constructed of brick daubed over with mud and stands about six feet high. People without yards set up a smaller but similar construction in the middle of the house in which to store their valuables when fires break out in the city. Since fires are a constant threat in the dry season, the government has instituted prevention and protection measures. Every householder is required during the dry period to keep a great jar of water on the roof and to have in the house a long dipper to throw water from the canals upon the fire. When these measures fail to halt the fire's spread, householders are under orders to cut the rattan straps which hold the thatched roof up and let it fall to the ground. For this purpose a long cutting hook is kept at the door to uncover the house as quickly as possible to make a fire-break. Those who fail to adopt these measures are severely punished. Fires nonetheless continue to break out and spread.[162]

The kings, who are constantly in residence, maintain two or three palaces, "such as they be," in the city. Two of them, built of timbers, are protected by great guns mounted on neighboring buildings. Nearby also are the stables and several large square parade grounds where the soldiers "draw themselves up regularly." The third, "called the Palace Royal," is also of timbers but "is more magnificently built than the other two." It is surrounded by a remarkable circular wall faced with brick which is fifteen to sixteen feet high and almost as wide. Its main gate faces the market and is

---

[161] Dampier in Masefield (ed.), *op. cit.* (n. 93), I, 590–94.
[162] Europeans of the late seventeenth century were particularly sensitive to the problem of urban fire. In 1666, when Dampier was fourteen years old, a great fire swept London. Plans were thereafter presented for rebuilding the city with bricks and wider streets.

opened only when the *vua* goes out. Two smaller gates adjoin it on each side, which are always open for regular traffic. Foreigners may never enter, but are permitted to ascend the stairs and walk around the wall. From here can be seen large fish ponds on which there are pleasure-boats "for the Emperor's diversion." [163]

The two foreign factory houses are located at the north end of the city where they front pleasantly on the river. The English, who recently moved here from Hien, have the best house in the city. On each end of it are little houses used for storage and kitchens. Each Sunday and on other special days the English flag is raised in the square open courtyard between the house and the river. The Dutch factory joins the English compound on the south, but is not as extensive. Little else about this city is worth mentioning, except for a huge, wooden bridge which is able "to resist the violence of the water in the rainy season." [164] The city, though it stands above the flood, is built on "a sort of yielding sand," a type of earth which permits the river to alter its course readily.

The Tonkinese of the capital are generally courteous and civil to foreign merchants, but the officials are haughty and the soldiers insolent. Poor people are given to thievery "notwithstanding the severe punishments." Since men customarily buy their wives, young women will offer themselves to strangers for a price. Even men of substance offer their daughters to the foreigners. Girls fathered by white men are fairer than others and bring higher prices. Some women who form liaisons with white men are able to save money and thus become more marriageable when the foreigner leaves. Others attach themselves loyally to Dutchmen who return annually. Some women are even entrusted with money and goods which they use to advantage by buying at the dull time of the year after the foreign ships have left. They are also able to employ workers more cheaply and to get better products when there is unemployment and no need for haste. [165]

Since no public cemeteries exist, a dead man of property is buried on his own land. Within one month after his death a great feast is held at his grave, at which the priests preside. To pay for the feast the family is obliged to sell a piece of land. For important men they erect a high wooden tower over the grave and nearby they put up little sheds in which they store the provisions for the feast. On the appointed day a priest mounts the tower and delivers "an Oration to the People below." Then they burn the tower to the ground and the feast begins. At the time of their New Year's festival, they do no business for ten to twelve days. They then dress in their best and spend their

---

[163] Dampier in Masefield (ed.), *op. cit.* (n. 93), I, 594–98. No vestiges of these palaces remain. They were replaced by new structures early in the nineteenth century. See L. Bezacier, *L'art Vietnamien* (2d ed.; Paris, 1954), p. 68.

[164] The Vietnamese like the Chinese were great builders of bridges. See J. Hejzlar, *The Art of Vietnam* (London, 1973), pp. 58–59, pls. 163–65.

[165] Dampier in Masefield (ed.), *op. cit.* (n. 93), I, 598–600.

time gambling, drinking, and otherwise making merry. Swings are set up in the crowded streets which are nothing more than a rope with a straight stick tied on the end which they stand on while being pushed to great heights.

The Tonkinese believe in a great overruling power and in the immortality of the soul. They represent the deity by man-like idols which show that they believe He excels in "Sight, Strength, Courage and Wisdom, Justice etc." In their countenances the idols show love, hatred, joy, or grief. Other images in the shape of horses and elephants stand in the rural pagodas. Most of the urban pagodas are wooden structures covered with pantiles. Many pagan priests are attached to these pagodas, who pretend to be skilled in telling fortunes. They have no set time for devotions except for their annual festivals. Laymen bring their written petitions to the priests, who read them aloud before the idol and burn them while the supplicant lies prostrate. Officials and rich men rarely visit the pagodas in person, but have their own clerks who read their petitions aloud in their own courts with eyes lifted up to heaven.[166]

The spoken language (Annamese) has a great affinity to the Fukien dialect of Chinese. The Tonkinese can read the Chinese characters even though they pronounce them differently. The language spoken by the scholar-officials of the court is quite different from the vulgar tongue. But Tavernier's brother is misinformed when he reports that the court language is "the Malayan tongue."[167] The Tonkinese have schools and special places where they teach the characters to the young. When writing they stand upright and hold the paper with one hand and the brush with the other. While they study mathematics and astronomy, they have learned much more about these sciences from the Jesuits. They are skilled in many crafts and so there are many who sell their services: smiths, carpenters, sawyers, joiners, turners, weavers, tailors, potters, painters, money changers, papermakers, lacquer workers, and bell-founders. Money changing is managed by women. Paper is made of both silk and wood pulp, the latter being the better type for writing. The local lacquerware is exceeded in quality only by that made in Japan. The lac of Tongking is a white "gummy Juice" from trees, which the country people daily bring to the market in great tubs.[168] Joiners who make the objects to be lacquered are not as skilled as those of Europe. Lacquer varnishing is considered to be a dangerous occupation because of the poisonous quality of the lac fumes. Work in this trade is limited to the dry season because each coat of varnish must be dry before the next can be applied. When the outside coat is dry they polish it. Lac can be made in any color by

---

[166] *Ibid.*, 600–603. A simple way of noting that the officials were Confucianists and only rarely Buddhists.

[167] On Tavernier and his brother regarding Tongking see above, pp. 1267–68.

[168] Resin of the *son tru* or *Rhus vernicifera,* commonly called the lacquer tree. This should not be confused with the lac of India, which is a resinous incrustation formed on the bark of the twigs of various trees through the action of the lac insect.

the addition of oils and other ingredients. From it they also make a good, cheap glue that may not be exported. The earthenware of Tongking is coarse and grey in color. Great quantities of their small dishes are taken by the Europeans for sale in the Malayan countries and Arakan. Despite all its commodities, the people of Tongking are generally poor.[169]

The government is an absolute monarchy "but of such a kind as is not in the World again." It is ruled by two kings, "each supreme in his particular way." The "Buoa" (*vua*) and his ancestors were sole monarchs for a long time and also rulers of Cochin-China. With its revolt the "Buoa" was also deprived of his power in Tongking by the general who commanded his armies. The usurper took the title of "Choua" (*chúa*), a term which means "Master."[170] Since then the "Buoa" lives like "a Prisoner of State" enclosed in the old palace, which he never leaves. Nonetheless he is revered by the people, who say they have no other king. The "Choua" seems to treat him with the utmost respect and makes formal calls on him two or three times annually. Ambassadors from China insist on delivering their messages to him alone. Otherwise he is left to his own devices with his family and the few servants assigned him. No officials report to him and he is allowed no guards. All state matters, even war and peace, are entirely in the hands of the "Choua." An "angry, ill-natured, leprous person,"[171] the "Choua" lives in the second palace with "his ten or twelve wives." Before the usurpation the "Choua's" family were great mandarins who controlled the northern province of "Tenchoa" (Thanh-Hóa). The present governor of this province is one of his principal eunuchs and he is in charge of the "Choua's" treasure, which is buried there "in great Cisterns full of Water, made purposely for that use."

Around the "Choua's" palace a strong guard of soldiers watches over the stables of his elephants and horses. On the parade ground in front are places for the mandarins to sit and watch the soldiers drilling. Across from these is a shed which houses the artillery mounted "on old and ill-made carriages." There is one brass gun much bigger than the rest which is more for show than for service. It was cast here twelve or thirteen years ago and mounted on a carriage with the help of the English. While it is a badly shaped and ordinary piece of workmanship, it should nonetheless be understood that the Tonkinese are "very expert in tempering the Earth, wherewith they make their Mould." While he has few great guns and no fortresses, the "Choua" maintains, it is said, between seventy and eighty thousand soldiers, of whom thirty thousand make up his personal bodyguard. Most are infantrymen armed with swords and thick, heavy matchlocks for which they make their own gunpowder. Each has a leather-covered box for car-

[169] Dampier in Masefield (ed.), *op. cit.* (n. 93), I, 604–12.
[170] Other contemporary European writers aptly compare the *chúa* to the shogun of Japan.
[171] Trịnh Căn, who ruled from 1682 to 1709.

tridges that are "small hollow canes, each containing a load or charge of Powder." They keep their guns clean and dry by covering them entirely with a lacquered bamboo cane. When they march, each file consists of ten men led by one officer. The men are lusty fellows whose strength is judged by the amount of rice they are able to eat; most are natives of the province of "Ngean" (Nghê).[172] After thirty years' service a soldier may petition for a discharge. Once it is granted, his native village must send another man to replace him. Both the infantry and the cavalry are expert with gun and bow, and practice by shooting at marks. Annually the king holds a match at which the best marksman wins a fine coat. Many soldiers are kept on the frontiers, especially on the Cochin-China border. These are defensive forces which make occasional forays into the enemy's territory. Armies take the field only in the dry season. Overland expeditions are led by officers mounted on elephants. Small field pieces with barrels six or seven feet long are carried on the backs of soldiers; other infantrymen carry the carriages on which these pieces are placed for firing. These guns are used to blast open a fortified mountain pass or to fire over a river at an enemy emplacement. Soldiers are assigned to guard the great roads and rivers and to act as customs officers. They check to see that no prohibited goods are imported or exported. All travelers are searched and strictly examined, "so that no disaffected or rebellious person can stir without being presently known."

The royal navy consists of flat-bottomed galleys in which soldiers are transported from place to place. From fifty to seventy feet in length, these vessels are from ten to twelve feet broad amidships where the men enter. The prow and stern stand about two feet out of the water, but the prow is not quite as high or as ornamented as the stern. The captain sits atop the covered stern on what looks like a little throne. Each galley carries a small brass gun which "looks out through a Port in the Bow." The oarsmen are always soldiers who stand behind the oars clothed only in a breechcloth. A rower pushes the oar forward which "lies in its notch on the Gunnal [gunnal or gunwale]." To set the rhythm a small gong or wooden instrument sounds before every stroke. The rowers respond with a yell; then stamp on the deck with one foot as they plunge their oars into the water. They go very slowly upstream if laden with a full complement of men. On an expedition the galleys are divided into squadrons with identifying flags of different colors. When not in service, the galleys are dragged ashore and stored in sheds on the riverside where they are cleaned and kept dry. Once the galleys are safely ashore, the soldiers who were oarsmen return to their land service.

Some of the soldiers act as security guards for private employers or as watchmen in villages and towns. In "Cachao" (Hanoi) every street is guarded

---

[172] These were soldiers of the first category (*uu binh*) who were recruited in the province of Thanh-Nghê, the place of origin of the dynasty, for the royal guard. See Lê, *op. cit.* (n. 2), p. 257.

at night by watchmen to maintain order and silence. Armed with staves they stand in the street by the watchhouses to examine all passersby. A rope is stretched across the street breast high to prevent people from escaping the examiners. Near every watchhouse is a "pair of Stocks" in which night prowlers may be detained. For a small bribe the guards will look the other way, so "for the most part only the poor are taken up." While corrupt and arbitrary, these soldier-watchmen are protected by the authorities and their other employers, who ignore all complaints against them.

Corporeal punishments are numerous and severe. Debtors are often imprisoned in the creditor's house, where they are beaten and barely kept alive until the debt is paid. Malefactors have iron chains or logs fastened to their legs and others carry two heavy planks about their necks. A similar instrument of punishment is the "Gongo" (cangue) which is a ladder-like yoke of bamboo worn constantly about the neck for prescribed periods of time. The owner of the house where a fire breaks out is forced to sit bareheaded in a chair twelve to fourteen feet in height for three whole days in the scorching sun. Lesser crimes are punished by whippings with a split bamboo, the number of blows depending on the seriousness of the crime. Magistrates issue warrants for the apprehension of malefactors and immediately try them. Sentences may not be appealed and are quickly executed. Capital crimes are punished by decapitation, and theft with the excision of an entire hand, a finger, or a finger-joint.

Most of the officials closest to the king are eunuchs learned in the laws of the land. While they enjoy easy access to the king themselves, they zealously keep others away from him. Some mandarins become so frustrated that they geld themselves to win the favor of the eunuchs and the king. Dampier claims to have heard that there were only three mandarins of any importance who were not eunuchs. Eunuch officials live "in great State" surrounded by their soldiers and guards. "They are generally covetous beyond measure, and very malicious." Once each year all officials swear an oath of loyalty to the king and their superiors. On this occasion they make a drink of arrack and chicken blood which each official solemnly drinks after swearing his oath as a proof of his sincerity. While bitter in their enmities, the eunuchs are friendly and hospitable to foreign visitors. At their entertainments and in eating their everyday fare, the Tonkinese pick up their food with two small sticks which "are called by the English Seamen Chopsticks."[173]

In mid-October, 1688, Dampier's English colleagues make up a fleet of small vessels to go to "Tenan" province to buy rice. It was in short supply and too expensive in Hanoi. As they thread their way eastward through the coastal islands they constantly watch out for pirates. Near the end of November they return and load the rice into the English ships at the anchorage.

---

[173] Dampier in Masefield (ed.), *op. cit.* (n. 93), II, 1–18. This is the earliest known usage (1699) in print of the word "chopsticks." See *OED.*

From here Dampier decides to follow the river to Hanoi on foot in the company of a native guide. Walking up its east side he notes that ferryboats cross the Red River. While there are no inns along the road, they are able to find lodging and food in private homes. He sees rural pagodas with animal idols looking out the doors. On the third day he sees a twenty-six-foot tower with a crowd of people around it, as well as what he takes to be stalls for the sale of meat and fruits. When he tries to buy some meat, he is assaulted, for he was not in a market but at a funeral feast. He stops at Hien two days later to rest and visit with the European missionaries living there. He describes the "Bishops's Palace" and its compound. He converses in Spanish with a French missionary who tells him that the people of Tongking are ready to accept Christianity but that the king and court are utterly opposed to it and to the missionaries. As a consequence the priests live in Hien in the guise of merchants. Despite these difficulties "they had about 14,000 converts, and more coming in daily" for the two French bishops, ten European priests, and three native priests to minister to. While they are not permitted to live at Hanoi, these priests are invited to go to the capital frequently to repair the clocks, watches, and mathematical instruments of the mandarins. The converts are mostly poor people who come to the Europeans for rice "in the scarce times." Christianity is hampered by the bad example set by the "loose livers" among the English and Dutch merchants. While the Catholics try to have the people exchange their pagan idols for the images of saints, they are not likely to succeed in making them give up their "Belief of the Goodness of their own Gods or Heroes."

Dampier leaves Hien on a ferry for Hanoi that proceeds upriver with the tide in the company of four or five other passenger boats. In his boat are twenty passengers and four or five oarsmen; the women and the men sit apart. At midnight they stop at a small settlement whose residents earn their living by entertaining passengers. Dampier gets off the ferry about five miles short of the capital and walks from there into the city. In Hanoi he stays a few days with an English private trader until a freighter leaves with the goods bought for his ship. In its cargo are two huge bells cast at Hanoi which were ordered by Constantine Phaulkon for the churches in Siam. At the instigation of the English factor, the bells are seized at Hien because the English were then at war with Siam. This factor "who was little qualified for the Station he was in" had failed in Dampier's view to use Tongking properly as an intermediary place for the development of English trade with China and Japan.[174]

In these European sources much more detail was given on Tongking than on Cochin-China, even though the traders and missionaries were more active in the south than in the north over most of the century. The Europeans

[174] Dampier in Masefield (ed.), *op. cit.* (n. 93), pp. 19–34.

were acutely aware of the greater size and wealth of Tongking and of its possible strategic value as a way of entry to China and Laos. They realized that both Vietnamese states had deep historical connections with China and were themselves almost identical in culture, religions, and language. As a consequence, much of what they said about the one, except for politics and economy, applied almost as well to the other. The distinctions they made were therefore mostly concerned with political organization, warfare, and conditions for trade. They understood that the Nguyễn, throughout their revolt, continued to pay tribute to the *vua* as lord of both Tongking and Cochin-China. The missionaries, because most of them spoke and read the Annamese language, and because a number remained in Indochina for extended periods of time, were generally better informed than the traders on native beliefs, customs, and institutions. Secular observers like Dampier provided graphic descriptions of topography, local industries, and everyday problems and practices.[175]

For their European readers the reports of the missionaries provided information on the names and numbers of the provinces in both states and of the provinces' role in government and justice. They described the legal system, the machinery of justice, and the punishments administered. They revealed that a written code existed which spelled out in minute detail with reference to innumerable customs and aspects of everyday life what was illegal and what punishments offenders might expect. Tight government control was thus maintained over both natives and foreigners. Education and the state examinations for civil service especially attracted the attention and admiration of the missionaries. Most observers stressed the growing importance of the court eunuchs and of their baneful influence upon the ruler, the mandarinate, and the civil order. They reported on the military and naval strength of both states and on the numbers of soldiers in the royal guard. They detailed the method of recruitment and gave the numbers of men available for military service, one such estimate being based on a military census prepared in 1641. Most Europeans agreed that the Vietnamese soldiers, unlike other Asians, were good gunners. Despite almost constant civil war, the only permanent fortifications were the walls built across central Vietnam as the line of division between Tongking and Cochin-China.

The strength of Vietnam centered in its numerous and productive coastal population; in the mountains of the interior lived primitive, black tribal peoples who were thought to be barbarians and were referred to by various derogatory names. Both states were self-sufficient in food and produced a few commodities for export. Only a few Vietnamese ships and traders went abroad. Generally their commerce was limited to local trade and to traffic

[175] On Vietnam's unique position as a "frontier between Southeast Asia and China," participating in both cultures but effectively hampering the spread of Chinese political influence in Southeast Asia, see A. Reid, *Southeast Asia in the Age of Commerce, 1450–1680*, Vol. I, *The Lands below the Winds* (New Haven, 1988), pp. 7–10 and *passim*.

with neighboring foreign countries that could be reached by coastal sailing. The economy was regulated and closed to maintain low and constant prices. Foreign traders were tolerated because of the regular need for arms and ammunition. In Cochin-China the Japanese and Chinese merchants lived at Fai-fo in separate settlements and under their own laws and leaders. In Tongking the foreigners were confined in their activities to the valley of the Red River from Hanoi to the sea. Foreign trading vessels, especially those of the Europeans, had to remain in port for extended periods awaiting a cargo of sugar, hemp, cottons, silks, and lacquerware. They paid for their purchases and their taxes in precious metals, arms, and foreign curios. Gold and pearls were both royal monopolies. While the court hoarded gold, the people suffered from unemployment. In times of shortages the city-dwellers were often forced to sell their children to survive.

Hanoi, the capital of Tongking, was a crowded but well-ordered city and the central market of the Red River delta. Each of its seventy-two sections had a wide main street and many narrow and unpaved side streets. Next to its market stood several palaces with courtyards, the one occupied by the *vua* being surrounded by a high wall. The royal guard was quartered near the *chúa's* palace. Watchmen patroled Hanoi's streets at night to maintain strict peace and order. The greatest threat to the capital was fire. Despite the strict enforcement of fire-prevention measures, it was often swept by fires in the dry season. On festival days, especially during *Tết,* people from the surrounding region flooded into the city. By the 1680's the Dutch and English had their factories in a compound at the north end of the city. Despite their abilities in the arts and crafts, the artisans of Hanoi were not interested in learning new or different foreign techniques. They had no incentives.

Traditional customs were maintained by law, and even minor infractions were punished. Certain festivals were celebrated on fixed dates set by the almanac drawn up by the Hindu astrologers at the court. Other printed books, particularly the Confucian classics, were also read and cited. Wedding ceremonies and burial and mourning customs were firmly fixed by tradition and enshrined in the law. Three religions were practiced, and the Vietnamese tended to believe in all of them, as well as in animism and evil and good spirits. Most officials were Confucians. Buddhist priests, idols, and pagodas were to be found everywhere. Many Taoists were physicians who practiced wizardry. The national heroes and the ancestors were worshipped regularly by everyone from the king to the lowliest of his subjects. Christianity, while periodically tolerated for the sake of the arms trade, was generally seen by the officialdom to be a threat to tradition and to internal peace and order.

CHAPTER XVII

Insulindia: The Western Archipelago

The Indonesian archipelago is the most important equatorial country and the greatest congeries of large and important islands in the world. Stretching around twenty-five hundred miles from the western tip of Sumatra to eastern New Guinea, the archipelago embraces some three thousand islands. Many efforts have been undertaken over time to subdivide the archipelago into groupings of islands based on topographical affinities, vegetational differences, economic connections, or political alliances. All such groupings are arbitrary and fail in one way or another to satisfy the requirements of specialists in the archipelago's past, present, or future. Perhaps this is so because it is the sea that unites and the land that divides the archipelago. For the purposes of this book an arbitrary maritime line is drawn, following the limits set by the Wallace line of the nineteenth century, between Bali and Lombok northward through the Makassar Strait which divides Borneo from Celebes. To the west of the line lie Borneo, Bali, Sumatra, and Java—the last two islands being at the foci of Indonesian history and civilization. To the east lie Celebes, the volcanic Moluccas, the Lesser Sunda islands, Timor, New Guinea, and the austral lands. Economically and politically, Borneo was closely related by trade to both the western and eastern reaches of Indonesia and even the Philippines. Celebes was likewise tied by trade to the western and the eastern parts of the archipelago.

Insular Southeast Asia's early history was characterized by successive waves of immigration or conquest in which the new people gained control of the coastal regions and drove the previous inhabitants into the interior mountains. With few exceptions, the Majapahit Empire (thirteenth to fifteenth centuries) on Java being one of the most notable, political power resided in the coastal cities. Ambitious princes competed with one another for control of the seaports and their trade, the most successful of them carving out impressive, if short-lived, maritime empires. Their control of the interior, however, was probably incomplete at best. Successive waves of cultural intrusion, ultimately coming from India or China, and carried both by the immigrants or conquerors and by the merchants who traded in the archipelago, affected the region throughout its history. Among the peoples of the interior—and especially on Java and Bali—Indian, Indochinese, and Chinese, Hindu and Buddhist influences can readily be found, syncretized with local, primitive traditions. The Malay-speaking, Islamic coastal peoples whom the first Europeans met everywhere in Southeast Asia represented the most recent cultural wave to wash ashore. Recent it surely was: Perlak and Samudra on Sumatra's north coast became Muslim in the late thirteenth century, Malacca in the early fifteenth century, Acheh in the late fifteenth century, and Java in the sixteenth century.[1] Some major powers, like Makassar, were not converted until the seventeenth century, and some, like Bali, never accepted Islam. Fear of the Portuguese and the hope of aid from other Muslim rulers probably abetted the new religion's spread during the sixteenth century.[2]

European readers had been introduced to most of the major islands of the archipelago during the sixteenth century. The Portuguese and Spanish writers seem to have been awed by the size of the area, the seemingly numberless islands and peoples, and the varieties of culture. Still, everywhere they met Malay-speaking Muslims who controlled the seaports and coasts and who were their formidable competitors in religion and trade. Consequently, their descriptions stress the importance and power of the Muslims and say very little about the interior of the islands or about their pre-Islamic traditions. Many reported the importance of the Chinese in the archipelago's economy and its past. The Javans, for example, were thought to have descended from Chinese immigrants. Sixteenth-century reports were most detailed for the Spiceries and for the Javan people whom the Europeans met in Malacca and other places. Less was written about Java itself or about Borneo and Sumatra, probably because they were dominated by the hated Moors and because the Iberians had no strongholds there. The location of the Moluccas, however, was a matter of dispute between Portuguese and Spanish writers. Little was written about New Guinea, and Australia was virtually unknown.[3]

At the beginning of the seventeenth century the Portuguese were in pos-

---

[1] For a series of authoritative studies regarding the introduction of Islam into Java see H. J. de Graaf, *Islamic States in Java, 1500–1700. Eight Dutch Books and Articles Summarized by T. G. Th. Pigeaud* (The Hague, 1976).

[2] See B. H. M. Vlekke, *Nusantara. A History of Indonesia* (rev. ed., Chicago, 1960), pp. 1–93; K. R. Hall, "Trade and Statecraft in the Western Archipelago at the Dawn of the European Age," *JRAS, Malaysian Branch*, LIV (1981), 21–47; and A. Reid, *Southeast Asia in the Age of Commerce, 1450–1680*, Vol. I, *The Lands below the Winds* (New Haven, 1988), pp. 1–10.

[3] For the sixteenth-century reports see *Asia*, I, 493–505, 646–50.

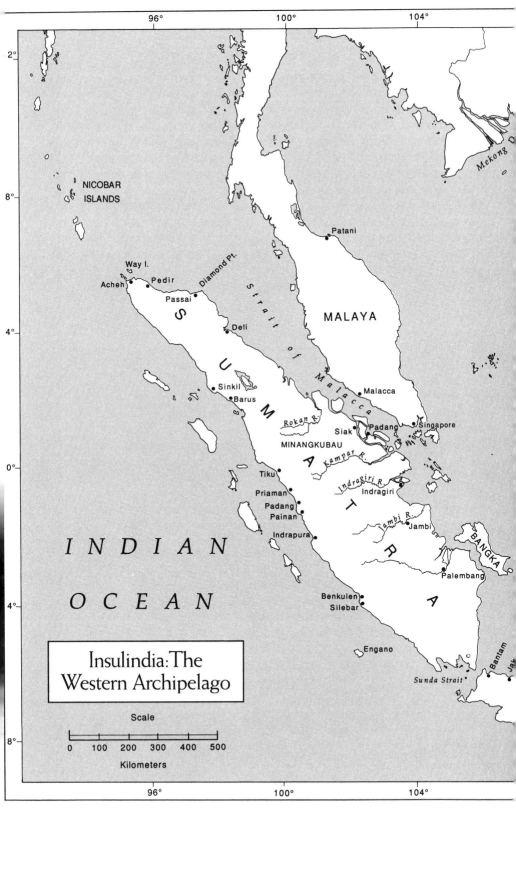

Insulindia: The Western Archipelago

Scale

0 100 200 300 400 500
Kilometers

session of Malacca, which involved them in rivalries with Acheh, the new Muslim power in northwest Sumatra, as well as with Johore on the Malay Peninsula.[4] From Malacca they traded in Sumatra, Java, and Borneo, but they had no secure base in these places. They were established in the Spiceries, but involved in a protracted war with a confederation of Muslim states and in a sporadic rivalry with the Spanish from Manila, who claimed that the Moluccas fell on their side of the Line of Demarcation. When the first Dutch ships arrived in the archipelago they traded first in Java and Sumatra where Portuguese influence was slight. They tried to cooperate with Portugal's enemies—Acheh, for example—and before long were making treaties with local princes which granted the Dutch exclusive trading privileges in return for protection against the Portuguese. Beginning with their second voyage (1599), the Dutch began to contest the Portuguese control of the Spiceries. They allied with the sultan of Ternate and other enemies of the Portuguese, and eventually tried with their allies to monopolize the spice trade. By the end of the century's first quarter the Spiceries were largely in Dutch hands. Following closely behind the Dutch in all this activity were the English, who quickly discovered that the newly established Dutch were as jealous of their position in the archipelago as the Portuguese, and soon began to entice local rulers to join them against the Dutch. Indeed, many local rulers soon found even the Portuguese preferable to the Dutch.

I

JAVA

A. DEVELOPMENT OF THE LITERATURE

The return of the first Dutch fleets from Indonesia in 1597 initiated what became a rich and growing stream of information about the archipelago— particularly Java—from European presses. Sixteenth-century reports about Java had been scant, both because the Portuguese and Spanish had failed to establish themselves on Java, and because of the Portuguese policy of secrecy.[5] Both the anonymous *Verhael vande reyse* (Middelburg, 1597) and the expanded *Journael vande reyse* (Middelburg, 1598), however, contained lengthy accounts of Java, especially of the port of Bantam (Banten). Still larger and more detailed is the description of Bantam and Java in Willem Lodewyckszoon's *D'eerste boeck* (Amsterdam, 1598); although Lodewyckszoon's description seems to depend more on a Portuguese manuscript than on firsthand observation, it nevertheless provided European readers with

---

[4] See above, pp. 12–13.
[5] On the sixteenth-century image of Java and its sources see *Asia*, I, 585–91.

much more and better information about the archipelago's main island than had previously been available.[6]

All the other Dutch fleets during the century's first decade stopped in Java, usually at Bantam, and the published reports of those voyages all contain brief descriptions of Java. *Het tweede boeck* (1601), the account of Jacob van Neck and Wybrand van Warwijck's voyage, for example, contains a brief but interesting description of Tuban and the island of Madura.[7] Olivier van Noort stopped at the east Javanese port of Jortan at Gresik in January, 1601, to repair his ship. The 1602 account of his voyage contains a brief description of the area.[8]

The publication in 1606 of Edmund Scott's *An Exact Discourse* provided English readers with a substantial firsthand description of Bantam in Java. Scott was among the English factors left in Bantam by James Lancaster in 1603, where he remained, attempting to buy pepper for the following three and one-half years.[9] Both Leonardo de Argensola's *Conquista de las islas Malucas* (Madrid, 1609) and François Pyrard's *Voyage* (Paris, 1611) contain some description of Java. Neither, however, is an eyewitness account.[10]

Captain John Saris, who replaced Scott as the English resident in Bantam in 1605, remained there until October, 1609. His account of those years was published in Purchas' *Pilgrimes* in 1625. It is not, however, as Purchas intended, an adequate continuation of Scott's narrative. Saris recorded the coming and going of ships and their cargoes but said little about Java or Javans. The most descriptive parts of his account have to do with East Indian drugs and with the weights and measures used in Bantam.[11] Some discussion of Java was included in the later editions of Sir Thomas Herbert's *A Relation of Some Yeares Travaile*, but all of it appears to have been culled from previously published works. Herbert also reproduced an English-Malay word list.[12]

Seyger van Rechteren arrived in Batavia on September 23, 1629, while the Dutch headquarters was besieged by a Javanese army from Mataram and just two days after Governor-General Jan Pieterszoon Coen died. He wrote a brief account of the siege and the events which led up to it, including the first siege in 1618–19 which attended the birth of Batavia. Van Rechteren's

[6] For complete bibliographical information about the published reports from the first Dutch voyage under Cornelis de Houtman see above, pp. 437–39.

[7] J. Keuning (ed.), *De tweede schipvaart der Nederlanders naar Oost-Indië onder Jacob Cornelisz. van Neck en Wybrant Warwijck, 1598–1600* (5 vols.; "WLV," XLII, XLIV, XLVI, XLVIII, L; The Hague, 1938–1951), III, 34–52. For bibliography of the voyage see above, pp. 439–41.

[8] J. W. Ijzerman (ed.), *De reis om de wereld door Olivier van Noort, 1598–1601* (2 vols.; "WLV," XXVII and XXVIII; The Hague, 1926), I, 141–42. For bibliography of the voyage see above, pp. 441–42.

[9] See above, pp. 551–52.

[10] On Argensola see above, pp. 310–12; on Pyrard see above, pp. 396–97.

[11] On Saris see above, pp. 560–61.

[12] Herbert, *A Relation of Some Yeares Travaile* . . . (London, 1634), pp. 202–5. See above, pp. 571–72 for bibliography.

Journael, first published in 1635, also contains a brief account of Batavia and its Chinese community.[13] David Pieterszoon de Vries also reports on the 1628–29 siege of Batavia in his *Kort historiael ende journaels aenteyckeninge* (Hoorn, 1655) but wrote little else about Java and its people.[14] Vincent Le Blanc, whose *Voyages* were published in 1648, also briefly described Java. Much of what he reported seems to be based on previously published accounts. Some of it is difficult to believe. Le Blanc appears either to have been gullible or imaginative—or both.[15]

Jacob Bontius' *De medicina indorum* (1642), augmented by Willem Piso in 1658, not only describes tropical Asian diseases and their treatment but depicts plants and animals as well.[16] While Dutch writers during the middle decades of the century added little to the earlier descriptions of Java, the Germans who served the VOC contributed some worthwhile reports. Johann Jacob Saar, whose *Ost-Indianische fünfzehen-jährige Kriegs-Dienst* was published in 1662, and Jacob Merklein, whose *Journal oder Beschreibung* appeared during the following year, each included firsthand descriptions of Batavia and Java.[17] Johann von der Behr's *Diarium; oder Tage-Buch,* published in 1668, repeated much of what Saar and Merklein had written.[18] Albrecht Herport's *Eine kurtze ost-indianische Reiss-Beschreibung* (1669) not only included a standard description of Java and Batavia but also a vivid account of a thirteen-day expedition into the jungle to the north of Batavia.[19]

The seventeenth century's most detailed information about Java's interior is contained in Rijcklof Volckertszoon van Goens' *Javaensche reijse gedaen van Batavia over Samarangh na de konincklijcke hoofdplaets Mataram,* published in 1666.[20] Van Goens had led five VOC embassies to the Susuhunan's court in Mataram between 1648 and 1654. His *Javaensche reijse* contains vivid accounts of central Java's mountains, streams, forests, and riceland as well as of the monarch, his court, and his government.

Several fresh descriptions of Java appeared during the last quarter of the century, many of which conveyed some glimpse of the changes in Javan life and politics resulting from the Dutch intrusion into the island's affairs. One of the best is found in Wouter Schouten's *Oost-Indische voyagie,* which ap-

---

[13] Seyger van Rechteren, "Journael . . . ," *BV,* IIb, 26–30. See above, pp. 453–55, for bibliographic details.
[14] See above, p. 482.
[15] See above, pp. 406–7 for bibliography.
[16] For bibliographical details see above, p. 457. The first four books of Bontius' work, with Piso's additions, was translated into English in 1769: *An Account of the Diseases, Natural History and Medicines of the East Indies.* . . . (London); this translation is reprinted in *Opuscula selecta Neerlandicorum de arte medica* . . . (Amsterdam, 1931), Vol. X. We have used the *Opuscula selecta* edition in what follows.
[17] For bibliographical details on Saar and Merklein see above, pp. 529–31.
[18] See above, pp. 531–32.
[19] See above, pp. 532–33, for bibliography.
[20] See above, pp. 484–85.

peared in 1676.[21] Schouten described events as well as the land and its people. Much of what he wrote was the product of his own observations, although he obviously augmented them with information from other sources. His description of the court of Mataram, for example, is not an eyewitness account; he apparently never visited it. Since the whole book is written in Schouten's lively style, however, it is difficult to distinguish between the firsthand portions of his account and that which came from other sources.

Several descriptions of the VOC headquarters at Batavia were published during the final quarter of the century, many by non-Dutch writers who were usually awed by its trade, wealth, and military power. The Frenchman François L'Estra, for example, was imprisoned there in 1673–74. He described the city, its various inhabitants, and the VOC government.[22] Frederick Bolling, a Danish soldier in VOC service, also described the Dutch headquarters and its trade in some detail.[23] All the German employees of the VOC who published their journals during the last two decades of the century included descriptions of Batavia and Java. Those written by Christian Hoffman (1680) and Christoph Schweitzer (1688) are brief and much like earlier reports.[24] Those of Elias Hesse (1687) and Christoph Frick (1692) are larger and contain some fresh, firsthand information, although most of Frick's description seems to have come from Saar.[25]

Perhaps the largest and surely the best-illustrated description of Batavia published during the seventeenth century is that found in Johann Nieuhof's *Gedenkwaerdige zee- en lant-reize* (1682).[26] It is a detailed description of the castle and of every major building, wall, gate, fortification, market, and street in Batavia. Furthermore, it contains beautiful plates made from Nieuhof's careful sketches of almost all the structures which he described, as well as drawings of the various peoples who lived in Batavia. Equally detailed are Nieuhof's discussions of Javan plants, trees, fruits, spices, birds, fish, and animals. These, too, are accompanied by engravings made from Nieuhof's sketches. Nieuhof's history of Batavia and his description of the rest of Java and its people, however, are much like those produced by earlier writers and do not seem to have benefitted much from his personal observations. Finally, in 1701 Nikolaas de Graaf included a sizable description of Batavia which was very similar to that of Nieuhof. De Graaf also described Japara, which he visited, and wrote a long diatribe about the behavior of Dutch and mestiza women in Batavia and other VOC settlements in Asia.[27]

[21] See above, pp. 496–97, for bibliography.
[22] See above, p. 418, for bibliography.
[23] See above, pp. 535–36.
[24] For bibliographical information on Hoffman and Schweitzer see above, pp. 538, 540–41.
[25] For bibliographical information about Hesse and Frick see above, pp. 539–40, 541–42.
[26] See above, pp. 500–501 for bibliography.
[27] See above, pp. 505–6.

B. GEOGRAPHY AND THE LANDSCAPE

The first and most commonly described place in Java was Bantam, the east-ernmost port on Java's north coast. European visitors recognized it as the best and largest seaport on the island.[28] It is situated on low—some say marshy—land at the foot of high mountains with a sheltered and convenient harbor. The earliest writers report that three shallow streams flow from the mountains, one on each side of the city, forming a natural moat, and one through the middle of the town.[29] Lodewyckszoon describes a red brick wall around the city about a stone's throw high and a fathom (about six Dutch feet) thick, with well-guarded gates, flanking gun emplacements, and many three-story, scaffold-like watchtowers. The cannons he thinks are useless, however, because the Javans know little about firing them and because they have no ammunition apart from what they can get in Portuguese Malacca, where there is a powdermill.[30] The *Verhael vande reyse* describes the wall as not more than two feet thick.[31] Pyrard reports that the watchtowers are about a hundred paces apart from each other.[32] According to Edmund Scott, some people think the Chinese built Bantam's wall while others credit the Portuguese with it. He concludes it must have been the Chinese because the wall looks old and has decayed in many places.[33]

Bantam is a populous city but has only three real streets. These lead from an open square—the "pacebam" (Javanese and Malay, *paseban,* or reception place)—on the north side of the sultan's palace in the center of the city, to three of the city's gates. None of the streets or paths in the city is paved, and no bridges cross the streams.[34] Pyrard reports that during the winter the streets are frequently flooded, forcing people to travel by boat.[35] Everyone describes Bantam's streams as polluted and foul-smelling. The land is marshy and the current is not swift enough to carry off the pollution result-ing from people bathing in the streams and throwing all sorts of refuse, in-

[28] For example, see Lodewyckszoon in G. P. Rouffaer and J. W. Ijzerman (eds.), *De eerste schipvaart der Nederlanders naar Oost-Indië onder Cornelis de Houtman, 1595–1597* (3 vols.; "WLV," VII, XXV, XXXII; The Hague, 1915–35), I, 105. Volume I of Rouffaer and Ijzerman's edition contains Lodewyckszoon's account. Volume II contains the *Verhael vande reyse,* the *Journael vande reyse,* and F. van der Does' previously unpublished account. Volume III contains other documents pertaining to De Houtman's voyage.
[29] Lodewyckszoon in *ibid.,* I, 105, and *Verhael vande reyse, ibid.,* II, 23. Actually the streams are branches of a single river, the Kali Banten. See our pls. 32 and 248 for illustrations from Lodewyckszoon's book that pertain to Bantam.
[30] *Ibid.,* I, 105–6.
[31] *Ibid.,* II, 23.
[32] Albert Gray (ed.), *The Voyage of François Pyrard of Laval to the East Indies, the Maldives, the Moluccas, and Brazil* (2 vols. in 3; "HS," o.s., LXXVI, LXXVII, LXXX; London, 1887–1890), II, 161.
[33] William Foster (ed.), *The Voyage of Sir Henry Middleton to the Moluccas, 1604–1606* ("HS," 2d ser., LXXXVIII; London, 1943), p. 169.
[34] Lodewyckszoon in Rouffaer and Ijzerman (eds.), *op. cit.* (n. 28), I, 106; *Verhael vande reyse* in *ibid.,* II, 24.
[35] Gray (ed.), *op. cit.* (n. 32), II, 161.

cluding animal carcasses, into them.[36] A city plan is included in several early descriptions of Bantam.[37]

Houses in Bantam are mostly built of wood and bamboo, roofed over with palm leaves. According to Lodewyckszoon, they stand on four, eight, or ten posts and are open underneath for cooling.[38] "Slight" buildings, Scott calls them. Still he reports good workmanship and fine carvings in the homes of wealthy or important people.[39] Lodewyckszoon reports that the homes of nobles have an outer court in which to receive visitors, also called a "pacebam" (*paseban*). The *paseban* usually contains a guard house, a water tank for bathing, and a small "mosque" for midday prayers. Slave quarters usually separate the *paseban* from the family living quarters. Wealthy families build square, brick, windowless storehouses with flat roofs, made of timbers, bricks, and sand to protect goods from Bantam's frequent fires.[40] The Chinese, who live in a distinct quarter on the city's west side, sometimes build such flat-roofed, brick houses in which to live.[41] Partitions in Javan houses are reportedly silk or cotton curtains, or latticed bamboo.[42]

Fires were apparently a constant threat in Bantam. Scott and his companions seem to have been so obsessed with the fear of fire that they hardly dared sleep at night.[43] Javan homes are inexpensive and easy to rebuild, however, and the frequent fires seem not to be personal or family disasters comparable to what they would be in Europe. Lodewyckszoon reports that new homes appear within a few days after a fire, and Frank van der Does claims that an entire house can be built for a cost of one piece-of-eight.[44]

Bantam is divided into four sections, each with a "nobleman" responsible for its protection during fires or war. In each quarter is a large drum for sounding alarms.[45] Wouter Schouten claims that these drums are eight feet across.[46] Fifty soldiers guard the sultan's court at night; nobles usually retain ten to twelve guards at their homes.[47] In addition to the royal palace most European visitors also mention the large mosque to the west of the palace, the residence of the "young king," and Bantam's three market places.

[36]Lodewyckszoon in Rouffaer and Ijzerman (eds.), *op. cit.* (n. 28), I, 106; *Verhael vande reyse* in *ibid.*, II, 24, 308.

[37]For examples, see Lodewyckszoon in *ibid.*, I, 104, or *BV*, Ia, 66.

[38]Rouffaer and Ijzerman (eds.), *op. cit.* (n. 28), I, 108.

[39]Foster (ed.), *op. cit.* (n. 33), p. 169.

[40]Rouffaer and Ijzerman (eds.), *op. cit.* (n. 28), I, 107-8. The storehouses are called *gedong* in Javanese, and *gudang* in Malay, from which the English term "godown" is derived.

[41]Scott in Foster (ed.), *op. cit.* (n. 33), pp. 169-70.

[42]Lodewyckszoon in Rouffaer and Ijzerman (eds.), *op. cit.* (n. 28), I, 108; *Verhael vande reyse* in *ibid.*, II, 24.

[43]For example, see Foster (ed.), *op. cit.* (n. 33), pp. 97-98.

[44]Lodewyckszoon in Rouffaer and Ijzerman (eds.), *op. cit.* (n. 28), I, 108; Van der Does in *ibid.*, II, 308.

[45]Lodewyckszoon in *ibid.*, I, 107.

[46]Wouter Schouten, *Reys-togten naar en door Oost-Indien* . . . (3d ed.; 3 vols. in 1; Amsterdam, 1740), III, 140.

[47]Lodewyckszoon in Rouffaer and Ijzerman (eds.), *op. cit.* (n. 28), I, 107.

Lodewyckszoon describes the markets and the products sold there in considerable detail.[48] It might be Java's premier city, but Van der Does thinks, considering its walls, fortifications, streets, buildings, and so on, that it cannot be compared to the least of Holland's towns.[49]

About Java's geography and landscape in general, the European accounts of the first half of the century say disappointingly little. Scott, for example, reports that while the land along the coast is low, frequently marshy, and its air unhealthy, most of Java's cities are located there. He names "Chiringin" (Cheribon), Bantam, Jakatra, and "Jortan or Greesey" (Gresik).[50] Few worthwhile crops other than pepper grow in the coastal lowlands. Inland are high mountains. Not so high, however, as to prevent people from climbing them. Much of the interior, Scott reports, is uninhabited. He locates Java at 9° south latitude and its center at 140° longitude. It is, he reports, 146 leagues from east to west and 90 leagues from north to south.[51]

The earliest visitors to Java occasionally included brief descriptions of other cities along its northern coast. Lodewyckszoon's many coastline sketches no doubt also gave his readers some sense of Java's coastal landscape. De Houtman's fleet visited Jakatra, which is described as a town of about three thousand houses, surrounded by a palisade, with a large and beautiful river running through it. The surrounding land, however, is low and poor, and there are many islands and bays in the area.[52] *Het tweede boeck,* the most popular report of the second Dutch voyage, describes Jakatra as the most beautiful city in Java.[53]

De Houtman's fleet also visited Tuban, a town situated on hilly land, with a broad beach, and high mountains behind it. It is very near three other cities: "Cidayo" (Sidayu), "Surbaya" (Surabaya), and "Joartam" (Gresik).[54] The discussion of Tuban in *Het tweede boeck* is much more substantial; it includes a long account of the king's palace, the separate buildings for his horses, dogs, elephants, women, and bedchamber. But it contains no real description of the city and its environs. The fanciful plates of the various buildings are of no help whatever.[55] The *Begin ende voortgangh* account of De Houtman's voyage contains an insert on Madura, which is described as a small island off the northeast corner of Java with very rich soil that produces an abundance of rice. Sandbars and shallows make it very difficult to approach with large ships, however.[56] Olivier van Noort's ship stopped at Jortan,

[48] *Ibid.,* I, 110–13.
[49] *Ibid.,* II, 308.
[50] Jortan or Jaratan was the harbor quarter of Gresik.
[51] Foster (ed.), *op. cit.* (n. 33), p. 168. Scott's figures are quite wide of the mark. Java lies between 105°12′ and 114°4′ east longitude and between 5°52′ and 8°40′ south latitude. It is between 575 and 622 miles long and from 48 to 121 miles wide.
[52] Lodewyckszoon in Rouffaer and Ijzerman (eds.), *op. cit.* (n. 28), I, 104; *BV,* Ia, 57.
[53] Keuning (ed.), *op. cit.* (n. 7), III, 35.
[54] Lodewyckszoon in *BV,* Ia, 58.
[55] Keuning (ed.), *op. cit.* (n. 7), III, 35–43; *BV,* Ia, 9–13. For the royal palace see our pl. 245.
[56] *BV,* Ia, 94.

which the published account of his voyage reports is built on a point of land, contains about one thousand houses, and has no wall.[57]

Lodewyckszoon's *D'eerste boeck* also contains brief descriptions of many north Javan towns, probably taken from an unpublished Portuguese work. It mentions "Ballambuan" (Balambangan), a "famous" walled city across the narrow strait from Bali; "Panarucan" (Panarukan), where many Portuguese live and which is shadowed by a large volcano (Raoen); and "Passaruan" (Pasuruan), six miles farther west, a strong, walled city, beautified by a fine river. "Joartan," ten more miles to the west, also on a beautiful river, has a fine harbor. West of the river is "Gerrici" (Gresik). Still farther west are "Surubaya" (Surabaya), on a "little river" (the sizable Kali Mas), "Brandaen" (?), and "Cidayo" (Sidayu), a strong, walled city recognizable from the sea because of the three long, low mountains behind it. Populous "Tubaon" (Tuban), ten miles farther west, lies on a large inlet. Still moving west, "Cajoano" (Jawana), also on an inlet, and "Mandalican" (Mandalika), with an islet in its bay, are fishing villages rather than seaports.[58] "Iapara" (Japara), however, five miles west of "Mandalika," is a powerful and busy seaport. Protected by a palisade, it is built on a point that stretches three miles out to sea, has a fine anchorage and a beautiful river nearby. Inland from Japara is Mataram, whose ruler is the most powerful on Java. Between Japara and "Charabaon" (Cheribon) stand "Pati" (Pati), "Dauma" (Demak), a strong, walled city, and "Taggal" (Tegal), all built on inlets near rivers. Cheribon is a fine city with a strong wall on a sweet river (the Ci Rebon or Shrimp River), recognizable at sea because of the two high mountains behind it. Between Cheribon and Jakatra, formerly called Sunda Kalapa, are "Dermayo" (Indramayu) and "Monucaon" (Pamanukan), both on rivers (the Ci Manuk or Bird River and the Ci Punagara), and "Cravaon" (Krawang), a large fishing village on a point where a river (the Ci Tarum) enters the sea through three mouths. Between Jakatra and Bantam, Lodewyckszoon lists a small village about a mile up the "Tonjonjava" River (Pangkalan Melayu on the Ci Sadane or Tanjung Untung Tonjonjava River), the "Punctan" River (Kali Pontang), also with a village about a mile upstream, and "Tanhura" (Tanara). Much pepper is grown in this region and its coastal waters are dotted with small islands.[59]

While the earliest descriptions are somewhat reticent about Java's landscape, Lodewyckszoon's *D'eerste boeck*, at least, is certainly thorough about the island's plants and animals. Four chapters are devoted to Javan plants and one to animals. These are also depicted in ten plates.[60] Among the animals

---

[57] Ijzerman (ed.), *op. cit.* (n. 8), I, 141.
[58] Contrary to what Lodewyckszoon implies, Surabaya is southeast of Gresik. The Mas is a major distributary of the Brantas, Java's second largest river. On "Cajoano" as Jawana see De Graaf, *op. cit.* (n. 1), p. 10.
[59] Rouffaer and Ijzerman (eds.), *op. cit.* (n. 28), I, 100–5.
[60] *Ibid.*, pp. 133–57.

on Java, Lodewyckszoon reports that elephants are used for labor and hired out by the day.[61] Javans told him that rhinoceroses are to be found on the island. He apparently had not seen one for himself; the plate in *D'eerste boeck* depicts a single-horned rhinoceros.[62] According to Lodewyckszoon, Java has many deer, wild oxen (probably buffalo), and wild pigs. Javans also raise cattle, buffaloes, sheep, and goats.[63] More exotic to Lodewyckszoon are the long-tailed monkeys and an animal he calls the weasel whose droll pranks he finds entertaining.[64] Of Java's birds he lists only peacocks, "parrots" (probably green parakeets), "sparrows" (by which he may have meant the *burung pipit,* which looks like a European sparrow), and a very large bird with a long neck, crooked beak, no tongue, very small or no wings, no tail, and long, thick, powerful feet. It will, he reports, swallow anything—eggs, apples, or tin, for example.[65] Javanese rivers teem with crocodiles, which are often hunted or even raised for food by the Chinese in Bantam.[66] Lodewyckszoon apparently has not eaten crocodile, although he was told that it was delicious. He has tried some of the many turtles and tortoises found on Java's coasts and thinks they taste very much like veal. The Chinese, he reports, buy tortoise shells and ship them to China. He also mentions civet cats on Java.[67] Finally Lodewyckszoon describes Javanese fighting cocks and how Javans tie lancets on their spurs and then let two such armed cocks fight to the death while onlookers lay bets on them.[68]

To Lodewyckszoon the most fascinating of Javanese plants is the areca palm and its fruit, which he describes in considerable detail. In Arabic, he reports, it is called "faufel," in Portuguese "arequero," and in Malay, "pinan" (*pinang*). It grows in many East Indian localities, including Java. Wherever it does not grow, it becomes an important article of trade. The areca nut looks like a date. When it first appears, the fruit is encased in a shell which falls off as it ripens, leaving the fruit hanging on a long thick branch. Everyone in the Indies chews areca nuts with white lime wrapped in a betel leaf. Betel leaves, writes Lodewyckszoon, grow on a vine like pepper or hops, and, like areca nuts, are offered for sale everywhere in Javanese towns. Wealthy people never go anywhere without servants to carry the ingredients for their quid. To offer betel to guests is an important part of Ja-

---

[61] *Ibid.,* p. 133. So far as we know, no one else reported that elephants were used for labor on Java.

[62] *Ibid.,* p. 134. It is an engraver's effort to copy the rhinoceros made so popular in Europe by Albrecht Dürer. For a Javan rhinoceros drawn from life see our pl. 273.

[63] *Ibid.*

[64] *Ibid.* Probably a red-brown echneumon or mongoose.

[65] *Ibid.,* and Lodewyckszoon's pl. 30. The last-described bird is probably the casuarius or Ceram emu. *Cf.* our pl. 276.

[66] *Ibid.,* pp. 134–35.

[67] *Ibid.,* p. 135.

[68] *Ibid.,* p. 136. See our pl. 260.

vanese courtesy. Also ubiquitous is the blood-red saliva which the chew produces.[69]

Lodewyckszoon also describes bamboo, used by Javans in place of wood for most building purposes. Mangoes, he reports, grow on spread-out trees with small leaves, similar to walnut trees. The yellow-green fruit with traces of red is somewhat crescent-shaped and hangs from a small twig. It is fibrous, with a rather large pit, and it tastes very good. Mangoes ripen in October, November, and December. Javans also pickle them with leeks and ginger and eat them the way Europeans eat olives. Lodewyckszoon thinks pickled mangoes are less bitter than olives.[70] He also describes pineapples in accurate detail. No finer fruit can be found, he asserts. Although they grow in abundance on Java, Lodewyckszoon realizes that the Portuguese introduced them to the archipelago from Brazil.[71]

Lodewyckszoon reports many tamarind trees in Java, large, spread-out trees with leaves shaped like those of the pimpernel which curl up and cover the fruit when the sun sets. Its blossoms are at first red, then white; its fruit when ripe is ash-gray turning towards red. Tamarind fruit is preserved in salt and shipped to Europe, where apothecaries use it in the treatment of fevers, constipation, and liver ailments. The "Assa" (Javanese, *asem;* Malay, *asam jawa*) tree, found in abundance on Madagascar, also grows on Java. The "excellent" fruit "Duriaon" (durian, *Durio zibethinus* Murr.; Malay, *durian;* Javanese, *duren*) grows on high trees like apples. It is about as large as a pineapple, and although its strong, unpleasant smell sometimes discourages the uninitiated, Lodewyckszoon reports that it is the best, healthiest, and tastiest fruit in the East. Later Dutch visitors call them stinkers (see pls. 272, 278). The "Lantor" (lontar, *Borassus flabellifer* L.) palm also grows on Java. Its long leaves are used like paper to write upon, and are bound together between two thin pieces of wood to make a book.[72] Lodewyckszoon also describes the "cubebe" (cubeb, *Piper cubeba* L.; Malay, *cuba chini;* Javanese, *kumukos*), in great demand by foreign traders; "Mangostans" (mangosteen, *Garcinia mangostana* L.; Malay, *manggistan;* Javanese, *manggis*), which he erroneously describes as growing like plums; the "Talasse" (Javanese, *tales;* Sundanese, *taleus*) plant which bears no fruit but is extensively used in Javanese cooking; and, of course, pepper.[73]

Lodewyckszoon provides shorter descriptions—but also illustrations—of what the Portuguese called "Iaca" (*Artocarpus intergrifolia* L.f.; Malay-Javanese-Sundanese, *nangka;* sometimes called "Jack Tree" in English); the

---

[69] *Ibid.,* pp. 136–38. On betel chewing see D. L. Umemoto, "The World's Most Civilized Chew," in the periodical *Asia,* VI (1983), pp. 25–27, 48. Also see our pl. 264.
[70] Rouffaer and Ijzerman (eds.), *op. cit.* (n. 28), I, 138–39. See our pl. 365.
[71] *Ibid.,* pp. 139–40.
[72] *Ibid.,* pp. 140–42.
[73] *Ibid.,* pp. 142–43.

salak, which grows primarily on Bali; the *Cassia fistula* L. (Javanese, *trengguli;* Malay, *tengguli*), which grows mainly in southwestern Sumatra and on the island of Krakatoa; wild cinnamon, which grows on Java but is not as good as that which comes from Ceylon; and delicious "carcapuli" (wild mangosteen; Malay, *manggis hutan*), which resembles cherries and is much in demand by the Chinese, as is "Calamus or diringuo" (*Acorus calamus* L.; Malay-Javanese, *deringu;* Javanese, *dringo;* Sundanese, *daringo;* popularly called rattan or canes). Long pepper or "chiabe" (*Capiscum annuum* L.; Javanese, *cabe*), actually chili pepper which the Spanish brought across the Pacific in the late sixteenth century, is abundant and cheap on Java and is often used instead of pepper by upper-class people in Bantam.[74]

"Zerumbet" or "canjor" (*Zingiber cassumunar* Roxb.; Javanese, *lempuyang* or *kaempferia rotunda* or *kaempferia galanga;* Malay, *kencur*), which Lodewyckszoon says is much like ginger but better, grows in west Java. "Galanga" or "lancuas" (*Alpinia galanga* Willd.; Malay, *langk(u) was* or *lengk(u) was;* Javanese, *lahwas* or *lahos*), similar to the lily, grows on Bali as well as on Java. He also mentions *Crocus indicus* or "curcuma" (turmeric), called *saffron da terrce* by the Portuguese, widely used in Javanese food; "fagara," a common drug which in fact does not grow on Java; the "caju lacca" (Malay, *kaju laka*), from which lacquer is made; large watermelons commonly called "batiec" (*Carica papaya* L.; Javanese-Malay, *kates;* Javanese, *katela;* Malay, *betik;* Portuguese, *pateca*), which may be another import from Spanish America; benzoin "mignan, or comignan" (Javanese, *menyan;* Malay, *kemennyan*), which grows on Java as well as several places on Sumatra; and camphor, which, he reports, comes from Brunei, Banjarmasin, and Lawai, on Borneo, most of which is shipped to China.[75] According to Lodewyckszoon both red and white sandalwood grows on Java (actually red sandalwood does not), but the more desirable white sandalwood, he reports, comes from Timor and Solor. Such white sandalwood as grows on Java lacks the distinctive aroma. Sandalwood on Timor and Solor, he reports, cannot be purchased with cash, but rather with Chinese beads and with "larins" (Persian, *lārīs*), small, double-bowed silver ingots from Lar in southern Persia.[76] The popular spice, ginger, grows abundantly on Java and so, according to Lodewyckszoon, does "anacardium" (*Semecarpus anacardium* L.).[77] "Podi" (Javanese, *podi*), Lodewyckszoon reports, is used against colds; cobra wood (Malay, *kayu ular*) is commonly used as an antidote for poisons. "Floers" or "caxumba" (*Carthamus tinctorius* L.; Malay-Javanese-Sundanese, *kasumba;* Javanese, *sombo*) is used both as a spice and as a dye for cotton cloth.[78]

---

[74] *Ibid.*, pp. 143–46.
[75] *Ibid.*, pp. 146–50.
[76] *Ibid.*, p. 150.
[77] *Ibid.*, p. 151. According to Rouffaer and Ijzerman anacardium (cashew) does not grow on Java.
[78] *Ibid.*, pp. 151–52.

Finally Lodewyckszoon lists a large number of drugs, herbs, and seeds, in most cases mentioning their origin and use: "Caju api" (Malay, *kayu api;* Javanese, *baku;* Sundanese, *katiga*) or fire wood, which Javans rub on their bodies; "Samparantaon" (*Sindora sumatrana* Miq.; Javanese, *saparantu;* Sundanese, *samparantu*), a root; "gato gamber" (Malay, *kacu;* Malay-Javanese, *gambir*), used to treat teeth; "ganti" (*Ligustrum glomeratum* Bl.; Malay, *ganti;* Javanese, *ganti*), a ginger-like root brought from China; "sabanah pute" (Malay, *sahang putih*) or white pepper, used in medicines; "sasani" (Sundanese, *sasawi;* Malay, *sesawi;* Javanese, *sawi;* black mustard), or "mustard seeds"; "doringi" (*Acorus calamus* L.; Malay-Javanese, *deringu;* Javanese, *dringo;* Sundanese, *daringo*), or the root of sweet flag used in a drink given to newborn babies; "galam" (*Eugenia michelii* Lam.; Malay, *gelam tikus*), a coolant which grows in the water; "tianco" (Malay, *cangkok*), taken with a drink if one feels ill; "madian maju corassani" (*Cannabis indica* Lam.; Malay, *mandian majuenun kurasani*) from Sumatra and used in drinks; "spodium," apparently an ash which is painted on the body, as is "sary" (*Mesua ferrua* L.; Javanese, *noge puspo* or *sara nogo*); "tagari" (*Dianella ensifolia* Red.; Javanese-Malay, *tegari;* Sundanese, *jamaka;* perhaps also *Dianella memorosa* Lam.) from Sumatra, used to wash the body; "surahan" (*Cedrela febrifuga* Bl.; Malay, *suriyan;* sometimes called red cedar); "sedowaya" (Javanese, *sidawayah*), also smeared on the body; "sambaja malays" or "geiduar" (*Curcuma zedoaria* Rosc.; Malay-Javanese, *temu-lawak*), imported from China and smeared on the body to counteract the venom of insect bites; "Ialave" (*Terminalia bellerica* Roxb.; Javanese, *joho*), which sick people use in their drinks; "paravas" (*Tetranthera brawas* Bl.; Malay, *daun perawas;* Javanese, *terawas*), a leaf used to alleviate fever; "tomon pute" (*Curcuma zerumbet* Roxb.; Malay-Javanese, *temu putih*), smeared on the body to alleviate fever; "queillor" (*Moringa pterygosperma* Gaertin.; Malay-Javanese-Sundanese, *kolor;* the ben-nut tree), whose fruit is used in Javanese food; "conduri" (*Abrus precatorius* L.), whose bean-like fruit is reputedly poisonous; and "aloes wood" (*Aquilaria malaccensis* Lam.; Malay, *kelembak;* Javanese-Sundanese-Balinese, *garu*), which is used to cure stomach disorders. Most of these are pictured in accompanying copperplates.[79] In his catalog of plants, Lodewyckszoon also lists several plants not native to the archipelago which came from India, southern Africa, or from islands in the Indian Ocean.

C. BATAVIA, THE METROPOLE AND ITS HINTERLAND

The most frequently described place in Java during the second half of the century is Batavia, the new VOC headquarters and town built after 1619 on

[79] *Ibid.*, pp. 152–57. Rouffaer and Ijzerman's notes are very good. They give Latin, Arabic, and Indian names when known; they refer to Orta occasionally.

the site of Jakatra or formerly Sunda Calapa. Several writers describe the siege of Jakatra in 1618–19 during which the Dutch garrison held out against the English and Bantamese until Governor-General Coen returned from the Moluccas with all the available Dutch warships to win the day. The victorious Dutch then destroyed most of the old town, including the English factory, and built a new castle and the new town of Batavia in its place. Van Rechteren arrived at Batavia in September, 1629, when the city and castle were being besieged, for a second time by a Javan army from Mataram. Coen died during this siege, just two days before Van Rechteren's arrival. Van Rechteren describes both the sieges of 1628–29 and that of a decade earlier.[80] A rehearsal of Batavia's origins and of the two sieges of 1628–29 became standard in most large descriptions of Batavia published during the second half of the century.[81]

Many visitors to Batavia report being impressed with their first glimpses of the town and castle, apparently a stunning sight from the sea (see pl. 17). Set against a background of dense forests and high mountains, its white coral walls gleam in the sunlight. Rows of coconut palms and mango and citrus trees line the walls and beautify even Batavia's bulwarks and gun emplacements.[82] At night the lantern atop the governor-general's residence is visible far out to sea.[83] Bolling describes two fortified islands in the bay, Onrust and Maron, from which flag signals or cannon shot alert the castle of approaching ships. VOC ships are also built and repaired on Onrust.[84] Taken altogether, says Frick, Batavia is "a man's sight . . . finer even than Amsterdam itself."[85]

The castle is on the east side of the harbor, its entrance to the north, its walls running to the water's edge. Not only is it beautiful, it is also large

---

[80]Van Rechteren, *loc. cit.* (n. 13), pp. 26–29.

[81]For example see Johann Jacob Saar, *Reise nach Java, Banda, Ceylon und Persien, 1644–1660,* NR, VI (The Hague, 1930), p. 31; Johann Jacob Merklein, *Reise nach Java, Vorder und Hinter Indien, China und Japan, 1644–1653,* NR, III (The Hague, 1930), pp. 14–16; Johann Nieuhof, *Gedenkwaerdige zee- en lant-reize door verscheide gewesten van Oost-Indien . . .* (Amsterdam, 1682), pp. 219–25; Johann Nieuhof, *Het gezantschap der Neerlandtsche Oost-Indische Compagnie, aan den grooten Tartarischen cham, den tegenwoordigen keizer van China . . .* (Amsterdam, 1665), pp. 28–30. On the founding of Batavia and the sieges also see J. S. Furnivall, *Netherlands India* (Cambridge, 1944), pp. 25–28; U. G. Lauts, *Geschiedenis van der veroveringen der Nederlanders in Indië* (2 vols., Kampen, n.d.), I, 45–50, 58–61; A. J. Eijkman and F. W. Stapel, *Leerboek der geschiedenis van Nederlandsch Oost-Indië* (Groningen, 1928), pp. 55–59, 66–68; H. Furber, *Rival Empires of Trade in the Orient, 1600–1800* (Minneapolis, 1976), pp. 43–45; C. R. Boxer, *The Dutch Seaborne Empire 1600–1800* (London, 1965), pp. 189–90. For an eyewitness account that was not published until the nineteenth century see P. A. Leupe (ed.), "Verhael van de belegeringhe der stadt Batavia in 't coninckrijck van Jaccatra, anno 1628, den 22 Augustij. (door en oogetuige)," *BTLV,* III (1855), 289–312.

[82]See especially Frederick Bolling, "Oost-Indisch reisboek, bevattende zijne reis naar Oost-Indië . . ." *BTLV,* LXVIII (1913), p. 330, and Christoph Frick and Christoph Schweitzer, *Voyages to the East Indies,* ed. C. Ernest Fayle (London, 1929), pp. 26–27.

[83]Nieuhof, *Zee- en lant-reize* (n. 81), p. 210.

[84]*Loc. cit.* (n. 82), p. 26.

[85]*Op. cit.* (n. 82), p. 26.

and strong. Most writers during the latter half of the century describe its fortifications and buildings. According to Van Rechteren, it is guarded by fifteen cannons and five or six companies of soldiers.[86] Saar thinks its portcullises and drawbridges resemble those of German castles. He describes each of its four bulwarks: the Pearl, the Diamond, the Ruby, and the Sapphire.[87] Bolling lists the number of soldiers stationed at each bulwark.[88]

Two main gates afford entrance to the castle; one, the Water Gate, faces the sea; another faces the city and is called the Land Gate or City Gate. Frick, who visited Batavia during the 1680's, mentions a recently built third gate, and De Graaf, writing later still, mentions four smaller gates in addition to the main gates.[89] Bolling, who wrote when there were only two gates, reports that each is guarded by one hundred soldiers.[90] A stone bridge of fourteen arches spans the moat separating the Land Gate from the city.[91]

Inside the castle are two great squares, on the larger of which stands the governor-general's residence, an impressive three-story brick structure whose high cupola affords a commanding view of the town and harbor. The governor-general's residence also houses the VOC auditor's offices, the secretariat, and the chambers in which the Council of the Indies meets. The councillors' residences stand nearby.[92] The castle houses many other high officials, among them the company's chief surgeon, the chief merchant, the chief of the armory, and the chief customs officer, as well as a great many bookkeepers, merchants, assistants, and craftsmen. Bolling estimates about 150 people.[93] The castle also contains many storehouses for VOC merchandise, foodstuffs, medical supplies, and military equipment. It is, in short, the political, economic, and military nerve center for the entire Dutch East India Company. Javans, according to Bolling, call the governor-general the "King of Jakatra." Indeed he lives like royalty, attended by elaborately uniformed guards, accompanied by processions whenever he leaves the castle, regularly reviewing his troops, and receiving Asian princes with great pomp and ceremony. Under the Diamond Point inside the castle stands a small, octagonal, stone church in which Dutch Reformed services are preached

---

[86] *Loc. cit.* (n. 13), p. 29.

[87] *Op. cit.* (n. 81), pp. 32–33.

[88] *Loc. cit.* (n. 82), p. 330.

[89] Frick and Schweitzer, *op. cit.* (n. 82), p. 27; J. C. M. Warnsinck (ed.), *Reisen van Nicolaus de Graaff gedaan naar alle gewesten des werelds beginnende 1639 tot 1687 incluis* ("WLV," XXXIII; The Hague, 1930), pp. 7–8.

[90] *Loc. cit.* (n. 82), p. 330.

[91] Warnsinck (ed.), *op. cit.* (n. 89), p. 7. Nieuhof, *Het gezantschap* (n. 81), pp. 28–29, has a fine copperplate depicting the castle, the town, and the connecting bridge. Frick reported twenty-one arches on the bridge: *op. cit.* (n. 82), p. 28.

[92] Bolling implies that the four ordinary councillors, one of whom is titled Director General, and the four extraordinary councillors all live inside the castle: *loc. cit.* (n. 82), p. 331; Frick reports that only two councillors live inside and that four live in the city: *op. cit.* (n. 82), p. 27. Nieuhof, *Zee- en lant-reize* (n. 81), pp. 208–9, provides a good sketch of the governor-general's residence.

[93] *Loc. cit.* (n. 82), p. 331.

twice each Sunday.[94] Across the stone bridge from the castle's Land Gate is a large field containing a gibbet, whipping post, and wheel, all frequently used. A small bridge on the other side of the field leads to a guarded gate and the city's main street.[95]

Like the castle, the city of Batavia is also encircled by a stone wall which in turn is ringed by a broad and deep canal. It has four gates and twenty-one bulwarks, all named after Dutch cities or provinces. One bulwark, Middlepunt, stands in the center of the city. Batavia's gates and bulwarks are guarded, according to Bolling, by four companies of soldiers, three hundred men to a company. All the gates, including the watergates where the river enters and leaves the city, are closed at 9:00 P.M. each night. The city is further protected by six small "castles" built about a quarter mile out from the wall on three sides of the city (see pl. 265). While the VOC uses many Asian soldiers in its military, only Europeans—mostly Germans—guard Batavia.[96]

Everyone describes Batavia as a beautiful city with broad streets meeting at right angles. The river which flows through the middle of the town from south to north provides water for Batavia's clear, deep canals (see pl. 263). Palm trees line the streets and canals; brick sidewalks flank the canals. It is a Dutch city in the tropics. Much of Batavia's architecture is Dutch: canal houses with beautiful enclosed gardens behind them, large stone and red-brick public buildings.

Both Nieuhof and De Graaf describe each major building in Batavia: the Kruiskerk or Cross Church, built of white coral in 1640, complete with bell tower and weather vane, inlaid ebony pulpit and pews; the three-story city hall with Corinthian columns at its entrance, standing in the middle of a spacious square; the hospital; the well-guarded, windowless Spinhuis, a correctional facility for wayward women. Batavia boasts a slaughterhouse, fish market, corn and rice market, poultry market, and fruit market, all built along the river so that the offal from these trades can easily be discarded in it, and a cloth market. Merchants—mostly Chinese—rent stalls or tables in these city-owned markets. Next to the Spinhuis stands the fine Chinese hospital and home for the aged, built in 1646, largely supported by contributions from the Chinese community and governed jointly by the Dutch and the Chinese. Batavia's orphanage is also maintained largely by private charity. Finally, both Nieuhof and De Graaf briefly mention the city stables, the Artisans' House, various city storehouses, and the Latin School. Nieu-

[94] This description of the castle is taken primarily from Bolling, *loc. cit.* (n. 82), pp. 330–32; Saar, *op. cit.* (n. 81), pp. 32–33; Frick and Schweitzer, *op. cit.* (n. 82), pp. 27–28; Nieuhof, *Zee-en lant-reize* (n. 81), pp. 209–12; and De Graaf in Warnsinck (ed.), *op. cit.* (n. 89), pp. 7–8.
[95] Frick and Schweitzer, *op. cit.* (n. 82), p. 24.
[96] For details about Batavia's fortifications and garrison see Bolling, *loc. cit.* (n. 82), pp. 332–34. Elias Hesse, *Gold-Bergwerke in Sumatra, 1680–1683* (NR, X; The Hague, 1931), p. 39, placed the extramural fortifications at about a half mile out from the city walls.

hof provides beautiful sketches of most of these buildings.[97] In addition to the Cross Church, where services are preached in Dutch, there is a Malay-language church and a church which holds services in Portuguese—all Reformed churches.[98] Bolling reports that there are all together four churches in the city and that they, in addition to the church in the castle, are served by eight preachers, two of whom are German, two English, two Dutch, and two French. There is no bishop or dean. One of the clergymen serves as rector, which office rotates among them. Bolling also lists the salaries paid to ministers by the VOC.[99]

Batavia is above all a commercial center. Almost all seventeenth-century visitors comment on the harbor choked with ships and boats and the streets lined with shops and restaurants. People from almost all Asian countries trade and live in Batavia. De Graaf, for example, lists Chinese, Malays, "Moors," Amboinese, Javans, Makassars, and "Mardykers," or Portuguese-speaking Indian Christians, in addition to Europeans.[100] Bolling's list is much longer. In addition to those mentioned by De Graaf he lists "Arowers" (Aru islanders), "Bancaneezen" (people from Bangka Island?), and people from Banda, Malabar India, Japan, Formosa, Siam, Manila, Persia, Ceylon, Borneo, Coromandel, Bengal, Syria, Greece, Turkey, and many other places. Europeans living in Batavia, according to Bolling, include Germans, Danes, Norwegians, Italians, "Babylonians," Maltese, Poles, Frenchmen, English, Scots, Irish, Spaniards, Portuguese, Swedes, and Dutch. In sum: "Here in Batavia live people from most nations in the whole world, except only Africans." Each practices his own religion, and each speaks his own language, although everyone can also understand Portuguese and Malay.[101]

Both Nieuhof and De Graaf describe Batavia's government as composed of six councils: the Council of the Indies, presided over by the governor-

---

[97] For a description of individual buildings see Nieuhof, *Zee- en lant-reize* (n. 81), pp. 196–208; Warnsinck (ed.), *op. cit.* (n. 89), pp. 1–8. For examples of Nieuhof's sketches see pls. 263–65.

[98] See Hesse, *op. cit.* (n. 96), p. 38; Bolling, *loc. cit.* (n. 82), pp. 333–34; Schouten, *op. cit.* (n. 46), III, 168.

[99] *Loc. cit.* (n. 82), pp. 334–35. See also Nieuhof, *Zee- en lant-reize* (n. 81), p. 219.

[100] Warnsinck (ed.), *op. cit.* (n. 89), pp. 9–11. On "Mardykers," or *mardijkers*, see Leonard Blussé, "The Caryatids of Batavia: Reproduction, Religion, and Acculturation under the V.O.C.," *Itinerario*, VII (1983), No. 1, pp. 57–85; Vlekke, *op. cit.* (n. 2), pp. 157n and 190; and J. G. Taylor, *The Social World of Batavia; European and Eurasian in Dutch Asia* (Madison, Wis., 1983), pp. 47–49. The word "Mardijker" is a Dutch rendition of *mardekar*, the Portugese version of *maharddika*, Sanskrit for "great man" or "high and mighty." In Dutch Insulindia it acquired the meaning of free(d) person. Mardijkers usually were emigrants from Malabar, Coromandel, Arakan, or Bengal, spoke Portuguese, and were baptized members of the Reformed Church.

[101] Bolling, *loc. cit.* (n. 82), p. 336. Legally only Dutch Reformed Christianity might be publicly or privately practiced in Batavia. In practice, however, Chinese and Muslims enjoyed freedom of religion. See Vlekke, *op. cit.* (n. 2), p. 150, and J. F. G. Brummund, "Bijdragen tot de geschiedenis der kerk te Batavia," *Tijdschrift voor Indische taal-, land-, en volkenkunde*, III (1864), 1–190.

general and wielding ultimate authority; the Council of Justice, whose chairman is usually a member of the Council of the Indies and which exercises general judicial, political, and fiscal authority over the town; the Council of Aldermen (Magistrates?), chosen from among the best citizens of Batavia and including two from the Chinese community; the Council of Hospitals and Orphanages, on which the Chinese are also represented; the Council of Minor Matters ("Kleine Saken"), chaired by a member of the Council of Justice; and a Council of Civil Defense. The appointed "captains" of the various peoples and their subordinates also have limited governmental authority, especially the "captain" of the Chinese. The VOC taxes all commerce coming in and going out of Batavia, sells licenses to merchants, collects poll taxes from the city's residents, and much more. Some of Batavia's seventeenth-century visitors list the taxes. Many also report that Batavian justice is harsh and give examples of commonly inflicted punishments.[102]

By far the most important and most numerous residents of Batavia are the Chinese. Van Rechteren, who visited Batavia in 1628, reports five or six thousand Chinese living in the city.[103] Everyone describes them as the most industrious of Batavia's residents, clever craftsmen, and involved in every sort of trade and commerce. Indeed, they dominate the city's commercial life. Most accounts of Batavia, therefore, include lengthy descriptions of the Chinese.[104]

The Chinese are distinct from other Batavians in their dress and appearance. They usually wear long blue coats, with sleeves so large that their hands are hidden, wide blue trousers, and broad soft slippers. In wet weather they wear wooden shoes. They are amazingly meticulous about

[102] Nieuhof, *Zee- en lant-reize* (n. 81), pp. 217–19; Warnsinck (ed.), *op. cit.* (n. 89), pp. 11–12. See also Merklein, *op. cit.* (n. 81), pp. 18–19; Van Rechteren, *loc. cit.* (n. 13), p. 29; Johann von der Behr, *Reise nach Java, Vorder-Indien, Persien und Ceylon, 1641–1650* (NR, IV; The Hague, 1930), p. 43; François l'Estra, *Relation ou journal d'un voyage fait aux Indes Orientales . . .* (Paris, 1677), pp. 230–32. For a selection of documents many of which deal with the early history of Batavia see J. A. van der Chijs (ed.), *Nederlandsche-Indisch plakaatboek* (Batavia, 1885), and J. K. J. de Jonge and M. L. van Deventer (eds.), *De opkomst van het Nederlandsch gezag in Oost-Indië* (20 vols.; Amsterdam and The Hague, 1862–95). See Taylor, *op. cit.* (n. 100), p. 10, for a brief sketch of the burger in Batavia's government. See also Boxer, *op. cit.* (n. 81), pp. 206–41.

[103] *Loc. cit.* (n. 13), p. 29. Vlekke, *op. cit.* (n. 2), p. 155, reports that in its first ten years (1619–29) Batavia's Chinese population grew from eight hundred to two thousand. See also Anthony Reid, "The Structure of Cities in Southeast Asia, Fifteenth to Seventeenth Centuries," *Journal of Southeast Asian Studies*, Vol. XI, No. 2 (Sept., 1980), 235–50.

[104] L. Blussé, "Batavia, 1619–1740. The Rise and Fall of a Chinese Colonial Town," *Journal of Southeast Asian Studies*, Vol. XII, No. 1 (Mar., 1981), 159–78, contends that Batavia was essentially an overseas Chinese town and that the VOC gave the Chinese a favored position in the city and encouraged their settlement there. Even the success of Batavia's often-praised public institutions—the orphanages, hospitals, public markets, etc.—resulted primarily from their congruity with Chinese practices. On the role of the Chinese in Batavia's government and their relationship to the VOC see B. Hoetink, "So Bing Bong: Het eerste hoofd der Chineezen te Batavia, 1619–1636," *BTLV*, LXXIII (1917), 311–43, and "Chineesche officieren te Batavia onder de compagnie," *ibid.*, LXXVIII (1922), 1–136. See also Victor Purcell, *The Chinese in Southeast Asia* (London, 1965), pp. 383–403.

their hair, which they wear very long, without the queue, even after the Manchu Conquest. Most Chinese go to a barber once a week to have their hair trimmed, washed, and plaited into a coil made fast on the back of the head with a bodkin. Over it all they wear a net made of black horsehair. Europeans profess difficulty distinguishing young men from women. Older men usually wear long thin beards. Everyone characterizes the Batavian Chinese as inveterate, indeed reckless, gamblers, often staking their homes, businesses, wives, and children. Only in the last extremity, however, will they wager their hair. "If one loses that he loses with it all his Credit and Reputation, and is lookt upon as a Slave, and is forced all his life long to work and sell for other People." [105]

The women in the Chinese community are mostly slaves from Bali or Makassar. It is exceedingly rare to see a Chinese woman. Men take as many wives as they wish. When a man dies, his wives are usually sold to others except in the rare instance that he stipulates in his will that a favorite wife be freed. Pyrard reports that Batavian Chinese also sell their women when they return to China but that they take their children with them. [106] Daughters are as rare as mainland Chinese women in Batavia's Chinese community. Many seventeenth-century writers contend that females are usually killed at birth.

Nevertheless, weddings are celebrated with much festivity by Batavian Chinese. The young couple parades through the streets accompanied by friends and relatives, carrying their gifts and most prized possessions. Sometimes wedding celebrations take place in boats on the canals or on ships in the harbor. In either case, they are accompanied by music, flowers, plays, feasting, and drinking. All European writers marvel at how skillful the Chinese are with their chopsticks.

Saar describes some Batavian Chinese medical cures, among them bleeding, which he says Chinese physicians do by half-choking the patient, tilting his head downwards, and lancing his forehead. [107] The Batavian Chinese wash their dead, wrap them in white cloth, and lay them in coffins together with money and other things thought to be of use in the next world. The coffin, accompanied by a procession of mourners, is then carried to the Chinese cemetery outside the city. Saar reports that the coffin bearers wear black. [108] Bolling describes the role of the priest at a funeral and speculates that the priests return to the grave after the funeral to retrieve the money

[105] Frick and Schweitzer, *op. cit.* (n. 82), p. 29.
[106] Gray (ed.), *op. cit.* (n. 32), II, 163. See Anthony Reid (ed.), *Slavery, Bondage and Dependency in Southeast Asia* (New York, 1983), pp. 26–27, on this practice. See also Reid, *op. cit.* (n. 2), pp. 154–56.
[107] *Op. cit.* (n. 81), p. 42. John Crawfurd, *History of the Indian Archipelago* (3 vols.; Edinburgh, 1820), I, 32, says Javans occasionally employed topical bloodletting, although never general bloodletting.
[108] *Op. cit.* (n. 81), p. 43. White is the usual color of mourning in China, but plainness of color is the most important consideration. In south China blue was often used in mourning clothes. See J. D. Ball, *Things Chinese* (5th ed.; London, 1926), pp. 403–4.

from the coffin.[109] Pyrard, however, contends that the Batavian Chinese never bury their dead, but that they embalm them and carry their bodies back to China for burial.[110]

Most European writers report that the Chinese in Batavia worship the devil, whom they call "Joosje."[111] Chinese keep images in their houses and also in a temple just outside one of the city gates. Frick's description of such a household "idol" and its worship is typical.

> In a corner of the Room they have an Altar set out with abundance of pretty little Trinkets, upon which is an Image made of Clay, about a span long. The face of it is very broad, with a large pair of Eyes; it is black, and painted with some round streeks of Red; a vast large Nose, and a long white Beard: On the head stand two Horns painted with all sorts of Colours. This Image they call Josgin; to this they bow, and make many salutations; clapping their hands altogether, begging it to keep them from all harms, and to take care that no evil may happen to them.
>
> They own that there is a powerful God, that hath made the Heavens and the Earth: But they say, that he is of a good nature and disposition, and that there is no fear of harm from him: But that all their fear is from the Devil, whom they appease by their Offerings and Prayers under the shape of that Image: Therefore they are very careful to please him, and will not fail at night to light Candles made of red or yellow Wax, which they set before it: And there they bring Meat and Drink, and all sorts of Fruit, which is all taken away the next day, and then it is eaten by the People of the house, and other fresh Meat is set in the room of it.[112]

Bolling describes a service in the Chinese temple: three altars inside, each with a gold image of "Satan," three priests wearing red mantles with little bells on their fringes, bell-ringers carrying bells behind the priests. Twelve large candles burn before the altars. The service begins with the ringing of bells and the people bowing their heads to the floor, repeating "Buizand Buizand Skielo . . . Eere zij God! [glory to God!]" The bell-ringers lay a dead goat with a grapefruit in its mouth on the altar as well as a variety of fruit. Then the priests begin to read the "mass," each word slowly, the end of each sentence accompanied by the ringing of bells and the "congregation" bowing. The service lasts more than an hour.[113] Bolling also describes a feast called "Weang" (?), held in "Josie's" honor at each full moon, and he describes Chinese New Year festivities which last eight days each March.[114]

---

[109] *Loc. cit.* (n. 82), pp. 346–47.

[110] Gray (ed.), *op. cit.* (n. 32), II, 163.

[111] *Jossie, Jossje,* or *Joosje* is apparently a corruption of the Portuguese *Deos.* The Dutch, however, thought they were using a genuine Chinese term. See H. Yule and A. C. Burnell, *Hobson-Jobson; Being a Glossary of Anglo-Indian Colloquial Words, Phrases, and Kindred Terms; . . .* (London, 1886), p. 353. The images described by the Dutch could have been any of a number of Chinese popular deities; see below, pp. 1648–51.

[112] Frick and Schweitzer, *op. cit.* (n. 82), p. 30 (*cf.* pl. 253).

[113] Bolling, *loc. cit.* (n. 82), pp. 344–45. On the *de facto* freedom of religion for the Chinese in Batavia see Brummund, *loc. cit.* (n. 101), pp. 69–71.

[114] *Loc. cit.* (n. 82), pp. 345–46.

De Graaf describes a "Wayang" (puppet theater) festival in Japara, where there was also a sizable Chinese community.[115] The suburbs which grew up outside Batavia's walls are populated mostly by Chinese. Also outside the city are beautiful gardens and parks, pleasure houses, and pleasant footpaths for all to stroll along.[116]

Between Nikolaas de Graaf's first visit to Batavia in 1640 and his last in 1687 there had evolved alongside Batavia's many races a new tribe which Frederick de Haan later called *Homo Bataviensis*—the free citizen of Batavia. These were Dutchmen and other Europeans who stayed on in Batavia after their terms of service with the VOC were completed, the Asian or Eurasian women they married, and their children. De Graaf describes them in a chapter entitled "The Rich and Excessive Lifestyle of the Hollanders in India, and Chiefly that of the Women."[117] He pictures them traveling through the streets in expensive horse-drawn coaches with slaves following behind. The women he describes as "so splendid, so haughty, so sensual and extravagant that they from voluptuousness scarcely know how to carry themselves." They are waited upon day and night, never lifting a finger for themselves, but cruelly abusing their servants should they spy even a piece of straw on the floor.[118] Too lazy to raise their own children they entrust them to slaves almost from the moment of birth. The children consequently grow up speaking the language of the slaves and can scarcely pronounce a Dutch word correctly much less construct a Dutch sentence.[119] Malay and a pidgin Portuguese, not Dutch, thus have become Batavia's dominant languages. The children of Batavia's free citizens grow up in idleness, spending their days chewing betel, smoking, drinking tea, or simply lying on a mat. Their conversation is only about slaves and food. They eat Javan food, with their fingers, scarcely knowing how to use European cutlery. De Graaf thinks they eat like pigs.[120] On rare occasions when they join a Dutch dinner party they behave awkwardly, knowing neither how to talk nor eat. De Graaf considers the women ugly (primarily, it seems, because of their dark skin), immoral, and unfaithful to their husbands; they are little more than whores.

---

[115] Warnsinck (ed.), *op. cit.* (n. 89), pp. 205–6. De Graaf must be referring to the *wajang kulit,* or Javanese puppet theater. The above description of Batavia's Chinese community comes primarily from Van Rechteren, *loc. cit.* (n. 13), pp. 29–30; Saar, *op. cit.* (n. 81), pp. 37–43; Schouten, *op. cit.* (n. 46), I, 21–27; L'Estra, *op. cit.* (n. 102), pp. 224–30; Frick and Schweitzer, *op. cit.* (n. 82), pp. 28–30; Bolling, *loc. cit.* (n. 82), pp. 343–47.

[116] See Merklein, *op. cit.* (n. 81), p. 19; Hesse, *op. cit.* (n. 96), p. 39; L'Estra, *op. cit.* (n. 102), p. 219; Schouten, *op. cit.* (n. 46), III, 169. For modern descriptions of seventeenth-century Batavia see Boxer, *op. cit.* (n. 81), pp. 206–14; Vlekke, *op. cit.* (n. 2), pp. 153–58, 185–99; and F. de Haan, *Oude Batavia* (Bandoeng, 1935).

[117] De Graaf, *Oost-Indise spiegel,* in Warnsinck (ed.), *op. cit.* (n. 89), separate pagination, pp. 13–22.

[118] *Ibid.,* pp. 13–14.

[119] *Ibid.,* pp. 14–15.

[120] *Ibid.,* p. 15.

Dutchmen who stay in Batavia and marry these Eurasian women, he thinks, can really never return to their families back home.[121]

Nowhere is Batavian conspicuous consumption so obvious and offensive as in church on Sunday. Women are overdressed in the most expensive clothes, laden with gold and jeweled chains, earrings, and broaches. Families parade to church attended by slaves holding their parasols and carrying their psalm books and betel boxes. During services the square outside the church is filled with slaves waiting for their masters and mistresses. De Graaf contrasts all this pretension with the modest place such people would occupy back in Holland.[122] He also complains about the general corruption of VOC employees in Batavia and elsewhere in Asia. He describes the large and growing illegal private trade carried on by VOC employees on Company ships, all to the serious disadvantage of the Company and made possible only by widespread bribery.[123]

The literature published during the last half of the century occasionally includes descriptions of other towns on Java's north coast. De Graaf, for example, describes Japara, and Bolling both Japara and Bantam. Van Goens includes a still larger account of Japara, emphasizing its defenses. Schouten briefly mentions each town from Balambangan to Bantam as Lodewycks-zoon had done earlier in the century.[124] None of these descriptions adds much to what was reported earlier.

Most Europeans report that Java's south coast was unknown and largely uninhabited. Schouten, however, relates the experiences of four Dutch sailors who, abandoned while searching for survivors of a shipwreck (the "Drake") on the Australian coast, sailed in an open boat to the south coast of Java and from there, accompanied by native guides, walked overland to Japara.[125] As Schouten describes it, the forest grows to the water's edge. Cliffs and caves on the shore, reefs and shoals off shore, make it very difficult to find a safe landing place even for a small boat. Visible inland are high mountains whose peaks protrude above the clouds. The four sailors walked very far along the shore before finding any sign of human life; the first person they met was a solitary hermit who survived by fishing. They stayed with

[121] *Ibid.*, pp. 16–17.
[122] *Ibid.*, pp. 18–20.
[123] *Ibid.*, pp. 22–48. Also see Hesse, *op. cit.* (n. 96), pp. 109–14 on the lifestyle of Batavian free citizens. De Graaf's picture of life among Batavia's free citizens is uncharacteristically negative and tinged with racial prejudice. Nevertheless it is not inconsistent with modern reconstructions of the seventeenth-century Batavian milieu. See, for example, Taylor, *op. cit.* (n. 100); Haan, *op. cit.* (n. 116); Boxer, *op. cit.* (n. 81), pp. 206–14; Crawfurd, *op. cit.* (n. 107), I, 139–49; and Blussé, *loc. cit.* (n. 100).
[124] Warnsinck (ed.), *op. cit.* (n. 89), pp. 204–5; Bolling, *loc. cit.* (n. 82), pp. 327–29; Rijckloff van Goens, "Reijsbeschrijving van het weg uit Samarangh, nae de konincklijke hoofplaets Mataram . . . ," ed. P. A. Leupe, *BTLV*, IV (1856), pp. 345–46; Schouten, *op. cit.* (n. 46), III, 134–39.
[125] Schouten, *op. cit.* (n. 46), I, 27–35.

the hermit for some days before they met the men who guided them across the island to Japara. Schouten's description, however, is not an eyewitness account and says relatively little about the landscape.

Two firsthand descriptions of Java's interior appeared during the second half of the century, one a brief account by Albrecht Herport, the other a more substantial account by Rijcklof van Goens. Herport was one of twelve soldiers, four sailors, and four Javans assigned to accompany a VOC ambassador whose task was to investigate a group of Javans who had recently settled to the south of Batavia. His account of the expedition's troubles conveys vivid impressions of Java's interior landscape. The expedition leaves Batavia traveling east in two boats. When they come to the mouth of the river "Megassi" (Bekasi) they travel upstream. Progress is slow. The riverbanks are underwater and it is difficult to find the mainstream. It rains continuously, and they are plagued with mosquitoes, especially at dusk. "There were so many, that we could not sufficiently defend ourselves against them; therefore we had to get drunk from arrack, which we had with us, so that we could forget the pain." [126] In the morning their faces, hands, and feet are swollen and bloody. Nothing but smoke and fire would drive the bugs away. Fires are the only effective nighttime protection against tigers as well, but they are exceedingly difficult to kindle, because there is no dry wood. One night they bed down on what appeared to be an island where they think they will be safer. During the night, however, their island begins to break apart and float downstream. The men scramble into the boats and make for shore. On another night they sleep sitting up around a fire while two men keep watch. One of the guards is attacked by a tiger. He later dies. As they inch upstream they regularly see tigers and rhinos on the banks and crocodiles in the water. Finally the current becomes too swift. The soldiers stand waist deep in the water and try to push the boats forward, but the sand and saltpeter in the swift current quickly wear their skin raw.

Sending two men to take the boats back downstream the rest of the party continues on foot. The rain also continues. Their provisions run low and get very wet. Some have to be thrown away. They fight their way through the thick rattan forest, thorns shredding their clothes and skin. They talk about turning back. Finally on the eighth day away from Batavia they spy a man at a distance. Following him they eventually see smoke, then discover a footpath which leads them to cleared land and a Javanese encampment. They have reached their destination. The Javans, who came from Mataram about a year earlier, have already built one hundred houses and are raising rice and sugarcane. When the Dutch envoy asks them if they wish to become subjects of the VOC they quickly agree. After feeding the Europeans and dry-

---

[126] Albrecht Herport, *Reise nach Java, Formosa, Vorder-Indien und Ceylon, 1659–1668* . . . (NR, Vol. V; The Hague, 1930), p. 89.

ing them out for a few days, a Javan guides them back to Batavia. The return trip takes only two days. They all become "deathly sick" after their return, Herport thinks because of the continuous rains and unhealthy air.[127]

Rijcklof van Goens' account of the route from Batavia to Mataram and of the Susuhunan's court contains even more vivid descriptions of the central Javanese landscape. The overland journey begins at "Samarangh" (Samarang), a seaport fifty-three to fifty-four miles east of Batavia and seven miles west of Japara. Semarang is unwalled, with twenty to twenty-five thousand households who make their living from fishing, woodcutting, farming, and a variety of other occupations. In Semarang the Dutch ambassadors are met by representatives of the Susuhunan and are conducted to the court with considerable pomp.[128]

The first day's journey south of Semarang covers about six miles through the foothills, past eight or ten villages of between sixty and one hundred households each, to the village of "Ongaran" (Ungaran). Ungaran contains about three hundred or four hundred households and is obliged to house and feed official travelers to the Susuhunan's court. It is situated at the foot of a beautiful mountain of the same name which, although so high that its peak frequently pierces the clouds, is cultivated almost to its summit with black sugar and fruit trees. Van Goens observes, "here the island begins to appear as a marvel and ornament of nature, with beautiful and splendid rice fields, the same with all sorts of fruits and berries, such that it cannot be too pleasantly depicted."[129] The six miles from Ungaran to the villages of "Chiandi" (?) and Salatiga takes them over higher terrain between the mountains through a two-and-one-half- to three-mile-wide valley. Rice fields cover its floor. Many small streams flow through it from the mountains to the river Demak (Tuntang). Villages become more numerous. The embassy sometimes passes three or four in an hour's time. They also pass through "unbelievable" *Jati* or teak forests with trees so large that three- to three-and-one-half-foot planks can be sawed from them.[130] Between Salatiga and "Selimbij" (Selimbi), on the third day's travel, the road crosses the river at the upper end of the valley over a massive bridge three hundred paces long, each plank of which is a beam ten or twelve inches square; strong enough, Van Goens thought, to march thousands of elephants and heavy cannon across.

Selimbi is the "first gate . . . of the province of Mataram," heavily fortified, with a guard that is changed with each new moon. Inside the gate is a large village of about one thousand or fifteen hundred households. No one is permitted to pass through the gate toward Semarang without a written permit from the sultan. Beyond Selimbi the road leads through a moun-

[127] *Ibid.*, pp. 89–94.
[128] Van Goens, *loc. cit.* (n. 124), p. 307.
[129] *Ibid.*, pp. 307–8.
[130] *Ibid.*, p. 308.

tainous forest for about a mile or a mile and one-half, after which the land opens up to reveal a large cultivated valley: Van Goens describes it as "the entrance to an earthly paradise." Paddies stretch as far as the eye can see, watered by many mountain streams and dotted by countless villages within a cannonshot of each other. Van Goens climbs part way up Mt. "Marbuou" (Merbabu) to see the view. Fatigue prevents him from reaching the top, but from where he stops he can survey the entire interior valley and see the ocean both to the north and the south. His ascent took him through at least a dozen hamlets of from fifteen to sixteen households. Up the road from Merbabu stands a second gate, "Tadie" (Taji), also well guarded, which admits travelers to the mountain-ringed central plain of Mataram. Lush rice fields crossed by clear rivers greet the eye. The foothills and even the faces of the encircling mountains are terraced for rice cultivation and orchards. Villages are everywhere; Van Goens estimates more than three thousand of them, varying in size from one hundred to fifteen hundred households. He traces the mountain ranges and names the peaks. Among them is "Belivangh" (?), Java's highest, visible for thirty-six miles out to sea. While the trail from Semarang to Mataram is about thirty miles long and that to the south coast another thirty-four miles, Java at this point is only about twenty miles wide.[131]

The toll gates of Mataram at Selimbi and Taji are made of wood and built into the steep mountainsides which function as walls. Van Goens thinks it unlikely that anyone could bypass the gates. Beyond Taji on the road that leads to the city of Mataram and the royal palace stand two more well-guarded gates. The city is surrounded by a very old stone wall two miles long, eighteen to twenty feet high, and eight to twelve feet thick. Breached in many places, it is an impressive ruin but no longer useful for the defense of the city. The royal castle, or *kraton*, is large, in a pleasant setting, with a large square before it and enormous enclosures behind it in which are kept all sorts of wild animals for the Susuhunan's hunts.[132] Van Goens mentions two other routes to Mataram: one approaching from the west and the seaport "Tagal" (Tegal), the other from the east originating in Balambangan with a spur from Gresik.[133] Wouter Schuten's description of Mataram obviously derives from Van Goens'. It contains no new information.[134]

Most descriptions of Java published during the last half of the seventeenth century contain some information about fauna and flora. Those of Bontius, Wouter Schouten, and Nieuhof are by far the most detailed.[135] Of animals, Schouten mentions oxen, cows, sheep, goats, horses, tame and wild buffaloes, tame and wild pigs, tigers, crocodiles, rhinoceroses, and snakes. He

[131] *Ibid.*, pp. 308–11.
[132] *Ibid.*, pp. 311–14.
[133] *Ibid.*, p. 348.
[134] *Op. cit.* (n. 46), III, 137–39.
[135] *Ibid.*, III, 161–67; Nieuhof, *Zee- en lant-reize* (n. 81), pp. 226–97; Bontius, *op. cit.* (n. 16).

notes that Javans raise chickens both for food and for cockfighting, to which they are much addicted.[136] He describes the casuarius or emu in much the same words as had Lodewyckszoon. The chameleon, Schouten observes, is reputed to change its color to conform to its immediate surroundings and is believed to live on air, requiring no food. Schouten was unable to verify the reports about the chameleon's diet, but after several experiments found it unable to change its color. He speculates that the reports probably resulted from seasonal changes. Bontius simply says the notion that chameleons live on air is false.[137] Everywhere, even in houses and occasionally running across your face as you sleep, are the harmless "egdissen," or as Bolling calls them, "hakedis" (Dutch, *hagedis,* lizard). Bolling contends that the frog-like *hagedis* actually guard sleeping humans from snakes, lizards, and scorpions by awakening them when in danger.[138] Much more troublesome are what Schouten calls cockroaches and the Portuguese call *barattes* (bookworms), but which he describes as a reddish flying insect which does much damage to books, paper, clothing, and food supplies. According to Schouten they smell bad if touched and even bite people. Older ships are usually infested with them.[139] Ships also carry poisonous centipedes or millipedes, some six or seven inches long, whose sting causes considerable pain.[140] Poisonous scorpions also abound on Java. Schouten says they crawl into cases and chests, even into books. He also saw many large poisonous spiders. Finally he briefly describes fireflies.[141] Bolling describes a salamander which the Javans call "jeccho" (gecko, a harmless lizard) in imitation of its call, whose urine is so poisonous that contact with it permanently ruins one's health.[142] Bontius mentions chickens, waterfowl, goats, buffaloes, deer, and pigs as providing the best meat on Java. Unlike European ducks and geese, Javan waterfowl live in rivers rather than lakes and marshes, which makes their flesh more wholesome.[143] His descriptions of rhinoceroses and tigers, both of which he apparently saw on Java, are particularly perceptive. The rhinoceros is about the same size as an elephant, but with shorter legs. Its skin is very rough and thick, with deep folds on the sides and back which have led some Europeans to think it was armor-clad. It is harmless unless provoked, eats herbs and twigs rather than flesh. If provoked it will kill, however, tossing a horse and rider up into the air as if they were flies and sometimes killing adversaries by licking the flesh off their bones with its rough tongue.[144] The tiger, on the other hand, is a very dangerous beast.

[136] Schouten, *op. cit.* (n. 46), III, 161–62. Bolling, *loc. cit.* (n. 82), p. 329, however, said there were no sheep on Java.

[137] Schouten, *op. cit.* (n. 46), III, 162; Bontius, *op. cit.* (n. 16), p. 65.

[138] Schouten, *op. cit.* (n. 46), III, 162–63; Bolling, *loc. cit.* (n. 82), p. 327.

[139] Schouten, *op. cit.* (n. 46), III, 163.

[140] *Ibid.*

[141] *Ibid.,* pp. 163–64.

[142] *Loc. cit.* (n. 82), p. 327. Bontius also described the gecko; see our pl. 269.

[143] Bontius, *op. cit.* (n. 16), pp. 65–67.

[144] *Ibid.,* p. 11. See our pl. 273 for Bontius' illustration of the rhinoceros.

Not because it is fast; most wild animals can outrun it. Tigers always attack their prey from ambush, rarely giving chase if they miss catching it on the first leap. For this reason they frequently prey on humans, who are not fast enough to escape. Tigers are exceedingly strong. They usually kill their prey with a single stroke, and a tiger can easily drag a buffalo three times as large as itself into the woods. Bontius describes a symbiosis or "friendship" between the tiger and the rhinoceros. The two frequently live near each other. Javans told him that tigers, regularly gorging themselves on flesh, frequently suffer stomach discomfort and use rhinoceros dung as a remedy. Bontius, however, reports having seen a young rhinoceros killed and eaten by a tiger. Bontius judges tigers to be members of the cat family, and he reports that they drink the blood of their prey before eating it.[145]

Bontius' description of the Ceram emu or "Casuary" is impressively precise. It walks erect, is about five feet tall and three feet from breast to tail. Its bald black-blue head is small in proportion to its body; its eyes are "large, shiny, and malicious." Two holes in the bill serve as nostrils and a yellow-brown ornament runs from the nostrils to the crown of the head. This ornament falls off when the emu sheds its feathers and grows back again like the feathers. The feathers are red and black. On the front of its neck are two red lobes similar to those of a turkey. It has long thick legs, covered with hard scales, and short toes without spurs. Its feet are not forked like those of the ostrich, but like the ostrich, the emu cannot fly. It eats anything thrown at it, simply passing later what is indigestible.[146]

Bontius also describes a "wood-pecker" or "Indian starling" which can imitate the human voice more accurately than a parrot; edible birds' nests, gathered by the Chinese, which are made from a soft substance originating from the sperm of whales and other fish; a kind of Indian codfish; flying fish with wings like bats; and the orangutan, which he claims to have seen cry, sigh, and display other human emotions. Javans told him that orangutans could speak if they wished, but chose not to for fear of being put to work. Bontius thinks this ridiculous, but he reports without comment that Javans believe orangutans are the progeny of apes and native women.[147]

Nieuhof's account contains many fine copperplate illustrations as well as written descriptions of Javan animals, birds, and insects.[148] Most Europeans were fascinated with crocodiles. Merklein, for example, reports crocodiles sixteen to eighteen feet long with skin so hard no gun can pierce it. The governor-general, he reports, offers a reward for dead crocodiles.[149] Merklein also describes Java's enormous snakes. He claims to have seen one swallow a woman; another which had swallowed a pig.[150] Herport reports

[145] *Ibid.,* pp. 217–19.
[146] *Ibid.,* p. 257. See our pl. 276.
[147] *Ibid.,* pp. 67, 249, 271, and 285. See our pl. 277.
[148] Nieuhof, *Zee- en lant-reize* (n. 81), pp. 265–97.
[149] *Op. cit.* (n. 81), p. 13.
[150] *Ibid.*

seeing orangutans, flying monkeys, flying rats and mice, "papaguyen" (parrots or parakeets), and the "year bird," which grows a new mark on its beak each year.[151] Schouten, Nieuhof, and Bontius describe a large number of Javanese plants as well. Schouten's descriptions of the various peppers, pineapples, coconuts, and bananas (whose leaves he thought must have been Adam and Eve's first clothing) are particularly vivid.[152] Nieuhof's catalog of plants is exhaustive, but it includes very few species not already described by Lodewyckszoon earlier in the century, and it includes many species not native to Java. It does contain, however, fine copperplate illustrations of most of the plants described.[153] Most of the plants included in Bontius' book had been described by Lodewyckszoon as well, although in many cases Bontius' description is superior. For example, he describes the *Crocus indicus* (turmeric) as having a red flower and a yellow root from which Javans prepare an ointment with which they rub the entire body to protect themselves against fevers, sunburn, and mosquito bites.[154] The benzoin tree is composed of a cluster of thick suckers. Because other plants often grow in the benzoin cluster, some observers have supposed that the benzoin tree produces several kinds of leaves.[155] Durians smell like rotten garlic but are among the most wholesome and medically useful fruits. Eating too many of them, however, heats up the liver and blood and causes facial eczema. The "jacca" (jackfruit) Bontius thinks is unhealthy and difficult to eat. A similar fruit called "champidaca" (Malay, *champĕdak,* another variety of jackfruit) tastes better and is more wholesome. Javans use the burnt ash of its rind instead of lye in washing clothes. Papayas he describes as melons growing on trees.[156] Bontius' account of pinang and betel leaves concentrates on the effects of chewing the mixture. The red juice, most of which is swallowed, eventually blackens the teeth. Frequent use causes the teeth to crumble and fall out. Most Malays, therefore, are missing teeth and some as young as twenty-five years old are already toothless. Chewing an unripened pinang nut causes dizzyness, and betel chewing is not good for nervous people. Still Bontius prefers chewing betel to smoking tobacco.[157]

Bontius never saw growing tea bushes. He studied the dried leaves, apparently talked with Chinese in Batavia, and relied on Governor-General

---

[151] *Op. cit.* (n. 126), p. 31. According to Herport's editor the orangutan is not native to Java. It is native to Sumatra and Borneo. The name of the man-ape was confusedly derived by Europeans from the Malay *orang utan,* a term applied to wild tribes of humans. See Yule and Burnell, *op. cit.* (n. 111), pp. 643–44. Bontius also describes an orangutan and a giant bat or flying fox; see our pls. 270 and 277.

[152] Schouten, *op. cit.* (n. 46), III, 164–67.

[153] Nieuhof, *Zee- en lant-reize* (n. 81), pp. 226–68.

[154] Bontius, *op. cit.* (n. 16), p. 345.

[155] *Ibid.,* p. 7.

[156] *Ibid.,* pp. 345–47. For Bontius' depiction of the durian see our pl. 272; for the papaya see pl. 271.

[157] *Ibid.,* pp. 301–3. *Cf.* our pl. 264.

Jacob Specx for his description of the plants. He reports that the tea plant is a shrub with leaves resembling the bruise-wort but with incised and crenulated edges. He finds the drink made from the tea leaves somewhat bitter; wealthier drinkers add sugar. Bontius is primarily interested in the medicinal properties of tea; he recommends it for people who suffer from consumption, shortness of breath, bladder and kidney stones, and as a diuretic. Willem Piso, Bontius' editor, added three or four pages of commentary to Bontius' one-page text, drawn from a wide variety of sources, for example François Caron, Matteo Ricci, Luis Fróis, and Luis d'Almeida, and resulting in one of the century's better descriptions of tea.[158]

Opium Bontius defends rather than describes. It is indispensable for treating dysentery, cholera, high fevers, and other bilious diseases. It should not be discredited simply because some misuse it.[159] On the other hand, he seriously questions the medicinal use of bezoar stone and "Hog Stone" (pigstone), a concretion similar to bezoar stone found in the gallbladder of hogs or in the stomach of porcupines. Javans use pigstone infused in wine to cure cholera. Bontius wonders why these animal concretions are so highly prized while human gallstones or bladder stones are not.[160] Bontius' account of the infamous Amboinese pox is probably the most thorough of the century. Its symptoms, which Bontius describes in detail, are very similar to those of "lues venera" (syphilis) except that they are attended with less pain. Its treatment is also very similar to that normally prescribed for syphilis. The disease is not, however, caused by sexual contact. Bontius thinks Amboinese pox is produced by Amboina's peculiar climate and soil and by the natives' poor diet of fish, sago, and a palm wine called "saguër."[161] Finally, Bontius lists several "marvellous works of nature" which he thinks should be investigated by subsequent physicians. Among them are volcanoes on Java and Banda which cast rocks larger than twenty men could move, high into the sky; naphtha on Sumatra which burns in water; the poison used on Makassarese javelins, the slightest amount of which kills instantly; and a small seed which placed in the mouth facilitates childbirth.[162]

D. CHARACTER, CUSTOMS, SOCIETY, AND CULTURE

The earliest accounts of Java—later accounts, too—report that the Javans thought themselves to have come originally from China. Lodewyckszoon found that easy to believe. Javans, like Chinese, have broad foreheads, large

---

[158] *Ibid.*, pp. 293–301. See our pl. 33 for the tea bush.
[159] *Ibid.*, p. 5.
[160] *Ibid.*, pp. 41–43.
[161] *Ibid.*, pp. 181–83. The disease is now known as yaws; see R. D. G. Ph. Simons (ed.), *Handbook of Tropical Dermatology* (Amsterdam, 1952), I, 270–73.
[162] Bontius, *op. cit.* (n. 16), pp. 287–89.

jaws, and small eyes. Marco Polo, he also observes, reported that Java paid tribute to the Mongol emperor of China.[163] The *Verhael vande reyse* describes the Javans in Bantam as having yellowish skin, and the men wearing loose-fitting cotton or silk garments which cover their bodies from waist to knees, and with nothing on their feet or above the waist. Some—the more devout Muslims—wear turbans or wear small cloth caps, but most go bareheaded. In the girdle around the waist every male Javan carries a dagger called a kris, often well made with an artfully carved or bejeweled handle. European observers seem fascinated with Javan krises and describe them repeatedly and in detail. Women wear cotton or silk garments reaching from just above the breasts to below the knees but bound around the waist with another cloth. They go barefooted and bareheaded except that on special occasions they wear gold or silver "crowns" on their heads and bracelets on their arms. Apart from the crowns and jewelry there is little difference in dress between rich and poor women.[164] Lodewyckszoon describes the dress of Javan "captains" as somewhat more elaborate: gold thread in their waist garments, turbans of fine Bengal linen (probably Dacca muslin), and jackets with sleeves of velvet, or of black or red cloth.[165]

Herport, later, describes Javans as somewhat brownish in color, with broad faces, flat noses, small eyes, short hair, and no beards. They are, he reports, rather small people but strong in body and limbs.[166] Saar thought the Javan's skin was yellow and observes that they rub their hair with coconut oil to make it glisten. Men, he reports, pluck out their beards by the roots with small tweezers.[167] Schouten, whose description is one of the most detailed, thinks Javans are "mostly black."[168] Their garments, he observes, are nothing more than a piece of cotton or silk cloth wrapped three or four times around their bodies. Women, he reports, rub their skin each day with a yellow ointment made from "borborry or Indian saffron" (turmeric), sandalwood, spices, and coconut oil.[169] Children under the age of eight or ten run naked.[170]

Almost all European writers comment on how frequently Javans bathe, especially the women: as often as five or six times a day. Some wealthier homes have water tanks or reservoirs in which to bathe. Those who live on

---

[163] Rouffaer and Ijzerman (eds.), *op. cit.* (n. 28), I, 91.

[164] *Verhael vande reyse,* in *ibid.,* II, 117–18. The editors contend that in the late sixteenth century, women in Bantam still wore nothing above the waist but a band just above the breasts. One of the plates in the *Verhael vande reyse* depicts a Javanese woman so dressed (II, 26, pl. 5), as does one of the plates in Lodewyckszoon's account (*ibid.,* I, 118, pl. 16).

[165] *Ibid.,* I, 116.

[166] *Op. cit.* (n. 126), pp. 28–29.

[167] *Op. cit.* (n. 81), p. 25.

[168] *Op. cit.* (n. 46), III, 152.

[169] On the use of turmeric in cosmetics see J. S. Pruthi, *Spices and Condiments* (New Delhi, 1976), p. 227.

[170] Schouten, *op. cit.* (n. 46), III, 154–56. On Southeast Asian clothing see Reid, *op. cit.* (n. 2), pp. 85–90.

the rivers or canals often build bathing boxes beside the water. Some are built out over the water with trap doors in the floor.[171] Most women, however, simply bathe in the rivers and canals, apparently with scant concern for modesty or privacy. Dutch observers thought that so much bathing befouled the streams and rivers. The author of the *Verhael vande reyse,* for example, is convinced that syphilis could be contracted from the water and reports that several Dutch crewmen died from drinking it. Bontius, however, does not think water from the river in Batavia is all that bad if drawn a little way upstream.[172]

Concerning Javan character and morals there was remarkable agreement among European writers. At the very beginning of the century Lodewyckszoon reports that "the Javans are a stubborn, dishonest, malicious, and murderous people. . . . They are so skillful in thievery that they surpass all others."[173] These characteristics are rehearsed again and again by later writers who also add untrustworthy, proud, lazy, jealous, vindictive, violent, merciless, heartless, and bloodthirsty to the list of unsavory adjectives and occasionally provide illustrative examples of these vices. Scott, for example, estimates that only about one Javan in a hundred is willing to work. Their laziness keeps them poor. "The gentlemen of this land are brought to be poore by the number of slaves that they keepe, which eat faster than their pepper or rice groweth."[174] Javanese pride frequently shows itself in what appears to the Europeans to be strange sensitivities. Javans cannot endure having someone stand over them while they are sitting, for example, or even allow someone of similar status to sit in a seat as little as one inch higher than the others. To lay a hand on a Javan's head is the worst insult of all.[175] Bolling observes that Javans never walk in pairs, not even when hundreds of them are together.[176] Their bloodthirstiness and violent tendencies make Javans good soldiers. Van Goens thought they surpassed all other nations as "desperate fighters."[177] Murder is common, and the official punishment for murder is slight, a small fine in Bantam. Relatives and friends always take revenge for murders, however, which greatly increases the number of killings—and the fines.[178] Almost everyone discourses on the practice of "running amok," apparently a Javan or Malay form of suicide. In Scott's words:

If any Javan have committed a fact worthy of death and that hee be pursued by any, whereby he thinketh hee shall die, hee will presently draw his weapon and cry

[171] Schouten, *op. cit.* (n. 46), III, 156.
[172] Rouffaer and Ijzerman (eds.), *op. cit.* (n. 28), II, 29; Bontius, *op. cit.* (n. 16), pp. 73–75. On drinking water see Reid, *op. cit.* (n. 2), pp. 36–40.
[173] Rouffaer and Ijzerman (eds.), *op. cit.* (n. 28), I, 117.
[174] Foster (ed.), *op. cit.* (n. 33), p. 171.
[175] *Ibid.,* pp. 159, 171.
[176] *Loc. cit.* (n. 82), p. 335.
[177] *Loc. cit.* (n. 124), p. 346.
[178] Scott in Foster (ed.), *op. cit.* (n. 33), p. 171.

Amucke, which is as much [as] to say: I am resolved; not sparing to murther either man, woman, or childe which they can possibly come at; and he that killeth most dieth with greatest honor and credit.[179]

Even the gruesome death penalties inflicted on amuck-runners by the VOC government in Batavia did not seem to discourage the practice.[180]

Van Goens, alone among seventeenth-century European reporters on Java, produces a list of Javan virtues: they are friendly and polite, never use abusive language, discuss serious affairs elegantly and efficiently, enjoy laughter and gaiety, love horses and treat them kindly, almost religiously respect their ruler, are loyal Muslims, and are generous to each other. Still, he concludes, their virtues are few because they are all hypocritically practiced. Javans are also, Van Goens observes, astoundingly like one another: so much so "that one would say, all Javans were raised in one house and descended from one father."[181] At the end of the century, European descriptions of Javan people show no greater appreciation for them than had the earliest descriptions. Frick, for example, confesses

that besides the pleasure I had out of a publick love for my Country, to see them in a fair way overcoming their Enemies and enlarging their Territories; I also had the secret satisfaction to see that they were Javians that were the objects of our Conquests; they being the most faithless, treacherous, and base of all the Indians. They are fit for all manner of mischief; but never fit to be employed in any action that's noble or generous. In short, they are skill'd in nothing, but in cheating, filching, and all manner of knavery.[182]

Only vague contours of the seventeenth-century Javan social structure emerge from the published European descriptions. They comment only upon the very top and bottom rungs of the social ladder. Society is hierarchical—perhaps even feudal. Javans of all ranks are jealous of their stations and very polite and subservient towards their superiors. Van Goens, for example, writes that in Mataram, Javans never speak to their superiors without attestations of service: holding oneself tense and rigid while the master talks, then leaping up with a shout and running out full tilt to do his bid-

---

[179] *Ibid.,* p. 171. From Malay *amoq.* According to Yule and Burnell, *op. cit.* (n. 111), pp. 18–23, the word means "to make a furious attack" rather than "I am resolved." See also John Crawfurd, *A Descriptive Dictionary of the Indian Islands and Adjacent Countries* (Varansi, 1974), p. 12.

[180] For example, see Schouten, *op. cit.* (n. 46), III, 152, or De Graaf in Warnsinck (ed.), *op. cit.* (n. 89), pp. 222–23.

[181] *Loc. cit.* (n. 124), pp. 346–47.

[182] Frick and Schweitzer, *op. cit.* (n. 82), p. 53. Crawfurd (*op. cit.* [n. 107], I, 38–73) provides a more favorable view of Javanese national character, although his account is influenced by social Darwinist notions of higher races. For an interesting discussion of seventeenth-century Dutch assessments of Javanese national character see Jörg Fisch, *Holland's Ruhm in Asien; Francois Valentyns Vision des niederländischen Imperiums im 18. Jahrhundert* (Stuttgart, 1986). On the influence of climate upon character see V. R. Savage, *Western Impressions of Nature and Landscape in Southeast Asia* (Singapore, 1984), pp. 170–75.

ding. When reporting to his superior a Javan always enters running hard and out of breath. According to Van Goens even the greatest lords of the land, the *pangerans*, behave in this way towards their superior, the Susuhunan.[183]

Slaves seem to have been common, for all European writers report on their large numbers. Some think Javans measure their wealth by the number of slaves kept. Others claim that ostentatious slave-owning impoverishes prominent Javan families. According to Scott, a free Javan in Bantam is required to keep ten female slaves for each wife he takes. Some Javans, he reports, keep as many as forty slaves per wife.[184] Slaves not only attend the persons of their masters or mistresses and accompany them when they go out but they perform all sorts of tasks both inside and outside the home: spinning, weaving, crafts, farm work, selling in the marketplace, and so forth.[185] Lodewyckszoon describes various kinds of slaves in Bantam, but in such a way as to raise questions about whether the term "slave" is appropriate for everyone so called in European reports. Some "slaves," for example, could be hired by the day for a stipulated sum of money. Some seem to have been required to serve their masters only half-time, working the other half for themselves and their families.[186] Hesse reports that industrious slaves could earn appreciable sums of money with which they themselves sometimes purchased slaves. Many enterprising slaves owned as many as five or six slaves. Governor-General Speelman had a slave who, according to Hesse, owned eighty other slaves. It is not clear whether only slaves of VOC officials were able to purchase other slaves or whether the slaves of rich Javans could do so as well.[187]

Few aspects of Javan society attracted more attention than marriage customs. Everyone reports that Javans are polygamous. One of the earliest Dutch reports, the *Verhael vande reyse,* states that Javans may marry as many wives as they wish, but that commoners usually have one or two wives and from ten to twenty concubines. Concubines are bought and sold.[188] Perhaps these concubines are the same as the mandatory ten female slaves per wife reported by Scott. The author reports that the concubines function as ladies-in-waiting and servants to the wives, and he observes that Javan men use their female slaves as concubines. Scott also reports that Javans are permitted only three wives.[189] Schouten also thinks that men may marry as many wives as they please, but Van Goens reports that nobles in Mataram are lim-

[183] *Loc. cit.* (n. 124), p. 314. Crawfurd (*op. cit.* [n. 107], I, 122–23) describes this as a "solemn dance."

[184] Foster (ed.), *op. cit.* (n. 33), p. 170.

[185] For example, see Rouffaer and Ijzerman (eds.), *op. cit.* (n. 28), I, 129, and Schouten, *op. cit.* (n. 46), III, 158.

[186] Rouffaer and Ijzerman (eds.), *op. cit.* (n. 28), I, 129–30.

[187] Hesse, *op. cit.* (n. 96), p. 41. See Reid (ed.), *op. cit.* (n. 106), pp. 1–43, and Bruno Lasker, *Human Bondage in Southeast Asia* (Chapel Hill, N.C., 1950). The description of slavery in the European accounts is essentially accurate.

[188] Rouffaer and Ijzerman (eds.), *op. cit.* (n. 28), II, 28.

[189] Foster (ed.), *op. cit.* (n. 33), p. 170.

ited to four wives. They may, however, keep as many concubines as they please.[190]

The earliest reports, Lodewyckszoon and the *Verhael vande reyse,* insist that Javan women—at least Muslim women—are closely secluded, which seems somewhat inconsistent with reports about public bathing.[191] The *Verhael vande reyse* reports that they are guarded by eunuchs. Apart from the repetition of that statement by Pyrard no other seventeenth-century description of Java mentions eunuchs.[192] All writers agree that Javans are exceedingly jealous of their wives, but several nonetheless assert that adultery is common. According to Van Goens, for example, a man justifiably may kill another for merely reaching out a hand towards his wife. In Mataram a man who suspects someone of dallying with his wife can complain to the sultan, who, if he thinks the plaintiff has reason to be suspicious, will issue a royal edict forbidding the suspect ever to come near the plaintiff's house. The sultan will also give the plaintiff a kris with which to kill the suspect should he ever approach his house.[193]

According to Schouten, children are promised in marriage at age thirteen or fourteen.[194] The Susuhunan and the great nobles contract marriages with great care, nobles always seeking the Susuhunan's approval for any match. Occasionally the Susuhunan selects a woman for one of his nobles from his enormous harem or staff of female servants. This is considered a high honor.[195] According to the *Verhael vande reyse,* wives can be returned to their father's home for very small offenses. Its author also reports that wives often poison babies born to their husband's concubines. Van Goens writes that the Susuhunan and the great nobles usually repudiate pregnant concubines and sometimes even wives until after the babies are born in order to avoid legitimizing a child whose parentage is not absolutely certain. Wives who bear deformed or ugly children are put away and forever forbidden any concourse with men. Those who produce healthy sons, however, are highly honored.[196]

Lodewyckszoon briefly describes a Javan wedding. Both bride and bridegroom remain secluded before the wedding. On the wedding day, friends, servants, and slaves carrying spears with colored banners on them gather in front of both the bride's and the groom's houses shouting, shooting guns, and in general making noise. After noon a saddled horse is brought to the

[190] Schouten, *op. cit.* (n. 46), III, 155; Van Goens, *loc. cit.* (n. 124), p. 343. Most Javanese nobles, like other Muslims, were limited to four wives by the tenets of Islam.
[191] Rouffaer and Ijzerman (eds.), *op. cit.* (n. 28), I, 114, and II, 28.
[192] *Ibid.,* II, 28; Gray (ed), *op. cit.* (n. 32), II, 163.
[193] Van Goens, *loc. cit.* (n. 124), p. 344. Reports about the seclusion of women and the jealousy of Javans for their wives are not supported by Crawfurd, *op. cit.* (n. 107), I, 73–82.
[194] *Op. cit.* (n. 46), III, 156.
[195] Van Goens, *loc. cit.* (n. 124), p. 343.
[196] *Verhael vande reyse* in Rouffaer and Ijzerman (eds.), *op. cit.* (n. 28), II, 28–29; Van Goens, *loc. cit.* (n. 124), p. 344. On sexual relations and marriage in Southeast Asia see Reid, *op. cit.* (n. 2), pp. 146–60.

bridegroom on which he rides slowly, followed by well-wishers, through the entire city, arriving early in the evening before his bride's house. There he is met by the slaves who will accompany his bride, each bearing a gift and also carrying the bride's gift. Then they eat the wedding feast, the parents of both the bride and the groom attending. Finally, after their parents have left, the bride and groom steal away together to a prepared room.[197]

Schouten's description of a rich Muslim Batavian wedding is much more detailed and varies somewhat from Lodewyckszoon's account. He claims to have attended it. It begins in the early evening with a procession led by torchbearers, dancers, acrobats, and musicians. Two Muslim "priests" (*penghulus*, or religious officials) dressed in white follow, after which come relatives of the bride and groom. The groom, mounted on a fine horse and accompanied by two of his close friends, follows a short distance behind. An elaborate fringed parasol is held over his head, two men on foot hold his horse and two others sprinkle him with rosewater while carrying a large perfumed and spiced cloth before him. The procession moves slowly through the town, finally stopping in front of the bride's house. There the bridegroom dismounts, assisted by his two friends. He and all the male guests then go inside a huge tent set up in front of the bride's house to eat the wedding feast. The women eat separately inside the house. There are cushions for the groom and the two groomsmen; everyone else sits tailor-fashion on a Persian carpet spread on the ground. A great many dishes are served, and the meal begins and ends with betel. When it is finished, the bride is brought in by her father and the ceremony begins. The wedding ceremony consists of questions asked by the "priests" of both the bride and groom, songs sung by the bride's attendants, and an exchange of rings and flower garlands.[198] The bride cries and has to be refreshed with some water before she can answer the questions, allowing Schouten a glimpse of her face. She wears rings in her nose, in her ears, and on her fingers, as well as a headdress of flowers and tinsel. Schouten thought she was beautiful. After the ceremony the groom with his bride mounts his horse, and the entire party conveys them to the groom's home. There the groom's mother prepares a single betel quid which they share, gives them her blessing, and shows them to their bedroom. By that time the first signs of dawn show in the east. According to Schouten the conduct of the principals and guests through the entire night is restrained, proper, and modest. There are no smirks, ribald jokes, drinking, or other tomfoolery. Schouten thought they put Christians to shame.[199]

Van Goens describes the royal banquets given by the Susuhunan of

---

[197] Rouffaer and Ijzerman (eds.), *op. cit.* (n. 28), I, 115. *Cf.* the wedding ceremony as described in R. M. Koentjaraningrat, *Javanese Culture* (Singapore, 1985), pp. 127–33.

[198] In modern times the questions are directed to the groom alone.

[199] *Op. cit.* (n. 46), II, 324–28. See also Crawfurd, *op. cit.* (n. 107), I, 86–93, on Javanese marriage customs.

Mataram. These are held in tents, open at one side and arranged half-moon fashion around the Susuhunan's tent, so that all the guests can see him. Food is brought in on banana leaves by servants who creep under the curtains at the back of each tent. As the meal begins each guest is brought water with which to wash his hands. Then comes an enormous number of dishes, which Van Goens does not describe in detail. Some he says are fried, others roasted, broiled, baked, or boiled, but all done in oil rather than butter. Whole chickens, sheep, and goats, and half oxen or buffaloes are the common roasts. There are spicy soups and vegetable dishes. Rice is the staple; it is brought out in interestingly shaped baskets which are inverted on banana leaves and removed. The rice retains the shape of the baskets, standing shoulder high to the diners seated cross-legged on the floor. Food is served in what Van Goens considers wasteful abundance; for each tent of 25 to 30 diners there is enough food for 150. Van Goens discovers, however, that the servants are fed from the excess, and that what the servants cannot eat they take home for their families. At the end of the meal, fruits and sweet cakes are served on clean banana leaves and finally tobacco and the inevitable betel quid. During the entertainment that follows dinner, guests chew betel and drink "brem" (Javanese, *brem*), a rice liquor which tastes like Spanish wine. Guests are careful to follow the Susuhunan in this, drinking only when he drinks. According to Van Goens, banquets of this sort are also regularly eaten in the homes of great nobles.[200]

Following a royal banquet the entertainment usually continues far into the night. First, as Van Goens describes it, there are musicians and dancing girls. The Susuhunan's women dance first, while he shouts approval and encouragement to them, sometimes promising them gold rings and bracelets. Then some of the noble guests send for their own dancing girls. Sometimes there are exhibitions of fencing, sometimes clowns and jesters, sometimes plays. Part of the entertainment is simply the merry repartee among the guests, each trying to outdo the other in making the Susuhunan and the other guests laugh. At other times the sultan and his court enjoy tournaments, hunting, and animal fights. Van Goens describes royal tournaments in great detail.[201] Most writers list music, dancing, drama, betel chewing, tobacco, and opium as favorite Javanese entertainments. According to Scott, some enjoy sitting cross-legged whittling sticks. They spend whole days at it, perhaps, Scott thinks, practicing their skill at carving kris handles.[202] About Javanese plays Scott observes:

The Javans use plays too; but they have no more but some history [*i.e.*, story], painted on a carde or mappe, the which one maketh relation of, with such jesture as

---

[200] *Op. cit.* (n. 124), pp. 325–27. On meat eating as ritual in Southeast Asia see Reid, *op. cit.* (n. 2), pp. 32–36.
[201] *Op. cit.* (n. 124), pp. 322–25, 327–29.
[202] Foster (ed.), *op. cit.* (n. 33), p. 173.

befitteth the matter. Likewise there be puppet playes, made by certain people of Clyn [Kling, Coromandel] which dwell there; the which puppets are apparrelled like unto the Christian manner; and they have lions and divers kinde[s] of beasts, artificially made, with which they performe their sport verie pretilie. But these hold the playes no poynt of religion or service to their gods, as the people of China doe.[203]

The music, dancing, and puppet shows frequently last all night.[204] Both the *Verhael vande reyse* and Lodewyckszoon describe the dancing as primarily consisting of the gentle swaying of bodies in rhythm with the music, synchronized arm and leg movements, but no leaping about. Lodewyckszoon includes a picture of a row of dancers moving in unison to the accompaniment of a marimba-like musical instrument.[205] Van Goens later describes the dancing girls and their costumes in some detail, but writes nothing about the dances.[206]

Most writers observe that the dancing is always accompanied by musical ensembles, and some describe what are obviously gamelans (orchestras). Van Goens, for example, reports that the orchestras are composed of many small gongs, larger gongs, a few flutes, and stringed instruments. Both in his and in other seventeenth-century descriptions, it is apparent that the percussion instruments are the most numerous and important in the gamelan. Lodewyckszoon pictures some of them (see pl. 257). Most European writers describe the music as sweet and pleasing.[207]

Apart from the many descriptions of ornately carved and bejeweled kris handles seventeenth-century European descriptions of Java do not mention any other arts, such as painting and sculpture.[208]

The first Dutch visitors reported that Javans spoke and wrote a language

[203] *Ibid.*, p. 176. In fact, much of the inspiration for Javanese puppet theater (the *wayang kulit*) seems to come from Hindu literature such as the Mahabharata and the Ramayana. But so far the origins of the Javanese puppet theater remain obscure. See Nena Vreeland, Peter Just, *et al.*, *Area Handbook for Indonesia* (Washington, 1975), p. 141; and Mantle Hood, "The Enduring Tradition: Music and Theater in Java and Bali," in Ruth T. McVey (ed.), *Indonesia* (New Haven, 1963), pp. 438–71. See also Crawfurd, *op. cit.* (n. 107), I, 127–32. *Cf.* Koentjaraningrat, *op. cit.* (n. 197), pp. 286–90.

[204] *Verhael vande reyse* in Rouffaer and Ijzerman (eds.), *op. cit.* (n. 28), II, 30. See Vreeland, Just, *et al.*, *op. cit.* (n. 203), pp. 138–41, and Hood, *loc. cit.* (n. 203), pp. 438–71, for recent descriptions.

[205] *Verhael vande reyse* in Rouffaer and Ijzerman (eds.), *op. cit.* (n. 28), II, 30, and Lodewyckszoon in *ibid.*, I, 124(4). See our pl. 258.

[206] *Loc. cit.* (n. 124), pp. 327–28. For a similar description of Javanese dance see Crawford, *op. cit.* (n. 107), I, 121–28.

[207] Van Goens, *loc. cit.* (n. 124), pp. 327–28; *Verhael vande reyse* in Rouffaer and Ijzerman (eds.), *op. cit.* (n. 28), II, 128(3) and (4). For a description of Javanese music see *Encyclopaedie van Nederlandsch-Indië*, II, 812–36. See also Crawfurd, *op. cit.* (n. 107), I, 332–41. On the orchestra itself see Suwandono, "Gamelan Orchestra in Wayang Kulit," in M. T. Osman (ed.), *Traditional Drama and Music of Southeast Asia* (Kuala Lumpur, 1947), pp. 290–97. See Reid, *op. cit.* (n. 2), pp. 201–15, on theater, music, and dance in Southeast Asia.

[208] Crawfurd (*op. cit.* [n. 107], I, 327) states, "of sculpture and painting the Indian islanders are at present absolutely ignorant." He supposes they once had sculptors, judging from the still-admired ruins of temples, but contends that they never painted. Curiously, no seventeenth-century observers mention the temples or the sculptures in them. But *cf.* our pl. 261.

unique to them and that most also spoke Malay which functioned as the international language of trade for most of Southeast Asia and even for many Indian seaports.[209] Very little was written about Javanese, however, in subsequent seventeenth-century European reports. Lodewyckszoon correctly reports that there are twenty characters in the Javanese script.[210] Schouten observes that, like the Chinese, the Javans require few characters to write their meaning. They laugh, he reports, at the Dutch for using so many letters to write something. A few Javanese characters can express the content of a whole page of Dutch.[211] Van Goens (in an account that was never published during the seventeenth century) thinks Javanese is a very old language and that its script has nothing in common with that of any other people. He also reports that unlike Southeast Asia's Malay-speakers, most Javans can read and write.[212]

Many of the European writers compare Malay to Latin because of its universality in India and Southeast Asia.[213] It is usually judged to be "sweet," "smooth flowing," efficient, and easy to learn.[214] Van Goens reports that Malay is written with Arabic letters, but again, the treatise in which he wrote this was not published during the seventeenth century.[215] Bolling observes that they write from right to left like the Hebrews, but he also thinks the lines on a page are written from the bottom of the page to the top.[216] Lodewyckszoon also mentions schools where some Javans study Arabic.[217]

Lodewyckszoon reports that the Javans do not print books, but that they write beautifully. They write on the leaves of a tree with an iron stylus. The leaves can then be rolled up like a scroll or bound between two pieces of wood like a book. Javans also, he observes, use Chinese paper and a sort of paper made from trees.[218] Bolling reports that he has seen no books but that

---

[209] Lodewyckszoon in Rouffaer and Ijzerman (eds.), *op. cit.* (n. 28), I, 119–20.

[210] *Ibid.,* p. 120. On Javanese script see Koentjaraningrat, *op. cit.* (n. 197), pp. 14–15. For a vocabulary see our pl. 246.

[211] Schouten, *op. cit.* (n. 46), III, 158–59.

[212] Van Goens, *loc. cit.* (n. 124), p. 356. Old Javanese script was of Indian derivation. For a brief account of Indonesian languages see *Encyclopedia of Islam,* 2d ed., III, 1215–17. For the differences between the pre-Islamic language (Old Javanese) and modern Javanese see B. Nothofer, *The Reconstruction of Proto-Malayo-Javanic* (The Hague, 1975), pp. 8–20.

[213] For example, see Merklein, *op. cit.* (n. 81), p. 14, and Bolling, *loc. cit.* (n. 82), p. 336.

[214] For example, see Lodewyckszoon in Rouffaer and Ijzerman (eds.), *op. cit.* (n. 28), I, 120, and Schouten, *op. cit.* (n. 46), III, 159.

[215] *Loc. cit.* (n. 124), p. 356. His observation is correct. See *Encyclopedia of Islam,* 2d ed., III, 1217.

[216] *Loc. cit.* (n. 82), p. 340. Obviously Arabic is written in lines running from right to left, but they are read from top to bottom.

[217] Rouffaer and Ijzerman (eds.), *op. cit.* (n. 28), I, 120. Perhaps the beginning of the *santri* (religious student) tradition described by C. Geertz, *Islam Observed: Religious Development in Morocco and Indonesia* (New Haven, 1968), pp. 65–70.

[218] Rouffaer and Ijzerman (eds.), *op. cit.* (n. 28), I, 119–20. The paper was made from the lontor tree. Paper was apparently manufactured in Java as early as the thirteenth century; see Reid, *op. cit.* (n. 2), pp. 227–28.

he has seen Javans write on the bark of coconut palms.[219] Several of the seventeenth-century reports from Java contain Malay, Javanese, and Dutch or Latin vocabulary lists.[220] No one describes Javanese education, schools, or literature.

All the seventeenth-century European visitors to Java report that most Javans are Muslims. They are, however, recent converts to Islam. Two reports date the coming of Islam to Java at 1560.[221] Some observe that there are still many Arab "priests" and teachers in Java.[222] Most European visitors report that while the Javans who live in the large cities and on the seacoast all seem to be Muslims, many of those who live inland have not been converted and are still "heathen."

Lodewyckszoon at the beginning of the century provides one of the longest descriptions of Islamic beliefs in Java. They hold to the teachings of the Koran, he reports, honor four prophets (Moses, David, Jesus, and Muhammad), and worship silently in mosques, facing west, bowing to the ground, and listening to readings from the Koran. They also fast twice a year. The great fast which begins each year on August 5 requires fasting from sunup till sundown for forty days, after which families, together with all their slaves and servants, eat the "passover" seated on the ground in a circle.[223] Most other seventeenth-century reports mention only that Javanese Muslims abstain from eating pork and practice circumcision. Circumcision apparently is regarded as a particularly holy act. Scott takes ten pages to describe the elaborate, month-long celebration surrounding the young "King" of Bantam's circumcision in June, 1605: the processions, entertainments, and the many rich gifts given both by his subjects and by foreign dignitaries.[224] Both Scott and Merklein contend that apart from circumcision and abstaining from pork they can detect few signs of the Islamic faith among the common people. Scott goes on to describe a popular belief in a remote god who created the universe and a devil who is worshipped so that he will not harm the people, all of which sounds more like the early Euro-

[219] *Loc. cit.* (n. 82), p. 340.
[220] Rouffaer and Ijzerman (eds.), *op. cit.* (n. 28), II, 162–68; Keuning (ed.), *op. cit.* (n. 7), III, 158–75; Bolling, *loc. cit.* (n. 82), pp. 337–40. See our pls. 36 and 246.
[221] See, for example, *Verhael vande reyse* in Rouffaer and Ijzerman (eds.), *op. cit.* (n. 28), II, 27, and Schouten, *op. cit.* (n. 46), III, 155. Islam apparently came to the area much earlier. It was introduced to northern Sumatra around 1112, and Persian missionaries were active on Java since 1400. Many of the commercially important seaports on Java's northern coast became Muslim during the fifteenth century. See *Encyclopedia of Islam*, 2d ed., III, 1218–21, and Vlekke, *op. cit.* (n. 2), pp. 80–86. Islam became dominant in Java only by degrees. See De Graaf, *op. cit.* (n. 1), p. 3.
[222] For example, see *Verhael vande reyse* in Rouffaer and Ijzerman (eds.), *op. cit.* (n. 28), II, 27, and Schouten, *op. cit.* (n. 46), III, 155.
[223] Rouffaer and Ijzerman (eds.), *op. cit.* (n. 28), I, 113. This so-called passover is *Rijaja,* a holiday devoted to asking for forgiveness.
[224] Foster (ed.), *op. cit.* (n. 33), pp. 152–62. See also Saar, *op. cit.* (n. 81), p. 27. On circumcision (*sunatan*) see C. Geertz, *The Religion of Java* (Chicago, 1960), pp. 51–53.

pean descriptions of popular Chinese religion than like the religion of the Javans.[225] Saar reports that Javanese Muslims try to send some pilgrims to Mecca each year to bring an offering to Muhammad. Also, according to Saar, they fast during daylight hours for eight days at each new moon and at the beginning of the new year in March.[226] Schouten adds that they keep Friday as a sabbath and hold their mosques in high respect. No Christian or other uncircumcised person may enter a mosque; should it happen, the mosque would have to be reconsecrated and the one who defiled it put to death. Schouten and some companions narrowly escaped death in the mosque in Japara only because they were stopped while still in the outer court. Schouten's book contains a full-page engraving of the mosque, which more closely resembles a pagoda than a traditional Near Eastern mosque.[227] Olivier van Noort describes what he calls a "principal priest," who holds court near Jortan. He is reputed to be 120 years old and a great enemy of Christians; he keeps many women to warm him and feed him milk.[228]

While ever more Javans were being converted to Islam, some who lived in the interior of the island remained "heathen." These apparently practiced the traditional Javan mixture of Hinduism, Buddhism, and earlier local beliefs.[229] Most seventeenth-century European writers report that Java's "heathens" follow the ancient teachings of Pythagoras; that is, they believe in metempsychosis.[230] Consequently, according to Lodewyckszoon, they eat nothing that has life, live soberly and peacefully, and wear white paper clothing made from trees.[231] Little else was reported by European visitors about pre-Islamic, Javanese religion. Frick, writing at the end of the century, however, describes his visit to the "Blue Pepper Mountain" south of Batavia where a community of holy men "devoted themselves to perpetual

---

[225] Merklein, *op. cit.* (n. 81), p. 14; Scott in Foster (ed.), *op. cit.* (n. 33), p. 172. That Indonesian Islam varied greatly from the Near Eastern varieties is true. There was also considerable variety within Indonesian and Javanese Islam. Islam came to Indonesia by way of traders and missionaries rather than by conquest, and these were quite tolerant of local traditions and beliefs. Islamic mysticism was soon integrated with the Hindu-Buddhist mystical traditions. Perhaps Islam on Java would have eventually become more orthodox in the Near Eastern sense if the Dutch intrusion and control of Javanese trade had not so seriously interrupted regular contacts with the Near Eastern Islamic world. For example, see C. C. Berg, "The Islamization of Java," *Studia Islamica*, IV (1955), 111–42; G. W. J. Drewes, "New Light on the Coming of Islam to Indonesia," *BTLV*, CXXIV (1968), 433–59; G. W. J. Drewes, "Indonesia: Mysticism and Activism," in *Unity and Variety in Muslim Civilization*, ed. G. E. von Grünebaum (Chicago, 1956), pp. 284–310; "Indonesia," *Encyclopedia of Islam*, 2d ed., III, 1215–35.

[226] *Op. cit.* (n. 81), pp. 27–28. Javanese Muslims were always eager for pilgrimages to Mecca. See, for example, *Encyclopedia of Islam*, 2d ed., III, 1227–28.

[227] *Op. cit.* (n. 46), I, 37–39; III, 155. See our pl. 261.

[228] Ijzerman (ed.), *op. cit.* (n. 8), pp. 141–42. Gresik or Jortan was the oldest center of Islam in Java and its mosque was much revered.

[229] On pre-Islamic Javanese religion see Vlekke, *op. cit.* (n. 2), pp. 59–79.

[230] For example, see Lodewyckszoon in Rouffaer and Ijzerman (eds.), *op. cit.* (n. 28), I, 113; Schouten, *op. cit.* (n. 46), III, 155.

[231] Rouffaer and Ijzerman (eds.), *op. cit.* (n. 28), I, pp. 128–128(2). The editors observe that old Javans wear clothing made from tree bark—"deloewang-dracht" (*deluwang* clothing).

austerity, mortification, and Self Denial." They believe that chastising the body will evoke God's special blessings. They wear long gowns, go about day and night with eyes and hands raised toward heaven, and eat only boiled herbs, roots, and beans. But according to Frick, on what he calls feast days they eat flies, mice, scorpions, and spiders, which seems inconsistent with Islamic, Hindu, or Buddhist asceticism. These holy men are much venerated by the Javans. After death they are cremated with "great solemnity," and usually "canonized."[232]

E. POLITICAL LIFE

When the Dutch first arrived in Java during the last years of the sixteenth century, the sultan of Bantam was clearly the most powerful ruler in the western part of the island. Further east the resurgent empire of Mataram was threatening the independence of the seaport principalities on Java's north coast. During the first quarter of the seventeenth century Mataram subdued most of these principalities. Nyakra-Kusuma, later known as Sultan Agung, who ascended the throne in 1613, claimed authority over the whole of Java, having, as he saw it, succeeded to the fourteenth- and fifteenth-century kingdom of Majapahit. Indeed when he assumed the title of Susuhunan in 1625 almost all of Java had submitted to him. Only Balambangan, supported by Bali, in the extreme east and Bantam in the extreme west remained independent. By 1619, however, the Dutch had subdued the prince of Jakatra and had established their headquarters in the new fort and city of Batavia.[233]

The earliest European reports accurately reflect Java's fluid politics during the first quarter of the seventeenth century. Lodewyckszoon, for example, claims that each city in Java has its own king, but that the king of Bantam is the most powerful.[234] The *Verhael vande reyse* notes that the various Javan princes readily make war on each other for slight causes. During trade negotiations in Bantam the sultan proposed that in return for a cargo of pepper the Dutch should send ships to Palembang on Sumatra to help kill its king.[235] Lodewyckszoon mentions a war between Balambangan and Pasuruan.[236] But he also reports that the king of Mataram is the strongest on Java, that he frequently threatens Bantam, and that the Bantamese are in a constant state of military preparedness for fear of him.[237] Pyrard thinks Ban-

[232] Frick and Schweitzer, *op. cit.* (n. 82), pp. 152–53. On Javanese ascetic, ethical, and mystical movements and orders see Koentjaraningrat, *op. cit.* (n. 197), pp. 404–10.
[233] Vlekke, *op. cit.* (n. 2), pp. 128–31.
[234] Rouffaer and Ijzerman (eds.), *op. cit.* (n. 28), I, 99–100.
[235] *Ibid.*, II, 28.
[236] *Ibid.*, I, 100–101.
[237] *Ibid.*, I, 103.

tam is the most renowned kingdom on Java but that there are other powerful kings as well: the king of Madura, for example, and the king of Tuban,
who can raise thirty thousand soldiers within twenty-four hours.[238] Scott
asserts that since the deposition and death of the emperor of Demak, the
king of Bantam is "held the principall king of that island."[239]

Only Bantam's government is described in any detail. Scott reports that
the "king," presumably the sultan, is absolute. He mentions other officials—"pangrans" (*pangerans* or nobles) and "petty kings," but he does not
describe their powers. That the *pangerans* were relatives of the sultan is apparent from Scott's description of the ceremonies attending the young sultan's circumcision: "on either of his [the sultan's] hands were placed the
sonnes of Pangran Goban [*Pangeran Gĕbang*], who is heire apparent to the
crowne, if the king should dye without issue."[240] The "pety kings who had
great troupes of men" appear to be vassals of the sultan.[241] The "king," Scott
observes, governs by "marshall law," which he does not define. Husbands,
however, may themselves execute unfaithful wives and their lovers, and
slaves can be executed by their owners for "any small fault." He also defines
a curious role for women as royal messengers:

If the King send for any subject or stranger dwelling or being in his dominions, if he
send a man, the partie may refuse to come; but if once he send a woman, hee may not
refuse nor make no excuse. Moreover, if any inferior bodie have a suit to a man of
authority, if they come not themselves, they always send a woman.[242]

During his stay in Bantam, Scott had to do with still other government
officials. He occasionally mentions the "protectour," the "saybyndar," and
the "admirall," but provides few clues with which to identify them. Lodewyckszoon also mentions the "capiteijn" (*pungawa*), the admiral Tomongon
Angabaya, the "panyeran" (*pangeran*), the "chenopate" or "chepaté" (*sen-
apati*), who is the "governor in the king's name," and the "sabandar" (*shahbandar*), the chief tollmaster, described as supreme next to the king, and he
continually refers to nobles.[243]

In addition, Lodewyckszoon describes Bantam's general assembly ("Gen-
erale Vergaderinge") called the War Council ("Krijghs Raet"), which meets
regularly in the "paceban" or "pacebam" (*paseban*), a large open square in
front of the sultan's palace, usually after the sun's heat has somewhat abated
in the afternoon. The major concern of the afternoon meetings seems to be
legal. Criminals are judged, and anyone may bring legal matters forward.

---

[238] Gray (ed.), *op. cit.* (n. 32), II, 160, 164.
[239] Foster (ed.), *op. cit.* (n. 33), p. 170.
[240] *Ibid.*, p. 153.
[241] *Ibid.*, p. 160.
[242] *Ibid.*, p. 170.
[243] Rouffaer and Ijzerman (eds.), *op. cit.* (n. 28), I, 104–7, 127–28; *BV*, Ia, 38b.

Charges must be brought and answered in person; the Javans use no lawyers. Legal cases take less time in Bantam's general assembly than they do in
European courts. Affairs of state are also presented and discussed in the afternoon assemblies, but these issues are resolved and decisions concerning
them taken at night, by moonlight, Lodewyckszoon suspects because of old
superstitions concerning the moon. The night assemblies, he reports, remain sitting until the moon has set. Military matters are also decided in
night assemblies.

It is not clear just who were members of the general assembly.
Lodewyckszoon reports that when military matters are discussed all of the
great nobles ("overste Heeren") or captains, three hundred of them, are invited, because protection of the entire population is divided among them. In
case of an attack, every citizen of Bantam is subject to one of the three hundred captains. Lodewyckszoon's journal contains a plate depicting the War
Council in session. Those who seem to be the captains are arranged in a
semicircle around the "Gouverner" (the regent, sometimes called protector,
during the sultan's minority) and the four "principal captains." They seem
to number far fewer than three hundred. Behind the regent and "principal
captains" sit a large number of servants and slaves. In several minor details
the plate seems inconsistent with Lodewyckszoon's description, thus raising
the possibility that its content was largely determined by the engraver rather
than the author. Lodewyckszoon reports that the members of the general
assembly sit on the ground around the "king or governor" and two or four
"principals," who present matters to the assembly and ask its advice. Members speak, advising the king in order, from the greatest lords to the least.[244]

Many European observers described Javanese soldiers; Lodewyckszoon's
was the earliest and remained one of the best. In addition to the ubiquitous
kris, soldiers employ long spears, swords, cutlasses, and blowguns whose
small, fish-tooth-pointed darts break off in the victim's flesh. The darts and
most of the other weapons are usually poisoned so that even a small wound
proves fatal. Some few have muskets, but usually lack ammunition and skill
in their use. They carry shields made of skin or leather stretched over a
frame. Some wear protective armor made of square pieces of iron held together with rings. Most Bantamese soldiers have long hair, long fingernails,
and file their teeth to sharp points.[245] European observers consider Javanese
soldiers to be among the bravest and most ferocious in Asia. The soldiers'
relationship to their lords or captains suggests a feudal organization of Bantam's military and perhaps also of its government. According to Lodewyckszoon, soldiers are obedient to death. They receive no salaries, but are armed

[244] Rouffaer and Ijzerman (eds.), *op. cit.* (n. 28), I, 127–28, pl. 22.
[245] On the traditional military arts and weapons of Java and Madura see D. F. Draeger, *Weapons and Fighting Arts of the Indonesian Archipelago* (New York, 1972), chap. ii.

and maintained by their captains. The man with the most soldiers is judged the wealthiest and most powerful.[246]

For the half century after 1625, three powers contested for control of Java: Mataram, Bantam, and the Netherlands. Sultan Agung of Mataram (r. 1613–45) was determined to make Bantam and Batavia submit to his rule, the VOC was determined to monopolize commerce with the Moluccas, and the sultans of Bantam were determined to resist both Mataram's threat to their territory and the Dutch threat to their trade. Agung's control over the eastern Javanese ports and his disdain for commerce probably helped the Dutch establish control over trade in the eastern archipelago by removing the east-Javan merchant-kings from competition. Meanwhile the Dutch in Batavia blocked the way to Bantam for the Susuhunan. Both Javanese sultanates claimed old Jakatra and both attacked Batavia during the late 1620's: Bantamese soldiers stormed the castle in December, 1627; twice during the following year Mataram's armies attacked and besieged the VOC headquarters. Mataram's defeat in 1629, however, secured the VOC's position on Java.

Dutch domination of Java was not immediately apparent. After 1629 the VOC sent regular embassies to the Susuhunan's court in an effort to secure peace and regular shipments of rice at fixed, low prices. In Mataram the embassies were understood to indicate the VOC's submission to the Susuhunan. The Dutch seemed not to mind. Meanwhile Agung turned his attention to the east and in 1639 attacked Balambangan and Bali, quickly overrunning Balambangan. The Balinese, however, repelled his attack on their island; later they regained parts of Balambangan as well. In the same year, attempting to enlist more powerful allies against the Dutch, Agung sent envoys to Mecca, which resulted in making Mataram a sultanate. Soon after his accession to the throne in 1645, Agung's son and successor, Amangkurat I (r. 1645–77), made a formal treaty with the VOC, couched in terms of Mataram's overlordship.

In 1674, however, a revolt against Mataram led by Trunajaya, a prince of Madura, seriously threatened its continued hegemony. Bantam meanwhile, under Sultan Abulfatah Agung (r. 1651–83), moved against Mataram's western provinces, thus threatening to surround Batavia. These were years of vigorous commercial expansion and prosperity in Bantam. The Dutch were reluctant to interfere, but in 1677 when Trunajaya burned the *kraton* and Amangkurat I died in flight, the VOC under its new governor-general Rijcklof van Goens defeated Trunajaya and placed Amangkurat II on his father's throne. From then on, the Susuhunan was totally dependent on the VOC. Bantam remained independent for only a few more years. During the

---

[246] Rouffaer and Ijzerman (eds.), *op. cit.* (n. 28), I, 117–18, pl. 15. See also Scott in Foster (ed.), *op. cit.* (n. 33), p. 171.

civil war (1682–84) between Sultan Abulfatah and his son Prince Hadji the Dutch interfered on the side of the young prince, insuring his victory and Bantam's submission to the VOC. Dutch control of Java thus became complete.[247]

Some of these events were reported by the Europeans who visited Java after 1625. Van Rechteren, for example, describes the last siege of Batavia by Mataram in 1629.[248] Wouter Schouten, whose book was first published in 1676—before the Bantamese civil war—observes that the sultan of Bantam has several times raised armies against the Dutch but that he has finally learned that it is better to live in peace.[249] Frick, published in 1692, describes the Bantamese civil war and the VOC's role in it in great detail.[250] All other seventeenth-century reports observe, accurately but in general terms, that while there used to be many separate kingdoms in Java all but the rulers of Bantam and Jakatra have submitted to Mataram, that Jakatra is under the control of the VOC, and that Bantam remains independent and hostile to both Mataram and the Dutch.[251]

Rijcklof van Goens, five times ambassador to Amangkurat I's court between 1648 and 1654, is the primary source of information about Mataram's government. What is said about it by others all seems to come from him, including Schouten's fairly substantial account.[252] As described by Van Goens, the empire of Mataram is basically a feudal state, modified by the despotic authority of a monarch who exercises some centralized control over the entire land. All Java is divided into fourteen provinces, twelve of which belong to the Susuhunan. The remaining two are, of course, Bantam and Jakatra, over which he nonetheless claims sovereignty. Each province is ruled by a *pangeran,* who appears to be either a prince of the royal family or of the family which ruled the province before it submitted to Mataram. The *pangeran*s all appear to reside at the Susuhunan's court, almost as hostages. Nevertheless they seem to be able to appoint lieutenants to govern the provinces in their absence. Perhaps the military provides the best clue to the *pangerans'* independent power. Van Goens lists the number of soldiers retained by each *pangeran.* They range from twenty thousand to one hundred thousand for each, while the Susuhunan personally maintains five hundred thousand. According to Van Goens, the Susuhunan maintains registers of all the

[247]Vlekke, *op. cit.* (n. 2), pp. 131–84. See also W. Fruin-Mees, "Een Bantamsch gezantschap naar Engeland in 1682," *Tijdschrift voor Indische taal-, land-, en volkenkunde,* LXIV (1923), 207–27, and Boxer, *op. cit.* (n. 81), pp. 190–94.

[248]*Loc. cit.* (n. 13), 27–29.

[249]Schouten, *op. cit.* (n. 46), III, p. 151. Several English pamphlets relating to the Bantamese civil war were published during the 1680's. See above, pp. 577–78.

[250]*Op. cit.* (n. 82), pp. 38–69.

[251]For example, see Saar, *op. cit.* (n. 81), pp. 25–26; Merklein, *op. cit.* (n. 81), p. 12; Herport, *op. cit.* (n. 126), pp. 27–28; Bolling, *loc. cit.* (n. 82), pp. 327–29; Nieuhof, *Zee- en lant-reize* (n. 81), p. 194.

[252]Schouten, *op. cit.* (n. 46), III, 141–51.

pangerans' soldiers and appoints commissioners to ensure that their number is neither increased nor decreased.[253]

Superior to the *pangerans'* lieutenants in each province is a royally appointed "tommagon" (*tumenggung*) or governor. The *tumenggung* of the inland province of Mataram functions as the Susuhunan's prime minister. In addition to the *tumenggung* each province has two *shahbandars* or tollmasters who are not subject to the *tumenggung* but rather to one of the two commissioners who supervise the coastal towns, one for the eastern part of the north coast, the other for the western. Van Goens thinks none of these royally appointed officials holds office for more than one year. Even the *tumenggung* of Mataram, the prime minister, usually does not hold office for more than two years. Finally, according to Van Goens, the king sends out four thousand undersheriffs "who run with whole troops through the country like hound dogs, to see and hear what is happening."[254] These report to the Susuhunan through four oversheriffs who reside at court and are much feared.[255]

The Susuhunan lives secluded in his *kraton,* guarded and served, according to Van Goens, exclusively by women. Counting wives, concubines, servants, cooks, handicraft workers, guards, dancers, and entertainers, Van Goens claims that at least ten thousand women work in the palace. Whenever the Susuhunan leaves the *kraton* he is accompanied by at least thirty women, some of whom are armed with spears and muskets while others carry those things necessary for his comfort and dignity.[256]

The Susuhunan comes out of the *kraton* three times each week: on Thursdays to hold court, on either Saturday or Monday to watch or participate in the tournaments, and on one other day to hold councils with the *pangerans,* *tumenggungs,* and other important officers of the realm. In fact, except for Fridays, all these great lords wait in the great square outside the *kraton* every morning from nine o'clock until twelve for him to appear or for him to call one of them inside. Not to be there each day, Van Goens surmises, would endanger one's life.

When the Susuhunan comes out to hold court, all the music and the drums suddenly cease playing. Once he is seated in an elevated summer house, the accused prisoners, usually with legs chained together and a wooden yoke around their necks to which their extended arms are lashed, are thrown on their faces about fifty paces from him. An official then presents the accusations to the king and calls up witnesses, at least three for each case. The monarch meanwhile sends one of his advisers to ask the prisoners why they are accused and what response they have to the accusations. He sends an-

---

[253] Van Goens, *loc. cit.* (n. 124), pp. 319–20.
[254] *Ibid.,* p. 320.
[255] This sketch of governmental structure comes from *ibid.,* pp. 317–21. On government see E. S. de Klerck, *History of the Netherlands East Indies* (2 vols.; Rotterdam, 1938), I, 177–84.
[256] *Loc. cit.* (n. 124), pp. 341–43.

other to examine the witnesses, threatening the Susuhunan's and heaven's wrath should they lie. When the two advisers return, the Susuhunan consults briefly with them and other advisers, after which he pronounces judgment. False witnesses are punished even more severely than condemned criminals. All criminal matters must be referred to the Susuhunan. Provincial officials may only arrest criminals and send them bound to the court. To Van Goens it seems that death is the only punishment ever ordered. Theft, murder, adultery, speaking ill of the ruler, all bring death sentences. Sometimes a whole family is executed for the crime of one of its members. Sometimes fathers are forced to execute their sons and the sons their fathers. Sentences are pronounced at the whim of the monarch.[257]

Royal council meetings are inquisitorial rather than deliberative. While most of the officials sit in the outer square waiting to be called, only the most powerful and closest advisers gather in the inner courtyard. When the Susuhunan appears they all sit in silence for a considerable time; the *pangerans* sit like slaves, on the ground, tailor fashion, hands on thighs, head bowed low with eyes to the ground. No one moves or talks. Then the Susuhunan begins to inquire of the *pangerans* and governors about the affairs of their provinces. They labor to flatter the monarch and to assure him that all his subjects are peaceful and obedient. The Susuhunan, daily informed of provincial conditions by his spies, then moves to harder questions about matters which displease him. His great subjects, who have spies of their own, are rarely caught off guard and answer him cleverly and in ways calculated to reassure him of their loyalty. In all, an exceedingly dangerous business, Van Goens thinks. Should the monarch be displeased with him, the least punishment a great lord can expect is the loss of his titles and lands. He may well lose his life.[258]

All the great lords and high officials, despite their apparent wealth and prestige, live in constant fear and are in fact little more than slaves to the Susuhunan. Should he ask for an official to be brought into a council meeting, for example, without designating who should do it, all the great lords leap to their feet, almost stumbling over one another to do his bidding.[259] Officials and even foreign ambassadors are constantly worried about where in the courtyard they are placed during audiences, proximity to the Susuhunan denoting greater favor—but also greater danger.[260] When the Susuhunan has his hair cut, every man in the kingdom follows suit. The undersheriffs roam the land, arresting anyone with long hair, subjecting the disobedient to hideous tortures which usually kill them. If the Susuhunan wears a turban, all the nobles do likewise; if he wears a traditional Javan cap, they all quickly change.

---

[257] *Ibid.*, pp. 315–17.
[258] *Ibid.*, pp. 317–22.
[259] *Ibid.*, p. 327.
[260] *Ibid.*, p. 347.

If at a banquet he does not drink coffee, no one does.[261] Van Goens is amazed by the Susuhunan's arbitrary power and by the slavish subservience of his subjects, even the greatest of them. The honor accorded him is more appropriate for gods than men, he thinks. Nevertheless Van Goens seems to be unaware of the sacred character of Mataram's ruler or of his reputed magical powers.[262]

Van Goens illustrates Amangkurat's absolute power and his cruelty by describing in considerable detail the death of his brother, "Wiera Gouna" (Vira Guna). Because they quarreled over a concubine when Amangkurat was just eighteen years old, he had long planned revenge. Not long after Amangkurat ascended the throne, Vira Guna thought he detected a growing suspicion and hostility towards himself. He attempted a showdown. With a group of his most loyal retainers Vira Guna attacked Amangkurat in front of the palace during a royal audience. Amangkurat's guards and vassals defended him, of course, first killing all of Vira Guna's companions, then his horse, but not daring to kill the king's brother. To keep Vira Guna from reaching the Susuhunan, one after another of his vassals threw themselves in the way and were killed by Vira Guna. Only after Amangkurat withdrew into the *kraton* was Vira Guna killed. After Vira Guna's death Amangkurat had several other great nobles and two thousand Muslim priests put to death for their suspected support of Vira Guna's revolt. According to Van Goens, over six thousand people were killed before the purge ended.[263] Awed as he was by the Susuhunan's power, Van Goens delightedly reports that the Dutch ambassadors are treated well in Mataram, continually advancing nearer the monarch during royal audiences and enjoying many extraordinary favors.[264]

F. ECONOMICS AND TRADE

The Europeans, of course, came to Java to trade, and their published accounts contain substantial information about commercial and economic matters. Since earlier writers all consider Bantam to be Java's best and busiest port, their accounts contain considerable detail on its trade and commodities. Three large markets are open each day, in which one can buy almost anything imaginable. They are thronged with people—as busy as

---

[261] *Ibid.*, pp. 344–45.
[262] See Vlekke, *op. cit.* (n. 2), pp. 145–52. On the conduct of government see also De Klerck, *op. cit.* (n. 255), II, 184–89.
[263] *Loc. cit.* (n. 124), pp. 329–41. Vlekke observes that Vira Guna's revolt and the subsequent bloodbath were not simply the result of a personal quarrel between Vira Guna and Amangkurat but rather a deliberate reversal of his father's policy of Islamization. Amangkurat never took the title sultan, preferring the traditional Javanese title Susuhunan. He also made administrative and judicial changes designed to reduce the influence of Islam in the kingdom. See Vlekke, *op. cit.* (n. 2), pp. 174–75.
[264] *Loc. cit.* (n. 124), 347–48.

any fairs in England.[265] The writer of the *Verhael vande reyse* lists some of the local products: chickens, deer, fish, rice, pineapples, bananas, coconuts, mangoes, durians, "iacca" (jackfruits), prunes, grapes, oranges, lemons, grenadines, cucumbers, melons, onions, leeks, and more.[266] Lodewyckszoon takes his readers for a stroll through the great market, observing the stalls where pepper and spices are sold and where weapons are on display. He notes the areas devoted to sandalwood, clothing and dry goods, jewels, meats, fish, fruit, rice, household utensils, cooking oil, drugs, and so on. All of these are also depicted in a large fold-out copperplate illustration.[267]

The century's earliest European visitors all emphasize the international character of trade in Bantam. It is the entrepôt for products from all parts of the archipelago and beyond. Merchants from all of Asia live in the city and can be seen in its markets (see pl. 249). Their ships fill its harbor. They come to buy cloves, mace, and nutmeg, which are shipped in from the Moluccas, and pepper, shipped in from Sumatra and other parts of Java. They buy porcelain, silk, damask, gold thread, and iron pans brought over from China.[268] Currencies can be exchanged in Bantam. Loans can be floated. Lodewyckszoon reports that some Javan, Malay, and Quilon merchants in Bantam are specialists in bottomry, loans advanced to sea-merchants with their ships as security.[269]

By all accounts the Chinese are the most aggressive and wealthiest merchants in Bantam. They sell a wide variety of Chinese products. The *Verhael vande reyse* reports that they distill brandy from rice or coconuts, which Javans buy under cover of darkness because of the Islamic prohibition against alcohol.[270] More important, the Chinese virtually control Bantam's pepper trade. Chinese merchants buy the pepper from Javan farmers and store it until January, when eight to ten large Chinese junks arrive to load the cargo. Europeans soon discover that they too have to buy the pepper from Chinese intermediaries.[271] Scott observes that less pepper from other places in the archipelago is brought to Bantam for sale since the Dutch are buying it in other ports.[272] The Chinese, according to the writer of the *Verhael vande reyse,* "are almost exactly like the Jews in our country: for they never go anywhere without taking a balance with them, and all things to their liking they pay close attention to any profit."[273] Scott reports, accurately, that the

[265] Scott in Foster (ed.), *op. cit.* (n. 33), p. 169. See also our pl. 250.
[266] Rouffaer and Ijzerman (eds.), *op. cit.* (n. 28), II, 25–26.
[267] *Ibid.,* I, 110–13. See our pl. 280.
[268] For examples, see Rouffaer and Ijzerman (eds.), *op. cit.* (n. 28), I, 105–21, and II, 24; Scott in Foster (ed.), *op. cit.* (n. 33), pp. 168–69.
[269] Rouffaer and Ijzerman (eds.), *op. cit.* (n. 28), I, 120–21.
[270] *Ibid.,* I, 24; II, 26.
[271] For example, see *Verhael vande reyse* in *ibid.,* II, 25–26, and Lodewyckszoon in *ibid.,* I, 122; "The Eighth Voyage Set Forth by the East-Indian Society . . . under Captaine John Saris," in *PP,* III, 506–8. Saris reported that the Chinese junks came in February or March (p. 508).
[272] Foster (ed.), *op. cit.* (n. 33), p. 168.
[273] Rouffaer and Ijzerman (eds.), *op. cit.* (n. 28), II, 26. See our pl. 251.

Chinese middlemen often adulterate the pepper by mixing in dirt and water because, he observes, the Chinese know that the Dutch will buy anything.[274] Indeed Chinese coins—"caixos" or cash—were standard currency in Bantam and on Java generally; the *Verhael vande reyse* calls them simply "Iavas gelt."[275] Lodewyckszoon describes cash in more detail. In Malay, he reports, they are called "cas," in Javanese "pitis." Individually they have little value—"less than a farthing"—and they are cast in a very poor alloy, Lodewyckszoon thinks lead in which copper dross is mixed. If you drop a string of them, eight to twelve will break, and if they lay in salt water overnight they all stick together and half will break. Cash, he reports, have square holes in their centers and are strung together in a bundle of 200 called a "satac" (*atak*). Five *ataks* bound together make 1,000, which the Javans call a "sapocou" (*peku*). The Dutch can buy twelve or thirteen strings for one real of eight. According to Lodewyckszoon, Chinese cash was first introduced to Java in 1590. Very few of these original coins can still be found, for they are more valuable than recently minted cash: 10,000 of them will buy a sack of pepper while ordinarily two or two and one-half sacks sell for 100,000 cash. Five or six Chinese porcelain dishes can be bought for a string of 1,000 cash in January when the Chinese ships come in; at other times 1,000 cash purchases only two or three dishes. The Chinese also send reals of eight to China, not as coins but melted down as silver "tayels" (taels).[276] Saris observes that cash strung in China rarely has the required number of coins on a string. Instead of 200 cash in an *atak* there will be only 160 or 170 and thus a *peku* or string of 1,000 will be 150 or 200 pieces short. The purchasing power of a string of cash also varies. Immediately after the Chinese junks come to Bantam in January, 34 or 35 strings can be purchased for one real of eight, but later in the year they sell for 20 to 22 strings per real of eight. A handsome profit can be made, therefore, by speculating on cash, although, Saris observes, the danger of losing them in a fire is also great.[277]

Saris provides considerable detail on Javanese weights and measures. Pepper, he reports, comes in sacks called "timbanges" (from Malay and Javanese, *timbang*, weight or balance), each of which contains 49½ "cattees" (catties) Chinese. Two "timbanges" equal a "peecull" (picul), three "peeculls" a small "bahar" (bahar), and 4½ "peeculls" a great "bahar," which contains 445½ "cattees." Javans, he writes, commonly use a volume measurement called a "coolack" (Malay, *kulak,* a local measure equal to one-half a coconut full) because they are not skilled in the use of balance beams. It contains 7¼ "cattees." Seven "coolacks" equal a "timbang," which is 1¼

---

[274] Foster (ed.), *op. cit.* (n. 33), p. 104.

[275] Rouffaer and Ijzerman (eds.), *op. cit.* (n. 28), II, 25.

[276] *Ibid.,* I, 122–23. The estimates of the value of cash and reals of eight in Dutch guilders are Rouffaer and Ijzerman's. Chinese cash are among the coins depicted in pl. 44 of Lodewyckszoon's journal, *ibid.,* I, 214.

[277] *PP,* III, 506–7.

"cattees" more than when the "timbang" is filled by weight.[278] Gold, bezoar, and civet Saris reports are weighed in "tailes" (taels) which equal two
reals of eight, or two English ounces. A Malay tael, however, equals 1½
reals of eight or 1⅓ English ounces. Ten Chinese taels equal six Javanese
taels. Saris observes that there is much deceit in weights, especially in the
Chinese markets.[279]

Saris also quotes prices for a great many of the products for sale in Bantam's markets. For example, Chinese raw silk from "Lamking" (Nanking)
sells for 190 reals per picul; Canton raw silk for 80 reals per picul. A bolt of
112 yards of Chinese taffeta sells for 46 reals. Thirteen-yard pieces of velvet
bring 12 reals each. The best musk brings 22 reals per catty.[280] He goes on to
describe the products brought to Bantam from other ports and in many
cases the prices of these products in Bantam.[281]

Although in large measure Batavia replaced Bantam as Java's entrepôt
during the second quarter of the century, at least in the eyes of Dutch reporters, Bantam continued to thrive and compete for trade. Later writers
provide occasional glimpses of Bantam's continued prosperity. Merklein,
for example, still lists Bantam and Japara as Java's major ports, where people
from all nations come to trade.[282] Schouten, writing in 1676, calls Bantam
"the principal seaport and commercial city on this island governed by the
inhabitants, one of the richest cities in all the Indies,"[283] although he observes that its commerce has "declined considerably" since the rise of
Batavia.[284] Even so, Schouten describes Bantam's three markets as overflowing with goods from all over the Indies and crowded with merchants from
all parts of Asia. Many foreigners still live in the town. In fact, the English
and even the Dutch still find it advantageous to maintain factories there.[285]
L'Estra, too, describes Bantam's bustling markets and harbor in language
similar to that of the earliest European visitors.[286] Finally, Bolling, whose
book was published in 1678, again reports that not only the Dutch and English maintain lodges in Bantam but so do the Portuguese and the Danes.
They purchase mostly pepper and agates.[287]

Nevertheless, most European accounts written after the first quarter of
the century convey the impression that Batavia had replaced Bantam as
Java's busiest port and most important entrepôt. Merchants from all Asian
nations live there; ships from all over the world trade there. Goods from all

[278] *Ibid.*, p. 506.
[279] *Ibid.*, p. 507.
[280] *Ibid.*, p. 508.
[281] *Ibid.*, pp. 506–16.
[282] Merklein, *op. cit.* (n. 81), p. 14.
[283] *Op. cit.* (n. 46), III, 139.
[284] *Ibid.*, pp. 140, 159.
[285] *Ibid.*, pp. 140–41.
[286] *Op. cit.* (n. 102), pp. 217–18.
[287] Bolling, *loc. cit.* (n. 82), p. 327.

other VOC factories are stored in Batavia while awaiting shipment to Europe or to other Asian ports. Most seventeenth-century visitors to Batavia were awed by the magnitude of its commerce. Bolling, for example, names every VOC factory in Asia and lists the products which are bought and sold at each: to Amboina the VOC sends reals of eight and cloth from China, Bengal, and Coromandel; in return they bring cloves, nutmeg, palm oil, and lemon preserves to Batavia. To Banda the Dutch send cloth from Surat and Coromandel in return for nutmeg, mace, preserved nutmegs, preserved lemons, and birds of paradise. From Solor and Timor the VOC in Batavia receives sandalwood, pigstone, honey, wax, tortoise shells, and mother-of-pearl, in return for all sorts of cloth and a variety of trinkets such as nails, mirrors, and knives. From the Moluccas come cloves and palm oil, again in exchange for reals of eight and cloth from Surat and Coromandel. In Makassar the VOC exchanges rice, cloth, and reals of eight for slaves and gold. In Ternate the Dutch exchange rice and cloth for tobacco and licorice.[288]

The VOC sends eight ships from Batavia to Japan each year, one of which is usually lost in a typhoon. Despite such losses, the Japan trade is the VOC's most profitable. Among the products sold in Japan are various kinds of cloth—Bolling quotes prices for each—as well as Turkish grosgrain, ivory, Morocco leather, sandalwood, ebony, fur clothing, pepper, cloves, linen from Guinea called *salpicades* (Portuguese, spotted), silk goods, especially taffeta, fine linen of several types, sugar, amber, "Raff" (dried halibut fins), blue cotton, and large dogs. From Japan the VOC ships take to Batavia silver, gold, lacquerware, copper, camphor, rhubarb, bamboo, pearls, sake, wheat, rice, chestnuts and other nuts, curved swords, and fur pelts. Most of the products sold to the Japanese can also be sold in Tongking, where the Dutch buy silk, gold, musk, and "Pelang" (?) silk. The Siamese buy the same sorts of goods as the Japanese; the Dutch purchase incense, lead, tin, gumlac, and ivory in Siam. In Sumatra the VOC exchanges Coromandel cloth and trinkets for incense, gold, pepper, and benzoin. VOC ships also bring various kinds of cloth, cloves and other spices, and Chinese porcelain to Malacca from where they carry "Philsbeen" (?), monkeys, tin, resin, ironstone, and gum.[289]

Even the VOC trade with Ceylon, India, and Persia was headquartered in Batavia, and Bolling describes what the VOC bought and sold in what they called "the West Quarter," as well. To Sinda (on Ormuz) they ship quicksilver, tin, pepper, tortoise shells, cinnamon, benzoin, amber, saffron, cardamom, Malaccan gum, indigo, sugar, porcelain, China root, mace, nutmeg, and chili pepper. From Sinda to Batavia they carry Persian cloths, cotton, silk, silk floss, saltpeter, and foodstuffs such as butter, rice, and wheat flour. Along the Coromandel Coast the VOC purchases cotton cloth,

[288] *Ibid.*, pp. 347–50.
[289] *Ibid.*, pp. 350–55.

rubies, diamonds, agates, pearls, indigo, opium, and "Callo Krud" (?); they sell sulphur, nutmeg, mace, cloves, alum, sappanwood, sandalwood, tin, quicksilver, pewter, preserved nutmeg, musk, gumlac, gold, China root, and, according to Bolling, most of the silk and porcelain at their factories along the Coromandel Coast. To Ceylon the VOC takes silver, gold, and cloth from China, Coromandel, and Surat. They ship cinnamon, ginger, pepper, elephants, rhubarb, and precious stones from Ceylon to Batavia. In Perak and Kedah on the Malay Peninsula the VOC buys tin in exchange for Coromandel cloth and reals of eight. In the island of Butung, off the coast of Celebes, they purchase horses, wax, honey, and slaves with all sorts of cloth goods. On the Malabar Coast the VOC buys primarily pepper and cardamom in exchange for Coromandel cloth and reals of eight. In Bengal they buy ginger, sugar, cotton, unspun silk, caraway, opium, and saltpeter in exchange for reals of eight, Chinese porcelain, and Moluccan spices. The Dutch sell all sorts of English cloth, cloves, nutmeg, brass, tin, red copper, sappanwood, sulphur, pepper, camphor, ivory, tortoise shells, benzoin, amber, saffron, Chinese silk, sugar, alum, turpentine, China root, sandalwood, quicksilver, cloth, and cut jewels in Surat, where they purchase primarily fine linens, saltpeter, indigo, carpets, musk, and white caraway. In Persia the VOC sells cochineal, colored cloth, amber, Coromandel cloth, Japanese copper, spices, sugar candy, preserved ginger, gumlac, indigo, cardamom, cinnamon, sappanwood, English tin, ebony, China root, and porcelain. From Persia they buy pearls, red silk, gold brocade, carpets, sulphur, saffron, sandalwood, alum, almonds and other nuts, raisins, "kismis" (Persian stoneless raisins), and Moorish ducats. Finally, according to Bolling, the Dutch obtain reals of eight, ducats, blue coral, ambergris, "Selisba" (?), amber, and civet from Mocha on the Red Sea, where they sell most of the same products that they take to Surat.[290] Bolling's long list of products shipped in and out of Batavia is limited to those which rode on VOC ships between VOC factories. In addition, considerable quantities of merchandise were carried on Chinese and Javanese ships. Goods from many islands in the archipelago where the Dutch had no establishments—primarily rice and other foodstuffs—were brought to Batavia in native boats.[291]

European writers also included some specific details about trade and commerce at other Javanese ports. Lodewyckszoon, for example, mentions villages along Java's north coast well known for their fishing industry. From Pasuruan, he reports, come prayerbeads for both Hindus and Muslims, made from the peppercorn-sized fruit of a tree. Merchants in Bantam also buy cotton cloth in Pasuruan and sell Chinese goods there.[292] The writer of *Het tweede boeck* describes a vigorous trade in silk, camlet, cotton cloth, and

---

[290] *Ibid.,* pp. 355–61.
[291] *Ibid.,* p. 350.
[292] Rouffaer and Ijzerman (eds.), *op. cit.* (n. 28), I, 100–103.

foodstuffs at Tuban.[293] Madura was known to most European writers as a rice-exporting area.[294] Olivier van Noort reports that the king of Jortan allows foreigners to trade without tolls or tariffs.[295] Saris mentions foodstuffs, cotton cloth, spun yarn, and pepper from Jambi for sale in Jortan, as well as mace and nuts from Banda.[296]

Mataram and Japara are major sources of rice and of wood for shipbuilding. Much of Batavia's rice and other foodstuffs come from there.[297] Apart from observing its rich rice lands, Van Goens reports almost nothing about Mataram's commerce. Schouten lists Java's premier products as rice, pepper, coconuts, coconut oil, salt, sugar, ginger, and arrack, but reports that almost anything imaginable from all over Asia and Europe can be bought in the great markets of Bantam, Japara, and Batavia.[298]

The Javans were also seen as a seafaring people. Many of the goods carried between the islands of the archipelago are carried in Javanese boats. They are able sailors, according to Lodewyckszoon, who do not use maps and who first learned to use the compass from the Portuguese. They usually sail in sight of land. He and many European observers after him describe and sketch Javanese ships and boats.[299] According to Lodewyckszoon the best "fusten" or galliots, called "cathurs," were built in "Lassaon" (Lasem) which he erroneously locates between Cheribon and Japara, where they have especially good wood.[300] These are single-masted vessels, manned by slave rowers and carrying many soldiers to board other ships or land on beaches. Most writers also describe large three-masted junks with high decks, a cabin aft hanging out over the water—like a farmer's outhouse, according to Schouten—and square sails made of straw or coconut bark, but without topsails. They are used for commerce rather than war. Javans and Chinese take long voyages on them, for weeks and even months, usually accompanied by their families.[301]

[293] Keuning (ed.), *op. cit.* (n. 7), III, 36.
[294] For example, see *ibid.*, III, 52.
[295] Ijzerman (ed.), *op. cit.* (n. 8), I, 142.
[296] *PP*, III, 510.
[297] For example, see Merklein, *op. cit.* (n. 81), p. 14; Bolling, *loc. cit.* (n. 82), p. 327; Schouten, *op. cit.* (n. 46), III, 136–37.
[298] Schouten, *op. cit.* (n. 46), III, 159.
[299] Rouffaer and Ijzerman (eds.), *op. cit.* (n. 28), I, 130–33 and pl. 27. See also Saar, *op. cit.* (n. 81), p. 28, and Schouten, *op. cit.* (n. 46), III, 160–61. Crawfurd (*op. cit.* [n. 107], I, 307–11) speculates that they may have learned about the compass from the Chinese but agrees that it was little used and that Javanese ships mostly sailed in sight of land.
[300] Rouffaer and Ijzerman (eds.), *op. cit.* (n. 28), I, 132, pl. 27. Rouffaer and Ijzerman identify the wood as *jati* (teak) wood. On teak in Java see A. L. Howard, *A Manual of the Timbers of the World* (3d ed., London, 1948), pp. 581–82. The origin of the word "cathur" or "catur" is uncertain. See Yule and Burnell, *op. cit.* (n. 111), p. 175. See also Schouten, *op. cit.* (n. 46), III, 160.
[301] Lodewyckszoon in Rouffaer and Ijzerman (eds.), *op. cit.* (n. 28), I, 132–33; Schouten, *op. cit.* (n. 46), III, 160.

Most numerous in Javanese waters are the smaller ships called "tynan-gen" (?), "prauwen" (proas), and "vliegers" (flyers) by the Dutch writers. These are pointed bow and stern, come in a variety of sizes, carry lateen sails but are sometimes rowed, and are maneuvered by means of a bamboo rudder that hangs off one side near the stern. The largest of these are equipped with tents or some other covering for the protection of the passengers. The smallest are often carved from a single log and are stabilized by outriggers made from thick bamboo logs. The Dutch call them "vliegers" because of their extraordinary speed. Javanese ships trade all over the archipelago with VOC permission.[302]

Not much is reported about Javanese peasants or artisans. Schouten lists some of their crafts. Java has, he asserts, good coppersmiths, ironworkers, and goldsmiths. Those who make krises are fine craftsmen. Apart from the krises, however, he does not describe any products of Javanese craftsmen. Nor does anyone else. But Schouten observes that Java could boast a great many sharp merchants. Echoing most European visitors he asserts:

The Javanese merchants are usually exceedingly crafty, dishonest, and very deceitful in the delivery of their goods and merchandise, especially towards the Christians. They adulterate the pepper with pebbles and brownish sand, are shrewd in the transaction of their business, assiduously looking around for a lucky chance at profit or advantage over others.[303]

During the seventeenth century the European image of Java emerged from the shadows with considerable clarity. The published reports were widely distributed and were rich in details concerning Javanese trade, political life, social customs, religion, and the landscape. By the last third of the century they were no longer confined to coastal towns but contained considerable information about the interior landscape and the empire of Mataram. A reader of all these reports could have obtained a fairly sophisticated understanding of seventeenth-century Java. But the accuracy of this image is difficult to assess. On some important topics it is not clear, for others there are too few observers, and the image changes in some respects during the course of the century. But for many aspects of seventeenth-century Javanese history, the published European reports are themselves the indispensable primary sources. Furthermore, the Europeans were no mere observers of Javanese realities, they were themselves changing Javanese society and politics in profound ways, often unaware of the changes they were effecting. Their descriptions, therefore, may be of conditions already con-

---

[302] Rouffaer and Ijzerman (eds.), *op. cit.* (n. 28), I, 133; Schouten, *op. cit.* (n. 46), III, 160–61. Rouffaer and Ijzerman identify them as "prahoe katirs" (*perahu katir*). On ships in general see Pierre-Yves Manguin, "The Southeast Asian Ship: An Historical Approach," *Journal of Southeast Asian Studies,* XI (1980), 266–76.
[303] Schouten, *op. cit.* (n. 46), III, p. 158.

siderably altered by the European presence in the archipelago. Nevertheless, they probably provide the earliest reliable comprehensive image of Java and its people available anywhere.

2

BALI

The published reports from the first Dutch voyage to Southeast Asia also contained some of the earliest European references to Bali and the first continuous description of that island in any language. Indeed these proved to be the most comprehensive notices about Bali written during the seventeenth century.[304]

The *Verhael vande reyse*'s report (1598) is brief: Bali is fruitful, although it produces no spices; Balinese dress like Javans and use the same weapons, especially krises and blowguns; they are enemies of both the Muslims and the Portuguese; and the king of Bali keeps a more magnificent court than the king of Bantam. According to the *Verhael vande reyse* the king rides in a wagon drawn by two white buffaloes and his guards carry spears with golden points (see pl. 254). The Balinese are "heathen," having no common religion. Some worship a cow, some the sun; each worships his own god. Balinese women, the *Verhael vande reyse* reports, practice suttee. They would be judged dishonorable if they refused it.[305]

Lodewyckszoon's description of Bali, also published in 1598, is the most detailed notice to appear. It locates Bali off Java's east coast, its northern point at 8.5° south latitude. According to Lodewyckszoon, Bali is twelve German miles in circumference, its north coast is very mountainous, and on its south coast a long, high point extends far out into the sea.[306] Bali's population is very large—he estimates it at six hundred thousand—a result, he speculates, of polygamy. In fact, he notes, the Balinese sell many of their people as slaves. Curiously, he describes them as black with curly hair.[307] They dress, however, like the people on Java and other neighboring islands.

---

[304]For bibliography see above, pp. 437–39. Rouffaer and Ijzerman (eds.), *op. cit.* (n. 28), I, 197. Thomas S. Raffles, *The History of Java* (2d ed., 2 vols.; London, 1830), II, Appendix K, contains the second continuous description of Bali; it first appeared in print in 1817.

[305]Rouffaer and Ijzerman (eds.), *op. cit.* (n. 28), I, 60–61. Van der Does' *Kort verhael* contains a similar, brief notice of Bali; see *ibid.*, II, 358–59.

[306]*Ibid.*, I, 197. Actually Bali lies between 8°4' (its northern point) and 8°51' south latitude (its southern tip). Its circuit is 400 kilometers or about 52 German miles.

[307]*Ibid.*, I, 197–98. Rouffaer and Ijzerman speculate that the black people whom Lodewyckszoon personally saw along the coast and aboard his ship were all Papuan slaves, who were still very numerous on Bali in the nineteenth century. Lodewyckszoon's estimate of Bali's population they judge to be plausible. Lodewyckszoon's 600,000 people roughly agrees with Raffles' 1817 report of 215,000 men on Bali.

The Balinese are heathen, according to Lodewyckszoon, by which he probably means nothing more than that they are not Muslims. Regarding the
content of Balinese religion Lodewyckszoon reports only that they worship
whatever they first meet in the morning.[308] He also describes suttee, which
he thinks is widely practiced on Bali. While the Dutch lay off the coast they
hear about fifty wives of a great noble who are to be burned alive on their
husband's funeral pyre. None of the Dutch, Lodewyckszoon reports, were
inclined to watch the spectacle. Lodewyckszoon thinks suttee is a moral obligation for Balinese women and that they believe it enables them to accompany their husbands to the next world. Although he mentions that Indians
also practice suttee, he seems not to understand it as a religious act and he
does not relate Bali's religion to India. He instead repeats the standard European story about the suttee's origin: that it was instituted by a king to keep
unfaithful wives from poisoning their husbands.[309]

Lodewyckszoon was most impressed by Bali's fruitfulness. The Balinese
raise an "overflowing" abundance of rice, but the king forbids its export. He
uses it to feed Bali's large population and to fill "forts" in the mountains
where surplus rice is stored against bad harvests or foreign invasion of the
rice-growing lowlands.[310] Bali also produces an abundance of coconuts
(from which the inhabitants make oil), oranges, lemons, limes—in fact, all
the fruits which grow on Java. Lodewyckszoon especially mentions "a fruit
the size of a pear covered with a thin shell shaped like a chestnut" (the *salak*)
and "a fruit that grows under the ground, the size of a walnut . . . which
they also use much in their food" (groundnuts or peanuts).[311] No spices
grow on Bali except ginger and some drugs which are also plentiful on Java
and other islands of the archipelago.[312]

The seas around Bali teem with fish, and fishing is one of the inhabitants'
major occupations. The Balinese raise chickens, ducks, partridges, peacocks, and turtledoves, as well as a variety of animals: oxen, water buffaloes,
goats, pigs, and a very large number of small horses. Few of the horses are
exported. They are used by the ordinary people for transportation. The
great nobles are carried by their slaves in sedan chairs or ride in carriages
drawn by buffaloes.[313] Lodewyckszoon also reports the existence of iron,
copper, and gold on Bali. The king forbids the mining of gold. The Dutch

[308] *Ibid.,* I, 197. This is a common Hindu custom.
[309] *Ibid.,* I, 202. For a description of a Balinese suttee see Crawfurd, *op. cit.* (n. 107), II,
241–53. See also Miguel Covarrubias, *Island of Bali* (New York, 1937), pp. 378–80.
[310] Rouffaer and Ijzerman (eds.), *op. cit.* (n. 28), I, 198–99. No other source mentions "forts"
in the mountains where rice was stored. *Cf.* the "ever normal granary" system of China.
[311] *Ibid.,* p. 199.
[312] *Ibid.*
[313] *Ibid.,* pp. 198–99. Rouffaer and Ijzerman note that on Java only the great rode horses,
while on Bali the common people used them—an indication of Bali's greater prosperity (*ibid.,*
p. 198n). See our pl. 255.

who visited the Balinese king's court, however, report seeing many golden drinking vessels; they are more numerous and more costly than any seen in any Javanese court including Bantam.[314] In addition to farming and fishing, the Balinese produce large amounts of cloth, woven from the cotton which grows on the island. Lodewyckszoon thinks it is a major export to Java and Sumbawa.[315] Apart from their cotton cloth trade with east Java, carried in small proas, the Balinese engage in little or no overseas trade. Ships from elsewhere, from Bantam, Amboina, Makassar, Timor, and Solor, however, regularly stop at Bali for food and water, and to buy cloth, cattle, and slaves. The Chinese, too, occasionally trade in Bali. They exchange porcelain and swords for cotton cloth. But Chinese strings of cash are not accepted as currency on Bali as they are in Java and Sumatra, although the Balinese use the larger Chinese coins. Chinese influence on Bali appears to be much less than in other parts of the archipelago.[316]

Balinese soldiers use krises, spears, swords, and shields like those of the Javans, but their favorite weapon is the blowgun. The small, thin darts of the blowgun have poisoned points which always break off in the victim's body causing great pain and very frequently death.[317]

Bali's king is absolute. He holds court in lavish pomp and splendor; even his greatest nobles dare speak to him only with folded hands. Day-to-day government appears to be in the hands of a governor called the "Quillor" (*Ki Lurah*), whom Lodewyckszoon compares to the great chancellor of Poland. Under him are many other nobles, each of whom governs his district in the name of the king. Lodewyckszoon reports an abortive conspiracy against the king about ten or twelve years earlier. The rebels, attempting to assassinate the king in his palace, were all quickly arrested and condemned to death. The king, however, mercifully changed the sentence and banished them to a small island southeast of Bali called "Pulo Rossa" (Malay, Pulau Rusa; Deer Island; Balinese, Nusa Penida). There they still live, quite prosperously, still subjects of the king, but not permitted to return to Bali.[318] The king of Bali comes down to meet the Dutch ship, riding in an elaborate carriage drawn by two white buffaloes and guarded by soldiers with gold-

---

[314] *Ibid.*, 201. Rouffaer and Ijzerman assert that the gold which the Dutch saw on Bali came from elsewhere, in the form of gold dust from Sumatra, Celebes, and Borneo in exchange for Balinese rice, cotton cloth, and slaves. They also use this report as evidence of the higher development of Balinese goldsmiths' art, compared to that of the Javanese seaports. (see *ibid.*, 200–201n.

[315] *Ibid.*, 198, 199.

[316] *Ibid.*, 199–200.

[317] *Ibid.*, 200.

[318] *Ibid.*, 201–2. Rouffaer and Ijzerman point out that this is the first European notice of "Deer Island" as a Balinese penal colony (*ibid.*, p. 201n). See also *Encyclopaedie van Nederlandsch-Indië*, III, 382.

pointed spears. The king thought they had been there before, because, Lodewyckszoon concludes, Francis Drake had visited the island.[319]

Several copperplates accompany Lodewyckszoon's text: one of a Balinese noble being carried in a sedan chair, one of a noble riding in a buffalo-drawn carriage, a map of the island, and a suttee. All are products of the engraver's imagination; the picture of the suttee was taken from Linschoten.[320] Lodewyckszoon's description of Bali, including the copperplate engravings, is also included in the *Begin ende voortgangh* account of De Houtman's voyage.[321]

During the remainder of the seventeenth century, Bali receives only short notices and from but relatively few European writers. Pyrard, for example, includes two pages about Bali which are almost identical in content with the notice found in the *Verhael vande reyse.*[322] The insert in Gerret Vermeulen's *De gedenkwaerdige voyagie* (1677) probably has the same origin or is culled from Lodewyckszoon's report. Vermeulen, a soldier in the VOC campaign against Makassar, visited the coast of Bali in 1667 or 1668. When the Dutch landed, looking for fresh water, local authorities told them they might not come ashore carrying weapons. The Dutch retreated to their ship but returned that night with more guards. A battle ensued. One VOC soldier was killed. Next morning, the Dutch who returned to retrieve his body carried guns. They met Balinese soldiers in battle formation, but no shots were fired. Later the Dutch bought many pigs from the Balinese. Vermeulen also relates a story about a European who plotted against the king of Bali and who was cut into little pieces for his trouble.[323]

Finally Frick, in 1692, includes a brief notice about Bali. In addition to what by then had become standard information, Frick observes that Balinese sold themselves as slaves; he bought a young girl. He also contends that the Balinese did not marry but held women in common. Still he mentions suttee—claims to have witnessed one—which would seem to imply marriage.[324]

The first Dutch visitors found the island and its people very pleasant, abundantly supplied with all things necessary for good living. Lodewyckszoon reports that they named Bali "New Holland." Two Dutch sailors jumped ship and remained there when the Dutch sailed away.[325] Still Bali did not fall under VOC control during the seventeenth century, probably because it produced no spices, had no seaport on its north coast, and had

---

[319] Rouffaer and Ijzerman (eds.), *op. cit.* (n. 28), I, 195–96. See our pl. 254.

[320] *Ibid.,* I, 196, 196(2), 202, 202(2). See our pls. 254, 255.

[321] *BV,* I, 98–101.

[322] Gray (ed.), *op. cit.* (n. 32), II, 165–66.

[323] Gerret Vermeulen, *De gedenkwaerdige voyagie . . . naar Oost-Indien in't jaer 1668 aangevangen, en in't jaer 1674 voltrokken . . .* (Amsterdam, 1677), pp. 61–66. For bibliography see above, pp. 498–99.

[324] *Op. cit.* (n. 82), pp. 108–10.

[325] Rouffaer and Ijzerman (eds.), *op. cit.* (n. 28), I, 203.

maintained its independence from Mataram. The Dutch built a lodging on the island in 1620, but it was destroyed during the following year. The VOC sent an embassy to Bali in 1633 attempting to enlist the king's aid against Mataram. Justus Heurnius, the missionary, was involved with the embassy and later wrote a report to the governor-general about the situation in Bali. No published description resulted from it, however.[326] VOC embassies were sent in subsequent years, as well, and some contracts were negotiated with the king of Bali for the purchase of slaves. Bali did not become a Dutch possession, however, until 1841, long after the demise of the VOC.[327] Europe's image of Bali during the seventeenth century, therefore, was formed almost entirely by Lodewyckszoon's report which, while it introduced European readers to the island, mentioned few of the Balinese cultural characteristics which nineteenth-century Europeans found so intriguing. It says very little about Balinese religion, for example, nothing about Bali's temples and art, nothing about its music, dance, and theater, nothing about its language and literature, and nothing about Bali's complex social structure and caste system.

3

SUMATRA

Sumatra had been frequently described in the sixteenth-century European literature, although relatively few of these descriptions were by eyewitnesses.[328] Fresh, firsthand notices of Sumatra became available during the last years of the sixteenth century (1597–99) when the several reports about the first Dutch voyage to Asia were published.[329] Much of the information in these reports, however, seems to have come from Portuguese Indian sources or from what the Dutch authors had seen in India. When describing coconut palms and pepper, which they had seen on Sumatra, for example, the authors used more Indian than Sumatran illustrations.[330] Detailed eyewitness information about Acheh appeared in the accounts of James Lancaster's first English East India Company voyage, published in 1603, and Joris van Spilbergen's voyage to Ceylon, published in 1605.[331] Bartolomé

---

[326] See P. A. Leupe (ed.), "Schriftelijck rapport gedaen door den predicant Justus Heurnius, aengaende de gelegentheijt van't eijlandt ende tot het voorplanten van de Christelijcke religie, en van wegen de gelengentheit van Bali, 1638," *BTLV*, III (1855), 250–62, and P. A. Leupe (ed.), "Het gezandtschap naar Bali, onder den Gouverneur-Generaal Hendrik Brouwer in 1633," *BTLV*, V (1856), 1–71.

[327] *Encyclopaedie van Nederlansch-Indië*, I, 108–9.

[328] See *Asia*, I, 571–78.

[329] For bibliography see above, pp. 437–39.

[330] For example, see "De eerst schipvaerd . . . ," *BV*, Ia, 33–36.

[331] For Lancaster's voyage see above, pp. 549–50; on Spilbergen's voyage see above, pp. 443–44.

Leonardo de Argensola's *Conquista de las islas Malucas* (Madrid, 1609) contains a brief general description of Sumatra, but it is not based on new, first-hand observations. Nor, apparently, is Pyrard's 1611 account, although it contains some fresh information about Achenese politics.[332]

Samuel Purchas' monumental *Pilgrimes*, published in 1625, contains several firsthand accounts of Sumatra, the most extensive of which is that by John Davis, the English pilot who accompanied Cornelis de Houtman's 1598 voyage to Acheh.[333] Notices of Acheh are also included in the journals of Thomas Best, John Milward, and Walter Payton's second voyage as published by Purchas; those of Payton, William Hore, and William Keeling also contain brief notices about other Sumatran ports, primarily the west coast towns of Tiku and Priaman.[334]

The reports of the first Dutch voyage as published in the 1646 *Begin ende voortgangh* collection are augmented by inserts taken from sixteenth-century literature. The *Begin ende voortgangh* also contains other firsthand notices of Sumatra, the most descriptive of which are found in the journals of Paulus van Caerden, Wybrand van Warwijck, and Pieter Willemszoon Verhoeff.[335] Two brief accounts, one by the Indo-Portuguese Franciscan Goncalo de S. Jose Velloso published in 1642 and the other by the Carmelite Francisco Agostino published in 1652, described the Portuguese embassy to Sultan Iskandar Thani of Acheh in 1638. The embassy was led by Francesco de Souza de Castro and included Father Pierre Bertholet and another Carmelite father who were seized and killed by the Achenese.[336]

Vincent Le Blanc's very popular travel tale, published in 1648, also contains a brief general description of Sumatra, certainly not firsthand.[337] The account, first published in Melchisédech Thévenot's *Relations de divers voyages curieux* (1664–66), of Augustin de Beaulieu's 1620–22 visit to Acheh is not only firsthand but one of the most perceptive and informative of the century. Beaulieu spent almost a year in Acheh attempting to purchase pepper and waiting for news from the vice-admiral of his squadron who ran afoul of the Dutch in Bantam. During his stay Beaulieu had many audiences with Sultan Iskandar Muda (r. 1607–36), and his description of this illustrious ruler is the most perceptive of the seventeenth century.[338] Wouter Schouten's *Oost-Indische voyagie,* published in 1676, contains one of the better descriptions of Sumatra, most of it apparently based on personal observations.[339] Johann Nieuhof includes a rather lengthy description in his 1682

---

[332] For bibliography see above, pp. 310–12 and pp. 396–97.

[333] See above, p. 558. On the voyage see W. S. Unger (ed.), *De oudste reizen van de Zeeuwen naar Oost-Indië, 1598–1604* ("WLV," LI; The Hague, 1948), pp. xviii–xl, 19–113.

[334] For bibliography see above, pp. 558, 562–64, 566.

[335] For bibliography see above, pp. 462–63, 466, 470–71.

[336] For bibliography see above, pp. 348, 381.

[337] See above, pp. 406–7.

[338] See above, pp. 410–11, for bibliography. See also D. Lombard, *Le sultanat d'Atjeh au temps d'Iskandar Muda, 1607–1636* (Paris, 1967), pp. 25–27, 193–96.

[339] See above, pp. 496–97.

Zee- en lant-reize. Although he had visited Sumatra, his report seems to depend heavily on earlier published accounts.[340] Several of the Germans and the one Dane who served the VOC and published their memoirs after returning to Europe describe Sumatra: for example, Frederick Bolling (1678), Elias Hesse (1687), Johann Wilhelm Vogel (1690), and Christoph Frick (1692).[341] Of these, Hesse, who accompanied a VOC gold-mining operation to Sillida, north of Painan on the west coast, provided the best description. Finally, in the last years of the century Jacob Janssen de Roy published some comments about trade and politics at Acheh and William Dampier discussed both Acheh and Benkulen in considerable detail. Nikolaas de Graaf, who visited Acheh on his first voyage in 1641, also included a brief description in his *Reisen,* published in 1701.[342]

A. PLACEMENT, CLIMATE, AND PRODUCTS

All of the seventeenth century reports locate Sumatra between 5° or 5°30′ north and 6° south latitude, straddling the equator. It is usually named as one of the world's largest islands. The earliest Dutch reports seem confused about its size. According to some it is 700 Dutch miles in circumference and 200 miles across. Others assert that it is 170 miles long and 60 miles wide.[343] Wouter Schouten and Elias Hesse, writing later in the century, say it is 195 and 200 miles long, respectively, and 50 miles wide. Schouten thinks it is 480 miles around, about the same as England and Scotland together.[344] The sixteenth-century speculations about whether Sumatra or Ceylon was ancient Taprobana and whether Sumatra was the Ophir from which King Solomon received gold were rehearsed in many seventeenth-century descriptions down to the end of the century.[345] Most writers also note Sumatra's

---

[340] See above, pp. 500–501.

[341] See above, pp. 535–36, 539–40, 541–42.

[342] For De Roy see above, p. 503; for Dampier see above pp. 582–85; for De Graaf see above, pp. 505–6.

[343] For example, see "De eerste schipvaerd . . . ," *BV,* Ia, 36. Scholars' estimates of how many English miles made a seventeenth-century Dutch mile range from three to six. For example, Boxer (*op. cit.* [n. 81], p. 305) says "The Dutch mile was very variable but usually taken as the equivalent of the English league (3 miles) in the 17th century." William Campbell (*Formosa under the Dutch* [London, 1903; reprinted Taipei, 1967], p. 541) estimates about six English miles to one Dutch mile in the seventeenth century. See also *Encyclopaedie van Nederlandsche-Indië,* II, 686.

[344] Wouter Schouten, *op. cit.* (n. 46), III, 46; Hesse, *op. cit.* (n. 96), p. 61. See also Beaulieu's similar description, "Relations de l'estat present du commerce des Hollandais et des Portugais dans les Indes Orientales: memoires du voyage aux Indes Orientales du General de Beaulieu," in *TR,* II, 96. Sumatra's length is actually 1,100 miles, its extreme breadth is 250 miles, and its area is 164,198 square miles. The circuit of the island is about 2,300 miles.

[345] For examples see "De eerste schipvaerd," *BV,* Ia, 36; Bartolomé Leonardo de Argensola, *Conquista de las islas Malucas* (Madrid, 1609), p. 141; Vincent Le Blanc, *The World Surveyed or the Famous Voyages of Vincent le Blanc . . . ,* trans. F. B. (London, 1660), p. 91; Merklein, *op. cit.*

proximity to the Malay Peninsula. They usually report the Straits of Malacca to be about ten miles wide. Schouten thought it was only six to eight
miles wide in some places.[346] Sumatra's beauty impresses most visitors. Schouten sketches the most
vivid images: "Sumatra displays soaring mountains, eternally green forests,
pleasant valleys, fruitful plains, bays and rivers abounding with fish, and
clear streams."[347] Everyone comments on the dense forests that grow down
to the water's edge, with trees hanging out over the sea. Frequently the
beaches are not visible from shipboard, nor are the towns and villages. It is
difficult to tell if the many smaller islands along Sumatra's coast are inhabited or not. De Houtman's men report that there are so many small islands
on the western side of the Sunda Straits that it is difficult to find the channel.[348] Beaulieu describes "Pulo Lancalhuy" (Lancahui or Langkawi, one of
the Pepper Islands), its mountains, forests, valleys, coastal plain, people,
and products.[349] Schouten describes many islands along Sumatra's east coast.
"Bangka" (or Bañak), for example, is large and fruitful; he is surprised no
one lives on it.[350] Hesse's ship sails close enough to Krakatoa in the Sunda
Straits in 1681 for him to survey the effects of the May, 1680, eruption. He
reports desolate charred forests with smoke still visible for many miles. No
one lives on it any longer.[351] He believes Sebesi, another uninhabited Sunda
Straits island, is the home of evil spirits, because of the continuous screech-
ing heard from it.[352]

William Dampier discusses the varieties of terrain and soils on Sumatra in
what appears to be expert detail. The mountains are rocky, especially along
the west coast; still they have enough thin soil to produce shrubs, small
trees, and good grass. Smaller hills sustain trees well enough to indicate
rather fruitful soil. On the plain the soil is frequently deep, sometimes
black, sometimes grey, sometimes reddish. The soil around Acheh is deep
and well watered by brooks and streams. In some places it is heavily forested, in others savannah, and in still other places swampy.[353] Sumatra is ex-

---

(n. 81), p. 21; Hesse, *op. cit.* (n. 96), pp. 61–62; Schouten, *op. cit.* (n. 46), III, 46. For a discussion of the sixteenth-century literature on this issue see *Asia*, I, 574. Regarding the name of the
island see William Marsden, *The History of Sumatra* (reprint of 3d ed.; Kuala Lumpur, 1966),
pp. 3–13, and N. J. Krom, "De naam Sumatra," *BTLV*, C (1941), 5–25.
[346] *Op. cit.* (n. 46), III, 46.
[347] *Ibid.*
[348] "De eerste schipvaerd," *BV*, Ia, 31.
[349] *Loc. cit.* (n. 344), pp. 80–82. Langkawi is the largest of a group of islets off the Malay
Peninsula near Kedah. See Crawfurd, *op. cit.* (n. 179), p. 207.
[350] *Op. cit.* (n. 46), III, 35–36.
[351] *Op. cit.* (n. 96), p. 54.
[352] *Ibid.*
[353] William Dampier, *Voyages and Discoveries,* ed. Clennell Wilkinson (London, 1931),
pp. 86–87. Marsden describes Sumatra's soils in similar terms but contends that it is mostly
sterile rather than rich: *op. cit.* (n. 345), pp. 25–33, 78–81. On Sumatra's alluvial swamps see
E. H. G. Dobby, *Southeast Asia* (9th ed.; London, 1966), pp. 198–99.

ceedingly fruitful, according to seventeenth-century European observers. It produces an abundance of rice, but also oranges, lemons, citrons, bananas, coconuts, ginger, honey, sugarcane, watermelons, balsam, indigo, camphor, sandalwood, and, of course, pepper. The Dutch first see pepper growing on Sumatra, and Lodewyckszoon's description of it is probably the first in Dutch. It is a vine, he reports, which grows around a thick reed stake. Its leaves resemble those of the orange tree, only smaller. The peppercorns hang in clusters like small grapes. They remain green until December or January, when they are picked.[354] Beaulieu's description of pepper is similar but provides additional details: Sumatrans often plant the pepper vines at the foot of trees on which they will climb. New vines usually bear fruit in the third year and reach peak yields in the fourth to sixth or seventh years. After ten or twelve years they are usually destroyed and new vines planted. Pepper vines bear small white flowers in April. The fruit looks like small green grapes in August, turns red in October, and black in November or December. Pepper in northern Sumatra is harvested between mid-December and the end of February.[355] Lodewyckszoon also describes banana trees, which he calls Indian fig trees, and coconut palms. He is fascinated by the many uses for the leaves, shells, meat, and milk of the coconut palm. These clear and detailed descriptions, however, do not seem to be based entirely on what he sees in Sumatra; they contain several references to India.[356]

Dampier's list of trees and fruits differs very little from that of earlier writers, although he also describes in detail mangosteens, which he particularly likes, "Pumple-noses" (pompelmooses or pomelos), and a plant called "Ganga" or "Bang" (Indian hemp or *Cannabis sativa*) which looks like hemp and which if infused in any liquid "will stupify the Brains of any Person that drinks thereof, making some very sleepy, some merry or silly, and some mad." According to Dampier, Sumatra also produces many medicinal drugs and herbs. He particularly mentions camphor, which is usually sent to Japan to be refined. Sumatrans also raise yams, sweet potatoes, and rice. Extensive rice culture on Sumatra he judges to be rather recent and he thinks they could raise much more of it if they wished.[357]

Sumatra's bays, rivers, and streams teem with fish of many kinds, but also with crocodiles. Inland there are elephants, rhinoceroses, small horses, cows, oxen, buffaloes, sheep, deer, tigers, wild hogs, goats, monkeys, chickens, ducks, and other fowl. Dampier thinks the herds of buffaloes which roam the savannah lands belong to specific people who milk them

---

[354] Lodewyckszoon in Rouffaer and Ijzerman (eds.), *op. cit.* (n. 28), I, 64, 68–69; "De eerste schipvaerd," *BV*, Ia, 35–36. See also W. S. Unger (ed.), *op. cit.* (n. 333), p. 53.

[355] Beaulieu, *loc. cit.* (n. 344), pp. 81–82.

[356] Rouffaer and Ijzerman (eds.), *op. cit.* (n. 28), I, 68–69; "De eerste schipvaerd," *BV*, Ia, 33–35.

[357] Dampier, *op. cit.* (n. 353), pp. 88–89. Most of the seventeenth-century reports about Sumatra's flora and agriculture appear reasonably accurate. *Cf.* Marsden, *op. cit.* (n. 345), pp. 65–84. On Sumatran camphor see below, p. 1386, n. 504.

and kill them for food. So far as he can tell, they are not used as draft animals.[358] Beaulieu, however, thinks they are used for work in the fields.[359] Hesse also describes orangutans (Malay, *orang utan*), which he contends look much like humans and indeed often rape women who stray too far into the jungle. Human women, he insists, can become pregnant by orangutans.[360] Most seventeenth-century European observers report that gold can be found in Sumatra's streams and that there are gold mines in the mountains. Indeed Hesse describes the mine at Sillada, south of Padang, which was once worked by natives and which he and other Saxon miners hired by the VOC attempt to reopen in 1671. But the mine did not produce enough gold to meet expenses. Europeans found it almost impossible to work the mines in Sumatra's climate, and it was very difficult to find natives to do the work. Slaves were used, but they required much supervision and soldiers to guard them. The mine was closed in 1694.[361] Dampier, too, reports that Sumatra, and Acheh in particular, are well supplied with gold. It was mined near what the English call "Golden Mountain" (Mount Luse), visible from the sea but quite far inland from the capital (Banda Acheh). He was told that the journey from Banda Acheh to the mines is exceedingly difficult and dangerous and that the mines are so unhealthy that only half of those who go there ever return. Furthermore, only Muslims are permitted in the area. Slaves, he reports, are used in the mines.[362] Jacob Janssen de Roy also contends that much gold can be had in Acheh. The Danes alone, he reports, ship between seventy and eighty bahars of gold each year from Acheh to their factory at Tranquebar on the Coromandel Coast.[363] European writers also report on the existence in Sumatra of other metals and minerals: silver, tin, copper, iron, sulphur, rubies, sapphires, and garnets. Schouten describes coral: "very elegant [*geestig*] stone-like plants which we found to be artfully formed by nature as tiny trees; some were red, although most were gray in color with their twigs grown very transparent and wonderful under water and on the ground, so that they provided a rarity for the curious."[364]

Despite Sumatra's beauty, fruitfulness, and potential wealth, its climate meets with general condemnation. To be sure, Le Blanc reports that Su-

---

[358] Dampier, *op. cit.* (n. 353), p. 89. See also Beaulieu, *loc. cit.* (n. 344), pp. 96–97, for his list of Sumatran plants and animals.

[359] Beaulieu, *op. cit.* (n. 344), p. 96.

[360] Hesse, *op. cit.* (n. 96), p. 75. Marsden's list of Sumatran animals is very similar to that of seventeenth-century writers, but also includes the hippopotamus, bear, otter, "stinkard," porcupine, armadillo, civet cat, and bat. He does not mention the orangutan: Marsden, *op. cit.* (n. 345), pp. 112–28. On the orangutan also see Yule and Burnell, *op. cit.* (n. 111), pp. 643–44, and above, p. 1327.

[361] Hesse, *op. cit.* (n. 96), pp. viii–ix. See also Marsden, *op. cit.* (n. 345), pp. 165–72.

[362] Dampier, *op. cit.* (n. 353), pp. 92–93.

[363] *Voyagie gedaan door Jacob Janssen de Roy na Borneo en Atchin, in't jaar 1691. en vervolgens: . . . Gedrukt volgens de copy van Batavia*, n.d., p. 126.

[364] Schouten, *op. cit.* (n. 46), III, 37. Marsden's list does not include gems: *op. cit.* (n. 345), pp. 28–29, 172–77.

matra's air is wholesome and its people healthy and long-lived.[365] But Europeans who actually visited Sumatra usually describe the intense heat and the many marshy areas, particularly on the eastern side of the island, which produce thick mists and generally unhealthy air, especially during the rainy months when thunderstorms and heavy rains visit the island every day.[366] The air seems especially bad for foreigners. Hesse, who spent six months in central Sumatra on the west coast, provides the most graphic account of its climate. The west coast, he asserts, could better be called the pest coast.[367] After the evening rainstorms at the mine, rank mists rise from the valley and become so thick that persons standing three or four paces apart cannot recognize each other.[368] Almost all the European miners succumb to terribly high fevers and many die. Hesse himself was delirious for three or four days, and Benjamin Olitz, the director of mines, died.[369] He pronounces Sumatra's "the unhealthiest climate in the world."[370] The English Captain Thomas Best anchors for eleven weeks in the harbor at Pasai, during which time twenty-five of his crew die. He recommends to the English East India Company that they never again send men or ships there, because of its contagious air and foul water.[371] Dampier similarly reports disease and high mortality rates at the English fort in Benkulen.[372]

B. ACHEH AND OTHER TOWNS

The most frequently and extensively described area of Sumatra was Acheh, on the island's northwestern tip. Seventeenth-century European writers agree that it is more populous than the rest of the island and that its ruler is more powerful than all the others. Most Europeans judge Acheh's climate to be better as well. Davis, for example, writes: "The whole country seemeth to be a garden of pleasure. The ayre is temperate and wholesome, having every morning a fruitful dew or small rain."[373] Johan de Moelre, who wrote up part of Admiral Pieter Verhoeff's voyage, describes Acheh's environs as pleasant and fruitful.[374] Schouten, who saw several other places on Sumatra, reports that Acheh is a populous, well-built city on a pleasant river about a half mile from the sea. "The air," he observes, "seemed much better and

---

[365] Le Blanc, *op. cit.* (n. 345), p. 91.
[366] For example, see Schouten, *op. cit.* (n. 46), III, 46–47; Hesse, *op. cit.* (n. 96), p. 69; Dampier, *op. cit.* (n. 353), p. 103. *Cf.* Dobby, *op. cit.* (n. 353), pp. 202–3.
[367] *Op. cit.* (n. 96), p. 61.
[368] *Ibid.*, pp. 69–70.
[369] *Ibid.*, pp. 64–65, 70, 81.
[370] *Ibid.*, p. 70.
[371] Thomas Best, "A Journall of the Tenth Voyage to the East India . . . ," *PP*, IV, 144.
[372] *Op. cit.* (n. 353), p. 123.
[373] Unger (ed.), *op. cit.* (n. 353), p. 53.
[374] "Journael ende verhael van alle het gene dat ghesien ende voorghevallen is op de reyse ghedaen door den E. ende gestrengen Pieter Willemsz. Verhoeven, . . ." *BV*, IIa, 37–38. Marsden (*op. cit.* [n. 345], p. 398) agrees, but with reservations.

more healthful there than in the south."[375] Beaulieu, however, complains about the unhealthy air, water, and food, which after about five months claimed the lives of forty crew members, mostly from dysentery and vomiting.[376] He also reports frequent earthquakes—three or four each year.[377]

According to Davis the city of Acheh is built in the forest and all its houses and buildings stand on wooden posts eight or more feet above the ground. People and animals can walk freely underneath the houses. Consequently the city cannot be seen from a distance. Once inside it, however, there seem to be so many houses and so many people that he thinks the city might spread over the entire land.[378] Nikolaas de Graaf estimates that the city is about two German miles in circumference, without walls or fortifications, although he reports seeing the ruins of Portuguese forts.[379] Beaulieu also comments on the absence of walls and speculates that they are unnecessary because of the difficult terrain around the city.[380] According to De Graaf, there are two large marketplaces in Acheh, several pagodas, a mosque, and a large royal palace with beautiful gardens.[381] Davis counts three large markets. The sultan's palace is about a half mile upstream from the city. It is built much like the other houses but higher, enjoying a commanding view. The mats that cover the walls of the palace are of damask or cloth of gold.[382] Schouten reports a moat around the palace and some gun emplacements.[383] Van Warwijck also mentions a moat and seven gates which must be passed in order to enter the palace.[384] Beaulieu describes it as oval-shaped with a moat about twenty-five or thirty feet wide. Instead of a wall there stands a thick hedge of bamboos through which no one is permitted to pass or look. He mentions only four gates, but also describes a branch of the river which has been diverted to run through the palace. Foreign visitors are received in the three great courtyards, conveyed there on their first visit with great pomp on royal elephants. For subsequent visits they walk or take boats from the town.[385] No Europeans visit the reputedly magnificent gardens and royal quarters. Acheh's harbor, according to Davis, is small but nonetheless a pleasant anchorage once one is inside; there is only about six feet of water

---

[375] *Op. cit.* (n. 46), III, 48. See also "Historische verhael vande reyse gedaen inde Oost-Indien . . . onder het beleydt van . . . Wybrandt van Waerwijck . . . ende Sebaldt de Weert . . . ," *BV*, Ib, 14.

[376] *Loc. cit.* (n. 344), p. 72.

[377] *Ibid.*, p. 57.

[378] Unger (ed.), *op. cit.* (n. 333), p. 53. Davis aptly describes what Anthony Reid (*loc. cit.* [n. 103]) calls the rural pattern of life in Southeast Asian cities. See also Marsden, *op. cit.* (n. 345), pp. 54–60. On the construction of houses see C. Snouk Hurgronje, *The Achehnese* (2 vols.; Leyden, 1906), I, 16, 34–44. See also Crawfurd, *op. cit.* (n. 107), I, 159–62.

[379] Warnsinck (ed.), *op. cit.* (n. 89), p. 13.

[380] *Op. cit.* (n. 344), p. 104.

[381] Warnsinck (ed.), *op. cit.* (n. 89), p. 13.

[382] Unger (ed.), *op. cit.* (n. 333), pp. 53–54.

[383] *Loc. cit.* (n. 46), III, 48.

[384] *Loc. cit.* (n. 375), p. 15.

[385] Beaulieu, *op. cit.* (n. 344), pp. 49–50, 103–4.

over the sandbar at its entrance. A poorly constructed stone fort guards the entrance.[386] Beaulieu, who lost an anchor getting in, is more impressed with the problems Acheh's harbor poses. His description of the fort, however, makes it seem much more imposing. It must have been rebuilt in the intervening years.[387] Van Warwijck observes many mosques in the city, but all poorly built.[388] Dampier describes the semicircular arch of small islands lying off Sumatra's northwest tip which forms the channels and outer harbor of Acheh.[389] He reports that the city is about two miles from the sea, has no walls—not even a ditch—and contains from seven thousand to eight thousand houses. It has several mosques, none very large and all without turrets or steeples. The queen's stone palace is "handsomely built," he thinks, but he is unable to get inside. He heard that it contains several large cannons, some of brass, which had been given to an earlier ruler by King James I of England.[390]

Seventeenth-century European writers report on other Sumatran towns as well. William Keeling, for example, describes the shoreline, reefs, and offshore islands near Priaman, but not the town itself apart from the trade he has driven there.[391] Walter Payton includes very brief notices of Priaman, Passai, and Tiku.[392] Merklein locates Jambi on the east coast.[393] Beaulieu visits Tiku in December, 1620, and describes it as located five minutes south of the equator, about a half league upriver from the sea, and containing about eight hundred houses. High mountains rise inland, but the land along the shore is low, fertile, and crossed by many streams. Its climate is exceedingly hot and unhealthy. It is, however, one of Sumatra's best sources of pepper. He also briefly describes Barus, although he does not stop there. He thinks little pepper can be obtained there.[394] Beaulieu also describes several north Sumatran coastal towns which he did not visit: Pedir, "the granary of Acheh," produces much rice and also some silk; Passai is rich in foodstuffs; "Dely" (Deli) is a source of oil (earth oil or liquid balsam) which, reputedly, once lit cannot be extinguished; Barus, a beautiful place on a large river, markets camphor and benzoin; "Passaman" (Pasaman), at the foot of a very high mountain visible for thirty leagues, produces fine pepper; and Padang, whose environs are thickly populated and cultivated up to the foot of the mountains, is a source of pepper, gold, and fine metal products.[395] Schouten names most of Sumatra's coastal towns, making one or two comments

[386] Unger (ed.), *op. cit.* (n. 333), p. 53.
[387] Beaulieu, *op. cit.* (n. 344), p. 5.
[388] *Loc. cit.* (n. 375), p. 14.
[389] *Op. cit.* (n. 353), pp. 85–86.
[390] *Ibid.*, pp. 90–91.
[391] William Keeling, "A Journall of the Third Voyage to the East India . . . ," *PP*, II, 518–20.
[392] Walter Payton, "The Second Voyage of Captaine Walter Peyton into the East-Indies . . . ," *PP*, IV, 301–5.
[393] *Op. cit.* (n. 81), p. 20.
[394] Beaulieu, *op. cit.* (n. 344), pp. 43–44.
[395] *Ibid.*, pp. 45, 98–100.

about each, usually regarding its trade and products. He mentions Pedir, Passai, Deli, Kampar, Indragiri, Jambi, and Palembang on the east coast. Of these Indragiri, Jambi, and Palembang are commercially the most important. On the west coast he lists Indrapura, Silebar, on a bay with a large river, ringed by deep jungles and framed by high mountains, Priaman, Tiku, Passai, Barus, Sinkil, "Labo" (?), and "Daya" (Daja).[396] Nieuhof mentions "Daya" and notes that Palembang was destroyed by the Admiral Johan van der Laen in retaliation for the murder of two Dutch yacht crews.[397]

In addition to Sillida, Hesse describes the pallisaded village (*pagar*) on the small island of "Poulo Chinco" (Pulau Chingkuk), as well as Indrapura, and mentions that the VOC also has warehouses and offices at Padang, Barus, Priaman, Bajung, Ajer, Lumpo, Tarusan, Jambi, and Palembang.[398] He, like most European observers, comments on Sumatran buildings. Houses, palaces, and even temples are all built on stilts. They are constructed of bamboo, roofed with palm leaves; their rooms are covered with mats.[399]

Dampier describes Benkulen on the west coast, where he stays for about five months serving as a gunner at the English fort. Benkulen is on a small river at 4° south latitude, about two or three leagues north of Silebar. The village is, like all Malay towns, built on a swamp with its houses on posts. Dampier thinks the Malays live on rivers because they love bathing, which he insists is an important part of their religion. Benkulen is easily recognizable from the sea because of a high slender hill behind the town (Gunungbengkok or Crooked Mountain). The townspeople are mostly fishermen or carpenters who work at the English fort. Farmers outside the town raise primarily roots, rice, and pepper. The English settle there in 1685 to gain access to the pepper after the Dutch drive them from Bantam.[400] Since Sumatran towns are always located on rivers upstream from the shore, it is very difficult to see them from the sea. Consequently many of the islands along Sumatra's coast which European observers think are uninhabited may have villages on them.[401]

C. POPULACE, CUSTOMS, AND BELIEFS

Sumatrans look very much like Javans. They are dark-skinned—some say black, some say yellow—about the same size as Javans, and according to some, ugly.[402] Hesse notes the women's long ears, sometimes hanging down

---

[396] Schouten, *op. cit.* (n. 46), III, 47–48.
[397] *Zee- en lant-reize* (n. 81), pp. 67–69.
[398] *Op. cit.* (n. 96), pp. 58–61.
[399] *Ibid.,* p. 73.
[400] Dampier, *op. cit.* (n. 353), pp. 122–26.
[401] See Reid, *loc. cit.* (n. 103), on Indonesian cities and towns.
[402] For example, see Verhoeff, *loc. cit.* (n. 374), p. 37. Hesse (*op. cit.* [n. 96], p. 73) calls them black.

to their shoulders. Sumatrans, he reports, consider long ears beautiful and decorate them with rings and precious stones.[403] Le Blanc contends that there are many hermaphrodites, caused, he supposes, by the drugs and spices which Sumatrans eat.[404] Christoph Frick, a physician, reports seeing many cases of elephantiasis, people with one leg as thick as a man's waist. The flesh on the affected leg feels spongy. Still, those who have it, he asserts, can run as fast as horses.[405] Dampier describes Sumatrans as "of a middle Stature, straight, and well shaped, and of a dark Indian Copper Colour. Their Hair is black and lank, their Faces generally pretty long, yet graceful enough. They have black Eyes, middling Noses, thin Lips, and black Teeth, by the frequent use of Betle."[406]

Lodewyckszoon reports that Sumatran women wear thick bracelets and dress in two-piece garments.[407] Schouten describes Sumatran clothing as light and simply made, of silk, cotton, or linen. Men of all ranks, even high officials, often leave their upper bodies bare. Most men wear shoes and stockings. Many wear turbans.[408] Van Warwijck, however, reports that they wear neither shoes nor stockings.[409] Dampier mentions that Sumatrans do not wear shoes or stockings, although he says "the better sort" wear sandals and brimless "woolen" hats of red and other colors. Most men, however, wear small turbans. In addition, the "better sort" throw a piece of silk over their shoulders.[410] Men always carry a kris at their waist, and several writers describe them in detail.[411] Hesse reports that Sumatran men squat to urinate.[412] Children, according to Verhoeff, wear no clothing except that young girls wear a silver plate over their genitals.[413]

Sumatran personal character is given uniformly low marks. Sinister, ma-

[403] Hesse, *op. cit.* (n. 96), pp. 73–74, 84–85.

[404] *Op. cit.* (n. 345), p. 92.

[405] Frick and Schweitzer, *op. cit.* (n. 82), pp. 106–7.

[406] *Op. cit.* (n. 353), p. 90. For comparison see Marsden, *op. cit.* (n. 345), pp. 40–49. Marsden describes the means used by Sumatrans to remove body and facial hair. He mentions the long painted fingernails grown by richer Sumatrans and the frequency of goiters among the hill people. Inlanders, he also observes, are bigger than the coastal Malays. In most other matters his description corresponds to those of seventeenth-century European writers. No seventeenth-century European described Sumatrans who lived in the interior.

[407] Rouffaer and Ijzerman (eds.), *op. cit.* (n. 28), I, 64.

[408] Schouten, *op. cit.* (n. 46), III, 49.

[409] *Loc. cit.* (n. 375), p. 15.

[410] Dampier, *op. cit.* (n. 353), p. 90.

[411] For example, see "De eerste schipvaerd," *BV,* Ia, 37. See also our pl. 256.

[412] *Op. cit.* (n. 96), p. 76.

[413] *Loc. cit.* (n. 374), p. 37. See Marsden, *op. cit.* (n. 345), pp. 49–53, for a general confirmation of seventeenth-century European descriptions of Sumatran dress and appearance, including the silver plate worn over the genitals. Marsden reports that young girls also wore a narrow silver plate across the front of their hair and that they wore silver bracelets. According to Marsden both sexes filed and blackened their teeth at puberty. No seventeenth-century writer mentions this practice. For a detailed description of the dress of modern Achenese see Snouk Hurgronje, *op. cit.* (n. 378), I, 25–30.

licious, haughty, wild, daring, deceitful, treacherous, unreliable, murderous, cruel, and lazy are the most commonly used adjectives.[414] Several writers cite examples. Davis describes in detail how after receiving Cornelis de Houtman's men graciously in September, 1599, agents of the *shahbandar* of Acheh lace the food and drink at a banquet with datura seed and then attack the Dutch when they are sufficiently intoxicated. Sixty-eight Dutchmen, including Cornelis de Houtman, are killed in that treachery.[415] His brother Frederick is imprisoned. Nieuhof describes the Dutch attack on Palembang in November, 1659, which he claims was done in retaliation for the treacherous murder of the crews of two Dutch yachts in 1658.[416] Wouter Schouten, who also mentions the seizure of the Dutch yachts in Palembang, describes a treacherous attack on a shore party from his own ship in Silebar which costs the lives of two interpreters.[417] According to Hesse, who spent half a year on Sumatra, Sumatrans lie continuously and can never be trusted.[418] Schouten thinks they make very good soldiers nonetheless—brave and cruel.[419] Dampier and De Roy, writing at the end of the century, are somewhat less negative. Dampier describes Sumatrans as "active and industrious . . . sociable and desirous of trade; but if . . . affronted, . . . treacherous and revengful."[420] De Roy describes them as "proud . . . unusually shrewd and clever" merchants, but "very slow and indolent" workers.[421]

Dampier comments frequently on the Sumatrans' love for bathing. The river in the city of Acheh, he reports, is always full of people, especially in the morning. Persons whose business takes them near the river rarely leave the area without bathing. Bathing is thought to be healthful, and the sick are

---

[414] For examples see Schouten, *op. cit.* (n. 46), III, 49; Nieuhof, *Zee- en lant-reize* (n. 81), p. 76; Hesse, *op. cit.* (n. 96), p. 73.

[415] Unger (ed.), *op. cit.* (n. 333), pp. 49–52.

[416] *Zee- en lant-reize* (n. 81), pp. 67–69.

[417] *Op. cit.* (n. 46), III, 16–18.

[418] *Op. cit.* (n. 96), pp. 80–81.

[419] *Op. cit.* (n. 46), III, 49.

[420] *Op. cit.* (n. 353), p. 123.

[421] De Roy, *op. cit.* (n. 363), p. 129. For comparison, Marsden's eighteenth-century description of the Malay-speaking coastal people on Sumatra is almost as reproachful as those of seventeenth-century Europeans. It contains words like indolent, stubborn, voluptuous, insidious, bloodthirsty, and rapacious. Inland peoples, whom he calls "native Sumatrans," fare somewhat better; they were, he wrote, mild, peaceable, forbearing, temperate, sober, hospitable, with simple manners, devoid of Malay cunning, modest, courteous. But they were also litigious, indolent, addicted to gambling, dishonest with strangers, superstitious, servile, careless, and improvident. See Marsden, *op. cit.* (n. 345), pp. 204–9. Snouk Hurgronje, writing in 1906, compiles no list of unsavory adjectives, but remarks that the "Achehnese are on their own confession indolent and ill-fitted for regular work" (*op. cit.* [n. 378], I, 22). Obviously these assessments of Sumatran character are shaped as much by the values of the observers and the character of their relationship to the Sumatrans as by the nature of the Sumatrans themselves. For an interesting but somewhat belabored discussion of this problem see Fisch, *op. cit.* (n. 182), pp. 1–8.

brought to the river. Dampier becomes convinced that daily bathing is help-ful in curing his own fevers and dysentery, but he believes that the primary reason for frequent bathing among the Sumatrans is religious.[422]

Everyone observes that Sumatrans are polygamous. Women and girls are described as very unchaste. Nieuhof, for example, thinks Sumatran women consider it no disgrace to prostitute themselves.[423] Hesse contends that pros-titution, by which he also seems to mean concubinage, is very common, and that it is not unusual for girls as young as eight years old to become pregnant. He extends his judgment about female promiscuity, however, to all "Indian women." Hesse's description of marriage and divorce among "Indian" slaves appears not to be taken from Sumatran practices.[424]

All of the seventeenth-century European visitors to Sumatra report that the Sumatrans speak Malay and that they are Muslims. Schouten, Nieuhof, and many other writers, however, note that while those who live along the coast are Muslim, most inland tribes are still pagan; some in fact are re-ported to be cannibals.[425] Beaulieu observes that the original inhabitants who were chased inland by the Malays also still live on many of the offshore islands.[426] Dampier seems to consider the Malay-speaking coast dwellers to be racially different from those who live inland. He observes that like the people of Johore, Malacca, and other places in the East Indies, Sumatrans are Muslim and speak Malay. They are also "alike in their haughty Humour and manner of living; so that they seem to have been originally the same people."[427] No one writing in the seventeenth century describes the people who lived in Sumatra's interior and no one notices any language other than Malay.[428]

Le Blanc believes the Sumatran kings are Muslims but that most Sumatrans are "idolators." The kings, he asserts, "warre continually with idolators." His description of the idolators' religion, however, sounds very much like the standard sixteenth- and early seventeenth-century European descrip-tions of Indian religion: they believe in metempsychosis, chiefly worship an idol called "pagode," practice suttee, and hate Christians. They will break a cup from which a Christian drank.[429] Hesse in 1687 reports that the Suma-

[422] *Op. cit.* (n. 353), pp. 95–96.

[423] *Zee- en lant-reize* (n. 81), p. 76.

[424] *Op. cit.* (n. 96), pp. 84–85.

[425] Schouten, *op. cit.* (n. 46), III, 49; Nieuhof, *Zee- en lant-reize* (n. 81), p. 76. Marsden, *op. cit.* (n. 345), p. 390, reports that ritual cannibalism against enemies or some criminals was still practiced among the Bataks in the eighteenth century. Also *cf.* Draeger, *op. cit.* (n. 245), pp. 118–20.

[426] *Loc. cit.* (n. 344), p. 98.

[427] *Op. cit.* (n. 353), pp. 89–90. Marsden (*op. cit.* [n. 345], pp. 40–42) points out that the dis-tinction between Muslim Malay-speaking coast-dwellers and the interior tribes was not consis-tent. Some coastal people were not Muslims, while some interior tribes were.

[428] See Lombard, *op. cit.* (n. 338), pp. 54–56, on Acheh's languages.

[429] Le Blanc, *op. cit.* (n. 345), p. 94. Beginning in the sixteenth century the sultan of Acheh launched a series of "holy wars" that brought most of the pepper-producing areas along the northwest coast under his control and by mid-century had also subjugated the coast of

trans' conversion to Islam was quite recent.[430] Merklein observes that Islam as practiced by Sumatrans is different from that of the Turks or Persians. Sumatrans retain superstitious beliefs and practices which appear "more heathen than Turkish," but he provides no examples other than that Sumatrans distill and drink liquor (*ajar putih* and arrack) despite Muslim prohibitions against alcohol.[431]

Earlier in the century, Davis described an Achenese royal ceremony which suggests a curious adaptation of Islam to a royal cult. Each year, according to Davis, the sultan, in lavish procession, rides an elephant to the "church" (mosque) to see if the Messiah has come. One richly outfitted elephant in the procession remains riderless, intended for the Messiah's use should he appear. Upon arrival, the sultan and several of his *orang kayas* look inside the mosque and, not finding the Messiah, remount their elephants to lead the procession back to the palace. On the return trip the sultan rides the elephant intended for the Messiah.[432]

Dampier thinks few of Acheh's people go to the mosque each day but that they are nonetheless zealous about making converts. He reports that a Chinese convert is paraded through the streets on an elephant, despite rumors that he was using his conversion to escape difficulties he had made for himself in the Chinese community. Dampier also sees bathing as "the chief Part of their Religion."[433] Most seventeenth-century European observers think Sumatrans are bitterly anti-Christian.[434]

Davis, already in the beginning of the century, reports that Sumatran Muslims claim descent from the biblical Hagar and Ishmael, that they use prayerbeads like Roman Catholics, and that they are zealous about the education of their children and have many schools. He also describes a highly honored "archbishop" who is also thought to be a prophet, probably the Sufi Syams ud-Din of Passai, who was the spiritual leader of the Achenese community and counsellor to its sultans until his death in 1630. Beaulieu reports that he can predict earthquakes.[435] According to Davis, Sumatrans

---

Minangkabau. Perhaps these are the wars to which Le Blanc refers. See B. H. M. Vlekke, *op. cit.* (n. 2), p. 93. See also *The Cambridge History of Islam,* ed. P. M. Holt, A. K. S. Lambton, and B. Lewis (2 vols.; Cambridge, 1970), II, 126–28.

[430] *Op. cit.* (n. 96), p. 73. Chinese sources record the establishment of Islam at Samudra (Passai), later part of Acheh's territory, as early as 1282. See *The Cambridge History of Islam* (n. 429), pp. 124–28.

[431] Merklein, *op. cit.* (n. 81), p. 20.

[432] Unger (ed.), *op. cit.* (n. 333), pp. 58–59. See Lombard, *op. cit.* (n. 338), pp. 146–47, for an interpretation and evaluation of this event.

[433] *Op. cit.* (n. 353), p. 96. Snouk Hurgronje, *op. cit.* (n. 378), I, 206–7, describes the ritual bathing on the "final Wednesday" of Achura-month still practiced in his day. See also Lombard, *op. cit.* (n. 338), pp. 139–51 regarding pre-Islamic elements in Achenese religion.

[434] This is generally believed regarding all of Indonesia. Some Indonesian princes seem to have accepted Islam largely in order to oppose the Europeans—for example, the ruler of Makassar in 1605. See Vlekke, *op. cit.* (n. 2), pp. 105–6, and *The Cambridge History of Islam* (n. 429), pp. 137–39.

[435] *Loc. cit.* (n. 344), p. 57. On Syams ud-Din see Lombard, *op. cit.* (n. 338), pp. 161–62.

bury their dead in family burial plots with their heads towards Mecca and place stones at both the head and the foot of their graves. The rulers of Acheh reputedly are honored with beautifully engraved golden stones.[436]

D. ECONOMY AND POLITY

Despite their reputation for sloth, the general impression conveyed by seventeenth-century European reports is that Sumatrans are able craftsmen and sharp merchants. Traders from all over Asia can be found in Sumatra's ports, especially in Acheh. Davis, for example, depicts Sumatrans as "cunning merchants and wholy dedicated thereunto." They also have able goldsmiths, gunfounders, shipbuilders, tailors, weavers, hat makers, potters, cutters, smiths, and distillers. In Acheh he finds merchants from China, Bengal, Pegu, Java, India, and Arabia.[437] Le Blanc reports much slave traffic in Acheh.[438] Schouten, who lists the products which can be purchased in each of Sumatra's important ports, notes that Sumatrans are particularly skillful shipbuilders and makers of knives. Sumatran krises are highly regarded.[439] Several Europeans comment on the beautiful work done by Sumatran goldsmiths from an alloy of gold and copper called "tembaga" (tombac; Malay, *tambaga*), which Sumatrans esteem more highly than gold.[440] Beaulieu reports some silk production in Acheh. Sumatran silk, he judges, is not as white or as fine as Chinese—it is yellow—but it nonetheless makes fairly beautiful taffetas.[441]

Dampier lists Acheh's chief tradesmen as carpenters, goldsmiths, fishermen, and money changers. The country people, of course, are farmers, raising cattle and fowl, roots and fruits. Sumatrans have little taste for the hard work involved in rice farming and therefore leave it largely to slaves. Most of Acheh's rice is still imported, he writes, and the new rice fields have increased the demand for slaves. Fishermen, he thinks, are Sumatra's most prosperous working people, especially if they can afford nets. Carpenters are particularly adept at building Sumatran style houses and proas. Blacksmiths are few, goldsmiths usually foreigners, and money changers usually women.[442] The cultural flowering associated with the reign of Iskandar Muda (1607–36) in Acheh is not mentioned by any European writers dur-

---

[436] Unger (ed.), *op. cit.* (n. 333), pp. 56–57.

[437] *Ibid.*, pp. 57–58. On foreign commerce in Acheh see Lombard, *op. cit.* (n. 338), pp. 112–25.

[438] *Op. cit.* (n. 345), p. 94.

[439] *Op. cit.* (n. 46), III, 47–48, 49. For a discussion of the products bought and sold in Acheh see Lombard, *op. cit.* (n. 338), pp. 109–11. On weapons see Draeger, *op. cit.* (n. 245), pp. 112, 124–26.

[440] For example, see Beaulieu, *op. cit.* (n. 344), p. 54; see also Lombard, *op. cit.* (n. 338), p. 50.

[441] *Loc. cit.* (n. 344), p. 99. See also Lombard, *op. cit.* (n. 338), p. 66.

[442] Dampier, *op. cit.* (n. 353), pp. 91–92. See also Beaulieu, *loc. cit.* (n. 344), pp. 99–100. Marsden's list of occupations corresponds quite closely to that of seventeenth-century writers;

ing the seventeenth century. They are for the most part silent regarding Sumatran literature generally.[443]

Dampier describes what he calls a "China camp" in Acheh, an area of the city near the sea where Chinese live during the trading season (from June to September). Each June the Chinese arrive with merchants and tradesmen and set up what seems like a continuous fair. As they sell their goods they occupy fewer houses and the "China camp" shrinks. As their business decreases their gambling increases. By the end of the summer the Chinese usually have sold everything, sometimes even their own ships, taking passage back to China on others' ships. While the Chinese are in town, Dampier observes, few other merchants do much business.[444] Davis describes the various coins used in Acheh (Chinese cash, the "mas" [mas], "coupans" [kupans], Portuguese pardaos, and taels), and Sumatran weights (the bahar and the catty).[445] Le Blanc describes the "mas" as a gold coin equal in value to a crown. Two thousand cash he thinks equal one mas. Le Blanc also mentions the tael.[446] Beaulieu implies that silver reals of eight are not used in Acheh.[447]

Dampier, writing at the end of the century, reports that cash used in Acheh is made of lead rather than copper and that fifteen hundred cash equal one "Mess" (mas). The "Mess" he describes as a thin gold coin stamped with Malay letters on either side and worth about fifteen English pence. Sixteen "Mess" equal one "Tale" (tael), about twenty English shillings. The tael, he correctly observes, is a weight. Five "Tale" weigh one "Bancal" and twenty "Bancal" weigh one "Catty" (catty). The gold "Mess," he observes, seldom holds its weight and thus the number of "mess" in a "catty" varies. The value of cash seems to vary at the discretion of the money changers. One hundred "cattys" Dampier reports equal a picul (132 English pounds), and 300 "cattys" equal a "bahar" or 396 English pounds. These weights also, he thinks, vary from port to port.[448] De Roy also reports that the most-used coin in Acheh is the gold mas. It is not as pure as unminted gold, he observes, and the queen controls its minting.[449]

---

he mentions goldsmiths, however, as among the best of Sumatra's craftsmen (*op. cit.* [n. 345], pp. 178–96). Iskandar Muda nonetheless was exceedingly eager to hire and keep Beaulieu's goldsmiths (see, for example, Beaulieu, *op. cit.* [n. 344], p. 52), and Lombard sees the presence of foreign goldsmiths as an indication of the decline of the craft in Acheh (*op. cit.* [n. 338], p. 51). Women were, and are, also money changers in Siam and elsewhere in Southeast Asia.

[443] On Achenese culture during the reign of Iskandar Muda see Lombard, *op. cit.* (n. 338), pp. 127–64.

[444] *Op. cit.* (n. 353), pp. 94–95.

[445] Unger (ed.), *op. cit.* (n. 333), pp. 57–58. Unger's notes identify the coins and their equivalents. See also Argensola, *op. cit.* (n. 345), p. 142.

[446] *Op. cit.* (n. 345), pp. 93–94.

[447] Loc. cit. (n. 344), pp. 57, 68–69.

[448] Dampier, *op. cit.* (n. 353), p. 92. For a quite similar eighteenth-century description of Sumatran coinage see Marsden, *op. cit.* (n. 345), p. 401. See also Lombard, *op. cit.* (n. 338), pp. 105–9 on Acheh's coinage.

[449] *Op. cit.* (n. 363), p. 127.

Seventeenth-century European readers were provided with fairly reliable information about Sumatran politics, including the impression that political relations on the island were, or recently had been, changing rapidly. The insert in the *Begin ende voortgangh* edition of De Houtman's voyage points out that there are several kingdoms on the island, many more than the two usually mentioned by the Portuguese: "Andragidan" (Indragiri) and "Aruan" (Aru), whose inhabitants are described as pagans and cannibals. The insert lists "Pedir" (Pedir), "Pacen" (Passai), "Comparan" (Kampar), "Manancabo" (Minangkabau), and "Achen" (Acheh). Acheh, it asserts, has become the most prominent, not only having subjugated Pedir and Passai but the entire northwest quarter of the island.[450] Davis mentions four kingdoms on Sumatra: Acheh, Pedir, Minangkabau, and Aru. All but Aru are tributary to Acheh; Aru is allied with the king of Johore.[451] Beaulieu amply describes Acheh's domination of northwest Sumatra's ports. He, for example, was unable to buy pepper in Tiku without permission from the sultan of Acheh. He paid duty to both the sultan and the king of Tiku. Beaulieu regularly reports the sultan's military expeditions. While in Tiku, before he had ever been to Acheh, he met three Achenese war galleys, each with three hundred men and an elephant aboard, which were used to enforce the sultan's will on rebellious princes.[452] Schouten, published in 1676, is more precise. The sultan of Acheh, he reports, also rules Pedir, "Pacem" (Passai), "Daya" (Daja), "Barros" (Barus), "Passaman" (Paseman), "Tycouw" (Tiku), "Pryaman" (Priaman), and Padang, as well as the kingdoms of "Queda" (Kedah) and "Perach" (Perak) on the Malay Peninsula. The "kings" in the southern part of the island—"Sillibar" (Silebar), "Dampin" (?), "Liampon" (Lampung), "Palimban" (Palembang), and "Jambay" (Jambi)—are either subservient to Bantam, as was Silebar for example, or under the patronage of Mataram.[453] Dampier is less specific about the extent of Acheh's power but reports that it stretches eastward along the northeast coast a long way towards the Straits of Malacca. He seems to sense the decline of Acheh's power at the end of the century when he observes that beyond Diamond Point, about forty leagues from the city "the inhabitants, though belonging to Achin are in less subjection to it." Dampier does not know how far Acheh's jurisdiction extends along the west coast or inland, but he thinks it includes many offshore islands including Pulau Way (or Wei) which is used as a penal colony.[454]

[450] "De eerste schipvaerd," *BV*, Ia, 37.

[451] Unger (ed.), *op. cit.* (n. 333), p. 59. See also Argensola, *op. cit.* (n. 345), p. 141. By the beginning of the seventeenth century the kingdom of Aru no longer existed. Deli was known to be part of it. On Aru's relation to Johore and Acheh see L. Y. Andaya, *The Kingdom of Johore, 1641–1728* (Kuala Lumpur, 1975), p. 65.

[452] *Loc. cit.* (n. 344), pp. 41, 91–96.

[453] Schouten, *op. cit.* (n. 46), III, 47–48.

[454] *Op. cit.* (n. 353), pp. 84–85. On precolonial Sumatran politics and the rise of Acheh see Hall, *op. cit.* (n. 2), pp. 21–47; A. Reid and L. Castles (eds.) *Pre-Colonial State Systems in Southeast Asia* (Kuala Lumpur, 1975); A. Reid, "Trade and State Power in Sixteenth- and Seven-

Sumatran rulers are always described as tyrannical, having absolute power over their subjects, inflicting harsh punishments for small crimes. Apart from the sultan of Acheh, however, few Sumatran rulers appear in the seventeenth-century European literature. Merklein includes only the briefest mention of Jambi, which he judges to be "not a very powerful kingdom." [455] William Hore describes a trial by ordeal in Tiku of a local man accused of killing an English seaman. The accused is able to extract a small ball from a large pot of boiling oil without being burned. Hore thinks the devil helped him. [456] Hesse describes two local rulers. One he calls the "emperor" of Indrapura and pictures him as a corpulent man dressed in red silk clothes with large golden buttons. He wears neither shoes nor stockings, but sandals on his feet. The *orang kayas* who attend him are barefoot and naked above the waist. They all wear turbans. [457] Hesse later eats dinner with the "petty king" of Sillida near the VOC gold mine. He compares the "petty king" to a German village schoolmaster—highly respected and feared rather than loved by the villagers, a petty tyrant. The meal, which Hesse also describes, is obviously a *rijstafel* (rice table): a large bowl of white rice with many small dishes of what he calls curry around it. Predictably, he did not like it. [458]

Much more is written about the sultan of Acheh, the most powerful of Sumatra's rulers. He, too, is repeatedly described as tyrannical; his subjects fear rather than love him. He rules solely by force, meting out cruel punishments such as gouging out eyes, cutting off hands, feet, or genitals for rather small crimes. [459] According to Davis the mutilated lawbreakers are frequently banished to the island of "Polowey" (Pulau Way). Criminals are put to death by impaling or by being trampled by elephants. Davis also reports many jails in Acheh. [460] Beaulieu discerns four judicial jurisdictions in Acheh—civil, criminal, religious, and commercial—for each of these, judgments are dispensed in a different location. [461]

Dampier, writing at the end of the century, when Acheh is ruled by queens, describes punishments in detail. He reports that small crimes are usually punished by whipping. Thieves, however, usually have their right

---

teenth-Century Southeast Asia," in *Proceedings of the International Association of Historians of Asia. Seventh Conference, Bangkok, 1977* (2 vols.; Bangkok, 1977); Lombard, *op. cit.* (n. 338); Vlekke, *op. cit.* (n. 2), pp. 93, 121–23; Marsden, *op. cit.* (n. 345), pp. 406–63.

[455] *Op. cit.* (n. 81), p. 20.

[456] "William Hores Discourse of his Voyage in the Dragon and Expedition, from Surat to Achen, Teco and Bantam . . . ," *PP*, V, 78–79.

[457] Hesse, *op. cit.* (n. 96), pp. 60–61.

[458] *Ibid.*, p. 73.

[459] For example, see Verhoeff, *loc. cit.* (n. 374), p. 37; Van Warwijck, *loc. cit.* (n. 375), p. 14; "Remembrances taken out of a tractate written by Master Patricke Copland Minister in the former Voyage," *PP*, IV, 151; Schouten, *op. cit.* (n. 46), III, 49; Nieuhof, *Zee- en lant-reize*, (n. 81), p. 76.

[460] Unger (ed.), *op. cit.* (n. 333), p. 56.

[461] *Loc. cit.* (n. 344), pp. 101–2. See also Lombard, *op. cit.* (n. 338), pp. 79–81.

hand chopped off for the first offense, the other hand or a foot for the second offense. Incorrigible offenders are banished to Pulau Way, an island colony of maimed thieves. Wounds from the judicial amputations are staunched with pieces of leather and heal rather quickly. Thieves are not put to death, although the death penalty is used for other crimes. Dampier reports seeing one man impaled, but he was unable to discover for what crime. Condemned noblemen, he reports, "are permitted to fight for their lives against large numbers of armed men."[462] Beaulieu reports seeing a woman impaled because a major fire started in her house.[463] De Roy thinks that punishments are determined by the amount stolen rather than the frequency of the offense and that those who steal very large amounts are impaled. Because of the harsh punishments for theft he regards Acheh as one of the safest cities for merchants in all of Asia.[464] Beaulieu, however, describes Acheh's trade as heavily taxed and dominated by the sultan. Much of his account is taken up by his difficult and frustrating negotiations with the sultan about the price of pepper, the quantity of pepper available, and the tariff to be paid on the trade.[465]

Seventeenth-century Europeans frequently comment on the prevalence of slavery in Acheh. According to Dampier, for example, almost everyone in Acheh owns slaves. The *shahbandar* reputedly has over a thousand. In fact, even slaves have slaves, who in turn have slaves. Slaves in Acheh are not meanly treated; they live in their own houses, often quite far from their masters. They can earn money and sometimes buy their freedom. It is difficult to tell free men from slaves, according to Dampier, "for they are all in a manner, slaves to one another; and all in general to the Queen and Oronkeys."[466] De Roy also describes a booming demand for slaves in Acheh, primarily satisfied by the English and Danes who sell them for gold.[467]

Davis reports that the sultan governs Acheh with the aid of five principal officers: a royal secretary and four *shahbandars* or harbor masters. Other officers are subordinate to these five. In all things, however, "the king's will is law. For it seemeth there is no free man in the land, for the life and goods of all is at the king's pleasure."[468] Most seventeenth-century European visitors talk about the *orang kayas*, by which they understand rich and powerful men

---

[462] *Op. cit.* (n. 353), pp. 96–98.

[463] *Loc. cit.* (n. 344), p. 71.

[464] *Op. cit.* (n. 363), p. 128. On justice, *cf.* Marsden, *op. cit.* (n. 345), pp. 404–5.

[465] Beaulieu, *loc. cit.* (n. 344), 58–60, and many other places.

[466] *Op. cit.* (n. 353), p. 98. Lombard (*op. cit.* [n. 338], pp. 57–58) suggests that the term "slave" is inappropriate for the obligations of Acheh's common people.

[467] *Op. cit.* (n. 363), pp. 126–27. Lasker (*op. cit.* [n. 187], pp. 27–28) says there was a strong tradition of slavery among the Batak people and that Acheh imported slaves from India and Africa, but treated them well. For a general discussion of bondage see Reid (ed.), *op. cit.* (n. 106), pp. 1–43.

[468] Unger (ed.), *op. cit.* (n. 333), p. 56. Van Warwijck's account is very similar: *loc. cit.* (n. 375), p. 14.

or great aristocrats who have political power.[469] Beaulieu reports that each *orang kaya* is in charge of an area of the city and dispenses justice in it. They also keep a close watch over their areas at night, devoting two hundred horses divided into four companies for that purpose.[470] Beaulieu also asserts that the sultan is heir to all his subjects' goods "as if there were no children," and that he also confiscates the goods of "those whom he daily executed." The possessions of any foreigners who die in Acheh also fall to the sultan, and he claims all shipwrecks along his coasts.[471]

Davis estimates that the sultan has about one hundred galleys, some of which carry up to four hundred men. These are open boats, paddled rather than rowed, and without cannons. But they seem sufficient to guarantee the obedience of neighboring kingdoms. According to Davis, Acheh's armies fight with bows and arrows, javelins, and swords; they fight naked and without shields. The sultan has some brass cannons, the largest Davis has ever seen, but they are without carriages, being fired as they lie on the ground. According to Davis the real power of the sultan's land forces is in his elephants.[472] Beaulieu also describes a system of conscription under Iskandar Muda which can raise forty thousand men. While the sultan provides weapons, which are returned to him after a campaign, the conscripts are responsible for up to three months' sustenance. The sultan also has many cannons and ample supplies of powder and shot. Nevertheless Beaulieu also judges the elephants—nine hundred of them—to be the backbone of the sultan's land forces.[473]

The sultan is immensely rich in gold, jewels, and elephants, and has several wives and a great many concubines, who are guarded by eunuchs.[474] Davis thinks the sultan's closest advisers are women and that even his admiral is a woman; he reportedly does not trust men.[475] Beaulieu also reports that the palace interior is served and guarded by a large company of women—he heard there were three thousand of them—who rarely leave the palace. They in fact keep their own markets and hold their own courts inside the palace.[476]

Acheh was not always ruled by sultans as powerful as Iskandar Muda. Beaulieu describes the period before 1589 as a golden age for Acheh during

---

[469] The term literally means "rich man." See Yule and Burnell, *op. cit.* (n. 111), pp. 644–45.

[470] *Loc. cit.* (n. 344), p. 102.

[471] *Ibid.*, pp. 108–9, 172. On Acheh's government during the reign of Iskandar Muda see Lombard, *op. cit.* (n. 338), pp. 74–76.

[472] Unger (ed.), *op. cit.* (n. 333), p. 56.

[473] *Loc. cit.* (n. 344), pp. 105–7. On Iskandar Muda's forces and military campaigns see Lombard, *op. cit.* (n. 338), pp. 85–100.

[474] For example, see Unger (ed.), *op. cit.* (n. 333), p. 56; Verhoeff, *loc. cit.* (n. 374), p. 37; Beaulieu, *loc. cit.* (n. 344), pp. 52–55; Schouten, *op. cit.* (n. 46), III, 48.

[475] Unger (ed.), *op. cit.* (n. 333), p. 56.

[476] Beaulieu, *loc. cit.* (n. 344), p. 102.

which political power was in the hands of the great commercial *orang kayas*, who seemingly made and unmade monarchs at will:

The orang kayas lived extravagantly, and following the affections of their nature were addicted to novelties, insolent, and proud. The great wealth their predecessors had left them, in lands and houses in the city, as well as gold and silver, supported this life; no kings have oppressed them nor foreign nation plundered them. The town was six times as populous as it is at present, and so crowded that it was difficult to move in the streets.

The orang kayas had beautiful, large, solid houses, with cannons at their doors, and a large number of slaves, both as guards and servants. They went out superbly dressed, with large retinues, respected by the people. Such great power very much diminished royal authority, and even safety, for the principal orang kayas had such authority and power, that when they tired of the domination of one king, they massacred him in order to install another. Thus a king was very lucky if he enjoyed his crown for two years.[477]

The power of the great *orang kayas* ended abruptly, however, after they chose 'Ala ad-din Ri'ayat Syah Sayyid al-Mukammil to be king in 1589. He was already quite old—seventy years old, according to Beaulieu—apparently a distinguished naval commander. Davis reports that he had been a common fisherman who because of his military valor was raised to the position of admiral and given a royal bride by the former sultan. When named regent for the sultan's heir and grandson he quickly killed the child, as well as thousands of the child's potential supporters.[478] Beaulieu describes the *coup d'etat* in detail; al-Mukammil gave a splendid banquet inviting a very large number of *orang kayas* whom he lured one by one into a back court of the palace where they were quickly killed. Eleven hundred were murdered that night, and in the days following their houses were demolished and their goods and weapons confiscated by the new ruler. Laws were made limiting the size and construction of new houses in the city.[479] Al-Mukammil reigned until he was ninety-five years old, and according to Beaulieu he reigned tyrannically. In the first year of his reign he was reputed to have had twenty thousand people put to death. The bloodshed continued in subsequent years. At his death he divided the kingdom between his two sons, one of whom took the title King of Pedir. Beaulieu describes in detail the misrule of these two and finally the wars between them and with the Portuguese, during which al-Mukammil's grandson ingratiated himself with the *orang kayas* and military leaders and was named king when his uncle died. As Beaulieu describes it, the new king, Iskandar Muda (r. 1607–36), is even more avaricious and bloodthirsty than his grandfather was.[480]

[477] *Ibid.*, p. 110.
[478] Unger (ed.), *op. cit.* (n. 333), pp. 54–55.
[479] Beaulieu, *loc. cit.* (n. 344), pp. 111–12.
[480] *Ibid.*, pp. 112–14. On the rise of royal absolutism in Acheh see A. Reid, "Trade and the

209. MAP OF SIAM

From Simon de La Loubère, *Du royaume de Siam*
(2 vols.; Paris, 1691), I, facing p. 1.

This was reduced in size from a larger map prepared
by the French royal engineer M. de la Mare who went
up the Menam to Siam's northern borders. It was corrected in Paris by Cassini, the Director of the Observatory, on the basis of other materials brought back from
Siam by La Loubère.

210. KING NARAI OF
SIAM ON THE ROYAL
ELEPHANT
From G. Tachard, *Second
voyage* . . . (Paris, 1689),
facing p. 288.

The elephant in this
picture is a grotesque
European beast of the
woodcut tradition; the
prostrate courtiers and
the king wear Siamese
ceremonial bonnets in
surroundings that look
like Versailles. The boy
on the back of the ele-
phant holds a clearly
recognizable elephant
hook.

le Roy monté sur son Elephant.

211. THREE-TIERED
VASE OF GOLD FILI-
GREE, ON WHICH THE
KING'S LETTER IS
CARRIED
From La Loubère, *op. cit.*
(pl. 209), I, facing p. 62.

Vase d'or de filigrane .   To.j.   *pag.* 62.

*Vase d'or à triple étage ou l'on portoit la lettre
du Roy*

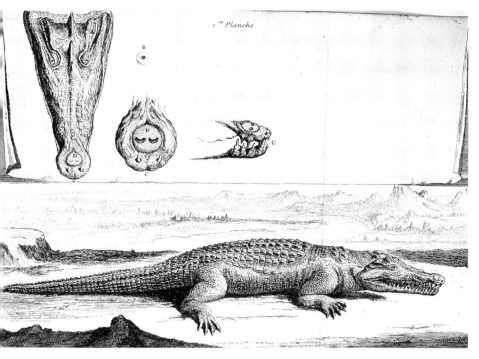

1.ᵉ Planche

B

D

C

C

212. THE UNKNOWN CROCODILE OF SIAM CALLED "TAKAIE" (*TAKHE*) IN SIAMESE: AN ANATOMICAL DESCRIPTION

From Thomas Goüye (or Gouge) *et al.,
Observations physiques et mathematiques . . .* (Paris, 1688), plate 1.

This is a portrait of the largest of three crocodiles captured by the Siamese for the French scientists to dissect and study. Here displayed are a few of its parts. King Narai ordered his people to collect all animals unknown to the Europeans to enable them to study the anatomy of these strange beasts. These crocodiles were taken from the Menam by Siamese fishermen in "baloons" (galleys). Pl. 2, not shown here, depicts the internal organs of the crocodile, and Pl. 3, also not shown here, displays its major bones.

OBSERVATIONS
PHYSIQUES
ET MATHEMATIQUES

POUR SERVIR

*A L'HISTOIRE NATURELLE,
& à la Perfection de l'Astronomie
& de la Geographie :*

Envoyées de Siam à l'Academie Royale des Sciences à Paris, par les Peres Jesuites François qui vont à la Chine en qualité de Mathematiciens du Roy :

AVEC LES REFLEXIONS

*DE MESSIEURS DE L'ACADEMIE,
& quelques Notes du* P. Goüye,
de la Compagnie de Jesus.

A PARIS,
Chez { la Veuve d'Edme Martin, } ruë Saint
{ Jean Boudot, } { Jacques,
{ & } { au Soleil
{ Estienne Martin, } d'or,

M. DC. LXXXVIII.
AVEC PRIVILEGE DU ROY.

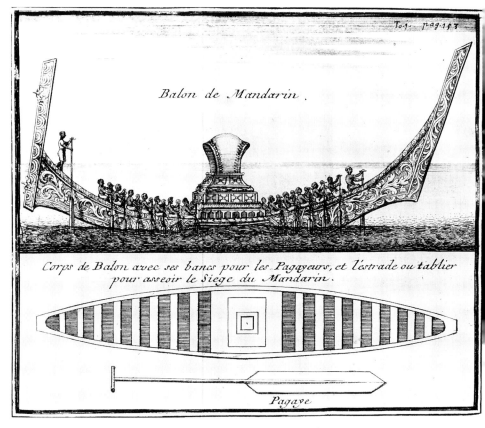

Balon de Mandarin.

Corps de Balon avec ses bancs pour les Pagayeurs, et l'estrade ou tablier pour asseoir le Siege du Mandarin.

Pagaye

214. MANDARIN'S "BALON" (GALLEY)
From La Loubère, *op. cit.* (pl. 209), I, between pp. 152 and 153.
   "The Body of a *Balon* is composed only of one single Tree, sometimes from sixteen to twenty Fathom in length. Two men sitting cross leg'd by the side one of another, on a Plank laid across, are sufficient to take up the whole breadth thereof. The one *Pagayes* at the right, and the other on the left side. *Pagayer* is to row with the *Pagaye,* and the *Pagaye* is a short Oar, which one holds with both hands, by the middle and at the end. . . . In a single *Balon* there are sometimes an hundred, or an hundred and twenty *Pagayeurs* . . . but the inferior Officers have *Balons* a great deal shorter." (La Loubère, *A New Historical Relation* . . . [2 vols., London, 1693; Wyatt facsimile edition, Kuala Lumpur and Singapore, 1969], I, 41).

215. NOBLEMEN'S "BALLON"
From Alexandre de Chaumont, *Relation* (Amsterdam, 1686), between pp. 26 and 27.
Pl. 229 is the title page of this book.

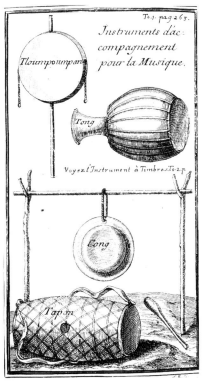

216. WATER-PIPE SMOKED BY THE
MOORS OF SIAM
From La Loubère, *op. cit.* (pl. 209), II,
between pp. 120 and 121.
 Its bamboo stem is said to be eight or
nine feet long.

217. SIAMESE RHYTHMIC MUSICAL
INSTRUMENTS
From La Loubère, *op. cit.*, I, facing
p. 263.
 Traditional Siamese musical instruments may be divided into stringed,
wind, and percussion groups. Most numerous are the percussion instruments,
particularly drums and gongs of the
kind shown here.

218. A SIAMESE SONG IN WESTERN NOTATION
From La Loubère, *op. cit.*, I, facing p. 262.

Thai music is similar to Chinese and Burmese music but with its own special diatonic scale of seven full tones. There is no native form of musical notation, for all music is learned by ear. Both singers and instrumentalists study with masters who teach the traditional music. Sporadic but unsuccessful efforts were made in the early twentieth century to have the traditional Thai music written down in symbols. See Phra Chen Duriyanga, "Thai Music," in *Thailand Culture Series*, No. 8 (3d ed., Bangkok, 1955), pp. 52–53.

Trois Alphabeth Siamois.

Ko Khò Khó Khô Khoo Khoo-ngo ‖ cho chó chò sò choo yo ‖ do to thó thò

1.

thoo no ‖ bo po ppó fo ppò fo ‖ ppo mo yo ro lo vo ‖ so só

só hò lo o

Kâ Kí Kĭ Keü Keü, Kou K û Ké Kê Káï Káai Ko

2.

Káou Kam Ka.

Keüy Kaáï Kâou Kíou Kýou Keüy Keüï Koüy Koüï

3.

Kéou Kéou Koüy Kôï Koüáï Kiáou Kía

La Suitte de cet Alphabeth est a la planche Suiuante.

Kia Keüa Keüà Koüà Koüà Ké Kê

Ko Kaou Koum Kam Karama Ko Koüáï Keüa

reu reû leu — lêü

Trois Alphabeth Balis

Ca Khá Khà ga— nga ‖ Tcha Tchá Tcha Tcha — ya ‖

1.

Ta thá tha da— na ‖ Ta thá tha da_na‖pa

ppá ppa ba_ma ‖ Ca ra la ua ta

ha la ang

Ka   Kaa   Ki   Kü   Kou   Kóu   Ke

2.

Kái   Ko   Káou   Kam   Ká

Ka – na   Ka – nâ   Ka-ni   Ka-nii   Ka-nou   Ka-ncû

3.

Ka – ne   Ka-nui   Ka-no   Ka – náou   Ka nang

Ka– nâ

Les Chiffres Siamois.

1   2   3   4   5   6   7   8   9

10

Les Noms numeraux Siamois.

1.   2.   3.   4.   5.   6.   7.   8.   9.   10.   11.
Neng. Song. Sam. Sii. haa. houK. Ket. peet. Caou. Sib. Sib-et.
12   20   30
Sib-Song. Tgii-Sib. Sam–Sib. &c.

219. THREE SIAMESE ALPHABETS, THREE PALI
ALPHABETS, AND THE SIAMESE NUMBERS
From La Loubère, op. cit. (pl. 209), II, between pp. 98
and 99.
   The Thai alphabet is of Indian and Cambodian origin and dates back to the late thirteenth century. On
the development of the Thai alphabets see Phyre Anuman Rajadhon, "The Nature and Development of the
Thai Language," Thai Culture, New Series, No. 10
(2d ed., Bangkok, 1963), pp. 18–30.
   Pali, derived from Sanskrit, is the language of Siamese Buddhism. In Siam it is pronounced "Bali" as it
is written here.

Talapat ou Para-sol des Talapoins.

220. A BUDDHIST MONASTERY IN SIAM

From La Loubère, *op. cit.* (pl. 209), I, facing p. 432.

This group of wooden religious buildings is called a *wăt* in Siamese. The large building in the center is the *bot* which generally houses an image of the Buddha and religious mural paintings. Around the *bot* stand eight *sima* (boundary stones) which indicate the holiness of the ground on which the *bot* stands. The houses of the monks stand in the rectangular enclosure between the inner and outer walls. This is probably a depiction of a community temple built and supported by the populace in its vicinity. The talipot parasol of the monk is at the bottom.

Statuës de Somnona-Codom.

To.9. pag. 531.

Statuë de cuiure

Statuë de brique dorée en demi-relief.

Statuë de cuiure dore.

221. SIAMESE IMAGES OF THE BUDDHA

From La Loubère, *op. cit.*, I, facing p. 531.

Statues of Somona Kotom, the Thai name for the Buddha: upper left, copper image (probably bronze); upper right, brick (probably stucco) image ornamented in bas-relief; bottom, gilded copper image.

In Siam the images of Buddha probably outnumber the human population. These images range in size from miniatures to great giants and are of various materials, as is indicated here. See Luang Baribal Buribhand, "Thai Images of the Buddha," in *Thailand Culture Series,* No. 9 (Bangkok, 1955).

222. THE THREE SIAMESE ENVOYS TO FRANCE, 1686

From a copperplate engraving by De l'Arrnessin, *Les augustes representations de tous les roys* (Paris, 1688), fol. 189. By courtesy of the Bibliothèque Nationale, Paris (B.N. N2 12 4°).

The figure in the middle holding the letter "to the king" is the ambassador Phra Wisut Sunthorn, commonly known as Kosa Pan. To his right is the second envoy named Ok Luang Kalayan Racha Maïtri and to his left is the young third envoy called Ok Khun Si Wisan Wacha. All three were received in audience at Versailles on September 1, 1686.

OOC, LOÜANG CALAYANARAA TCHAMAÏTRIOUPATHOUD.
Premier adjoint de l'Ambassadeur de Siam envoyé au Roy, homme âgé et qui a beaucoup d'Esprit.
Il a été Ambassadeur du Roy de Siam vers l'Empereur de la Chine, et s'acquita fort bien de cette
Ambassade. Ces Ambassadeurs partirent de Siam le 22 Decembre 1685, sur les trois heures du
matin dans le Vaisseau du Roy nommé l'Oiseau, commandé par Mr de Vaudricourt.

223. THE SECOND SIAMESE EMISSARY TO LOUIS
XIV OF FRANCE (1686)
Sketched from life. Original in Bibliothèque Nationale,
Paris.

"Ooc, Loüang Calayanaraa Tchamaitrioupathoud"
was an older man who had previously acted as Siamese
ambassador to China. He left Siam on the "Oiseau" on
December 22, 1685.

His name in modern transcription was Ok Luang
Kalayan Racha Maïtri, an official title also transcribed
as Luang Bovorn Kalaya Rajmaitri. See M. Jacq-
Hergoualc'h, "Les ambassadeurs siamois à Versailles,"
Journal of the Siam Society, LXXII (1984), p. 32, n. 1;
and L. Sitsayamkan, *The Greek Favourite of the King of
Siam* (Singapore, 1967), p. 92, n. 6.

224. THE THIRD SIAMESE EMISSARY TO LOUIS
XIV OF FRANCE (1686)
Bust by the engraver Hainzelman. Original in Biblio-
thèque Nationale, Paris.
    According to the caption, this is a portrait of "Tan
oc-Cun Srivi Sarauacha tritud." According to Chau-
mont (see pl. 229) he was called "Ockhun Jurin Ocman
Viset Ppubaan," which may be transcribed as Ok
Khun Si Wisan Wacha or Khun Srivasar Vacha. See
Jacq-Hergoualc'h, *op. cit.* (pl. 223), p. 33, n. 2; and Sit-
sayamkan, *op. cit.* (pl. 223), p. 92, n. 7.

225. RECEPTION OF THE SIAMESE EMISSARIES BY
LOUIS XIV, SEPTEMBER I, 1686
Original in Bibliothèque Nationale, Paris.
  Notice the ceremonial hats of the envoys, and the
golden vase for carrying the king's letter (*cf.* pl. 211).
See E. W. Hutchinson, *1688 Revolution in Siam: The
Memoirs of Father de Bize, S.J.* (Hong Kong Univ.
Press, 1968), pl. 10.

HISTOIRE
DE LA
REVOLUTION
DE SIAM.
ARRIVE'E EN L'ANNE'E 1688.

A LILLE,
chez JEAN CHRYSOSTOME MALTE,
Imprimeur juré, ruë Equermoife,
au bon Pafteur 1691.

Avec Permiffion.

226.

JOURNAL
DU
VOYAGE
DE SIAM
FAIT
en 1685. & 1686.
Par M. L'ABBE' DE CHOISY.

Seconde Edition.

A PARIS,
Chez SEBASTIEN MABRE-CRAMOISY,
Imprimeur du Roy, ruë Saint Jacques,
aux Cicognes.

M. DC. LXXXVII.
Avec Privilege de Sa Majefté.

227.

HISTOIRE
De Monfieur
CONSTANCE,
Premier Miniftre du
ROY DE SIAM,
ET
DE LA DERNIERE
Revolution de cet Etat.

PAR
Le Pere d'ORLEANS,
de la Compagnie de
JESUS.

A PARIS,
Chez DANIEL HORTHEMELS,
ruë S. Jacques, au Mecenas.

M. DC. XCII.

228.

RELATION
DE
L'AMBASSADE
de Mr. le Chevalier
DE CHAUMONT
A LA COUR DU ROY
DE SIAM,
Avec ce qui s'eft paffè de plus
remarquable durant fon
voyage.

A AMSTERDAM,
Chez PIERRE MORTIER, Libraï-
re fur le Vygendam, à la Ville de Paris.
M. DC. LXXXVI.

229.

A Prospect of the Hall of Audience in the Pallace of Siam.

230. THE AUDIENCE HALL OF THE KING OF SIAM
From the facsimile of the English translation (1693) of
La Loubère, introduced by D. K. Wyatt (Kuala Lum-
pur and Singapore, 1969), facing p. 72.

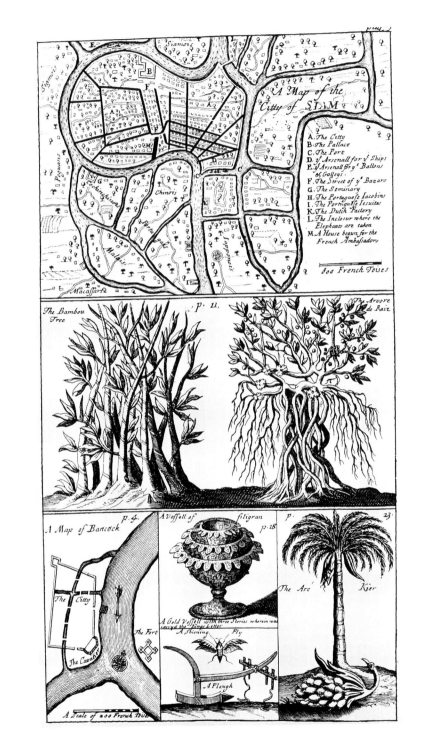

A Map of the
City of SIAM

A. The City
B. The Pallace
C. The Port
D. y^e Arsenall for y^e Ships
E. y^e Arsenall for y^e Ballons
&c Galleys.
F. The Street of y^e Bazars
G. The Seminary
H. The Portuguese Iacobins
I. The Portuguese Iesuites
K. The Dutch Factory
L. The Inclosur where the
Elephants are taken
M. A House begun for the
French Ambassadors

800 French Toises

The Bambou
Tree

p. 11.

The Arvore
de Raiz

A Map of Bankock

p. 4.

The Citty

The Fort

The Cavalier

A Scale of 200 French Toises

A Vessell of

filigran

p. 18

A Gold Vessell with three Stories wherein was
carryd the Kinge Letter
A Shining   Fly

A Plough

p.   23.

The Are   Kier

Kingdome brought to fuch trade and beauty as it had formerly. But to facilitate our travells, and to point you out the way the eafier, accept an adjoning Map, to that in fol. 300 : This defcribing *India extra Gangem.*

232. MAP OF *INDIA EXTRA GANGEM* (OR FAR EAST)

From Thomas Herbert, *Some Yeares Travels into Divers Parts of Asia and Afrique . . .* (rev. ed.; London, 1638), p. 321.

231. (FACING PAGE) THE MAPS OF AYUT'IA AND BANGKOK WITH SIAMESE TREES, PLOUGH, INSECT, AND THE GOLDEN IMPERIAL VASE USED IN DIPLOMACY.

From La Loubère, *op. cit.* (pl. 230), facing p. 7.

233. INSULINDIA: WESTERN ARCHIPELAGO
From Nicolas Sanson d'Abbeville, *L'Asie en plusieurs
cartes* (Paris, 1652).

Sanson d'Abbeville reports (incorrectly) that the
Portuguese call these islands the "Isles de la Sonde" because they are to the south of Malacca. He cites Pyrard;
he probably also used Purchas and some of the Dutch
authors. Actually, early geographers used the term "islands of the Sundas" for the great chain stretching
from Sumatra to Timor. Sunda is now the name of the
western, mountainous part of Java whose people speak
a language that is different from Javanese. The strait
between Sumatra and Java is named for these people,
as are the islands (Lesser Sundas) between Java and
Timor.

234. MAP OF BORNEO (1601)

BV (facsimile ed., Amsterdam, 1969), II, facing p. 50, n. 24.

This was published to illustrate the world tour of Olivier van Noort. From the rendition of the place-names it is clear that the cartographer depended upon Portuguese and/or Spanish sources. The placement of the equator in the East Indies, a subject much debated in Europe, runs east to west through Borneo in roughly the correct place. The north is to the reader's left.

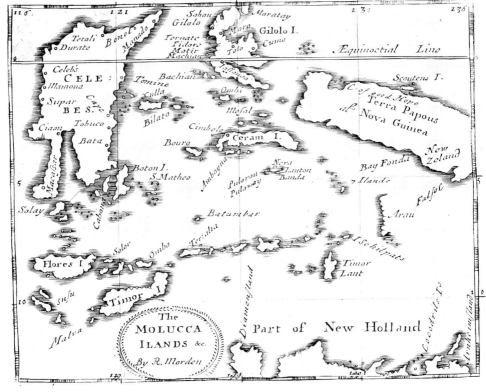

235. MAP OF THE MOLUCCAS
From Robert Morden, *Geography Rectified* (London,
1688), p. 438.
    Text cites no sources.

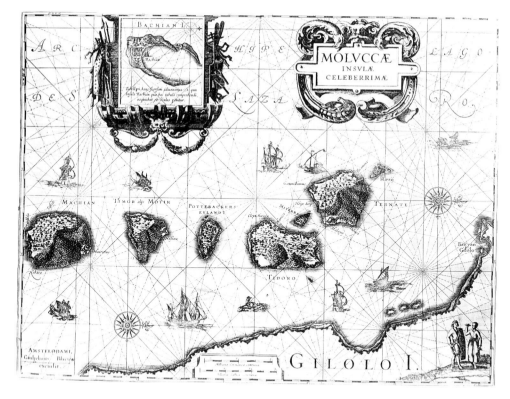

236. THE MOLUCCAS

From Johan Blaeu, *Atlas Maior, Asia* (Amsterdam, 1662), Vol. X, Bk. 1, between pp. 89 and 90.

Blaeu printed this map from plates acquired by his father, Willem Blaeu, from Joost de Hondt (Hondius) in 1629 for the *Theatrum orbis terrarum* (1635 to 1655). See I. C. Koeman, *Joan Blaeu and His Grand Atlas* (Amsterdam, 1970), pp. 31, 83.

Banda excede toutes les Isles des Moluecques en Noix Muscades, Macis, voire nulle autre côtree il n'y a des Noix qu'icy, & a Poelepetaeque, Polletin, Puloway & Gunanapi. A Gunanapi il y a une Montagne featente en Soulphres & toufiours brustante. Icy a Banda a vous laisse 10 de nos Compagnons pourveuz des marchandiles & argent, qui acheteront les fruits en faifon, & les garderont jufques a noftre venuë.

A Nera se fait la plus grande trafique, & il y a grande converfation des eftrangers, comme

Iavans, Chirefes & maints autres, entre Ortatan & Comber il n'y a qu'une maifon, & n'ont nulle converfation enfemble, a caufe qu'ils prennent les Sangliers qui fe tiennent illec, ceux de Labbetacq, e, Combex & Wayer menent une guerre fanglante contre ceux de Nera, Lontor & Poeleron, laquelle n'elt jamais a reconcilier, a caufe qu'ils ont pillez & endommagé leurs Forts, & ceux d'Ortatan (qui font au milieu d'eux) vivent en paix.

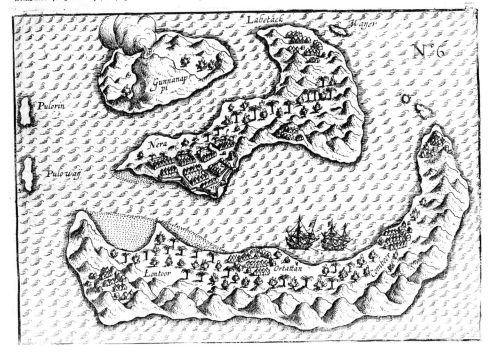

237. MAP OF BANDA, THE NUTMEG ISLANDS
From *Le second livre de l'histoire de la navigation aux Indes orientales* (Amsterdam, 1609; bound as one volume with Lodewyckszoon's *Premier livre* [see pl. 246]), p. 111. Pls. 245 and 259 are also from this book.
Around 1860 Alfred R. Wallace wrote: "Banda is a lovely little spot, its three islands inclosing a secure harbor from whence no outlet is visible, and with water so transparent that living corals and even the minutest objects are plainly seen on the volcanic sands at a depth of seven or eight fathoms. The ever-smoking volcano rears its bare cone on one side, while the two larger islands are clothed with vegetation to the summit of the hills" (*The Malay Archipelago . . . with an Introduction by John Bastin* [Singapore, 1986], p. 293).

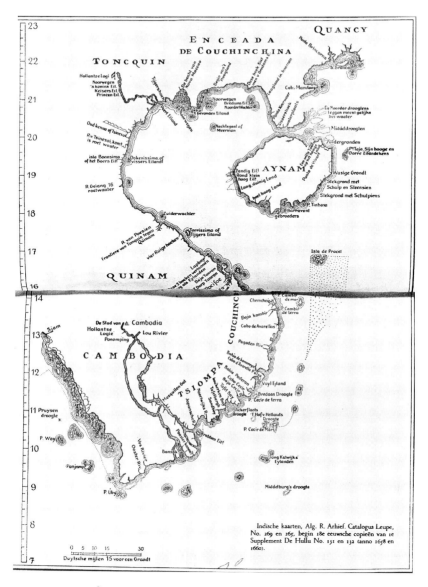

238. DUTCH MAP OF VIETNAM AND HAINAN
ISLAND AROUND 1660
"Quinam" equals Annam; "Aynam" equals Hainan;
"Tsiompa" equals Champa. See Wilhelm J. M. Buch,
De Oost-Indische Compagnie en Quinam (Amsterdam,
1929).

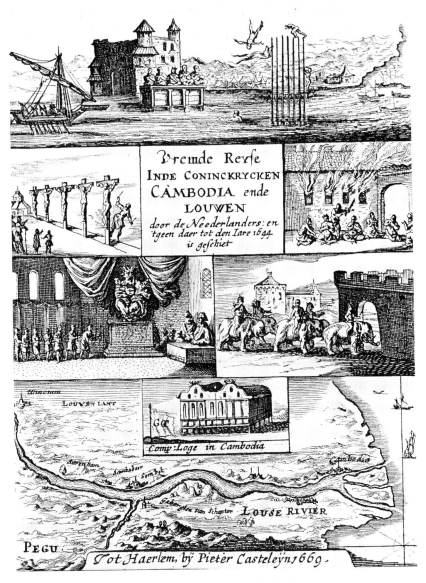

239. THE DUTCH IN CAMBODIA (1644)

Frontispiece, *Vremde Geschiedenissen in de Koninckrijcken van Cambodia en Louwen-Lant* (see pl. 282).

See H. P. N. Muller, *De oost-indische Compagnie in Cambodja en Laos,* IV, Vol. XIII (The Hague, 1917), Pt. I.

The "Louse River" is the river of Laos, or the Mekong.

240. MAP OF TONGKING

From J. B. Tavernier, *Recueil de plusieurs relations et traitez singuliers et curieux* (Paris, 1681), between pp. 168 and 169.

Map made by Daniel Tavernier, the brother of Jean-Baptiste, who presumably made eleven or twelve voyages to Tongking. The captions on the map contain a mixture of good and bad information.

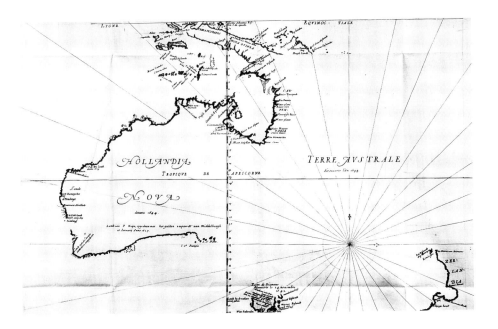

241. MAP RECORDING THE GRADUAL UNCOVER-
ING OF THE AUSTRAL LANDS
From "La terre australe descouvertes par le Capitaine
Pelsart, qui y fait naufrage," between pp. 50 and 51 in
Melchisédech Thévenot, *Relations* (TR), Pt. I (Paris,
1666). Pl. 275 is also from this book.

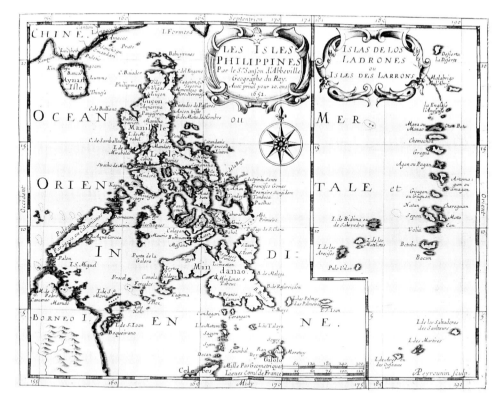

242. THE PHILIPPINES AND THE LADRONES
(MARIANAS) (1652)

From Sanson d'Abbeville, *op. cit.* (pl. 233).

Engraved by A. Peyrouin.

Text mentions Linschoten on the Philippines. Nothing mentioned about sources for the Ladrones, except he admits to knowing next to nothing about them. Whatever the Iberians and the Dutch knew about the Pacific region, they did not generally make it available to the rest of Europe. Nonetheless, this is a rather specific map, whatever its sources. The Philippine part of this map is also reproduced in Carlos Quirino, *Philippine Cartography (1320–1899)* (2d rev. ed.; Amsterdam, 1963), p. 82, fig. 30.

243. MRAUK-U, THE ROYAL CAPITAL OF
ARAKAN, IN 1660

From Wouter Schouten, *Reistogt naar en door Oostindien*
(Amsterdam, 1780), Pt. I, between pp. 158 and 159.
Pl. 261 is also from this book.

The view is from the Portuguese quarter of Daingri-
pet, a suburb on the western side of the capital. See
M. Collis, *The Land of the Great Image* (New York,
1943), pp. 143–44, and plate facing p. 150.

IV.
DELINEATIO PROCESSIONIS REGINÆ
PATANIENSIS.

Iuitas Patane à Regina quadam defuncti Regis vxo-
re̦, cum Hollandi ibi essent, gubernabatur. Hæc si
quando animi oblectandi gratia prodire in publicum
constituit, Elephanti regium in morem splendide ex-
ornato insidet, habetq̦ secum gynæceum suo virgines
suas pulcherrimè exornatas, Elephantib. similiter in-
sidentes, nobilibus vero & satellitibus stipata, Elephantes aliquot se-
cum ducit, arma defuncti sui Regis gestantes.

B   V. DELI·

244. PROCESSION OF THE QUEEN OF PATANI
From Johann Theodor de Bry and Johann Israel de Bry
(comps.), *India orientalis,* VIII (Frankfurt, 1607), pl. 4.
Pls. 260 and 262 are also from this book.
   More than a century of female rule in Patani
(1584–1688) involved four successive queens who occupied the throne during the period when Patani was a
major entrepôt. On female rule in the commercial
states of Southeast Asia see Anthony Reid, *Southeast
Asia in the Age of Commerce 1450–1680,* Vol. I, *The
Lands below the Winds* (New Haven and London, 1988),
pp. 170–72.

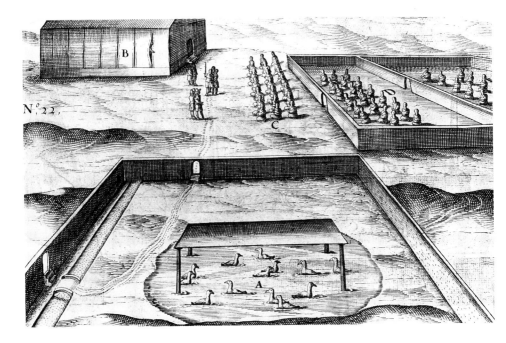

245. THE ROYAL PALACE OF TUBAN

From Lodewyckszoon, *op. cit.* (pl. 237), appendix.

A, Pool for Oriental birds that look like large European ducks and lay bigger eggs; *B,* The residence of the king's four wives; *C, D,* In addition, the king keeps three hundred concubines.

Tuban was a port and a wealthy royal center in eastern Java and a site of weekly tournaments (*senenan*). For an illustration of a *senenan* in Tuban see Anthony Reid, *op. cit.* (pl. 244), p. 188.

VOCABVLAIRE DES MOTS
IAVANS ET MALAYTS, QV'AVONS
MESMES ESCRIT A TERNATI, SERVANT DE PROMPTVAIRE

a ceux qui y defirent naviger ; car la langue Malayte s'ufe par toutes les Indes Orientales, principalement ez Molucques. Lefquels avons voulu mettre icy pour fatisfaire au curieux Lecteur.

François.	Malayts.	Javanß.	François.	Malayts.	Javanß.
Hauffer	Packhoe	Rngßo	Lier	Icat	Bunfgaefa
defubler	kaelwaer	Gaffap panna	arroufer	zieron	Bonfgaefa
refpondre	miniaot	ara raffana	aprefter	boat adar	gavenay abeere
adorer	backaffe	carna afa (18	faire credit	petfchaya	anbac
porter en bas	batturon cabauwa	gavanay Rinfcßox	amender	bocaet bae	gave fanay
detenir	carratan pangal	Baffafa fongac	cogiter	battau doelou	Gexu bumyy
accepter	tariman	Baffambof	fauver	femoeny	Zaparof
arer	bangala tana	—	garder	femoeny	Zaparof
cultiveur	oran gouno	Gvoncarya faua	defplaire	tida bifhouka	Bvza Zoucka
arriver	fampe	Gvoffaka (fcßox	employer	zouda balanga	anfyy kaffar
defcendre	turan cababe	monga ißine	enfumer	baaffap	affap gimne
ouir	badangat	Badangar	nager	trayzion	Bafrapzioy
labourer	backarga	mangaue	rompre	peytzia	potof
couper	karat	figafr	payer	bayar	mangafo
autre	laing	manne	commencer	moullay	mangavekay
ainfi	bigitou	mackono	defirer	mauncka	arap
toufiours	farian	faßandina	piper	bodoy	gaue Bobo
illec	difornna	ankana	enfevelir	tanam	fanamy
povre	caffian	Gvoucaffiay	guetter	batiagay	mandafankay
derriere	balacan	Boure	enchanter	tackana	—
trop tard	lambaet	—	mocquer	barmayn	BofRpobox
trop tempre	arry galab	pagitina	defendre	papodan	goue paday
vuide	abis	antyy	mordre	giget	fiokof
regardez	liat	Befay	aggraver	mangoro, ou fourou	kvukoy
manifacture	pande	pangaua	offrir	batavaer	manavaer
ouche	bavan mira	Bauay aßay	prier	mintacan	fafonkay
vin aigre	thouka	Gvack	feuiles	tiop	fiop ana
refponce	britou	paraffanna	faigner	kalwaer darat	mattou giffe
terre	tava,ou darat	fava,ou Saraf	diligenter	betachinta	maniva gugadf
furgir a terre	piggy darat	monga baraf	trembler	goumattaer	Bagoumaffaer
foir	malan	malay	promettre	tavar	gßafouka
tout	famonga	kobbe	retenir	manaroo	Bafavoo
ancre	favou	fauou	commandement	fourouan	coukonay
povreté	kaffion amat	voy kaffiana amat	aveugle	bouta	Boufa
ancrer	labo faou	Bafianfiay	large	lebar	feBar
rabatre	tarre kaelwaer	—	homme courtois	kyaey agum	kiay fvza
voftre Seigneurie	candati packanira	—	dedans	dalang	Safang
bras	tangan	fangay	dehors	lonaer	fiaBa
amore	oupan	oupay	bleu	idgo	pßgo
feul	fendiri	Beveck	en haut	attas	affaß
tirer les vaines	kaelwaer darot	afa panay gife	en bas	di bava	BinfcBox
accorder	badimme	gaue fubaf	meilleur	bayck	Bezzeyck
aventurer	bamanarou onuton	—	amer	payit	payif
arrefter	bapaffou	—	pain	rotty	futfe
ceffer	yangan	gava	beurre	minga fappi	fanga fappi
amener	bawa	manko	Chirurgien	oran pande thicor	pande minyoucox
attendre	nanty	gßynny mangafa	boulenger	oran pande rotty	papavßay
brufler	backara,ou mangala gungoy	—	fire de nopfes	cave cavyan	mangaue caue
abayer	mangala	fatly mana	nopfes	macanan minum	Sz vzay panganfa
					François.

246. INITIAL PAGE OF A FRENCH–MALAY–JAVAN VOCABULARY

From Willem Lodewyckszoon [G.M.A.W.L.], *Premier livre de l'histoire de la navigation aux Indes orientales par les Hollandois* (Amsterdam, 1609), appendix. Pls. 248–58 are also from this book.

Renderings of Malay shown here are based on the usage then prevailing on Ternate.

G: Waem. Vander Gaawen fe.

Makassar Souldiers who blow poison'd darts out of Trunks

247. MAKASSAR SOLDIERS WITH BLOWPIPES
From Nieuhof, *Voyages and Travels*, in *CV* (3d ed.; 6 vols.; London, 1744), II, between pp. 258 and 259 (reproduced there from Nieuhof's *Zee- en lant-reise*, engraving no. 35). Pls. 263–65 are also from this book.

When the Europeans first arrived in Insulindia, the blowpipe (*sumpitan*) was the weapon used by most of the wild tribes of Sumatra, Borneo, and Celebes for hunting and for war.

Engraved by Gilliam (or Willem) van der Gaawen (or Gouwen) of Haarlem, who also did the engraving in pl. 172.

248. SKETCH OF BANTAM (BANTEN) (1596)
From Lodewyckszoon, *op. cit.* (pl. 246), p. 26r.
   An engraving made in Holland that is based on the text.
   Notice that the merchants in the foreground carry krises in their waistbands.
And behind them, observe the big-tailed sheep.

249. FOREIGN MERCHANTS AT BANTAM (1596)
From Lodewyckszoon, *op. cit.* (pl. 246), p. 30r.
　Left to right: Peguan, Persian, and Arab. (*Cf.*
pl. 29.)

250. JAVANESE OF BANTAM ON THEIR WAY TO
MARKET (1596)
From Lodewyckszoon, *ibid.*, p. 29r.
    The man and woman on the left are dressed as ordi-
nary Javanese and are naked above the waist. To the
right walks a wealthier Javanese followed by his servant. Both men carry a kris in the waistband, for it was
a part of the male dress of all classes. The woman has
her hair gathered at the back of her head and twisted
into the customary large knot. For a thorough description of native dress see Sir Thomas Stamford Raffles,
The History of Java (2d ed.; 2 vols.; 1830), I, 96–99.

251. THE PRINCIPAL CHINESE MERCHANTS AT
BANTAM (1596)

From Lodewyckszoon, *op. cit.* (pl. 246), p. 31r.

Notice that the merchant on the right carries a balance scale or *timbangan*. The woman on the left is probably one of those bought by the Chinese to stay with them during the period of their residence in Java.

252. A MUSLIM LEGATE FROM MECCA WITH
GOVERNOR "CHEPATE" OF BANTAM AND THEIR
ENTOURAGES (1596)
From Lodewyckszoon, *ibid.*, p. 27v.
   The fully clothed figure is evidently the legate from
Mecca.

253. A CHINESE SHRINE IN BANTAM (1596)
From Lodewyckszoon, *op. cit.* (pl. 246), p. 31v.
An example of the popular religion practiced by the
overseas Chinese.

Le pourtrait du Roy de Bali, qui nous monſtra beaucoup d'amitie : lequel ainſi aſſis ſur un char Royal, eſt tiré par deux Buffles blancs : ſa garde por-
tant picques longues a fers eſmouluz & dorez, & ſont auſſi comme ſarba:aines, par leſquels ils ſoufflent petites fleſches : ce que bien apperçeumes le 2 jour
de Novembre dernier, a l'eſcarmouche, quand neuf des noſtres en furent navrez.

254. THE KING OF BALI IN HIS ROYAL
OX-DRAWN CHARIOT (NOVEMBER, 1596)
From Lodewyckszoon, *ibid.*, p. 50r.

The oxen (*buffles blanc*) are white Brahman cattle introduced from India possibly along with Hinduism.
Alfred Wallace noted that "they are large and handsome animals, of a light-brown color, with white legs,
and a conspicuous oval patch behind of the same color"
(*op cit.* [pl. 237], p. 162).

The king's guards carry long iron pikes and
blowguns.

255. (TOP) A GENTLEMAN OF BALI ON THE MOVE IN 1597
From Lodewyckszoon, *op. cit.* (pl. 246), p. 44v.

256. (BOTTOM) SUMATRAN CHIEF AND HIS PEOPLE
From Lodewyckszoon, *ibid.*, p. 18r.

257. JAVANESE GONG ORCHESTRA (1596)

From Lodewyckszoon, *ibid.*, p. 34r.

This is a Dutch impression of a small marketplace gamelan at Bantam. Here the gongs of the ensemble are played outdoors by men. Our word "gong" probably derives from the Javanese language. See Reid, *op. cit.* (pl. 244), pp. 210–13.

258. JAVANESE DANCERS (1596)
From Lodewyckszoon, *op. cit.* (pl. 246), p. 36v.
   The man on the left accompanies the dancers on
what appears to be a metal xylophone (*demung*). Notice
the finger movements of the dancers on the right. This
appears to be a performance by unmasked *teleḍek* dancing girls. See Koentjaraningrat, *Javanese Culture* (Singapore, 1985), pp. 200–201.

Pourtra t de leur maniere de jouër a la paume, comme ils fe tiennent en maniere d'un cer- | mundi, de certains cerclets des Cannes de Sucre, bigarrez, & celuy qui ne le touche du pied,
cle & celuy du milieu jette l'efteuf en haut , & le donnent icy par rangs & l'abatent du pied, | eft en grande ofprobre, voire grandemет mocqué, jeu certes bien eſtimé entre eux , aucuns
voire il haut qu l'on le ſcauroit jetter de la main , les eſteufs ſont faits en forme d'une Sphera- | fautellent & le frappent en fautellant, aucuns qui fe tournent & le frappent,

259. *TAKRAW* OR *SEPAK RAGA* ("KICK BASKET" IN MALAY), THE MALAY GAME OF FOOTBALL

From Lodewyckszoon, *op. cit.* (pl. 237), fig. 12.

This sport or exercise was observed at Banda by the Dutch in 1599. It was played with a hollow ball of plaited rattan. The object was to pass the ball with the foot or leg, from one player to the other in the circle without letting it hit the ground. A variation on *takraw*, the Thai word for the game, is still played throughout southeast Asia. In the modern version it is a competitive sport that resembles volleyball. For a fascinating discussion of *takraw*'s history see Reid, *op. cit.* (pl. 244), pp. 199–201.

V.
QVO PACTO IAVANI GAL-
LOS GALLINACEOS IN PVGNAM
committant.

 IN GVLARI *Iauanis voluptati est, gallos educatos in conflictum pugnamque insti-*
tuere. Quoties enim familiaritatis gratia conueniunt, tum inter cætera plerunque ipsis
contentiuncula nascitur, vter eorum pugnacissimum & bellicosissimum gallum alat.
Certa quoque pecunia interdum deposita, de sui galli victoria concertant. Quo facto,
quilibet sui galli pedibus calcaria in hunc vsum fabrefacta innectit. Sic ergò his armati,
ex oppositis in publico locis committuntur. Qui confestim congressi, tanta alacritate
& pertinacia depugnant, vt eos humano more q. quadam victoriæ laude inflammari existimare queas.
Nec duellum deserunt remittuntue prius, donec alter alterum confecerit & obtruncarit.
Hac ipsa quoque icone Gatto Dalgalia siue catus zibeticus depingitur. Similiter & animalculum
aliud quod plerunque in Tamarindorum arboribus degit, cuius fructibus victitat.

b 2

260. JAVANESE COCKFIGHT
From De Bry, *op. cit.* (pl. 244), IV (1601), pl. 5.
    Cockfighting in its origins had religious significance as a
blood sacrifice to the gods. In more recent times it became
the most popular form of gambling. Individual males cultivate and cherish fighting roosters. A certain type of private
magic is thought to protect the fighting cocks and their
masters. For an analysis of the symbolism of the modern
cockfight see Reid, *op. cit.* (pl. 244), pp. 189–91, 193–94.
    Notice the civit cats and tamarind trees in the background.

261. THE MOSQUE OF JAPARA IN JAVA
From Wouter Schouten, *op. cit.* (pl. 243), Pt. I,
between pp. 40 and 41.

XIII.
DESCRIPTIO CIVITATIS
GAMMÆ LAMMÆ.

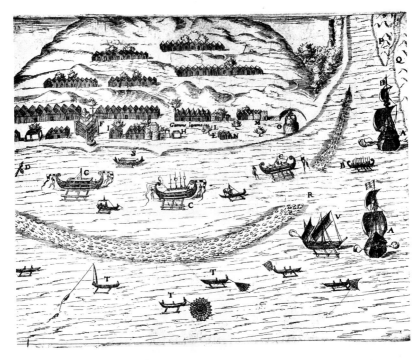

CIVITAS dicta in Ternate Insula sita est. In illa Hollandi sua quoque commercia agitauerunt. Domus eorum ex crassa arundine confecta aut fissa, intorta sunt. A. Hollandorum binæ naues sunt. B. Karkolla est, exploratum ad illos veniens, qualesnam homines essent, quamente appellerent. Quo cognito gaudere visi sunt. C. Karkolla bellica est. D. Palus in vnda erectus, ex quo caput hostis propendebat. E. Forum, propter solis vehementiam sub arbore agi solitum. F. Musquita seu templum. G. Palatium Regis, ex lapidibus structum. H. Ædicula, in qua tormentum positum est, quod capitaneus Franciscus Draco quondam valida tempestate concussus in mare exturbauerat. Hoc deinde à Barbaris extractum, eo collocatum est. I. Domus est, à Rege Hollandis illis, qui remanserunt, data & concessa. K. Domus est Hollandorum mercatoria. L. M. Cœnobium S. Pauli, ex lapidibus olim extructum à Lusitanis. N. Interpretis regij domus. O. Turris est, tormento munita. P. Insula intra Ternatem & Tidorem sita. Q. Insula Tidore. R. Aditus est ciuitatis, aliàs vndiquaque breuijs & scopulis interiectis inaccessæ. Hoc loco defluæ vnda piscatores pisces captant. S. Nauis est ludicra seu ambulatoria. T. Naues sunt, quibus iis modis, vt in historia commemoratum est, pisces captant. V. Nauis vectoria, qua merces ab vna insula in aliam transuehunt.

d 2

262. THE HARBOR OF GAMULAMO (OR GAMMO-
LAMMO) IN TERNATE
From De Bry, *op. cit.* (pl. 244), V (1601), pl. 8.
  In the Malay of Ternate *gamu* means village or town; *lamo* means big. After Ternate's conquest by the Spanish in 1606, this town was officially called Rosario. Near its fort the Portuguese Jesuits established a residence. In their religious work they were aided by Spanish Franciscans. See H. Jacobs, S. J. (ed.), *Documenta Malucensia* (3 vols.; Rome, 1974–84), III, 14*–15*; 659.

263. THE TYGERS GRAFT [*GRACHT*, OR A CANAL STREET] OF BATAVIA

From Nieuhof, *op. cit.* (pl. 247), between pp. 252 and 253.

Of Batavia's fifteen streets with water channels in them, "the *Tygers Gracht* is the most stately and most pleasant, both for the goodliness of its buildings and the ornament of its streets" (p. 253).

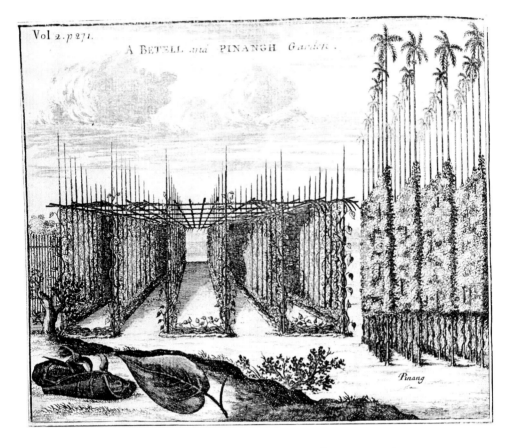

264. BATAVIA: BETEL AND PYNANG (ARECA PALM) GARDEN

From Nieuhof, *op. cit.* (pl. 247), facing p. 271.

Betel "resembles at a distance the black pepper, and runs up with its branches, round trees, stalks, posts, or any other thing it meets with, like our hops. . . . The leaves have a spicy taste, very penetrating and somewhat astringent. They are so generally used in the Indies, as if the inhabitants could not live without them. They take a single leaf and a small quantity of lime made of burnt oyster shells, then folding the leaf together, they put into it the lime, and the fourth part of the nut Areka (or Pynang), which augments the astringent quality of the Betel, and draws the spittle" (*CV*, II, 271).

This is the recipe for making betel quids. "Pynang" is the Malay word for areca, a name generally adopted by the Dutch writers.

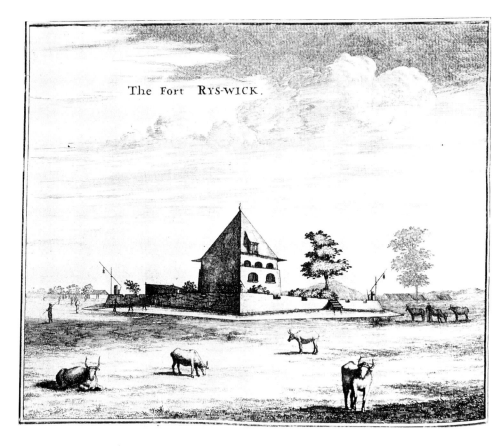

The Fort RYS-WICK.

265. BATAVIA: FORT RYSWICK
From Nieuhof, *ibid.*

Fort Ryswick was built as an outer redoubt in the summer of 1656 in the middle of rice fields on the south side of the city. It was evacuated in 1697 and by 1729 had fallen into ruins. See *Oud Batavia. Gedenkboek uitgegeven door het Bataviaasch Genootschap van Kunsten en Wetenschappen* (2 pts.; Batavia, 1922), Pt. 1, pp. 131–32, 392.

Liurea de Soldati della
Guardia del Re detto Bua
in Tumkino

266. A SOLDIER OF THE IMPERIAL GUARD IN TONGKING

From Giovanni Filippo de Marini, *Historia et relatione del Tunchino* (Rome, 1665), between pp. 62 and 63.

A guardsman in full regalia at the court of the "Bua" (*vua* or emperor) of Tongking. He displays a fan inscribed with Chinese characters, only some of which are legible.

Habito de Mandarini
letterati che uan calzati
in Casa del Re detto Bua
in TumKino

267. A MANDARIN OF TONGKING

From Marini, *op. cit.*, between pp. 270 and 271.

A mandarin in full dress at the court of the "Bua" in Hanoi. *Cf.* his black gauze cap to the cap of the Ming Chinese official on the map in pl. 302, below.

II.
DELINEATIO PISCATVRÆ TERNATENSIS,

268. FISHING AT TERNATE
From De Bry, *op.cit.* (pl. 260), VIII (Frankfurt, 1607).

269. (FACING PAGE, TOP) THE INDIAN SALAMANDER OR GECKO
From J. Bontius (Jacob de Bondt), *Historia naturalis et medica* in Piso, *De Indiae utri-usque re naturali et medica* (Amsterdam, 1658), p. 57. Pls. 270–74 and 276–77 are also from this book.
  "There exists an extremely dangerous sort of lizard, of which I show you here a picture, drawn after the living model; its bite is so dangerous, that without any doubt the sufferer is done for, when the wound is not cut out immediately or burnt out with a hot fire" (as translated in *Opuscula selecta Neerlandicorum de arte medica*, X [Amsterdam, 1931], 229.
  The gecko, a house lizard, is harmless. Bontius is here repeating a common belief of his day. The word "gecko" is probably derived from Malay *gēkoq*.

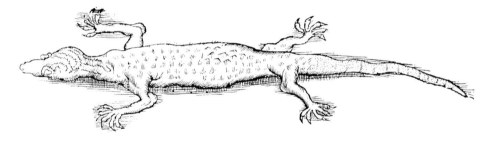

HIST. NATVRAL. & MEDIC. L IB. V.

V E S P E R T I L I O   V O L A N S.

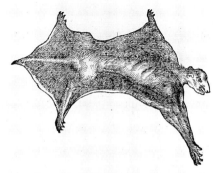

V E S P E R T I L I O   arte   E X T E N S V S.

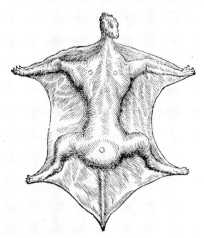

270. A STRANGE BAT, OR THE FLYING FOX

From Bontius, *op. cit.*, p. 69.

"All strangers are amazed, when seeing their size and strange form. Therefore the Dutch . . . called them rather illogically winged monkeys. Since they use a membranous skin as wings, have long ears and nails and four legs, bring forth living young, which they suckle, and do not lay eggs, they must be counted among the other beasts" (*Opuscula*, X, 253).

These are indeed giant fruit bats, commonly called flying foxes. Westerners, beginning with Marco Polo, have been astounded by these impressive bats, particularly when vast hordes of them skim the ocean or inland waters at sunset.

271. *ARBOR MELONIFERA:* THE
MELON TREE, OR THE PAPAYA

From Bontius, *op. cit.* (pl. 269), p. 96.
Cf. our plate 170.

"How would one, who never has visited these countries, believe that melons
grow on trees? They are like melons,
in regard to their pulp as well as their
taste" (*Opuscula* [see pl. 269], X, 313).

A native of the Americas, the papaya
probably was introduced to the East
Indies via the Philippines. The word
"papaya" is of Carib origin. Today the
papaya is widely distributed throughout
the tropics.

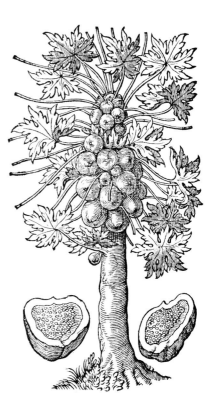

272. CLOSE-UP OF THE DURIAN
FRUIT

From Bontius, *op. cit.,* p. 118.

"The fruit is called doerian after the
hard rind or thorns [Malay, *duri*, thorn].
When tasted for the first time they are
nauseous, for they smell like rotten garlic, but they must be counted among the
most wholesome Indian fruit. . . .
When one is used to this fruit it does not
pall as quickly as other fruit" (*Opuscula,*
X, 346–47).

This globular fruit is about the size of
a giant coconut (about eight pounds in
weight) and is covered with a hard shell
armored with sharp spines. The edible
part is the fleshy glutinous covering of
the seed called the aril. Today the pulp is
eaten as it comes, or is used in making
ice creams, jams, and candies.

Cf. pl. 278, below.

F ʀ ᴠ ᴄ ᴛ ᴠ s   D ᴠ ʀ ɪ ᴏ ɴ ɪ s   Majoris I ᴀ ᴀ ᴄ ᴀ.

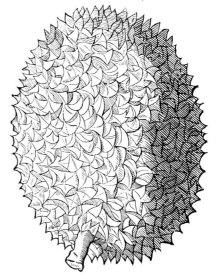

273. THE JAVANESE RHINOCEROS

From Bontius, *op. cit.*, p. 51.

Bontius wrote: "As far as I am able, I will describe this animal, as I saw it, in order to make clear the error of the artists, who picture it with a shield and with scales" (*Opuscula*, X, 211).

One of the first attempts to draw a rhinoceros from life. It owes nothing to Dürer's marvelous beast. See T. H. Clarke, *The Rhinoceros from Dürer to Stubbs, 1515–1799* (London, 1986), p. 41. This is also one of the first efforts to study the rhinoceros' anatomy scientifically. See F. J. Cole, "The History of Albrecht Dürer's Rhinoceros in Zoölogical Literature," in *Science, Medicine and History: Essays . . . in Honour of Charles Singer,* ed. E. A. Underwood (London and New York, 1953), I, 349.

274. THE DODO

From Bontius, *op. cit.*, p. 74.

On the island of Mauritius "the bird Dronte [*Dod-aers*], with its curious appearance, is found abundantly. Its size is between that of an ostrich and a chicken. . . . It has a large, ugly head, covered with a thin skin and similar to that of a cuckoo. . . . The body is fat and round and it is covered with soft grey feathers, like that of the ostriches. . . . The legs are yellow, thick and very short, and have four long firm toes that are as scaled, and bear as many black, strong nails. The bird walks slowly and is stupid and is therefore an easy prey for the hunter" (*Opuscula*, X, 255).

The dodo (*Raphus cucullatus*), a clumsy and flightless bird, became extinct, apparently around the end of the seventeenth century. The Dutch and English sailors took living birds to Java and Europe as curiosities. See the drawing by Roelant Savery in *Asia*, Vol. II, Bk. 1, pl. 142. A dodo which arrived in England in 1637 was, after its demise, stuffed and given to the Ashmolean Museum (Oxford), where it was on display until 1755. The name "dodo" is derived from *doudo,* the Portuguese word for "simpleton." For further discussion see *Encyclopaedia Brittanica,* 11th ed., Vol. VIII; Patrick Armstrong, "The Dodo and the Tree," *The Geographical Magazine,* Vol. LVIII, No. 10 (Oct., 1985), pp. 541–43; and W. R. Sanford and C. R. Green, *Gone Forever. The Dodo* (New York, 1989).

HIST. NATVRAL & MEDIC. Lib. V.

RHINOCEROS.

CRANIVM RHINOCEROTIS.

DRONTE.

Dronte Alijs Dod-Aers.

275. ANIMALS OF THE INDIAN OCEAN ISLANDS

From TR, I (Paris, 1666), "Voyage de Bontekoe," p. 5.

These are supposedly portraits of the animals eaten by Bontekoe and his companions on their way to the East Indies in 1619.

The one-horned goat in the middle is probably a throwback to old European ideas about unicorns in Asia.

The text reports that the dodo's wings are so small that the bird cannot fly, and that it is so fat that it can barely walk—easy prey!

Judging from the text, the small bird on the left is possibly supposed to be a parakeet.

E M E V vulgo C A S O A R I S.

276. EMU, COMMONLY CALLED CASSOWARY

From Bontius, *op. cit.* (pl. 269), p. 71.

"This well-known bird is found in the island Ceram and in the neighboring islands of the Molucs [Moluccas]. It walks with its head erect and its neck slightly curved and reaches then about five feet. The length of the body, from the breast to the arse, is three feet" (*Opuscula* [see pl. 269], X, 257).

"These birds wander about the vast mountainous forests that cover the island of Ceram, feeding chiefly on fallen fruits, and on insects or crustacea. The female lays from three to five large and beautifully shagreened green eggs upon a bed of leaves, the male and female sitting upon them alternately for about a month" (Wallace, *op. cit.* [pl. 237], p. 403).

277. THE ORANG-UTAN

From Bontius, *op. cit.*, p. 84.

"And the most curious thing is, that once I saw myself some of both sexes walking upright, and the female satyr (of which I give a drawing here) hid her person with great shyness for the strange men, covering her face with her hands (when I am allowed to express myself in that way) and she cried and sighed and showed other human emotions, therefore, one is inclined to say that no human quality failed her, except for the speech. . . . They [the Javanese] call them Ourang-Outang, which means wood man" (*Opuscula*, X, 285).

Bontius was the first to introduce the name of this great manlike ape to European literature. It is from the Malay, *orang-utan,* man of the woods. See H. Yule and A. C. Burnell, *Hobson-Jobson* (rev. ed.; London, 1968), pp. 643–44. Certainly this portrait bears no resemblance to *Pongo pygmaeus,* the long-armed ape of Borneo and Sumatra to which we now commonly apply the name orangutan. For the relationship of this "satyr" to other contemporary European illustrations see William B. Ashworth, Jr., "The Persistent Beast: Recurring Images in Early Zoölogical Illustration," in *The Natural Sciences and the Arts. An International Symposium* ("Acta Universitatis Upsaliensis," n.s. 22; Uppsala, 1985), pp. 55–57.

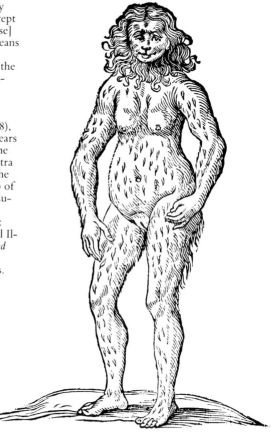

OVRANG OVTANG.

XII.
DE ALGA SEV ARVNDINE
INDICA, BAMBVS DICTA, ITEM DE
arbore radicofa: & tandem de arbore
Duryoens.

RVNDINIS *quoddam in India genus prouenit, quod Indi Bambus vocant, craſsi-*
tiem femoris virilis occupans.
   Arbor quoque alia ibidem prouenit, Arbore de Rays .i. de radicibus nuncupata,
è cuius ramis filamenta plurima deſcendunt, quæ terram attingentia illi ſe denuò
inſinuant, & radice ſagentia ramos viciſsim alios ſurſum parturiunt, qui & ipſi la-
tius propagati tandem arborem conſtituunt, ambitu ſuo quartam partem milliaris
vnius complexam.
   His quoque iunctim appicta cernitur alia quædam arbor, quæ fructum Duryoens dictum fert, in
ſola Malacca cognita. Fructus iſte à guſtantibus fructuum omnium, quos vniuerſus terrarum orbis gi-
gnit, longè optimus & ſuauiſsimus cenſetur. De qua re vberius hiſtoria euoluatur.

d

278. DURIANS, BANYAN TREES, AND BAMBOOS
From De Bry, *op. cit.* (pl. 260), IV, plate 12.
   Each durian, a giant fruit, dangles from its tree at the end of a long string. Once it
ripens and drops, the durian divides into a number of sections, as shown here. One
eats the odorous, custard-like pulp which surrounds the seeds in these sections.
   The banyan is a fig tree whose aerial roots (extra trunks) help support its super-
structure. Like the tree itself, the name "banyan" has been spread throughout the
tropical world.
   Sections of bamboo were made into containers to carry water and palm and fruit
juices.

SVCESOS DE LAS
ISLAS FILIPINAS.
DIRIGIDO.
A DON CRISTOVAL GOMEZ DE
Sandoual y Rojas, Duque de Cea.

POR EL DOCTOR ANTONIO DE MORGA,
Alcalde del Crimen, de la real Audiencia de la Nueua Es
paña, Consultor del santo Oficio de la Inquisicion.

EN MEXICO.
En casa de Geronymo Balli. Año 1609.
Por Cornelio Adriano Cesar.

279.

280. THE MARKET AT BANTAM (*CA.* 1596)

From the facsimile of *BV,* I, "De eerste Schipvaerd der Hollandsche Natie naer Ost-Indien," between pp. 68 and 69.

This market was held daily in the great open square before the sultan's palace and close to the mosque. The Dutchmen can be located by the parasols they carry.

COCHIN-CHINA:

Containing many admirable Rarities and Singularities of that Countrey.

Extracted out of an Italian Relation, lately prefented to the P O P E , by CHRISTOPHORO BORRI, *that lived certaine yeeres there.*

And publifhed by R O B E R T A S H L E Y.

Cum hac perfuafione viuendum eft ; Non fum vni angulo natus : Patria mea totus hic mundus eft. Seneca.

L O N D O N.
Printed by *Robert Raworth* ; for *Richard Clutter-buck,* and are to be fold at the figne of the Ball in *Little-Brittaine.* 1 6 3 3.

281.

Vremde
GESCHIEDENISSEN
In de Koninckrijcken van
CAMBODIA en
LOUWEN-LANT,
IN OOST-INDIEN,
Zedert den Iare 1 6 3 5. tot den Iare 1 6 4 4.
aldaer voor-gevallen.

Mitfgaders de Reyfe der Nederlanders van Cambo-dia de Loufe Revier op, na Wincjan, het Hof van de Loufe Majefteyt.

Ende ten laetften de wreede Maffacré in Cambodia door de Indianen, Anno 1 6 4 3. gefchiet.

T O T H A E R L E M,
Gedruckt by *Pieter Cafteleyn,* Boeckdrucker woonende op de Marckt in de Keyzers Kroon, 1669,

282.

ITINERARIO
DELAS MISSIONES
DEL INDIA ORIENTAL
Que hizo el P. Maeftro Fra Sebaftian Manrique Religiofo Eremita de S. Aguftin.

Miffonario Apoftolico treze años en varias Miffiones della dicha India
Y al prefente Prefecto Apoftolico de la Million Calaminenfe efpecialmente delegado por la Santidad de INNO-CENTIO X. nueftro Señor.

Procurador , y Diffinidor General della Prouincia Au-guftiniana de Portugal en efta Curia de Roma .

Con una Summaria Relacion del Grande y Opulento Imperio del Emperador X-ahabam Correombo Gran Mogol y de otros Reis Infieles en cuios Reynos affiften los Religiofos de S. Aguftin.

AL EMINENTISS. SEÑOR
CARDENAL PALLOTTO
Protector de la Religion Aguftiniana.
CON PRIVILEGIO

IN ROMA A la inftancia de Guilielmo Halle Sub figno
Salamandra Regia . M. DC. LIII.
Con licencia de los Superiores.

283.

Those who wrote at the end of the century, when Acheh's power had declined and queens sat on its throne, describe its government quite differently from those who had visited during the first half of the century. Dampier reports that the queen rules with the aid of twelve great lords called "Oronkeys" (*orang kaya*s), of whom the "Shabandar" (*shahbandar*) is one. The queen is always an old maid, chosen from the royal family. Once chosen, she is secluded in her palace except for an annual procession to the river for a ceremonial bath. She has little real power, the actual government being in the hands of the *orang kaya*s. Dampier heard that Acheh was ruled by kings in the beginning of the century, but he also repeats speculations that Acheh was originally governed by women and that the Old Testament's Queen of Sheba who visited King Solomon was from Acheh. Dampier describes a succession crisis in 1688 resulting from the opposition of several *orang kaya*s to the newly chosen queen.[481] De Roy calls Acheh a republic. The queen, he reports, has much honor but little power. Power is in the hands of a royal council, any member of which can frustrate its proceedings if it is in his or his family's interest to do so. He compares Acheh's government to that of Poland.[482]

Because it was necessary for them to negotiate with the sultans regarding trade, many European visitors to Acheh during the first part of the century were received by the sultans, talked with them, and later wrote descriptions of them. Davis' depiction of al-Mukammil is one of the most detailed and colorful. When Davis met him he was reputed to be one hundred years old but still vigorous. Davis describes him as "exceedingly grosse and fat," sitting cross-legged in his palace, wearing four jewel-encrusted krises, "a sword lying upon his lap." Forty women attend him, fanning him, drying his sweat, serving him drinks, and singing. He does little all day but eat and drink, "and when his bellie is readie to breake, then he eadeth arreca betula [chews betel] . . and procureth a mighty stomach," after which "he goeth with a fresh courage to eating." For a change of pace he sometimes bathes in the river to revive his appetite. "Hee, his great men and women, doe nothing but eate, drinke, and talke of venerie."[483] Those who enter the sultan's presence first remove their shoes and stockings and then bow deeply hold-

---

Problem of Royal Power in Aceh. Three Stages: c. 1550–1700," in Reid and Castles (eds.), *op. cit.* (n. 454), pp. 45–51.

[481] *Op. cit.* (n. 353), pp. 98–103.

[482] De Roy, *op. cit.* (n. 363), pp. 128–29. Dampier's and De Roy's descriptions of Acheh's government during the second half of the seventeenth century seem generally accurate. While royal prestige seemed intact during the reigns of Iskandar Thani (1636–41) and Iskandar Muda's daughter, Taj al-Alam, who was the first queen (1641–75), the queens who reigned during the remainder of the century seem indeed to have been under the control of the *orang kaya*s. For the decline of royal power in Acheh after 1676 see Reid, *loc. cit.* (n. 480), pp. 52–55. See also Marsden, *op. cit.* (n. 345), pp. 446–48.

[483] Unger (ed.), *op. cit.* (n. 333), pp. 54–55. Beaulieu, *loc. cit.* (n. 344), p. 113, reports that al-Mukammil was ninety-five years old when he died in 1603.

ing their palms together over their heads—the *sembah*—after which they may sit cross-legged on the floor. Davis concludes: "He doth only spend the time in eating with women and cock-fighting. And such as is the king, such are his subjects, for the whole land is given to no other contentment." Van Warwijck's description of al-Mukammil is very similar.[484]

Van Warwijck also mentions the "young king," most likely 'Ali Ri'ayat Syah or Sultan Muda (r. 1604–7), who lives in a separate palace not guarded exclusively by women. The young king's favorite pastimes are swimming in the river and hunting elephants.[485] Later Van Warwijck describes the young sultan sitting cross-legged under a canopy, surrounded by armed women, eating and drinking. His journal contains a rather fanciful engraving of the scene.[486]

Sir James Lancaster, who commanded the first English East India Company voyage, also visited the old sultan, al-Mukammil, in 1602. He describes the procession of elephants that takes him to the palace, the royal reception, the gifts exchanged, and the cockfight which he is invited to watch, but he does not describe the king himself.[487] Pyrard, whose *Voyage* was first published in 1611, reports that the young king has recently usurped the throne from his father, that he favors the Dutch, and hates the Portuguese.[488]

Beaulieu provides the most detailed picture of the great Iskandar Muda. From his report emerges a monarch with a high sense of duty, proud of his accomplishments, but given to quick changes in temper and to seemingly irrational rages. He could be gracious, as when he personally escorts Beaulieu around parts of his palace showing off his gold and jewelled treasures. He could be almost unbelievably cruel, sometimes personally torturing suspected criminals. He reputedly had his own mother killed and personally executed the young son of the king of Johore. Scarcely a day passes, according to Beaulieu, but someone is put to death by the sultan; sometimes several people are executed in the same day. Beaulieu thinks Iskandar Muda has executed almost all of the old *orang kayas*.[489]

Both Thomas Best and Patrick Copeland, who in 1613 also visited Acheh during Iskandar Muda's reign, describe royal banquets of four or five hundred dishes. One, which lasts for an entire afternoon, is served to diners who sit in the water at the sultan's favorite bathing place about six miles upstream from the town. Iskandar Muda also entertains them with cock-fights, elephant fights, ram fights, water buffalo fights, and even antelope fights.[490] Beaulieu describes in much detail the dancing girls who entertain

---

[484] Unger (ed.), *op. cit.* (n. 333), p. 55; Van Warwijck, *loc. cit.* (n. 375), pp. 14–15.
[485] Van Warwijck, *loc. cit.* (n. 375), p. 15.
[486] *Ibid.*, pp. 31–32.
[487] Sir William Foster (ed.), *The Voyages of Sir James Lancaster to Brazil and the East Indies, 1591–1603* ("HS," 2d ser., LXXXV; London, 1940), pp. 90–99, 129–36.
[488] Gray (ed.), *op. cit.* (n. 32), II, 157–60. See Marsden, *op. cit.* (n. 345), pp. 437–38.
[489] *Loc. cit.* (n. 344), pp. 56–59, 101–2.
[490] Best, *loc. cit.* (n. 371), pp. 137–40; Copeland, *loc. cit.* (n. 459), pp. 150–54.

after a royal banquet, their cloth-of-gold costumes, their jewelry, and their dances.[491] Royal receptions of foreign ambassadors and other dignitaries follow a rather rigid routine, parts of which most Europeans describe.[492] John Milward, visiting in 1614, witnesses a procession of elephants, carrying the sultan with his women and eunuchs. Bystanders along the route are hustled out of sight; doors and windows are tightly closed. Milward also reports the arrival and departure of the sultan's galleys for Malacca and Pedir. Altogether, he heard, the sultan has over three hundred war galleys, some of which can carry one thousand men.[493] De Graaf was in Acheh during February, 1641, when Iskandar Thani (r. 1636–41) died. He describes the funeral: the lavish procession of 260 elephants draped in costly silk, tusks covered with gold and silver, rhinoceroses and Persian horses covered with gold and silver, the sultan's body in a casket made of tombac, laid to rest beside his ancestors in the garden behind his palace where he is mourned by his wives and concubines for one hundred days.[494] Later still, Schouten and Nieuhof report that a woman, no doubt Taj al-Alam (r. 1641–75), ruled Acheh, and that it was rumored that she wanted to marry a Dutchman but that the governor-general and the Council of the Indies would not allow it.[495] Few men had access to the ruler during the reigns of Taj al-Alam and her successors. No Western writers describe them or their courts.[496]

During the seventeenth century many European travelers visited Sumatra. Many more sailed along its coasts and described their appearance, often augmenting their descriptions with information gleaned from previously published accounts. From the reports of those who actually visited Sumatra's coastal towns a fairly clear and detailed image of the island's geography, climate, products, people, rulers, and politics emerged. The image is clearest for Acheh, the most powerful of Sumatra's coastal states and its most frequented port; it almost entirely fades out for Sumatra's interior. Apart from brief, vague, and general references to gold and other inland products, and the different language and religion of the inland peoples, little was written about Sumatra's interior during the seventeenth century. Less was known about it than was known about interior Java or perhaps even interior Borneo. Significant improvement in Europe's knowledge of inland Sumatra had to wait until the 1783 publication of William Marsden's *History of Sumatra*. As for the rest of insular Southeast Asia, the descriptions written by seventeenth-century European visitors to Sumatra not only provide information and images of a far-off corner of the world for their literate contemporaries, but are

[491] *Loc. cit.* (n. 344), pp. 54–55.
[492] For example, see *ibid.*, pp. 49–51. *Cf.* Lombard, *op. cit.* (n. 338), pp. 139–43.
[493] John Milward, "Memorials of a Voyage Wherein Were Employed Three Shippes," *PP*, IV, 284–85.
[494] Warnsinck (ed.), *op. cit.* (n. 89), pp. 13–14.
[495] Schouten, *op. cit.* (n. 46), III, 48; Nieuhof, *Zee- en lant-reize* (n. 81), p. 73.
[496] On Taj al-alam and the queens who ruled for the rest of the century see Reid, *loc. cit.* (n. 480), pp. 52–55. See also Marsden, *op. cit.* (n. 345), pp. 446–47.

themselves indispensable primary sources for the precolonial history of Sumatra, given the paucity and quality of native sources.

4

BORNEO

Borneo could be discerned only in hazy outline through sixteenth-century European reports. Several trading towns, such as Brunei, Tanjungpura, and Lawai, were mentioned, as were Borneo's major products, but only Brunei emerges with any clarity.⁴⁹⁷ Apart from Brunei, most towns mentioned in the sixteenth-century accounts seem to drop from view during the seventeenth, to be replaced by places not mentioned in the sixteenth century: Sukadana, Landak, Sambas, Cotawaringin, Banjarmasin, Martapura, and others, on the west and south coasts of the island. Most of the new information came from Dutch reports. The Dutch, however, never really established themselves on Borneo during the seventeenth century. They maintained a factory at Sukadana from 1608 until 1622, and in Sambas during 1610; they signed several treaties and sporadically traded with Banjarmasin. But they were unable to monopolize the trade anywhere on Borneo, their relationship with local rulers was usually uncomfortable, and trade was never very profitable. Consequently, while the image of Borneo becomes much more distinct during the seventeenth century, it remains considerably less detailed than that of Java, Sumatra, or the Spiceries.

The earliest seventeenth-century notices of Borneo, like those of the sixteenth century, relate almost entirely to the sultanate of Brunei on the north coast. The first of these, Olivier van Noort's *Beschrijvinghe vande voyagie* (1601), is the most detailed and very likely the only eyewitness account.⁴⁹⁸ Van Noort's ship anchored in the "Bay of Borneo" (Brunei) on December 26, 1600. Upon his arrival he sent one of his Chinese pilots to the "King of Borneo" in the capital, also called "Borneo" (Brunei), three miles upriver from the coast. The pilot was to assure the "king" that the Dutch came in friendship and to ask for permission to trade and to buy provisions. The Chinese pilot soon returned with emissaries from the "king," who was afraid that the Dutch were Spanish, with whom he was at war.⁴⁹⁹ Some pains and the help of Chinese intermediaries were required to convince the

---

⁴⁹⁷ See *Asia*, I, 579–85, and R. Nicholl (ed.), *European Sources for the History of the Sultanate of Brunei in the Sixteenth Century* (Brunei, 1975).

⁴⁹⁸ For bibliography see above, pp. 441–43. For an English translation of the materials on Borneo see Nicholl (ed.), *op. cit.* (n. 497), pp. 82–87.

⁴⁹⁹ Ijzerman (ed.), *op. cit.* (n. 8), I, 121–22. The "king" was probably Sultan Saiful Rijial (r. 1575–1600?). The Spanish in Manila laid formal claim to northern Borneo in 1578. See F. Blumentritt, "Spain and the Island of Borneo," *Brunei Museum Journal*, Vol. IV, No. 1 (1977), p. 85. Actually a letter from the sultan of Borneo in 1599 had requested peace and friendship of Manila.

king that they were not Spanish; thereafter the Dutch were able to buy provisions and some pepper from resident Chinese merchants. The Chinese merchants also warned Van Noort of a plot against his ship; the appearance in the bay of almost one hundred proas on January 1, 1601, put the Dutch on guard. Their vigilance apparently prevented an attack on the ship and frustrated an attempt by four swimmers to cut its anchor cable. Nevertheless, Van Noort maintained the appearance of friendship with the king until he sailed on January 5.[500]

Van Noort reports that Borneo is one of the largest islands in the East Indies and that it is well populated. The capital city, also called "Borneo," is built on a swamp; its inhabitants travel from house to house in boats called proas. The city contains some three hundred houses. Many people live further inland who are idolators. "Brown like other Indians," they clothe themselves with a long cloth which they "wind about their bodies in various ways." They wear thin cotton turbans on their heads. The men are large and strong ("groote en cloecke") and always carry weapons, "even the poorest farmer or fisherman." Their weapons are bows and arrows and long, iron-tipped javelins. His further description of the bows and arrows, however, suggests that he means blowguns. The arrows, he says, are poisoned and can be "blown" with great force. Anyone wounded by them deeply enough to draw blood will die from the poison.[501]

The coastal people are generally Muslims and they "would sooner suffer death than eat pork," which is why there are no pigs on the island. Men keep "as many wives as they can feed," and are intensely jealous of their women. Van Noort also describes the women as brave, many of them coming aboard to trade with the Dutch. But whenever one of the crew makes a suggestive gesture towards the women the men become furious and threateningly draw their weapons. Van Noort describes the "king" as a young man, still under the guardianship of his uncle, who holds a large and magnificent court. The officials who come to visit the Dutch are richly dressed, speak gravely, and travel in covered proas which contain tables set with fine silver dishes to hold the ingredients for betel quids.[502]

Van Noort reports that Borneo raises no spices, but that it produces the best camphor in the East. The price, however, is very high. Pepper in Borneo also seems expensive, and the Chinese from whom he buys it want pieces of eight, not merchandise: thirteen pieces of eight per picul. In fact, most of Brunei's trade seems to be in the hands of Chinese from Patani who live in Brunei but claim to be subjects of the "King of Patani."[503]

Pedro Teixeira visited Brunei in 1604. In his *Relaciones* (1610) he describes

[500] Ijzerman (ed.), *op. cit.* (n. 8), I, 122–25.
[501] Blowguns are still used in Borneo to kill small game. On their construction see Fung Yee Ping and Kinawa, "Blowpipes," *Sabah Society Journal*, Vol. III, No. 4 (March, 1968), pp. 294–96.
[502] Ijzerman (ed.), *op. cit.* (n. 8), I, 126–27, contains most of Van Noort's descriptive material.
[503] *Ibid.*, I, 124.

Borneo as rich in provisions and desirable products, especially camphor. The natives scrape camphor with iron claws from the heart of a large tree. It is not shipped to Europe because it brings such high prices in India.[504] Teixeira also mentions tortoise shells, wax, and gold. Brunei is not well populated, nor are its people very healthy. He thinks the kingdoms on the other side of the island—"Lave" (Lawai) and "Maiar Magem" (Banjarmasin) are richer. There is little trade in Brunei. The Spanish controlled it at one time, he reports, but they "abandoned it as unhealthy and little fit for traffic, the land unsuitable, and the folk unserviceable." Brunei's harbor is large and safe. The city is built in the river. Its houses are constructed of wood atop wooden pilings and can easily be moved from one side of the river to the other for protection against typhoons. Brunei's inhabitants are Muslims, of an olive complexion, and good-looking, especially the women. Most of them wear nothing but a cloth wrapped around their waists. They are addicted to thievery, especially at sea, often sailing to the coast of Pegu, four hundred miles away, on piratical raids. In addition to blowguns and lances, they use shields made from rattan and charred wooden spears which are as hard as iron but which break, leaving splinters in the wounds of those struck by them.[505]

As published in Commelin's *Begin ende voortgangh* (1646), Van Noort's account contains an insert further describing Borneo which comes primarily from Teixeira. It adds, however, some additional information about bezoar stones, describing how they are found in the stomachs of sheep and goats and how they are used to counteract poison.[506] It reports that Borneo's circuit is variously estimated at two hundred and fifty miles and twenty-one hundred miles.[507] Van Noort's account in almost all of its editions also contains three plates pertaining to Borneo: one of the bay with the Dutch ship surrounded by native proas, another of a royal proa, and a map of Borneo, containing place-names probably derived from sixteenth-century descriptions (also see pl. 234).

The Dutch never established an office or factory at Brunei, nor did they

[504] Borneo camphor is a secretion of the kapur tree (*Dryolealanopa aromatica*), which grows prolifically in northern Borneo. Camphor crystals are formed in the trunks of decayed trees. These huge trees are cut down and the scales of pure camphor either shaken or scraped from the heart of the tree. Borneo camphor, the most coveted and the highest in price, should not be confused with the inferior camphors produced from plants in Sumatra and other parts of Southeast Asia and from another large tree (*Cinnamomum camphora*) native to East Asia. See R. Nicholl, "Brunei and Camphor," *Brunei Museum Journal*, Vol. IV, No. 3 (1979), pp. 52–74.

[505] William F. Sinclair (trans.), *The Travels of Pedro Teixeira; with His "Kings of Harmuz" and Extracts from his "Kings of Persia"* ("HS," 2d ser., IX; London, 1902), pp. 4–6. For bibliography see above, pp. 323–24. Also see the report of the Jesuit Antonio Pereira, who was shipwrecked off Borneo in 1608, as translated in Nicholl (ed.), *op. cit.* (n. 497), pp. 87–90.

[506] On the bezoar stones see Carl Bock, *The Head Hunters of Borneo* (London, 1881; reprinted in Singapore, 1986), pp. 205–6.

[507] "Beschrijvinge van de schipvaerd by de Hollanders ghedaen onder 't beleydt en generaelschap van Olivier van Noort, door de Straet oft Engte van Magallanes, ende voorts de gantsche kloot des aertbodems om," *BV*, Ib, 50–51.

trade there with any regularity during the seventeenth century. Merchants from Brunei traded freely at Batavia, however, and after 1641 at Malacca. Common antipathy towards the Spanish kept relations between the VOC and the sultan of Brunei amicable; letters and a few embassies were exchanged and the Dutch promised aid to the sultan should he be attacked by the Spanish from Manila.[508]

The *Begin ende voortgangh* also contains a report about Dutch activities on Borneo's west coast—primarily at Sukadana and Sambas—during 1609 and early 1610.[509] The author, Samuel Bloemaert, was sent to Sukadana in 1607 or 1608 with instructions to negotiate exclusive trade agreements with as many native princes as possible, among them the queen of Sukadana, the king of "Borneo" (Brunei), and the king of Banjarmasin. The Dutch were primarily interested in the diamonds which were shipped to Sukadana by the "savages" (Dayak tribesmen) of Landak, upriver and north of Sukadana. But they were also interested in gold, rice, and bezoar stones. The gold, however, they judged to be of very poor quality. Wybrand van Warwijck in 1604 had also touched upon Borneo's west coast and had sent a sloop to buy diamonds at Sukadana. Later the king of Brunei released eight Dutch prisoners to him at Patani, prisoners who had been taken by Bruneians from one of Admiral Heemskerk's boats. Van Warwijck's report published in the *Begin ende voortgangh*, however, contains no description of Borneo.[510]

From Sukadana, Bloemaert and his associates negotiated with the king of Banjarmasin for trade and the release of a Dutchman imprisoned there; with the queen of Sukadana for toll-free trade in diamonds without competition from other Europeans; with "Quiay Area" (Kiai Aria), one of the chiefs of Landak where the diamonds were found; with the king of Sambas, north of Sukadana, for free, exclusive trade; and with Landak and Sambas to induce the Dayaks of Landak to ship the diamonds downriver to Sambas instead of Sukadana.[511] Bloemaert's "Discours" is a detailed account of these negotiations. It contains no description of the places or the peoples of western Borneo—a pity, since Bloemaert traveled much in the area, including trips up the rivers to Landak. Nevertheless, his readers learned considerably more about Borneo's geography and politics than was available during the sixteenth century.

[508] For Dutch relations with Brunei see L. C. D. van Dijk, *Neerland's vroegste betrekkingen met Borneo, den Solo-Archipel, Cambodja, Siam en Cochin China* (Amsterdam, 1862), pp. 209–317. For an English translation of Van Dijk's materials on Borneo see R. Nicholl (ed.), "Relations of the East Indies Company with Borneo (Brunei), the Sulu Archipelago, Mindanao etc.," *Brunei Museum Journal*, Vol. V, No. 3 (1983), pp. 61–80; Vol. V, No. 4 (1984), pp. 6–34.

[509] "Discours ende ghelegentheyt van het Eylandt Borneo, ende 't gene daer voor ghevallen is in 't Iaer 1609. ghestelt door S[amuel]. B[loemaert]. . . . ," *BV*, IIa, 98–107 (appended to the account of Pieter Verhoeff's voyage). For bibliography see above, pp. 471–72.

[510] "Historisch verhael vande reyse . . . . ," *BV*, Ia, 70–71, 75. See above, p. 466, for bibliography. See also Van Dijk, *op. cit.* (n. 508), p. 211.

[511] On diamonds in Landak see *Encyclopaedie van Nederlandsch-Indië*, I, 597. On the mines of Martapura see Bock, *op. cit.* (n. 506), pp. 170–71.

Bloemaert points out that the king of "Borneo" (Brunei) governs in the far north while the king of Banjarmasin rules an area on Borneo's south coast. Negotiations with both of them he thinks will require an entire year.[512] The best chance to trade in the diamonds from Landak is through Sambas. The queen of Sukadana is a usurper who killed her husband and seized control of the government. Bloemaert describes her as a "stingy wife," who tries to buy up all the diamonds that come downriver from Landak, saying that she is old and wants to keep them for her children. Her "Orankays" (*orang kayas*) dare not oppose her for fear of their lives. Landak, Bloemaert observes, is about forty miles upstream from Sukadana. From "Quiay Area" he learns that it can also be reached by way of "Teyen" (Tajan), a village on the "Lauwe" (Lawai or Kapuas) river from where a small branch of the river extends towards Landak. He learns that Landak can also be reached overland in one day from the "Sandongh" (Sadong) river, north of Sambas. Landak is subject to Sukadana, however, and "Quiay Area" dares do nothing without the queen's permission. Most of Bloemaert's efforts are aimed at detaching Landak from Sukadana by arranging a treaty with the king of Sambas who would protect Landak and allow the diamonds to be shipped through his territories to the Dutch. He also thought trade with Landak might be carried on through "Manpana" (Mempawa) south of Sambas. Bloemaert saw some of the diamonds. One he guessed was thirty to forty karats. Should the VOC negotiate an agreement with Sambas, Bloemaert thinks the Dutch will not need Banjarmasin. Trade there, he judges, is spoiled by the Chinese who come once a year bringing everything the local people need. Furthermore, merchants from Banjarmasin trade regularly at Malacca, where they can obtain cloth more cheaply than the Dutch can sell it. The prices of pepper and of other commodities in Banjarmasin, he reports, are too high.

Bloemaert's negotiations are complicated by other political rivalries, for example, by the quarrel between Landak's two chiefs, "Quiay Area" and his enemy "Tommegon" (Temenggong; probably Temenggong Boroxa). The queen of Sukadana tries to settle it, and when she learns about the Dutch negotiations with Landak and Sambas she sends a war fleet upriver. Furthermore, the "savages" of Landak distrust Muslims, and both Sukadana and Sambas are Muslim. Nevertheless, when Palembang on Sumatra threatens Sukadana, the queen appears willing to negotiate with the Dutch; but no treaty is signed because she will not grant a monopoly. Such a contract was made with the king of Sambas in 1609, but at the end of Bloemaert's account, trade with Landak through Sambas had not yet begun.[513]

From Bloemaert's account we also learn that Sambas is dominated by the sultan of Johore on the Malay Peninsula, that three areas north of Sambas— "Calca" (the Kaluka or Krian River), "Seribus" (probably Sarawak or

---

[512] *Loc. cit.* (n. 509), p. 100.
[513] For the text of the treaty see *ibid.*, pp. 103–4.

Saribas), and "Melanouge" (Malanau?)—had fallen away from the sultan of Brunei and had placed themselves under the protection of the sultan of Johore. In retaliation the sultan of Brunei prepared a war fleet of 150 proas to attack Sambas. Later Bloemaert heard that the sultan of Johore was dispatching a fleet to attack Brunei. At one point Bloemaert tries to use the influence of the "King of Surabaya" on Java to help him negotiate with Sukadana, which he thinks is under Surabaya's suzerainty. From this account readers could obtain a rudimentary understanding of Borneo's major political jurisdictions, the rivalries between them and overseas states such as Johore, Palembang, and Surabaya, and the influence of Java and Malaya in Borneo. Most of the towns, territories, and rivers mentioned by Bloemaert were new to European readers, but were described by him with sufficient accuracy to be located today.[514]

The VOC established a factory at Sambas in 1610, but it was looted and all its personnel massacred during the same year, apparently on orders from the king who was angry because the Dutch had not delivered the cannons they had promised. The VOC sent a retaliatory expedition in 1612, about which very little is known. The Dutch seem not to have had any relations with Sambas after that. In 1611 the English also appeared at Sukadana and their competition drove up the price of diamonds. The Dutch factory in Sukadana was destroyed by a mysterious fire in 1622 during Mataram's invasion of the city. Thereafter Sukadana appears to have continued under Mataram's hegemony, its king living in Mataram. Neither the Dutch nor the English seem to have resumed regular trade there. Merchants from Sukadana brought their goods to Batavia instead.[515] No new published descriptions of Borneo's west coast resulted from these activities. Between 1646 and 1692 no continuous accounts of Borneo appear to have been published, although the island and places along its coast were occasionally mentioned in the travel literature.[516] In 1692, Vicente Barbosa (1663–1721) published a brief account celebrating the opening of a Theatine mission to the "Biadjoes" (more correctly Ngadjus or "uplanders") near Banjarmasin in 1687.[517] Barbosa describes the experiences of the missionaries, their first

---

[514] For place-name identifications see J. O. M. Broek, "Place Names in sixteenth- and seventeenth-Century Borneo," *Imago Mundi*, XVI (1962), 129–48. Note also the importance of rivers as arteries of trade, centers of population, seats of political power, etc. See *Encyclopaedie van Nederlandsch-Indië*, I, 359–68.

[515] Van Dijk, *op. cit.* (n. 508), pp. 130–99.

[516] Spaniards from Manila raided Borneo in 1648–49, and left several Jesuits behind. Embassies from Brunei were sent to Manila in 1679–80 and 1680. See Nicholl (ed.), *op. cit.* (n. 497), pp. 94–96. This story is continued from unpublished Spanish documents in English translation included in R. Nicholl, "Relations between Brunei and Manila, A.D. 1682–1690," *Brunei Museum Journal*, Vol. IV, No. 1 (1977), 129–75.

[517] Vicente Barbosa, *Compêndio da relação, que veio da India o ano de 1691* . . . (Lisbon, 1692). See above, p. 363. The Ngadju Dayaks are called "Biadjoes" by the other tribes on the Barito. See Hans Schärer, *Ngaju Religion: The Conception of God among a South Borneo People*, trans. by R. Needham (The Hague, 1963), p. 1.

converts, and their activities during a conflict between the "Biadjoes" and the Muslims. His descriptions of Borneo and of the "Biadjoes," however, are very brief. The "Biadjoes" worship one God, who rewards good and punishes evil. They do not sacrifice to idols.[518] They are extremely jealous; any personal offense must be avenged by death. They hold goods in common and are exceedingly generous to those who have done good to them. They are at war with the Muslims.[519] Despite Barbosa's optimistic report, the Theatine mission languished after 1692–93.[520]

Much more and better information about Banjarmasin and the "Biadjoes" became available in 1698 with the publication of Jacob Janssen de Roy's *Voyagie*, the largest single description of Borneo printed during the century.[521] De Roy was a VOC skipper who lost his ship on the south coast of Borneo in February, 1692, when his largely Chinese and Javanese crew mutinied. His *Voyagie* is the story of his adventures on Borneo and later as a free trader in Borneo, Acheh, and Siam, a period of over six years. His reliability has been questioned because the VOC declared him an outlaw for absconding with the ship's money, and the *Voyagie* obviously strains to demonstrate that its author worked tirelessly for the Company's benefit in Banjarmasin even when it failed to respond to his several appeals to exploit the commercial and political opportunities he had created. While his story may be too self-serving to trust, his descriptions of Borneo seem authentic.[522]

Although there was no Dutch residence in Banjarmasin while De Roy was there, relations between its ruler and the VOC were amicable and some trade between the two occurred, most frequently in Batavia. Earlier in the century the VOC had come to regard Banjarmasin as commercially more important than other parts of Borneo. Relations with the Banjars had always been difficult; already in 1607 the sultan had imprisoned and executed a Dutch envoy, and some time between then and 1612 the Dutch appear to have burned the capital city in retaliation. The details surrounding the burning of old Banjarmasin are shrouded in mystery—or official secrecy. In 1612

---

[518] In contrast to other Asians—particularly Indians and Chinese—the Ngadjus are not worshippers of idols. On the manifestations of their deities and supreme spirits see Schärer, *op. cit.* (n. 517), p. 235.

[519] Barbosa, *op. cit.* (n. 517), p. 6.

[520] Father Antonino Ventimiglia, a Sicilian and the founder of the Theatine mission, died in the midst of his Ngadju converts in 1692. Sporadic and fruitless efforts were undertaken thereafter, until 1761, to reopen the mission to the Ngadjus. The story of Ventimiglia and his Portuguese cohorts from Macao is told in the massive work of Bartolomeo Ferro, *Istoria delle missioni de' Clerici regolari Teatine* (2 vols.; Rome, 1705), II, 405–22, 501–675. These materials have been summarized and commented upon in R. Nicholl, "The Mission of Father Antonino Ventimiglia to Borneo," *Brunei Museum Journal*, Vol. II, No. 4 (1972), 183–205. See also above, p. 218.

[521] See above, p. 503, for biographic and bibliographic details.

[522] See also Broek, *op. cit.* (n. 514), p. 30. See *Encyclopaedie van Nederlandsch-Indië*, I, 355–81, 556–67, for a general description of Borneo and the Dayaks. In its light De Roy's account seems quite accurate.

the sultan established a new capital at Martapura, the diamond producing center, several days' journey upriver from the coast. Not long thereafter the Dutch resumed trading at Martapura, and the sultan then seemed receptive to the negotiation of a treaty. The VOC wanted pepper, rice, bezoar stones, camphor, and gold from Banjarmasin and they hoped to sell Indian cloth there. But, as usual, they demanded that the sultan sign a contract granting the Dutch a monopoly of the trade. The sultan, on the other hand, wanted Dutch protection against Mataram on Java. An exclusive treaty was finally signed in 1635 after years of negotiation. Both before and after the treaty, however, VOC agents continually complained to the sultan that most of the pepper was being sold to the Portuguese or the English, usually through Makassar, but sometimes directly. The sultan repeatedly promised cooperation, but the Dutch never trusted him. The Banjars could send the pepper down any number of small streams to the sea and Dutch attempts to stop or slow the illicit trade were always ineffective.

The year 1637, however, saw important changes in Banjarmasin. The old king rebuilt the old capital and moved there. The officials whom he left in charge at Martapura negotiated a treaty with Mataram. On April 16, 1638, all the Dutchmen in Martapura and in old Banjarmasin were killed except seven who professed Islam and accepted circumcision—sixty-four Dutchmen, twenty-one Japanese and other Asian employees of the VOC. A few days later all the Dutch in Kotawaringin, to the east and also subject to the sultan of Banjarmasin, were killed—another forty people. When the news reached Batavia, VOC officials issued a condemnation of Banjarmasin and vowed revenge. But while the Dutch wreaked awful vengeance on the crews of some Banjarmasin boats, the threatened massive retaliation never materialized, although the threats were renewed several times between 1638 and 1660. The culpable officials in Martapura eventually died, the VOC became concerned not to appear as high-handed as the Portuguese had been, and a trickle of trade gradually resumed. Finally in 1660 a new treaty was signed between Martapura and the VOC which did not mention revenge, restitution, or compensation.[523]

De Roy's account includes brief descriptions of both Brunei and Sukadana although most of his description concerns Banjarmasin. He also provided European readers with their first published description of Borneo's interior and of the peoples who lived there. He describes the "Biagies" (Ngadjus) who live along what he calls "Biagies" River (the Barito River) and other large streams he observed during a journey with the king of Banjarmasin from "Caijetinga" to "Tatas" and to "Banjer Massingh" (Banjarmasin). Their religion, laws, and commerce, De Roy observes, conform to those of

---

[523] For the story of VOC relations with Banjarmasin see Van Dijk, *op. cit.* (n. 508), pp. 1–129. John Saris in *PP*, III, 494, reported the massacre at Banjarmasin.

the rest of Borneo's inhabitants, but the "Biagies" who live along the Barito River are considered more powerful and bolder than other Borneans.[524] According to De Roy they are headhunters, occasionally surprising pepper traders or people from Banjarmasin by attacking their boats as they travel upriver. The Dayak men are alert and strong, with long hair and yellowish skin. They are industrious and as courageous as Javans. Headhunting appears to be a ritual among them. A young man cannot marry until he has taken a head. When he is successful, he brings it to his intended bride, after which they can be married. The head is stuck on a pole, gongs are beaten, and the whole village—even neighboring villages—turn out in their finest clothes to celebrate.[525] De Roy does not describe the finery worn at weddings. The Dayaks' ordinary dress, he reports, is "like that of the Malabars," a piece of tree bark fastened over the privates and another piece worn on the head. Dayak women are "reasonably beautiful and well-shaped." They live under the authority of their husbands.[526]

Dayak religion, according to De Roy, is "full of superstition." They worship the sun and the moon and pay close attention to omens in their daily life; for example, to bird cries. If a man, on leaving his house to go somewhere, meets a bird judged to be more powerful than the others flying towards him, he will immediately return home and remain there for the rest of the day. If he sees such a bird flying in the direction he wants to travel, however, he will regard it as a good omen.[527] Regarding most of their customs, manners, and morals, De Roy thinks the Dayaks are not much different from the Moluccan "Alphoeresen" (Alfurese).[528]

As De Roy puts it, "these silly naked people actually possess considerable wealth because of the gold and other merchandise which happens to be in their land." They love to trade, he reports, but merchants with a little experience can obtain the Dayak's treasures for trifles. Above all, the Dayaks esteem red agate rings and also coral and copper bracelets for their women. On his river trip with the king, De Roy also visited the pepper villages of "Compay" (?), "Borrangbaha" (Barabai?), and "Moranpijouw" (Muara-

---

[524] The "Biagies" (Ngadjus) are a specific tribe of Dayaks living in the lower and middle reaches of the Barito River. Today they number around fifty thousand. See *Encyclopaedie van Nederlandsch-Indië*, I, 557.

[525] See *ibid.*, p. 566, for a discussion of Dayak headhunting. The heads of enemies graced all rites, including marriage. See Bock, *op. cit.* (n. 506), pp. 215–16. *Cf.* to headhunting in Taiwan, below, pp. 1806–8.

[526] De Roy, *op. cit.* (n. 363), pp. 48–49. For some excellent illustrations of Dayaks see Bock, *op. cit.* (n. 506).

[527] Borneans have seven omen birds in common. See Edward Banks, "A Note on Iban Omen Birds," *Brunei Museum Journal*, Vol. V, No. 3 (1983), pp. 104–7. Pictures of the birds appear at the end of the article.

[528] De Roy, *op. cit.* (n. 363), pp. 49–50. "Alfurese" is a term used by coastal people in the Moluccas to refer to the uncivilized, pagan tribesmen of the interior. See *Encyclopaedie van Nederlandsch-Indië*, I, 30. It was probably derived from Portuguese or Arabic and was part of the vocabulary of the Europeans. Generally it was applied to peoples not subject to European authority.

pulau?), where he reports the Portuguese from Macao trade. He also describes a large fishing village in which "an unusual abundance of the familiar fish Cabos" (Portuguese for chub, frosh-fish) is dried and shipped to surrounding areas. Here the king stayed for some time. De Roy describes in detail a large sort of castle built at the water's edge near the village.[529] Dayak villages and houses are unusually large; often as many as one hundred related families live in a single great house, each having its own apartment, with their pigs, chickens, and ducks being kept beneath the house. The larger houses apparently dominate the smaller, and occasionally rivalries or quarrels between houses result in the loss of a few heads.[530]

According to De Roy the king of Banjarmasin owes his power to the "Javan Pangerang," a bastard son of the Susuhunan who was driven from Java during a rebellion. The people of Banjarmasin speak Malay mixed with Javanese, Dayak, and other words. He correctly observes that the Malay spoken by most of the coastal people in the Indonesian archipelago is a mixed language having incorporated into it words from all the native languages where it is spoken. The inhabitants of Banjarmasin are also Muslims and occasionally they try to spread their religion to the people inland—not with much success, however, because the Dayaks outnumber them by about a thousand to one. The Dayaks do not attack the Muslims on the coast, because they are afraid of their firearms. On the other hand, the king of Banjarmasin tries to live in friendship with the Dayaks, despite occasionally losing some of his people to Dayak headhunters, because of the rich merchandise under their control: gold, jewels, camphor, bezoar stones, "sarnangh" (Malay, *sárang,* cloths of many colors), wax, rattan, and most provisions except salt and rice. De Roy reports that the Dayaks have rich gold mines. He has often seen them bring shipments of twenty to one hundred catties of gold dust to Banjar and especially to Sukadana, which they exchange for cloth, porcelain, copper bracelets, coral, and a certain kind of long red agate stone which they wear on their arms and shoulders.[531]

The "Rivier van Banjer" (the Barito) is deep and easily navigable, with some high islands in it which are easy to avoid. The king's chief residences are in the villages of "Tatas" and "Cajoe Tenga," several miles up from the coast. Good pepper grows in this area, and gold can be found in the nearby hills, although it is of poor quality. The natives often use it to adulterate better gold. De Roy lists these and several other nearby villages (sixteen of them altogether) and the number of armed men each could muster—a total of 5,900 soldiers.[532]

[529] *Op. cit.* (n. 363), pp. 50–51.
[530] *Ibid.,* p. 103. On the Iban multifamily longhouse see D. Freeman, *Report on the Iban* (New York, 1970), pp. 1–7. See also *Encyclopaedie van Nederlandsch-Indië,* I, 559.
[531] De Roy, *op. cit.* (n. 363), pp. 102–3. This was alluvial gold panned from the rivers. On the necklaces of red and white agates worn by the Dayaks see Bock, *op. cit.* (n. 506), p. 153.
[532] De Roy, *op. cit.* (n. 363), pp. 103–5.

De Roy briefly describes the streams and coastal areas to the west of the "Banjer" River: the large deep "Biadjies" River (another branch of the Barito), "along whose banks live an endless number of heathen," unbelievably rich in gold and other costly goods. The Portuguese from Macao trade here and established a mission which was initially very successful—recording over three thousand converts. Left without a pastor, they are hopelessly superstitious and know nothing about Christianity beyond wearing crosses.[533] Further west along the coast is the river and village of "Tabanjouw" (Tabanio?), whose people were well known as boat builders, and the "Mandaway" (Mendawai) River, where gold, wax, "jermang" (Malay, *jernang*, dragon's blood, a red resin used in dyeing, which is found in certain rattans), rattan, and bezoar stones are traded. Still further west lies the river, bay, and town of Sampit, a good sheltered harbor with considerable trade. De Roy reports that the mountain people bring cloves, which smell and taste as good as those from Amboina, as well as nutmeg to Sampit. He claims to have seen cloves and nutmegs floating down the river and concludes that if the natives were not so lazy many more spices could be had there. For each village De Roy lists the number of its soldiers, moving west until he comes to the river and town of "Ponboang" (Pembuang on the Serujan), the "frontier of Banjar's kingdom."[534] Beyond Banjarmasin to the west De Roy mentions Kotawaringin and Sukadana which, although not as large as Banjarmasin, are uncommonly rich because of the diamonds and camphor which the natives upstream sell there. The king of Sukadana permits no foreigners to trade with the natives.[535]

Finally De Roy briefly describes "Borneo" (Brunei), "whose inhabitants surpass all of the others in riches." Their gold is of better quality and they have more camphor and other valuable goods. De Roy reports that villagers in Brunei often marry Dayak women, who are preferred because of their light-colored skin and their intelligence. The king of Sukadana, he reports, also takes Dayak wives.[536] At the end of his description of Borneo De Roy asserts that he has seen a diamond belonging to the king of Sukadana the size of a dove's egg.[537] Whether or not he actually saw it, he must have been writing about the famous Sukadanese diamond called *Ibn Inbam* or *Intan Uby* in the seventeenth century and later called *Danau Radje,* a stone reputed to have weighed 367 karats.[538]

A very brief notice about Borneo appears in Ambrose Cowley's "Voyage

---

[533] Obviously refers to the Theatine mission (1687–93) and its converts. See above, p. 218.
[534] De Roy, *op. cit.* (n. 363), pp. 105–6.
[535] *Ibid.,* pp. 106–7.
[536] *Ibid.,* pp. 107–8.
[537] *Ibid.,* p. 108.
[538] See Van Dijk, *op. cit.* (n. 508), pp. 180–82. *Encyclopaedie van Nederlandsch-Indië,* I, 598, reports that modern scholars regard it as crystal, not a real diamond.

Round the Globe," published as part of the Hacke collection (1699).[539] His ship touched on Borneo's coast in 1683. He mentions Borneo's products—diamonds, pepper, camphor, ebony—and the abundance of food and animals. He reports that there is one king over the island; there formerly had been two, but the king of the north defeated the king of the south. The king, he thinks, has a treaty with the Spanish at Manila. He says nothing about the land or the people other than that the natives are Muslims who abstain from pork and wine.[540]

While it was not as well described as Java and Sumatra, the image of Borneo which emerges from the seventeenth-century travel accounts is a marked improvement over what was known during the preceding century. The major political powers on the island are identified and their relations with other powers in the archipelago touched upon. Brunei, it is clear, had four lines of external communication and trade with Malacca, Manila, Batavia, and Macao. Borneo's major products are accurately itemized. Many towns and rivers along the south and west coasts are identified, the Kapuas and Barito rivers and their many branches and distributaries are described in some detail. A European reader could soon grasp the importance of rivers to the people of Borneo: for food, travel, defense, and so on. All the towns were built close to the rivers' banks. Despite the difficulty of traveling inland, the seventeenth-century notices of Borneo clearly distinguished between the Islamic, Malay-speaking people on the seacoast and the Dayaks of the interior. Barbosa and De Roy, in fact, provided what are probably the first European printed descriptions of a Dayak tribe—the "Biadjoes"—of the Barito River: a description which, while frustratingly brief, seems quite accurate when compared to modern descriptions of the Dayaks. In fact, De Roy's account and all the other seventeenth-century notices about Borneo are indispensable to reconstructing the early history of the island.

[539] "Cowley's voyage Round the Globe," in W. Hacke, *A Collection of Original Voyages* (London, 1699). See above, pp. 585–86, for bibliography.

[540] Hacke, *op. cit.* (n. 539), pp. 24–25. A treaty was being negotiated between Brunei and Manila in 1683.

CHAPTER XVIII

Insulindia: The Eastern Archipelago and the Austral Lands

The eastern reaches of Insulindia were opened by European vessels that followed the traditional direct route through the Straits of Malacca, by Dutch
navigators who sailed the indirect route south of Java, and by those who
braved the trans-Pacific crossing. Here, as in the Philippines, the European
voyagers met those of their own kind who came from the opposite direction. Here they also met indigenous peoples of diverse backgrounds, many
of whom had lived for aeons in relative seclusion. While itinerant Arab, Indian, Chinese, and Japanese merchants had appeared irregularly at many of
the inhabited islands, it was the Europeans—Portuguese, Spanish, Dutch,
and even the English—who began the systematic exploration and exploita-
tion of these previously remote islands which stretch from the Wallace Line
to Australia and into the vast expanse of the south Pacific. The European
Christians learned as they proceeded that they were confronted here, as in
western Insulindia, with the challenge posed by Islam and the competition
offered by Arab, Chinese, and Indian merchants. Nature, too, presented its
share of obstacles and trials: typhoons, volcanic eruptions, earthquakes,
excessive heat, dangerous and pesky animals and insects, and endemic
diseases.

The eastern Indonesian archipelago can be treated as comprising four
somewhat distinct groupings of islands: the Moluccas (Ternate, Tidore,
Motir or Moti, Makian, Bachan, and the larger island variously called Hal-
mahera, Gilolo, or Batochino do Moro), Amboina (Ceram, Buru, and
Amboina), Banda (Gunung Api, Neira, and Lonthor or Great Banda), and
Celebes together with the largest of the Lesser Sunda chain (Celebes, Sum-

bawa, Flores, and Timor).[1] These are the renowned Spiceries with their dependencies, which had been the ultimate goal of so many Portuguese expeditions in the sixteenth century and remained so for the Dutch and English into the seventeenth century. Consequently the Spiceries, or at least parts of them, were described in the accounts of most seventeenth-century voyages. Frequently, even the accounts of voyages that did not visit them included descriptions of the Moluccas, Amboina, or Banda. Interest in the Spiceries continued through the century, although Dutch control of the spice trade after the second decade tended to confine Europe's information about them to Dutch reports and to reduce the total number of descriptions. News of the austral lands likewise came mainly from Dutch reports, although some earlier Portuguese notices were reprinted and contemporary Spanish and English accounts also appeared. Many of the "unnamed nations" of the sixteenth century thus received names and descriptions (slight as some of these descriptions were), during the course of the seventeenth century.

I

THE MOLUCCAS

The Moluccas had been a very important, but troublesome, corner of the Portuguese maritime empire throughout the sixteenth century. From the beginning, in 1521, the Portuguese had become involved in the inter-island rivalries and wars, especially those between the rulers of Ternate and Tidore. Vigorous mission activity evoked still more native hostility. That and the high-handed conduct of several Portuguese governors resulted in the foundation of a Muslim confederation, headed by the sultan of Ternate, which was determined to drive Christianity and the Portuguese from the Spiceries. After Governor Diogo Lopez de Mesquita had Sultan Hairun (r. 1535–45; 1546–70) of Ternate treacherously murdered in 1570, the Portuguese were almost constantly at war with the confederation of Muslim princes. Furthermore, the Spanish claimed that the Moluccas fell within their half of the overseas world, and especially after the establishment of Spanish power in Manila (1565), they sporadically contested Portuguese control of the Spiceries.[2]

At the end of the sixteenth century the rivalries between the Portuguese, the Spanish, and the Muslim confederation were further complicated by the intrusion of the English and the Dutch into the Moluccan world. In 1579,

---

[1] A rationale for these divisions is presented in *Asia*, I, 592–93.
[2] For the sixteenth century in the Spiceries see *ibid.*, pp. 286–90, 592–623.

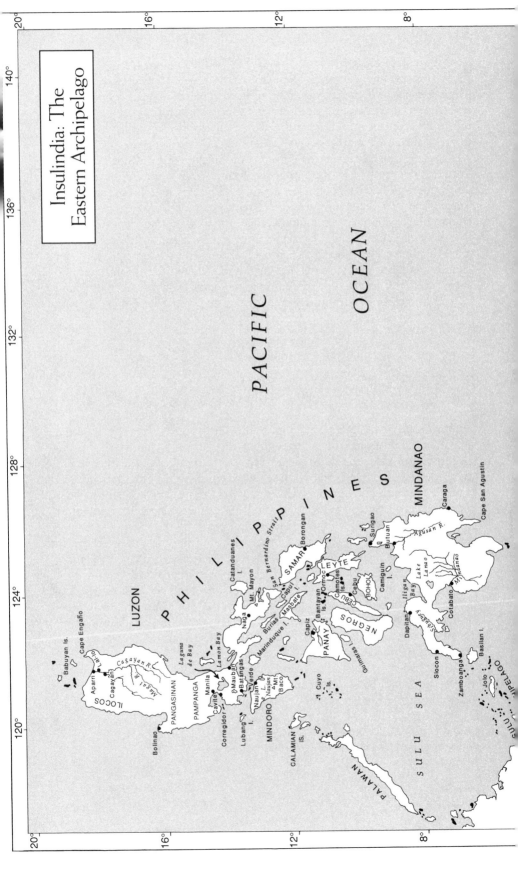

Insulindia: The
Eastern Archipelago

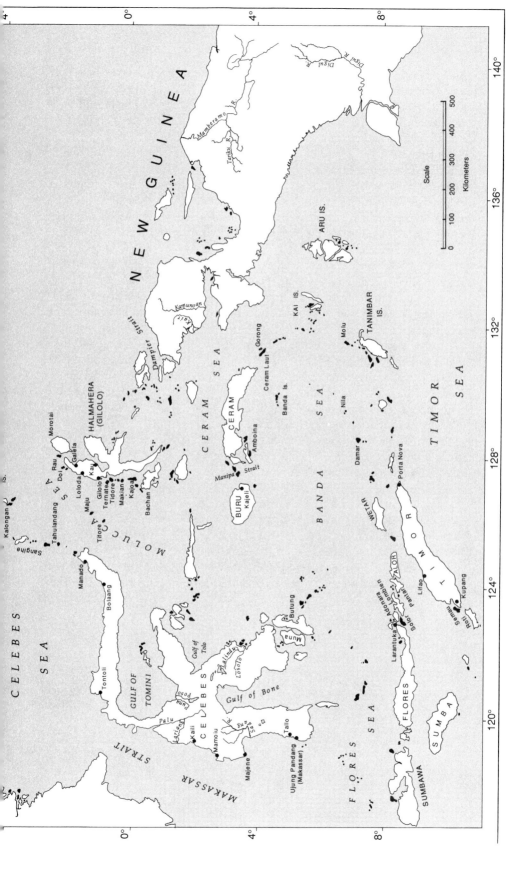

Sir Francis Drake visited Ternate and was apparently regarded by the sultan as a potential ally against the Portuguese.[3] In 1599 ships from the second Dutch expedition to the east, under Jacob Corneliszoon van Neck and Wybrand van Warwijck, arrived in the Spiceries leaving factors on Banda, Amboina, and Ternate.[4]

During the first decade of the seventeenth century, therefore, the Dutch contested Iberian control of the Spiceries, often with the support of Moluccan rulers who hoped the Dutch would help rid them of the Portuguese, while the English played on all sides, hoping somehow to achieve an independent presence. Changes were rapid and the story became exceedingly complex. For example, Van Neck ousted the Portuguese from Amboina in 1599 when he established a Dutch factory there, but in 1601 André Furtado reclaimed it. Steven van der Hagen, however, drove the Portuguese from Tidore and Amboina in 1605. In 1606, under Pedro de Acuña, the Spanish expelled the Dutch from all their positions in the Spiceries except for Amboina in an expedition which was celebrated in Manila and in Spain as the "conquest of the Moluccas." During the following year, however, Admiral Cornelis Matelief strengthened the Dutch position on Amboina and Ternate, and by the end of 1611 the VOC had made monopolistic treaties with the sultan of Ternate and several other Moluccan princes and had decisively defeated an attempted Spanish counterattack. During the second decade the Dutch worried more about the English than the Iberian competition in their attempts to monopolize the spice trade.[5]

Information about the Moluccas continued to appear in Iberian accounts during the first decade of the seventeenth century. Diogo do Couto's continuation of João de Barros' *Décadas,* published between 1602 and 1616, discusses Portuguese activities in the Moluccas and contains some description.[6] Fernão Guerreiro also gathered materials on affairs in the Moluccas for his *Relaçam annual* (1603–11).[7] He describes the wars between the Iberians, the Muslim confederation, and the Dutch, but he was primarily interested in the effects of these struggles on the Jesuit mission and on the Moluccan Christians. The *Relaçam* contains considerable detail on local events and on the fate of the Jesuit mission but relatively little description of the islands or

---

[3] See *ibid.,* pp. 622–23.
[4] See J. Keuning (ed.), *De tweede schipvaart der Nederlanders naar Oost-Indië onder Jacob Cornelisz. van Neck en Wybrant Warwijck, 1598–1600* (5 vols.; "WLV," XLII, XLIV, XLVI, XLVIII, and L; The Hague, 1938–51), I, xvii–xxiii.
[5] On European activity in the Spiceries during the first decade of the seventeenth century see above, pp. 13–14, 46; Albert Gray (ed.), *The Voyage of François Pyrard of Laval to the East Indies, the Maldives, the Moluccas, and Brazil* (3 vols.; "HS," o.s., LXXVI, LXXVII, LXXX; London, 1887–90) II, i–xvi; and especially Bartolomé Leonardo de Argensola, *Conquista de las islas Malucas* (Madrid, 1609).
[6] See above, pp. 314–15, for bibliographic information.
[7] For bibliography see above, pp. 315–16.

their people.[8] The most detailed account of events in the Moluccas from the beginning of European commerce there to Pedro de Acuña's expedition is contained in Bartolomé Leonardo de Argensola's *Conquista de las islas Malucas* (1609).[9] While Argensola's main concern was to celebrate the Spanish victory of 1606, he includes descriptions of the islands, the people, the rulers, the cloves, and other products, much of which, however, appears to come from Barros. Antonio de Morga's *Sucesos de las islas Filipinas* (1609) also recounts military activities in the Moluccas, including De Acuña's victory and the return of the Dutch shortly thereafter. It contains, however, no description of the Moluccas.[10] Spanish successes in the Moluccas were again celebrated in Antonio de Herrara y Tordesillas' *Historia general de los hechos de los Castellanos . . .* (1601–15), again with very little description of the islands themselves or of the people.[11] Apart from Manuel de Faria y Sousa's three-volume *Asia portuguesa* (1666–75)[12] and Francisco Colin's *Labor evangélica* (1663),[13] no Iberian accounts of the Spiceries appeared after the first decade of the century.

The first two decades of the seventeenth century also saw the publication of the first Dutch and English reports from the Moluccas. Accounts of the Van Neck and Van Warwijck fleet, the first Dutch expedition to visit the Moluccas, were published in 1600 and 1601. The second of these, called *Het tweede boeck,* contains ample descriptions of the Moluccas and was reissued or translated ten times before 1620.[14] Some of Argensola's description of the Spiceries appears to come from it, although he mentions Linschoten as his only Dutch source.[15] The first published account of two Dutch circumnavigations, that of Joris van Spilbergen and that of Jacob Le Maire and Willem Corneliszoon Schouten, appeared in 1618 and these, too, became exceedingly popular during the second decade of the century. The journals of both circumnavigations were frequently published together, and while each circumnavigator landed in the Moluccas, neither journal contains much description of them. An informative "Discourse" on the Moluccas, however, written by Appolonius Schotte is appended to the combined pub-

---

[8] For examples see Artur Viegas (ed.), *Relação anual das coisas que fizeram os padres da Companhia de Jesus . . .* (3 vols.; Coimbra, 1930–41), I, 267–72; II, 126–32, 302–12. For the Jesuit letters themselves see H. Jacobs, S.J. (ed.), *Documenta Malucensia* (3 vols.; Rome, 1974, 1980, 1984), II (1571–1606), 483–740; III (1606–82), 55–210. These Jesuit volumes are extremely valuable for making identifications of the place names in other sources.

[9] See above, pp. 310–12.

[10] See above, pp. 326–28. For Barros' description of the Moluccas see *Asia*, I, 603–8.

[11] See above, p. 323.

[12] See above, pp. 354–55 for bibliography.

[13] See above, p. 353.

[14] For bibliography see above, pp. 439–41. *Het tweede boeck* is also reprinted in Keuning (ed.), *op. cit.* (n. 4), III, 1–186.

[15] Argensola, *op. cit.* (n. 5), p. 241. He mentions Linschoten in connection with his discussion of Banda.

lication in all of its editions.[16] The published report of Henry Middleton's voyage, the second English East India Company voyage, appeared in 1606.[17] Middleton was in the Moluccas during 1605, at the same time as Steven van der Hagen. Middleton negotiated with everyone—the Portuguese, the native princes, and the Dutch—in an effort to secure a place for the English in the face of Portuguese and Dutch attempts to monopolize the spice trade. The anonymous account of his voyage describes these negotiations and other events in the Moluccas in great detail. But it contains little description of the islands themselves or of the people.

A few other European visitors to the Moluccas published reports during the first two decades of the seventeenth century. François Pyrard, who came to the Moluccas on a Portuguese ship in 1607, published an account of his voyage in 1611. It contains descriptions of the islands as well as of the struggles between the Dutch and the Iberians for control over them.[18] Events in the Moluccas and their effects on the Jesuit mission there were also described in an Italian Jesuit letterbook, *Raguagli d' alcune missione fatte . . . nell' Indie Orientali . . . ,* published in Rome in 1615.[19] Of all these reports about the Moluccas during the first two decades of the century, *Het tweede boeck,* Argensola, and Schotte are by far the most informative.

They report that five main islands comprise the Moluccas: Ternate, Tidore, Motir, Makian, and Bachan. These all lie on the same meridian just west of the large island Halmahera, also called Gilolo or Batochino do Moro. According to Argensola, Ternate, the northernmost island, lies at one-half degree north latitude, and Bachan, the southernmost, at one degree south, altogether twenty-five leagues (one hundred miles) from north to south. They are within sight of one another. Bachan, he observes, is really several islands separated from one another by small channels navigable only by small vessels.[20] On these small islands, and nowhere else in the world, grow cloves. The author of *Het tweede boeck,* however, reports that cloves also grow on "Meau" (Mayu), about eleven Dutch miles from Ternate, on "Marigorang" (?), "Sinomo" (?), "Cabel" (Pulau Cabale), and Amboina.[21] Apart from Amboina, these appear to be among the "numberless islands" visible from the top of the volcano on Ternate.[22] The islands are very small, the largest less than seven leagues (twenty-eight miles) in circumference,

[16] For bibliography see above, pp. 445–48.
[17] For bibliographical details see above, p. 551.
[18] See above, pp. 396–97.
[19] See above, p. 373.
[20] Argensola, *op. cit.* (n. 5), pp. 8–9. *Het tweede boeck* locates Ternate at forty minutes or about two-thirds of a degree north latitude. See Keuning (ed.), *op. cit.* (n. 4), III, 132.
[21] Keuning (ed.), *op. cit.* (n. 4), III, 131. The small island of Mayu lies between north Celebes and Halmahera in the Molucca Sea. Argensola, *op. cit.* (n. 5), p. 56, says "Meaos" is twenty leagues (about 66 miles) from Ternate, which appears more accurate.
[22] Argensola, *op. cit.* (n. 5), p. 56.

and they are all almost round, which accounts for the paucity of good harbors on them. Only on Ternate's eastern shore, according to Argensola, are two ports available, "Talangame" (Telinggamme) and "Toloco" (?), whose anchorages are protected by coral reefs.[23]

Although small, the islands are all mountainous with a "dry and spongy" soil which sucks up all the water regardless of how much it rains. In many places streams gushing from the mountains never reach the sea.[24] Almost every European visitor mentions the volcano on Ternate, but Argensola's description of it is the most vivid, even if not entirely credible. It is, he asserts, two leagues high.[25] Trees and other vegetation cover it up to about two-thirds of its height; its summit is barren and devoid even of birds, although plagued by flies. The crater is broad—a man can scarcely be seen across it—and deep. Argensola reports that it is measured to be five hundred fathoms (three thousand feet) deep. At its bottom a square, flat area "like a threshing floor" and a beautiful clear spring can be seen. Also at the top, he reports, is an "abundant sweet pool, surrounded by trees, in which there are blue, and gold alligators, more than one fathom [six feet] long." Argensola thinks eruptions result from the sun passing over the equator, kindling its flames. It smells bad and spews out smoke, sulphur, and red stones as if "from a cannon's mouth."[26]

The Moluccan climate is unpleasant: hot, the air heavy, and unhealthy for foreigners. There are no seasons, not even a discernible rainy season, although it usually rains more with the northeast wind than with the south wind.[27] The author of *Het tweede boeck* observes that it rains every day, followed by hot sunshine.[28]

The trees are always green and the vegetation lush, yet all the European writers remark that the Moluccas produce very little food. The people there grow neither rice nor any grain from which bread can be made. They raise no cattle, only a few goats and some chickens.[29] The surrounding seas are not very rich fisheries, according to *Het tweede boeck;*[30] Argensola, however,

---

[23] *Ibid.*, pp. 54–55. For two very different seventeenth-century maps of the Moluccas see our pls. 235 and 236.

[24] Argensola, *op. cit.* (n. 5), pp. 9, 54–55.

[25] It rises to 5,750 feet above sea level; the island itself is merely a pedestal for the mountain. See John Crawfurd, *A Descriptive Dictionary of the Indian Islands and Adjacent Countries* (London, 1856), p. 430.

[26] Argensola, *op. cit.* (n. 5), pp. 55–56.

[27] *Ibid.*, pp. 9, 56.

[28] Keuning (ed.), *op. cit.* (n. 4), III, 114. The climate of this region, particularly rainfall, is almost entirely controlled by the monsoon. See M. Sukanto, "Climate of Indonesia," in H. Arakawa (ed.), *Climates of Northern and Eastern Asia,* Vol. VIII, *World Survey of Climatology* (Amsterdam, 1969), pp. 215–29.

[29] Argensola, *op. cit.* (n. 5), p. 9; Keuning (ed.), *op. cit.* (n. 4), III, 115; Gray (ed.), *op. cit.* (n. 5), II, 166.

[30] Keuning (ed.), *op. cit.* (n. 4), III, 116.

seems to disagree.[31] Pyrard reports that food is very expensive, since so much of it must be imported.[32]

The staple food in the Moluccas is a white "bread" called sago, the flour for which is made by beating the pith of the sago palm with cane hammers. The Moluccans bake it into square cakes about the size of a man's palm. Pyrard says these are very tasty.[33] According to *Het tweede boeck* sago bread also functions as money in the islands.[34] Most European observers report that coconuts and bananas are plentiful and that there are some orange and lemon trees.[35] Palm wine is made from the sap of both the coco and sago palm, and, according to Argensola, another liquor comes from the hollow stalks of bamboo.[36] *Het tweede boeck* reports that palm wine must be purchased secretly because of the Islamic law against wine drinking.[37] In addition, Argensola mentions "lignum-aloes, sandalwood, cinnamon, mace, and mastic trees" as products of the Moluccas.[38] *Het tweede boeck* also contains the description of what its author calls a large sort of almond tree.[39] Argensola notes that there is neither gold nor silver—in fact, no metals at all—in the Moluccas.[40]

While cloves seem to grow nowhere else on earth, these small islands are literally covered with them. Argensola's *Conquista, Het tweede boeck,* and Pyrard's *Voyage* each contains detailed descriptions of the clove tree.[41] The cloves grow, without cultivation, in the interior of the islands, both on the hillsides and in the valleys. Contrary to Linschoten's report, says the author of *Het tweede boeck,* they do not grow along the seashore.[42] Argensola notes that on Tidore the natives do some pruning and watering to increase

---

[31] Argensola, *op. cit.* (n. 5), p. 10. On fishing in Ternate see our pl. 268.

[32] Gray (ed.), *op. cit.* (n. 5), II, 166.

[33] *Ibid.* On sago see A. R. Wallace, *The Malay Archipelago* (New York, 1962), pp. 289–92 (first published in 1869).

[34] Keuning (ed.), *op. cit.* (n. 4), III, 115.

[35] For example, see Argensola, *op. cit.* (n. 5), p. 9; Keuning (ed.), *op. cit.* (n. 4), III, 115; Gray (ed.), *op. cit.* (n. 5), II, 166.

[36] Argensola, *op. cit.* (n. 5), p. 10. Bamboo stalks were frequently used as containers for liquids. Perhaps Argensola's source misunderstood and thought the liquid was produced by the bamboo.

[37] Keuning (ed.), *op. cit.* (n. 4), III, 116. In the Moluccas as elsewhere in Southeast Asia, Islam was never able to suppress the use of alcohol for entertainments and feasts. See A. Reid, *Southeast Asia in the Age of Commerce, 1450–1680,* Vol. I, *The Lands below the Winds* (New Haven, 1988), pp. 39–40.

[38] Argensola, *op. cit.* (n. 5), p. 9.

[39] Keuning (ed.), *op. cit.* (n. 4), III, 116. It is the Kanari tree (*Canarium commune* L. fam. *Burseraceae*). See also J. Crawfurd, *History of the Indian Archipelago* (3 vols.; Edinburgh, 1820), I, 383, and *Encyclopaedie van Nederlandsch-Indië* (2d ed., 8 vols.; Leyden, 1917–39), I, 435.

[40] Argensola, *op. cit.* (n. 5), p. 10.

[41] *Ibid.,* pp. 51–54; Keuning (ed.), *op. cit.* (n. 4), III, 111–15. The description in *Het tweede boeck* was derived largely from Linschoten's *Itinerario.* See also Gray (ed.), *op. cit.* (n. 5), pp. 357–58.

[42] Keuning (ed.), *op. cit.* (n. 4), III, 115–16. Clove trees do not grow well too near the sea or at altitudes above one thousand feet. See W. M. Gibbs, *Spices and How to Know Them* (Buffalo, N.Y., 1909), p. 108.

yields.[43] The clove tree resembles the European bay tree, its leaves resemble those of the laurel. The leaves taste very much like the fruit. The cloves grow quickly. Trees destroyed by fire or cutting are rapidly replaced. Argensola repeats the story of the ring dove which feeds on cloves and from whose droppings new trees spring up. Wherever the clove tree grows, it destroys other vegetation by sucking up the available moisture. In fact, sacks of cloves will attract and diminish the water standing in nearby pails or dishes. Clove trees take eight years to mature. They live up to a hundred years and bear cloves every two or three years.[44]

Clove flowers are at first white; then they turn green, and finally red. When the cloves are in bloom, the air over the entire island is perfumed. When ripe, the cloves fall to the ground. Moluccans harvest them, however, by first cleaning the ground beneath the trees and then shaking the branches with poles or ropes to make the cloves fall. Cloves are red when ripe, black when dried. They are harvested between August and December, according to *Het tweede boeck;* between September and February, according to Argensola.[45]

Argensola, who is concerned to place the Spanish "conquest" of the Moluccas in a global context, provides a historical sketch of the clove trade. In ancient times, he reports, the trade was controlled by the Chinese. Persians and Arabs transshipped cloves to the Greeks and Romans. For a time Egypt controlled the route between Asia and Europe; the Venetians were the most important importers. With the fall of the Byzantine Empire, the clove trade fell into the hands of the Turks, after which the Portuguese, sailing around the Cape of Good Hope, came to dominate the trade and the Moluccas.[46] After this general sketch he describes in detail the more recent rivalries of the Portuguese, Spanish, Dutch, and English in the Moluccas, concluding with Pedro de Acuña's victory in 1606.

The clove, as Argensola points out, has been known in the West for a very long time. Pliny called it "Garyofilo" and the Persians called it "calafur." Formerly the Spanish called it "girofe" but now "clavos" because the cloves look like nails. Moluccans, however, call the tree "Siger" (?), the leaf "varaqua" (?), and the fruit "chamque" (Malay, *chěngkeh*).[47] To obtain the cloves, people traveled long distances and fought many wars. Writes Argensola, the clove is "really the fruit of discord, more than the fabulous apple of the three goddesses, since for it there has been, and still is, more fighting than for mines of gold."[48]

---

[43] *Op. cit.* (n. 5), p. 96.
[44] They take from four to five years to begin bearing. Normally they yield one crop annually. Records exist of clove trees that have lived for 150 years. See Gibbs, *op. cit.* (n. 42), p. 116.
[45] Argensola, *op. cit.* (n. 5), p. 53; Keuning (ed.), *op. cit.* (n. 4), III, 114; Gray (ed.), *op. cit.* (n. 5), pp. 357–58.
[46] Argensola, *op. cit.* (n. 5), pp. 12–13.
[47] *Ibid.*, p. 52. "Calafur" is probably Arabic, *kerunful;* the Persian is *meykuk.*
[48] *Ibid.*, p. 58.

Among the birds and animals of the Moluccas both Argensola and *Het tweede boeck* describe colorful parrots which imitate other animals and which learn to talk easily.[49] *Het tweede boeck* also mentions the bird of paradise.[50] Argensola lists a variety of birds, fishes, and crabs, but also describes some which seem quite fanciful. For example, there are snakes over thirty feet long which feed on fish, but do so by chewing a certain herb which, after they spit it into the sea, renders the fish drunk and helpless so that they can be easily caught. He reports crocodiles in the sea so timid that they can be bound under water, strange reddish sticks that burn like coal, and a bush or tree called "catopa," whose leaves are transformed into butterflies when they fall.[51]

The author of *Het tweede boeck* finds the Moluccan people of all ranks very goodhearted although "beggarly." Argensola considers them "officious and courteous to strangers," but when more familiar, "importunate and troublesome in their requests." He adds jealous, fraudulent, false, poor, proud, "and to name many vices in one, ungrateful." *Het tweede boeck*, however, depicts Ternatan nobles as abler, more reliable, and less deceitful than their Javan counterparts. Both report that the islanders hate theft, which on Ternate is never pardoned. *Het tweede boeck* describes the imprisonment and severe public humiliation imposed on an eleven-year-old boy who stole a couple of tobacco leaves. Adultery, however, is easily pardoned. The islanders are valiant in battle. In Argensola's words, "they are strong, much addicted to war, and lazy in all other tasks." *Het tweede boeck* illustrates this with an account of the king of Ternate's attack on Tidore of July 20, 1599.[52]

The women are fair and beautiful, the men darker. They have large eyes, long eyebrows and eyelashes, which they blacken, and straight hair, into which they rub sweet-smelling oil. They live long but their hair becomes grey early.[53] The writer of *Het tweede boeck* thinks the grey-bearded nobles at court look majestic, and he adds that, unlike Javans, some Moluccans let their beards grow. In general, he finds Moluccans superior in physical appearance and condition to Javans.[54]

Ternatan men wear turbans of several colors, usually with feathers in them, short jackets, and trousers "like the Portuguese" of blue, red, green, or purple. According to *Het tweede boeck* the clothes are made of cotton or tree bark. Argensola reports that they also wear silk, even common

[49] *Ibid.*, p. 57; Keuning (ed.), *op. cit.* (n. 4), III, 116.
[50] Keuning (ed.), *op. cit.* (n. 4), III, 116. On birds of paradise see Wallace, *op. cit.* (n. 33), pp. 431–32.
[51] Argensola, *op. cit.* (n. 5), pp. 56–57. "Catopa" may be from Malay, *kĕtapang, Terminalia catappa,* the Indian almond tree. On this region as a scene of marvels see V. R. Savage, *Western Impressions of Nature and Landscape in Southeast Asia* (Singapore, 1984), chap. ii.
[52] Keuning (ed.), *op. cit.* (n. 4), III, 117, 136; Argensola, *op. cit.* (n. 5), pp. 10–11.
[53] Argensola, *op. cit.* (n. 5), pp. 10–11.
[54] Keuning (ed.), *op. cit.* (n. 4), III, 136. *Cf.* J. Prins, "Location, History, Forgotten Struggle," in *idem, The South Moluccas* (Leyden, 1960), p. 15.

people.[55] Women are proud of their hair, wearing it in a variety of ways, but always with ribbons and flowers. Women also wear bracelets, necklaces, pendants of diamonds and rubies, and sometimes long strings of pearls, all of which come to Ternate in trade from other lands. Women are clad, Argensola reports, after the Persian and Turkish fashion.[56]

Many languages are spoken in the Moluccas. People in one town sometimes cannot understand the people in the next town. But Malay is the most commonly used. Argensola thinks the diverse languages result from the waves of foreign occupation; first the Chinese, later Javans and Malays, and lastly "Persians and Arabs."[57]

Trade with Muslims, Argensola realizes, brought Islam to the Moluccas. Most Moluccans are Muslims. In fact, as both Guerreiro and Argensola describe them, the wars of resistance against the Portuguese were at least partially inspired by Muslim opposition to Portuguese religion, and the persecution of Christians is part of the story. *Het tweede boeck* depicts the sultan of Ternate always attending the mosque on their sabbath day.[58] Argensola observes that Islam in the Moluccas is mixed with earlier religious practices. Although the Koran forbids sacrifices, Argensola includes a description of one made in the mosque by Sultan Hairun's son "Babu" (Bab-Ullah, r. 1570–83). He describes a procession with incense, water pots at the door for washing hands and feet, prayers made kneeling on white carpets, and drums rather than bells.[59] *Het tweede boeck* also mentions sacrifices of goats in the mosque and describes a procession to and from the mosque for a circumcision ceremony.[60] No writer in the first two decades of the seventeenth century mentions non-Muslims in the Moluccas.

The preservation of pre-Muslim beliefs is apparent in the ceremonies attending an eclipse of the moon.[61] Ternatans believe that an eclipse foretells the death of the king or some other great person. To prevent such a calamity the people make an awful noise during the eclipse, shouting, crying, praying, and beating on drums or pots and pans. If the eclipse passes without mishap to the king or other high dignitaries, the people celebrate with feasting and processions of thanksgiving to the mosques and through the streets. When the Dutch tell Ternatans that people in Europe can predict eclipses, no one believes them.

[55] Keuning (ed.), *op. cit.* (n. 4), III, 136; Argensola, *op. cit.* (n. 5), pp. 11–12.
[56] Argensola, *op. cit.* (n. 5), pp. 11–12.
[57] *Ibid.*, p. 12. The indigenous languages spoken in the Moluccas belong to the Austronesian family. Member languages are spoken from the eastern coast of Africa to the western edge of America except for parts of New Guinea and a number of adjacent islands. See. J. T. Collins, "The Historical Relationship of the Languages of Central Maluku, Indonesia" (Ph.D. dissertation, Dept. of Linguistics, The University of Chicago, 1980), p. 1.
[58] Keuning (ed.), *op. cit.* (n. 4), III, 136.
[59] Argensola, *op. cit.* (n. 5), pp. 79–80.
[60] Keuning (ed.), *op. cit.* (n. 4), III, 136–37.
[61] Argensola, *op. cit.* (n. 5), p. 354; Keuning (ed.), *op. cit.* (n. 4), III, 118–19. Argensola appears to have taken it from *Het tweede boeck*.

The most powerful monarch in the Moluccas is the king or sultan of Ternate. Argensola describes the extent of his empire—seventy-two islands in the archipelago, many of which he names—and lists the number of soldiers in each place who will fight for him.[62] Many of these places have their own "kings" (rajas), who pay tribute to Ternate. According to Argensola there are fourteen kings in the Moluccas, several of whom, the ruler of Ternate and his archrival of Tidore among them, claim divine origin. He recounts the story, earlier printed by Barros, of the ancient prince Bicocigara, who, upon seeing a fine stand of rattans along the shore of Bachan, ordered his men to cut them. Once ashore they could not find them, so Bicocigara personally went ashore to supervise. The rattans, however, bled when cut and a voice from them ordered Bicocigara to preserve what appeared to be four snake eggs at their roots, promising that great princes would be born from them. He obeyed and later three princes and one princess hatched from the eggs. One ruled in Bachan, one in the land of the Papuas (New Guinea), and one in Butung. The princess married the ruler of the Lolodas, west of Halmahera, and from them came the rulers of Halmahera, Tidore, and Ternate. The son of one of the ancient kings of Tidore was honored as a prophet who foretold the coming of iron men from the remotest parts of the world to settle and rule the islands. According to Argensola, the Portuguese were taken as fulfillment of this prophecy when Francisco Serrão, dressed in white armor, landed on Ternate in 1513.[63]

Argensola goes on to describe subsequent Portuguese relations with Ternate and Tidore, especially the treacherous murder of Sultan Hairun of Ternate, his son Bab-Ullah's vow of revenge, and the wars of the Muslim confederation against the Portuguese and Tidore.[64] Bab-Ullah's son Modafara, (r. 1606–27) ruled Ternate when the first Dutchmen arrived. They describe him as a short, squat man, about thirty-six years old, high-spirited and insatiably curious about the world. He is fascinated with Linschoten's *Itinerario*, a prepublication copy of which the Dutch show him.[65] He is less jovial with his subjects, however, who greatly fear him. No one enters his presence without hands folded together, continually raising them above the head and letting them slowly fall. They perform this obeisance all the while they are talking to the sultan or in his presence.[66]

The sultan above all hates the Portuguese and the king of Tidore, although the latter is his uncle. He is valiant in battle and spares himself neither effort nor danger. He impressively demonstrated this to the Dutch

---

[62] Argensola, *op. cit.* (n. 5), p. 82.
[63] *Ibid.*, pp. 2–8. Cf. *Asia*, I, 607, for Barros' account.
[64] Sultan Said Berhat was taken captive by the Spanish in 1606 and carried to Manila, where he died in 1627. See Jacobs (ed.), *op. cit.* (n. 8), p. 5*.
[65] Keuning (ed.), *op. cit.* (n. 4), III, 133–36.
[66] *Ibid.*, p. 136.

during the attack on Tidore in 1599. The Dutch, therefore, think he will be a useful ally against the Iberians in the Moluccas.[67]

The sultan's soldiers are also courageous. Their principal weapons are hand-thrown spears of wood or reeds, large broad swords, and four-foot-long shields. Some use muskets obtained from the Portuguese. The sultan commands thirty-four "Karcollen" (*cora-coras*), vessels which carry four or six guns each and are propelled by between forty and sixty rowers. The sultan spends much of his time on his elaborate *cora-cora* moving about from town to town. In each town, however, he maintains houses and wives so that he is always at home. Altogether he has over forty wives.[68] Argensola describes the king's *cora-cora:* it has a gangway all around it, large, spoon-shaped paddles rather than oars, two slaves to each paddle, musicians on the top deck to set rhythms for the rowers, seven brass cannons, and a richly adorned bed on which the sultan lies or sits, fanned and attended by his servants.[69] Argensola also observes that Moluccan kings frequently row their own boats and that this is considered no more demeaning than for Spanish kings to ride horses.[70]

Ternate was the most frequently visited island in the Moluccas, and much that early seventeenth-century European writers said about the archipelago was based on what they had seen in Ternate. *Het tweede boeck* contains a brief description of "Gammelamme" (Gammolammo, or "Big Town"), Ternate's principal city and the sultan's residence. It is a surprisingly large city; its main street is as long as the longest distance across the old city of Amsterdam, "from the Haarlemmer Poort to the Reguliers Poort" (about two miles), but it is unpaved. Most of the houses are of reeds, although some are of wood. The mosque is built of wood. Some Portuguese buildings are still standing when the Dutch visit: the castle, the sultan's house, Saint Paul's church, the ruined Dominican monastery, a stone wall, and three or four stone houses. Gammolammo has no harbor for large ships because the passage through its reef is too small. The author of *Het tweede boeck* apparently thinks the reef man-made and of stone; he compares it to the wooden pilings that protect Amsterdam's harbor. Larger ships anchor at "Telingamme" (Telinggamme). Nearby is a small walled town named "Maleyo" (Malayu), which became a Dutch fortress.[71] Concerning Tidore, *Het tweede boeck* merely observes that it is at the same latitude as Ternate and that the Por-

---

[67] *Ibid.*, pp. 118–19, 132. Tradition seemed to require that the ruler of Tidore marry his daughter to the sultan of Ternate, perhaps as an acknowledgment of Ternate's suzerainty. See Jacobs, *op. cit.* (n. 8), I, 4*.

[68] Keuning (ed.), *op. cit.* (n. 4), III, 118, 136.

[69] Argensola, *op. cit.* (n. 5), p. 81.

[70] *Ibid.*, p. 151.

[71] Keuning (ed.), *op. cit.* (n. 4), III, 132–33. For a view of Gammolammo's harbor see our pl. 262.

tuguese control it.[72] Argensola notes that Tidore is as fruitful as Ternate, larger and more populous.[73] The only other place in the Moluccas described by Argensola was Halmahera. It is 250 leagues (1,000 miles) in circumference and subject to two kings, at Gilolo and Loloda. The king of Loloda is the most ancient ruler in the Moluccas and used to be the strongest. Now he is the weakest. The people in northern Halmahera are savages who live in deserts without kings, laws, or towns. On the east coast, called "Morotia" (Moro), there are populous towns.[74] The people there speak several different languages but seem to understand one another. Offshore from Moro are islands called Morotai where live "deceitful, brutal, and dastardly men," without "laws, weights, measures, coin, gold, silver, and other metals, or a king." Women till the land and each town is governed by a magistrate chosen by the people. They pay no taxes. Some Morotai towns are controlled by Ternate, others by Tidore.[75]

Appolonius Schotte's *Discours*, published in 1618, describes the political state of the Moluccas in 1610 and comments extensively on the character of the Moluccans. The Dutch have, he reports, three forts in Ternate: one called "Maleya" (Malayu), or "Orangien" (Orange), at the east end of Ternate; Fort "Tolucco" (?), or Hollandia, about a half-mile north of the village of Malayu; and Fort "Tacome" (Takome), or "Willemstadt," on the northwest side of the island. These forts protect many Ternatans who earlier fled from the Spanish to Halmahera and have now returned. Motir, according to Schotte, had been completely depopulated during the wars between Ternate and Tidore. The Dutch built a fort at the north end of the island and brought people back from Halmahera to live there. Over two thousand people live on Motir in 1610.[76]

Three forts insure Dutch control of Makian: "Taffasor" (Tufasoho) on the west side, "Noffigina" (Ngofakiaha) on the north side, and "Tabelole" (Tabilolo) on the east side. About nine thousand people live on the island. It produces more food and more cloves than any of the other islands because, Schotte asserts, the people of Makian and Motir work harder and take better care of their land than those of Ternate and Tidore, who live "more by warfare than by agriculture."

Bachan is also fertile, rich in cloves, sago, and fruit, but it is thinly populated by a "lazy, careless people, who are addicted to nothing but voluptuousness and a wanton life." Cloves on Bachan are often left to rot. The Spanish and Portuguese fort at "Laboua" (Labuha) was conquered by the

---

[72] *Ibid.*, p. 132.
[73] Argensola, *op. cit.* (n. 5), p. 96.
[74] The term "Moro" includes both the coastland (Morotia) of northeast Halmahera, whose main town was Tolo, and the island opposite, called Morotai.
[75] Argensola, *op. cit.* (n. 5), pp. 70–71.
[76] Like the other Moluccas, Motir was a volcanic island which produced cloves. After the Dutch destroyed its clove trees in 1650, Motir was rapidly depopulated.

Dutch in November, 1600. Schotte reports that seventeen Portuguese and eighty native Christians still live there.

The Dutch control only the village of "Gamma-duorre" (Gani Diluar or Outer Gani) in southeast Halmahera, but it is heavily populated because people from some Spanish-controlled parts of Halmahera have fled there.[77] The Spanish, on the other hand, have several fortresses on Halmahera: "Sabougo" (Sabugo), which was taken from the Dutch in 1611 along with another called "Gilolo" (Gilolo) and one called "Aquilamo" (?), all on the west coast of the island. The Spaniards also control several forts on the Moro coast, the east side of the island, from which they obtain rice, sago, and other foods with which to supply their forts in Tidore and Ternate. The whole of Tidore is in Spanish hands; they have three forts on the island: "Taroula" (Tomanyira?) in the large city of Tidore, a rebuilt Portuguese fort which the Dutch held for a short time, and a third called "Marico" (Marieko). On Ternate the Spanish still control a large town which they call "Neustra signora del rosario." It is walled and heavily fortified. Between it and Malayu they hold another fort named "San Pedro y Pablo."[78] Schotte fears that once the threat of Spanish and Portuguese domination recedes, the Ternatans may find that they have promised the Dutch more in tolls and trade than they will want to deliver. They are, he points out, a brave nation, accustomed to ruling other peoples. They will, he fears, chafe under Dutch domination. What is more, he judges them faithless because their Muslim religion permits the breaking of oaths and promises. They are brave, "addicted to war and pillage," credulous, unstable, and under their new young sultan, poorly governed—"a wanton, lascivious, fierce, greedy, tyrannical nation of perjurers." He advises settling Dutch colonists and Christians in the Moluccas gradually to bind the natives to the Dutch.[79] He does not expect the Spanish to remain content with Dutch control of so many Moluccan islands. Schotte advises a massive attack on the Spanish at Manila as the best means of driving them from the Moluccas.[80]

Two more English reports about the Moluccas appeared in 1625 as part of Purchas' *Hakluytus Posthumus:* the report of John Saris, who traded in the Moluccas in 1612 and 1613, and Humphrey Fitzherbert's "A Pithy Description of the Chiefe Ilands of Banda and Moluccas."[81] Saris primarily describes his efforts to trade in the Moluccas. Everywhere he went—to Bachan, Makian, Tidore, and Ternate—natives were eager to sell cloves to him but were usually prevented from doing so by the Dutch. As Saris de-

---

[77] Apollonius Schotte, "A Discourse," in J. A. J. de Villiers (trans.), *The East and West Indian Mirror, being an Account of Joris van Speilbergen's Voyage around the World (1614–1617) and the Australian Navigations of Jacob le Maire* ("HS," 2d ser., XVIII; London, 1906), pp. 134–37.
[78] *Ibid.*, pp. 142–44.
[79] *Ibid.*, pp. 137–42.
[80] *Ibid.*, pp. 145–49.
[81] For bibliographical details see above, pp. 560–61, 566.

scribes it, the long wars in the Moluccas have caused much destruction, dislocation, and misery; Dutch domination is not improving conditions. In Bachan and Makian, for example, rich crops of cloves are allowed to rot on the ground.[82] The wars continue. While Saris was anchored at Tidore, the "Prince of Tidore" returned with the heads of one hundred Ternatans, the king of Ternate's son among them.[83] Saris describes several of the islands, but adds little to what was available in earlier reports. He provides much careful description of the smaller islets, shoals, reefs, anchorages, channels, and coasts, collected as he sailed north between Halmahera and the clove-producing islands. He reports the annual yield of each Moluccan island.[84] Saris includes a brief history of the wars and rivalries in the Moluccas and a list of the Dutch forts. His list is identical to Schotte's except that he reports Marieko, the Spanish fort on Tidore, to be in Dutch hands.[85] Fitzherbert's brief description of the five main clove-producing islands mostly repeats what was published earlier. Bachan is the most fruitful but still underpopulated. The Dutch receive their greatest profit from Makian, with its high cone touching the clouds and with no plains at all. On Makian grows a special tree called the king's clove, whose fruit differs from other cloves and is never sold but given to friends by handfuls.[86] These two, Saris' and Fitzherbert's, prove to be the last English descriptions of the Moluccas until William Dampier's at the end of the century.[87]

After the first two decades Dutch control over the Moluccas continued to tighten, and after 1625 Europe's information about the Moluccas came overwhelmingly from Dutch accounts or from the accounts of Germans who served the VOC. A large number of Dutch accounts appeared in 1645 and 1646 as part of Isaac Commelin's *Begin ende voortgangh* collection.[88] They include Roelof Roelofszoon's report of Jacob Corneliszoon van Neck's second voyage which landed at Ternate in 1601; reports of Steven van der Hagen's Moluccan campaigns in 1605 and those of Cornelis Matelief in 1607, Paulus van Caerden in 1608, and Pieter Willemszoon Verhoeff in 1609; as well as Gillis Seys' 1627 report on the state of the Moluccas and the report of Hendrick Hagenaer's brief visit in 1635.[89] None of these accounts contains extended descriptions of the Moluccas; they primarily record the consolida-

[82] "The Eighth Voyage set forth by the East-Indian Societie . . . under the Command of Captaine John Saris," *PP*, III, 416.
[83] *Ibid.*, pp. 429–30.
[84] *Ibid.*, pp. 431–32.
[85] *Ibid.*, pp. 432–34. Pieter van den Broecke in 1634 produced a list of the five islands, their annual productivity, and the Dutch forts on them, but his figures for annual productivity are considerably lower than Saris'. See Pieter van den Broecke, "Historische ende journaelsche aenteyckeningh," in *BV*, IIa, 27–28.
[86] Humphrey Fitzherbert, "A Pithy Description of the Chiefe Ilands of Banda and Moluccas," *PP*, V, 178–80. On the scarce royal clove see Gibbs, *op. cit.* (n. 42), p. 109.
[87] See below, pp. 1420, 1439–41.
[88] For bibliography see above, pp. 461–62.
[89] For bibliographical details see above, pp. 463–65, 466–70, 472, and 461.

tion of Dutch power there, the battles with the Spanish and Portuguese, the treaties with Moluccan rulers, and the attempts to enforce the treaties. Most descriptive passages repeat what was written in earlier accounts. Nevertheless they contribute a few new shadings to the European image of the Moluccas. Roelofszoon's account, for example, contains a small insert on Halmahera: a large island, rich in rice, sago, chickens, and sea turtles; it is inhabited by a well-proportioned but wild people, some of whom have been cannibals.[90] Roelofszoon also describes an elaborate wedding feast in Ternate, and his editor provides an imaginative plate to accompany it.[91] Matelief describes the city of Tidore as seen from the sea: so wooded that only three or four houses could be seen from a musket shot away, with a reef a stone's throw from shore that is dry at low tide and only three feet under water at high tide, effectively preventing an amphibious attack.[92] The account of Verhoeff's voyage describes one of the parts of Bachan as an uninhabited territory with a good anchorage. It has fresh water, plenty of sago, fruit, buffaloes, chickens, and pigs, as well as cloves.[93]

Seys' report describes the state of VOC affairs in the Moluccas at the time of his official visit in 1627. He lists the various Dutch forts, their personnel, weapons, defenses, supplies, and expenses, and the villages dependent on each fort. He reports events: the king of Tidore died on May 23, 1627;[94] the king of Ternate on June 16. The new king of Ternate does not have the Dutch governor's approval.[95] Some of Schotte's earlier fears are realities by 1627. For example, Seys reports that the Ternatans near the Dutch fort at Malayu harvested no cloves this year, explaining that they were too busy farming and fishing. He suspects they are selling the cloves to the Spanish in violation of their treaty with the Dutch. Not much can be done about it except to refuse aid to Ternate when its king needs help against Tidore.[96] At the moment, Tidore and Ternate are at peace. Something could be done about the plot to capture Fort Barneveldt on Bachan and turn it over to the Spanish. Five conspirators are arrested and executed, and their heads stuck on poles. Others flee to the mountains; the Dutch offer rewards for their heads.[97] The conspiracy elicits considerable description of Bachan and its people: an island rich both in cloves and in foodstuffs, but inhabited by a lazy, careless people. They wreck the trees when they harvest the cloves. Much of the crop goes unharvested because the king of Bachan keeps his

[90] Roelof Roelofszoon, "Kort end waerachtigh verhael . . . ," *BV*, Ib, 5–6.
[91] *Ibid.*, pp. 7–8.
[92] Cornelis Matelief, "Historische verhael . . . ," *BV*, IIa, 64.
[93] "Journael ende verhael . . . ," *BV*, IIa, 60–61.
[94] G. Seys, "Verhael vande Mollucs Eylanden . . . 1627 . . . ," *BV*, IIa, 162.
[95] *Ibid.*, 183. As a prince, Hamja (r. 1627–48) of Ternate had been baptized in Manila. He became king only after he renounced his Catholicism. See Jacobs (ed.), *op. cit.* (n. 8), III, 5*. Mole of Tidore died in 1627 and was replaced by Naro (r. 1627–34). See *ibid.*, p. 6*.
[96] Seys, *loc. cit.* (n. 94), 165.
[97] *Ibid.*, p. 167.

men busy hunting or rowing at harvest time. Population is meager; the king can man only two large *cora-coras*. The king wants Dutch help in subduing some of his rebellious subjects, but Seys thinks the VOC should use the rebellion as an excuse to settle other people on Bachan who would at least harvest the cloves.[98] Makian by contrast is well populated—twenty-two hundred armed men can be mustered there. Only seven miles in circumference, it produces more cloves than any island except Bachan. The people of Makian, subject to the king of Ternate, also sell cloves to the Spanish.[99]

Francisco Colin's *Labor evangélica,* published in 1663, brings the story of the Jesuit mission in the Philippines down to 1616.[100] The Moluccas as part of the Jesuit Philippine province appear both in his historical account of the Spanish in the Philippines and in his record of the Jesuit mission.[101] Colin describes each of the five main clove-producing islands, although he devotes more attention to Ternate and Tidore than to the others. His description is not as detailed as those found in *Het tweede boeck* or in Argensola's *Conquista,* and most of what he reports can be found in those earlier publications. There are some differences, however. For example, he lists maize and yams along with sago as staple foods grown on the island and he reports that soldiers on Ternate raise maize, yams, legumes, and other garden vegetables for recreation. He also reports an abundance of fish in Moluccan waters. Ternatans, he thinks, are mostly healthy and long-lived. They cure most of their maladies with herbs and roots.[102] Tidore's climate is more healthful than Ternate's, and Tidore is more fruitful because it is better cultivated and the military obligations of its people are not as heavy. It is also heavily populated. The king can outfit thirty *cora-coras* and muster six or seven thousand men in case of war. The king also claims six thousand tributaries on nearby islands. Tidore's landscape is rocky and craggy, good for building fortifications. The volcano in the south of the island is more conical than Ternate's. The natives call it a water volcano and ascribe curative powers to baths taken in its waters. While Tidore's main crop is cloves—five to six hundred bahars per year—Colin reports that it also produces nutmeg.[103]

Motir, Makian, and Bachan Colin describes very briefly, and notes that some tobacco is grown on Bachan. "Batochinas del Moro" (Halmahera) is large, high, and mountainous. Its name comes from Bata, which means rocky or mountainous, and China, which empire once dominated the Moluccas. He lists several places in Halmahera: Gilolo, Sabugo, Morotai, "San Iuan de Tolo" (Tolo), Galela, "Rao" (Rau), "Chao" (Kau), "Seguita" (Sakita on Morotai), "Nira" (?), and "Doy" (Doi), but says nothing about

[98] *Ibid.,* pp. 171–72.
[99] *Ibid.,* p. 182.
[100] For bibliography, see above, p. 353.
[101] Paulo Pastells (ed.), *Labor evangélica* . . . (3 vols.; Barcelona, 1900–1902; covers dated 1904), I, 105–15. Also see below, p. 1512.
[102] Pastells (ed.), *op. cit.* (n. 101), I, 107.
[103] *Ibid.,* pp. 108–9.

them other than that Gilolo has its own king, and that it and Sabugo are both very populous and maintain eight *cora-cora*s each, besides a large number of smaller vessels. The other places, he reports, are all vassals of the king of Ternate.[104]

Colin also mentions islands between Ternate and Mindanao in the Philippines which are not properly part of the Moluccas. His descriptions of them are very brief. "Meaos" (Mayu), mentioned earlier in *Het tweede boeck,* is very small, has no anchorage and no shelter, is unfruitful, and has no cloves.[105] The natives live by fishing and are friends of the Dutch. "Tasures" (Tifore), only three leagues around, has a large lake at the top of its cone. It produces sago and several fruits, but is largely depopulated because of wars with Mayu.[106] "Tagolanda" (Tabulandang), sixteen leagues north, is volcanic, has a good anchorage and a good fresh river, produces sago and fruit, and has it own king. Its warlike people speak a language different from those of the Moluccans and different from Malay.[107] Finally, he describes an island called "Calonga" (Kalongan in the Talaud group?), which is six or seven leagues in circumference, has an active volcano, is fruitful and populous, and has three kings, the most important of whom is Christian.[108]

Accounts of two Dutch voyages to the Indonesian archipelago were published during the late 1670s: Wouter Schouten's *Oost-Indische voyagie* in 1676 and Gerret Vermeulen's *De gedenkwaerdige voyagie* in 1677.[109] Vermeulen includes only a very brief description of Ternate, which provides no information not already well known.[110] Schouten's description of Ternate, on the other hand, is one of the century's most vivid. His first glimpse of the Moluccas is of "the wonderfully high peaks . . . their blue crowns sticking up through the clouds."[111] Sailing through "Patience Strait" from Ternate to Amboina, so called because of the many shoals, reefs, and narrows to be navigated on the inter-island passage, Schouten obviously revels in the beauty of the blue sea and myriad green-covered, volcano-crowned islands.[112] Ternate's anchorage teems with fish, with waters so clear the ship's anchors are visible seven fathoms below. Its sparkling brown sand beaches shimmer in the sunlight.[113] Schouten's ship anchored there in June, 1659, and

---

[104] *Ibid.,* p. 109.

[105] *Ibid.* The author of *Het tweede boeck* described it as one of the small islands which also produced cloves. See n. 21, above.

[106] Pastells (ed.), *op. cit.* (n. 101), I, 109.

[107] *Ibid.,* I, 110. Robert F. Austin, "A Historical Gazetter of Southeast Asia" (Dept. of Geography, University of Missouri, Columbia; April, 1983), p. 82, identifies it with Roang but is unsure whether it is an island and whether it is in the Philippines.

[108] Pastells (ed.), *op. cit.* (n. 101), I, 110. *Cf. Asia,* I, 621.

[109] For bibliography see above, pp. 496–97, 498–99.

[110] Gerret Vermeulen, *De gedenkwaerdige voyagie . . .* (Amsterdam, 1677), pp. 81–83.

[111] Schouten, *Reys-togten naar en door Oost-Indien . . .* (3d ed.; 3 vols. in 1; Amsterdam, 1740), I, 42.

[112] *Ibid.,* p. 51.

[113] *Ibid.,* p. 50.

he spent his days hiking with an old friend who was stationed there. They visited the Spanish fort at "Calamette" (Kalamata) and had a congenial conversation with its captain, who wished the Spanish and Dutch would live peaceably together in the Moluccas so as to provide the Muslims with an example of Christian love and morality.[114] The Spanish still maintain forts on Ternate and Tidore, and a Spanish governor resides in "Gammolamma," (Gammolammo), but all the Moluccan islands are now under Dutch control. Schouten briefly recounts the history of the wars between Ternate and Tidore, the Iberians and the Dutch; in his opinion, these were caused by the other island princes' jealousy of Ternate's power, which rivalries the Europeans exploited and intensified. The king of Ternate rules over seventy-two islands, including parts of Celebes, and is an ally of the VOC.[115]

While much of what Schouten says about Ternate duplicates earlier published descriptions, most of it seems to come from what he observed on his visit there. The island is seven miles around but from the sea looks like a single mountain, flaming and smoking from its top. The sultan's walled palace is very near Malayu. Schouten glimpses its gardens, planted with a large number of exotic plants and the home of a wide variety of tropical birds. There are three kinds of parrots: the three-colored lory bird (*Psittacus lori*), parakeets, and snow-white cockatoos. Houses in the village of Malayu are mostly built of a reed called "adap" (*atap*, roof of palm leaves), roofed with coconut palm leaves. They have doors and windows and are divided into rooms, but the windows have no glass, the doors are not locked at night, and the houses contain very little furniture. Malayu's mosque reminds Schouten of the mosque at Japara on Java (see pl. 261); it has five roofs one above the other. The people are all Muslims and must wash their hands before entering the mosque. They practice circumcision and abstain from eating pork. A procession of priests dressed in white accompanies the sultan whenever he goes out. The present sultan's name is "Manderzaha" (Mandar Syah, r. 1648–75). Sometimes he walks down the street with a few attendants, greeting people as he goes. In his presence even the highest nobles bow with folded hands raised over their heads and slowly lowered.

Ternatans are "heroes in combat," but otherwise kind-hearted and courteous. They hate splendor and excess and will not tolerate theft, but they love leisure and are not much given to work or study. They seem to be self-sufficient: each builds his own house, makes his own clothing, carves his own boat from a thick tree trunk, fishes or hunts for his own food. They dress lightly; most wear only a cloth around the waist, with no jacket or shoes. Some wear a cloth of silk or cotton on their heads. Men marry as many women as they want and can support. Schouten seems attracted to

[114] *Ibid.,* pp. 44–45.
[115] *Ibid.,* pp. 45–46. *Cf.* Argensola's list of the seventy-two islands in vassalage to Ternate, mentioned above, p. 1406.

Ternatan women although, he reports, they are seldom seen in the streets. They wear their "gleaming black" hair long, down to the shoulders, and keep it in place with strings and bows. They are generally "attractive in appearance, lovely of face, essentially brown, but not all black; very sweet, courteous, and friendly of speech; small of person, lightly clothed." Some wear only a cloth wound around the middle, others wear a thin veil over their breasts. Some throw a cotton or silk cloth over their shoulders. They spend their time preparing betel and do only a little sewing or spinning. Some sell fruit in the town to help their lazy men support the household. Ternatans bury their dead with little ceremony but in the Muslim manner in brick graves.[116]

The last seventeenth-century Dutch writer to publish an account of Ternate was Nikolaas de Graaf who visited there on his sixteenth and last voyage (1683–87).[117] He was probably over sixty-five years old when he visited Ternate. Like most European visitors, De Graaf was impressed with Ternate's volcano: about 4,540 feet high, it is wooded almost to the top. Caves and sulphur pools can be found on the mountain. He hears that many people climb it, but he does not understand how they can, because it is very steep and the crater spews out rocks and lava. It always smokes; sometimes it glows.[118] De Graaf recalls the earthquake and eruption of Makian's volcano in 1646 and he describes the eruption of "Gamma Knor" (Gamkonorah) on Halmahera in 1673.[119] De Graaf records changes on Ternate since Schouten's account. The Spanish castle at Gammolammo is in ruins now and there is a sort of lake between it and Fort Oranje where the Spanish had tried to make an inner harbor.[120] Castle Oranje, on the other hand, is strong: four stone bulwarks, thick walls, a deep moat, and many cannons. Visitors are housed there and its hospital cares for the sick. Few cloves are harvested now; each year the trees are cut down and burned. Amboina produces enough cloves for the VOC.[121] The village of Malayu seems to be divided into two parts. In the southern part are the VOC gardens and the homes of free Dutch residents and mixed-race company employees. The sultan's palace, the mosque, the cemetery, and the Muslim markets are located in the northern part of the town.

[116] Schouten, *op. cit.* (n. 111), I, 47–50; there is a good picture of Ternate between pages 46 and 47. Marketing and trade were women's work in traditional Southeast Asia. See Reid, *op. cit.* (n. 37), pp. 162–65.

[117] For bibliographical information on his *Reisen* (Hoorn, 1701), see above, pp. 505–6.

[118] J. C. M. Warnsinck (ed.), *Reisen van Nicolaus de Graaf, gedaan naar alle gewesten des werelds beginnende 1639 tot 1687 incluis . . .* ("WLV," XXXIII; The Hague, 1930), p. 208. The volcano is actually 1,537 meters high.

[119] *Ibid.*, p. 210.

[120] Ruins of this fortress may still be seen, as well as a breakwater that is still intact. See Jacobs (ed.), *op. cit.* (n. 8), III, 659, n. 3. For a 1933 photograph of the ruins of the fortress see C. R. Boxer and F. de Vasconcelos, *André Furtado de Mendonça (1558–1610)* (Lisbon, 1955), facing p. 70.

[121] Warnsinck (ed.), *op. cit.* (n. 118), pp. 209–10.

2

AMBOINA (AMBON)

In contrast to the Moluccas, Amboina was the subject of only a few extended descriptions published during the first quarter of the seventeenth century. Argensola does not mention Amboina, and while Geurreiro devotes many pages to it, most of them describe Furtado's armada and his victory over the Dutch and the Ternatans at Amboina in 1601; the rest are devoted to an account of the missioners' efforts to care for the native Christians.[122] Henry Middleton visited Amboina in February, 1605, but the account of his voyage describes nothing but his attempts to trade, his negotiations with the Dutch, Portuguese, and Amboinese, and Steven van der Hagen's seizure of the Portuguese fort; it does not describe the islands or the people.[123]

Het tweede boeck briefly describes Amboina: the island is about twenty-four miles northeast of Banda and is very fruitful. Cloves grow there, as well as oranges, limes, lemons, coconuts, bananas, and sugarcane. The natives are "bad people." They dress like the people of Banda or the Moluccas; they earn their livelihood by harvesting and selling cloves. For weapons they have long, iron-tipped spears, like harpoons, which they can throw far and with deadly accuracy; they also use sabers and shields. Poor people carry a large knife which they use in their work. The Amboinese bake large cakes of rice, sugar, and dried almonds which they sell in the surrounding islands. The cakes are a very good remedy for diarrhea. They also bake a bread from rice. *Het tweede boeck* does not report whether or not rice grows on Amboina. The Amboinese travel in "galleys" called *cora-coras*, which are shaped somewhat like a drake, decorated with flags and pennants, and can be rowed very fast. Some are beautifully constructed and appear costly. The "admiral of the sea," for example, meets the Dutch with three large and elaborate *cora-coras*, which circle the Dutch ships while people aboard them sing and beat drums or copper cymbals. The drums and cymbals keep a rhythm for the "slaves" who row and sing. Each of the admiral's *cora-coras* carries three guns which are fired as a salute to the Dutch.[124] Commelin inserted another brief description of Amboina in his *Begin ende voortgangh* edition of *Het tweede boeck*.[125]

By far the most substantial account of Amboina published during the first quarter of the seventeenth century was Sebastiaen Danckaerts' *Historische ende grondich verhael van de standt des Christendoms int quartier van Amboina*

[122] Viegas (ed.), *op. cit.* (n. 8), I, 273–83.
[123] William Foster (ed.), *The Voyage of Sir Henry Middleton to the Moluccas, 1604–1606* ("HS," 2d ser., LXXXVIII; London, 1943), pp. 20–25.
[124] Keuning (ed.), *op. cit.* (n. 4), III, 55–59.
[125] *BV*, Ia, 18–19.

(The Hague, 1621).[126] Danckaerts was hired by the VOC as a minister (*predicant*) to VOC employees and the native Christians on Amboina in 1617. His appointment was perhaps the first serious attempt by the VOC to assume some responsibility for the Amboinese Christians, who had been almost totally neglected since Van der Hagen's conquest of the Portuguese fort in 1605.[127] Danckaerts preached in Malay as well as Dutch, and revived the school for Amboinese young people. His *Verhael* is intended primarily to describe the state of Christianity in Amboina. In doing so he discusses the Amboinese people, their culture, and way of life, but he does not describe the physical aspects of the islands or even their products.

Once all the Amboinese were "heathen," according to Danckaerts. Some later became Muslim when Javan and Ternatan traders came to the islands, just as some became Catholic Christians when the Portuguese controlled the islands. Danckaerts implies, however, that most Amboinese are still heathen and that most Amboinese Muslims and Christians retain many heathen, superstitious beliefs and practices and rather easily slip back into heathendom. He says almost nothing about Islam, but describes "heathen" beliefs extensively.

The "heathen," he contends, have no knowledge of God whatever, but instead serve the devil, or, more accurately, devils. While there seems to be a supreme devil called "Lenthila" (?) and other principal devils named "Lanithe" and "Taulay," every village, town, and even family seems to have its own special devil or evil spirit which they generally call "Nito" (*nitu,* or spirits of the dead), a word which also applies to certain dead people such as murderers or sorcerers whose spirits still wander around.[128] The devil sometimes appears, usually in a person rather than in an animal, so they can speak with him. Some say he has appeared in, among others, the three "kings" of the Amboinese islands—"Rossiniven," "Soijen," and "Kielangh."[129] In the Amboinese ceremonies in which they call on or serve the devil, there are candles, drums, readings, chants, and the setting out of food and drink. Most people have places in their homes where they set out food and drink and burn candles for the devils. They usually call on the devils when they are about to do something important like hold a council meeting, build a house, or take a journey, so that the devils will not hurt or hinder them. Whenever they eat a special meal they set part of it out for the devils. They

---

[126] For bibliographic details see above, pp. 448–49.

[127] On the Catholic mission on Amboina under the Portuguese see C. J. Wessels, S.J., *De geschiedenis de R. K. missie in Amboina, 1546–1605* (Nijmegen-Utrecht, 1926). For conditions under the VOC between 1605 and 1616 see his last chapter, pp. 161–71. See also above, pp. 215–18.

[128] On the spirits of the dead see G. A. Wilken, *Het animisme bij de volken van den Indischen Archipel* (2 pts.; Amsterdam, 1881), Pt. 2, pp. 168–69.

[129] Amboina had no sultan who ruled the entire island. The small Islamic state of Hitu on its north coast was ruled by five *perdanas* under the *kapitan* appointed by the sultan of Ternate. See Jacobs (ed.), *op. cit.* (n. 8), II, 12.

attribute misfortune, sickness, and death to their failure to propitiate the devils. According to Danckaerts they live in constant fear of the devils, indeed are slaves to them.[130] Most aspects of life on Amboina, Danckaerts observes, are affected by the people's devil worship. Nevertheless he thinks that above all other peoples in the East Indies, the Amboinese are profane and irreligious.[131]

The Amboinese practice a kind of circumcision which seems unrelated to that practiced by Muslims. Instead of removing the entire foreskin as the Muslims do, they split only the top part of it with a certain reed. Danckaerts cannot discover the origin of the practice. People merely tell him that women will not marry a man who has not been circumcised.[132] Amboinese marriages are rare and are easily broken. The ceremony is simple: the father of the groom presents gifts to the father of the intended bride. If these are acceptable, the father of the bride gives a banquet or a party and the couple is considered married. Marriages are broken over trifling disputes. Gifts are returned, some water is thrown over the man's feet to signify the cleansing of any pollution, and the couple is divorced. Sometimes the children are sold to the highest bidder.[133]

Danckaerts is certain that the Amboinese ritual for swearing oaths, called "Mattacau" (*matakau*), stems from devil worship. They place things such as some gold, earth, or a bullet in a cup of water, or dip the tip of a knife or spear in it, and "after some mumbling" drink the water, thereby calling for damage or loss to those things should they not keep the oath. Such an oath-swearing is always done in the name of "Lenthila," the chief devil.[134] The Amboinese greatly fear and hate sorcerers and poisoners called "Zwangij," whom they believe cause all sorts of trouble. When someone dies, a shield and sword are placed by the corpse at night lest the "Zwangij" steal its heart and eat it. Danckaerts never saw one or heard any reliable report of one, but the fear is so intense that merely the suspicion that someone is a "Zwangij" could easily result in his being killed, along with his entire family. Danckaerts does not like the Amboinese. They are "by nature a very faithless, timid or faint-hearted, dull, and intractable people."[135] They bury their valuables in the ground because they do not trust one another, sometimes leaving things so long that they rot. They have little courage, will scarcely

---

[130] Sebastien Danckaerts, *Historisch ende grondich verhael van den standt des Christendoms int quartier van Amboina* as reprinted in *BTLV*, VI (n.s., II) (1859), pp. 110–13. On shamanism in Indonesia see M. Eliade, *Shamanism. Archaic Techniques of Ecstasy* (New York, 1964), pp. 344–54.

[131] *Op. cit.* (n. 130), p. 118.

[132] *Ibid.*, pp. 113–14. Danckaerts may have confused what he called circumcision with the ritual of inserting small penis bells, widely practiced in Southeast Asia; see Reid, *op. cit.* (n. 37), pp. 149–50.

[133] Danckaerts, *op. cit.* (n. 130), pp. 114–15. Divorce was easily obtained in most Southeast Asian societies; see Reid, *op. cit.* (n. 37), pp. 151–53.

[134] Dankaerts, *op. cit.* (n. 130), p. 115. On *matakau* see O. D. Tauern, *Patasiwa und Patalima* (Leipzig, 1918), pp. 53–54.

[135] *Op. cit.* (n. 130), p. 116.

defend themselves, but can be viciously cruel when they have the upper hand. They have no crafts of any kind apart from the poorly made sack-like dresses which the women wear. They do not learn new things easily and are not curious. They have preserved nothing of their past and have no written language. Their houses are poorly built, and they eat so little that Danckaerts wonders how they stay alive. Nevertheless he admits that they are healthy, lively, and fairly strong. They spend most of their time fishing or gardening. They carry on no trade other than that in cloves. It seems to Danckaerts that there is very little love or affection between Amboinese husbands and wives, but that they dote on their children and raise them permissively. They would rather receive blows from their children than punish them.[136]

Danckaerts reports a fairly large number of Christians, Amboinese who were converted by the Catholic missionaries under the Portuguese, still living in the islands. Those in the village of "Hativa" (Hatiwi) close by the castle are very loyal to the Portuguese, largely because they are hated and persecuted by the Muslims. Since the departure of the Portuguese and the missionaries they have become negligent about their Christianity and some have fallen back into devil worship. According to Danckaerts they were never adequately instructed in Christian doctrine but held in the church by the authority of the priests. What is true for Hatiwi is even more true of the Amboinese Christians in other villages. Some have fallen back into devil worship, most still retain some heathen practices, and even those who do not have a very inadequate grasp of Christian teachings.

Among the foreigners who live in Amboina are people from the Moluccas and elsewhere who were brought there by the Portuguese. These "Mardecas" (Dutch, *Mardijkers,* or freemen),[137] as they are called, used to work for the Portuguese, but are now free and are intermarrying with the Amboinese. Many of them are still Christian, although they were all "heathen" at one time. They are quite different from the Amboinese, however, and even when heathen they do not worship devils. The Chinese living in Amboina are also heathens, but unlike the Amboinese they do not worship devils. Also unlike the Amboinese they are tractable, curious, and eager to learn. Some have recently become Christians, and Danckaerts has high hope for the mission to the Chinese on Amboina if only someone could be found to teach them in their own language. All of the Christians and former Christians in Amboina need more instruction in the faith. Danckaerts places the most confidence in the school which he reopened and reformed. He has more hope that young people can be converted and taught than that their elders can be genuinely converted.[138]

---

[136] *Ibid.,* pp. 116–18.

[137] See Jacobs (ed.), *op. cit.* (n. 8), II, 352, n. 26. On the Mardijkers see above, chap. xvii, n. 100.

[138] *Op. cit.* (n. 130), pp. 118–36.

The year 1624 saw the publication of the first of the many pamphlets pertaining to the famous, or infamous, Amboina massacre of 1623.[139] The English condemnations and Dutch justifications continued almost to the end of the century. The pamphlets contain details of the events of 1623 and of Dutch and English activities in the Spiceries and elsewhere which led up to the massacre, but they do not describe Amboina or its people.[140] After 1623 the English withdrew from the Spiceries and consequently contributed nothing to the European image of Amboina until the end of the century when William Dampier briefly described part of the coast of Ceram and Buru.[141]

After the first quarter century, Europe's image of Amboina was shaped by Dutch writers or by Germans in the employ of the VOC. As in the case of the Moluccas, Commelin's *Begin ende voortgangh* (1646) included several descriptions of Amboina. Those in the accounts of Van der Hagen's two voyages and in that of Verhoeff's voyage are very brief.[142] Those in Cornelis Matelief's "Historische verhael" and Gillis Seys' "Verhael van den tegenwoordigen staet inde quarteren van Amboyna," however, are substantial.[143]

Matelief visited Amboina in March, 1607, while Frederick de Houtman was still governor and the king of Ternate was still begging the Dutch to help him against the Spanish. Matelief learned that many of the Amboinese on the outlying islands refused to accept the new young king of Ternate as their overlord. The leaders of the Amboinese who lived near the Dutch fort, mostly Christians, complained to Matelief about soldiers' riots after the Dutch victory in 1605, about the lack of church services and Christian instruction, and about the dissolute lives of VOC soldiers and the fact that they were not permitted to marry native women as the Portuguese soldiers had done. Matelief reopened the school and appointed a teacher, allowed Dutch soldiers to marry native women, and selected three young native men, two of them sons of "Captain Hittou" (Hitu), to take back to the Netherlands with him so that they could see how the Dutch lived at home and return to teach the Amboinese.[144] Matelief describes the sago palm called "Lepia" by the Amboinese, and how bread is made from its pulp, drinks from its sap, and clothing from its leaves.[145] He reports another tree,

[139] On the Amboina massacre see above, p. 51.
[140] See above, pp. 555–56, for bibliography of the Amboina pamphlets.
[141] James Spencer (ed.), *A Voyage to New Holland; The English Voyage of Discovery to the South Seas in 1699* (Gloucester, 1981), p. 162.
[142] For bibliography see above, pp. 465–67, 470–72.
[143] See above, pp. 467–70, 472.
[144] Matelief, *loc. cit.* (n. 92), pp. 54–57. "Captain Hitu" was the sultan of Ternate's representative in Amboina; his name should probably be rendered as "Captain of Hitu."
[145] Sago is made from at least five varieties of palm, among which the bamban, or *Sagus laevis,* and the prickly sago palm, or *Sagus metroxylon,* are two of the most common. See Crawfurd, *op. cit.* (n. 25), pp. 371–72. See also L. S. Cobley, *An Introduction to the Botany of Tropical Crops* (London, 1956), p. 190.

called "Nava" (Nina?) by the Amboinese, which was also used to make sago bread. Its quality is inferior, however.[146]

Matelief includes a general description of Amboina. It lies four degrees south of the equator, three Dutch miles south of "Ceiram" (Ceram), and twenty-four miles northwest of Banda. It is about twenty to twenty-four miles around. The term Amboina embraces several islands: Amboina itself, Ceram, Buru to the west, and several smaller islands such as "Manipa Liliboy" (Manipa) between Buru and Ceram eight or nine miles north of Buru. Ceram is a large island which, like all the Amboinese islands, belongs to the king of Ternate. Most of its inhabitants are heathen and wild, known for their thievery; some are cannibals. Across from Amboina, however, are some Muslim villages—"Cambalou" (Ambelan) and "Lougo" (?)—where cloves grow. Amboina has a safe deep harbor on its west side, with a good anchorage in front of the Dutch fort. There is also a safe harbor on the east side of the island. Amboina is populated by families or tribes, each of which lives in a separate village, with its own leaders. For example, close to the Dutch fort live the families "Ateyves" (Hativi), "Tavires" (Tawiri), "Halon" (Alang), "Baguale" (Bagula), "Putu" (Paso?), and "Rossanives" (Rumah?), among others, each in its own village.[147] These are all Christians. The villages on the north side of the island are all Muslim. Amboina is fertile and healthful, with excellent water. There are enough sago trees, fruits, and fish that they do not have to import food. Rice grows on Amboina, but the constant wars between the villages frequently destroy the crops. The island yields about six hundred bahars of cloves each year, including those produced on the south coast of Ceram. If the land remained at peace and if the people would pluck the cloves, Matelief estimates it would produce twice as much. Much of the land is desolate, but he thinks clove trees could be planted on it. Amboina also grows ample wood for shipbuilding, and cordage can be made from coco palms.[148]

Following Matelief's description of Amboina in the *Begin ende voortgangh* is another brief description written by Frederick de Houtman, the governor.[149] He provides many details about the villages not found in Matelief's account. The island of Amboina is divided into two parts. The Dutch fort is on the smaller part, which has twenty villages and about two thousand able-bodied men, all Christians. The larger part has twenty-eight villages, four larger towns, and about fifteen hundred men, mostly Muslims and all under the control of "Hitto" (Hitu). "Captain Hitto," as he is called in most Dutch reports, is a vassal of the VOC. The Amboinese villages are divided into two alliances or parties, the "Olisivas" (*ulisivas*) and the "Olilimas" (*uli-*

---

[146] Matelief, *loc. cit.* (n. 92), pp. 55–56.
[147] For these identifications see the map in Jacobs (ed.), *op. cit.* (n. 8), I, facing p. 36*.
[148] Matelief, *loc. cit.* (n. 92), pp. 57–58.
[149] *Ibid.,* pp. 58–61.

limas). Most Muslims are "Olilimas"; the "Olisivas" party includes Muslim, heathen, and Christian villages. Each village, says De Houtman, has its own language. He goes on to list each of the villages on each island, the party to which it belongs, its religion, and the number of its fighting men.

Gillis Seys' "Verhael" resulted from his official inspection tour of Amboina in 1627.[150] It is a mine of detailed information about the Dutch establishment on the island. He describes the fort in fine detail, its redoubts, cannons, food supplies, personnel, and so forth. He lists each village on each island, the religion of each village, the number of able-bodied men, and the amount of cloves produced annually. He lists each Dutch establishment in the islands and the personnel of each. Some of this duplicates the reports of Matelief and Frederick de Houtman, but it is more thorough and shows some of the changes which had occurred between 1607 and 1627. For example, Seys reports that few cloves are being produced, but that many new trees have been planted during the last five or six years which are beginning to mature.[151] He reports that the Ternatans tyrannize some of the villages on Ceram, where they as well as the Dutch have an establishment. Then he describes how the people of Ceram flee to the mountains to avoid Company service, living on snakes, roots, bats, and the like, clothing themselves with leaves, killing anyone who comes looking for them. Both Muslim and Christian Amboinese are unbelievably afraid of these mountain people.[152]

Seys' report indicates how restive both the sultan of Ternate and the Amboinese had become under Dutch rule and under the VOC clove monopoly. There are constant attempts to circumvent the monopoly, usually by shipping the cloves in *cora-coras* to villages and beaches on the north coast of Ceram where they are sold at night to merchants from Makassar. The Makassarese will pay 100 to 120 pieces of eight per bahar; the VOC's monopoly price is 60. No Amboinese leader is more effective in circumventing the monopoly than "Captain Hittoe." He is never guilty of any provable violation of the treaty with the VOC, but he is most effective in arranging for the sale of the cloves to Makassarese, Malays, and Javans. As Seys sees it, Captain Hitu is the VOC's public friend but private enemy. His goal is to convert all Amboinese to Islam, detach them from the Dutch, and sell all the cloves to Makassarese for 100 to 120 pieces of eight per bahar. Seys recommends burning villages, raiding beaches, harrassing leaders, and destroying cloves on Ceram until it is widely known that no cloves can be purchased there.[153]

The religious situation on Amboina has improved a little. Services are regularly held in both Dutch and Malay, but rather poorly attended by the

---

[150] "Verhael van de tegenwoordigen staet inde quartieren van Amboyna, ende omleggende plaetsen," appended to Verhoeff's voyage, *BV*, IIa, 130–51.

[151] *Ibid.*, p. 133.

[152] *Ibid.*, pp. 134–35.

[153] *Ibid.*, pp. 137–38, 140–42.

Dutch. Seys complains that the VOC employees and free citizens generally set a poor example for the Amboinese Christians. Malay services are better attended, usually by two hundred to three hundred people, and they include a question from the catechism for the children to answer. Seys observes that no Christian mission to the Muslims on Amboina has been undertaken. One problem is that the pastors and schoolmasters do not stay on Amboina very long, and it takes replacements one year before they know enough Malay to work effectively. Sixteen schools are now open on the islands, but the schoolmasters complain that they have no paper for the students and that the Amboinese frequently withdraw their children from school to work at home when they are ten or eleven years old.[154]

During the early 1660's three non-Dutch works carried brief descriptions of Amboina: Johann Jacob Saar's *Ost-Indianische fünfzehen-jährige Kriegs-Dienste* (1662), Merklein's *Journal oder Beschreibung* (1663), and Colin's *Labor evangélica* (1663).[155] Saar and Merklein were both employees of the VOC; both served in Asia between 1644 and 1659.[156] Saar's is the largest description of the three, but none of them adds anything significant to Europe's image of Amboina. Colin thinks Amboinese cloves are less perfect than those grown in the Moluccas and that the people are thinner than Moluccans or Bandanese.[157] Saar thinks the Amboinese are darker—"blackish brown"—than Javans.[158] Saar, like most Europeans, describes sago bread and how it is made. He is perhaps more candid about its flavor than most: even freshly baked it is poor food, like wool. Only need drives one to it. When it becomes old it can only be eaten when soaked in water or soup. White sago from Ceram is somewhat more palatable than other varieties.[159] He also describes, in vivid detail, the Amboinese pox, for which he contends the islands are infamous. It afflicts some on the forehead, some on the limbs, or neck. To treat it they wrap the lesions with datura leaves or wash them in seawater and rub them with lemon juice. Victims must avoid all hot foods. Some people get it every year; some two or three times a year; Saar does not speculate about the cause of the Amboinese pox.[160]

Merklein reports the Amboinese revolts against the Dutch in 1651. Some Dutch soldiers were killed and some forts and outposts seized. Arnold de Vlamingh van Oudshoorn was sent with a fleet of ten ships and fourteen

[154] *Ibid.*, pp. 149–51. The *Begin ende voortgangh* also includes the text of two 1609 contracts between Captain Hitu and Dutch authorities, *ibid.*, pp. 197–99, as well as a 1638 contract between the Dutch and the sultan of Ternate and his Amboinese subjects, *ibid.*, pp. 209–14.
[155] For bibliography see above, pp. 353, 529–31.
[156] Both left the Netherlands in 1644. Merklein returned to Europe in 1653, Saar in 1659.
[157] Pastells (ed.), *op. cit.* (n. 101), I, 113.
[158] Johann Jacob Saar, *Reise nach Java, Banda, Ceylon, und Persien, 1644–1660* . . . (NR, VI; The Hague, 1930), p. 46.
[159] *Ibid.*, pp. 46–47. On Ceram sago see Wallace, *op. cit.* (n. 33), pp. 289–92.
[160] Saar, *op. cit.* (n. 158), p. 47. This is the skin disease now known as yaws. The early physicians saw a relationship between it and the "Spanish pox" (syphilis). See R. D. G. Ph. Simons (ed.), *Handbook of Tropical Dermatology* (Amsterdam, 1952), I, 270–73.

hundred men to restore order. Although progress had been made the task was not yet completed when Merklein left for Europe in 1653.[161] Vlamingh had become governor of Amboina in 1647, but was in Batavia when the revolt broke out in 1651. He and his predecessors had heavy-handedly tried to enforce the VOC monopoly of the spice trade for decades before 1651, usually by destroying villages and food supply on the north coast of Ceram where much of the smuggling took place and by destroying clove trees in areas outside the Company's control. These tactics were intensified by Vlamingh when he returned to Amboina in 1651, and Amboinese opposition and smuggling were ruthlessly suppressed. Order was restored by 1659, although "smuggling" continued to plague the VOC until the final conquest of Makassar in 1669.[162]

Most of the descriptions of Amboina published during the last quarter of the century—all written either by Dutchmen or German employees of the VOC—reflect post-1659 conditions. Gerret Vermeulen, whose book was published in 1677, visited Amboina during the 1670's. He mentions no troubles with the natives. The Dutch governor of Amboina, he reports, has jurisdiction over all of the Moluccas. He mentions the usual natural products of Amboina but seems most intrigued by the legless birds of paradise which die if they alight on the land, and a kind of parrot which cleverly builds its nests in tall dead trees which men dare not climb because of the red ants which infest them. Regarding the Amboinese people, Vermeulen observes that when a woman marries, the bridegroom gives money to her father, and that young couples sleep together for a year before marriage to see if the woman is fruitful. Vermeulen thinks Amboina is a healthful place except for the pox, which he thinks is spread by a certain kind of fly and cannot be cured.[163]

Although his book was published in 1676, Wouter Schouten had visited Amboina in 1659, before the complete suppression of the rebellion. In fact, the ship on which he served participated in punitive expeditions to Buru and Ceram. Schouten provides detailed accounts of them. Native princes are required to provide soldiers for the expeditions. Schouten describes the process on Buru. When the Dutch attack "Arakky" (Hatuwe?) on Ceram, for example, the inhabitants flee to the mountains. The Dutch burn the village, cut down all fruit and sago trees, and kill or carry off as slaves whomever they find. Their Amboinese allies take the heads of fallen enemies as trophies with which to decorate their *cora-cora*s or to give to their wives. They

---

[161] Johann Jacob Merklein, *Reise nach Java, Vorder- und Hinter-Indien, China und Japan, 1644–1653* (NR, III; The Hague, 1930), p. 91.

[162] Bernard H. M. Vlekke, *Nusantara; A History of Indonesia* (rev. ed., Chicago, 1960), pp. 166–68; E. S. de Klerck, *History of the Netherlands East Indies* (2 vols.; Rotterdam, 1938), I, 242–44, 255–57. On the conquest of Makassar see below, pp. 1442, 1446–48.

[163] Vermeulen, *op. cit.* (n. 110), 81–84. For bibliography see above, pp. 498–99. On the birds of paradise, see Wallace, *op. cit.* (n. 33), pp. 419–40.

also roast and eat parts of their bodies, but in secret because the Dutch commanders forbid it. Everywhere they go, the Dutch burn villages, ruin fruit and sago trees, and cruise to intercept any boats from Makassar attempting to buy cloves.[164]

Because he accompanied the expeditions, Schouten was able to visit parts of the Amboina islands other than the area around Victoria Castle on Amboina. The small island of "Goram" (Gorong) on the southeast coast of Ceram, for example, is heavily wooded and mountainous, with deep valleys, morasses, and caves in the interior. Its people are naked except for loincloths, live in reed huts, and subsist on dried fish and sago. They are untrustworthy, bloodthirsty, and stubborn.[165] Buru, too, has high mountains and deep forests, but also clear pure streams and fruitful farms which produce coconuts, pinang (areca nut), bananas, beans, cajan (a legume), tobacco, sweet potatoes, and green vegetables. The people, mostly brought in by the Dutch, live in fourteen small villages around the "Bay of Cayelle" (Cayeli) on the northeast coast. They wear only loincloths. Women wash their newborn babies in the river, lay them in a sort of hammock, and return to their work. After funerals they hold a feast, eating, drinking, singing, and dancing late into the night. Some of the people are beginning to follow Islam, although many still worship crocodiles. They tell the story of a large crocodile which came ashore each day to eat people but which fell in love with the king's daughter. It promised to harm the people no longer but instead to protect them if they would give it the king's daughter. Which done, the island became safe and fruitful and its people still revere all crocodiles. They are much distressed and afraid when the Dutch kill them.[166]

Schouten's description of Amboina itself is vivid, as are all of his descriptions, but it adds very little to what was already in print. He revels in the scenery: high mountains, deep forests, clear streams, spectacular views. Victoria, the Dutch fort, is built on a good, deep harbor; it has a fine market town and many villages nearby. People from many nations live there. He of course describes cloves and comments on the paucity of food, which he thinks results not from the poverty of the land but from the laziness of its people, who would rather live poorly than work hard.[167] Schouten's account also contains descriptions of many other islands as seen from the sea, as well as of terrible storms, an earthquake, and waterspouts, some of which are a bit repetitious. Johann Christian Hoffman, although he never visited Amboina, included a very vivid account of a severe earthquake which shook

---

[164] Schouten, *op. cit.* (n. 111), I, 53–61.

[165] *Ibid.*, p. 60.

[166] *Ibid.*, pp. 72–73. Wild crocodiles have become virtually extinct in many parts of today's Indonesia. *Cf.* the reverence for crocodiles in the Philippines, below, p. 1505.

[167] *Ibid.*, pp. 76–78. Wallace, *op. cit.* (n. 33), pp. 226, 230, agrees regarding Amboinese laziness.

Amboina on February 17, 1674. It was taken from a letter written by an eyewitness.[168]

Johann Nieuhof also visited Amboina in 1659. His account includes a brief historical sketch of how the islands came into Dutch hands, but does not detail any military expeditions. Nieuhof describes the Dutch castle, cloves, sago, *cora-coras*, weapons, and the nature of the people, all in familiar terms. He describes the Amboinese pox (yaws) in much detail and insists that although it is similar to the Spanish pox (syphilis), it is not contracted through sexual intercourse. He thinks it is caused by a combination of the hot damp climate with a diet of sea fish and sago. The only unique features about Nieuhof's description of the Amboinese people are what he says about the women: wives are purchased from the woman's parents, they are lascivious and prefer Christians, and they use a poison which kills very slowly, makes the victim impotent, but can be reversed if the antidote is given by the same woman who administered the poison.[169] Nieuhof's description of Buru seems to have come from Schouten.[170]

Johann Sigmund Wurffbain visited Amboina in 1632 and 1633, during which time he took part in punitive expeditions to Manipa, Ceram, and Ceram Laut or Little Ceram off the east coast. His account of these actions resembles Wouter Schouten's. The Dutch always burned the villages, destroyed the clove, fruit, and sago trees, and burned the villagers' boats. Wurffbain also reports cannibalism among the VOC's Amboinese allies; he claims to have actually witnessed it.[171] Wurffbain's description of Amboina mostly repeats what, by 1686, was well known. He credits the Dutch for the large number of Christians on Amboina and describes the special felt hats given by the Dutch to "Radjas" and "Orang Kajas" who have become Christian. They trail ribbons on which are written in gold or silver letters "Subject of the illustrious high and mighty lords, States [General] and Nassau." Over or under the last word is depicted a pair of folded hands. Despite these honors, Wurffbain reports, some still desert the faith and revert to heathen practices. Wurffbain also lists what he calls the peculiar troubles and diseases of Amboina: earthquakes, the Amboinese pox,

---

[168]Johann Christian Hoffman, *Reise nach dem Kaplande, nach Mauritius, und nach Java, 1671–1676* (NR, VII; The Hague, 1931), pp. 67–71. For bibliography of his *Oost-Indianische Voyage* (1680) see above, p. 538.

[169]Johann Nieuhof, *Gedenkwaerdige zee- en lant-reize door de vornaemste landschappen van West en Oostindien* (Amsterdam, 1682), pp. 27–38. For bibliography see above, pp. 500–501. Nieuhof's description of the Amboinese pox is very similar to that of Jacob Bontius: *An Account of the Diseases, Natural History and Medicines of the East Indies*, in *Opuscula selecta Neerlandicorum de arte medica* (Amsterdam, 1931), X, 181–83.

[170]Nieuhof, *op. cit.* (n. 169), pp. 24–27.

[171]Johann Sigmund Wurffbain, *Reise nach den Molukken und vorder-Indien* (2 vols.; NR, VIII, IX; The Hague, 1931), I, 80–91; see p. 88 for cannibalism. For bibliography see above, pp. 523–25.

beriberi, and a peculiar kind of night blindness and painful swelling of the face thought to be caused by the moon shining on one's face.[172]

Nikolaas de Graaf visited Amboina twice, once in 1644 and again in 1683. His description of the 1644 visit is very brief and contains no new information. His observation about the laziness of the Amboinese—"they would rather live in poverty than do hard work"—may well have been taken from Schouten.[173] His account of his 1683 visit is not much more informative, but it suggests the extent of Dutch control. He lists forts on most of the islands and describes Fort Victoria on Amboina in detail. The town outside the fort now contains a city hall, a house of correction for women (*Spinhuis*), a hospital, and an orphanage, as well as the two churches—the essential ingredients of a Dutch colonial town.[174]

3

THE BANDAS

While the Portuguese landed in the Banda Islands early in the sixteenth century, they did not establish themselves there. The Moluccas, Ternate and Tidore, became the major focus of their attention in the Spiceries, and Banda appears to have been outside the imperial claims of both these Moluccan powers. Nevertheless, Portuguese merchants traded in Banda throughout the sixteenth century, and in 1529 Portuguese soldiers began building a fort on Banda Neira. The fort was never completed, however, and for the rest of the century the Portuguese purchased nutmegs and mace from local traders who brought them north to Ternate and Tidore.[175] The Iberians, consequently, wrote little about Banda. Barros included a very brief account,[176] but even Argensola's 1609 description is largely dependent on the earliest Dutch accounts.[177] Colin, as late as 1663, essentially repeated Barros' description.[178]

In the seventeenth century the Bandas quickly became a Dutch preserve. Two ships under the command of Jacob van Heemskerk, part of Van Neck and Van Warwijck's fleet, traded for nutmegs there in 1599. They left

[172] Wurffbain, *op. cit.* (n. 171), I, 71–80. For a later description of the Amboinese mixture of Catholic, Protestant, and pagan religious practices, see Wallace, *op. cit.* (n. 33), pp. 230–31.
[173] Warnsinck (ed.), *op. cit.* (n. 118), pp. 24–25.
[174] *Ibid.*, pp. 212–15.
[175] W. E. Hanna, *Indonesian Banda; Colonialism and Its Aftermath in the Nutmeg Islands* (Philadelphia, 1978), pp. 1–11.
[176] See *Asia*, I, 609.
[177] *Op. cit.* (n. 5), pp. 238–44.
[178] Pastells (ed.), *op. cit.* (n. 101), I, 112–13.

twenty-two men in two lodges to continue the trade after the fleet departed. The first monopolistic contract between the VOC and the *orang kayas* of several Bandanese villages was signed in May, 1602. In the Bandas the Dutch met competition and opposition not from the Spanish or Portuguese but from the English, who first arrived there in 1601, and from the Bandanese, who refused to honor the monopolistic contracts with the VOC either because they did not understand what they had promised or because they gradually realized that exclusive trade with the Dutch threatened their independence and indeed their livelihood.

The Dutch repeatedly tried to enforce the monopoly. The Bandanese made and broke agreements but generally seemed determined to evade the monopoly. The English encouraged Bandanese resistance, sometimes supplying the Bandanese with arms. Hostilities became intense after 1609 when Admiral Pieter Willemszoon Verhoeff and his entire council were ambushed and killed after having been invited to confer with the Bandanese *orang kayas* about the terms of a new treaty. The Dutch built forts and took reprisals: seizing and burning coastal villages and boats and blockading ports to deprive the Bandanese of foodstuffs. The Bandanese sometimes resisted valiantly, sometimes besieged the Dutch fort at Neira, and sometimes made peace and signed new contracts which they quickly disregarded. The English meanwhile fortified themselves on some of the smaller islands (Pulau Run and Pulau Ai), traded with the Bandanese in violation of their agreements with the VOC, and in many other ways provoked the Dutch. Finally in 1621 VOC Governor-General Jan Pieterszoon Coen massively invaded the islands, killed or deported most of the Bandanese, executed the leading *orang kayas*, and drove the English out.[179] Coen then divided the islands, except for Pulau Run, into allotments called *perken* and leased them to Dutch free burgers, former VOC employees who had remained in the Indies after their terms of service were completed. The *perkeniers,* as the leaseholders were called, were required to maintain the land and to deliver the nutmeg crop at fixed prices. The VOC provided rice and other imported necessities at cost and provided slaves to work the nutmeg plantations.[180]

The earliest Dutch descriptions of Banda, therefore, are crucially important not only to the seventeenth-century European image of Banda but also, after 1621, to any history of the Banda Islands. Dutch occupation changed the islands considerably. Visitors after 1621, for instance, could learn little

---

[179] Coen allowed the English to remain on Pulau Neijalakka, a coral islet just off Pulau Run, and seemed to half acknowledge their claim to Pulau Run. He cut down all the nutmeg trees on Pulau Run, however. The English remained there until 1628 but were unable to trade. They continued to claim Pulau Run, however, and occasionally tried to reestablish themselves there. Not until the Treaty of Breda in 1667 did they formally cede Pulau Run to the Dutch. See Hanna, *op. cit.* (n. 175), pp. 64–66.

[180] *Ibid.,* pp. 11–78. See also Luc Kiers, *Coen op Banda; de conqueste getoetst aan het recht van den tijd* (Utrecht, 1943), and De Klerck, *op. cit.* (n. 162), I, 211–12, 229–30.

about the Bandanese people, because so few of them remained in the islands and those who did were enslaved. Unfortunately, most of the accounts written by Europeans who visited the Bandas before 1621 contain little description of the islands and the people. Of these *Het tweede boeck,* the earliest Dutch account, is the most extensive.[181] The writer of *Het tweede boeck* locates Banda at 4½° south latitude, twenty-four miles from Amboina. It is divided into three parts which taken together are about five square miles in area.[182] Banda's principal city is "Nera" (Neira), and merchants from many surrounding islands and places as far away as Java, Malacca, and China come there to purchase nutmegs. Merchants often stay for two or three months before they have a cargo, for which time they usually purchase local women to serve them. When they leave, the women are left free until the merchants return.[183]

Nutmegs grow nowhere in the world except on the Banda Islands. The writer mentions "Lontor" (Lonthor), "Nera" (Neira), "Gunnanappi" (Gunung Api), "Pulovvay" (Pulau Ai), and "Pulore" (Pulau Run). He also mentions "Ortatan" (Orantatta), "Comber" (Combir), and "Wayer" (Wajo), which are not islands but villages (*kampongs*) on Lonthor. He does not mention Rozengain. Nutmegs ripen three times each year: in April, August, and December. The April crop is the largest and the best. The nutmeg tree looks much like a peach tree, although its leaves are shorter and rounder.[184] The fruit is covered with a thick shell which breaks open when it is ripe—exposing the red mace and the nut itself. When dried, the mace separates from the nut and turns almost orange. Nutmeg strengthens and warms the stomach, reducing stomach gas. It helps digest food and "consumes all cold dampness." A plaster made from pulverized mace mixed with rose oil placed on the chest also aids digestion. *Het tweede boeck* also contains a sketch of the nutmeg leaves, blossoms, and fruit, as well as a map of Banda.[185]

The Bandanese are devout Muslims, frequently going to the mosque for prayers. Soldiers pray in the mosque before and after guard duty. The prayers are so loud they can be heard as far as twenty houses away. No one goes into the mosque without washing their feet. Outside the mosque they use prayer rugs on which to say silent prayers in their homes, on the streets, on the beaches, or in their *cora-coras*. These prayers follow a routine: after spreading the rug on the floor they stand on it and cast their eyes upwards

---

[181] For bibliography see above, pp. 439–41.
[182] Keuning (ed.), *op. cit.* (n. 4), III, 76. The distance from Amboina is in fact thirty German miles. Banda Neira lies at 4°32′ south latitude. The area of the three islands is forty-four square kilometers. The three islands referred to are Neira, Lonthor or Great Banda, and Gunung Api; this entire group is comprised within a space seven miles long and three miles wide.
[183] *Ibid.,* p. 77.
[184] Argensola, *op. cit.* (n. 5), p. 239, says it is like a pear.
[185] Keuning (ed.), *op. cit.* (n. 4), III, 77–82. For the map see our pl. 237.

two or three times, after which they fall to their knees and touch their heads to the rug two or three times.[186] They eat frequent common meals in the mosque, each one paying for his share of the food. Such common meals are also eaten in the woods, especially when there are governmental affairs to discuss. Sometimes as many as a hundred people attend, and they seem to enjoy themselves a great deal.[187] They also enjoy a football game in which the players stand in a circle with one in the center who throws a ball made of reeds to the others who must then kick it in the air. The Dutch are impressed by the players' ability to twist, turn, and leap kicking the ball at the same time. Sometimes the ball soars almost out of sight. If a player misses it, however, the others laugh and ridicule him.[188]

Life on Banda is not all idyllic, however. Villages less than a mile apart, Neira and "Labbetacke" (?), make constant war on each other. Their quarrel apparently began many years ago when people from "Labbetacke" cut down some trees in the area tended by the people of Neira. The war is viciously fought and the enemies offer each other no quarter. They keep constant watch during the night for fear of attack. While the Dutch were at Neira, the people from "Labbetacke" attacked the town, killing and wounding several people. Early the next morning, soldiers from Neira in five *cora-coras* attacked not "Labbetacke," but the little island of "Wayger," whose people were allies of "Labbetacke." They killed most of the people, except for a few women whom they took back to Neira. One was cruelly cut down as the Dutch watched. They also returned with the heads of their slain enemies which, after displaying them, they wrapped in white cloth and ceremoniously buried. Incense was burned at the grave just as if they had been people from Neira, although no relatives came to mourn and pray at the grave, which the Dutch discovered was ordinarily done at Bandanese burials. The Bandanese are brave warriors. They fight with guns, long shields, large swords called "padangs" (Malay, *pedang*), small wooden spears which they throw, and small harpoon-like weapons with cords attached to them. They wear helmets like coxcombs with bird of paradise plumage to protect themselves, or so they believe. Some wear back- and breastplates. At sea their *cora-coras* become formidable weapons, carrying two small brass cannons and rowed very swiftly by slaves who sit in the outriggers. Soldiers pride themselves on how far they can leap out from the boat with all their weapons, all of which is accompanied by much shouting and beating of drums.[189] There are some very old people on Banda; one, whom the Dutch saw frequently, is claimed to be 130 years old. Women do most of the work,

---

[186] *Ibid.*, pp. 82–83.
[187] *Ibid.*, p. 83.
[188] *Ibid.*, pp. 84–85. This game is called *sepak takraw*, the most universal indigenous amusement in Southeast Asia. See Savage, *op. cit.* (n. 51), p. 117. Also see Reid, *op. cit.* (n. 37), pp. 199–201, and W. W. Skeat, *Malay Magic* (London, 1900), p. 483. See our pl. 259.
[189] Keuning (ed.), *op. cit.* (n. 4), III, 73, 83–90.

harvesting and drying the nutmeg and many other tasks. The men do the soldiering and "walk along the street." [190] The other Dutch reports about Banda written during the first half of the seventeenth century concentrate on events: on the negotiations with Bandanese *orang kayas* and the monopolistic treaties signed with them, on Bandanese perfidy and their continuous violation of the treaties, on the constant English interference and provocation, on Admiral Verhoeff's tragic experience and the subsequent events culminating finally in Coen's 1621 conquest of the islands. Paulus van Solt, who commanded one of the ships of Van der Hagen's fleet, visited the Bandas in 1607. His account, first published in the *Begin ende voortgangh,* describes many of the earlier negotiations. [191] The *Begin ende voortgangh* account of Verhoeff's voyage contains a detailed account of the tragic events of 1609 and 1610. [192] Finally an overview of the events between 1609 and 1621 and a detailed account of Coen's invasion, stressing throughout the hostile role of the English, was published as the *Waerachtich verhael van't geene inde eylanden van Banda . . . inden jaere sestien-hondert eenentwintich . . .* in 1622. [193] It was translated into English during the same year and was also appended to the *Begin ende voortgangh* account of Jacques L'Hermite's voyage. [194] A similar report of Coen's conquest of the Banda Islands and the events leading up to it was published in Nicolaes van Wassenaer's newspaper in 1622. [195] Of these, only Solt's account contains a very brief descriptive insert. [196] It correctly names all the islands, adding Pulau Pisang, and briefly describes nutmeg, observing that at any time during the year the trees carry blossoms, green nutmegs, and ripe nutmegs simultaneously. Banda, Solt reports, is very deficient in foodstuffs. Nevertheless durians, "Nances" (ananas or pineapples), bananas, oranges, and coconuts grow there. Rice and other necessities are imported from Makassar and sago is obtained from Ceram.

The German Johann Verken was stationed in the Bandas from 1609 to 1611, and his 1612 *Beschreibung* provides a very detailed account of Dutch activities there, including Verhoeff's death. It contains, however, almost no mention of the islands or the people, apart from naming the islands and contending that they are the best and most valuable in all of the Orient because of the nutmegs. He estimates that from ten to twelve thousand people live in the islands. [197]

---

[190] *Ibid.,* p. 90.
[191] For bibliography see above, pp. 466–67.
[192] For bibliography, see above, pp. 470–71.
[193] See above, p. 449.
[194] See *BV,* IIb, 75–79.
[195] Wassenaer, *Historisch verhael alder ghedenck-weerdichste geschiedenisse . . . ,* II (Feb., 1622), 81–85. See also G. Seys, *loc. cit.* (n. 94), pp. 191–95.
[196] Paulus van Solt, "Verhael ende journael vande voyagie. . . . ," *BV,* IIa, 79.
[197] Johann Verken, *Molluken-Reise, 1607–1612 . . .* (NR, II; The Hague, 1930), pp. 73–74. For bibliography see above, p. 519. The population of the pre-Dutch era is usually estimated at around fifteen thousand. See *Encyclopaedie van Nederlandsch-Indië* (n. 39), I, 133.

Many English ships traded in the Banda Islands prior to the 1621 Dutch conquest. Accounts of several of these voyages were published by Samuel Purchas in 1625. William Keeling was there in 1609–10, John Saris in 1613, and Thomas Spurway in 1616–17. Nathaniel Courthop commanded the English forces on Pulau Run and the islet of Neijalakka from 1616 to 1620, when he was killed by a Dutch bullet. His account was continued by Robert Hayes. Humphrey Fitzherbert was there in 1621.[198] These pieces contain voluminous detail about English trade negotiations with the Bandanese and about Dutch activities in the Bandas, but they contain very little description of the islands or the people. Even Fitzherbert's "Pithy Description" contains more recitals of events than discussion of the islands. Nevertheless he remarks on the "very fair and spacious Harbour" formed by Lonthor, Neira, and the volcano Gunung Api. The latter he describes as barren, "at the top yeelding nothing but cinders, fire and smoake; on the surface below, woods without water or fruit for the sustenance of the life of man."[199] The volcano's eruptions often destroy forests on Gunung Api, and they sometimes throw ash and boulders on Neira as well. All of the Bandas suffer frequent earthquakes. The Dutch castle at Neira is large and strongly built, but poorly situated with a high hill rising behind it. To overcome this disadvantage the Dutch have built a smaller fort on the hill, but it, too, is vulnerable because still another hill overlooks it.[200] Lonthor is the largest and richest of the Bandas but is almost inaccessible from the sea. Since the Dutch have conquered it, they have been building a fort on it.[201] Pulau Ai is a paradise: "There is not a tree on that Island but the nutmeg, and other delicate fruits of superfluitie; and withall, full of pleasant walkes, so that the whole country seems a contrived Orchard with varieties." But it has no water; its people must either collect rainwater or carry water from the other islands. Its coast is steep and dangerous, having only one possible anchorage and that not at all safe. The Dutch have built a strong castle on it. Pulau Run is neither beautiful nor fruitful, but the Dutch have conquered it also.[202] Fitzherbert does not mention Rozengain. Thomas Spurway's account in Purchas contains a very brief account of Pulau Run. It is judged to be the worst island, he reports, but it nonetheless produces "a prettie store of Mace and Nuts" and would produce still more if better tended. Lonthor and Rozengain produce the most nutmegs, the largest amount coming from Rozengain. What is more, he reports, if the English could continue to hold Pulau Run the Bandanese would bring all the nutmegs they needed over from Lonthor.[203]

[198] For bibliography see above, pp. 558, 560–61, 565–66.
[199] Fitzherbert, *loc. cit.* (n. 86), p. 174.
[200] *Ibid.*, p. 175.
[201] *Ibid.*, pp. 174–75.
[202] *Ibid.*, pp. 176–77.
[203] "A Letter from Master Thomas Spurway, Merchant, touching the wrongs done at Banda to the English by the Hollanders . . . Bantam . . . 1617," *PP*, IV, 532.

Concerning the Bandanese people, one characteristic emerges clearly from all of the pre-1621 accounts, both Dutch and English: their stubborn independence. Against overwhelming Dutch power they seem determined to maintain their freedom. They fight courageously, make peace with the enemy when they must, but break the treaties to fight again when they can. They try to enlist English support by formally surrendering their lands to the English king; they smuggle the nutmegs off the islands to sell them to the English or even to the Portuguese at Makassar; they ambush the Dutch when they find an opportunity and sometimes even besiege the Dutch fort on Neira. But by 1622 most of them have either been killed or enslaved, and their islands are firmly in Dutch hands.

Those who visited the Banda Islands after 1621 had far fewer interesting events to report. To the VOC chaplain Seyger van Rechteren, who served at Celamme on Lonthor during 1630 and 1631, the outstanding events were the rice shortage in 1630 when the supply ship from Batavia was wrecked, and the earthquakes that took place on June 21 and July 17, 1630, and in April, 1631.[204] Wurffbain, who spent five years on Banda, also reported earthquakes, as well as a twenty-four-foot snake that ate a slave woman and her two children, a tidal wave, an unusual catch of fishes, and an English ship anchoring off Pulau Run.[205] For the most part, however, Wurffbain's noteworthy events are the arrival and departure of ships and the arrest and punishment of malefactors.

Van Rechteren's description reflects the changes which accompanied VOC occupation. He names and locates the six main islands but then describes the Dutch forts and strongholds on each of the islands: two forts on Neira, a fort and five strongholds on Lonthor, a fort on Pulau Ai, and a stronghold on Pulau Run and on Rozengain.[206]

No one lives on Gunung Api, whose volcano smokes day and night. An eruption some years ago threw so many rocks into the channel between Gunung Api and Neira (the Sonnegat) that sailing ships can no longer navigate it. It used to be twenty fathoms deep.[207] Van Rechteren describes not only nutmeg and mace but also the *perken* and the VOC system of nutmeg production.[208] He describes large snakes, parrots, cockatoos, "Indian ravens" (*corwue coras?*), and a bird called "Lo" by the natives which eats only nutmegs.[209] Concerning the people on Banda, Van Rechteren says very little. He briefly describes the funeral practices of both the Muslims and the "Indian Christians." But he reports that the native Bandanese, because they

---

[204] Seyger van Rechteren, "Journael gehouden . . . ," *BV*, IIb, 31, 33. Van Rechteren's *Journael* was first published in 1635; for bibliography see above, pp. 453–55.

[205] Wurffbain, *op. cit.* (n. 171), I, 96, 94, 139–40, 95, 157.

[206] Van Rechteren, *loc. cit.* (n. 204), p. 32.

[207] *Ibid.* Probably a reference to the eruption of 1629. See below, p. 1435.

[208] Van Rechteren, *loc. cit.* (n. 204), p. 33.

[209] *Ibid.*, p. 35. Wallace, *op. cit.* (n. 33), p. 233, calls the "Lo" a fruit pigeon, *Carpohaga concinna*.

always dealt so treacherously with the Dutch, have been "completely dispersed, leaving no child nor even suckling in the whole land but was carried away, killed, or enslaved."[210]

Johann Jacob Saar was in the Bandas in 1646; his book was published in 1662.[211] He describes the inhabitants as dressed like the Amboinese, except for a roll or coil on their heads. They are strong with curly hair and long beards; they are excellent warriors, using long shields, short broad swords, and blowguns. Saar describes the Dutch forts and garrisons, VOC nutmeg production, and methods of shipping. He reports widespread night blindness on Banda during June, July, and August, which can be cured by eating the liver of a fish called "Hay." A plant which looks like flax, called "chini" (Malay, *ginji*, or Indian hemp) on Banda, is pulverized and rolled in a "Pisan" (areca) leaf and smoked. Inhaling it causes hallucinations and giddiness. Under its influence, people seem especially prone to leap into any water and swim, which they ludicrously attempt even on wet ground. A little salt in the mouth, however, restores the senses. Excellent wild horses roam the island. When tamed, they are as fine as any Persian horse. The VOC maintains three hundred of them at their headquarters in Batavia.[212] In the Aru Islands live native Bandanese, driven there by the Dutch. They are mortal enemies of the Dutch and interfere with Dutch activities there. During an expedition to Aru which Saar accompanied, several Dutchmen were killed and beheaded by these Bandanese.[213] Gerret Vermeulen's *Gedenkwaerdige voyagie* (1677) also contains a brief description of the Banda Islands, the weather, and the nutmegs. About the people he merely reports that they look and dress like the Amboinese.[214]

The most thorough description of post-conquest Banda published in the last half of the seventeenth century is that by Wurffbain. He served in the Fort Nassau garrison on Banda Neira from 1633 until 1638, although his journal was not published definitively until 1686.[215] Like previous post-conquest writers Wurffbain describes each island, each Dutch fort and stronghold. He reports some things, however, which earlier writers had not mentioned. Pulau Ai, for example, has a fine castle but no water. At the castle they collect rainwater, but they also ship water in from other islands. Pulau Run is still claimed by the English, but it is of little use to them. The Dutch have destroyed all its nutmeg trees, and no one lives there. Because it was so difficult and costly to control, they also devastated Rozengain, the producer of the largest and best nutmegs. Gunung Api, the volcano, is unfruitful and unpopulated, although the VOC has established some tobacco

[210] Van Rechteren, *loc. cit.* (n. 204), pp. 32, 33.
[211] See above, pp. 529–30.
[212] Saar, *op. cit.* (n. 158), pp. 48–51.
[213] *Ibid.*, p. 56.
[214] Vermeulen, *op. cit.* (n. 110), pp. 84–86.
[215] His account of Banda is found in *op. cit.* (n. 171), I, 92–161. Most of it reports his day-to-day experiences.

plantations on one side of the island. A very small uninhabited islet between Gunung Api and Neira, "Frauen Insul" (Pulau Kraka), is famous for an exceedingly rich catch of fish—he calls them mackerel—which lasts for an entire month. The islands suffer repeated earthquakes and tidal waves; Wurffbain describes one in 1629 which destroyed homes, broke walls at the castle, and tossed a ship up on land. Natives believe the islands lie on the horns of a great ox which causes the earthquakes when it shakes its head.[216]

Nutmeg production is confined by the VOC to just three islands—Neira, Lonthor, and Pulau Ai—but these are almost unbelievably productive. In 1634, these three islands produced 666,744 pounds of nutmeg and 178,170 pounds of mace. During Wurffbain's five-year residence there the VOC shipped 3,097,209 pounds of nutmeg and 890,754 pounds of mace to Batavia.[217] Wurffbain, like most European visitors, describes the nutmeg trees and their fruit. In contrast to earlier writers, however, he reports that the third harvest of the year is the best. Once harvested, the mace is dried in the sun, the nuts over fire. The mace is mixed with salt or seawater to keep it from spoiling; the nuts are preserved in strong lime water. Then they are shipped to Batavia. Wurffbain also describes the *perken* and the obligations of the *perkeniers,* and observes that the VOC enjoys a total monopoly of nutmegs. Some cloves also grow in the Bandas, but the VOC regularly destroys the trees because enough of these are grown in the Moluccas and Amboina.[218]

Coconuts grow on the Banda Islands, some other fruit trees, and according to Wurffbain, tobacco. Banda's fauna includes both wild and tame cattle, small parrots called "lourys" (lories), cockatoos, and fruit pigeons. The pigeons are good to eat. There are many large snakes, five to ten feet long, but they are not poisonous (pythons). Pigs, goats, and chickens run wild. They have all been brought in from other lands, and they cause considerable damage. Wurffbain does not mention horses. From the surrounding seas are taken many kinds of fish unknown to Europeans. Many fishing techniques are used: some fisherman build fires in their boats at night to attract the fish; some drag iron or copper hooks along the bottom; some set out woven fish baskets; some use a poison which causes the fish to rise to the surface and die, although its use is now forbidden.[219]

Clothing and food are mostly imported from Batavia, Java, Ceram, and the Aru and Kai islands; they are mostly brought in VOC ships. Only from Kai and Aru is native trade with the Bandas permitted. Each year sixteen to twenty boats with eighty to one hundred men come from the Kai and Aru islands carrying sago, coconuts, coconut leaves, beans, peas, slaves, parrots, and birds of paradise. Contrary to popular belief, the birds of paradise have

[216] Wurffbain, *op. cit.* (n. 171), I, 92–98.
[217] *Ibid.,* p. 98.
[218] *Ibid.,* pp. 98–100.
[219] *Ibid.,* pp. 100–102.

feet. The people from Aru and Kai trade these products for cloth, iron, silver, and gold. Rice, salted meat, lard, olive oil, vinegar, wine, and the like are all imported from Batavia.[220] Wurffbain sketches the recent history of the Banda Islands. They used to be ruled by the king of Ternate, but the Bandanese frequently rebelled. Once free of the king of Ternate, each Bandanese village had its own chiefs or elders. Then came the Portuguese, English, and Dutch to trade for nutmegs. The Bandanese frequently stole their merchandise and killed their merchants. The Dutch then conquered the islands. Many Bandanese fled to surrounding islands. The rest were either killed in the war, carried off to Batavia, or enslaved. Thus the Bandanese people were completely scattered. Prior to the conquest they were Muslims in religion and expert warriors, especially with the sword and shield. They had good-looking bodies and were moderately intelligent—not much different from Javans.[221]

Since the conquest, the VOC has tried from time to time to set up an ecclesiastical and civil government on the model of Batavia. Efforts were made to evangelize the remaining population, and free schools were set up for that purpose. Initially quite a few became Christians and some learned to read and write Dutch. Most of these, however, have slipped back into the "blind heathendom" of their forefathers. Wurffbain does not describe the contemporary population of the Banda Islands, but he reports their numbers. In 1638, 3,842 people lived in the islands, not counting children under twelve years of age. He lists the population of each island and of each village on the large island of Lonthor. He also reports the numbers of Europeans, old-Bandanese, and other nationalities, and within each category the number of men, women, and children and whether they are slaves or free. Of the 3,842 people there are 560 old-Bandanese men, women, and children, of whom 280 are slaves.[222] Nikolaas de Graaf visited Banda some time after 1683, but his description of the islands is very brief and adds nothing to the other post-conquest descriptions.[223]

4

CELEBES

The large island of Celebes remained largely unknown during the seventeenth century. Some writers were even uncertain as to whether the name

---

[220] *Ibid.,* pp. 102–4, 108.
[221] *Ibid.,* pp. 104–5.
[222] *Ibid.,* pp. 105–7.
[223] Warnsinck (ed.), *op. cit.* (n. 118), pp. 215–17. For a much later description of the Bandas under Dutch rule see Wallace, *op. cit.* (n. 33), pp. 219–23. Most of his description of the islands and the nutmeg plantations agrees with those written during the seventeenth century. He con-

Celebes was applied to one island or to a group of islands.[224] Olivier van Noort did not describe Celebes, but the map of Borneo included in his account locates Makassar as the largest of several small islands off the east coast of Borneo, another of which is labeled "Bogis" (Bugis).[225] Wouter Schouten's 1676 account appears to be one of the earliest to describe Celebes unambiguously as a single island estimated to be three hundred Dutch miles in circumference.[226]

Argensola describes the inhabitants of Celebes as "filthy and vile in their behaviour." Each family or clan lives together in a single house, and the island "is full of little towns." The towns are "horrid stews of sodomy." They hang the hair of those whom they have killed in battle on their houses.[227] Argensola seems to include the natives of Celebes in a general description of people who live on the islands to the west of the Moluccas, who frequently wear no clothes, paint their bodies, wear their hair long in back or coiled but cut short over the forehead, and have well-shaped but blackened teeth and pierced ears. He further describes a strange tree of Celebes, the shade of which would kill any person who lies under its west side but which dire consequence could be avoided by quickly moving to the shade of its east side.[228] The insert in Roelofszoon's account of Van Neck's second voyage describes the inhabitants of Celebes as white-skinned people, formerly cannibals, idolators, and pirates, who run naked except for a small loincloth. "The King of the Moluccas torments those who have been condemned to death by sending them there [Celebes] for the inhabitants to eat."[229] None of these descriptions is firsthand.

Among the specific places on Celebes, apart from Makassar, Menado on the island's northeast promontory was frequently mentioned although seldom described. Colin calls it very populous—thirty to forty thousand people—and possessing abundant rice, legumes, crabs, and flocks, as well as copper and bronze. The people he reports are whiter than those of the Philippines or the Moluccas. The men go naked; women wear a cloth made from reeds that covers them from the waist to the knees. The women he describes as well featured. The people are heathen and very superstitious,

---

tends that the native Bandanese were Papuans. He also strongly defends the Dutch monopoly of the nutmegs, even their destroying trees on islands they could not effectively control.

[224] For example see Argensola, *op. cit.* (n. 5), pp. 71–72; Roelofszoon, *loc. cit.* (n. 90), pp. 5–6; and Colin in Pastells (ed.), *op. cit.* (n. 101), I, 2.

[225] J. W. Ijzerman (ed.), *De reis om de wereld door Olivier van Noort, 1598–1601* (2 vols.; "WLV," XXVII, XXVIII; The Hague, 1926), II, 127–28. See also Van Noort in *BV*, Ib, 50–51. For bibliography of Van Noort's account see above, pp. 441–43. Some of the Bugis possibly originated on the southwestern limb of Celebes in the area of Bone. For discussion see D. E. Sopher, *The Sea Nomads* (Singapore, 1964), pp. 357–58.

[226] *Op. cit.* (n. 111), I, 74–75.

[227] Argensola, *op. cit.* (n. 5), p. 72.

[228] *Ibid.* The legendary "poison" or "upas" tree of Makassar, *Arbor toxiaria*. See E. M. Beekman, *The Poison Tree. Selected Writings of Rumphius . . .* (Amherst, Mass., 1981), pp. 135–39.

[229] Roelofszoon, *loc. cit.* (n. 90), p. 5. See also Vermeulen, *op. cit.* (n. 110), pp. 37–39.

but friends to the Portuguese. They are cruel in warfare, killing all their captives.[230] Colin goes on to mention "Cauripe" (Kaidipan), on a large river where the warlike people dress like those of Tidore and Ternate. Kaidipan is well stocked with fruit, beans, and fish.[231] Not far away is "Bulan" (Bolaang), a town of about three hundred people, some of whom are Christians. They are enemies of Kaidipan and allies of the Dutch. They produce much rice but little fruit.[232]

Friar Domingo Navarrete's ill-starred voyage from Manila to Makassar in 1657 took eight months, from February 14 to October 17, much of which time was spent in towns along the north and west coasts of Celebes. He describes these towns and his experiences in them in the sixth book of his *Tratados* (1676).[233] After about six weeks of violent storms and navigational uncertainty, Navarrete's ship anchors at Tontoli on the north coast, where they find another ship at anchor. There is plenty of sago bread at Tontoli, although Navarrete does not like it very much. He recalls pitying poor Filipinos when scarcity forced them to eat it; now he and his shipmates are so hungry they consider it a "dainty." It is, he reports, "very like yellow Sand . . . sometimes it was insipid, sometimes had a taste; it is so tough it never breaks, tho it be drawn out a yard in length."[234] Navarrete meets the "king" of Tontoli, whose "Palace was a little House made of Canes and Straw, and in that Hovel he carry'd himself with unbelievable Majesty and all his People spoke to him prostrate on the Ground."[235] At the funeral of his son, the king wears wooden clogs and the queen walks barefoot. Small cannons are fired every half hour for twenty-four hours; the king secludes himself for several days and offers all his possessions for sale. No one, however, dares buy anything.[236]

From Tontoli, Navarrete sails to Kaili, on the west coast of Celebes which he locates at 1° south latitude.[237] At Kaili, Navarrete meets men who dress in women's clothing and are publicly married to other men. These transvestites are reportedly very rich, holding a local monopoly on the goldsmiths' craft.[238] Both men and women in Kaili wear paper clothing made from the

---

[230] Pastells (ed.), *op. cit.* (n. 101), I, 111. On the fair-skinned, head-hunting people of Menado, see Wallace, *op. cit.* (n. 33), pp. 185–86.

[231] Pastells (ed.), *op. cit.* (n. 101), I, 110–11. Kaidipan was the name of a *kampong* and its surroundings on the north coast. See Jacobs (ed.), *op. cit.* (n. 8), I, 414, n. 15.

[232] Pastells (ed.), *op. cit.* (n. 101), I, 111. Bolaang was the central town of the Bolaang-Mongondow country at the mouth of the Lombagin River. See Jacobs (ed.), *op. cit.* (n. 8), I, 414, n. 12.

[233] For bibliography see above, pp. 358–60.

[234] J. S. Cummins (ed.), *The Travels and Controversies of Friar Domingo Navarette* (2 vols.; "HS," 2d ser., CXVIII, CXVIX; Cambridge, 1962), I, 106–7.

[235] *Ibid.*, p. 107.

[236] *Ibid.*

[237] Kaili or Kajeli is the common name for the coastal strip along the Strait of Makassar.

[238] Cummins (ed.), *op. cit.* (n. 234), I, p. 109. Navarrete apparently encountered the transvestite *Bissu* who enjoyed an official status in Bugis society and religion. They functioned in a variety of religious ceremonies as sexually neutral intermediaries between the people and their

bark of a tree (the paper mulberry, *Broussonetia papyrifera*). The women seem continuously to be beating the bark into paper cloth of varying degrees of fineness and dying it in a great variety of colors. The paper clothing is warm in cold weather but rain destroys it. Consequently, when it rains, people strip and carry their clothes under their arms. The men seem to be kept busy making coconut oil, both to sell and to ship as tribute to the king of Makassar. The Kaili area also produces a great number of bananas—the best in the world, Navarrete reports. Bananas are the staple of Kaili's diet; they grow no rice or other grain. They also raise buffaloes, goats, and horses, which they sell. At public meetings they roast a couple of buffaloes, some of which is eaten half-roasted, some raw. According to Navarrete the people of Kaili would happily submit to the Spanish in order to escape the tyranny of Makassar.[239] En route from Kaili to Makassar, Navarrete mentions Mamoiu and Mandar, towns on the west coast, and observes that the nearer one comes to Makassar the more civilized the people seem to be.[240]

William Dampier's description of Celebes' location and shape is the most detailed and accurate of the century. The island stretches from about 1°30' north to 5°30' south latitude, about seven degrees, and it spans about three degrees in breadth. He describes its long narrow promontory running eastward towards Halmahera and the large sea or gulf, seven or eight leagues wide and forty or fifty leagues long, which runs northward from the island's southern end—the Gulf of Bone. Dampier actually coasted only the eastern shore of Celebes, which he describes as low, with deep black soil, many inlets and streams, and thick forests of tall trees. "Indeed all this East-side of the Island seems to be but one large Grove of extraordinary great high Trees." Offshore are many small islands.[241] Dampier and his shipmates land frequently to hunt turtles and shellfish, but they see no people or houses and only once do they see native boats. Dangerous shoals offshore towards the southern end of the island are marked by small huts built on tall posts which act as beacons. Along the shore Dampier finds huge "cockles" sufficient to feed seven or eight men, and a vine which grows on the trees whose leaves have medicinal value.[242]

Butung, the large island off the southeast coast of Celebes, was also frequently mentioned in seventeenth-century European accounts. Appolonius Schotte visited there in December, 1612, and negotiated a treaty between

---

gods. Some of these pre-Islamic rites are still followed today, and a collegium of ritual transvestites still exists in Segeri on the coast north of Makassar where Naverrete met them. See Gilbert Hamonic, "Travestissement et bisexualité chez les 'bissu' du pays Bugis," *Archipel*, X (1975), 121–34. Ritual transvestitism was also practiced in the shamanism of coastal Borneo. See Eliade, *op. cit.* (n. 130), pp. 351–52.

[239]Cummins (ed.), *op. cit.* (n. 234), I, 109–10.
[240]*Ibid.*, p. 111.
[241]Albert Gray (ed.), *A New Voyage Round the World* (London, 1927), pp. 301–2. For bibliography see above, pp. 582–85.
[242]Gray (ed.), *op. cit.* (n. 241), pp. 302–3.

the VOC and Butung's "powerful king." Schotte's account contains no description of the island or of its people, beyond reporting that they use piece goods for money and want the Dutch to bring copper cash for them on subsequent visits.[243] Van Rechteren landed there on April 20, 1632, and accompanied the VOC ambassador Anthony Caen on a visit to the king. Van Rechteren describes the ruler as very old with a white beard, a friend of the Dutch and an enemy of the king of Makassar. Butung, Van Rechteren reports, is about eighty miles in circumference. Little rice grows on it; the natives eat roots called "oby" (Malay, *ubi,* yams), and "anjames" (possibly from Malay, *anjang,* herbs) instead of rice or bread. The best parakeets and cockatoos come from Butung, but there is little else to buy on the island apart from slaves.[244] Earlier, Van Rechteren told of the difficulty his ship experienced picking its way through the Strait of Butung.[245] Saris also describes the strait and provides nautical advice concerning it, but he does not describe the island. In a *cora-cora* sent out from the island to Saris' ship, Saris met an Englishman named Weldon who was employed by the king of Butung.[246]

The VOC merchant Hendrick Hagenaer stopped at Butung in 1635 on his way from Batavia to the Moluccas. He briefly describes his reception by the king. The city is on a high mountain, so steep that one must climb it hand over foot. Once on top, the travelers pass through an opening beyond which stand several bamboo and reed houses. Beyond them stands the king's rather large residence. The king, a young man, sits on a Bengal carpet. Salutes are fired, gifts are exchanged, they drink some arrack, and the king complains to Hagenaer about the Dutch seizure of a junk bringing sago and other foodstuffs to Butung.[247]

Wurffbain's ship anchored at Butung in 1632, but he does not appear to have gone ashore. All he reports is that trade with Butung is limited to slaves and food. The people are agriculturalists. He describes the troubles between the VOC and Butung, and the recent treaty between the two. Wurffbain also complains about the difficult channel between Butung and "Cabona" (Muna) to the west.[248]

Dampier's description of Butung is the most informative of the century. Butung lies about three or four leagues from Celebes, is more than twenty-five leagues long, and about ten leagues broad. The land is high, but fairly

---

[243] "Schot's verhael, wegens sijn voyagie gedaen van *Bantam,* naer Botton, Solor ende Tymor . . ." appended to Verhoeff's voyage, *BV,* IIa, 116–17. This is but one of several instances in which the Dutch seem to be spreading the use of cash to new areas in the archipelago.
[244] Van Rechteren, *loc. cit.* (n. 204), pp. 40–41. The sultanate of Butung, like those of Sulu and Tidore, developed a profitable slaving business during the seventeenth century. See Reid, *op. cit.* (n. 37), I, 133.
[245] Van Rechteren, *loc. cit.* (n. 204), pp. 36–37.
[246] Saris, *loc. cit.* (n. 82), p. 413.
[247] Hendrick Hagenaer, "Verhael vande reyze . . ." *BV,* IIb, 79.
[248] Wurffbain, *op. cit.* (n. 171), I, 66–70.

flat and heavily wooded. The harbor, a rather poor one, is at 4°54' south latitude on the east side of the island. The large town, "Callasusung" (Kalingsusuh), is less than a league from the anchorage on top of a "small hill" (rather than Hagenaer's high, steep mountain), encompassed by coconut trees and a strong, stone wall. Dampier does not know if there are any other towns on the island. He judges the town clean and pleasant, its homes built like those he saw on Mindanao, but neater. The people, too, resemble those of Mindanao in both appearance and dress, "but more neat and tight." They are Muslims and they speak Malay. They are ruled by a sultan, a small man about forty or fifty years old who has a great many wives and children. While they are anchored there, the sultan comes aboard the ship twice, and Dampier accompanies the captain to the sultan's house once. The sultan wears a silk turban edged with gold lace, a broad piece of which hangs down on one side, sky-blue breeches, and a piece of red silk thrown loosely over his shoulders. He wears neither shoes nor stockings. He comes out to the ship in "a very neat Proe [proa], built after the Mindanao fashion." It flies a large white silk flag edged in red, in the center of which a green griffin tramples a winged serpent. He is accompanied by his three young sons and sixteen musketeers. The sultan's house stands at the far end of the town, and as the Englishmen pass, people line the streets to look at them. The house is "pretty neat," built on the ground rather than on stilts, guarded by about forty soldiers. As they sit on mats, the sultan entertains them with tobacco, betel, and coconuts. According to Dampier, the ruler complains about the Dutch and is especially pleased to have a visit from Englishmen. The Dutch buy slaves in Butung, who are heathen people from the island's interior who have not submitted to the sultan's rule. The sultan's subjects hunt them to sell as slaves. Before Dampier's ship leaves Butung, the sultan presents its captain with a young slave who has two rows of teeth in each jaw. He also gives the Englishman a couple of goats. Dampier, like earlier visitors, reports that no rice grows on Butung and that the natives eat mostly roots. The Englishmen buy many beautiful parakeets and cockatoos, the finest Dampier has ever seen.[249]

The most frequently described part of Celebes was Makassar, on the island's southernmost extremity. Of the four ethnic groups living in what is today called South Sulawesi (Bugis, Makassar, Toraja, and Mandar), Makassar was by the beginning of the seventeenth century clearly the strongest. Its lands were along the western shore of the peninsula, and it was challenged only by the Bugis kingdom of Bone on the eastern shore. By 1611, however, the twin Makassar kingdoms of Gowa and Tallo had subjugated Bone and dominated the entire peninsula. Indeed, Makassar's power extended over the entire southern half of Celebes, to eastern Borneo, and to Sumbawa in the lesser Sundas. Earlier, between 1605 and 1607, Makassar

---

[249] Gray (ed.), *op. cit.* (n. 241), pp. 305–9.

had accepted Islam and some of its early seventeenth-century expansion was ostensibly intended to spread the new religion. During the seventeenth century, Makassar's port became a major trading center for the eastern archipelago. The sultan, or king, as the Europeans usually styled him, freely welcomed all traders; his own subjects traded over the entire archipelago. As the Dutch gradually tightened their control over the Spiceries they recognized Makassar as perhaps the most serious challenge to their monopoly.

Merchants from Makassar regularly sailed to the outlying islands of the Spiceries, especially to Ceram and Buru, where they obtained the precious cargoes which could be sold to the Portuguese, Danes, or English in Makassar. The Dutch regularly raided the suspected rendezvous and frequently seized Makassarese ships, but with little effect. The Makassarese, in turn, encouraged native resistance in Banda and Amboina and, in fact, openly aided the Amboinese rebellion of the early 1650's. The Dutch responded by seizing more Makassarese ships and blockading Makassar's harbor. A treaty was signed in 1656, but it had no apparent effect on Makassar's activities in the Spiceries. The rulers of Gowa apparently regarded the VOC monopoly not only as a threat to international trade at their port of Makassar—the lifeblood of their kingdom—but as a challenge to their own tribute rights and to their status as the dominant power in the region. Gowa and the VOC were rivals for control of the spice trade and for political hegemony.[250] In 1660, therefore, a large fleet under Johann van Dam bombarded Makassar and seized a fort, Pa'nakkukang, at the southern edge of the city, ostensibly in retaliation for the seizure of the cargo of a shipwrecked VOC ship and the murder of its crew. Another treaty followed, but relations between the VOC and Makassar continued to deteriorate until in 1666 the VOC launched a full-scale war against Makassar which ended in 1669 with Makassar subjected to a monopolistic treaty, a Dutch fortress established in Makassar, and Makassar's government in the hands of a Bugis prince, La Tenritatta (his personal name), or Arung Palakka (his appanage title) as the Dutch called him, who had aided the Dutch in the conquest.[251]

---

[250] For Gowa's view of the VOC monopoly and the treaties see Leonard Y. Andaya, *The Heritage of Arung Palakka: A History of South Sulawesi (Celebes) in the Seventeenth Century* ("Verhandelingen van het Koninklijk Instituut voor Taal-, Land-, en Volkenkunde," XCI; The Hague, 1981), pp. 45–49.

[251] For background see Andaya, *op. cit.* (n. 250); Andaya, "A Village Perception of Arung Palakka and the Makassar War of 1666–1669," in Anthony Reid and David Marr (eds.), *Perceptions of the Past in Southeast Asia* (Singapore, Kuala Lumpur, and Hong Kong, 1979), pp. 360–78; Andaya, "The Nature of Kingship in Bone," in Anthony Reid and Lance Castles (eds.), *Pre-Colonial State Systems in Southeast Asia; The Malay Peninsula, Sumatra, Bali-Lombok, South Celebes* ("Monographs of the Malaysian Branch of the Royal Asiatic Society," VI; Kuala Lumpur, 1975), pp. 114–25; C. R. Boxer, *Francisco Viera de Figueiredo; A Portuguese Merchant-Adventurer in South-East Asia, 1624–1667* (The Hague, 1967); W. E. van Dam van Isselt, "Mr. Johan van Dam en zijne tuchtiging van Makassar in 1660," *BTLV*, LX (7th ser., VI) (1908), 1–44; De Klerck, *op. cit.* (n. 162), I, 218, 256–59, 275–78.

Reports from Europeans during the first years of the seventeenth century already depicted Makassar as a powerful kingdom and a major commercial entrepôt. Wybrand van Warwijck, for example, met a Makassarese ship near Malacca in August, 1603. He reports that the Makassarese trade principally in cloves, nutmegs, and mace from the Spiceries, that they speak Malay, and that they are a "good, earthy, and friendly people" who fight valiantly against their enemies. The king and his people, Van Warwijck reports, are heathen, although many Muslims and Christians live in Makassar, as well.[252] Admiral Matelief in 1607 actually landed at the village of "Kakeka" (?), part of the Makassarese kingdom of "Tello" (Tallo). The area he visited is thickly populated, flat, beautiful, green, and not as densely forested as other islands in the archipelago; he judges the land to be the "most fruitful and pleasant of all that they have seen so far." Makassar's king is a powerful prince and his land overflows with rice and foodstuffs. Matelief talks about making a treaty with him for the purchase of nutmeg and mace.[253] Paulus van Solt's account, which likewise resulted from a 1607 visit, contains a fairly informative descriptive insert on Makassar.[254] He too reports an abundance of food: rice, all sorts of fruits, coconuts, goats, pigs, and buffaloes. He reports that the king had become a Muslim only four years earlier and was determined to convert the entire land. Prior to the king's conversion the Makassarese were heathens like the people of Pegu and Siam, to whom they bear some physical resemblance. Like the Siamese, Makassar's men used to wear small metal bells in their penises, but do so no longer since they have become Muslims. The women used to cut their hair; since accepting Islam they let it grow long and coil it like Malay women. Female slaves still walk down the streets naked above the waist. Both men and women can be seen standing naked by the wells to wash themselves. Because of the long monsoon rains, November through March, houses in Makassar stand on poles one-and-a-half fathoms (nine feet) above the ground. The king of Tallo (Sultan Alauddin, r. 1593–1639), is a light-skinned man about forty years old and very industrious. His houses and *cora-coras* are large and beautifully made. The Dutch carpenters believe no craftsmen in Holland would be able to make such things. The king has his nobles and other subjects firmly but gently under his control. He treats the king of Gowa, for example, like a father because he is really of higher nobility than the king of Tallo. The king maintains storehouses for rice in all the villages, which may not be emptied until a new crop is in, so that there will be no shortage if the crop is poor. The king is particularly eager to attract trade to Makassar and keeps an

---

[252] Wijbrand van Warwijck, "Historische verhael vande reyse gedaen inde Oost-Indien," *BV*, Ib, 34–35. For bibliography see above, p. 466.

[253] Matelief, *loc. cit.* (n. 92), pp. 53, 73–74. Makassar was a rice surplus area, the Maros plain having been developed to produce rice for export. See Reid, *op. cit.* (n. 37), pp. 24–25.

[254] See above, p. 467.

agent in Banda for that purpose.[255] Although Van Warwijck, Matelief, and Solt visited Makassar in the first decade of the century, none of them was published until the *Begin ende voortgangh* collection in 1646.

Seyger van Rechteren visited Makassar in March, 1632, on a Dutch-Portuguese prisoner-exchange mission. Makassar was ideal for such an exchange because it was an open port and because the Danes, English, and Portuguese all maintained factories there. Van Rechteren observes, however, that the king of Makassar is no friend of the Dutch, because they had cut off his active trade with Amboina. Nevertheless, he and the Dutch ambassador are received by the sultan at his palace. Van Rechteren vividly describes the scene. The palace is very large with many costly decorations of carved and gilded wood. It stands three fathoms (eighteen feet) above the ground on forty-six high columns. Van Rechteren is amazed that such a heavy building can be built so high above the ground. The king sits on an expensive mat, leaning against velvet cushions, attended by about one hundred nobles and servants, all wearing ornate krises. Twenty to twenty-two women sit tailor-fashion with him and serve him tobacco and betel. The king seems about fifty-eight to sixty years old. He is beardless, corpulent, and naked above the waist; his skin color is between yellow and brown. In addition to a gold-threaded garment around his lower body, the king wears a small white cap on his head. The Dutch are served tobacco, betel, and coconuts. A twenty-two-year-old prince talks religion with Van Rechteren, impressively displaying his familiarity with the Old Testament. Van Rechteren promises to send him a Hebrew Old Testament.[256] The royal palace is surrounded by a stone wall about one-half mile in circumference. Four strong bulwarks on the sea side contain twenty large cannons, all donated by Christian nations. The Makassarese make their own powder. According to Van Rechteren, their ordnance is managed by an Englishman turned Muslim who pompously rides around town on a horse followed by his slaves. The king's galleys are the finest Van Rechteren has ever seen. They are beautifully carved with ebony and ivory inlays, and very large. The sultan maintains two or three galleys for his personal use. Each one carries five hundred to six hundred oarsmen. The galleys are pulled up on shore and covered to protect them from the rain, but they can be made ready to sail or fight in less than one-half hour. If necessary the sultan can muster one hundred thousand soldiers in six hours' time. Their main weapons are spears and blowguns with poisoned darts.[257]

More generally, Van Rechteren describes the Makassarese as good sol-

---

[255] Van Solt, *op. cit.* (n. 196), pp. 82–83. Andaya, *op. cit.* (n. 250), pp. 32–33, places the conversion of Tallo and Gowa to Islam in 1605. Others state that Makassar had accepted Islam by 1607. See Jacobs (ed.), *op. cit.* (n. 8), III, 245, n. 16; and Boxer, *op. cit.* (n. 251), p. 3, n. 6. *The Encyclopedia of Islam* (5 vols.; Leiden, 1960), I, 830, indicates that Islam came to Celebes by way of Ternate.
[256] Van Rechteren, *loc. cit.* (n. 204), 37–39.
[257] *Ibid.*, p. 40. For Makassarese soldiers with blowguns see our pl. 247.

diers, strong and brave; religiously they are Muslims. Women work at agriculture; men at fishing. Men wear only a garment around the waist. Women wear a loose sack-like garment over their trousers, large enough to hide another person in it. Sodomy is common in Makassar. It goes on unpunished and with little or no shame attached to it.[258] Van Rechteren's account was first published in 1635.

The French Jesuit Alexandre de Rhodes visited Makassar in 1647, or about fifteen years after Van Rechteren. He was also received at court, not by the sultan, but by his chief minister "Carim Patingaloa" (Karaeng Pattingalloang, d. 1654), whom Rhodes describes as

exceedingly wise and sensible, and apart from his bad religion, a very honest man. He knew all our mysteries very well, had read with curiosity all the chronicles of our European kings. He always had books of ours in hand, especially those treating with mathematics, in which he was quite well versed. Indeed he had such a passion for all branches of this science that he worked at it day and night.[259]

Rhodes frequently talks with him about mathematics, science, and religion. He speaks Portuguese like a native. Not only is Karaeng Pattingalloang wise and well informed about Western science, he is uncommonly virtuous as well. He ruled as regent for the underage Sultan Hasanuddin, refusing the crown when the nobles offered it to him and voluntarily relinquishing power to the sultan when the latter became capable of ruling. Although Karaeng Pattingalloang seems genuinely interested in Christianity, listens to sermons, and follows Holy Week processions, all of Father Rhodes' efforts to convert him prove futile.[260]

Rhodes' general description of Makassar differs little from Van Rechteren's except that it appears to emphasize the consolidation of Islam in the kingdom: that all the pigs have been exterminated for religious reasons, and that while men go naked above the waist women are covered from head to toe, not even showing their faces.[261] Rhodes also tells what became a widely circulated story describing Makassar's submission to Islam: that the king sent ambassadors both to the Christians in Malacca and to the Muslims in Acheh asking for religious instruction with the concealed intention of accepting the religion of whoever arrived first. The Muslims won, to Rhodes' great regret.[262]

---

[258] Van Rechteren, *loc. cit.* (n. 204), p. 40.

[259] Solange Hertz (trans.), *Rhodes of Viet Nam; The Travels and Missions of Father Alexander de Rhodes in China and Other Kingdoms of the Orient* (Westminster, Md., 1966), p. 208. For bibliography see above, pp. 408–9.

[260] Hertz (trans.), *op. cit.* (n. 259), 208–10. On Karaeng Pattingalloang see Boxer, *op. cit.* (n. 251), pp. 4–5, and Andaya, *op. cit.* (n. 250), pp. 33–39. The Dutch poet Joost van Vondel wrote a laudatory ode to Karaeng Pattingalloang. See Vondel's *Volledige dichtwerken*, ed. A. Verwey (Amsterdam, 1937), p. 982.

[261] Hertz (trans.), *op. cit.* (n. 259), pp. 206–7.

[262] *Ibid.*, pp. 207–8.

Navarrete, who arrived in Makassar in 1657, also told the story about Makassar's conversion, adding that since accepting Islam, the Makassarese had become very strict Muslims.[263] Navarrete, like Rhodes, had several conversations with the chief minister, "Carrin Carroro" (Karaeng Cronon), Pattingalloang's son, who showed Navarrete his father's books, maps, globes, and clock. The sultan was present at one of the meetings. On that occasion, reports Navarrete, "their Garb was the most ridiculous that can be express'd; they were both in their gay dress, had European Cloth Coats over their bare Skins, their Arms naked, the Sleeves hanging down, and their Bellies uncover'd after their fashion."[264] The meetings are held at the home of Francisco Viera de Figueiredo, a wealthy and influential Portuguese merchant adventurer.[265] Figueiredo is not the only Portuguese resident of Makassar. Navarrete reports that thousands of Portuguese have moved to Makassar since the fall of Malacca to the Dutch in 1641 and that Portuguese trade there increases every day. The sultan has assigned a part of the city for Portuguese habitation.[266] In addition to his own experiences in Makassar, Navarrete describes a few prodigies: a huge crocodile whose stomach contained, among other things, human heads, daggers, and bracelets; some unusually beautiful birds of paradise; a bird, the *tabon,* whose eggs, which seem larger than the bird itself, are buried deep in the sand and are hunted by the natives as a delicacy; and a child with twenty-four fingers and toes, who was also reputed to be a hermaphrodite.[267] Navarrete reports seeing a funeral procession in which four boys carry the bier, each with a fan in his hand which is used to cool the dead person's soul.[268]

Those who described Makassar during the last quarter of the century mostly concentrated on its troubles with the Dutch and the eventual Dutch conquest of the kingdom. Wouter Schouten, for example, participated in Johan van Dam's 1660 attack on Makassar, which he describes in minute detail. He has little good to say about the people: they are fierce warriors, for many years either sworn enemies or disloyal friends of the Dutch, forever stirring up trouble in the Moluccas, Amboina, and Bandas, and often allying with the Portuguese. He then goes on to describe the plans for the expedition, the assembling of the fleet, the strategy, the naval bombardment of the city, seizure of the port, and the peace negotiations. He includes some brief general description of the landscape in his account of the attack. The shoreline is beautiful, with inviting beaches and impressive homes. Inland are lovely fields, farms and pleasure gardens, and pleasant plains with high

---

[263] Cummins (ed.), *op. cit.* (n. 234), I, 113. Cummins says the "ecclesiastical boat race" took place in 1620 and that the loser was the Jesuit Manuel de Azevedo. No wonder Rhodes regretted having to report it.

[264] Cummins (ed.), *op. cit.* (n. 234), I, 115–16.

[265] On Figueiredo see Boxer, *op. cit.* (n. 251).

[266] Cummins (ed.), *op. cit.* (n. 234), I, 113–14.

[267] *Ibid.,* pp. 116–18, 126. On the *tabon* see below, pp. 1521–22.

[268] Cummins (ed.), *op. cit.* (n. 234), I, 118.

blue mountains in the background. It looks like a green heaven.[269] The Muslim priests, he reports, are clothed in white from head to foot, live moral lives, and are diligent in their religious duties. The Makassarese generally are better and more fully clothed than most other people in the archipelago. They are also mannerly, more industrious, very clever builders, and the most courageous of soldiers.[270]

Vermeulen's account of Makassar is primarily concerned with the Dutch-Makassar war of 1666–69 and its antecedents. Vermeulen participated in its last stages. He provides what might be the earliest published biographical sketch of Arung Palakka, the VOC's Bugis ally in the Makassar war. Vermeulen reports that Arung Palakka's father was a fisherman from Bone, on the east side of the peninsula, that he had joined that sultan's army, distinguished himself, and rose in power to become a royal favorite. He once saved the sultan's life. Nevertheless he twice plotted against the sultan, and was executed when the plots were discovered. Arung Palakka was kept at the palace as a royal slave; he carried the sultan's betel box. As he grew older he determined to avenge his father's death. Eventually he stole aboard a VOC ship and went to Batavia, where he offered to help the Dutch against Makassar. Arung Palakka's honesty and ability were tested by the VOC in a campaign on Sumatra, after which the governor-general called him king of the Bugis and put him in command of five hundred Bugis soldiers in the invasion of 1666.[271] Vermeulen then goes on to describe Speelman's campaign against Makassar in fine detail, noting all the while Arung Palakka's very important role. It ends with the defeat of Makassar and a treaty between Makassar and the VOC, the text of which Vermeulen reproduces. The VOC is ceded a monopoly of Makassar's trade and its port is closed to all other peoples. Lands captured in the war are to remain in VOC hands, and all his goods, lands, and possessions are restored to Arung Palakka, who is called the king of Butung. Arung Palakka cuts his hair to celebrate the victory; he is crowned and honored with a golden chain. Later he makes war on the "Wayers" (Wajo) on the other side of the peninsula.[272] There is

---

[269] Schouten, *op. cit.* (n. 111), I, 85–86.

[270] *Ibid.,* I, 98. Schouten's entire account of the attack on Makassar is found on pp. 74–98.

[271] Vermeulen, *op. cit.* (n. 110), pp. 39–45. There are some inaccuracies in Vermeulen's account. Arung Palakka's father was a minor lord in the Bugis kingdom of Soppeng, his mother the daughter of the king of Bone. Arung Palakka and a small band of Bugis warriors fled to Butung in 1660 after an unsuccessful Bugis uprising against the Makassar kingdom of Gowa. Constantly fearing an expedition from Makassar, they appealed to the Dutch who settled them along the Angke River near Batavia. Arung Palakka and his Bugis comrades had sworn to return to South Sulawesi and free their people from Makassar's rule. The Dutch found them a troublesome group, but finally in 1666 used them to fight the Minangkabau in Priaman on Sumatra where they distinguished themselves and, consequently, became allies of the Dutch in the war against Makassar. See Andaya, *op. cit.* (n. 250), chap. iii, and "A Village Perception of Arung Palakka," (n. 251), p. 363.

[272] Vermeulen, *op. cit.* (n. 110), pp. 45–73. Reid, *op. cit.* (n. 37), p. 81, thinks Arung Palakka cut his hair as a sacrifice in fulfillment of a vow to do so in return for divine aid in the conquest of Makassar.

little description of the land or people to be found in Vermeulen's account of the conquest, and the brief general description at the end of his account contains almost nothing new. He comments on the gold teeth of the Makassarese, on their practice of wearing orange blossoms in their hair, and on the absence of furniture in their houses.[273]

By far the most detailed work on Makassar written during the seventeenth century was Nicolas Gervaise's *Description historique du royaume de Maçaçar* (1688).[274] Gervaise, who spent four years as a missionary in Siam, returned to France in 1685 with two orphaned sons of "Daën Ma-Allé," a refugee prince of Makassar who had died in Siam. It does not seem that he personally visited Makassar. His account is rich in details about Makassar's history, government, religion, social customs, and products, but contains almost nothing specific about the landscape or about anything that one would have to see for himself in order to describe. Furthermore, while his account is certainly the largest seventeenth-century description of Makassar, indeed the only book devoted entirely to the kingdom, it contains many inaccuracies; he, in fact, seems rather gullible.

Gervaise begins with Makassar's history, observing that although it had long been considered a powerful kingdom, its control over the entire southern peninsula of Celebes had been accomplished only about sixty years before by the present ruler's grandfather; prior to that time the kingdoms of "Mandar" (Mandar) and "Bouguis" (Bugis) were still independent.[275] Presumably Gervaise meant Sultan Alauddin (r. 1593–1639), although he was not the present ruler's (Karaeng Bisei's) grandfather. Other details of the conquest of South Sulawesi as related by Gervaise are equally confused; for instance, he attributes the subjugation of Toraja (1683) to Karaeng Bisei (r. 1674–77) but dates it "about seven years ago," which would place it in the reign of Sultan Hasanuddin (r. 1653–69) or Sultan Amir Hamzah (r. 1669–74), after the Dutch conquest in 1669.[276] Gervaise reports that Toraja refused to submit to Islam, although its people were no longer pagans and believed in a creator God.[277] Gervaise's chronology of the Dutch conquest of Makassar is likewise vague and somewhat confused; he is clearer on tales of personal valor by Portuguese or Makassarese participants than on the events. He does not mention Arung Palakka. He describes Dutch intrigues with the king's favorite concubine against the king's brother, "Daën Ma-Allé," who fled first to Java and finally, in 1664, to Siam, where he became involved in Muslim plots against the king of Siam in which he was

---

[273] Vermeulen, *op. cit.* (n. 110), pp. 75–78.
[274] See above, pp. 422–23.
[275] Nicolas Gervaise, *An Historical Description of the Kingdom of Macassar in the East Indies . . .* (London, 1701), pp. 1–4.
[276] *Ibid.*, pp. 6–9. See Andaya, *op. cit.* (n. 250), pp. 258–63.
[277] Gervaise, *op. cit.* (n. 275), p. 9. In fact, the people of Toraja were, or had been, Christians.

killed. Presumably Gervaise's information about Makassar came from "Daën Ma-Allé" or his sons.[278]

According to Gervaise, Makassar's climate is very hot and wet, although the air is healthful because the wind usually blows from the north; "the greatest part of the Men enjoy a perfect Health to a hundred or sixscore years of age."[279] It is a rich and productive land, the source of many precious stones, gold, copper, tin, ebony, "calambas" (calambac or aloeswood), sandalwood, and bamboo. Lemons and oranges grow there, as do mangoes, watermelons, bananas, walnuts, cotton, sugarcane, pepper, betel, and good rice. Makassar produces no wine, but the liquor from palm trees tastes "as good as the best wines of France" and gives indulgers no headaches, although too much will cause dysentery. The natives also produce arrack.[280]

Gervaise mentions a fragrant, lily-like flower called "Bougua Gené Maura" (?), which is used medicinally and in embalming, several edible roots including sweet potatoes, and opium, a shrub from which a very intoxicating liquor is made which the natives mix with tobacco. "'Tis dangerous therefore to contract a Habit of smoking Tobacco thus sprinkl'd with this Tincture of Ophyon, for in a short time it will become so necessary, that there will be no living without it. Seeing that they who leave it off, presently grow lean, languish, and soon after die of a Consumption." Too much will make you die in your sleep. Makassarese soldiers mix a pinhead's quantity with a pipe of tobacco before going to battle.[281]

The land supports fowl, parrots, oxen, cows, deer, boars, an unusually beautiful fishing bird called "Ten Rou Joulon," huge snakes, many monkeys, and baboons. Some of the apes have no tails. White apes are particularly dangerous, frequently attacking and killing women. Because they feed on a certain shrub, both monkeys and goats produce bezoar stones which can be found in their excrement. Those from monkeys are preferred, being both larger and more effective. No elephants are found in Makassar, but many horses, although they are not as good as European horses. The rivers are home to dangerous crocodiles which sometimes attack boats, and to mermaids "of a prodigious bigness."[282]

Gervaise distinguishes Makassar's seaport which he calls "Tompandam" or "Jompandam" (Ujung Pandang) from "the Metropolis of the Kingdom, and the most usual Residence of the Kings," which he calls "Mancasara" (Mangkasara).[283] Ujung Pandang is a busy port with an excellent harbor,

[278] *Ibid.*, pp. 31–54.
[279] *Ibid.*, p. 11. Reid gives an estimate, based on the court chronicle *Lontara'-bilang Gowa,* that the average lifespan of men in seventeenth-century Makassar who survived infancy and died naturally was about fifty years; see *op. cit.* (n. 37), p. 49.
[280] Gervaise, *op. cit.* (n. 275), pp. 13–21.
[281] *Ibid.*, pp. 21–24.
[282] *Ibid.*, pp. 25–29. The mermaids are probably dugong. See below, p. 1521.
[283] Gervaise, *op. cit.* (n. 275), pp. 29, 42, and 56. Mangkasara is more correctly the local name of the people whom we call Makassarese.

sustaining trade with many lands such as Borneo, the Spiceries, Siam, Cambodia, Cochin-China, Tongking, and the Philippines. For over thirty years the Dutch have been masters of the port. Despite the difficulties in subjecting the Makassarese, the Dutch now fear them so little that their port is guarded by only about twenty Dutchmen and some ill-disciplined natives.[284] The metropolis, "Mancasara," is located on a fertile plain a short distance inland from the mouth of a river (probably the Garassi). Its streets are large and neat, but not paved. The king's palace and some mosques are built of stone, but other houses are of wood, often beautifully carved and inlaid. Windows are narrow and the roofs are of broad leaves thickly layered. Houses are built on pillars with ladders that can be pulled up lest a dog should follow someone inside. This, because of the Muslim fear of defilement from touching a dog. There are many shops, and public markets are held twice a day, during the hour before sunrise and the hour before sunset. Only women go to market; it would be disgraceful for a man to be seen there. "Mancasara's" population was once over 160,000, but since the war with the Dutch and an epidemic twenty-five years ago, it is only about 80,000.[285] Gervaise mentions several other cities in Makassar: "Bone," a busy port with an excellent harbor sustaining trade not only with other parts of Celebes but also with "Vagiou" (Wajo), "Soppen" (Soppeng), and "Penecqui" (Peneki) in the province of "Beuguis" (Bugis); Mandar and "Mamoya" (Majene) in the province of Mandar; Toraja in Toraja; and "Tallou" (Tallo), "Tourate" (Turatea), and "Borobassou" (Barru?) in the province of Makassar. He does not discuss these places other than to report how many days distant they are from Makassar.[286]

Makassar's people are strong and vigorous, very interested and skilled in military affairs. They are not as dark as the Siamese and they have flatter noses because they work to make them flatter from birth. "Tho' the *Makassarians* are not naturally addicted to Endearment and Caressing, their friendship however, is very steadfast and very faithful." They are quick-tempered, however. Children are weaned after a year. Boys are raised away from home from five or six years of age on. At age seven or eight they attend schools where Muslim priests teach them reading, arithmetic, and the Koran for two hours each day. "Two years are sufficient to make 'em as learned as any in the Country; for those Agguys [priests] are a sort of People that are infinitely severe." Children are kept continually busy learning trades—or, for nobles, at sports—lest they should become lazy.[287]

---

[284] *Ibid.*, pp. 29–31. The Dutch controlled Makassar's trade only since 1669.
[285] *Ibid.*, pp. 56–60. Those who earlier visited the sultan's palace reported that it was built of wood, on pillars, although surrounded by a stone wall. See, for example, Van Rechteren, *loc. cit.* (n. 204), pp. 37–39.
[286] Gervaise, *op. cit.* (n. 275), pp. 60–61.
[287] *Ibid.*, pp. 62–63.

"A Man can hardly imagine the Modesty of the Women, nor how chaste they are, and reserved in all their Actions." They are closely secluded, not daring to visit even their brothers. The men are extremely jealous and the law allows them to kill a man found alone with someone else's wife. Men, however, take several wives, thinking it shameful to have only one or to have few children.[288]

Marriages are arranged, often contracted by parents when their children are only three or four years old. At age sixteen the betrothed children may see each other with their parents present. A prospective groom builds a house before the wedding. His parents, meanwhile, send gifts to the bride's family in fulfillment of the original marriage contract. If the gifts are accepted, the groom, elaborately dressed, goes to the mosque, where the priest exhorts him and then leads him to the bride's house holding his thumb. The bride usually makes them wait for a while after they knock on her door. Once inside, the priest takes the bride's thumb and exhorts her, after which the newly married couple are confined to a small room for three days while their guests feast outside, sometimes shouting suggestive remarks to the couple. An old woman sits at the door to fetch the couple anything they might need. On the morning of the fourth day the bride and groom dress and come out. They stand with their bare feet on a "Barr of Iron, whereon are engrav'd certain mysterious Ciphers"; a servant throws a pail of water over them; they dress and go to the banquet hall. At noon they go to the groom's parents' home with all the guests, where they feast and dance until nightfall, after which they go to their new home, the new bride immediately assuming all of her domestic responsibilities. "And indeed so soon as a Woman enters her Husband's House, she may be said to enter into Slavery."[289]

Concubinage frequently causes problems in Makassarese families. Upper-class women usually insist that their husbands keep their concubines in a separate house, but strife between wives and concubines is common. Men consult a priest before taking or dismissing a concubine. Men can rather easily divorce their wives by complaining to the priest about their conduct. If the priest approves, a secular judge will divorce them. The divorced man usually takes a favorite concubine to wife. Divorced women may also remarry if they can find husbands. Makassarese are meticulous about wills and inheritances. If a woman survives her husband but has no children, she and her parents share one-half of her husband's possessions, the rest going to his family. If she has children and remarries, she gets one-third; if she has children and does not remarry, she gets everything. Her sons share what is

---

[288] *Ibid.*, pp. 67–69.
[289] *Ibid.*, pp. 103–12. Reid, *op. cit.* (n. 37), pp. 159–60, concludes that the average age of marriage for women was between fifteen and twenty-one years.

left when she dies; daughters inherit nothing unless there are no sons. Surviving husbands inherit all their wives' goods.[290]

Makassarese girls remain home and learn to cook and sew. Women make all the family's clothes; there are no professional tailors. Nor are there male cooks. The Makassarese eat two meals a day, one at eight or nine o'clock in the morning, the other at sunset. Between meals they chew betel, smoke tobacco, and drink arrack, sherbet, tea, or coffee. The whole family eats together sitting on the ground at low tables. They eat with their hands, and all drink from the same glass. They use a lot of pepper and cloves in their food.[291]

Upper-class men wear breeches underneath a long waistcoat of gold or silver brocade or of scarlet, which hangs to the knees. It has long sleeves, buttoned at the wrist. A vest is added on top when they go out. They have neither shoes nor stockings, although upper-class men will sometimes wear small slippers. They wear no hats and wear turbans only on festival days: white for priests and old men, colors for the young. Women wear full-length, narrow-necked shifts with sleeves to the elbow and calf-length pantaloons underneath. Over all of this they wear a garment called a "Jippo" (Malay, *jipun,* a kind of coat). They wear no hats and few jewels. Men wear most of the jewels. Married women wear a gold chain denoting submission to their husbands. Men do not cut their hair. Priests wear long beards. Makassarese bathe two or three times a day and rub their bodies with an ointment made of mash and sandalwood powder. They trim their nails short and dye them red. They color their teeth black, green, or red. At age eleven or twelve they file their teeth to separate them from each other, a painful and bloody process. Sometimes they extract a tooth to replace it with one of gold, silver, or "tambac" (Malay, *tambaga*), an alloy of gold, silver, and copper.[292]

Gervaise reports that there are very few slaves in Makassar. Parents are not permitted to sell their children, and prisoners of war are usually sold to other lands. On the other hand, he reports that upper-class women "have a great number of Servants and female Slaves to do the druggery" and to attend them when they go out. They are usually carried in a palanquin with considerable display.[293] Nobles, ranked "Daëns" (Malay, *daing* or *daeng,* a Bugis title), "Cares," and "Lolos," are very haughty. Some of them receive

[290] Gervaise, *op. cit.* (n. 275), pp. 112–16. According to Reid, *op. cit.* (n. 37), pp. 152–53, most marriages in Makassar, and in Insulindia generally, were monogamous. Divorce was easy and could be initiated by women as well as men.

[291] Gervaise, *op. cit.* (n. 275), pp. 74–76. Male and female domains were sharply distinguished in Insulindia; in addition to weaving and cooking, transplanting, harvesting, and marketing were usually considered women's work. See Reid, *op. cit.* (n. 37), pp. 162–72.

[292] Gervaise, *op. cit.* (n. 275), pp. 76–80. While cutting the hair was a sign of conversion to Islam in most of Southeast Asia, most Makassarese continued to wear long hair until the nineteenth century. See Reid, *op. cit.* (n. 37), pp. 81–82.

[293] Gervaise, *op. cit.* (n. 275), pp. 81–85.

lands and titles because of great service to the king. The lands, however, are inalienable, although the nobles must pay a yearly sum to the king, attend him, and serve in his army. The noble families are all old. No new ones are being established.[294]

Visits are very brief. A guest is ushered into the host's house and seated on a carpet with cushions. After about fifteen minutes he is served betel and some liquor. Usually after another fifteen minutes the guest leaves and is conducted to the door or, if he is of higher rank, to his home. The Makassarese are very class-conscious. Nevertheless their visits and chance meetings in the streets are not excessively formal.[295]

Makassar's king is an absolute monarch, although he seems to be advised by a council and his chief minister has considerable power. According to Gervaise the chief minister actually appoints most officials in the kingdom; the king always approves of the appointments. The king personally judges accused princes or "Daëns." These and all trials are conducted in an orderly fashion employing accusations, witnesses, and interrogations. A provost of the merchants judges commercial disputes, although the important cases are always referred to the king and his council. There are no advocates. Registrars or notaries are very important. Most contracts and agreements are drawn up by them. Few people found guilty of great crimes are publicly executed; most such either kill themselves or die resisting arrest. Anyone may kill a thief or an adulterer if he catches him. Thieves are numerous but they are not very cruel. Most of them are also sorcerers who charm their victims.[296] In his description of Makassar's government, Gervaise does not mention Arung Palakka or the Dutch.

The reigning king is called "Craen Biset" (Karaeng Bisei), the twentieth of his line. As yet he has no brother or child. He was educated by Jesuits.[297] The king spends much of his time hunting and drilling his army. Soldiers are equipped by the king but not paid. Therefore they are not all on duty at the same time. One hundred thousand Makassarese soldiers participated in the last war. The king usually leads his troops into battle. During a war, rewards are offered for the heads of the enemies. Booty is divided three ways among the king, the princes and officers, and the soldiers. Gervaise includes much detail about flags, formations, and the like. Traitors, deserters, and cowards are severely punished. Few young men will marry until they have become accomplished soldiers; they think it "indecent" to farm or follow a trade once they have become soldiers. They spend much of their time hunting. Their most common weapon is a kris, "made like a Dagger,

---

[294] *Ibid.*, pp. 87–90.
[295] *Ibid.*, pp. 86–87.
[296] *Ibid.*, pp. 90–91, 98–103.
[297] After the Dutch capture of Malacca in 1641, a number of Jesuits took refuge in Makassar. This station was finally assigned to the Japan Province of the Society. See Jacobs (ed.), *op. cit.* (n. 8), III, 574–75. The Jesuits left after the Dutch conquered Makassar in 1667.

about a foot and a half long, and the Blade is shap'd as our Painters represent a Beam of the Sun"; krises are usually poisoned. They also shoot light wooden arrows tipped with the tooth of a fish from blowguns seven or eight feet long.[298]

Several games are played by the Makassarese: one somewhat like western chess called "Toupie" (?), kite-flying, and cockfighting.[299] They also play musical instruments, but never use them to accompany singing; "for they have none but Trumpets, that have no variation of sound; Drums not half so good as ours, and a sort of Violin, which they touch with a Wand, and a small Bushel made of very thin Wood, upon which they beat very prettily with two Sticks, which make it yield several different Sounds, pleasing enough the first time you hear 'em, but not to be endur'd the second."[300]

"It is not above sixscore years ago that the Macasarians were all Idolators." They worshipped the sun and the moon, praying at their rising and setting. The first and fifth day of each moon were festival days. They believed in the transmigration of souls and opposed taking any life. Nevertheless they sacrificed animals to the sun and moon and even sacrificed children if they had no cattle. They ate pork and fowl, apparently because they believed no soul was so bad as to be reborn as a pig or fowl. Gervaise describes a cosmology in which the heavens had no beginning and the sun chased the moon, wounding her, and thus giving birth to the earth. Every hundred thousand years the moon gives birth to another world, the old one being consumed by the sun's heat.[301]

Gervaise devotes considerable space to the story of Makassar's conversion to Islam. During the sixteenth century already two Makassarese merchants become Christian under the instruction of the Portuguese governor of Ternate, Antonio Galvão. These preached and made converts when they returned to Makassar. Many of the princes were interested in Christianity but only the "King of Soppen" (Datu Soppeng) accepted baptism. Francis Xavier resolved to go to Makassar but was never able to do so. Meanwhile the king of Makassar sent for priests from Malacca and from Acheh vowing to accept the religion of those who arrived first. When the Muslim priests arrived first, the king submitted and built a mosque, the people were circumcised, and Makassar became Muslim. Later visits by Jesuits failed to change the situation, although the king allowed trade and freedom of religion to the Portuguese. He even built them a church. Islam has since spread to most of Celebes, even to Soppeng. The Portuguese continued to worship freely in Makassar, however, until the Dutch conquest. Gervaise accuses the

---

[298] Gervaise, *op. cit.* (n. 275), pp. 70–71, 92–97.

[299] On kite-flying in Indonesia see C. Hart, *Kites, an Historical Survey* (Mount Vernon, N.Y., 1982), pp. 44–47. On chess see Skeat, *op. cit.* (n. 188), pp. 485–86.

[300] Gervaise, *op. cit.* (n. 275), pp. 69–70, 72–73.

[301] *Ibid.*, pp. 118–22.

Dutch of destroying the Portuguese churches and scattering the native converts.[302]

The Makassarese are very devout Muslims, never neglecting a ceremony or holy day, going beyond what is required. They are "far more devout than all other Mahometans." Circumcision is practiced with much ceremony. The boy is bathed for an hour, sits between the horns of a sacrificial ox or buffalo while the priest lectures him, blood is smeared on the child's forehead, and the child repeats the confession. After the circumcision the boy is kept in bed for forty days, bathed frequently, and watched by physicians. The family meanwhile celebrates, unless the child becomes ill. The Makassarese also circumcise girls, according to Gervaise, but it is done quietly and few people know much about it.[303]

Funerals are particularly elaborate. The body is washed five times, clothed in a long white robe and a white turban, and laid on a board in the best room of the house. After the widow receives mourners in another place, priests carry the body to the mosque, scattering money as the procession moves through the streets. White turbans are worn as a sign of mourning. In the mosque, water and ashes are thrown on the corpse and the mourners pray for about two hours. Then the procession continues to the burial ground. There is no coffin. In the grave the body is covered with the plank on which it was carried. Earth is shoveled in and a priest throws a pail of water on the corpse, after which the mourners return home to purify themselves. Later a mausoleum is built, attended by more ceremonies and a feast. The day after Lent is also a day of prayer for the dead.[304] Mosques are built of stone. They contain no altars, images, or ornaments. The people worship in bare feet. Women worship in a separate mosque. In Makassar there are three orders of priests: "Labes" (*lebes*), who may marry; "Santari" (*santri* or teachers), who are celibate and live in the mosque; and the "Toun" (possibly from Malay, *tuan,* lord), who have been to Mecca. Gervaise includes details about other Muslim ceremonies as practiced in Makassar, noting that they are very strictly observed.[305]

5

THE LESSER SUNDAS

In addition to Sumatra, Java, Borneo, Celebes, and the Spiceries, literally hundreds of other islands and coasts were described in the published reports

---

[302] *Ibid.,* pp. 121–32.
[303] *Ibid.,* pp. 133–40. On female circumcision see Reid, *op. cit.* (n. 37), pp. 148–49.
[304] Gervaise, *op. cit.* (n. 275), pp. 140–47.
[305] *Ibid.,* pp. 147–58. Indonesians still make pilgrimages to Mecca in relatively large numbers.

of Europeans who had sailed through the Indonesian archipelago during the seventeenth century. Some can easily be identified; some cannot. The Lesser Sundas (Lombok, Sumbawa, Flores, Sumba, Savu, Roti, Solor, and Timor) and the many surrounding islands are particularly difficult for modern scholars to handle. The seventeenth-century descriptions, usually written by someone who viewed the islands from shipboard, make them appear quite similar to one another. The islands are intensely green, usually heavily wooded, with surprisingly high peaks which frequently pierce the clouds. Volcanoes abound, and it seems a rare European visitor who was not treated to some display of nature's fireworks. Those who land on the smaller islands usually report vegetation similar to that of the more frequently visited places. Even the people on those islands which were inhabited are described as being similar to Javans, Moluccans, Amboinese, or Filipinos. The reader of these accounts eventually becomes numbed to vistas of emerald islands in a deep blue sea, to spectacular volcanoes, colorful birds, and tawny islanders in their proas or outriggers.

Some islands, however, because they were mission stations or were important commercially or politically, received regular attention during the century. Solor and Timor, for example, were important as sources of sandalwood, and the Portuguese had established a fort on Solor and converted many of the natives during the sixteenth century.[306] Pedro Teixeira in one of the many digressions in his *Kings of Persia* (1610) briefly describes Timor's sandalwood and notes that Timor produces other medicinal woods which are less well known because they are not major articles of trade: "vidáre pute" or "white apple" and "vidáre lahor" or "sea apple," for example. He also mentions "Solor wood" from the nearby island of Solor, which is valued as an antidote for poison. What he says about how sandalwood grows and about the people of Timor is obviously secondhand; Teixeira had never been there.[307]

Detailed information about Solor appeared in a book of three short relations of the Dominican mission there, written by António da Encarnação (d. *ca.* 1672) and Miguel Rangel (d. 1645), published together in 1635.[308] Encarnação's first treatise is a brief overview of Dominican activities in Asia. In his second treatise Encarnação briefly describes the founding of the Dominican mission on Solor in 1561, its destruction by the Dutch in 1613, its reestablishment by Rangel and others in 1616, and the visit of Governor Nuno Alvares Botelho's fleet in 1629. In addition to recounting the history of the

---

[306] See *Asia*, I, 599–601. Also see above, pp. 14, 138–39.
[307] William F. Sinclair (ed.), *The Travels of Pedro Teixeira; With His "Kings of Hormuz" and Extracts from His "Kings of Persia"* ("HS," 2d ser., IX; London, 1902), pp. 215–16. For bibliography see above, p. 323.
[308] *Relações summarias de alguns serviços que fizerão a Deos . . .* (Lisbon, 1635). A modern edition of these relations is found in Artur Basilio de Sá (ed.), *Documentação para a história das missões do padroado português do oriente* (5 vols.; Lisbon, 1958), Vol. 5, *Insulindia*, pp. 277–347. See above, pp. 343–44.

Christian church on Solor, he extols Solor's pleasant climate, healthful air, and fertile land. All fruits appropriate to that part of the world could be grown there in abundance but for Solor's lazy people. He notes four different languages on Solor.[309]

Rangel's relation is intended to demonstrate that the Dominican fort on Solor is necessary to insure free access to Timor's sandalwood and to protect the Portuguese and native Christians living there and on the neighboring islands of Timor, Flores, and Ende.[310] To that end, Rangel glowingly describes the original fort and the nearby churches, the awful damage done to both the fort and the churches by the Dutch in 1613, and how the Dominicans rebuilt the fort and some of the churches after the Dutch abandoned Solor. The Dutch attacked the rebuilt fort in 1620, and although they were repelled by the fort's defenders, much damage was done. Rangel was in Europe during the second Dutch attack but returned to Solor with Nuno Alvarez Botelho's fleet in 1630. His enthusiasm for rebuilding the fort was met by opposition from the Portuguese at Larantuka, who wanted it razed, fearing that the Dutch would return if they rebuilt it. Rangel chides them for being insufficiently angry over the affront given to the church and thus to God by the heretic Dutch. The remaining chapters of his book relate details of the rebuilding and strongly argue for the necessity of rebuilding and maintaining the fort.[311]

Rangel prefaces his account of the fort with a general description of Solor which, while somewhat rosy, is the most detailed and informative of the century. Solor, he reports, has an abundance of those things necessary for human life and for commercial profit. For example, good and inexpensive rice is available at the fort, grown not on lowlands in flooded paddies but among the mountains with the dew of heaven.[312] In the absence of vegetables, yams are a staple of the people's diet. Knowledgeable people say that there is no better wine in all India than that made on Solor. Rangel does not tell how the wine is produced. Good meat is readily available: sheep give birth three times a year, goats produce three healthy young each time they give birth, and in addition there are many deer, pigs, buffaloes (which taste as good as beef), and a large variety of good fish. Good fruit is even more abundant: muscatel grapes are available all year (they are pruned monthly); there are oranges as good as those from China, melons, pomegranates, figs, lemons, pineapples, mangoes, jackfruits, plums, almonds, and many others. Among the many plants and flowers which serve as condiments, marjoram grows wild like rosemary in Portugal. All the materials for making gun-

---

[309] Encarnação, *Relaçam do principio da Christandade das ilhas de Solor, e da segunda restauração della,* . . . , in Sá (ed.), *op. cit.* (n. 308), V, 308–9.

[310] His treatise is entitled *Relaçam das Christandades, e ihas de Solor, em particular, da fortaleza,* . . . , in Sá (ed.), *op. cit.* (n. 308), V, 318–45. For a sketch of Rangel's career see A. T. de Matos, *Timor português, 1515–1769* (Lisbon, 1974), pp. 47–48, n. 27.

[311] Sá (ed.), *op. cit.* (n. 308), V, 327–46.

[312] *Ibid.*, V, 322.

powder are available on Solor. There is ample stone for building and excellent lime or "chumbo" (*chunam,* lime made from calcified seashells). Firewood is plentiful, as is good wood for building houses and ships; boxes and chests made from it last a very long time. Rangel mentions several medicines found on Solor: pigstone (a kind of bezoar stone), "lucerragem" (?), "belile" (?), "bidarupes" (?), tamarinds, and cane.[313]

Solor's climate is not unhealthy as some imagine because of Solor's supposedly unhealthy breezes. Rangel does not think the breezes make the land unhealthy, but that the natives use them to explain disorders or problems which they do not understand. He contends that many people living near the fort reach 100 years of age, some as much as 120 years. He finds the breezes fresh and the climate pleasant, comfortable for all sorts of recreation.[314]

The region's most important export is the precious sandalwood from Timor. Other exports include wax, turtles, slaves, cattle, and fine cinnamon from Ende. Its more important imports are gold, silver, ivory, iron, and finished cloth, especially silk. Rangel thinks trade with Solor and the surrounding islands is unusually profitable both for the natives and for foreigners. Even the perils of the sea and from thieves are fewer here than in most other places, and an enterprising merchant can very quickly enrich himself. Rangel cites a recent letter from Macao in which reliable merchants report profits as high as 200 percent on the sandalwood traded in China during the last monsoon. Still other credible merchants reported profits of at least 150 percent. For money, Solor's merchants clip gold as Chinese merchants clip silver. For smaller transactions they use "laris" (larins) from Goa.[315]

Solor's people, except for those called "Gunos" (from Malay, *gunung,* or mountain?), who live high in the mountains, are lazy; Christians as well as pagans "are not born to work." They are not interested in farming or fishing; they do not look for ways to make a living. They see no advantage in study, or even in becoming wealthy. They do not work to achieve anything or to have anything. Consequently they have no professions or skills; they rely on foreigners for these. They are wholly devoted to war, arms, vanity, honor, and recreation. As a result most of them are poor and miserable, although they do not like to admit it or to ask for charity even when very hungry. Nevertheless they seem grateful, in their way, if they are given something.

They are governed by lords, called by some "ataquabiles" (?), by others

---

[313] *Ibid.,* V, 323–24. "Pedras de porco espinho" (pigstone), sometimes called "pedra de Malaca," appears to be a kind of bezoar stone used as an antidote for poisons. "Lucerragem," "belile," "bidarupes" we have not been able to identify. Rangel, however, also refers to a town on Flores as "Lussarragem"; see *ibid.,* p. 320.

[314] *Ibid.,* V, 324.

[315] *Ibid.,* V, 324. According to Rangel the larin is like the Portuguese vintem.

"alalaque" (?), and by others kings. Most crimes, even murder, theft, and adultery, are punished by bondage rather than death. Sorcerers, however, are so universally hated that they are put to death and their children defamed and enslaved.[316]

The people of Solor, especially the nobles, treasure pieces of gold, silver, ivory, and pearls, with which they buy women to marry. Women are thus like slaves to their husbands, and because of the treasure they bring when they marry, daughters are much desired. Rangel regrets that regarding the purchase and sale of wives and concubines there is little difference between the native Christians and the others, expecially among the nobles. They marry their daughters to Muslims, pagans, and apostates as readily as to Christians, despite the church's opposition. Older and richer men are the worst offenders.[317]

The original fort on Solor Rangel describes as beautiful and strong, with five bulwarks, three on the seaside and two on the land. Outside the walls were beautiful gardens, a town, and three beautiful churches. The Dutch were not able to destroy Solor's Christian community despite their destruction of the town and the churches. The town has been rebuilt and trade flourishes; as many as five thousand souls, Portuguese and natives, come to confession in its churches.[318]

Detailed descriptions of Timor and Solor are also contained in Appolonius Schotte's account of the Dutch seizure of Solor from the Portuguese in 1613.[319] Schotte's ships arrived at the Portuguese fort on Solor in mid-January, 1613, began shelling it, landed troops to attack it from the rear, and burned the town around it. He negotiated treaties of trade and friendship with several kings on Timor including the "King of Coupan" (Kupang) on the western tip of Timor, who promised trade, land for a Dutch fort, and the conversion of all his people. Schotte was aware that the king of Kupang had promised the same things to the Portuguese. The Dutch finally captured the fort on Solor in April, 1613, after which Schotte sailed to Timor to complete negotiations with the kings on the "inside" of the island and to make preparations for building a fort at Kupang.[320]

Schotte describes the Portuguese fort on Solor as well located, close to the shore but on high ground with deep valleys on either side. After its capture the Portuguese and mestizos, including seven Dominican priests, were sent to Malacca. The native Christians submitted to the Dutch. On Solor there are three villages of new Christians: "Cherebate" (Querivatu?), with about forty families; "Pamancaye" (Pamacaio), containing about eighty families; and "Louolaingh" (Levahojong), with about thirty families. Four more vil-

[316] *Ibid.,* V, 325–26.
[317] *Ibid.,* V, 326.
[318] *Ibid.,* V, 330–31.
[319] Schotte, *loc. cit.* (n. 243), pp. 116–25.
[320] *Ibid.,* pp. 116–21.

lages on a nearby island are also under Dutch control: "Carmangh" (?), with about one thousand families; "Louococol" (?), with about three hundred families; "Louonamangh" (?), also with three hundred families; and "Louoongin" (?), with about one hundred families. Then he lists "Mimba" (?), about three hundred families; "Siki" (Sika on Flores), about two hundred families; and "Larentocal" (Larantuka on Flores), about one hundred families. Each of these Christian villages is ruled by a military officer—"overste"—and a priest. They arm themselves with bows and arrows, shields, and swords, although some also carry muskets.[321] In addition to the Christian villages, five Muslim villages of Solor now find themselves under VOC rule: "Lamakera" (Lamaqueira), "La Male" (Lamala on Adonara), "Toulon" (Tulão?), "Adenare" (the Island of Adonara), and "Pratololy" (?).[322] Many peasants are still heathen, however, as are the people of "Aude" (?) and "Sallelauvo" (?).[323] The sultan of Makassar also seems to claim some jurisdiction over Solor; while Schotte was there, a fleet of thirty-three *cora-cora*s arrived from Makassar to collect tribute. The people of Solor, however, contend that they are subjects of the sultan of Ternate rather than of Makassar.[324]

The Dutch are primarily interested in Timor as a source of sandalwood, most of which is shipped to China and to the Coromandel Coast of India. Dutch interest in Solor is primarily to strengthen their position on Timor. In addition, both Solor and Timor can serve as a nearby source of food for the Bandas and the Moluccas. In exchange, the people of Timor and Solor buy Coromandel cloth, Chinese trinkets, such as coral, and products from Gresik ("Gressickse waren").[325] Schotte's account contains no description of Solor or Timor's landscape or of the people beyond naming their religions.

Schouten visited Solor and nearby islands in 1660 with Johan van Dam's fleet just before the attack on Makassar. His account includes a bit more description. They apparently sailed in to Solor between "Lombatte" (Lombata or Lomblen) and Adonara, which he calls "Serbiete." Lomblen has a high active volcano but is otherwise very pleasant: many trees, sand dunes, beautiful valleys, and pleasant villages. He mentions that the Portuguese of "Larytauke" (Larantuka on Flores) fled to Timor. The "Queen of Solor" and many *orang kaya*s come out with two large boats to welcome the fleet, singing and playing pipes, flutes, and gongs. The Dutch fire salutes. The fleet seems to have anchored closer to Adonara, and the Dutch apparently traded there. It sports beautiful farms and plantations, villages protected by palisades, a high mountain, and a river with clear water. The people wear

[321] *Ibid.*, pp. 119–20.
[322] On the "islands" which comprised the Solor archipelago of the Portuguese see the map (fig. vii) in H. Leitão, *Os Portugueses em Solor e Timor de 1515 a 1702* (Lisbon, 1948); and Matos, *op. cit.* (n. 19). Also see Boxer, *op. cit.* (n. 251), for the period from 1640 to 1688 in Makassar and Timor.
[323] Schotte, *loc. cit.* (n. 243), p. 120.
[324] *Ibid.*, p. 123.
[325] *Ibid.*, pp. 121–22, 125.

only small loincloths and use no money. The Dutch trade tin, old iron, and spoons for food. The people of Solor are bolder than those of Adonara; they canoe out to the fleet each day with food which they hope to trade for cotton cloth.[326] Vermeulen, whose account, like Schouten's, was published in 1676, includes a brief, general description of Timor. It is a fruitful island, sustains many animals and a large population, even contains gold, but has an unhealthy climate. The people are black-skinned with long black hair. Women wear many large rings, bracelets, and armbands; their ears are pierced with large holes. They are not Muslims and they eat all kinds of meat.[327]

The most detailed seventeenth-century description of Timor was that written by Dampier at the century's end. Dampier first saw Timor in December of 1687 when he sailed through the straits between Alor and Pantar and along the northwest coast of Timor on his way to Australia. He mentions many fires on Pantar and a large town on its northeast side. Timor he describes as a "long high mountainous island stretching N.E. and S.W." It is about seventy leagues long, fifteen to sixteen wide, its center at about 9° south latitude. He has heard that the Portuguese trade there, but he does not know what they trade unless it is coir for making ropes.[328] He apparently does not know about sandalwood, probably an indication of how little Dampier depended on previously published material.[329]

Dampier visited Timor again in 1699 on the way north from his not-too-successful voyage of discovery to Australia. He stayed for three months, September to December, trying to repair his ship, and he included an account of Timor in his *A Voyage to New Holland*.[330] As always, Dampier's description of the landscape is richly detailed. The beach along the south side of the island, where Dampier made his first landfall, is "low and sandy, and full of tall straight-bodied trees like Pines, for about 200 yards inwards." Beyond this beach, extending to the foot of the mountains, about three miles inland, is a "Tract of swampy and Mangrovy Land" which is flooded at high tide.[331] The south shore of the island is fairly straight, without points or inlets in which to anchor and with shallow water extending about a mile or a mile and one-half from the beach. The mountains inland are partially covered with woods interspersed with savannah. Dampier sees some coconut plantations. He sailed along the south coast to the west end of

---

[326] Schouten, *op. cit.* (n. 111), I, 80–82.

[327] Vermeulen, *op. cit.* (n. 110), pp. 78–79. Wallace, *op. cit.* (n. 33), p. 142, contends that the natives of Timor are more like the Papuans of New Guinea than like Malays. He describes their hair as "frizzly." The Timorese differ from both the Indonesians and the Melanesians in stature and language.

[328] Gray (ed.), *op. cit.* (n. 241), pp. 309–10. Wallace, *op. cit.* (n. 33), p. 141, reports Timor's length as three hundred miles and its width as sixty miles. The mountains of Timor reach heights of 7,300 feet.

[329] See for example J. C. Shipman, *William Dampier, Seaman-Scientist* (Lawrence, Kans., 1962), pp. 9–11.

[330] For bibliographic details see above, pp. 384–85.

[331] Spencer (ed.), *op. cit.* (n. 141), pp. 152–54.

the island, sighted "Rotte" (or Roti) to the south ("dry and barren, only here and there a Spot of Trees"), and then sailed between the western tip of Timor and "Anamabao or Anabao" (Semau) into Kupang Bay, where he discovered the Dutch Fort Concordia on the south side of the bay.[332] The Dutch were none too friendly, apparently suspecting that Dampier was a pirate.

Semau, reports Dampier, is only about ten leagues long and four leagues wide but contains two kingdoms: "Anamabao" in the east and "Anabao" in the west. They are enemies of each other. The natives are "of a swarthy copper-colour, with black lank Hair." They raise roots and coconuts, fish, and hunt turtle and buffalo. They frequently hunt for four or five days at a time, drying the fish or meat which they catch over a fire in order to carry it back home with them.[333] Leaving Kupang Bay, Dampier coasted Timor's north shore, which he describes as higher land than that on the south but not as lush. The grass in the savannahs seems dry and the trees seem small and withered, as if they lacked water.[334] Dampier was graciously received at "Laphao" (Lifao) Bay, the Portuguese settlement on the north coast. He stayed there until the northwest monsoon made the Lifao anchorage unsafe. He then sailed back to Kupang Bay, anchoring off Babao on its north side, where he began scraping the ship's bottom.[335]

While Timor has many bays in which ships ride during certain times of the year, it has few good harbors; Kupang Bay is the best. Dampier describes all its shores and anchorages in close detail. The Dutch fort, Concordia, is built on the south side of the bay on a rock close to the water. It is small, but built of stone. A small river runs alongside it, beyond which is a small sandy bay. Near the bridge is a fine walled garden which supplies fruits and vegetables for the fort. There are fifty to sixty native houses nearby and the fort is manned by about fifty soldiers.[336]

Lifao Bay, the Portuguese settlement, has forty to fifty houses and a church. The houses are low and poorly built, the walls made of mud or wattle with boards on the sides, and the roofs thatched with palm or palmetto leaves. The church is small, boarded to the top on its east end, but enclosed only three or four feet above the ground on the other three sides. It also has a thatched roof. The church contains a small altar and a couple of images. Each house has a yard around it enclosed by nine- or ten-foot-high canes, containing fruit and coconut trees and a well. By the sea a decaying platform holds six small, deteriorated cannons, attended by a few armed

---

[332] *Ibid.*, pp. 154–56.

[333] *Ibid.*, pp. 158–59.

[334] *Ibid.*, p. 162. See Wallace, *op. cit.* (n. 33), pp. 142–43, 152, for similar observations on the general appearance of Timor's vegetation.

[335] Spencer (ed.), *op. cit.* (n. 141), pp. 165–71.

[336] *Ibid.*, pp. 172–75.

men.[337] The people of the town look like others on Timor but are Catholic and speak Portuguese. They are proud of their religion and Portuguese descent; in fact, they would become very angry if anyone said they were not Portuguese. But Dampier saw only three white men there, two of them priests. A few Chinese also live at Lifao. There is considerable trade, especially with the Chinese, who, Dampier reports, come from Macao. The Chinese bring rice, adulterated gold, tea, iron, tools, porcelain, and silks, which they exchange for pure gold, which is collected in the mountains, beeswax, sandalwood, and slaves. Occasionally a ship comes from Goa.

These "Portuguese" claim to be able to muster five to six hundred men, armed with guns and swords, and boast of being able at any time to drive the Dutch from the island, if only the viceroy of Goa would give them permission to do so. Their chief on Timor is a man named Antonio Henriquez whom they call "Captain More or Major" (*Capitão-mor,* or commander). They say he is white, sent by the viceroy of Goa, but he lives at Porta Nova (Dili) on the eastern tip of the island. He seems to be involved in Timor's tribal rivalries, at war with some native princes, and allied with others. A man whom the people at Lifao call lieutenant lives about seven miles away. He looks native but is Catholic and speaks Portuguese. Another "lieutenant" lives at Lifao. He, too, looks like a native but speaks Portuguese; he is old and infirm. For all their boasting and their pride in being Portuguese, Dampier judges them a lawless people and not effectively under Portuguese control. Some time before, when the viceroy sent a ship to Timor with a governor aboard, "Captain More" put the governor in irons and sent him back to Goa. No supplies or arms have come from Goa since. They buy guns and ammunition from the Dutch in Batavia.[338] A chain of high mountains runs through the center of Timor along almost its entire length. Since the island is narrow, the streams are short and small. There are no great rivers. The soil is loose, in places sandy, and only moderately fertile. Many of the mountains are rich in gold and copper. The natives collect gold from the streams. Dampier does not know how they obtain the copper.[339]

Dampier describes many of Timor's trees: white, red, and black mangroves, calabash, cotton trees, locust, cana-fistula, tamarinds, wild fig trees, sandalwood, and several sorts of palms. He usually notes the differences between those on Timor and similar species in the West Indies. Some he has not seen before, such as the variety of palm which has a trunk seven to eight feet around, grows to eighty or ninety feet high and produces oval-shaped

---

[337] *Ibid.,* pp. 175–76. After 1668 the Portuguese began to build up Dili as their main location on Timor.

[338] *Ibid.,* pp. 176–78, 183–84.

[339] *Ibid.,* pp. 178–79. Concerning the persistent belief that Timor contained rich gold and copper deposits and the discovery that it contained little of either see Wallace, *op. cit.* (n. 33), pp. 147–49.

nuts about the size of a duck's egg. The husk is soft and yellow, the kernel too hard to eat, and it contains no liquid at the center. The nuts are smashed when they fall to the ground and soon begin to smell. Another kind of palm grows short branches which divide into small twigs rather than long branches at the top. Its fruit hangs from the twigs like ropes of onions, each of which is about the size of a plum. Its trunk is of constant diameter up to the branches, about fifty to sixty feet aboveground, above which it tapers to a point. Nothing on the tree except its fruit is green. Timor also produces many straight timber trees, some of which resemble pine. The wood is hard, heavy, and reddish in color.[340] Among Timor's fruits, Dampier lists guavas, mangoes, jackfruits, coconuts, plantains, bananas, pineapples, citrons, pomegranates, oranges, lemons, limes, muskmelons, watermelons, and pumpkins, some of which had been brought to the island by the Dutch or the Portuguese. "Indian corn" (maize) is the staple food for most of the islanders, although the Portuguese and their friends grow some rice. Dampier also mentions parsley, samphire (glasswort), and an herb called "calalaloo" in the West Indies, which tastes something like spinach.

Buffaloes, cows, horses,[341] hogs, goats, sheep, monkeys, guanos, lizards, snakes, scorpions, centipedes, and snakes abound on Timor. Dampier thinks the cows, horses, goats, and sheep probably came with the Portuguese and Dutch. There are many birds: wild cocks and hens, eagles, hawks, crows, two kinds of pigeons, turtle doves, three or four sorts of parrots, parakeets, cockatoos, blackbirds, and many more. One he calls the ringing bird because of its repeated six-note song. It is about the size of a lark, has a small sharp black bill, blue wings, pale red head and breast, and a blue stripe around its neck. Water birds include man-of-war birds, boobies (gannets), fishing hawks, herons, goldens, crab-catchers, and others. The forests are full of bees; honey and wax are items of trade. The surrounding seas are rich in fish. Dampier lists mullet, bass, bream, snook, mackerel, "Parracoots," garfish, ten-pounders, scuttlefish, stingrays, whip rays, "Rasperages," "Cockle-merchants or Oyster-crackers," cavallies, conger eels, rockfish, and dogfish. Rays are plentiful; every net has some in it. Dampier caught one whose tail was thirteen feet long. In addition there are several sorts of oysters, cockles as big as a man's head, crawfish, shrimp, green turtles, grand pisces, and some alligators.[342]

Dampier describes Timor's "original natives" as of middle height, straight-bodied, slender, long-faced, having very swarthy skin, with straight black hair. They are nimble and dextrous but very lazy. "They are

---

[340] Spencer (ed.), *op. cit.* (n. 141), pp. 179–80.
[341] On the Arabian horses raised on Timor see Matos, *op. cit.* (n. 310), p. 17.
[342] Spencer (ed.), *op. cit.* (n. 141), pp. 180–82. Dampier's book contains sketches of many plants collected in Brazil, Australia, Timor, and New Guinea (*ibid.*, pp. 126–34) and of some fish (pp. 135–37). Wallace, *op. cit.* (n. 33), p. 144, could not identify Dampier's ringing bird. See also Wallace, pp. 155–62, on the natural history of Timor and its relationship to that of Australia.

said to be dull in every Thing but Treachery and Barbarity." Their houses are low and poorly built; their clothing merely a cloth about the middle. Some wear thin, oval-shaped pieces of mother of pearl, gold, or silver, five in a row, on their foreheads above the eyebrows. Some wear palmetto caps of various shapes. They marry as many women as they can afford, sometimes even selling children to purchase more wives. When Dampier asks about their religion he is told that they have none. They eat primarily maize, clearing the land by burning off the grass and shrubs during the dry season. Most of all they enjoy hunting. Some few are fishermen. They hunt and fight with lances, thick short truncheons, and shields.[343]

Although the natives seem to be of one race and culture, they are divided into many kingdoms each with its own language. Dampier lists "Cupang" (Kupang), "Amabie" (Amavi), "Lortribie" (Lorotova), "Pobumbie" (Boboque?), "Namguimal" (Naimute), "Anamabao" (Amanubāo), and "Anabao" (Ambeno).[344] "Each of these hath a Sultan who is supreme in his Province and Kingdom, and hath under him several Raja's and other inferiour officers." They are mostly enemies of each other, stirred up, Dampier thinks, by the Dutch, whose fort was in the kingdom of Kupang, and the Portuguese. "Amabie," "Pobumbie," "Namguimal," and "Lortribie" are allies of the Portuguese.[345] They take enemy heads in battle, carrying them back to their villages on poles where they stick them on the tops of their houses.[346]

On Timor, as in all the islands of the archipelago, Malay is the common language. "The greater the Trade is, the more this Language is spoken: In some it is become their only Language; in others it is but little spoken, and that by the Sea-side only." Islam spread with the Malay language, observes Dampier, although in areas where Islam has declined because of Portuguese or Dutch occupation, the Malay language persists. In areas where the Dutch and Portuguese are weak, however, as in Solor and on the east of "Ende" (Flores) Islam is still the major religion and Malay the chief language. Dampier heard that "Lorantuca" (Larantuka) is a large town, larger than any on Timor, also ruled by a "Captain More," who was as independent and absolute as his namesake in eastern Timor.[347]

When the Dutch arrived in the Spiceries at the beginning of the century, the Portuguese were still established there, although their position was being contested by the Spanish from Manila and by the sultan of Ternate's

---

[343] Spencer (ed.), *op. cit.* (n. 141), pp. 182–83.

[344] Most of these "kingdoms" were in Servão in southwestern Timor. See the map in Matos, *op. cit.* (n. 310), facing p. 16.

[345] Spencer (ed.), *op. cit.* (n. 141), pp. 183–84.

[346] *Ibid.*, p. 185.

[347] *Ibid.*, pp. 185–86. Probably refers to António de Hornay, the Eurasian "prince" of Larantuka, Solor, and Timor from 1673 to 1693. See C. R. Boxer, "Portuguese Timor," *History Today*, X (1960), 351–52.

Muslim league. During the first two decades the Dutch swept the Iberians from the Spiceries, negotiated monopolistic trade agreements with Ternate and most other princes, and staved off British attempts to claim a share of the trade. The VOC's determination to monopolize the spice trade provoked considerable native opposition, which ranged from smuggling spices to other buyers to armed rebellion against the Dutch overlords. One by one, however, they all fell before Dutch power: the Ternatans, the Bandanese, the Amboinese, and finally the Makassarese. For the most part, with minor exceptions such as the Portuguese on Timor, the Spiceries became a Dutch preserve.

Printed information about the Spiceries also became overwhelmingly Dutch during the course of the century. With very few exceptions—Colin, Rangel, Gervaise, and Dampier, for example—Portuguese, Spanish, and English reports disappear after the first half of the century. Few Europeans other than the Dutch and their German employees visited the Spiceries any longer. The European reports describe the islands and the appearance, character, customs, religions, politics, commerce, and society of the islanders, as European reports did everywhere in Asia, and they certainly convey the impression of the Spiceries as a coherent unit. But they also describe the changes which resulted from Dutch occupation. Not only changes in society, politics, and commerce, but also in the people themselves and in their islands. Populations were mixed and moved about; some groups, like the Bandanese, almost ceased to exist. The fauna and flora of the islands were changed by the extirpation of clove and nutmeg trees from many islands and the importation of new plants. For the Spiceries, more so than for anywhere else in Asia, the European reports are essential for the early history of the region, because there are so few native sources. The image of the Spiceries produced by the Europeans who wrote before the Dutch conquests or by those later writers who looked back to pre-conquest conditions is virtually the only image we have.

6

INSULAR SOUTHEAST ASIA'S EASTERN AND SOUTHERN
PERIPHERY: NEW GUINEA, THE PACIFIC ISLANDS, AND
AUSTRALIA

During the seventeenth century, Europeans ventured south and east of the Indonesian archipelago to New Guinea, the Papuan and South Pacific islands, and Australia. Here they found a world quite different from that of the archipelago, although parts of it, such as the Papuan Islands and western New Guinea, had some commercial and political contacts with the Spiceries. Here they met people who were racially very different from the peoples of the archipelago, who appeared to be uncivilized, were not Muslims, and could not understand Malay. Their reports sketched the frontiers of insular Southeast Asia and introduced their readers to unknown places in their environs.

A. NEW GUINEA AND NEIGHBORING ISLANDS

The earliest seventeenth-century reports of New Guinea and its offshore islands appear to be derived from the secondhand Jesuit descriptions published during the sixteenth century.[348] Argensola (1609), for example, reports that the rival kings of Ternate and Tidore "went on to establish possessions in the Papuas, east of the Moluccas, islands little frequented, because of the many flats and shoals. The natives are black, like the Kaffirs"; in fact, reports Argensola, the word "Papua" means black.[349] The Papuans wear their hair "wound in large curls." Most seventeenth-century observers, however, describe Papuan hair as kinky or frizzly. Their faces, writes Argensola, are "lean and ugly." They are "a stern people, accustomed to labor, capable of any kind of treachery." Their islands are "subject to kings, and each abounds in gold, which they do not transport elsewhere, because no one stores more than is needed for their jewellry." Argensola has heard that there are some albinos among the Papuans and that many of the Papuans are deaf. "In regard to the size of this country, if we may believe the accounts of the Spanish pilots who have sailed there, these islands run along a vast land which ends at the Straits of Magellan."[350]

Argensola was obviously referring to reports about the several Portuguese and Spanish expeditions that had touched upon the northern coast of New Guinea and its adjacent islands between 1526 and 1545 and perhaps that of Alvaro de Mendaña y Neyra's 1567 expedition in search of the southern continent.[351] No published reports resulted from these voyages, but some firsthand observations from Mendaña and Pedro Fernandez de Quiros' 1595 expedition and from Quiros' 1605 expedition may have appeared in the 1610 publication of Quiros' eighth memorial to Philip III concerning the exploration and colonization of the austral continent.[352] Mendaña and Quiros had touched on the Marquesas, Solomons, and New Hebrides; Quiros thought these islands were very near to the southern continent. He describes them and their people as part of the Australian world. Some of Europe's earliest descriptions of those islands therefore may be em-

---

[348] For the sixteenth-century descriptions see *Asia*, I, 616.
[349] Papua (Malay, *papuwah*) actually means "frizzle-haired."
[350] Argensola, *op. cit.* (n. 5), p. 71. Later explorers also report on the presence of albinos in these populations.
[351] See Günter Schilder, *Australia Unveiled* (Amsterdam, 1976), pp. 27–28 and above, pp. 6–8.
[352] For the bibliography of Quiros' publication see above, pp. 307–8.

Australia, New Guinea, and Surrounding Islands

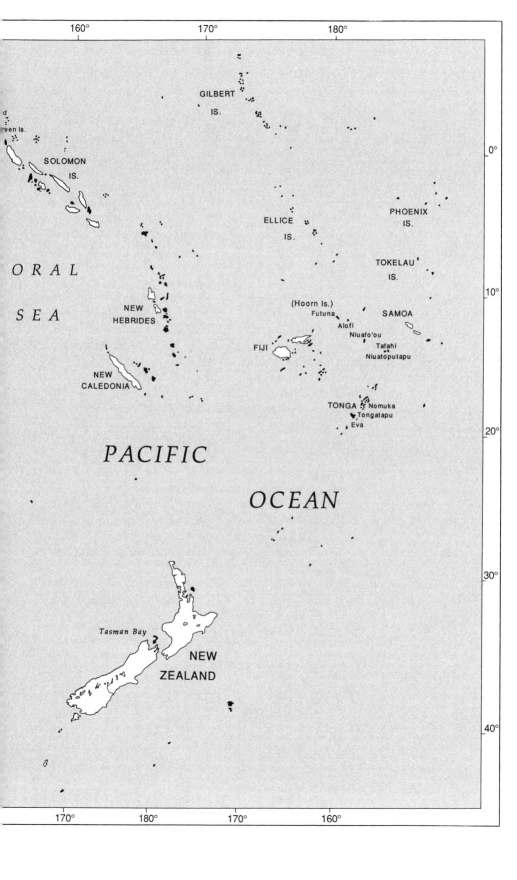

bedded in Quiros' account of the austral continent, but it is very difficult to distinguish the firsthand observations from the products of Quiros' enthusiastic imagination.

Quiros' estimate of the austral continent's size—"as great as all of Europe and Asia the Lesse, unto the Sea of Bachu [Caspian Sea], Persia, and all the Isles, as well of the Ocean, as of the Mediterranean Sea, taking England and Island [Ireland]"—and his general description of its population—"an incredible multitude . . . some . . . white, others black . . . and others of a mingled complexion"—are obviously not based on firsthand observations.[353] When he reports that the people know few trades; live in small unfortified communities of wooden houses with palm-leaf roofs; fight with bows and arrows, clubs, pikes, and darts; wear only a small garment which covers them from waist to mid-thigh; and are clean, cheerful, tractable, and grateful, he may be describing the people he observed in the Solomons or the New Hebrides. So, too, with Quiros' report that the natives make bread from large roots and use coconuts for many purposes. But his list of products such as silver, pearls, gold, nutmeg, mace, cloves, pepper, cinnamon, anise, ebony, nuts, most fruits, and sugarcane seems to be based on what was found in America and the Spiceries in the latitudes he imagined were embraced by his Southern Continent.[354] Perhaps the same extrapolations inspired his report about the Southland's climate: it is healthful—none of his crew became ill, the natives live long, and build their houses on the ground rather than on stilts—temperate, neither swampy nor barren and sandy, and free from thistles, marshes, snow, snakes, crocodiles, worms, fleas, caterpillars, and gnats.[355]

Europe's earliest reliable firsthand descriptions of the Tongas, the Solomons, and the islands off New Guinea's northern coast appeared in the published journals of Jacob Le Maire and Willem Corneliszoon Schouten's 1615–17 voyage of discovery.[356] Inspired by Quiros' description, Le Maire believed these islands to be very near the mainland of the austral continent. His descriptions of them, however, do not seem to be embellished by any preconceived notions about the Southland.

After landing on several atolls of the Tuamotu archipelago, Le Maire's ship anchored in May, 1616, at what he called Coconut Island (Tafahi in the

[353] "The Copie of a Petition presented to the King of Spaine, by Captaine Peter Ferdinand de Quir . . .," *PP*, XVII, 219–20; "Verhael van seker memoriael, gepresenteert aen Sijne Majesteyt den Koningh van Spangien, by den Capiteyn Pedro Fernandez de Quir, . . .," appended to "Journael van de Nassausche Vloot . . .," *BV*, IIb, p. 69.

[354] *PP*, XVII, 220–24; *BV*, IIb, 69–71.

[355] *PP*, XVII, 228–29; *BV*, IIb, 72–73.

[356] For a description of the voyage and its publications see above, pp. 445–48. See also Schilder, *op. cit.* (n. 351), pp. 32–37; P. A. Leupe, "De reizen der Nederlanders naar Nieuw-Guinea en de Papoesche eilanden in de 17 en 18e eeuw," *BLTV*, XXII (1875), 175–79; A. Wichmann, *Entdeckungsgeschichte von Neu-Guinea* (2 vols.; Leiden, 1909–12), I, 60–72; and C. Jack-Hinton, *The Search for the Islands of Solomon, 1567–1838* (Oxford, 1969), pp. 190–97.

Tonga archipelago).[357] This he describes as a high mountain, like the Moluccas, covered with coconut trees. The natives trade coconuts, yams, bananas, and pigs for coral and pieces of iron, especially nails, stealing whatever possible from the Dutch ship. Their "king" comes out to the Dutch ship with a flotilla of canoes, seems to welcome the strangers, and sends gifts aboard. The Dutch also trade briefly at "Traitors' Island" (Niuatoputapu) and "Good Hope" (Niuafo'ou) before anchoring for about two weeks at what Le Maire called the Hoorn Islands (Futuna and Alofi islands).[358] Before anchoring at Futuna and Alofi, however, the ship's council, over Le Maire's objections, decided to abandon the quest for Terra Australis and to turn north in order to reach the Moluccas by sailing along New Guinea's north coast rather than to risk being trapped south of New Guinea unable to find a passage to the west and unable to return to the east because of the steady strong easterly winds.[359] Obviously no one on board Le Maire's ship knew that Luis Vaez de Torres, the captain of one of Quiros' ships, had sailed between New Guinea and Australia's Cape York Peninsula in 1606.[360] Le Maire nevertheless seems to have thought they had discovered Terra Australis when they anchored at Futuna and Alofi.[361]

The Dutch visit of almost two weeks to Futuna and Alofi seems to have been entirely pleasant. Le Maire, Schouten, and other of the officers were received with great ceremony and respect. The local "kings" as well as the people bowed their heads to the ground and kissed their hands and feet. The king placed his crown on Le Maire's head. The Dutch were well supplied with food and entertained. Dutch sailors even danced with the natives in the evenings. As described by Le Maire, the Tonga Islanders are large and strong, yellowish brown in color, and proud of their hair, which they wear in a variety of styles, cut short and frizzly, bound up, or braided. They wear no clothes other than a small covering over the genitals. Tonga women are ugly, with long hanging breasts and short-cropped hair. They appear poor, living in conical hovels about twenty-five feet in circumference, containing few furnishings and having doors so low one must crawl through them. They appear to have few rules regarding chastity, no religion, and no familiarity with commerce. They live, he concludes, without cares like the people in the golden age of the poets. All they need they gather from the

---

[357] For details see A. Sharp, *The Discovery of the Pacific Islands* (Oxford, 1960), p. 74.

[358] W. A. Engelbrecht and P. J. Herwerden (eds.), *De ontdekkingsreis van Jacob le Maire en Willem Cornelisz. Schouten in de jaren 1615–1617, journalen, documenten en andere bescheiden* (2 vols.; "WLV," XLIX; The Hague, 1945), I, 54–58; "Australische navigatien, ontdeckt door Jacob le Maire ende Willem Cornelisz. Schouten inde jaeren 1615, 1616, 1617," *BV*, IIb, 90–94. See the map facing p. 1 in E. N. Ferdon, *Early Tonga* (Tucson, 1987).

[359] "Australische navigatien" (n. 358), p. 94; Schilder, *op. cit.* (n. 351), p. 36.

[360] On the lack of knowledge in northern Europe about Torres' feat see Jack-Hinton, *op. cit.* (n. 356), p. 192.

[361] Engelbrecht and Herwerden (eds.), *op. cit.* (n. 358), I, 63. These two islands are separated by a narrow channel about one mile wide.

trees. The fish they occasionally catch are eaten raw.[362] Le Maire also describes the islanders' feasts, exotic birds held in great honor by the islanders, and a drink called "kava" made from chewing a certain green leaf and making a narcotic infusion from the chewed quids.[363] Despite their idyllic existence, Le Maire noted frequent wars between the islanders.[364]

The peoples of the Solomons (Le Maire and Schouten's next landfall in June, 1616), and of the islands along the coast of New Ireland and New Guinea, all of which the Dutch believed to be New Guinea, are described as racially different from those of the Tongas.[365] Like the Tonga Islanders, they wear only a leaf or other small covering over the genitals, some not even that much, but they are much darker skinned; in fact, they are black like Africans, with thick lips and flat noses. Most of them wear rings though holes bored in their earlobes, through each side of their noses, and through the nasal septum. Many wear rings around their upper arms, decorate their necks and shoulders with shells or boars' teeth, or wear feathers in their hair. Their hair is kinky, but not as wooly as Ethiopians'. Beards are common, but not mustaches. Some groups streak their hair and beards with lime. Some scar their faces and bodies. Many have blackened teeth. The women are exceedingly ugly, with short hair like men, breasts like intestines hanging down to their navels, protruding stomachs, spindly legs and arms, and humps on their backs large enough for babies to ride upon.

Their language seems totally different from that of the Tonga Islanders and from Malay.[366] Also, unlike the Tonga people, they build their houses on poles eight or nine feet above the ground.[367] Some wear small caps made of bark which they raise above their heads as a sign of respectful greeting. Some break arrows or wooden spears over their heads as a sign of peace or friendship. Some sing songs before they eat a meal, perhaps in thanksgiving. Not all are friendly. The Dutch ship is frequently attacked and the Dutch sometimes fire to frighten the islanders off, occasionally killing them. They fight with blowguns, wooden spears, bows and arrows, wooden swords, and clubs. Some of those whom the Dutch took captive

---

[362] *Ibid.*, p. 73. "Australische navigatien" (n. 358), p. 101.

[363] "Australische navigatien" (n. 358), pp. 97–100. On *kava*, a drink for all occasions derived from the pepper plant and prepared in this manner, see Ferdon, *op. cit.* (n. 358), chap. iii.

[364] "Australische navigatien" (n. 358), p. 98.

[365] The Tongas are Polynesians and the others are Melanesian, "the two main complexes of Pacific peoples," according to W. Howells in his article on "Physical Anthropology" in J. D. Jennings (ed.), *The Prehistory of Polynesia* (Cambridge, Mass., 1979), p. 272.

[366] Around fourteen hundred indigenous languages were spoken in Oceania and insular Southeast Asia. More than one language was spoken in the Solomon Islands alone. For a discussion of recent linguistic scholarship on the complexities of the Austronesian and Papuan languages and their subgroups see P. Bellwood, *Man's Conquest of the Pacific* (New York, 1979), chap. v.

[367] Evidently some houses were built on piles from five to eight feet above the ground, but this custom was far from being universal. See H. B. Guppy, *The Solomon Islands and Their Natives* (London, 1887), p. 60.

chewed their ropes loose and attacked their captors by biting them. As the Dutch move slowly westward they find signs of contact with other civilizations: articles of Spanish origin, pieces of Chinese porcelain, less curiosity about the ship, more experience with trade, more interest in cloth than nails or coral in exchange for food, canoes decorated in the Moluccan fashion, and finally, lighter-skinned people who wear clothing and speak Malay.[368] Not only did Le Maire and Schouten's voyage chart a new route across the Pacific but it also provided what might be the first comparative eyewitness description of the major ethnic groups encountered across the southern Pacific: the Polynesian, Papuan, and Malay.[369]

The earliest published report of Jan Carstenszoon's 1623 voyage of discovery appeared in the May, 1625, issue of Wassenaer's *Historisch verhael*.[370] Carstenszoon sailed along the south coast of New Guinea past the entrance to the Torres Straits, which he mistakenly judged to be a shallow bay, and down along the west coast of Australia's Cape York Peninsula, which he took to be part of New Guinea.[371] The report of his expedition published in Wassenaer's newspaper, therefore, contains some description of New Guinea's south coast, although it is not clearly distinguished from the Cape York Peninsula. It is a low, flat, densely wooded coast, broken by many rivers, creeks, and inlets. Its numerous people, the report calls them Papuans, are wild, totally naked cannibals, who fight with bows and arrows, darts, and wooden spears. At first they are not afraid of guns but become terrified when they realize they can be killed by them.

On his way to New Guinea, Carstenszoon stopped at the Kai and Aru islands to obtain their submission to the Dutch. The treaty between the VOC and the *orang kayas* of Aru, signed February 4, 1623, is appended to Paulus van Caerden's account in the *Begin ende voortgangh* (1646). The treaty lists the villages represented by the *orang kayas*—"Wodgier [Wokam?], Tutewanagh, Salguadingh, Bocun, Guamar, Bagambel, Maycoor, Rato, Tarangan [Trangan]"—allows the islanders free trade in Banda and Amboina, and forbids any other trade. It contains no descriptions of the islands or the people.[372]

Johann Saar, however, included some description of the Papuan Islands in his 1662 account. Saar, a soldier, accompanied Adriaen Dortsman on a 1645 expedition to baptize new Christians in the Arus and to build a fort on Pulau Damar.[373] Saar's first meeting with the Papuans is at the island of "Tenem-

[368] Engelbrecht and Herwerden (eds.), *op. cit.* (n. 358), I, 76–84; "Australische navigatien" (n. 358), pp. 104–10.
[369] On the races of insular Southeast Asia see Wallace, *op. cit.* (n. 33), pp. 446–57; on the Papuans see pp. 449–52. See also Crawfurd, *op. cit.* (n. 39), I, 1–36, especially pp. 23–36.
[370] *Op. cit.* (n. 195), IX, 68–69.
[371] On Carstenszoon's expedition see Schilder, *op. cit.* (n. 351), pp. 84–98, and Leupe, *loc. cit.* (n. 356), pp. 8–10.
[372] Paulus van Caerden, "Kort verhael ofte journael . . . ," *BV*, Ib, 19–20.
[373] On Dortsman's expedition see Leupe, *loc. cit.* (n. 356), pp. 44–47.

ber" (Tanimbar or Timor Laut), where the fleet stops for provisions. The Dutch are greeted by sixty *cora-coras*, each containing forty to fifty men, shouting, beating gongs, and breaking arrows over their heads as a sign of friendship. They are, he reports, strong men, completely black, wearing their hair tied behind their heads like a horse's tail. Their staple food is a very large potato-like root (yams) which tastes better than sago. Their clothes resemble Javans'; they live in straw-roofed houses. They trade fish and fruit for cloth, red caps, knives, red coral, and other trinkets. Saar judges them a dishonest people; he was cheated by one.[374]

Saar was among those chosen to accompany the Reverend Jacobus Vertrecht to Aru in order to baptize new Christians in response to a request made the previous year. They go ashore in a skiff while the fleet sails to the "Key" (Kai) islands to cut timber for the fort they intend to build on Damar. Vertrecht's party is at first received in very friendly fashion by the villages on either side of the river. The Papuans bring gifts: birds of paradise, parrots, East Indian ravens, which are green, and "Luris" (lories), which are colorful birds about the size of a blackbird: they have a beautiful blue head, red feathers, green wings, red to dark green breast, and reddish feet, and they can easily be taught to talk and to laugh. But when Vertrecht prepares to baptize the people they balk, fearing they will surely die if they submit. The fleet has left for the Kais intending to return for Vertrecht and his party in four or five weeks. Meanwhile many Bandanese exiles stir up the Papuans against the Dutch and lead an attack on some of them while they are trading. Two Dutchmen are beheaded, another dies later from a poisoned dart. The Dutch withdraw in their skiff to the river's mouth, where they wait until the fleet returns to rescue them.[375]

From Aru, Saar went to Damar, where he helped build a new Dutch fort—Fort Willemsburg. The people on the coast of Damar are friendly to the Dutch, but those who live in the mountains prove implacable enemies, regularly killing soldiers or workmen who stray too far into the forest. In addition, Saar reports, Damar is an unhealthy land. During seven weeks on the island the Dutch lose 127 men. Almost everyone is ill, although Saar blames Dortsman's cruelty and the brackish water for some of the problems. They are afraid to go inland for fresh water. About Damar itself, Saar says little, other than to report that nutmeg trees grow there.[376]

New descriptions of Tonga, Fiji, the Solomons, and the islands along the coast of New Ireland and New Guinea became available in 1671 with the first published notice of Abel Tasman's explorations.[377] Tasman, in 1642–43,

[374] *Op. cit.* (n. 158), pp. 52–54.
[375] *Ibid.,* pp. 54–57. On Aru see Wallace, *op. cit.* (n. 33), pp. 327–75; see pp. 369–71 on Aru's "rivers."
[376] *Op. cit.* (n. 158), pp. 57–61.
[377] For bibliography see above, p. 492. For an account of Tasman's explorations with an analysis of the manuscript and printed sources concerning it see Schilder, *op. cit.* (n. 351), pp. 139–205.

sailed south of Australia and charted about half of Tasmania's coast, which he called Van Diemen's Land, and the west coast of New Zealand before landing at "Amsterdam" (Eva), "Middelburch" (Tongatapu), and "Rotterdam" (Nomuka) islands in the Tonga group.[378] From there he went to "Prins Willems Eijlanden" (the Fiji Islands) and then to the Solomons, "Marcken," and the Green Islands, earlier sighted by Le Maire and Schouten.[379] From here he retraced Le Maire and Schouten's route along the north coast of New Ireland and New Guinea to the Moluccas, sighting or landing on many of the coastal islands earlier noted by Le Maire and Schouten.

The first account of Tasman's voyage, apparently written by the ship's physician Hendrik Haelbos, contains some interesting description of the peoples encountered but little precise geographic information. It is impossible to tell, for example, whether the round windowless houses made of reeds and mud are found in the Tongas, in Fiji, or in the Solomons. He entered one of them and found several young men and women sitting around apparently tending an old blind woman. Thinking the Dutchmen were interested in their women, the men all left the hut. When the Dutch made no advances towards them, the women danced around the Hollanders singing strange songs. The men here have decorative scars on their chests and shoulders, some of which are fresh and still bleeding. They do not cultivate food, but seem to subsist on what grows naturally, especially on coconuts. They eat meat almost raw, merely warming it a little. They sleep on mats laid on the ground, their heads resting on small wooden four-legged stools. They take great pride in their hair.[380]

Haelbos' description of the natives along the coasts of New Ireland and New Guinea is similar to that of Le Maire and Schouten. They vary in color from dark brown to pitch black. None wear clothes except a very small covering over the privates. Most groups braid or in other ways dress their hair; some use wooden combs, some stick feathers or flowers in it. Some groups wear necklaces and girdles of hogs' teeth or seashells. Some groups paint their bodies; one group paints red stripes on their foreheads. Many wear bone rings through their ears. Some wear bones sharpened at each end through their noses. Many groups break arrows over their heads as a sign of friendship.[381]

Wurffbain includes a brief description of the Papuans from Aru and Kai who traded in Banda each year, although he apparently had not visited these

---

[378] Schilder, *op. cit.* (n. 351), pp. 174–77; R. Posthumus-Meyjes (ed.), *De reizen van Abel Janszoon Tasman en Franchoys Jacobszoon Visscher ter nadere ontdekking van het Zuidland in 1642–43 en 1644* ("WLV," XVII; The Hague, 1919), pp. 57–76; Leupe, *loc. cit.* (n. 356), pp. 179–84; Wichmann, *op. cit.* (n. 356), pp. 85–101.

[379] Schilder, *op. cit.* (n. 351), pp. 178–79; Posthumus-Meyjes (ed.), *op. cit.* (n. 378), pp. 94–96.

[380] Haelbos' account in Arnold Montanus, *De nieuwe en onbekende weereld; of beschryving van America en 't Zuid-land, vervatende d'oorsprong der Americanen en Zuidlanders . . .* (Amsterdam, 1671), pp. 581–82. On hair styles in the Solomons see Guppy, *op. cit.* (n. 367), pp. 116–18.

[381] Montanus, *op. cit.* (n. 380), pp. 582–85.

islands himself. They are, he reports, "poor, simple, black, and by nature mostly heathen people." Wurffbain reports that some have been converted to Islam by the Bandanese who fled there after the Dutch conquest, but he thinks their conversion is quite superficial. They do not cover their heads and they eat pork. In fact, they seem to be "complete savages." They wear no clothes except a leaf over the genitals. They defend themselves with bows and arrows, wooden swords and shields; and they are terrified by musket or cannon shots. On Banda, large groups of them—fifty, sixty, or more—run through the streets, singing, jumping, and in other ways exuberantly enjoying themselves. Still Wurffbain is impressed by their cleverness in trade. They test the purity of gold, for example, by rubbing it in their hair and then smelling it.[382] Wurffbain also reports that Dutch officials persuaded the people of Aru, Kai, and Damar to destroy the clove and nutmeg trees on their islands.[383]

A rare notice about New Guinea mainlanders is included by Wurffbain in what is apparently the seventeenth-century's only published report of an unsuccessful VOC voyage to New Guinea and Australia in 1636.[384] Several Dutchmen, including the expedition's commander, Gerrit Thomaszoon Pool, were killed by about one hundred natives when they went ashore at a place they called Murderers' Bay on the south coast of New Guinea. As Wurffbain describes it, the "savages" were black like the Kaffirs of Angola, but larger and taller than Europeans. They had long black hair and were naked except for their "privates." One had an animal skin over his shoulders. They fought with clubs, blowguns, and bows and arrows. They charged out of the forest on either side of the beach, screaming as if crazy and paying no attention to the Dutch musket fire. They shot so many darts that it looked like a hailstorm. After Pool and his comrades fell, the "savages" took Pool's Japanese sword and cut the Dutchmen into pieces. Wurffbain thinks they are cannibals.[385]

The last European to visit the north coast of New Guinea in the seventeenth century was William Dampier. Leaving Timor in December, 1699, Dampier sailed northeast, threading his way through the islands off New Guinea's northwestern extremity and rounding Cape Mabo. From there he sailed east along the coast, raised the coast of New Ireland, following it south until he picked up the coast of New Britain, which he thought to be connected to New Ireland. He followed New Britain's coast through the passage between it and New Guinea (Dampier's Passage), thus discovering that these islands were not part of New Guinea. He then sailed west along the coast back to Cape Mabo, sighting and landing at many islands never

[382] Wurffbain, *op. cit.* (n. 171), I, 102–3.
[383] *Ibid.*, I, 100.
[384] On the expedition, commanded by Gerrit Thomaszoon Pool, see Schilder, *op. cit.* (n. 351), pp. 129–38; Wichman, *op. cit.* (n. 356), I, 80–85; and Leupe, *loc. cit.* (n. 356), pp. 10–38.
[385] *Op. cit.* (n. 171), I, 108–9, 144–46.

before visited by Europeans. As usual, his account as published in his *Voyage to New Holland* contains careful notations of latitude, longitude, and distances, coastal sketches, and detailed descriptions of the landscape, people, fauna, and flora.

Dampier's first impression of New Guinea's coast near Cape Mabo is of "a high even land, very well clothed with tall flourishing trees, which appeared very green and gave us a very pleasant Prospect." [386] Further east Dampier traded at "Palo Sabuda" (Pulau Pisang), 2°43' south latitude and 486 miles from Baba Bay on Timor. It is rocky on the coast but has good soil above the rocks. Tall trees and many useful products grow on it. He mentions plantains, coconuts, pineapples, oranges, papayas, potatoes, jackfruits, and the "Libby Tree," from which the natives make sago cakes. [387] He sees sea and land birds, especially large sky-colored birds, and a large number of bats. The islanders are "very tawny," with long black hair, somewhat similar to the people of Mindanao and other islands. They seem to dominate the black, curly-haired people who also live on the island, who may be their slaves. They are naked except for breech clouts, but the women wear "a Sort of Callicoe-Cloathes." Many wear blue and yellow beads around their wrists. They fight with bow and arrow, lances, and broad swords. They spear fish with wooden gigs, luring the fish to the surface by means of a carved and painted decoy—"much like a Dolphin." They have outrigger canoes like those of the Malayans. Dampier cannot determine their religion but he doubts that they are Muslims because they readily drink brandy from the Englishmen's cups. [388] On what he calls King William's Island, Dampier describes sixty- to seventy-foot-tall, straight trees, very green, many bearing white, purple, and yellow flowers which make the whole island smell fragrant. [389] All along the way, Dampier tries to trade with people. Judging from the smoke of cooking fires and the patches of cleared land on the hillsides, he concludes that the mainland and many of the offshore islands are quite populous. There seem to be many languages. Words Dampier learns in one place quickly become useless as he travels east. Signs of friendship vary, but usually involve holding something over the head: a tree branch, hands, arrows, a club, or other weapon. In one place the natives throw arrows into the sea, scoop water in their hands which they pour over their heads. In some places, however, they seem treacherous, suddenly attacking the ship with stones. Sometimes Dampier frightens them by shooting guns; sometimes natives are killed or injured. At what is called Garret Dennis Island on the Dutch charts, Dampier describes the natives as a "very black, strong, and well-limb'd People," with large round heads and short curly

[386] Spencer (ed.), *op. cit.* (n. 141), pp. 190, 198.
[387] This probably refers to the prickly sago palm (*Metroxylon rumphii*), a native of New Guinea and the Moluccas. See L. S. Cobley, *op. cit.* (n. 145), p. 190.
[388] Spencer (ed.), *op. cit.* (n. 141), pp. 194–95.
[389] *Ibid.,* p. 200.

hair which they groom into various shapes and dye red, white, or yellow. They have large faces with bottle-shaped noses which they stretch by wearing large things, four inches long and as thick as a man's thumb, though the nostrils. They also wear ornaments in their ears and paint their faces. Dampier admires the beautifully curved high bows and sterns of their outrigger canoes. They do not seem to know about iron.[390] On New Britain the men wear colored feathers in their hair and carry lances, while the women walk behind them and carry large baskets of yams on their heads. The women wear only a bunch of small green branches tucked under a string around their waist. When he discovers that the land he was coasting is not joined to New Guinea, Dampier names it Nova-Britannia and describes it as having

about 4 deg. of Latitude: the body of it lying in 4 deg. and the Northernmost part in 2 deg. 30 min. and the Southernmost of 6 deg. 30 min. South. It has about 5 deg. 18 min. Longitude from East to West. It is generally high, mountainous Land, mixed with large Valleys; which as well as the mountains, appeared very fertile; and in most Places that we saw, the Trees are very large, tall and thick. It is also well inhabited with strong well-limb'd Negroes, whom we found very daring and bold at several Places.[391]

Most of Dampier's descriptions of the places he saw as he sailed back westward along the coast are similar to those made earlier by Le Maire or Haelbos, although Dampier is always more precise about geographical details. Readers of his account and those of his seventeenth-century predecessors who described coastal New Guinea may have wished for more concrete details or for some description of the island's interior, but nevertheless through these writings they were offered a glimpse of the Papuan world beyond the Spiceries and the eastern archipelago, a variegated world whose people and products differed markedly from those of the Malay-dominated archipelago and which was only minimally involved in its trading patterns.

B. AUSTRALIA AND NEW ZEALAND

The seventeenth century began with Europe's ancient belief still intact that a large undiscovered continent lay somewhere to the south of the Cape of Good Hope, Java, and the Straits of Magellan. Among the century's major accomplishments, therefore, were the actual discovery of Australia, the development of a realistic conception of its location and size, and the charting of about half its coastline. Manuel Godhino de Héredia claimed that the Portuguese had discovered Australia in 1601, but it seems that in fact the Dutch

[390] *Ibid.*, pp. 210–12.
[391] *Ibid.*, p. 224.

discovered it in 1605. The further exploration of its coasts during the seventeenth century is overwhelmingly a Dutch story.[392]

The first adequately documented European visit to Australia is that of Willem Janszoon and Jan Lodewyckszoon van Roossengin on the Dutch pinnace "Duyfken" in 1605. They were sent out from Bantam to "discover" New Guinea and other islands south of the Bandas, and they raised the west coast of the Cape York Peninsula near the Pennefather River. They sailed south along the coast for a while, then doubled back, sailing along the same coast further to the north. They landed at Batavia River in Albatross Bay, where they were attacked by aborigines who killed several Dutch crewmen. Janszoon and Lodewyckszoon called the coast New Guinea. Although they sailed past it, they did not recognize the Torres Strait as a passage south of New Guinea. Their discoveries soon appeared on charts as a southern extension of the New Guinea coast, but no published account of their voyage appeared during the seventeenth century.[393] The English factor John Saris, however, reported from Bantam both the departure of the "Duyfken" and its return to Banda in 1606. When published by Purchas in 1625 it was probably Europe's first printed notice of Australia:

The eighteenth of November 1605 here departed a small Pinnasse of the Flemmings, for the discovery of the Island called Nova Guinea, which, as it is said, affordeth great store of Gold.[394]

The fifteenth of June 1606, here arrived Nockhoda Tingall a Cling-man [*Kling*, Malay for Indian] from Banda, in a Java Juncke, ... he told me that the Flemmings Pinnasse which went upon discovery for Nova Ginny, was returned to Banda, having found the Island: but in sending their men on shore to intreate of trade, there were nine of them killed by the Heathens, which are man-eaters; so they were constrained to return, finding no good to be done there.[395]

The discovery of Australia's west coast, which could not be confused with New Guinea, resulted from the new route across the Indian Ocean followed by many Dutch ships after 1611. In that year Hendrik Brouwer demonstrated that much faster voyages to Java could be made if ships would sail east in the 35°–40° latitudes instead of turning north after they rounded the Cape of Good Hope. In these latitudes, where steady westerly winds prevailed, Brouwer sailed about one thousand miles east of the Cape of Good Hope before turning due north and reaching Bantam by way of the Sunda Straits. Given the difficulties of measuring long distances at sea and of cal-

---

[392] On the possible sixteenth-century discovery of Australia and the cartography of Godhino de Héredia see Schilder, *op. cit.* (n. 351), pp. 20–23, and above, p. 328. On the ancient and medieval belief in Terra Australis and on European explorations in the southern Pacific prior to the discovery of Australia see Schilder, pp. 5–31.
[393] For the voyage of the "Duyfken" see *ibid.*, pp. 43–53.
[394] Saris, *loc. cit.* (n. 82), p. 491.
[395] *Ibid.*, p. 492.

culating longitude in the seventeenth century, it was inevitable that some ships following Brouwer's course would sail too far east and raise the Australian coast.[396] The first to do so was the "Eendracht," commanded by Dirck Hartogszoon, in 1616. No published report of Hartogszoon's discovery appeared and the log of the "Eendracht" has not survived. Hartogszoon, however, nailed a pewter plate, inscribed with the date and the name of his ship, to a pole which he planted on one of the offshore islands. The plate was discovered by Willem de Vlamingh at the end of the seventeenth century.[397]

In the years following Hartogszoon's discovery many Dutch ships sighted the Australian coast on their way to Batavia. The new route became mandatory for VOC ships in 1617. No descriptions of it were published, but since the coast was dangerous, VOC officials in Batavia carefully charted all the sightings, and contemporary charts and maps began to show fairly long stretches of the Australian coast, usually labeled Southland or *Land van d'Eendracht*. In 1622 an English ship, the "Tryall," was wrecked along the coast, and in the following year a Dutch ship narrowly escaped a similar fate. VOC officials became convinced that they should send ships to chart carefully the coast with its offshore islands and shoals.[398]

The hoped-for voyage of discovery was several times postponed, and early in 1623 Herman van Speult, VOC governor of Amboina, sent two small ships, the "Pera" and the "Arnhem," under Jan Carstenszoon to explore further the south coast of New Guinea. Carstenszoon sailed southeast along the New Guinea coast, where the commander of one of his ships and several crewmen were killed by Papuans, to the Torres Strait, which he took to be a shallow bay. From there he left the coast and sailed straight south until he raised the Cape York Peninsula, which he thought was still part of New Guinea. He sailed along the Peninsula's west coast to 17°8′ south latitude, several times landing and meeting people. The ships separated on the return voyage, the "Pera" returning along the New Guinea coast and the "Arnhem" exploring land along the northwest shore of the Gulf of Carpentaria. The journal of the "Pera" has survived and contains what might be the first western descriptions of Australia and of the people Carstenszoon encountered on the Cape York Peninsula.[399]

The brief account contained in Wassenaer's *Historisch verhael* (May, 1625) is probably the earliest published description of Australia and its people, although it is difficult to determine in Wassenaer's general description what

---

[396] On the new course and the nautical problems it entailed see Schilder, *op. cit.* (n. 351), pp. 54–60, and Jaap R. Bruijn, "Between Batavia and the Cape; Shipping Patterns of the Dutch East India Company," *Journal of Southeast Asian Studies*, IX (1980), 251–65.

[397] Schilder, *op. cit.* (n. 351), pp. 60–70.

[398] *Ibid.*, pp. 70–84.

[399] On the Carstenszoon expedition see *ibid.*, pp. 84–98. See also above, p. 450.

relates to New Guinea and what to the Cape York Peninsula. The coast is low, level, heavily forested, broken by many rivers and streams. There are many people, who are called Papuans; they are black, wear no clothes except over their privates, and do not seem to have seen guns before.[400] His description of the aborigines captured by Carstenszoon, however, can be determined by the log of the "Pera" to have come from Australia. They are difficult to capture; the Dutch had to entice them with colorful pieces of coral. Even so one got away. There must be many languages. Two captives taken from places along the coast only twenty-five miles apart cannot understand each other. Both are black with black curly hair. One has a long beard. They apparently have never seen iron and are very curious about it. One prisoner is able to make a cap for his head from some cloth which his captors give him, using thread and a tiny stick. They make fine canoes out of single logs by burning away the unwanted wood. On the return trip north one of the captives is able to recognize the place from which he came; he leaps overboard and attempts to swim ashore.[401]

Unintentional sightings along Australia's west coast continued and, as a consequence, more and more of the coast was charted. One ship, the "Gulden Zeepaerdt," which was commanded by Frans Thyssen and had Pieter Nuyts, a high VOC official, aboard, fell in with the southwestern tip of Australia and then sailed east, charting the south coast to about 133° east longitude. By 1630 almost all of the west coast and about half of the south coast had been charted. While the new information appeared on printed maps and globes, no literary descriptions appeared.[402]

The first published descriptions of the west coast resulted from the tragic shipwreck of the "Batavia" on a reef in the Walabi Group of Houtman's Abrolhos in 1629. After evacuating crew and passengers to one of the islands the commander of the "Batavia," François (or Francisco) Pelsaert, sailed to the mainland in the ship's boat, searching for water. The coast was inhospitable, there were few places to land, and no water to be found on shore. What began as a search for water ended in an open-boat voyage to Batavia, where a rescue ship was quickly outfitted to pick up the survivors. A popular account of the misadventures of the "Batavia," based on Pelsaert's journal, was published in 1647 (a brief notice had already appeared in Seyger van Rechteren's *Journael* in 1635).[403]

The story of Pelsaert's adventures was popular and exciting, but not because of its description of the Australian coast. At first sight this coast appeared low, barren, and rocky, like the coast near Dover. Beyond the coast

---

[400] See above, p. 450, and p. 1471.
[401] Wassenaer, *op. cit.* (n. 195), pp. 68–69.
[402] Schilder, *op. cit.* (n. 351), pp. 99–110. See our pl. 241.
[403] For the story of the shipwreck of the "Batavia" and subsequent events and for the bibliography of Pelsaert's journal see above, pp. 475–77, and Schilder, *op. cit.* (n. 351), pp. 111–28.

the country appeared pleasant and fruitful, but the surf was too heavy to land.[404] Further north the coast seemed a continuous reddish-colored rock against which the waves crashed making it impossible to land.[405] Some days later, six of the Dutchmen swam ashore and spent the whole day searching for water. They found none, but they saw four black, totally naked men, who fled at their approach. Subsequent landings were no more productive. The only water they found was the rainwater that collected in shallow indentations on some of the rocks. They saw only a dry barren plain, dotted with anthills so large that from a distance they looked like natives' huts. They saw only a few more people, all naked, who also ran from them, and they were plagued by flies.[406]

Tasman's 1642–43 voyage was of crucial importance in determining the size and location of Australia. He virtually sailed around it, thus disproving the existence of a large antipodal continent. He did not, however, even see the Australian coast on that voyage, and thus the published accounts contain no description of it. They contain, however, the first European descriptions of Tasmania and of New Zealand, both of which he coasted and extensively charted.[407]

On Tasmania, which he called Van Diemen's Land, Tasman thinks he hears sounds, like those of a trumpet, which he assumes are made by humans. Two large trees have footholds cut into them, presumably to enable men to climb up to the birds' nests in the branches, some sixty to sixty-five feet above the ground. The toeholds are about five feet apart, suggesting that either the people are extremely large or they have some peculiar way of climbing trees. Some of the toeholds are freshly cut. Tasman finds no men or animals, however; only some smoke in the distance and some paw prints resembling those of a tiger in the sand.[408]

Along the coast of New Zealand, however, Tasman finds an abundance of people: extremely large, tawny, seemingly fearless folk, with loud, hoarse voices. Their hair is long and thick, like that of the Japanese, which they comb upwards into a tuft on the top of the head, held in place with a sort of quill. They cover only the middle of their bodies, some with a sort of mat, others with what looks like woolen cloth. They walk swiftly, taking prodigiously long steps. Some come aboard the ship and barter in friendly fash-

---

[404] "La terre australe descovverte, par le capitaine Pelsaert, qui y fait naufrage," TR, Vol. I, No. 21, p. 51.

[405] *Ibid.*, p. 52.

[406] *Ibid.*, pp. 52–53.

[407] See above, p. 492. For Tasman's navigations and their cartographical consequences see Schilder, *op. cit.* (n. 351), pp. 139–205, and Posthumus-Meyjes (ed.), *op. cit.* (n. 378).

[408] Abel Tasman, "The Voyage of Captain Abel Jansen Tasman for the Discovery of Southern Countries by Direction of the Dutch East India Company," in J. Pinkerton (ed.), *A General Collection of The Best and Most Interesting Voyages and Travels in All Parts of the World* (17 vols.; London, 1808–14), XI, 441–42. Pinkerton's is a translation of the account found in Dirck Rembrantszoon van Nierop, *Eenige oefeningen* . . . (Amsterdam, 1674). See above, p. 492.

ion, but others attack a Dutch sloop, killing three crewmen. The Dutch then call the anchorage Murderers' Bay.[409]

Haelbos, in what must be the first published description of Maori tribesmen, adds some details to Tasman's picture, some of which may have actually come from depictions of Tonga Islanders. Many men, he reports, wear a white feather in their hair, a square plate hanging from their neck, and a white stripe on their chest. Some wear a square mantle that ties at the throat. Some wear their hair in a tuft, which they color red, while others let it hang down in long braids. Men shave their mustaches with fish teeth attached to little sticks, but wear square beards on their chins. Beardless youths, however, paint a black stripe over their upper lip to look like a long mustache. Most men go bareheaded, although a few wear a square sunshade of coconut leaves over the eyes. Haelbos describes two kinds of waist garments: one a grass skirt, the other a small mat over the genitals made from coconut shells. Some of the islanders are tattooed or scarred in various places on their bodies. Women's dress differs from men's only in that their grass skirts hang a little longer. Some older women and a few older men cut off their little fingers. Haelbos is unable to learn why. According to Haelbos, the women who came aboard the Dutch ship made overt and persistent sexual advances towards the crewmen, obviously encouraged by their men.[410]

Tasman does not mention this. He reports, however, that New Zealand is high and mountainous, but appears rich and fertile. It does not appear to be cultivated.[411]

Tasman's second voyage of discovery, in 1644, began by retracing Carstenszoon's route along the south coast of New Guinea, passing the Torres Strait without recognizing it for what it was, and continuing down the west coast of the Cape York Peninsula. He continued to follow the coast beyond where Carstenszoon turned back, however, and when the voyage was completed he had charted most of the Bay of Carpentaria and Australia's north coast. Evidence of his accomplishments survive only in maps and charts, however; no published accounts of this voyage appeared and no ship's log or journal has been preserved. That there had been such papers is suggested by a brief note in Nicolaas Witsen's *Noord en Oost Tartarye* (1692) describing attacks on Tasman's ships by naked black men with curly hair, armed with bows, arrows, javelins, and spears, at 17°12' south latitude, and again by stone-throwing natives in latitude 19°35' and longitude 134°. The natives, reports Witsen, eat roots, wear no clothes, and "seem to lead a miserable

---

[409] Tasman in Pinkerton (ed.), *op. cit.* (n. 408), pp. 442–43. These were Polynesians usually called Maori, who first settled New Zealand. They probably migrated there from the Society, Cook, and Marquesas islands. See J. M. Davidson, "The Polynesian Foundation," in W. H. Oliver and B. R. Williams (eds.), *The Oxford History of New Zealand* (Oxford, 1981), pp. 3–5. Murderers' Bay appears to be on the eastern shore of present-day Tasman Bay.

[410] Montanus, *op. cit.* (n. 380), pp. 579–81. On Maori dress *cf.* Davidson, *loc. cit.* (n. 409), pp. 24–25.

[411] Pinkerton (ed.), *op. cit.* (n. 408), pp. 441–42.

life." They drink from wells and paddle bark canoes. They seem to communicate over long distances with smoke signals.[412]

Small notices about the Southland continued to appear in published travel literature during the last quarter of the seventeenth century, despite the cessation of systematic VOC exploratory expeditions. Frederick Bolling, for example, claimed to have seen the west coast on his voyage out to Batavia. He seems much too fascinated with seeing all five parts of the world, the Southland being the fifth, to be accepted without question. All he reports is that "this land looks like Seeland in Denmark, with white sand along the sea."[413] Wurffbain retold the story of Pelsaert's adventures along the west coast, but provided no additional description of the land or people.[414] He also reported the death of Commander Gerrit Pool on New Guinea's south coast in 1636, but did not mention the subsequent voyage of Pool's ships to Melville Island and the Coburg Peninsula in North Australia.[415]

The last Dutch voyage of discovery to Australia was that commanded by Willem de Vlamingh in 1696–97, which explored the west coast from about 34° to 20° south latitude. In addition to charting the coast, De Vlamingh was supposed to assess the commercial potential of the Southland. Consequently he made several short trips inland, but the results were disappointing. He found no valuable commodities, fruitful areas for colonization, or people with whom to trade. The journal of his voyage, published in 1701, only adds corroborative details to the seventeenth-century image of Australia: that of an inhospitable land and a barbarous people, with little potential.[416] The land is mostly sandy and rocky; "a coast similar to that of Holland."[417] The trips inland are anything but pleasant; De Vlamingh and his men are constantly struggling with brushwood, sand, sore eyes, and flies. The vegetation seems strange: unusual plants, some aromatic wood. They eat some fruits which resemble beans, probably from the zamia palm, and begin to vomit violently. There are a few birds, which seem very shy, and no animals other than a rat about the size of an ordinary cat. But they see black swans, two of which they capture and take back with them. The people seem as shy as the birds. Although they regularly see footprints, smoke, fires, and even huts, "as bad as those of the Hottentots," only once do they see a few naked black men, who immediately flee from them.[418] They are not sorry to leave:

[412] Nicolaas Witsen, *Noord en Oost Tartarye* (2d ed.; Amsterdam, 1705), pp. 175–76, quoted in Schilder, *op. cit.* (n. 351), pp. 184–87.
[413] Frederick Bolling, "Oost-indische reisboek, bevattende zijn reis naar Oost-Indië . . . ," *BTLV*, LXVIII (1913), p. 324
[414] Wurffbain, *op. cit.* (n. 171), I, 40–45.
[415] *Ibid.*, 109, 144–46. See above, p. 1474.
[416] See above, pp. 504–5, for details of the voyage and for bibliography.
[417] G. G. Schilder (ed.), *De ontdekkingsreis van Willem Hesselsz. de Vlamingh in de jaren 1696–1697* ("WLV," LXXVIII, LXXIX; The Hague, 1976), II, 210.
[418] *Ibid.*, pp. 209–15. The "huts" may have been anthills.

The 21st [February, 1697] made sail in the morning, the latitude 21 degrees; held once more a council. Put out to sea in a N.W. direction. Got from de Vlamming three half barrels of water. One glass after Sun our skipper came from de Vlamming's ship and five shots were fired and from our vessel three as a signal of farewell to the miserable South-land.[419]

Not surprisingly, the most detailed and informative seventeenth-century descriptions of Australia where those of William Dampier. He first visited Australia in 1688, spending the first two months of that year on the north coast. His description of that visit, the first in English, appeared in his *A New Voyage around the World* (1697).[420] The land, he reports, is low and level; the shore is sandy except for the points, which are rocky. The soil inland is dry and sandy, yet it produces a variety of trees, the most common of which is the "Dragon tree." The woods are thin, however, and the trees fairly small. He finds no fruit or berry trees. Nor are there any animals; only once does he see the tracks of an animal, which he judges might be the size of a large dog. Few birds are seen and these not very large. There seem to be few fish in the sea, although there are plenty of "Manatee" and turtles.[421] While Dampier provides more details about the aborigines, he does not make them appear any more attractive than did the earlier Dutch accounts. They are, he concludes,

The miserablest People in the World . . . They have no Houses, and skin Garments, Sheep, Poultry, and Fruits of the Earth . . . And setting aside their Humane shape, they differ little from Brutes. They are tall, strait-bodied, and thin, with long Limbs. They have great Heads, round foreheads, and great Brows. Their Eyelids are always half closed, to keep the Flies out of their Eyes; they being so troublesome here, that no fanning will keep them from coming to one's Face; and without the assistance of both Hands to keep them off, they will creep into ones Nostrils, and Mouth too, if the Lips are not shut very close; so that from their Infancy being thus annoyed with these Insects, they do never open their Eyes as other People: And therefore they cannot see far unless they hold up their Head, as if they were looking somewhat over them. . . . They have great Bottle-noses, pretty full Lips, and wide Mouths.[422]

They are all, young and old, missing the two front teeth of their upper jaw. Dampier cannot tell if they are born without them or pull them out. They have long beardless faces and short, black, curly hair. Their skin is coal black. They wear no clothes but a tree-bark belt from which hang bunches of grass or small leafy branches to hide their genitals.[423]

They seem to have no houses but sleep out in the open. They live in

---

[419] *Ibid.*, p. 220. Translation by C. H. Robert in C. H. Robert (ed.), *The Explorations, 1696–1697, of Willem de Vlamingh* . . . (Amsterdam, 1972), p. 135.
[420] See above, pp. 582–85.
[421] Gray (ed.), *op. cit.* (n. 241), p. 312.
[422] *Ibid.*
[423] *Ibid.*, pp. 312–13.

groups of twenty or thirty. What sort of family structure they have Dampier cannot tell. Their only food seems to be small fish which they catch by making stone weirs across small coves and inlets, picking up the fish when the tide runs out. They also gather shellfish at low tide. They have neither fishing not hunting equipment, and they do not seem to eat any grains, roots, birds, or animals. Whatever they gather from the shore at low tide they broil and eat in common. Wooden swords and lances appear to be their only weapons; they have no metal. Nor do they have boats or canoes. They swim to and from the offshore islands. Their speech is throaty and Dampier cannot recognize any words. He finds no evidence of religion or worship. The aborigines they see on the mainland all flee when the English approach. On one of the islands where they could not easily escape, Dampier tries unsuccessfully to persuade some to carry water by giving them clothing.[424]

Dampier visited Australia again on his voyage of 1699, this time on the west and northwest coast, from Shark Bay (which he named) northward, surveying some of the same coast that De Vlamingh had surveyed only two years earlier. His account of this voyage, *A Voyage to New Holland,* was published in 1703.[425] As usual, Dampier's description of the coastline is very detailed and precise. He records latitudes, longitudes, compass directions, wind directions, depths, and the nature of the ground at each anchor drop. He includes some sketches of the coastline. In many places he corrects Tasman's chart, which he has with him. He apparently is uninformed about De Vlamingh's voyage. His description of the appearance of the coast merely confirms what earlier writers reported: the land is rather low and even but with steep cliffs to the sea. Some of the cliffs appear reddish, some white. Within Shark Bay the land slopes gently to the water. It is sandy on the beach, but the earth is a reddish color further inland. Some thin grass and small plants or shrubs can be seen, but nothing over ten feet high. Farther north, where he is able to walk inland, he observes that the land is lower than that along the sea. The sand is coarser and mixed with clay in some places. The forest begins still further inland. There are several sorts of small trees, none more than three feet in circumference, none more than twelve or fourteen feet high.[426] He has no more success finding water than Pelsaert or De Vlamingh had.

Dampier's descriptions of flora and fauna are more vividly detailed than any earlier descriptions. The grass grows in scattered tufts, each about as big as a bushel. Trees or shrubs of several kinds grow about ten feet high and have trunks about three feet in circumference which are bare to about five or six feet, where the small dense branches begin. Long narrow leaves are green on one side and whitish on the other. Some trees have a sweet smell and are reddish inside the bark. In the woodlands the trees are a little

---

[424] *Ibid.,* pp. 313–16.
[425] See above, pp. 584–85.
[426] Spencer (ed.), *op. cit.* (n. 141), pp. 105, 108, 124–25.

taller, but thinner, all still having a head of small branches. There are a few small black mangrove trees along the creeks and near the sea. Like De Vlamingh, Dampier is fascinated with the flowers and blossoms. He arrives in August, which is early spring there. Trees and bushes bear blossoms of red, white, yellow, and blue. Tall flowers are blooming, as well as very small flowers which grow along the ground. Many are unlike any flowers he has seen before; all are very beautiful and fragrant.[427]

Dampier sees few land birds: some eagles and five or six sorts of small birds ranging in size from sparrows to larks. Of seabirds there are ducks, with young now in the early spring, curlews, galdens, crab-catchers, cormorants, gulls, pelicans, and some that he has not seen before. He includes sketches. Further north he sees crows, small hawks, kites, and turtle doves, as well.[428]

There are few land animals: some lizards, one that looked like a hungry wolf, an ugly, scaly "sort of Guano" that had a stump of a tail which made it appear two-headed, and kangaroos. Dampier's description of kangaroos is disappointing: "A Sort of Raccoons, different from those of the West-Indies, chiefly as to their Legs; for these have very short Fore-Legs; but go jumping upon them as the others do, (and like them are very good Meat)."[429]

The bay and the sea yield a variety of fish: sharks, skates, thornbacks, rays, garfish, bonitas, whales, rockfish, oldwives, and "parracoots." There are watersnakes and huge green turtles, some weighing about two hundred pounds. Along the shore can be found many kinds of good shellfish. The beach is strewn with beautiful shells, many of which Dampier has never seen before.[430]

Like Pelsaert and De Vlamingh, Dampier sees few people, all of whom run away as soon as they spy the white strangers. Attempts to contact them or to catch one of them finally result in violence. One of Dampier's men is wounded with a wooden sword, and Dampier shoots one of the aborigines. They seem to be the same sort of people Dampier met in 1688 on the north coast. They look the same, although Dampier is unable to see if they are missing their two front teeth. Of the group that fought with the English, one young black man appears to be chief. He has a white circle painted around his eyes, a white stripe on his nose and forehead, and white stripes on his arms and chest. The aborigines seem to live chiefly on shellfish. Wherever they have built fires there are heaps of shells. They have no houses. What at first looked like huts, Dampier reports, proved to be rocks. He apparently does not realize that these are anthills.[431]

[427] *Ibid.*, pp. 108, 124–25.
[428] *Ibid.*, pp. 108, 125.
[429] *Ibid.* Pelsaert's manuscript journal contains a detailed and accurate description of kangaroos, but it does not appear to have been published.
[430] Spencer (ed.), *op. cit.* (n. 141), pp. 108–9, 124–25.
[431] *Ibid.*, pp. 120–23.

His crew developing scurvy, continually pestered by flies, always short of water, and finding little to encourage further exploration, Dampier sailed away from Australia with as little reluctance as had De Vlamingh.[432] His descriptions, like the several Dutch descriptions earlier in the century, certainly do not sketch an enticing picture of the Southland. They are a far cry from what Quiros had hoped to find. Nevertheless, Dampier and his Dutch predecessors provided Europeans with a reasonably detailed and quite accurate image of the Australian west and north coast and of the aborigines who lived there. That both the scenery and the people along the east coast might be different is suggested by Tasman's descriptions of Tasmania and New Zealand. Attractive or not, Europe's image of the overseas world at the end of the seventeenth century included a real Australia in place of the fabled Antipodes and a first glimpse of New Zealand and its Maori people.

Many other islands and coasts were described in the published reports of seventeenth-century European visitors to insular Southeast Asia. Most of them were observed from shipboard; many of them are not identifiable. Authors of travel journals and the ships' logs from which so many of them were taken described the islands, along with reefs, rocks, volcanic eruptions, typhoons, waterspouts, tidal waves, and ordinary weather conditions. It is impossible to report them all.

By the close of the seventeenth century, European readers had available immeasurably more and profoundly richer information about the archipelago than when the century began. They could have read about literally hundreds of islands and about the religion, politics, customs, arts, appearance, and character of scores of ethnic groups, much of it in rich detail produced by firsthand observations. They could have read careful, scientific descriptions of plants, birds, animals, flowers, soil, clothing, houses, boats, crafts, musical instruments, weapons, and the like. The literature carrying all this information was voluminous, repetitious, widely distributed, and translated into most European languages. It was, in short, widely available in sufficient quantities to become deeply familiar to many European readers.

During the seventeenth century, Europe's image of insular Southeast Asia was no longer confined to its littoral. Considerable information about the interior of many islands and the tribes which inhabited them became available. Some of it was still based on what coastal Malays told the Europeans about the interior, but some of it, especially in Java, Borneo, and the Spiceries, was the result of firsthand observation. Europe's image of Southeast Asia consequently grew richer and more complex. The periphery of the Malay Archipelago was also explored during the seventeenth century, and by the end of the century, European readers had available their first eyewitness glimpses of the world beyond Southeast Asia—of the Papuan Islands,

[432]*Ibid.*, p. 125.

New Guinea, the South Pacific islands, New Zealand, and a real Australia to replace the long-imagined Antipodes.

The Europeans who were describing insular Southeast Asia in the seventeenth century were also changing it. In the literature available to them, seventeenth-century readers could have traced the fortunes of powerful maritime states such as Acheh, Bantam, Brunei, Ternate, Tidore, Mataram, and Makassar, and watched each of them finally succumb to VOC hegemony before the century was out. They could have read about the depopulation of several Moluccan islands, the destruction of clove and nutmeg trees, the near annihilation of the Bandanese, the resettlement of other peoples in the Banda Islands and elsewhere, and the resettlement of Chinese captives on Java. In the end the archipelago became a Dutch preserve. Their Iberian and English competitors were effectively squeezed out. More and more, the books describing it were written by Dutchmen, with the consequence that Dutch priorities and Dutch evaluations of the subject peoples colored the image produced by the seventeenth-century literature. In it, for example, Java is more thoroughly described than any other part of the archipelago, in part because of its traditional cultural and political predominance, but also because it was the heart of the VOC empire.

The image formed from this massive body of firsthand reports and descriptions is not simply that of a confusing welter of islands large and small ruled by hundreds of petty autocrats, often at war with one another, and populated by a large variety of people with varied customs, religions, dress, and social structures. Many unmistakable elements of unity emerge from the literature which were frequently detected and noted by the seventeenth-century authors. Many of them seem to have regarded insular Southeast Asia as a coherent entity. The physical appearance of the region gave it a unity in the minds of the Europeans who traveled there during the seventeenth century. They all, with widely varying degrees of eloquence, describe the blue waters, the green coasts, the high mountains, the volcanoes, the lush vegetation, and the tropical, monsoonal climate. While differences between Java and Sumatra on the one hand and the Moluccas on the other are noted (Wallace's zones and divisions can be ascertained from these seventeenth-century descriptions), the similarities are far more striking.[433] Only Australia's landscape—and to a lesser extent, that of the eastern Sundas— seems markedly different. Even the ships and boats which ply the waters of the region bear noticeable similarities to one another. Oceangoing vessels, usually called junks, all seem to have several masts, reed or bamboo sails, multiple planking, high sterns, and twin side rudders.[434] Smaller boats, from Sumatra to New Guinea and beyond, whatever their differences in

---

[433] Wallace, *op. cit.* (n. 33), pp. 1–15.
[434] On oceangoing junks see Pierre-Yves Manguin, "The Southeast Asian Ship: An Historical Approach," *Journal of Southeast Asia Studies,* Vol. XI, No. 2 (Sept., 1980), 266–76.

size, decorations, and workmanship, all seem to be versions of the outrigger canoe. The people provide another major element of unity for insular Southeast Asia. Seventeenth-century Europeans describe them as of varying shades of brown or yellow-brown, not black, and with straight black hair. They of course detected physical differences between the various islanders, but most frequently they streamline their descriptions of a new people by reporting that in many respects they are similar to Javans or Ternatans, for example. Seventeenth-century Europeans immediately recognized the black-skinned, curly-haired Papuans and Australian aborigines at the very eastern and southern edges of the area to be racially different from all the other peoples of the area. Those who had used "black" to describe darker-skinned Javans or Sumatrans used "coal black" and similar terms to describe Papuans or Australians. Even the character of the people as described by seventeenth-century Europeans displays a large number of common features. With small variations the long list of negative characteristics so frequently used to describe Javans and Sumatrans seems applicable to the peoples of the eastern archipelago as well. These judgments, of course, may result as much from the prejudices, purposes, and relationships of the Europeans as from the common behavior of the islanders. Nevertheless, quite different characteristics were ascribed to the Papuans.[435]

As described by seventeenth-century Europeans, the coastal regions of insular Southeast Asia were inhabited by Malay-speaking people. Malay, they reported, was the *lingua franca* for the entire area. Many European observers realized that the Malays had displaced earlier inhabitants who had fled to the interior mountains. Islam, they reported, came along with the Malay language. Those who lived in the interior—old Javans, Bataks on Sumatra, Dayaks on Borneo, Alfuros in the Moluccas, and the like—retained their old religions and their old languages. Only in the Papuan Islands, New Guinea, and Australia was the pattern broken of a Malay-speaking, Muslim coastal population together with a less civilized, pagan, inland population. The process was continuing, however, and was unwittingly abetted by the European intrusion. The Bandanese, for example, who fled the Dutch were becoming influential in the Kai and Aru Islands, were introducing Malay words and practices to the Papuans, and were converting some of them to Islam. At the same time Banda's new population, largely imported by the Dutch overlords, was becoming more like that of other parts of the archipelago.

Insular Southeast Asia was dominated by highly urbanized populations. Apart from interior Java and Makassar, where settled agriculture prevailed,

---

[435] For a perceptive discussion of the problems attending seventeenth- and eighteenth-century Europeans' generalizations about the character of Southeast Asians see Jörg Fisch, *Holland's Ruhm in Asien, François Valentyns Vision des niederländischen Imperiums im 18. Jahrhundert* (Stuttgart, 1986).

the inland areas of the region seem sparsely settled. Attempts to encourage rice agriculture in Acheh were described as ineffective. Acheh still imported most of its rice. Most people seem to have lived in fairly large coastal towns, near the mouths of rivers. Some of the cities were surprisingly large. Furthermore, they were described as similar to one another, built on stilts along the rivers, amidst fruit and coconut trees. Many large cities were scarcely visible from the sea; some towns simply could not be seen. The cities obtained marketable products from inland tribes which were rarely effectively under their control, and they traded these commodities with merchants from other places, especially with Indian, Chinese, or European merchants. Towns which did not trade directly with foreign merchants usually traded with one or another of the major emporia—Bantam, Batavia, Makassar, Acheh, or Malacca—where foreigners bought their products.[436] Consequently, as seventeenth-century Europeans described it, insular Southeast Asia was not only highly urbanized, it also formed a commercial unity. Products from all over the area were available at its great markets. Many parts of the region were not self-sufficient. The Spiceries, for example, imported much of their food and clothing, exchanging it for cloves, nutmeg, and mace. Dutch attempts to monopolize the spice trade and to localize spice production were destructive of the region's commercial unity and disastrous for some of the people in the Spiceries. The Dutch promised to bring in food and clothing. The natives distrusted their ability or willingness to do so, and indeed the Dutch were unable to meet the demands. They tried to supplement their food shipments by allowing the Papuans of Kai and Aru to trade freely with Banda and Amboina. One result was to speed the Papuans' integration into the Southeast Asian commercial network. All this emerges quite clearly from the published seventeenth-century European descriptions, and a wide-ranging and perceptive seventeenth-century reader probably would have been able to recognize it.

The nature of Southeast Asian cities and commerce helps explain the politics of the region. Except in central Java, ambitious rulers sought to expand not by conquering inland territories but by controlling riverine towns through which the products of the interior were marketed. While none of the authors in the seventeenth century described it in exactly these terms, many of their published descriptions trace the rise and decline of such Southeast Asian empires as Acheh, Johore, Bantam, Mataram, Ternate, Tidore, Brunei, and Makassar, and the rivalries among them. Perhaps the VOC should be considered simply the last and most successful of these basi-

---

[436] On Southeast Asian cities see A. Reid, "The Structure of Cities in Southeast Asia, Fifteenth to Seventeenth Centuries," *Journal of Southeast Asian Studies,* Vol. XI, No. 2, (Sept. 1980), 235–50; and Bennet Bronson, "Exchange at the Upstream and Downstream Ends: Notes toward a Functional Model of the Coastal State in Southeast Asia," in Karl L. Hutterer, *Economic Exchange and Social Interaction in Southeast Asia* (Ann Arbor, 1977), pp. 39–52.

cally seaborne commercial empires. Even the political structure of Southeast Asian cities displayed common features. Everywhere local princes controlled the trade in their cities and taxed it. Everywhere the Europeans met comparable officials: a king or sultan, a *shahbandar, orang kayas,* and so forth. Sometimes they applied the titles inaccurately, but in fact the port cities contained a fairly large number of common features. Even comparable social institutions such as slavery and the control of manpower as a measure of wealth appear throughout the area.[437] The absence of many of these common features in New Guinea, Australia, and the South Pacific islands clearly delineates the region's eastern and southern frontiers. Western New Guinea and the islands off its western coast, however, were a regular source of slaves for Southeast Asia.

Elements of unity in insular Southeast Asia, stressed or assumed in much recent scholarship, were already visible in the image of the area to be derived from seventeenth-century descriptions. Indeed, for most of the area, these seventeenth-century descriptions and travel accounts, together with the unpublished European materials, are the indispensable sources on which any reconstruction of the region's history depends.

---

[437] See A. Reid, "Trade and State Power in Sixteenth and Seventeenth Century Southeast Asia," *Proceedings of the Seventh IAHA Conference, Bangkok, August, 1977* (Bangkok, 1979), pp. 391–419; Kenneth R. Hall, *Maritime Trade and State Development in Early Southeast Asia* (Honolulu, 1955); A. Reid (ed.), *Slavery, Bondage and Dependency in Southeast Asia* (New York, 1983), especially the introduction, pp. 1–43.

CHAPTER XIX

The Philippines and the
Marianas (Ladrones)

Printed books and maps of the Pacific region published in the sixteenth century revealed to Europe for the first time the existence of the Philippines and
the Ladrones (Marianas) and of the Spanish interests in these two archipelagos.[1] In the early years of the seventeenth century a rash of publications
appeared in Europe which contained substantial eyewitness accounts by seasoned observers as well as briefer reports on the appearance of the Dutch
in the western Pacific and on their clashes with the Spaniards. Olivier van
Noort's description of his voyages around the globe (1598–1601) and his
battle with the Spaniards off Manila first let the world at large know that
the Spanish monopoly of the Pacific was being challenged by the aggressive Netherlanders.[2] Contemporaneously the Spanish Franciscan missionary
Marcelo de Ribadeneira published his *Historia,* which promises in its title to
give a description of the Philippines and other places in the East.[3] Primarily
a polemic against the Jesuits in Japan and an account of the Franciscan activities in China, Siam, and elsewhere, Ribadeneira's large volume devotes only
the first of its six books to the Philippines and the Franciscan successes there.
Distressed by a new growth of problems for Christianity in Japan and by the
appearance of the Protestant Dutch in the Pacific, Rome itself began to pay
more attention to the missions in the strategically located Philippines. The

---

[1] See the summary account in *Asia,* I, 623–46.
[2] Van Noort's journal was published shortly after his return home in 1601 as *Beschryvinghe
vande voyagie om den geheelen werelt cloot . . .* (Amsterdam). For its bibliographical history see
above, pp. 441–43. A portion of it was published in English translation in *PP,* II, 187–206.
[3] *Historia de las islas del archipiélago Filipino y reinos de la gran China, Tartaria, Cochin-China,
Malaca, Siam, Cambodge y Japon* (Barcelona, 1601). Reprinted in Spanish with an English translation by P. G. Fernandez as Vols. XVI and XVII of the publications of the Historical Conservation Society (Manila, 1970). The references which follow are to this English translation.

Jesuits, for example, started to publish separately certain of their Annual Letters from the Philippines to let the faithful in Europe know of the victories still being won in the Pacific despite setbacks in Japan.[4] They also include mission statistics and warnings about Dutch activities and ambitions in the Pacific area.[5]

The best Jesuit account of this period is Pedro Chirino's *Relación de las islas Filipinas* (Rome, 1604).[6] In the Philippines from 1590 to 1602, he went to Rome as procurator, where he wrote down his relation in 1603. Jesuit General Acquaviva was so taken with this account that he ordered its immediate publication in Rome. In Spain, meanwhile, pamphlets began to appear telling of the Chinese revolt of 1603 in Manila and of the efforts being undertaken by the authorities to control and placate the Chinese.[7] In his book celebrating the Spanish conquest of the Moluccas, Bartolomé Leonardo de Argensola supplied bits of fresh information on the Philippines, the staging ground for the Spanish military expedition.[8] The best book of this period was prepared by Antonio de Morga, lieutenant-governor of the Philippines from 1595 to 1598 and senior judge of its *audiencia* from 1598 to 1603. His *Sucesos de las islas Filipinas* (Mexico, 1609) became a standard work on the islands widely quoted and plagiarized by Morga's contemporaries and successors and used still as a basic account of the condition of Filipino culture at the beginning of the Spanish period.[9] Except for memorials to the crown and martyrologies, very little more was published in Europe on the Philippines before 1640.

[4] Until the early seventeenth century the Philippines were usually mentioned in the letter-books concerning Peru and Japan. See W. E. Retana (comp.), *Aparato bibliográfico de la historia general de Filipinas* (3 vols.; Manila, 1906; reprinted [Manila] in 1964), I, 45; and A. Viegas (ed.), *Relação anual . . . nos anos de 1600 à 1609* (3 vols.; Coimbra, 1930–42), I, 169–70. Separate letterbooks on the Philippines were first published in 1604, 1605, and 1610; these were quickly translated and reissued at various Jesuit presses in Europe. See Streit, V, 237–49, 253–54. Letterbooks were published in the Low Countries and at Dillingen and Lyons in 1618–19 which contain summary materials on the progress of the Jesuits in the Philippines from 1602 to 1614. Copies of these five exceedingly rare letterbooks are preserved in the Regenstein Library of the University of Chicago. For an evaluation of the Jesuit letters from the Philippines see H. de la Costa, S.J., *The Jesuits in the Philippines, 1581–1768* (Cambridge, Mass., 1967), p. 629.
[5] See, for example, the letter of Gregorio Lopez, S.J., regarding events of 1609 and 1610, which concentrates on the Dutch threat to the Philippines; the English translation is in BR, XVII, 100–43.
[6] Translated into English in BR, XII, 175–321; XIII, 29–217. For a recent summary of what is known about his life and writings see M. R. Jurado, S.J., "Pedro Chirino, S.J., and Philippine Historiography," *Philippine Studies*, XXIX (1981), 354–59. For further bibliographical detail see above, pp. 318–19.
[7] For example, see *Relación del levantamiento de los Sangleyes . . .* (Seville, 1606). Translated in BR, XIV, 119–39.
[8] *Conquista de las islas Malucas* (Madrid, 1609). Excerpts relating to the Philippines are translated in BR, XVI, 217–317.
[9] For further bibliographical detail see above, pp. 326–28. The most recent critical edition is J. S. Cummins (trans. and ed.), *Sucesos de las islas Filipinas* ("HS," 2d ser., CXL; Cambridge, 1971).

I

"INDIOS" (FILIPINOS) AND SPANIARDS

Most of what Europeans knew about the Philippines before 1600 came to them from authors who were primarily intent upon reaching the Spice Islands, China, or Japan via the Pacific route. As a consequence, much of what they report about the Philippines is of secondary or merely coincidental importance. It was only with the appearance of Chirino's and Morga's books that the Philippines became objects of study in their own right.[10] The works of these two commentators, supplemented by materials provided by a few of their contemporaries, brought the Philippines for the first time into sharp focus for European readers of the earlier half of the seventeenth century. In these two works, more than in any of the others, can be discerned the confrontations between the indigenous culture, the Christian religion, and the Spanish civil and military administration. From their accounts it becomes clear also that the Spanish secular administrators and the missionaries were not always in agreement about the best methods to follow in pacifying and Christianizing the islanders.

Much had been reported in the sixteenth century on the location of the Philippines and their geographical relationship to neighboring island groups and continental East Asia. Nonetheless both Chirino and Morga remind their readers that the Philippines are placed between the Moluccas and Japan and notice that they extend south of the equator and terminate with the island of Borneo.[11] The archipelago includes innumerable islands, large and small, though the Spanish administer only forty of the larger islands.[12] There are from sixteen to nineteen chief islands; Luzon, the largest, extends from the San Bernardino channel northward to Cagayan Province, and its width varies markedly. Luzon and Borneo are each larger than Spain, and Mindanao is no smaller. The islands are close one to the other and "not one

[10] In his dedication Morga remarks (*ibid.*, p. 43): "For since those parts are so remote, no account has been published which deals specifically with them from their beginnings down to their present state." Chirino, who had seen Morga's unpublished work before publishing his own, calls it "a complete and copious history" (BR, XII, 176). This relieves Chirino of the need to write a historical background for his own report on the missions.

[11] Borneo was possibly included as part of the Philippine archipelago because of its trading connections, its slave raids, and its export of Islam to the Sulu islands and Mindanao. But Chirino also remarks that the southern terminus is not known. See BR, XII, 177, 202. For example, Mindanao was not always considered to be a part of the Philippines proper according to Argensola in *ibid.*, XVI, 225. Ribadeneira, who is notably inaccurate on geographical locations, seems to think that Cebu and Luzon are alternative names of the same island. See Fernandez (trans.), *op. cit.* (n. 3), I, 331.

[12] Morga in Cummins (trans. and ed.), *op. cit.* (n. 9), p. 245. Argensola (BR, XVI, 233) claims that the archipelago "called Filipinas" includes 11,000 islands. More frequently this number is used with reference to all the islands of Southeast Asia. The Philippines proper actually number around 7,100 islands.

so small that it is not in reality large."[13] According to Morga, "much that is said of Luzon is true of, and applies in general terms to, the other islands."[14]

The weather of Luzon varies from the more temperate north to the hotter south, and from lowlands to uplands. Winter (the wet season) and summer (the dry) are generally the reverse of those seasons in Europe. It rains and storms from June to September and is clear and fair from October through May. But these seasons are not everywhere the same; in northernmost Luzon, for example, the seasons are about the same as those of Spain. Tornadoes and heavy storms (typhoons) sweep both land and sea; they ordinarily originate in the north, veer towards the west and south, and "move around the compass in the space of twenty hours or more."[15]

Blessed by a sunny climate and ample water, these islands abound in plants and animals of all sorts. In both the flatlands and the mountains, trees of various kinds provide shade, lumber, masts, and fruits throughout the year. While most trees never shed their leaves, the "balete" (*Ficus balete*) and the "dabdab" (*dapdap,* or the *Erythrina variegata*) are exceptions to this rule; the leaves of both these trees are used in cooking.[16] Aside from the numerous and valuable coco palms, there are many native trees which produce a wide range of edible fruits including oranges, lemons, and bananas "of some ten or twelve varieties." Vegetables of all types flourish. Grapes have been successfully introduced, but olive and quince trees from Spain do not fare well. In the Cagayan province of Luzon, chestnuts and pinenuts grow profusely; its mountains also produce fine woods, including cedar, various grades of ebony, and redwood. Bamboo canes provide membranes for writing material, carry clear drinking water in their hollow interiors, and are readily made into strong ladders. In the fertile flatlands the people cultivate yams, rice, and cotton. Honey and wax are plentiful, for beehives abound in the mountains.[17]

The fields and hills are full of wild fowl, deer, swine, and goats. The islanders breed and raise these and many other animals, including some imported from abroad. Water buffaloes called "carabaos" are native breeds with long horns which roam wild in the mountains and are domesticated in

---

[13]Chirino in BR, XII, 204. Spain is actually much larger in area than any of the Philippine Islands. Luzon is comparable in area to Guatemala.

[14]Cummins (trans. and ed.), *op. cit.* (n. 9), p. 246. Ribadeneira (Fernandez [ed.], *op. cit.* [n. 3], I, 340) writes only about the native customs and habits of the Tagalog area.

[15]Cummins (trans. and ed.), *op. cit.* (n. 9), pp. 247–48; and Chirino in BR, XII, 183. The climate of the Philippines is even and mild in temperature throughout the year and the seasons less pronounced than those of continental Southeast Asia. The weather varies, as Morga says, within the island of Luzon. Typhoons hit the Philippines, particularly the islands north of Mindanao, with great frequency. On the climate of the Philippines see E. H. G. Dobby, *Southeast Asia* (9th ed.; London, 1966), pp. 320–23.

[16]These trees shed their leaves during the hot dry period. See Science Education Center, Univ. of the Philippines, *Plants of the Philippines* (Quezon City, 1971), p. 4.

[17]Chirino in BR, XII, 187–91, 214–16; and Morga in Cummins (trans. and ed.), *op. cit.* (n. 9), pp. 253–54. Ribadeneira claims incorrectly that "the islands are replete with wheat" (Fernandez [trans.], *op. cit.* [n. 3], I, 333). In fact, wheat does not grow well in the Philippines.

the flatlands. Smaller and gentler cattle are imported from China which have large humps on their shoulders and are kept for the milk they give.[18] Horses, mares, and asses, not being native to the Philippines, have been introduced from New Spain, China, and Japan. Horses and mares thrive in this climate and become fat from being fed on a maize-like plant and on rice in the husk. Mules, asses, and sheep imported from America "never increase because so far the climate and pasturage seem unsuitable."[19] Monkeys, parrots, parakeets, and large venomous snakes are everywhere. In the rivers and estuaries live deadly scorpions and the bloodthirsty crocodiles which the *Indios* venerate. Rivers, lakes, and seas provide all kinds of fish and shellfish for food. The *Indios* trap the fish in bamboo enclosures, catch them in reed baskets, or on fishing lines with hooks.[20]

Morga, whose personal experience was limited to Luzon and its immediate environs, claims that the inhabitants of its southern and northern provinces "are the aboriginals of the island." Those of the Manila area are Malays and other migrants from afar.[21] Both sexes are "of average height," endowed with fine features, and have the bronze color "of cooked quinces." They have black hair; men keep their beards scanty by pulling out the hairs. Sharp, hot in spirit, and determined, these *Indios* are clever at agriculture, fishing, and trading. They deport themselves with elegance, and the rich commonly walk the streets followed by a train of servants. In certain parts of Luzon live black, barbarous people with kinky hair. Of limited ability, these small people have no fixed abodes and so roam about the mountains and rough country. They support themselves by catching game, planting rice in temporary plots, and generally living off the country. Periodically they attack the settlements of the other natives; they resist all efforts to subdue them.[22] The inhabitants of Cagayan Province in northern Luzon are braver and more warlike than their neighbors and have risen at least twice against their Spanish governors.[23]

The males of Luzon usually wear a short collarless linen garment like a

[18] On cattle raising after the coming of the Spanish see J. L. Phelan, *The Hispanization of the Philippines. Spanish Aims and Filipino Responses, 1565–1700* (Madison, Wis., 1959), pp. 111–12. The Spanish learned quickly that animals from other Eastern countries acclimatized better than those from America.

[19] Mules are sterile.

[20] Chirino in BR, XII, 188–89; Morga in Cummins (trans. and ed.), *op. cit.* (n. 9), pp. 255–58. Although these two authors say little about it, severe strains were imposed on the subsistence economy of the islands, as is indicated by the food shortages suffered in Manila during the end years of the sixteenth century while Chirino and Morga were there. See Luz Ausejo, "The Philippines in the Sixteenth Century" (Ph.D. diss., Dept. of History, University of Chicago, 1972), pp. 354–58.

[21] On the prehistory of the Philippines see Ausejo, *op. cit.* (n. 20), Pt. I.

[22] Called Negritos or Negrillos by the Spaniards, small, black peoples were found in the interior reaches of Negros and in the mountains of Mindoro, Luzon, and Mindanao. See *ibid.*, pp. 267–68, and below, pp. 1522, 1536.

[23] Morga in Cummins (trans. and ed.), *op. cit.* (n. 9), pp. 247–48; also see Ribadeneira in Fernandez (trans.), *op. cit.* (n. 3), I, 341.

short-sleeved jacket, which reaches slightly below the waist and is called a "cangan" (Tagalog, *kangan*). Ordinary jackets are blue or black, but those of the chiefs are red and called "chinana" (possibly from Malay, *chincha*, a rich cloth fabric). Around the waist they wear a red loincloth called "bahaques" (*bahag*) and around the head a narrow turbanlike cloth called a "potong" (*putong*). Many bedeck themselves with gold necklaces and bracelets; others wear strings of carnelians and other stones twisted on cords around their legs. In the mountains of Zambales in central Luzon they shave the front half of the scalp and let a long mane of loose hair hang from the back. Women in Luzon generally wear a short jacket with sleeves of different colors called "varos" (*báros*). Around the waist they wrap a white cotton skirt which falls to the feet. Also they dress in other colored garments, the principal women wearing graceful and decorative crimson mantles of silk and other rich materials.[24] They adorn themselves with gold necklaces, bracelets, earrings, and finger rings, and tie their black hair in a knot on the back of the head. Only the chieftains and their women have footwear; all others leave their feet and legs bare.[25]

Both sexes are personally very clean and neat, and tidy about their garments. Particular about their hair, they wash it in *gogo* (bark of a climbing vine)[26] and make it very shiny by applying a lotion of oil of sesame and musk. They take care of their teeth by washing them regularly, by filing them down when young to equal size, and by coloring them black; they insert gold between their teeth for ornament. Brought up in the water, the islanders swim like fish and bathe regularly for cleanliness and recreation. Newborn children and their mothers are bathed in cold water. Everyone bathes at sunset after the day's work is done. Modesty leads them to submerge themselves in a squatting posture when bathing. A vessel of water is kept at the door of every house for washing the feet. In the famous hot springs near Lake Bay baths are taken as treatments for particular maladies. At no time do they consider bathing to be harmful.[27]

[24] In Luzon the cotton skirt is called *sáya* and the outer mantle is the *tapis*. See G. F. Zaide, *The Pageant of Philippine History* (2 vols.; Manila, 1979), I, 107.

[25] Morga in Cummins (trans. and ed.), *op. cit.* (n. 9), pp. 248–49. *Cf.* Ribadeneira in Fernandez (trans.), *op. cit.* (n. 3), I, 341. Colored drawings, possibly by a contemporary Chinese artist, show Filipinos in costume. These are found in the unpublished "Boxer Codex" described in C. Quirino and M. Garcia, "The Manners, Customs, and Beliefs of the Philippine Inhabitants of Long Ago; Being Chapters of 'A Late Sixteenth Century Manila Manuscript,' Transcribed, Translated, and Annotated," *Philippine Journal of Science*, LXXXVII (1958), 325–449. A photostat copy of the "Boxer Codex" is in the Ayer Collection of the Newberry Library; four of the colored drawings of its Filipinos have been reproduced in black and white in Phelan, *op. cit.* (n. 18), between pp. 32 and 33. For a complete description and history of the codex see C. R. Boxer, "A Late Sixteenth Century Manila MS," *JRAS*, April, 1950, pp. 37–39.

[26] Gogo is still considered in the Philippines to be the best old-fashioned shampoo for cleansing long hair.

[27] Morga in Cummins (trans. and ed.), *op. cit.* (n. 9), pp. 249–50. Chirino in BR, XII, 186–87, 212–13. The missionaries vainly tried to deprive their converts of the daily bath as an act of penitence; the Filipino Christians also took enthusiastically to the use of holy water. See

Household chores and the tending of children, poultry, and pigs are women's work. While the women weave cloth, spin cotton, and do needle-work, their men farm, fish, sail, or trade. Female chastity and virginity do not possess any particular merit for the *Indios;* even adultery brings little or no censure.[28] When the *Indios* go walking through the streets their slow and stately processions are led by the ladies under their umbrellas, followed by the men and their attendants. The women pound rice in wooden mortars, which they then cook in water; the staple of their diet, cooked rice, is known as *morisqueta* in Filipino Spanish. For meat they eat boiled fish, pork, venison, and carabao. Vegetables and fruits are abundant, especially tubers and beans, as well as plaintains, guavas, pineapples, custard-apples, and many kinds of oranges. They eat at small, low tables and have no hesitation in all plunging their hands into the same dish or in all drinking from the same cup. *Tuba,* a distilled and clear palm wine, is drunk in all the islands. At their feasts and celebrations they drink it incessantly. While they are heavy drinkers, the Filipinos rarely get drunk enough to lose their senses. To them there is nothing disgraceful in being tipsy or drunk.[29]

The Filipinos fight with bows and arrows, but more commonly arm themselves with iron-headed spears. They protect themselves from head to foot with wooden shields called "carasas" (Tagalog, *kalásag*). At the waist they carry a dagger with a pointed blade, a gold or ivory hilt, and an open pommel with two crossbars. These double-edged daggers called "bararos" (*barong?*) are carried in scabbards of wood or buffalo-horn. With this weapon they are able to cut off an enemy's head with a single blow. Heads severed in war are hung up in their houses as trophies. Before the advent of the Spanish they defended their settlements with fortresses mounted by primitive artil-lery. From the Spaniards they quickly learned to handle with dexterity the European arquebuses and muskets.[30]

Heavily dependent on water transport, the Filipinos construct various kinds of vessels for use in the rivers and along the coast and for more distant travel from one island to the other. On the rivers and creeks they travel in-land in large canoes made of single logs, equipped with keels and lined with plank benches. Long ships called "vireyes" (*vireys*) and "barangayes" (*baran-gays*) are used in war. These slender ships are propelled by many oarsmen who row on either side of the vessel with paddles, sometimes as many as one hundred on each side. Some men sing chants to pace the rowers. Above

---

Phelan, *op. cit.* (n. 18), p. 75. Many Europeans, especially Protestants, regarded frequent bathing, especially in rivers and streams, as unhealthy and this-worldly. River bathing was banned by Cambridge University in 1571!

[28] *Cf.* Ausejo, *op. cit.* (n. 20), pp. 292–93.

[29] Morga in Cummins (trans. and ed.), *op. cit.* (n. 9), pp. 250–51; Chirino in BR, XII, 308–10. On drinking as a ritual see Phelan, *op. cit.* (n. 18), p. 23.

[30] Morga in Cummins (trans. and ed.), *op. cit.* (n. 9), pp. 251–52. On the practice of head-hunting in Cagayan see Quirino and Garcia, *loc. cit.* (n. 25), p. 393. The Borneans are credited with introducing artillery use and manufacture. See Ausejo, *op. cit.* (n. 20), pp. 303–4.

the oarsmen, soldiers stand on a bamboo platform ready to fight. A square linen sail supported by two thick bamboos is hoisted on this same platform; larger ships have foresails which are similarly set up. Both types of sail are lowered by windlasses with a tackle. The entire platform is protected from sun and rain by an awning made of palm-leaf mats. An outrigger or bamboo framework is tied securely to each side of the ship. The length of the vessel itself, the outrigger serves as a counterbalance to keep the ship from capsizing in heavy seas or in gales. The Filipinos also construct larger and roomier vessels to carry bulk merchandise along the coasts. Ordinarily all vessels are put together with small wooden bolts and splices, though they sometimes use iron nails.[31]

In Luzon and the islands neighboring it, there are many bays, rivers, bars, coves, and other sheltering places for vessels large and small. But reefs, shifting shoals, strong currents, and fierce winds make navigation tricky and sailing hazardous for the inexperienced. Manila lies on a bay with a narrow entrance, in the middle of which an island called "Miraveles" (Corregidor) lies crosswise. Seagoing vessels can enter the bay through the channels on either side of this island. While the whole bay has good anchorages, the spacious harbor of "Cabis" (Cavite) is protected from the winds by a point of land. The river of Manila itself is not much good for anchoring, since its bar and shifting shoals make entrance difficult even for ships that draw little water. As a consequence most seagoing vessels anchor at Cavite just to the south of Manila.[32]

These insular coasts produce mother-of-pearl, seed pearls, large oyster and turtle shells, ambergris, and cowry shells, from which curios are made. Many of these products are exported to other Eastern areas and to Mexico. Cotton threads and cloths along with carabao horns are traded to China. Prominent among the exports to Japan are redwood, deerskins, and antique earthenware jars (*tibores*) in which tea is preserved. The Japanese prize these jars, pay huge prices for them, and put them on display in their homes. Foreign and internal trade is facilitated by the presence of gold. Placers and mines at Paracole on Luzon island yield gold mixed with copper. In the island's mountainous interior the unsubdued "Ygolotes" (Igorots, Tagalog for mountaineers) mine gold mixed with silver. Reputedly they extract only as much as they need. This partially refined gold is traded in Ilocos for living necessities, and here it is further refined before entering general commerce as a commodity and medium of exchange.[33]

[31] Morga in Cummins (trans. and ed.), *op. cit.* (n. 9), pp. 252–53. For a general discussion see P. Y. Manguin, "The Southeast Asian Ship: An Historical Approach," *Journal of Southeast Asian Studies*, XI (1980), 266–76.
[32] Morga in Cummins (trans. and ed.), *op. cit.* (n. 9), pp. 264–65.
[33] *Ibid.,* pp. 261–63. On the Igorot gold mines see Quirino and Garcia, *loc. cit.* (n. 25), pp. 391–92, n. 10. On gold coins see Zaide, *op. cit.* (n. 24), pp. 145–46. On gold in the southern islands see below, pp. 1516, 1533.

"Indios" (Filipinos) and Spaniards

The Bisayan islands of the central Philippines, where the early Spanish explorers first landed, lie between Luzon and Mindanao. Of these numerous and heavily populated islands the most important are Leyte, "Babao" (Ibabao, or East Samar), Samar, Bohol, Negros, Cebu, Panay, the Cuyo group, and the Calamians between Palawan and Mindoro. Their Bisayan-speaking inhabitants are called "Pintados" (*i.e.,* painted or tattooed people) by the Spaniards "because they adorn their bodies with figures from head to foot." Beginning when a boy is young, he is tattooed by degrees. Designs and lines are drawn on the body by a tattoo artist. These lines are pricked until blood comes. On the bloody surface they apply a black powder (soot or ink) which never fades out. Young children are not tattooed and the women tattoo only one hand and part of the other. Even when covered with pictures, they do not wander about naked. They dress from shoulders to ankles in collarless cotton robes bordered with colors. Under these outer garments they wear a breechclout. Chirino, who saw these tattooed Bisayans himself, believed that much money could be made in Europe by exhibiting one of them.[34]

The Bisayans are better natured and more noble in their bearing than the natives of Luzon. The men cut their hair except for a short pigtail which they retain following the old Spanish style. Around the head they wind a distinctive turban-like headdress. While they follow the same occupations as other Filipinos, they are less inclined to agriculture than to navigation, war, and piracy.[35] Their boats and weapons are similar to those of Luzon. In color they are darker and in their manners less polite than the inhabitants of Luzon. The island of Leyte, like Luzon, exhibits climatic differences between its southern and northern parts.[36] When the northerners are harvesting the southerners are sowing; as a consequence the island produces two abundant crops annually. In Panay most of the males are highly skilled carpenters who specialize in ship construction.[37] The Bisayans sell rice to one another at a fixed price and always offer generous hospitality to travelers.

No universal language unites the Philippine Islands. While the tongues are many and different, they exhibit strong similarities and any of them may be learned and spoken in a short time. If one is learned, the others come readily.[38] Only the language of the Negritos is very different from the rest.

[34]Chirino in BR, XII, 205–6. Morga observes that they do not tattoo the face (Cummins [trans. and ed.], *op. cit.* [n. 9], pp. 266–67), but a contemporary illustration shows tattooing on part of the face. See pl. 2 in Nicholas P. Cushner, S.J., *Spain in the Philippines from Conquest to Revolution* (Quezon City, 1971), facing p. 62.
[35]On the Bisayan attitude towards war see Ausejo, *op. cit.* (n. 20), pp. 287–88.
[36]Leyte is divided more accurately into northeastern and southwestern zones by a mountain ridge.
[37]Morga in Cummins (trans. and ed.), *op. cit.* (n. 9), pp. 266–68.
[38]Filipinos today speak around 55 languages and 142 dialects. Since they are all derived from the Malayo-Polynesian and are of the agglutinative type, if one is learned it is easy to learn the others. See Zaide, *op. cit.* (n. 24), p. 131.

There is not even a single language for each island. On Luzon itself there are six different languages, that of Manila being Tagalog (the language of the river men).[39] It is the dominant language of the islands of Luzon, Mindoro, Lubang, and others; the language spoken in some regions is more polished than others. Bisayan is the language of most of the "Pintados," but in some villages Harayan is spoken.[40] Both Chirino and Morga conclude that Tagalog is a rich, highly developed language "fully capable of expressing whatever a person wishes to say elegantly and in many ways and manners."[41]

These languages, according to the Spaniards, are written in native letters which resemble those of the Arabs and are entirely different from the characters used in China and Japan or the alphabets of India. The alphabet of the *Indios* has fifteen characters made up of three vowels and twelve consonants.[42] Every consonant is pronounced with the vowel A. To change the vowel sounds from A to E, I, O, or U, certain comma-like points (*avelits*) are placed above or below the consonant. Chirino provides a sample alphabet and illustrations of how the vowel sounds are changed.[43] Most men and women are able to read and write correctly.[44] Formerly they wrote from top to bottom and from left to right with a stylus on bamboo or palm leaves.[45] Now they write with ink on paper and horizontally in the Spanish manner. To illustrate the similarities and differences between Tagalog, Bisayan, and Harayan, Chirino gives translations of the Ave Maria in those three languages. Although they have books of simple poetry which they call *golo* (charms for lovers), they have no written works on science, philosophy, or religion.[46]

[39] The others are Ilokos, Bikol, Pangasinan, Pampanga, and Ibanag.
[40] Harayan or Waray-waray is a Bisayan dialect spoken mainly on Samar and Leyte. The three major languages of the Bisayan group are Waray, Hiligaynon (in Panay and eastern Negros), and Cebuano. Together they form the largest Philippine language group. Cebuano and Hiligaynon are not mutually intelligible.
[41] Morga in Cummins (trans. and ed.), *op. cit.* (n. 9), p. 269; *cf.* Chirino in BR, XII, 235–36. Between 1593 and 1648 the missionaries published twenty-four books in Tagalog while only five were issued in Bisayan. Like Chirino, the other missionaries saw Tagalog as the best developed of the native languages. See J. L. Phelan, "Philippine Linguistics and Spanish Missionaries," *Mid-America, XXXVII* (1955), 159.
[42] Another contemporary writer, the author of the "Boxer Codex" (see above, n. 25), claims that seventeen letters were in use. See Quirino and Garcia, *loc. cit.* (n. 25), p. 424. Modern Tagalog uses seventeen letters. This alphabet, called *baybaying*, was probably derived from the Asokan alphabet of India. See Zaide, *op. cit.* (n. 24), p. 132. Philippine writing traveled from India via Indonesia.
[43] Compare Chirino's alphabet to that given in Zaide, *op. cit.* (n. 24), p. 133. Also see the alphabet in Bobadilla's *Relation* in BR, XXIX, 289.
[44] They read and write slowly as "when schoolchildren do their spelling," according to the anonymous author in Quirino and Garcia, *loc. cit.* (n. 25), p. 425.
[45] It is now thought that they always wrote horizontally and from left to right. See Zaide, *op. cit.* (n. 24), p. 133. The pre-Hispanic script is now virtually extinct, but it is still used by native groups in Mindoro and Palawan.
[46] BR, XII, 237–39, 242–44, 254; also Morga in Cummins (trans. and ed.), *op. cit.* (n. 9), p. 269; and Ribadeneira in Fernandez (trans.), *op. cit.* (n. 3), I, 342.

Located on the seashore between rivers and creeks, their settlements are small economic units devoted to agriculture or fishing. The dwellings of commoners and other buildings are all alike throughout the islands. They are detached houses raised high above the ground on stakes and piles and roofed with timber and bamboo covered with palm leaves. On the ground below the house they fence in their animals and pound their rice. They climb into their small, low living quarters by bamboo ladders which can be pulled up. Parents and children live together in these homes which are almost devoid of *bahandi,* or ornaments. Their simple beds and floors are made of bamboo canes held tightly together by bamboo strips. The houses of chiefs are similar in construction but roomier, more substantial, and better furnished than the others. Neither commoners nor chiefs live in the lower quarters of their houses because of flooding and because of the huge rats which damage both their houses and their crops. At times, flooded village streets can be traversed only in boats.[47]

No central government existed in the Philippines before the coming of the Spanish.[48] In every island there were numerous recognized chiefs of varying power who warred or allied with one another. For ruling, aiding, and protecting his followers, the chief received veneration, services in war and peace, and tribute known as "Buiz" (*buwis*). Inheritance of chiefdoms was from father to son; failing a direct heir the domain and authority passed to brothers and collateral relatives. Both male and female descendants and relatives of the chief, even those not heirs, were regarded as nobles and were not obligated to perform the services required of the "Timaguas" (freemen or commoners). Lesser chieftains who paid homage to greater chiefs retained control of their own group, or *barangay* (Tagalog word for a small ship, adopted as the term for the smallest political unit). For example, the village of Taytay, which included four hundred families, was divided into four *barangays.* The chiefs of the *barangays* were called "Datos" (*datus*). They handled the special problems of each *catongohan* (the population of a *barangay*) even in Spanish times.[49]

Datus possessed life-and-death powers over their subjects and often acted arbitrarily in their administration of justice. Civil suits were heard and judged by appointed elders from the same class as the litigants. Judges made their decisions on the basis of precedent. The legal system derived from oral tradition and customs (*ugali*) rather than written law.[50] Nonetheless the same

[47] Morga in Cummins (trans. and ed.), *op. cit.* (n. 9), pp. 270–71; Chirino in BR, XII, 210; Ribadeneira in Fernandez (trans.), *op. cit.* (n. 3), I, 341.
[48] The exception was the sultanate of Sulu.
[49] Morga in Cummins (trans. and ed.), *op. cit.* (n. 9), p. 271; Chirino on Taytay in BR, XII, 211. For a summary description of the *barangay* system in pre-Spanish times see Ausejo, *op. cit.* (n. 20), pp. 272–80.
[50] Laws written by the *datus* of Panay presumably survived in two codes of *ca.* 1250 and 1433. The second of these was discovered by the Spanish in 1614. See Zaide, *op. cit.* (n. 24), pp. 117–22. Other scholars doubt the authenticity of these codes.

practices were followed throughout the islands with only minor variations from place to place.[51]

Three social classes exist in the islands: chieftains and their families, freemen, and slaves, who are subject to the other two groups. All the slaves are natives who were forced into servitude by being captured in raids, by failing to repay loans, or as punishment for crimes and infractions. In the Tagalog country there are many types and categories of slaves. Those called "Saguiguilires" (*aliping saguiguilir*) and their children are household servants. Others known as "Namamahayes" (*aliping namamahay*) live separately and perform services for the master on a regular basis and without stipend. Children of slaves always inherit servile status. In the two groups just mentioned, there are persons who are only partial slaves. If one parent is free and the other a slave, an only child is half free and half slave. When there is more than one offspring of such a mixed marriage, the eldest has the status of the father, whether free or slave, the second has the mother's status, and so on. Should there be an odd number of children, the last child is half slave and half free. The children of a free parent and a half slave become one-quarter slaves. Half and quarter slaves serve their masters one month and work the next one for themselves. Similarly, the status of slaves is governed by inheritance customs. In a division of property a slave may fall to several masters, each of whom he serves for his proportionate share of time. Half and quarter slaves may purchase their complete freedom by paying to the master a fair price established by others; masters cannot be forced to exchange or free a complete slave. Slaves are regularly sold, exchanged, and traded, for they constitute the chief capital of the free natives. The usual price for a "Saguiguilir" is twice that for a "Namamahay."[52]

Marriages ordinarily are contracted within the same social class, but occasionally marriages occur across class lines. Bisayans are more averse to intermarriage than Tagalogs and usually seek a wife who is closely related. Uncle and niece or first cousins commonly marry. While polygamy is practiced it is not common. Chirino lived in the Philippines for almost ten years before he learned that polygamy existed in the islands. He found it in those parts of the south most influenced by Islam. Even where polygamy exists, it is by no means general. Most Filipinos marry just one wife, although concubinage is

---

[51] Morga in Cummins (trans. and ed.), *op. cit.* (n. 9), p. 272.

[52] *Ibid.*, pp. 272–74; Chirino in BR, XIII, 56–58. Phelan, *op. cit.* (n. 18), pp. 20–22, argues that slavery is a misleading term to apply to what was essentially a system of labor performed by a dependent class. The Spanish, especially Chirino and other missionaries, denounced the treatment accorded this dependent class, and the government tried without complete success to reform the traditional labor system (Phelan, pp. 113–16). Most Filipino historians, despite Phelan's admonition, continue to use the term "slave" with reference to this class. See Ausejo, *op. cit.* (n. 20), pp. 280–87. The European terms are misleading, since no equivalent class existed in Western society. For a thorough study see W. H. Scott, "*Oripun* and *Alipin* in the Sixteenth-Century Philippines," in A. Reid (ed.), *Slavery, Bondage, and Dependency in Southeast Asia* (New York, 1983), pp. 138–55.

not uncommon. Certain ceremonies, rituals, and conventions are followed in contracting marriages. On the wedding day the groom's parents pay a dowry (*bigagkáya,* or bride price) to the bride's father in the presence of her kinsmen; the amount of the dowry is fixed by the contracting parties to accord with the means of the groom's family. Gifts are sometimes showered on the bride's kinsfolk by a rich groom. The dowry paid, the wedding ends with a rousing party.

The legal wife, called "Ynaaba" (Tagalog, *asawa,* consort), is mistress of the house, and her children are the only legitimate children and heirs of the father; adopted children also are legal heirs. All legal heirs share their parents' property equally. The other women of the household are concubines, and their children, not being heirs, receive an inheritance only by special bequest. A will is made by oral statement before witnesses. Divorce is easy for both husband and wife. An assembly of the couple's relatives determines which of the two is at fault. If the husband is judged responsible, he loses the dowry; when the wife is at fault, the dowry is returned to the husband's family. Adultery on the wife's part is a sufficient reason for the husband to obtain a divorce; adultery need not necessarily result in divorce, for the offender may simply pay a fine to the offended. Any property acquired jointly is divided equally on divorce and both dispose of their own shares as they see fit. Children and slaves are also divided equally. Female slaves who have offspring by freemen are themselves freed and their children are also free. Such children, as well as the illegitimate children of married women, have no rights of inheritance.[53]

Indigenous mores are readily tolerated by the Spanish authorities and churchmen so long as they do not conflict seriously with European Christian morality. Chirino, the staid missioner, is even somewhat bemused by the customs followed in the adoption of names. In these practices he finds another illustration of the elegance and courtesy embodied in the Tagalog language. At birth the child is given a name by the mother, usually one which reflects the mother's experiences in pregnancy or delivery, or her aspirations for the child; at other times the name given is the first word, whatever it is, that occurs to the new mother. The child is known only by this single name until after marriage. The firstborn child then gives its name to the parents: the father thus becomes "the father of So-and-so," and the mother the "mother of So-and-so." Female names are distinguished from those of males by the addition of "in." When speaking of children, diminutives are often used, as well as other affectionate appellations. A child in speaking to another of his father refers to the parent as "ang amaco" or "my father," the word "ama" meaning father. In addressing the father directly, the child does not use "ama" but the more intimate "bapa." Mothers and

[53] Morga in Cummins (trans. and ed.), *op. cit.* (n. 9), pp. 274–76; Chirino in BR, XII, 293–96. *Cf.* Ausejo, *op. cit.* (n. 20), pp. 289–95, and Phelan, *op. cit.* (n. 18), pp. 18–20, 64.

children are also directly addressed by personal names of endearment. Children hold their parents' proper names in such high respect that they never dare to utter them. To name the parents of another person is to insult him. While the Filipinos traditionally have no special family names or distinctive titles, the Christian converts, aping the Spanish, quickly learn to place the title "Don" before the given name so "there are even more Dons among them than among our Spaniards."[54]

The Tagalogs, while not as formal as the Chinese and Japanese, are well bred and "very civil and courteous in word and action." Upon meeting one another, they uncover their head. In conversing with superiors they bare their head, throw the head covering over their left shoulder, and squat on the ground. Their mode of salutation is to bow and place one or both hands on their cheeks. Then they sit down and await a question; it is bad manners to speak to a superior before being spoken to. In addressing others they always use the polite third person and never a familiar form. Even when conversing with equals, they lace their speech with honorifics. Their letters, which are their only form of literary expression, begin and end with extravagant terms of courtesy and affection. Sensitive to all forms of communication, they are able to impart messages by their skillful playing of the guitar called the "cutyapi" (*kudyapi*). The Bisayans, when compared to Tagalogs, are not as civil and polite in manners or speech. Their language, which has borrowed its alphabet from Tagalog, has fewer developed terms of courtesy and polite expressions.[55]

While the Filipinos are naturally polite and personally neat, their morals leave something to be desired. They quietly accept concubinage, incest, and rape unless the victim is a woman chieftain. Bachelors called "Bagontaos" (*bágungtao*) and unmarried girls known as "Dalagas" (*dalága*) mingle and openly have sex together. Virgins are deflowered by men who make this task their occupation; they see virginity as an impediment to marriage. Men commonly have sexual relations before marriage with their intended wife's sister and mother. The Bisayans, especially the women, are "very vicious and sensual." To satisfy these women the young males insert a peg into their penis which is called the "sagra." The Chinese and Spanish introduced the islanders to sodomy.[56]

The religious beliefs and practices of the *Indios* are vigorously denounced as blind idolatry invented by the devil. Chirino, out of compassion for their ignorance, seeks to "reduce to order" this "false heathen religion." Their faith, like their government, is based on native tradition, a set of customs and beliefs which they have never bothered to record in writings. They have

[54] Chirino in BR, XIII, 200–203.
[55] *Ibid.*, XII, 240–42. Cf. Zaide, *op. cit.* (n. 24), pp. 113, 130.
[56] Morga in Cummins (trans. and ed.), *op. cit.* (n. 9), pp. 277–78. On the penis peg or pin see Tom Harrisson, "The 'Palang,' Its History and Proto-history in West Borneo and the Philippines," *JRAS*, Vol. XXXVI, Pt. 2 (1964), 162–74. On this dubious assertion about the introduction of sodomy see Phelan, *op. cit.* (n. 18), pp. 64, 186–87.

successfully preserved these traditions in songs "which they know by heart and learn when children." [57] These songs they sing at work or while sailing, feasting, or mourning their dead. [58] In these litanies they retell the genealogies and deeds of their gods. They believe in a single Supreme Being whom the Tagalogs call "Bathala Mei capal" (*Bathálà May kapál*) or "God the Creator" and the Bisayans name "Laon," or "The Old One." Their songs tell "of the creation of the world, the origin of the human race, the deluge, paradise, punishment, and other invisible things." In brief, they believe in spirits, good and bad, as well as in heaven and hell.

The Supreme Deity is inaccessible, remote, and protected by a vast pantheon of gods and goddesses who are more immediate and approachable. They adore and deify their ancestors, and even make idols called "Larauan" (*laráwan*) in memory of the departed. [59] They also worship the sun, moon, rainbows, animals, and birds. The Tagalogs adore a bluebird whom they name "Bathal" (*Bathálà,* god). [60] They also worship a crow called "Mei lupa" (*May lúpa*) which means "master of the soil," or god of the earth. Some venerate the crocodile and call it "nono" (*núno*), or grandfather. Others make offerings to ancient trees, reefs, cliffs, headlands, and special rocks. Omens by the "thousand" guide them in their everyday decisions.

Common places for worship or public festivals do not exist. Within their own houses they make sacrifices to the images (*anitos*) kept there. While they have no temples, they do have priests and priestesses called "Catolonan" (*katolonan*) by the Tagalogs and "Babailan" (*baylan*) by the Bisayans. Priests sometimes dress as women while performing rites. They are trained as medicine men and sorcerers and obtain their priestly offices "through special friendship, or kinship, or as a legacy." Highly revered by the others, these priests officiate at sacrifices and receive rich gifts for their services. Ordinarily they sacrifice a cock or a hog, but never a human being. At their feasts these priests and priestesses become more intoxicated than the others.

---

[57] Philippine native religion seems to have been affected only slightly by the rites and ceremonies of the other people with whom they had long trading contacts. Hinduism and Buddhism, extremely important in other parts of Southeast Asia, made relatively little impression upon Luzon, the Bisayan islands, or Mindanao. Besides the Tagalog alphabet, the pre-Hispanic Filipinos incorporated a number of Indian religious terms, concepts, and customs into native beliefs and practices. For example, see M. H. Churchill, "Indian Penetration of Pre-Spanish Philippines: A New Look at the Evidence," *Asian Studies,* XV, 21–45. Islam and Christianity were the only world religions which finally and successfully rooted out native beliefs in all but a few remote places.

[58] On the types of traditional songs see Felipe Radilla de Leon, "Philippine Music," in A. S. Lardizabal and F. Tensuan-Leogardo (eds.), *Readings in Philippine Culture and Social Life* (Manila, 1970), pp. 157–59.

[59] For a few pictures of surviving figurines see Juan Roger, *Estudio etnológico comparitivo . . . de Filipinas* (Madrid, 1949), appendix.

[60] They also called it Villiarayani and Tigmamanuquin; its scientific name is *Irena cyanogastra cyanogastra,* and its common name is the Luzon fairy bluebird. For a scientific description see the Marquess Hachisuka, *The Birds of the Philippine Islands* (2 vols.; London, 1931–35), II, 377. Morga in Cummins (trans. and ed.), *op. cit.* (n. 9), p. 279, makes this deity a yellow bird.

Certain of the priestesses, some of important and wealthy families, terrorize villages and compel the Christian converts to seek their services.[61] In cases of illness a sacrifice is offered to the *anitos,* or the images called *divatas* by the Bisayans.[62] While offering this sacrifice, the priest or priestess dances furiously and rings a bell. These ceremonies halt abruptly when death occurs. Dirges and lamentations are then played and sung to the accompaniment of much weeping, some of it by professional mourners. With these sad sounds in their ears, they wash and perfume the body. Then they embalm it with "aromatic balsams," especially "buyo" which is injected through the mouth to penetrate the body.[63] The corpse is then clothed in its best garments and a three-day mourning period begins. At its end they enclose the corpse in an airtight coffin of hard wood; some bodies so treated "have been found uncorrupted after a lapse of many years." They put gold in the mouth of the corpse and place many other articles of value in the coffin, including clothing and food for the next world. Usually the coffin is buried in a pit dug under the deceased's own house or in the open fields roundabout. White is the color of mourning for Bisayans, and black for the Tagalogs; close relatives are sometimes required to fast during a mourning period. After the burial the mourning is ended with a feast.[64] When a chief dies, the entire *barangay* mourns officially. Villages must be utterly silent for the period of mourning, infractions being severely punished.[65]

Muslims (Moros), much to the dismay of the Spaniards, were already active in the Philippines when they arrived at Luzon in 1565. Traders from Borneo had settled in the Manila area and had married Filipino women. Through these Muslim merchants, "gazizes" (*kazis*) began to introduce Islam to the people of Luzon, including its leading chiefs. They were followed by "Marabites" (Arabic, *murābit,* Muslim monks) who came all the way from the Red Sea to teach and manage the Muslims and their converts.[66] The Spaniards were quick to learn that the Moros were much more numerous in southern Mindanao and the Sulu Islands than in Luzon and Mindoro. The Muslims, inspired by Ternate, are the enemies of both the Spaniards and the *Indios.*[67]

---

[61] Chirino in BR, XII, 262–71. On "animo-deism" see M. G. Santamaria, "The Religion of the Filipinos," in Lardizabal and Tensuan-Leogardo (eds.), *op. cit.* (n. 58), pp. 126–34.

[62] Written in various ways, the word "divata," meaning "demigod" in modern Cebuano, derives from Sanskrit. See Churchill, *loc. cit.* (n. 57), p. 37.

[63] *Buyo, Piper betle,* was also used as a stimulant in the Philippines by both Spaniards and *Indios.*

[64] Cf. the Celtic wake or death festival.

[65] Chirino in BR, XII, 302–4.

[66] Morga in Cummins (trans. and ed.), *op. cit.* (n. 9), pp. 280–81. The introduction of Islam into Southeast Asia and the Philippines is one of a host of unsolved problems relating to the early history of the area. Its advent in the southern Philippines is usually dated in the fourteenth century or later. See Ausejo, *op. cit.* (n. 20), pp. 310–11, and below, p. 1536.

[67] Chirino in BR, XII, 313–14. The presence of Christians in the southern Philippines and in the Moluccas inspired the Muslim leaders of the region to work together. See Ausejo, *op. cit.* (n. 20), p. 312.

Manila, the "city of cities," was founded on a site at the mouth of the Pasig River where it flows into the bay. On either side of this river had been located the settlements and forts of two local chieftains, called "Rajamora" (the "young rajah," named Soliman) and "Rajamatanda" (the "old rajah").[68] After the Spanish conquest in 1571, this area was divided into equal plots of land and given to the Spaniards. A new and well-laid-out town was rapidly built, which became by royal decree the capital of the islands with its own coat of arms. Manila's central plaza contained the city's cathedral and administration buildings. Another square was left as a parade ground, in the center of which stood the fortress and other royal buildings. For its protection the city is enclosed in a wide stone wall, a fortress at the river's bar, and another fortress at "the end of the curtain-wall that runs along the shore of the bay"; ramparts on the landward side command with artillery all the approaches to the wall. The gates to the city are locked each night before dark and the key deposited in the guardroom. The royal arsenals and the powder house in the parade ground have their own administrators and workmen. At the foundry in another part of the city the cannons are cast. The Augustinians, Dominicans, Franciscans, and Jesuits now have their own establishments. The Jesuits operate a college and minister to a royal sanctuary for women and girls in distress. There is also a royal hospital for the Spaniards, a *Misericordia* devoted to works of charity, and a hospital for natives administered by the barefooted Franciscans.

As the seat of government the royal offices are stationed in Manila: the *audiencia* (high tribunal of justice), the royal chancery, the governor, and the captain-general. The city is administered by a *cabildo* (council), two resident *alcaldes* (judges), twelve permanent *regidores* (notaries), and other lesser officials. The ecclesiastical organization is headed by a resident archbishop and three suffragan bishops with dioceses in Cebu, Cagayan, and the Camarines. The Holy Office of the Inquisition keeps its agents in Manila and the other bishoprics. Attached to the cathedral are the usual canons, full- and half-prebends, chaplains, and sacristans. In the ornate cathedral, a choir sings accompanied by an organ and wind instruments. For short recreational excursions there are two drives outside the city.[69]

But Manila is mainly a port where the royal galleys, soldiers, and trade officers are stationed. Most of its residents engage in insular and international trade or in related occupations. The annual galleons land and depart for New Spain from Manila's bay. Local vessels throng its harbors along with merchant ships from China, Japan, insular Southeast Asia, Siam, Cambodia, Malacca, and India. Every year, thirty or forty large junks come from south China, usually in March. Laden with wares, merchants, and factors employed by Chinese mercantile establishments, these are trading voy-

---

[68] Both were Muslims, probably with some relationship to the Brunei royal family. See Zaide, *op. cit.* (n. 24), p. 248.

[69] Morga in Cummins (trans. and ed.), *op. cit.* (n. 9), pp. 281–87.

ages licensed by the Chinese authorities. Not "even masses of paper [would] suffice for the task" of listing the variety of goods brought in these junks for sale in Manila. A 3 percent duty is immediately paid to the royal exchequer on the value of the China goods. Then the merchandise is unloaded and taken to warehouses and markets in the city "where it is sold freely." The Chinese insist on payment in silver and require quick sales so that they are able to leave by the end of May. Dispatch is also required on the Spanish side because the galleons leave for New Spain at the end of June. Not all transactions are hurried. Some of the Chinese remain in Manila to work out quantity sales of silks and other textiles as well as credit arrangements with the bigger merchants.

Japanese and Portuguese merchant ships sail from Nagasaki for Manila in October and March. Mainly they bring food, especially "good quality wheat flour and highly rated salt meats." Only a small part of the merchandise imported from Japan is transshipped to New Spain; most of it is consumed or retained in the Philippines. Perhaps this is so because the Japanese, unlike the Chinese, do not insist on taking home silver; rather, they purchase Chinese raw silks and the products of the Philippines, New Spain, and Spain itself. The Portuguese ships from the Indies bring spices from the islands as well as textiles and precious stones from India; royal duties are not collected from these vessels since they belong to subjects of the same king. Small vessels from Borneo sell camphor and other of their local products right off the decks of their ships to the Filipinos. Occasionally ships from Siam and Cambodia arrive with pepper, ivory, precious stones, rhinoceros horn, slaves, and trinkets.

The cargoes for the Acapulco galleons are made up of these Asian imports as well as Philippine products: gold, cotton textiles, cloth for padding (kapok), and cakes of white and yellow wax. Before the galleons set sail, the owners pay a 2 percent duty on the value of their exports in addition to freight charges; at Acapulco they pay a 10 percent entry fee. Because the space aboard these ships is limited, the governor appoints commissioners to divide and allocate it. The galleon trade is easy to conduct and profitable to all concerned. Since the ships remain in Manila for only three months annually, the trading period is hectic and short. The Spaniards profit so much from this enterprise that they disdain all others. Preoccupation with trade has helped to limit developments in agriculture, mining, and other noncommercial activities; the natives, too, because they indirectly profit from shipping and commerce, abandon agriculture and other forms of necessary labor. Since most commodities must be paid for in silver, the trade, especially that with China, draws silver from New Spain into the coffers of "heathens" who will never again return it.[70]

---

[70] *Ibid.*, pp. 304–10. On the silver drain see above, pp. 38–39.

Most of the menial and everyday labor in Manila is performed by the "Sangleyes"[71] (Chinese) for "they are skilled in every trade, are very hard workers, and satisfied with moderate wages." Indeed Manila could not survive without them. Since jobs are scarce and wages low in south China, each year large numbers arrive with the junks. Many Chinese remain in the islands to work in the Spanish settlements. While some farm, fish, and trade from island to island, the majority work as shopkeepers or in service occupations. In Manila most have their shops and dwellings in a special market quarter called the "Parian."[72] A "wicked and vicious people," the Chinese heathens undermine the morals of the *Indios,* commit crimes, stir unrest, and spy "out the land . . . which they know better than do the Spaniards themselves." To restrict the number of Chinese, the Spanish require them to obtain a "written license to remain" from a specially appointed official. He limits the number of permits issued to the number requested by the city council; all others are supposed to return to China with the annual fleet. The Parian has its own *alcalde* (judge) to provide for its better security and good order. Those "Sangleyes" who cannot find room in the Parian live across the river in two small settlements administered by the town of Tondo. There the Dominican friars learn the Chinese language to help in their work of evangelizing; the friars also maintain a special hospital for the Chinese. The Christian "Sangleyes," numbering five hundred households, live apart in their own settlement, with a Christian governor of their own race. Legally the "Sangleyes" may not reside or own property outside these special settlements. They may not travel outside the city or to other islands without special permission. Natives are not allowed to live among them or even near them.[73]

The Japanese, both Christian and heathen, also have a special settlement and area in Manila. Not nearly as numerous as the "Sangleyes," the Japanese

---

[71] Probably derives from Chinese *Shang Lü,* meaning "merchant-traveler," according to Y. Z. Chang, "Sangley, the Merchant-Traveller," *Modern Language Notes,* LII (1937), 189–90. For a long and scholarly note on this word and for the Chinese characters see C. R. Boxer (ed.), *South China in the Sixteenth Century* ("HS," 2d ser., CVI; London, 1953), p. 260, n. 2 and illustration opposite. Also see Albert Chan, "Chinese-Philippine Relations in the Later Sixteenth Century and to 1603," *Philippine Studies,* XXVI (1978), 55–56, n. 8. See our pl. 31.

[72] This word, whose origin is obscure, probably derives from the Tagalog word *Dian* or *Diyan.* See A. Santamaria, O.P., "The Chinese Parian (El Parian de los Sangleyes)," in A. Felix, Jr. (ed.), *The Chinese in the Philippines 1550–1770* (Manila, 1966), p. 71. The first Parian dates from late 1581 or early 1582.

[73] Morga in Cummins (trans. and ed.), *op. cit.* (n. 9), pp. 314–17. Argensola (BR, XVI, 226–34 *passim*) repeatedly makes the point, as did other contemporaries, that the Chinese had once governed insular Southeast Asia, including the Philippines. They abandoned this enterprise as being too costly but continued the trade. They were only too happy to accept Spanish silver and gladly permitted the Spanish to bear the burden of empire. Located nearby, the Chinese watched closely the developments in the islands and especially the treatment of the "Sangleyes." Some of these points were advanced at this time by those in Spain who advocated abandonment of the Philippines.

total around five hundred persons. They are "a spirited people of good disposition and courageous." Unlike the "Sangleyes," they return home without undue delay, cause no trouble, show no desire to go to other islands, and when converted are "truly devout" Christians.[74] In the Philippines the Japanese are treated "very courteously," for they are a resolute people who "demand nothing less." The Spanish authorities also require that they be treated as "people of quality" because of their wish to maintain good relations with Japan. Other Asians, who come only infrequently to Manila, return home with the ships in which they came.[75]

The five religious orders work diligently for the conversion and training of the natives in Christian and Spanish ways. They are supported by a secular hierarchy which is trying to supervise a growing church widely scattered over a number of islands. The spread of Christianity is aided by the governor and the *audiencia,* and particularly by the requirement that the *encomenderos* (holders of assigned districts) faithfully meet their obligation to provide temporal and spiritual protection to the *Indios* from whom they collect taxes. Because of this extension of Spanish and Christian authority, the islands enjoy peace and justice. The tyranny of the native chiefs has been mitigated; now the *datus* and their retainers work together for the common good. The *datus* collect the taxes of their subjects and pass over what is required to the *encomenderos.* Each settlement annually elects a local governor as well as justices who hear minor civil suits between natives. In such suits the native traditions govern the decisions so long as custom does not contravene natural law.[76]

Indios may move about freely, providing only that they do not transfer from one *barangay* to another in the same township or from a Christian to a non-Christian settlement, or go on trading expeditions without permission. While Spaniards are forbidden to own slaves, the natives continue to practice traditional slavery. The owner must pay "their tributes" for the *saguiguilirs;* the *namamahays* are responsible for meeting their own tribute payments, since they possess independent means of livelihood. Natives of all classes are obligated to render to the Spaniards labor services known as the *polo.* Paid a token wage by officials and ecclesiastics, the *Indios* are required to perform domestic services, act as pilots and crews on war vessels, and work in the

---

[74] In contrast to the Chinese converts, who are regularly suspected by the Spanish writers of lacking sincerity and of being motivated by their material interests to accept Christianity.

[75] Morga in Cummins (trans. and ed.), *op. cit.* (n. 9), pp. 317–18. The Spaniards had earlier feared an invasion from Japan because Hideyoshi had sent an embassy to the islands in 1592 demanding their subjection. Ieyasu, on coming to power in 1601, promised to maintain friendly relations with the Philippines. The Tokugawa ruler also wanted to establish direct commercial relations with Mexico, and paid little heed to the welfare of his subjects in Manila. See N. Murakami, "Japan's Early Attempts to Establish Commercial Relations with Mexico," in H. Morse Stephens and H. E. Bolton (eds.), *The Pacific Ocean in History* (New York, 1917), pp. 467–80. On Japanese residents in the Philippines at this time see E. M. Alip, *Philippine-Japanese Relations* (Manila, 1959), pp. 22–25.

[76] Morga in Cummins (trans. and ed.), *op. cit.* (n. 9), pp. 291–94.

royal foundry, magazines, and shipyards. Since the Spaniards themselves do not work in agriculture or mining, *polo* labor is not recruited for these activities.[77] Natives also are obligated to provide rice and other supplies to the Spanish on a quota basis and at prices "current amongst themselves."[78]

Five classes of Spaniards live in these islands: ecclesiastics, *encomenderos*, soldiers and sailors, merchants and business men, and royal officials. Most Spaniards live in Manila and its vicinity, but some *encomenderos* reside in the provincial cities of Nueva Segovia, Nueva Cáceres, and Cebu. Officials are permitted to go into native settlements only when it is the specified time to collect tribute. In addition, they must be constantly on the move; every fourth month they shift their residence to a different circuit to "make it less onerous for the natives who have to maintain and serve these officials." All appointments to public office and to military posts are made by the governor; some offices are sold by royal decree for the lifetime of the purchaser. Elections for the officials of the Spanish towns are held annually on New Year's Day. The revenues of Manila derive from fines, weighing charges, rents of the Parian, and the playing-card monopoly.[79] Official salaries, maintenance of fortifications, and festival expenses come out of the city's budget.[80]

2

DEEPER PENETRATIONS

The works of length which follow in time the accounts of Chirino and Morga add many details but do not significantly alter the general picture outlined by these two early commentators. All of the later writings were by regular ecclesiastics bent primarily upon recording the victories of their orders. Friar Sebastião Manrique, the Portuguese Augustinian, published his *Itinerario* in Rome during 1649. It includes several short chapters relating to his stopover in Manila for fourteen months in 1637–38.[81] The Dominican

---

[77] At the beginning of the seventeenth century the requirement of *polo* labor was relatively mild. Under the impact of the Hispano-Dutch wars between 1621 and 1648, draft labor needs became constantly greater, particularly in naval and naval-related occupations. See Phelan, *op. cit.* (n. 18), p. 99.

[78] Morga in Cummins (trans. and ed.), *op. cit.* (n. 9), pp. 297–99. On the compulsory sale of products to the government, known as the *vandala,* see Phelan, *op. cit.* (n. 18), pp. 99–100.

[79] Gambling was a common form of recreation, especially for the Spanish and Chinese wives.

[80] Morga in Cummins (trans. and ed.), *op. cit.* (n. 9), pp. 299–301. On Spanish objectives and methods in the Philippines see Phelan, *op. cit.* (n. 18), pp. 8–14, and Zaide, *op. cit.* (n. 24), chaps. xiii–xiv.

[81] Chaps. xli–xliv in Vol. II of C. Eckford Luard and H. Hosten (trans. and eds.), *Travels of Fray Sebastien Manrique, 1629–1643* (2 vols.; "HS," 2d ser., LX, LXI; Oxford, 1926–27). These chapters have been reproduced and further edited as an appendix to Mauro Garcia (ed.), *A Voyage to the Philippines by Giovanni Francisco Gemelli Careri* (Manila, 1963). Manrique went to Manila in the hope of getting into Japan. While he was there, the governor, on the request of Macao, forbade any further attempts to enter Japan.

bishop Diego Aduarte (1569–1636), in the balanced chronicle of his order's Province of the Holy Rosary, provides new materials on the remote places and people of northern Luzon and on the "Sangleyes."[82] A rare pamphlet (Mexico, 1662), probably by Bartholomé de Letona, a Franciscan, describes anew the physical features of the islands.[83] Far more important is the Jesuit Francisco Colin's *Labor evangélica* (Madrid, 1663), which he intended to be a continuation of Chirino's unpublished *Historia*.[84] After thirty-five years in the Philippines, Colin sent his manuscript to Europe in 1656 for publication. Using the books and documents available to him, Colin brought together the materials telling the story of the Jesuit mission in the Philippines down to 1632. The first book includes a geographical and historical description of the islands, as well as brief essays on native languages, customs, religions, and government, and on the early Spanish voyages to the Moluccas and the Philippines. The second and third books review the founding, growth, and difficulties of the Jesuit mission to the Philippines. The two supplements that follow include reproductions of many relevant documents of the sixteenth century. The fourth book recounts the history of the Jesuit enterprise from 1600 to 1632 in the Philippines and in other insular regions of Southeast Asia. The work concludes with a statistical appendix on the state of the Jesuit province as of 1656, the year when Colin completed his manuscript.[85] Throughout, he attempts to integrate his special knowledge of the geography and the natural world of the Philippines into the European scholarly traditions exemplified by Ptolemy and Clusius, the biologist. In brief, this is a work of scholarship as well as observation.

Volume II of Melchisédech Thévenot's *Relation de divers voyages curieux* (Paris, 1666) contains six brief accounts translated from Spanish manuscript and printed sources.[86] In his preface Thévenot claims that these are the first general accounts of the Philippines to become widely available; they are all dated from 1640 or before. The most important of these is the *Relation* by a

[82] *Historia de la provincia del Santo Rosario de la orden de predicadores en Filipinas, Japon, y China* (Manila, 1640). Reprinted at Zaragoça in 1693, as Vol. I of a two-volume history of the Dominican province. The second volume was written by Baltasar de Santa Cruz. The first edition is translated, partly in synopsis, in BR, XXX, 110–321, XXXI, XXXII. References hereafter are to this English translation.

[83] Translated in BR, XXXVI, 189–217.

[84] Portions translated in *ibid.*, XL, 37–98. See above, p. 353 for bibliography. The critical edition of Colin's work was issued by Pablo Pastells in three volumes (Barcelona, 1900–1902; covers dated 1904). Pastells added copious notes and a number of helpful maps.

[85] For the place of this work in the official history of the Jesuit Philippine Province see De la Costa, *op. cit.* (n. 4), p. 623.

[86] Thévenot's collection was printed in sections and issued at different dates; the arrangement and collation of the copies vary. In the edition dated 1666 there are three separately paginated sections which include translations from a book or pamphlet printed in Mexico in 1638. The *Relation* of Admiral Don Geronymo de Bañuelos y Carillo regarding the Philippines as of 1637–38 is the first of these accounts. It is translated into English in BR (XXIX, 66–85) from Thévenot's French version; no copies of the original appear to exist. In this section Thévenot also prints abridged translations of the memorials on the Philippines prepared by Hernando de

religious who lived in the Philippines for eighteen years. This unsigned and undated account has been attributed to Father Diego de Bobadilla, S.J. (1590–1648), who was Jesuit procurator in Europe from 1637 to 1641; from internal evidence it may be dated *ca.* 1640–41.[87] Bobadilla avers that he wrote this relation on the request of a friend—possibly Carlo del Pezzo, the Roman collector. From internal evidence it is clear that Bobadilla consulted Chirino's and Morga's accounts while preparing this manuscript. But much of it, particularly those parts relating to the Bisayans and Mindanao, records Bobadilla's own experiences and observations.[88] These literary accounts are followed by a Portuguese map of the east centered on the Philippines.

More materials on Manila and its environs around mid-century are to be found in the *Tratados históricos* (Madrid, 1676) of the Dominican friar Domingo Navarrete, who was in the Philippines for almost a decade (1648–57).[89] In 1698 the first part of Gaspar de San Agustín's *Conquistas de las islas Philipinas* (Madrid) appeared, which reviews the South Sea discoveries and the history of the Spanish in the Philippines to 1614, with special reference to the activities of the Augustinians. This chronicle, just the first part of which was published in the seventeenth century, is important only for the history of the mission, since it includes little that is new about the Philippines.[90] Finally there are the observations of Gemelli Careri, the Neapolitan world-traveler, who visited Manila and its environs briefly in May–June, 1697.[91]

Colin provides a comprehensive geographical survey of the islands. Starting at Manila on Manila Bay, he moves southward to Cavite and then iden-

---

los Rios Coronel and by Juan Grau y Monfalcón, as well as the relation attributed to Diego de Bobadilla and an anonymous account of Mindanao that contains a letter by Marcello Mastrilli. These materials were reprinted in the 1695 edition of Thévenot; for its contents see T. H. Pardo de Tavera, "Biblioteca Filipina," in A. P. C. Griffin *et al., Bibliography of the Philippine Islands* (Washington, D.C., 1903), Pt. 2, pp. 414–15.

[87] Translated into French from a Spanish manuscript in the cabinet of curiosities of Don Carlo del Pezzo, a Roman gentleman. Translated into English in BR, XXIX, 277–311.

[88] A textual comparison of these three accounts reveals that Bobadilla is most original on native religious beliefs and on natural history.

[89] For his materials on the Philippines in English see J. S. Cummins (trans. and ed.), *The Travels and Controversies of Friar Domingo Navarrete* (2 vols.; "HS," 2d ser., CXVIII, CXIX; Cambridge, 1962), I, 52–102. Cummins' translation, which is limited to Navarrete's sixth book of the travels, is based on the anonymous translation included in Churchill's 1704 *Collection (CV)* (I, 238–57), with insertions from certain of Navarrete's unpublished writings as well as from other parts of the *Tratados*.

[90] The second part of the *Conquistas* was left in manuscript until it was published at Valladolid in 1890; it surveys the progress of the Augustinians in the Philippines from 1616–98. The materials from the *Conquistas* translated into English in BR are all from this second part.

[91] For bibliographical detail on his *Giro del Mondo* (6 vols., Naples, 1699–1700) see above, pp. 386–87. Vol. V, on the Philippines, includes the journal of his personal observations and a general description derived from the writings of others. For instance he copied Colin on the technique of giving personal names in the Philippines and even provides the same example. For an English translation see *CV*, IV, 416–500; his journal entries are on pp. 416–26, 475–78. On the authenticity and limits of Careri's work on the Philippines also see Garcia (ed.), *op. cit.* (n. 81), p. xix.

tifies the main places along the southern coast. In passing, he mentions the volcano of Albay, its eruptions, and its importance as a landmark for sailors.[92] From Albay, near the tip of Luzon's southern arm, he proceeds northward to the Spanish town of Nueva Cáceres next to the native town of Naga. From here he takes the reader northward to the region of Paracole, where gold and other metals are found. Two to three days' journey northward along the eastern coast is Mauban, a port on the great bay (Lamon Bay) across the narrow middle of Luzon from Manila. The lengthy eastern coast from here northward to Cape Engaño is lightly populated and is within the jurisdiction of Cagayan, the largest province of the island. Its capital of Nueva Segovia (Aparri) is situated at the mouth of a great river which rises in the mountains of Santor in the Pampanga region and is called Tajo by the Spanish. The principal *Indios* of this region are the "Irayas" (Irrayas). Cape Engaño on the northern tip is called the "Cape of Deceit" because many ships have been wrecked by its treacherous waters and furious winds. To the west of the fertile Cagayan valley is the long, narrow province of Ilocos, which is considered to be the most heavily populated, most independent, and richest part of the island. In its mountain fastnesses live the "Igolotes" (Igorots), a bellicose people of large stature who mine gold.[93] To the south of Ilocos is the province of Pangasinan on whose coast is the port of Bolinao and the Playa Honda where the Spaniards defeated the Dutch heretics. The next province to the south is Pampanga; it includes a great plain as well as the Zambales Mountains which have hostile tribes in their western portion. Its lowland peoples, who were readily pacified, fight side by side with the Spanish. It exports rice as well as wood for the naval yards at Cavite.[94] The two provinces immediately adjacent to Manila are "Bahy" (Bay), with its great lake, and little Bulacan, which stands between Pampanga and Tondo, the Tagalog town across the river from Manila.[95]

Colin then lists and comments on the small islands around Luzon. Catanduanes, almost triangular in shape, is one of the largest of the islands which command the San Bernardino Strait, the entryway to the archipelago used by the galleons from Acapulco. This island of many rivers produces rice, palm products, wax, honey, and gold. Its men, many of whom are tattooed like Bisayans, are great shipbuilders, seamen, and rowers of various kinds of boats. Within the strait is Capul and several other small islands whose peaceful peoples follow Bisayan customs. Close to the exit from the strait is the lightly populated island of Ticao, one of the places where the galleons

[92] Mount Mayon in Albay Province of southern Luzon is one of the most spectacular sights in the Philippines. Southeast of Laguna, Luzon becomes a varied country of volcanoes from the Taal volcano to Mayon Mountain. See Dobby, *op. cit.* (n. 15), p. 320.

[93] The Ilocos rebellion of 1661 was punished by sentencing thirty persons to death and five hundred to slavery. See Bartolomé de Letona in BR, XXXVI, 193.

[94] *Cf.* John A. Larkin, *The Pampangans. Colonial Society in a Philippine Province* (Berkeley, 1972), chap. ii.

[95] Colin in Pastells, *op. cit.* (n. 84), I, 20–24.

bound for America take on water. To the west of Ticao lies Burias, and to its south, Masbate, two islands important to navigation which were pacified by 1579. Marinduque is another island passed by the galleons on their way to Manila; it boasts five hundred families of Tagalog background who have their own dialect which they use among themselves. To the southeast is the much larger island of Mindoro, a rough mountainous country whose *Indios* of the coast opposite Manila are Tagalogs while those of the coast facing Panay are Bisayans; its principal town is "Nauhan" (Naujan) on the north coast. The interior is populated by "Manguianes" (Mangyans), a half-naked people who use different languages.[96] Between Batangas in southern Luzon and the north coast of Mindoro is the islet named Verde, which gives its name to the nearby strait, through which the ships pass on their way from Cavite. At the eastern end of the Verde Island Passage is the small island of "Luban" (Lubang) with its extensive lowland areas that surround a volcano-like mountain. Lubang is one of the most populous of the smaller islands and for a time was the center of native resistance to the Spanish conquest. Northward from Lubang there are no island groups off Luzon's western coast. Off the northern tip of Luzon lie the "Babuyanes" (Babuyan Islands), a chain of low, small islands on the sea route to Formosa. Only the largest and nearest of these has been pacified.[97]

Southwest of Mindoro are the seventeen small islands and the single large island of Calamian Province. "Paragua" (Palawan), the third largest island in the Philippine archipelago, is only partially under the control of the Spanish.[98] The inhabitants of its southern tip and those of the small islands farther south continue to pay tribute to Borneo. Not far distant from its north coast are the three most important islands of the Calamian group, whose pacified *Indios* export wax.[99] To the west of the Calamians, the five islands of the Cuyo group can be seen from the heights of Mindoro. Farther to the west, Panay, a triangular island, is the first of the larger islands in terms of population and fertility. Its three principal points or promontories are called "Potol" (Pucio), "Naso" (Naso), and "Bulacabi" (Bulacaue). Many rivers flow from its mountainous interior to water the coastal lowlands, especially the famous Panay River, at whose mouth the Spanish have built the port called "Lutaya."[100] On the southern and opposite end of the island, in the Iloilo region between the "Tigbanan" (Jalaud?) and "Iaro" (Jaro) rivers, the Spanish have erected a beautiful and strong stone fortress. Nearby are the people called the Oton who are divided into two groups of five hundred tributaries

[96] On the Mangyans today see F. L. Wernstedt and J. E. Spencer, *The Philippine Island World. A Physical, Cultural, and Regional Geography* (Berkeley, 1967), p. 433, and V. B. Lopez, *The Mangyans of Mindoro: An Ethnohistory* (Manila, 1976).
[97] Colin in Pastells, *op. cit.* (n. 84), I, 24–29.
[98] It is actually the fifth largest in area.
[99] The three principal islands are Culion, Busuanga, and Coron.
[100] Built on the extensive delta land created by the Panay River, "Lutaya" is now called Roxas City.

each. While both are Bisayans, one group speaks "Harayas" (Waray-waray) and the other "Harigueynes" (Hiligaynon). In the vicinity of Panay are a number of smaller islands: "Imaras" (Guimaras) opposite Iloilo, Sibuyan, Romblon, Bantayan, and Tablas.[101]

In the eastern Bisayan islands of Samar, Leyte, and "Bool" (Bohol), the Jesuits find the peoples who are most responsive to their Christian message. The west coast of this first island is called Samar and its eastern side is known as Ibabao.[102] The promontory nearest to Luzon, called "Baliguaton" (Balicuatro), is on the south side of the San Bernardino channel; its southern point is named "Guiguan" (Guiuan). Between Guiuan and Cape Espirito Santo in the north is Borongan, the east coast port often used by the Dutch to prey upon the galleons from Mexico. In the north are the towns of Palapag and Catubig and on the west coast facing Leyte the settlements of Ibatan, Bangahon, Catbalogan (the regional administrative and Jesuit mission center), Paranas, and "Caluiga" (Calbiga). Ibatan is one of the places where the galleons are built. Very near to Samar and just to the south of Panamao Island is Leyte. To Leyte's south is the island of "Panahon" (Panoan), opposite Leyte's ports called Sogor and Cabalian, to which Magellan came in 1521. In the north is "Ogmuc" (Ormoc), one of the entryways to Leyte's fertile valley regions.[103] Leyte's west coast ports of Ormoc and Baybay send boats southward to Bohol, whose southeastern coast looks towards Mindanao. Most of Bohol's population live in the southern towns of "Lobog" (Loboc) and Baclayon and on the nearby small island of Panglao. Its population has been reduced in numbers considerably by wars with the Moros of Ternate and with the Portuguese, and by the rebellions against the Spanish. Bohol produces no rice but is rich in gold workings and mines. It abounds in palms, several kinds of root crops, and fishing grounds. Cotton is cultivated, from which Bohol's women make fine cloths for tribute payments. Courageous and arrogant on both land and sea, the Bohols under their principal *datu* called "Varay Tupuing" (Warai Tupuing, or the Peerless One) fought against all comers until finally they were forced to appeal to the Spanish for protection.[104]

Between Bohol and Panay lie the islands of Cebu and Negros. The administrative headquarters for the Spanish before the founding of Manila, Cebu is an island of special religious, political, and commercial importance despite its small size. Cebu city, a town of about five thousand people, is a replica of Manila with its ecclesiastical establishments, government houses, and even its own Parian. Lacking rice, the people of Cebu produce "bo-

[101] Colin in Pastells, *op. cit.* (n. 84), I, 29–32.
[102] The east coast was called Ibabao until 1768.
[103] For Leyte's geography see F. S. Tantuico, Jr., *Leyte, the Historic Islands* (Tacloban City, Philippines, 1964), chap. i.
[104] *Ibid.*, pp. 32–36. On Bohol *cf.* De la Costa, *op. cit.* (n. 4), pp. 163–64.

rona," a grain resembling maize that is made into a kind of bread.[105] In addition, Cebu produces abaca, garlic, onions, tobacco, cotton, wax, and civet. From the cotton they make all sorts of textiles and certain of the abacas are woven with cotton into striped and mixed cloths.[106] Near to Cebu are the small Bantayan and Camotes island groups, which also pay tribute to the Spanish. Close to Cebu's southern Point "Tanion" (Tañon) and across a narrow strip of water, lies the large island of Negros. This mountainous island produces rice, which is sold in and around Cebu as well as given in tribute. Negros derives its name from the black inhabitants of its mountains, most of whom live as savagely and rebelliously as their ancestors did; its coasts are peopled by Bisayan-speaking *Indios,* most of whom live in the western part of the island in a river valley.[107]

Aduarte, who was in the Philippines in 1595–96, 1597–99, 1600–1602, 1606–7, and 1628–36, acted as bishop of Nueva Segovia during the last eighteen months of his life. It was during this last tour of duty that he wrote his history of the first fifty years of the Dominican enterprise in the Philippines, Japan, and China. His discursive history, sometimes maddeningly obtuse, is especially valuable for the light it throws on the ethnohistory of the Pangasinan-Ilocos and Cagayan regions of northern Luzon.[108] About these backward regions, some of whose mountainous areas still remain virtually unexplored, Aduarte is the first to record the natural features and the names of settlements, tribes, and even chieftains. Although penetration of this region had been undertaken sporadically beginning in 1572, it was not until the early seventeenth century that the Spaniards began to acquire a substantial knowledge of it. The reports of the Dominicans, who first became active in northern Luzon in 1587, were compiled by Aduarte and combined with his personal experiences to produce a vivid portrait of local conditions and customs as the missionaries saw and understood them.

The Dominican province of Nueva Segovia is in the Cagayan valley of northeast Luzon. It is named for Segovia in Spain because its climate is also relatively cool, mild, and refreshing.[109] Located close to China, it produces a similar abundance of fish, rice, and game.[110] Pine and oak are native to its cooler and higher parts. Spanish plants introduced here have returned high yields. The Spaniards of Manila became interested in this region during

---

[105] Probably Italian millet or *Setaria italica.*

[106] Abaca (*Musa textilis*), popularly known as Manila hemp, is indigenous to the Philippines. These tough fibers of palm are woven into cords, cloth, rings, and bags.

[107] Colin in Pastells, *op. cit.* (n. 84), pp. 36–40. A reference to the Jesuit missions in the Tanay valley of Negros. See map in De la Costa, *op. cit.* (n. 4), p. 432.

[108] It is used extensively as a source in F. M. Keesing, *The Ethnohistory of Northern Luzon* (Stanford, 1962).

[109] "Valley temperatures, although still very much tropical, show greater diurnal and seasonal ranges than do those encountered in other parts of the Philippines" (Wernstedt and Spencer, *op. cit.* [n. 96], p. 316).

[110] Aduarte was in China during 1599–1600.

1581 when it was attacked by a Japanese fleet. The Japanese were interested in the Cagayan valley because of their need for its crops and timber. But the Spaniards, whose numbers were small, feared that the numerous and "audacious" Japanese would make bad neighbors and so determined to keep them out of this fertile and strategic valley by going there themselves.[111]

The Augustinians, the first of the orders sent to Christianize this region, met resistance so fierce that the missionaries beat a hasty retreat and left the pacification to the military. Manila sent expeditions northward from the Pangasinan plains across the mountains into the valley; to the upper valley they gave the name of "Ituy" (the modern province of Nueva Vizcaya). Other Spanish efforts were launched upriver from the port and settlement of Nueva Segovia and to the east of the valley from Abulug up the Apayao River. The Dominicans were thus gradually enabled to establish ecclesiastical control over Spanish centers along the middle reaches of the Cagayan River to the point where the Magat flows into it. Missionaries of all the orders made occasional crossings of the mountains from the south to work among the local people of "Ituy." Even in the most pacified parts of the lower Cagayan valley revolts were frequent against the Spanish tribute collectors and their missionary allies.[112]

Worst of all are the wars the *Indios* are "constantly waging among themselves" and the great oppression being inflicted on the lower classes by those superior in rank.[113] Dominicans are sent from the Cagayan settlements in 1604 to the country of the "Ytabes" (Itaves) in the "estuary of Lobo" to convert these people "from bloodthirsty wolves to gentle sheep."[114] Others brave the land route northward from the plains of Pangasinan through the swamps and lowlands of Ilocos and from there over the "rough and lofty" Caraballo mountains.[115] In the region known as "Yrraya" (Irraya) lives in relative isolation a bellicose mountain tribe called the "Gadanes" (Gaddangs), who stir up the other *Indios* against the Spanish.[116] Missionaries did not work in "Ituy" on a regular basis until 1633 when the Dominicans established a permanent mission in its main village of the same name. In exploring the high country of the Caraballo mountains, the missionaries report on its barter economy, give a precise account of its system of dry rice cultivation, and laud the cleanliness and fraternal spirit of its peoples. The Dominicans nonetheless plan to resettle their converts in larger communities in the river valley so that they "may be visited and helped in their nec-

[111] Aduarte in BR, XXX, 272–74.
[112] See Keesing, *op. cit.* (n. 108), pp. 176–77, and accompanying maps.
[113] Aduarte in BR, XXX, 193.
[114] *Ibid.*, XXXI, 204–5. The Itaves of the lower Chico River area in the Cagayan valley today number almost twelve thousand, most of whom are Christians. See Keesing, *op. cit.* (n. 108), p. 221.
[115] Aduarte in BR, XXXII, 65–66.
[116] *Ibid.*, pp. 113–14. Also see Keesing, *op. cit.* (n. 108), pp. 250–52. The Gaddangs live in the middle and upper Cagayan area and have a language of their own.

essities" by the few available missionaries.[117] The Dominicans meanwhile begin to take charge of the missions in Ilocos, while others go to the "remote and craggy mountains in the province of Nueva Segovia" to win the "Mandayas" back to the faith.[118] Hope is also held out for the conversion of the islands called "Babuianes" (Babuyan and Batan islands) which are stepping stones on the route to Formosa and Japan.[119]

Hostility to the Christians is generally fomented by the priestesses called "managanito" who serve "Ana Gaoley," their "greatest idol."[120] The presence of the Christians and their cross angers this god and it punishes the *Indios* by refusing to answer their prayers or to give oracles to their priestesses. No sacrifice is too costly to appease this devil-god. Even when its servitors are mourning a loved one, it requires that they wear a golden neck chain for the entire period, or until the bereaved commits a murder. Mourners fast the first three days, during the next three they eat a little fruit, and for a long time thereafter have only boiled herbs or roots. Once a homicide is committed, the mourning and the fast end and the feasting begins.[121] The *Indios* believe implicitly that there are good and bad *anitos* whom they must follow or propitiate. At illnesses the *aniteras,* or priestesses, perform rites and sacrifices to the spirits. Before sowing their fields they feast for three days. All believe in omens, auguries, and divinations.[122] In Nueva Segovia province the *Indios* keep idols in secret places or sacred huts to which they make pilgrimages.[123] The gods nonetheless act with severity to punish the *Indios*. In 1631 the lower Cagayan valley suffered a plague of locusts "which were more in number than the natives had ever seen before."[124] Frequent epidemics of smallpox also occur, which are particularly fatal to young children.[125]

Bobadilla reports that the *Indios* reveal by their songs that they "are not far from our belief on . . . the creation of the world." According to them, the first human couple, once they emerged from a bursted reed (bamboo) on the island of Sumatra, quarreled at their marriage.[126] When the soul leaves

---

[117] Aduarte in BR, XXXII, 192–203; also *cf.* Keesing, *op. cit.* (n. 108), pp. 280–83. The Dominicans also invited the neighboring Alaquetes to join these communities.

[118] Aduarte in BR, XXXII, 210, 226–30; also *cf.* Keesing, *op. cit.* (n. 108), pp. 194–96. The Mandayas fled *ca.* 1625 from the missions on the Apayao River to their original mountain homes.

[119] Aduarte in BR, XXXII, 91.

[120] "Anagaloey" in the Pangasinan area is the god to whom they offered sacrifices of pigs and humans. See Roger, *op. cit.* (n. 59), p. 73.

[121] Aduarte in BR, XXX, 190–93; *cf.* Keesing, *op. cit.* (n. 108), p. 58, and Zaide, *op. cit.* (n. 24), pp. 127–28. Probably a reference to the revenge murder of the killer of a deceased, or an "eye for an eye."

[122] Aduarte in BR, XXX, 285–91; on superstition *cf.* Zaide, *op. cit.* (n. 24), pp. 129–30.

[123] Aduarte in BR, XXX, 155–56. For photographs of *anitos* see Roger, *op. cit.* (n. 59), appendix.

[124] Aduarte in BR, XXXI, 203.

[125] *Ibid.,* XXXII, 93–94.

[126] This appears to be an abbreviated version of a story still preserved in the oral tradition. See Zaide, *op. cit.* (n. 24), p. 31.

the body at death, they believe it travels to an island where everything is black; from here it passes on to another island where all things are of different colors; and finally it arrives at one where everything is white.[127] A chief form of idolatry is the adoration of their "humalagar," those ancestors remarkable for their courage or intelligence. Whenever possible, each person ascribes divinity to their own father immediately at his death. One old man of Leyte, in anticipation of being a deity after death, had himself placed conveniently on the seashore to be revered by passing sailors.[128] In addition to animals and birds, the *Indios* venerate ancient trees, which they refuse to cut down. Their domestic sacrifices are named for the offering being made to the god. Some priestesses at these sacrifices are possessed by the devil and "say and do things that fill the bystanders with fear."[129]

Women are generally held in high esteem. Most married couples have children. In some islands the head of a newborn child is pressed between two boards "so that it would not be round, but long;" they also flatten the forehead as a mark of beauty.[130] At the birth of high-ranking children, a week-long festival is held, at which the women sing joyful songs. Women are generally hired as mourners at funerals "as they are most apt for that music." Like the men the women swim so well that bridges are not needed to cross the rivers. At their menstrual periods the women bathe in hot springs.

Most men are good sailors and navigate readily from one island to the other to carry on trade. They are not equally good on the open sea, since they do not use the compass. Generally they are cowards who prefer to fight from ambush. To protect their animals and crops from beasts and human thieves, they scatter caltrops (star thistles) around them. Many have learned how to fight with firearms, especially the Pampangos who are recruited to fight side by side with the Spanish. While most *Indios* readily accept Christianity, "their meager intelligence does not permit them to sound the depths of its mysteries." Their two chief vices are usury and intoxication, habits which they persist in despite the best efforts of the missionaries.[131]

While the islands lack wheat, grapes, olives, and the ordinary fruits of Europe, they are rich in rice. In the flatland, rice is grown under water, but on the mountains it is watered only by the rain. Horses and cows have been introduced from Mexico and China, but the people's usual meat is pork and the innumerable fowl, deer, and goats native to the islands. Sugar is plentiful and many mills for its processing have been built since the advent of the

---

[127] On the belief of the early Filipinos in a future life see *ibid.*, p. 127.

[128] *Cf.* Roger, *op. cit.* (n. 59), pp. 126–27.

[129] Bobadilla in BR, XXIX, 283–86.

[130] *Cf.* J. Hewitt, "Head Pressing amongst the Milanos of Sarawak," *JRAS, Straits Branch*, LX (December, 1911), pp. 69–72.

[131] Bobadilla in BR, XXIX, 286–96 *passim*. On Bobadilla and other Jesuit theologians as moralists see De la Costa, *op. cit.* (n. 4), pp. 354–57.

Spanish. Beans, strawberries, and cinnamon are readily available, although the cinnamon of Mindanao is inferior to that of Ceylon. The commonest fruits are bananas (fifteen or sixteen kinds), "santors," and "birinbines."[132] Because they are tart, the last two of these fruits are made into preserves. Oranges, including a variety with red pulp, are grown in abundance. In the mountains the *Indios* gather for food certain wild roots called "pugaian" and "corot."[133] They cultivate other plants especially for their roots: "apari," "ubi," "laquei," and "camote."[134] Throughout the islands the trees, especially the coco palm, provide food, shelter, and materials for ship construction. A certain tree grows in high dry areas which yields water like a perpetual spring.[135]

Snakes are a menace in the Philippines; especially dangerous is the bite of the one called "omodro" (*Hemibungarus collaris*). Other snakes called "saua" (*Python reticulatus*) hang from the branches of trees along the road. They wind their huge bodies several times around their prey to break its bones before devouring it.[136] Wild roots and herbs grow in the mountains which are used as specifics for the treatment of snakebite.[137] Civet cats, which look like small tigers, roam the mountains. These animals are captured and bound while the musk is removed from a small sack under the tail. The rivers swarm with fierce, scaly crocodiles which audaciously attack boats as well as men; when they are ashore sunning themselves they are not so voracious. The "woman fish" (dugong) is as large as a calf and its flesh tastes like beef. While reputed to be mermaids, "they have nothing of the beauty of face and of the voice that is attributed to sirens." Finally there are the ashen-colored birds as large as a hen called the "tabon."[138] Their eggs, three times as large as hen's eggs, are laid in holes which they dig in the sand and

---

[132] "Santor" or santol is the *Sandoricum koetjape,* a tree which produces a thick-skinned fruit. "Birinbines" or balimbings are star-fruit, the *Averrhoa carambola* of Linnaeus. See *Plants of the Philippines* (n. 16), pp. 119–21.

[133] "Pugaian" or *pukingang* (Tagalog) is the butterfly-pea or the *Clitoria ternatea,* a common vine. See T. H. Pardo de Tavera, *The Medicinal Plants of the Philippines* (Philadelphia, 1901), pp. 92–93. "Corot" or *korot* (Bisayan) is the *Dioscorea hispida,* whose tuberous roots are fleshy, yellow yams often called *namé.* See *Plants of the Philippines* (n. 16), p. 71.

[134] "Apari" is possibly *paria* (Ilocano), the balsam apple or *Momordica balsamina;* it is usually the fruit which is eaten. "Ubi" (Tagalog) is the *Dioscorea alata,* the most popular of the yams. "Laquei" is possibly *laktag* (Tagalog), or *Anamirta corculus.* See Pardo de Tavera, *op. cit.* (n. 133), p. 24. "Camote" or *kamote* is the generic name in most dialects for the sweet potato, which comes in several varieties. It was probably introduced from New Spain (*cf.* Aztec, *camotl*).

[135] Bobadilla in BR, XXIX, 296–300. The tree that gives water is probably the Australian pine *Casuarina equisetifolia.* See E. A. Menninger, *Fantastic Trees* (New York, 1967), p. 231.

[136] Ordinarily pythons do not attack people.

[137] Bobadilla (BR, XXIX, 302) gives a list of the local names of twelve different remedies. A comparison of his romanizations with those in Pardo de Tavera, *op. cit.* (n. 133), produced no identifications.

[138] According to the Tagalog dictionary, this is the name of a bird which lays but one large egg. According to Hachisuka, *op. cit.* (n. 60), p. 60, the name *ta-bon* in Tagalog refers to a bird of the order *Galliformes* and of the genus *Megapodius freycinet pusillus.*

cover over; "sometimes one hundred and fifty of the eggs are found in the same hole."[139]

The native peoples of the Philippines, according to Colin, are of three types: "Moro-Malay," Bisayans, and Negrillos (Negritos).[140] The first and most advanced group originated in the Malay peninsula and entered the Philippines from Borneo, as is indicated by the analogues in the Malay and Tagalog languages, in bodily color and features, in costume, and in customs and ceremonies. The Bisayans possibly came from Makassar where it is reported that other tattooed people live.[141] But not enough data or "even a well founded conjecture" exists to indicate their origin. The Negrillos, an uncivilized people, live in the mountains and thick forests away from the sea. They go about naked except for tree-bark clouts called "bahaques" (Tagalog, *bahág*). Their ornaments are limited to rattan armlets, anklets, and bracelets, and head decorations of flowers, leaves, and bird plumes. They have no laws, letters, or government, but simply follow the lead of a chief clansman. As the first inhabitants of the islands, the Negrillos have been forced into the interior by the later migrations of more advanced peoples. Some appear to have intermarried with these later migrants to produce a mixed breed called by different names in the various islands.[142] Generally these mixed breeds live at the sources of rivers and trade downstream with the Tagalogs and Bisayans of the coast. Although they are not Christians, they pay tribute to the Spaniards and run their own affairs. Since the *Indios* are of such varied backgrounds, it is possible that in the past people from Indo-China, India, and Japan also settled there, as is borne out by artifacts found in graves uncovered in northern Luzon.[143]

The Tagalog alphabet is derived from the Islamic Malays who took it from the Arabs.[144] *Indios* who know the Latin alphabet are trying to write Tagalog in its letters. But most men and women, even when Christian, still "cling fondly to their own method of writing and reading." They read prayerbooks in their own language and compose prayers and poems on divine subjects in it; some are even able to translate Spanish plays into elegant Tagalog poetry. Many have learned how to write enough Spanish to work as clerks and secretaries; a few have learned enough Latin to help students

[139] Bobadilla in BR, XXIX, 301–3. For a confirmatory description of the nesting habits of the *ta-bon* see José Montero y Vidal, *El archipielago filipino* . . . (Madrid, 1886), pp. 97–98.

[140] Malays, Indonesians, and Negritos are today discerned as the three basic groups which peopled the Philippines in pre-Spanish times. See Zaide, *op. cit.* (n. 24), p. 65.

[141] *Cf.* above, p. 1499. Several of the Dayak tribes of Borneo reportedly practiced tattooing. See John Crawfurd, *A Descriptive Dictionary of the Indian Islands and Adjacent Countries* (London, 1856), pp. 426–27.

[142] In Mindoro, for example, they are called Mangyans or mountaineers by others. On their designations of themselves see John M. Garvan, *The Negritos of the Philippines* (H. Hochegger [ed.], "Wiener Beiträge zur Kulturgeschichte und Linguistik," XIV; 1963), pp. 6–7.

[143] Colin in BR, XL, 38–48.

[144] Probably derives ultimately from the Asokan alphabet of India. *Cf.* above, p. 1500.

edit their rough drafts. Others are competent enough to work as printers in Manila's two printing houses. While the native languages are many, they resemble one another because they have a common origin in Malay. Colin seeks to show their affinity with Malay and with one another by setting down in a comparative table the words for sky, sun, and moon in Malay, Tagalog, Pampanga, and Bisayan. He also revises Chirino's Tagalog translation of the Ave Maria, since it was written "in the old style, which has changed here somewhat since then."[145] The languages of the "uncivilized nations" are even more numerous, though the people are fewer; almost every river valley has its own language. At a meeting of Mangyans in Mindoro those from different but nearby places were "not able to understand one another." This multiplicity of languages greatly hinders the instruction and conversion of these primitive peoples.[146]

The Tagalogs, much more than the others, are exceedingly courteous and correct in their use of names. They are embarrassed to name another person baldly and usually add honorifics to a name. Influential persons who have no children from whom to obtain their surnames are formally assigned a new name at a banquet.[147] An assemblage of friends and relatives coins a *pamagat* (Tagalog, meaning "title") for the honoree on these occasions. It is usually contrived from a play on words or metaphor of excellence based on the name given at birth. For example, if the given name is "Bacal" (Tagalog, *bakál*) meaning "iron," the title assigned might be one which means "not to spoil with time." It is also customary in daily life to call friends or chums by nicknames recalling a mutually notable experience or event. "These are all," Colin pronounces, "arguments in favor of the civilization of these Indians."[148]

Both men and women throughout the islands are well built, good-looking, and of the same yellowish brown complexions; among the Bisayans some of the women are of a lighter color. The men, who have no pride in beards or mustaches, pull out their facial hairs with bamboo or shell pincers. Both sexes, but the women more so than the men, pierce their ears and wear circular gold earrings. Women stretch the openings in their ears as much as possible for beauty's sake and some even have two holes in each ear for different sorts and sizes of earrings. Males cover the head with a narrow and thin turban which they tie in various modes. Their rank is indicated by the color they wear, red being reserved to those who have killed at least one person. Embroidered turbans may be worn only by those who have killed seven. Like the Bisayans, the Ilocanos of Luzon tattoo themselves, but not

---

[145] On Chirino's translations see above, p. 1500.
[146] Colin in BR, XL, 48–56. On the nature of the Negrito dialects see Garvan, *op. cit.* (n. 142), pp. 188–91.
[147] For the surnames of parents, see above, p. 1503.
[148] Colin in BR, XL, 59–60.

so elaborately; both sexes of the Ilocos dress in the same or similar costumes. However, most of the *Indios* have been quick to adopt Spanish clothes, ornaments, and even shoes.[149]

The Spanish call their boiled rice "morisqueta" as if to call it "food of the Moors." *Indios* eat it with small, whole boiled fish and fish sauce. At banquets they serve venison, pork, and beef, which they prefer to eat when the meat begins to spoil. When dining they sit on the ground around small and low square or round tables which will accommodate four persons. They have no nappery or utensils and eat in common from the various plates laid on the tables. They eat sparingly and most relish salty, spicy, and acid foods. Banquets are invitations to drink, the food being secondary. They drink either palm wine called *tuba* or that made from sugarcane which they call "quilong" (Tagalog, *kilang*). The Bisayans also make *pangasi* or a yeast from rice; on this fermented mash they pour water, which is then converted into a liquor that they suck up through a tube.[150]

At their banquets they sing traditional songs in which one or two take the lead and the rest respond. They also dance to the accompaniment of metal bells. Their dances are "warlike and passionate," but with steps that are measured and patterned. Generally they hold a cloth, a spear, or a shield in their hands with which they make meaningful gestures in time with the music. When their hands are empty their foot movements are alternately slow and rapid, portraying attacking and retiring, inciting and pacifying. Their folk dancers are so graceful and elegant that they are invited to participate in Christian festivals. The youths and children are so apt in music and dance that they learn quickly to sing, play, and dance quite acceptably in the European manner.[151]

Songs and stories preserve their traditions about the creation of the world and the human race. They say that in the beginning there was only sky and water and a kite which flew between them. Tired of flying and not having a resting place, the bird "stirred up the water to splash against the sky." To restrain the water the sky burdened it with islands. The sky then ordered the kite to alight on the islands, to build its nest there, and to let sky and water remain in peace.[152] Man is said to have come from the stem of a large bamboo which had just two nodules. While floating on the water it was carried onto a beach to the feet of the kite. Angered by what had hit its feet, the kite pecked the bamboo open and "out of one nodule came man and from the other woman." The god of the earthquake asked the fish and birds to con-

[149] *Ibid.*, pp. 60–64.
[150] *Ibid.*, pp. 64–67. *Cf.* the production of sake and arrack in D. H. Grist, *Rice* (3d ed.; London, 1959), pp. 323–24.
[151] Colin in BR, XL, 67–68. On traditional dances see R. L. Villa, Jr., "Filipino Identity in Folk Dances," in Lardizabal and Leogardo (eds.), *op. cit.* (n. 58), pp. 164–68. The dance here described is a common one on the theme of combat, possibly the "Moro-Moro."
[152] This myth of origin is still preserved in the oral tradition. See Zaide, *op. cit.* (n. 24), p. 2.

sent to their marriage even though they were brother and sister. From this couple's many children originated "the various kinds and classes of people." Angered by having so many idle and useless children around the house, the father one day decided to whip them with a stick. The frightened children fled into various parts of the house. Those who took refuge in the innermost chambers became the chiefs, those who escaped outside became the free-men, and those who fled to the kitchen and other lower rooms became the slaves. Those who fled to distant places founded the other nations.[153]

Ceremonies for making sacrifices vary with the occasion. Ostentatious celebrations for chieftains are called "the feast of the great god." Near the chieftain's house they erect a leafy bower around which cloths of various colors are hung in the Moorish fashion. Once the guests assemble there, the presiding *katolonan* (priestess) orders the best-looking girl present to stick the animal, usually a pig, while the others perform a ceremonial dance. After the animal is dead, they cut it into pieces which are passed out to the people "as is the blessed bread." When the sacrifice is for a critically ill per-son, a new and large house is quickly built at the patient's expense. The sick individual is moved to his new lodging and laid down on a palm mat. The sacrifice—a slave, turtle, large shellfish, or hog—is placed on the floor near the sick person along with small tables of food. Dancing to the ringing of gongs the *katolonan* wounds the victim and anoints with its blood the ill per-son as well as some of the bystanders. After killing and skinning the victim, the *katolonan* takes out and examines its entrails for signs of the patient's fate. After going through a prophetic frenzy, the priestess predicts the pa-tient's future. If the prophecy is recovery, they sing and celebrate until they collapse from sheer exhaustion. If the prophecy is death, the priestess pro-claims that the *anitos* have chosen this virtuous person to become one of them and entreats him to remember her in the other life. All regard him hereafter as an *anito*. Sacrifices always end with feasts and with offerings to the priestess from each person in attendance. Because they are greedy, the *katolonan*s are not highly regarded unless they unite "with their office no-bility or power."[154]

Omens and auguries are what these people live by: an owl on the roof is a sign of death; a serpent in the road or the chirp of a lizard portend danger, and so forth. Their oaths are taken in the form of terrible curses, such as "May I die," or "May I be eaten by a crocodile." When the chiefs of Manila pledged allegiance to the Spanish in 1571, they asked "the sun to pierce them through the middle" if they failed to keep their word. For solemn oaths they perform the "pasambakan," a ceremony in which they present a

---

[153] Colin in BR, XL, 73–74. This is a slightly longer and different but clearly recognizable version of the myth still preserved in the oral tradition. See Zaide, *op. cit.* (n. 24), p. 31.

[154] Colin in BR, XL, 74–77. On sacrifices in northern Luzon *cf.* Quirino and Garcia, *loc. cit.* (n. 25), pp. 394–95.

portrait of a monstrous beast "asking that they might be broken into pieces by it" if they fail to keep their promise.[155] They also follow a "barbarous kind of vengeance" called *balata,* which involves repaying violence with equal violence. Mourning for a murdered person cannot end until the murderer is caught and killed.[156]

Their laws, traditions, and customs are "not very barbarous for barbarians." To break with tradition and proprieties is considered unacceptable, no matter what the circumstances. Respect for parents and elders, even by small children, is religiously maintained by the custom of never uttering one's father's name. In civil and criminal suits the *datu* and the elders act as judges. In civil contests the litigants are first summoned before the judges to work out an agreement. When arbitration fails, each of the parties swears an oath to abide by the decision of the court. Witnesses are then called and examined. If a clear-cut decision is impossible, "the difference is split equally." If the decision favors one of the parties, the other must accept it. Should the convicted one break his oath, the judges attack him, even with arms, to enforce obedience. In such cases, the judges and witnesses for the successful litigant receive a major part of the fine. In murder cases, distinctions are based on the ranks of the murderer and the victim. If the victim is a chief, his kinsmen hunt down the murderer and his relatives in what amounts to war. Mediators then step in to impose a fine in gold upon the murderer. One-half of the fine goes to the mediator, with the rest being divided among the wife, children, and relatives of the deceased. The death penalty is never imposed by law unless the victim was a commoner and the murderer is also a commoner unable to pay a fine in gold. Death in these cases is carried out by his own chief or other chiefs by lashing the murderer to a stake and spearing him to death. Persons suspected of thieving are subjected to trials by ordeal. Suspects are first given an opportunity to make restitution. Each is ordered to put together a heap of cloths, leaves, or any other material. If the stolen article is found in the heap, the trial ends. If it is not recovered, one of three ordeals is ordered. The suspects, each with a wooden spear in hand, are plunged underwater; the one to come out first is adjudged guilty. Or each is required to take a stone out of boiling water; the one who refuses pays the penalty for the theft. Or each is given a lighted candle; the one whose candle burns out first is deemed the culprit.[157]

Chiefs usually attain to this status by descent or by personal strength, courage, and ingenuity. There is no higher authority to appoint or elect a chief. Succession by heredity is not automatic, for everything depends on the abilities of the claimant. Men of low extraction may attain authority through a display of ability and force.

[155] Colin in BR, XL, 77–79.
[156] *Ibid.,* p. 82.
[157] *Ibid.,* pp. 84–86. *Cf.* Zaide, *op. cit.* (n. 24), pp. 122–24.

The manner of life and everyday conduct of all classes reflect their preoccupation with trade. Most of the products of the earth are sold personally by
the producers. Fishers sell or barter their own catch, hunters their own
game, and farmers their own crops. Women, almost all of whom can read
and write, are particularly shrewd in trading their needlework, weaving,
and embroidery. When husband and wife set out on a trading junket, they
walk in single file with the wife leading the way. Even groups of people will
walk down a wide road in single file. Commerce is not always peaceful.
Maritime peoples regularly make profitable raids on other islands and interior peoples ambush traders. The adoption of children is another form of
commerce, the natural parent paying to have the child adopted. Adultery is
punished by the payment of a fine. Persons are enslaved when they are unable to pay their debts and the interest on them. A partial slave has the right
to buy his freedom for a just price. In addition to dowries or bride prices, a
present called "panhimuyat" is given to the mother of the bride as a payment for rearing her.[158]

The Dominicans, who have made the "Sangleyes" their special charge,
preach to them in the Chinese language and take care of their sick and aged.
In 1617 the friars took up residence in "Binondoc" (Binondo), the Chinese
Christian community, and built a church there in the Chinese style;[159] now
Chinese plays and operas are not allowed to be performed there, for they are
"full of superstitions and idolatries." Between 1618 and 1633 the Dominicans baptized 4,752 Chinese adults and continue to make converts at this
rapid rate. News of these successes and of the Dominicans' services to the
Chinese are relayed to China by those returning there. The Dominicans,
who long for a mission of their own in China, prepare to send friars to the
waiting harvest in Formosa, Korea, and China itself.[160]

The city of Manila in 1637–38 includes 150 Spanish households within its
walls and about 20,000 Chinese in the Parian. "Sangleyes" are an omni-
present danger to the city which they exploit so freely. Although the Parian
is only a settlement of unprotected wooden structures, the Spanish forbid
the Chinese to carry weapons and always have artillery pointed at the Parian. The Chinese would readily take Manila over, were it not in their interest to drain the silver of Peru into their own hands and into China. In this
commerce, which involves smuggling, they are aided by the Spaniards in
the Philippines and Mexico and by the Portuguese in Macao. Manila, constantly under threat from the Dutch and the Muslims, is seriously affected
economically by this growth of illicit trade. Of its Spanish families "there

---

[158] Colin in BR, XL, 86–97 *passim.*
[159] Binondo was a permanent settlement of Chinese and Chinese *mestizos* north of the Pasig
River.
[160] Aduarte in BR, XXXI, 68–69, 216–18; XXXII, 76–87, 204. On the Dominicans in Formosa and China see above, pp. 190–91, 197, 358.

are not two who are very rich." These grave conditions are exacerbated by the failure of the galleons to appear in some years with reinforcements from Mexico. Surrounded by enemies, the Spaniards in the Philippines "can muster scarcely eight hundred men."[161]

Domingo Navarrete, the Dominican theologian, was in Manila and its environs from 1650 to 1657. He reviews the many setbacks suffered by the Spaniards during the governorship (1635–44) of Don Sebastian de Corcuera: numerous deaths of Manila's gentry in the expeditions (1637–39) against Jolo, the loss of Formosa (1642), and Corcuera's peculations. Corcuera is reviled for inventing the tax called the *vandala* by the natives.[162] The revolt of Pampanga (1660) is attributed to the unjust exactions required by the *vandala*. Pampanga is required to pay a tax of twenty-four thousand bushels of rice at a fixed price; the government on its side postpones payments for many years while meeting its other obligations with relative promptness. Discouraged, the *Indios* migrate or refuse to sow rice. Even when natural disasters strike the crops, the unyielding Spanish demand the *vandala* without regard to the sufferings of the *Indios* or the welfare of the islands. The local authorities are equally arbitrary in taking the exactions with which some of them fill their own purses.[163]

The friars learn Tagalog "without much difficulty." They find the *Indios* "civil and tractable" and less "harsh and stern" than the Indians of Mexico. They are submissive to the priests, and quick to learn any manual art. Some are excellent "Penmen, Painters [and] Carvers." They love to read the religious books printed in their own language. Women are especially devout, and both sexes enjoy and participate in the religious festivals by dancing, singing, playing instruments, and decorating the churches. The *Indios* particularly adore the cross and fill their settlements with crosses.[164]

Daily life is far from comfortable for the friars, who grow sickly in the excessive heat and humidity. They are frightened by the violent storms, earthquakes, and floods. Travel into the interior is a hardship because of rock slides, the lack of roads, and leech-ridden mountains. "Fierce and terrible Alligators" terrify people on land and water. To escape these monsters the *Indios* attack their eyes to force them to flee. The female alligator lays its eggs in a current of water; when the young hatch they are carried downstream by the current, where the mother waits to eat as many of them

---

[161] Bañuelos y Carillo in BR, XXIX, 69–76. Friar Manrique was also in Manila at this time, awaiting an opportunity to go to Japan. He stresses the dependency of Manila on the galleon trade. See M. Garcia (ed.), *op. cit.* (n. 81), pp. 201–2. In 1639 the Parian was burned and many of its inhabitants killed by Spanish and Filipino forces in what is referred to as the "second great insurrection." See Felix (ed.), *op. cit.* (n. 72), pp. 24, 78.

[162] On the *vandala*, or the compulsory sale of goods to the government, see Phelan, *op. cit.* (n. 18), pp. 99–102, 108–9.

[163] Navarrete in Cummins (trans. and ed.), *op. cit.* (n. 89), I, 52–58.

[164] *Ibid.*, pp. 58–60, 89.

as she can catch in her mouth.[165] Worse even than the wild animals are "the Robbers they call Camucones" and the Muslims, who periodically raid the Christian islands to take captives.[166] Even the devil sends "witches and fairies" to make mysterious noises and to throw things around to vex and torment the missionaries.[167]

Not all is gloom. The *Indios,* even the primitives of the mountains, are kind and gentle. The land and waters yield an abundance of food. In Bataan the "Lechia" (litchi fruit) grows, one of the best fruits in the world. On Mindoro the "Mountain-Blacks" "look like Devils" because the males are painted white and the females other colors; nonetheless, they prove to be friendly. Mount Baco on Mindoro looks "like a Mountain of Cristal" because a river tumbles down its side. On this island grow "an infinite number of Cedars, whose Blossom . . . exhales a most fragrant scent," a tree (Spanish, *cabo negro*) from which they make black hemp for rigging ships, and another called the abaca, which "is excellent for Cables for the more it is wetted, the stronger it grows." The surrounding seas and the mountain rivers abound in excellent fish. The "Lisas" (skates) are so numerous in Lake Nauján that "sometimes they take them with their hands." The roe of these fish are salted and eaten with rice. On the islands around Manila the "Swallows Nests" are found in the rocks which are bought for high prices and eaten in Manila and China. The Portuguese make a practice of buying them cheaply in Cambodia and Siam to sell for great profit in China. In Manila the old cathedral which was wrecked by the earthquake of 1645 is in process of being rebuilt in 1657. In their books the Chinese call the island of Manila "Lin Sung" (Luzon) and rightly claim that it abounds in gold.[168] Gold is found most readily in Luzon's provinces of Pangasinan and Ilocos. One type of rice grows remarkably fast, "so that in the space of forty days it is sow'd, grows, ripens, is reap'd, and eaten."[169] Wheat might grow well and become cheap in Luzon if only the farmers had an incentive to plant it. Native buffaloes have been mated with imported cows to produce a "third Species very fine to look upon." Grazing land is spoiled by the spread of "Guayava" (*Psidum gaujava,* or guava) whose fruits are eaten with meats and preserved in jelly.[170] Guava is spread by birds who eat the fruit and drop the seeds.

---

[165] Obviously a myth. Alligators lay their eggs on land.

[166] Camucones were heathens of Palawan and Brunei who hunted human quarry in the northern Bisayans and in southern Luzon. See De la Costa, *op. cit.* (n. 4), p. 321.

[167] Navarrete in Cummins (trans. and ed.), *op. cit.* (n. 89), I, 52–88 *passim.* Many of the missionaries report on being visited by poltergeists.

[168] For a translation of what the Ming Annals have to report about Luzon see Felix (ed.), *op. cit.* (n. 72), pp. 246–51.

[169] Very unlikely, since the maturation period of rice in Southeast Asia varies from 90 to 260 days. See Grist, *op. cit.* (n. 150), p. 67.

[170] Guava trees and shrubs introduced from tropical America now grow throughout the Philippines. See E. D. Merrill, *An Enumeration of Philippine Flowering Plants* (4 vols.; Manila, 1922), III, 155.

Fruits which are "equal to the best of ours" are the "macupas" (Tagalog, *makópa*), "bilimbins" (*balimbing*), "pahos" (*páho*), "santols" (*santol*), and "papaws" (Spanish, *papaya*).[171] The "Nanca" (Tagalog, *nangka*), the "largest Fruit that is known in the World," contains "Nuts or Kernels" which are "delicious whether eaten raw or roasted.[172] Small "zapotes" (*sapota*), as well as black ones, are plentiful and very good, but for delicacy of taste and aroma the best fruit of all is the "Ates."[173] A thousand varieties of fragrant flowers and sweet herbs grow wild in the fields. The waters abound in fish, especially "olaves" (Spanish, *alosa*, or shad) and pompano. "Wondrous" oysters and horrible-looking iguanas are eaten as great delicacies. Certain places in the islands are so fertile that they will produce anything. Wheat planted in "Tunazan" (Tunasan in Laguna Province near Manila) produces one hundred and thirty bushels for each one sown.[174]

In Manila there is a college called "of the children of St. John Lateran" which was founded by a Dominican lay brother for the training of Filipino boys. Educated in a traditional European manner, these youths become soldiers, priests, and members of the Dominican, Franciscan, and Augustinian orders. Although the city is small and the Spaniards few, it supports thousands of Chinese, native Filipinos, and mixed breeds. In the Parian there live two hundred Chinese carpenters and "a proportionate number of other trades" including at least two hundred Chinese and *mestizo* barbers. In the Chinese hospital of the Dominicans there is a Chinese physician who administers Chinese medicines. A Dominican who interprets Chinese is always available in the Parian church; a Franciscan performs similar services in the Japanese church in Dilao. When the Christians were banished from Japan, many of the converts sought refuge in Manila, where they were looked upon as saints and esteemed "as Relicks of inestimable Value."[175]

Careri was in Manila and its environs from May 8 to June 28, 1697. During this time he made a brief side-trip to Cavite (May 17–19) and was there again for twelve days (June 16–28) immediately before his departure for Mexico. From June 2 to 7 he made a sightseeing excursion to the "Lake of Bahi" (Laguna de Bay) on horseback. Included with his description of Manila's gates, foundry, and ecclesiastical and government buildings are estimates of the numbers of Chinese in its variegated population. He claims that only three thousand live in the Parian, with a like number scattered about

---

[171] These fruits were probably all introduced from tropical America. For their scientific designations in order see *ibid.*, III, 168; II, 324, 467–8, 361; III, 119. For additional discussion see BR, XXXVIII, 49, n. 17; XIII, 141, n. 20.

[172] Merrill, *op. cit.* (n. 170), II, 41. This is the jackfruit. Also see H. Yule and A. C. Burnell, *Hobson-Jobson* (rev. ed., London, 1968), pp. 440–43.

[173] BR, XXXIII, 50, nn. 20–21. "Ates" (*Anona squamosa*) is the custard apple or sweetsop. See Merrill, *op. cit.* (n. 170), II, 177.

[174] Navarrete in Cummins (trans. and ed.), *op. cit.* (n. 89), I, 91–98. Laguna is the garden province of the Philippines. See BR, XXXVIII, 53, n. 23. Wheat was not generally cultivated.

[175] Navarrete in Cummins (trans. and ed.), *op. cit.* (n. 89), I, 99–102.

the other islands.[176] The Chinese in the Parian are ruled by a governor, a magistrate "who acts as their protector," and by a steward and other officials "whom they pay." At their lunar New Year, the Chinese pay a special tax for the privilege of playing "metua," an even-and-odd game.[177] Besides the Parian, Manila has fifteen other suburbs in its immediate vicinity with housing comparable to that of Siam. Between these suburbs and Laguna de Bay, farms are interspersed between the hamlets, all of which are ministered to by the Franciscans, Augustinians, and Jesuits. Near the lake is another deeper lake and hot springs. Cavite is a semicircular port town whose houses "have no beauty in them." Its major industry is shipbuilding, more than six hundred natives being forced to labor in its yards.[178]

3

MINDANAO AND JOLO

South of the Bisayan islands, the peoples called "Moros" by the Spanish resisted stoutly the incursions of the Europeans. To Chirino, Morga, and Argensola they are Muslim enemies allied with the Islamic ruler of Ternate to form a united front against the Spanish Christians. While the natives are generally inclined to be friendly, those who live around the "river of Mindanao" are enemies of both the Spanish and those natives who work with the Christians.[179] The sixteenth-century attempts of the Spaniards to pacify and colonize this region had failed when its Raja Sirongan was sent reinforcements and funds by Ternate. In retaliation for the Spanish invasions, wrathful Moros began raiding the Christian villages of the Bisayas. Spanish pacification of Mindanao was successful by 1600 only in the north around "the river of Botnan [Butuan or Agusan] [and at] Dapitan and in the province and coast of Caragan [Caraga]" in the southeast. After the conquest of

---

[176] After the withdrawal of the Spaniards from the Moluccas in 1662, a decline in silver exports from Mexico, and the growing competition of Coromandel traders, the sampan trade began to decline after 1670. No longer so dependent on Chinese commerce, the Manila city council ordered the expulsion of all non-Christian Chinese in 1689. This policy was pursued without great success until 1700, thus perhaps resulting in the decline of the total Chinese population here reflected in Careri's figures. See Felix (ed.), *op. cit.* (n. 72), pp. 172–73, 189–90. Careri's figures also coincide with the alleged legal situation which limited the Chinese residents in the Philippines to six thousand (*ibid.*, p. 34). Perhaps Careri is merely repeating here what he was told by the Spanish authorities.
[177] "Metua" is possibly *má tséuk*, a Cantonese slang term for playing cards which literally means "hempen birds." See Catherine P. Hargrave, *A History of Playing Cards* (Boston and New York, 1930), p. 9.
[178] Careri in *CV*, IV, 420–26, 475–78. On the Cavite shipyards see De la Costa, *op. cit.* (n. 4), pp. 343–45.
[179] The Spanish "river of Mindanao" is the Rio Grande. At its mouth is the town of Cotabato. The center of Muslim strength in this area was in the town of Buhayen (Bwayan, near the modern town of Dulawan on the Mindanao River).

Ternate in 1608 the Spaniards were able to mount new invasions of Moroland.[180] Still, it was not until 1635 that they took Zamboanga and built a fortress there. Over the next several years Governor Hurtado de Corcuera conquered Maguindanao in central Mindanao and the island of Jolo. Following these conquests Europe began to learn more about the southern islands, particularly from the writings of the missionaries.

Corcuera's exploits are celebrated by the Jesuit Father Bobadilla in his *Relación de las gloriosas victorias de . . . Corcuera . . . contra Cuchil Curralat* (Mexico, 1638).[181] Much more important accounts of Mindanao and Jolo with their adjacent small islands are to be found in the works of two other Jesuits: in Colin's *Labor evangélica* (1663) and in Francisco Combés' *Historia de las islas de Mindanao, Iolo, y sus adyacentes. Progressos de la religion y armas catolicas* (Madrid, 1667).[182] Like Colin's book, Combés' centers on the victories of the Jesuits in advancing the Christian faith. In the process he provides in his eight books descriptions of the geography, peoples, and products of Moroland, the conquest of the "Malanao" (Lake of Lanao) region (Bk. III), and the government of "Diego Faxardo" (Fajardo) during which a peace settlement was concluded in 1645–46 with the Maguindanao people and the Sulus. Combés' *Historia* was probably written at Manila between 1662 and 1664 to celebrate Spain's conquests and to explain and deplore the decision of 1662 to withdraw from the Spiceries and the south. Glimpses of life in Mindanao after the Spanish retreat can be obtained from Captain William Dampier's *A New Voyage around the World* (London, 1697).[183] The Englishman was there on a buccaneering expedition from July, 1686 to January, 1687. From Moroland, Dampier threaded his way northward to Manila, but his journal adds little of relevance to the earlier available information on the Christian Philippines.

Mindanao is roughly triangular in shape with a jagged coast and three renowned promontories: "Samboangan" (Zamboanga), Cape of San Agustin (Batulah Point), and "Suligao" (Surigao). Between Surigao and San Augustin on the east coast is the land of the Caraga.[184] In the north, Caraga extends inland to the river of "Butuan" (Agusan). Between Butuan and Pangil (Iligan) Bay live the idolatrous people called "Manobos," as well as the Bisayan Christians of Camiguin Island. On the northern coast of the

---

[180] See Chirino in BR, XII, 313–21; Morga in Cummins (ed.), *op. cit.* (n. 9), 268; and Argensola in BR, XVI, 270–74.

[181] Translated in part in BR, XXIX, 86–101, as the *Relation of the Glorious Victories against the Moros of Mindanao.*

[182] A critical edition of Combés' work was published at Madrid in 1897 by P. Pastells and W. E. Retana (referred to hereafter as Pastells-Retana). Cols. 27–75 and 489–98 were translated into English in BR, XL, 99–182. For further material on Combés see H. Jacobs, S.J., "The *Discurso Politico del Gobierno Maluco* of Fr. Francisco Combés and Its Historical Impact," *Philippine Studies*, XXIX (1981), 309–44.

[183] John Masefield edited *Dampier's Voyages* (2 vols.; London, 1906); his journal entries and recollections of Mindanao appear in I, 318–76.

[184] On Caraga see Crawfurd, *op. cit.* (n. 141), p. 83.

Zamboanga peninsula between Iligan and Dapitan live the "Subanos" (Subanons), who were among the first to become converts in this island.[185] In the interior near Bayug, south of Iligan, are eight thousand bellicose Moros called "Malanaos" (Maranaos) who live around Lake Lanao.[186] Northwest of Pangil Bay on a high hill stands the town of Dapitan whose inhabitants are the descendants of the first people pacified on this island. Of Bisayan background, these docile people live on the northern coast of Zamboanga. Farther south is "Puerta de Santo Maria" (Siocon), and the peninsula terminates with "Punta de la Caldera," so called because it possesses a deep bay which looks like a cauldron from the sea. La Caldera is happily situated at almost equal distances from the Moluccas, Makassar, Borneo, and other important islands. The Spanish maintain a fort here, for it is on the frontier with their Moro enemies in Mindanao and Jolo, and its port is a vital stopover for the ships sailing from Manila to Ternate. Along the south coast, the territory of the Mindanao Moros begins at the Sibuguey River and extends eastward to the Caraga country. The land of the Moros runs northward to Pangil Bay and is dominated by "Cachil Corralat" (Kachil Kudrat, r. 1619–71), to whom all the Moro lords pay tribute. South of Mindanao lies a chain of islands which stretches almost to Borneo. Closest to Zamboanga is Basilan, a large island garden spot almost circular in shape. Between Basilan and Jolo are numerous small islands, some uninhabited. Jolo is peopled by the bellicose Lutaos (Lutaus, or Samals) who came originally from Bohol. Its Muslim ruler holds in vassalage many of the nearby islands.[187]

Mindanao is a well-watered island with twenty copious and navigable rivers; more than three hundred of its streams are large enough to have individual names. It has two large and famous lakes, Lanao and "Mindanao"; indeed, in the common language *danao* means "laguna" (lake).[188] Two of its best-known rivers, the "Buhayen" (Bwayan or Mindanao River) and the "Butuan" (Agusan River), have common sources in mountain lakes. The flat land is fertile, especially the coastal region of Dapitan and the valley of the Sibuguey. Here they grow potatoes, "gabes" (*gabi*, or taro), "apanes" (?), and other produce. Sago palms grow everywhere, from whose starchy pith they make bread flour. Cinnamon grows in twenty-five locations in the valleys of Zamboanga and Dapitan. In Caraga gold is collected from the streams.[189] Sulphur is gathered from volcanic vents, but saltpeter for making

---

[185] On the Subanons see F. M. Lebar (ed.), *Ethnic Groups of Insular Asia* (2 vols.; New Haven, 1975), II, 32–34.

[186] See *ibid.*, pp. 36–39.

[187] Based on Colin in Pastells (ed.), *op. cit.* (n. 84), I, 40–42, and Combés in Pastells-Retana, *op. cit.* (n. 182), col. 104. On the Samals see Lebar (ed.), *op. cit.* (n. 185), pp. 5–6.

[188] Colin in Pastells (ed.), *op. cit.* (n. 84), I, 40; and Combés in Pastells-Retana, *op. cit.* (n. 182), col. 4. Refers here to Lake Maguindanao or Buhayen north of Mount Apo. See Montero y Vidal, *op. cit.* (n. 139), p. 373.

[189] In northeastern Mindanao gold is found in the vicinity of Butuan.

gunpowder is in short supply. Eruptions from nearby volcanoes becloud Zamboanga and turn day into night; rivers of fire run down the mountains and sterilize the soil in the valley for many months after an eruption. Birds peculiar to Mindanao are the green "Errero or Carpintero" (woodpecker) and a black bird of prey the size of a kite called "Colocola." [190] Wild boars roam in its forests. On Basilan, the garden island, enough rice of various varieties is grown to feed the entire Samal-Laut nation as well as an abundance of durians, plantains, and "Lancones" (santols). In Jolo, the Muslim emporium and fishing center, are found many elephants and spotted deer. Its small migratory birds called "Salangan" (*sa-lac-sá-can*) are much esteemed by the Chinese merchants. [191] Special to Jolo is the "fruit of paradise" eaten only by royalty; it is purple in color and the size of an apple. [192] Jolo produces pepper and a medicinal herb called "Punayaman" (?), which acts like opium. The Dutch call Jolo the "Isle of Pearls" because of the pearls found in its seas. [193] Amber is found on the shores of this rich island. Huge tortoises called "Punos" are eaten by the natives, who sell their shells to the Chinese for high prices. [194]

An estimated half-million people live on Mindanao. [195] They are divided into four main "nations": the "Caragas" (Caragas), the "Mindanaos" (Maguindanaos or "people who come from the lake"), the "Lutaos" (Samal-Lauts or "Samals of the sea,"), and "Subanos" (Subanons, or "men of the rivers"). [196] While the smallest in total numbers, the Caragas are renowned for their bravery and warlike activities on land and sea. Before being subdued by Christianity, they were "the scourge of the islands" and raided Leyte regularly. The Muslim Maguindanaos who rule over the several political units of Buhayen are "one in customs and language." Scattered about on the waters of Mindanao, Basilan, and Jolo are the houseboats of the Samal-Lauts. These boat people refuse to farm the land and live exclusively from fishing and trade. In Mindanao they center their activities along the coast from the tip of Zamboanga to the mouth of the Rio Grande (Mindanao River). Although fewest in number, the Samals are highly regarded by the other groups for their skill in building and managing ships of war. Alert and intelligent, they are considered to be "the most capable, the most

[190] Probably Hargitt's pygmy woodpecker and the Philippine white-collared kingfisher. See Hachisuka, *op. cit.* (n. 60), II, 135, 234.

[191] Probably the broad-billed roller known throughout the Philippines. See *ibid.*, p. 122.

[192] In Hinduized cultures the durian was reserved to royalty. See *Plants of the Philippines* (n. 16), p. 122.

[193] On pearl fishing in the Sulu archipelago see R. E. Huke, *Shadows on the Land: An Economic Geography of the Philippines* (Manila, 1963), pp. 391–92.

[194] Combés in Pastells-Retana, *op. cit.* (n. 182), cols. 4–27.

[195] Colin in Pastells (ed.), *op. cit.* (n. 84), I, 43.

[196] The Caragas, if they ever comprised a separate "nation" on Mindanao's east coast, no longer enjoy an individual existence. Caraga was the name applied to the inhabitants of Surigao, a people of Bisayan stock. The name is possibly derived from *kalag* (spirit) plus *an* which may mean "region of brave people." See M. Garcia (ed.), *op. cit.* (n. 81), p. 101, n. 2.

clear-sighted, and the most crafty people of these islands." They are employed as warriors and pirates by the others; indeed, power is measured by the number of Samals a ruler can command. Since many are Christians, the Samals also fight for the Spaniards. Many others fight for Muslim Jolo and are the major source of its military power. The Subanons are a passive people and the least esteemed. They live in isolated settlements along the rivers. Extremely poor and generally hostile towards others, the Subanons for protection build their houses like nests in the high trees. Every one of their villages pays tribute to a Samal chief (*timoly*) who is master "of their entire freedom."[197]

Dapitan, where a Christian population of seven thousand lived in 1656,[198] receives more than its fair share of attention from the missionary authors. Its inhabitants are extolled for being "superior to all those [others] discovered in nobility, valor, fidelity, and Catholicism." Originally from Bohol, these Bisayans were renowned for their military prowess. As rulers of Bohol they were the only group in the islands important enough to receive embassies from Ternate and Borneo. In a war with Ternate the Bisayans were vanquished by firearms which they then saw for the first time. Led by their chief, named Pagbuaya, one thousand families of Bisayan freemen crossed to Mindanao and seized a small rugged hill on its north coast that could be easily defended and from which they could continue to participate in the inter-island trade. Datu Pagbuaya of Dapitan allied himself with the Spaniards and his descendants became Christians. His Christian son and successor, "Manooc" (Manook), aided the Spaniards in the capture of Manila and in the conquest of Camarines in Luzon. The Dapitans also supported the Spaniards in their campaigns in Mindanao and Jolo. "Laria," the cousin of Manook, served with the Spanish in the conquest of the Moluccas. The power of Dapitan thereafter rose and fell with the fortunes of the Spanish. It is now (*ca.* 1665) reduced to being a very small town constantly under attack by the Moros. Still the Dapitans work as guides and guards of the Jesuits as they make their rounds to minister and evangelize the neighboring Subanons. Hispanicized in their customs, the Dapitans, despite their new weakness, continue strong in the faith.[199]

The aboriginals of these islands are called Subanons in the Iligan country and in Zamboanga; "Marrobas" (*man-uba,* or *man-suba,* meaning "river people") and "Mananapes (*man-anap,* or beast), which is equivalent to "brutes," in the rest of Mindanao; "Guinuanos" (Guimbanos) in Jolo; and "Sameacas" (?) in Basilan. Geography and language testify to the fact that

---

[197] Combés in BR, XL, 100–111. The Subanons are shifting cultivators who generally live and work in the mountains. See Lebar (ed.), *op. cit.* (n. 185), pp. 32–34.

[198] See De la Costa, *op. cit.* (n. 4), p. 434.

[199] Combés in BR, XL, 111–22. The Spaniards abandoned the fort and mission of Zamboanga in 1662, but the Jesuits maintained their residence in Dapitan and continued to work for the conversion of the Subanons. See De la Costa, *op. cit.* (n. 4), pp. 451–52.

these aboriginals are of Malay background. The Samal-Lauts, who dominate the aboriginals, are boat people who dress in Moorish fashion, speak in a polished manner, embrace Islam, and intermarry with the Borneans, all of which indicates that they are "new to these islands." Negritos, who resemble the natives of Negros and the upland Aetas of Luzon, pay tribute to nobody in Mindanao. Around the Bay of Pangil they "live more like brute beasts than like men." They walk about naked and arm themselves with arrows dipped in poison. Despite their "wretched mode of life," they retain their freedom, for no outside power has been able to subjugate them. While they may well have been the original inhabitants, nothing of substance is known about their origin.[200] Jolo and Basilan tradition has it that their rulers and nobility originated in Mindanao at the Bisayan village of Butuan, which is in sight of the island of Bohol.[201]

Paganism is at the base of the beliefs and superstitions prevailing in these southern islands. Along the coast of southern Mindanao the law of the Prophet reigns. It also prevails in Basilan and Jolo, the latter being the Mecca of the Sulu archipelago. In Jolo there is the tomb of "their first master about whom Muslim teachers relate many fables."[202] One story claims that he came from paradise with three others. One went to Java, one to Borneo, and the two others to Jolo. From Jolo one went to Mindanao where he was not well received. In Jolo, the other converted the "barbarians" by deceit, telling them that he could get fresh water from the sea, sail on land, and catch fish on the mountains. Among the relics they preserve are the staff and cap of this first teacher; the cap is a hereditary possession of the sultan and on it he swears his solemn oaths. When the Spanish captured Jolo in 1638, they desecrated and destroyed the elegant mausoleum of this first master. Despite all their pretenses, the Moros are not good Muslims. Their religion consists merely in not eating pork, insisting on circumcision, and having several wives. Even though they are forbidden to drink wine, they revel in drunkenness. No matter what they pretend to be religiously they prefer to follow their native customs, laws, and superstitions. Most are atheists who believe in omens, ancestor worship, and sorcery.[203]

Like other Filipinos, the natives of the southern islands are "content with little" and ignorant of the "niceties of art." Even the wealthy prepare their own simple dishes of rice or roots. From fish, venison, or pork they make stews flavored with sharp herbs. Their "puches" (preserves) and "poleadas"

---

[200] These are the Negrito-like people of northeastern Mindanao called the Mamanua. They have a language of their own. See Lebar (ed.), *op. cit.* (n. 185), pp. 29–31.

[201] Combés in BR, XL, 122–30.

[202] A grave of a foreign Muslim dated A.D. 1310 is located in a sacred grove on Bud Dato a few miles from Jolo town. This venerated place is the usual site for the coronations of the sultans of Sulu. See P. G. Gowing, *Muslim Filipinos—Heritage and Horizon* (Quezon City, 1979), p. 18.

[203] Combés in BR, XL, 130–38. On the "little tradition" in Filipino Islam see Gowing, *op. cit.* (n. 202), pp. 64–69.

(a sort of fritter) for great feasts are made from coconut milk and sugar syrup. At the court of Jolo they serve terribly rich small cakes of rice flour and coconut milk baked brown and garnished with durian preserves and syrup. Like their food, their clothing is simple and homemade. All classes dress in everyday clothes made of the same fabric and follow the same fashion. Innovation in dress is frowned upon, so all men wear similar-looking white breeches and skirts (*ropilla*); some occasionally don a jacket that is worn open. For special events they wear breeches of silk trimmed with gold borders or fringes and styled in the Malay fashion. Ashamed to appear in public with the head uncovered, they invariably wear a turban in the Moorish style. Women wear sacks (the *malong*) of local fabrics which they hang around the waist. At night this sack serves as quilt and cover to "protect them from the cold and the mosquitos." On gala occasions the women also wear a shirt (*sayuelo*) with long sleeves and load their arms with gold bracelets; their cloaks are made of "patolas," a very rich kind of silk. Their houses on piles provide shelter but little else. Constructed of bamboo and roofed with thatch, these dwellings are suitable to a country which suffers from frequent earthquakes. They have no benches or chairs, for they feel more secure when seated on the floor. The tables from which they sometimes eat are round and hollowed out in the middle; they put their dishes in the hole to prevent them from spilling. Their jars and bowls are made from lengths of bamboo taken from between the knots of the tree. Coconut shells serve as their cups.[204]

In their daily life the Filipinos brutally and tyrannically enslave one another without regard to family or class relationships: fathers enslave sons, and sons "subject their mothers to whatever they choose." Genuine charity is unknown and all benefits given by one to another are reckoned as debts. Orphans and abandoned persons become slaves to pay for their rearing and sustenance. These practices are even more pernicious in Muslim regions than they are elsewhere. For in Moroland there is no middle class of freemen, but only chiefs and slaves.[205] Justice works in one direction only, in favor of the rich and powerful. Not only offenders are punished, but their relatives as well are enslaved or punished for the crime of one of their number. All penalties, including capital punishment, can be pardoned or mitigated by payments. Husbands and wives own their possessions separately and may even pay fines to each other for offenses committed. Theft is especially abhorrent and, as an example to others, the fingers of a thief are cut off, "more or fewer according to the crime." But even this penalty may be escaped by payments. Unnatural sexual crimes, especially incest, are always

---

[204] Combés in BR, XL, 139–46. *Cf.* Gowing, *op. cit.* (n. 202), pp. 83–86, 90–92.

[205] A freeman in traditional Muslim Filipino society is a person without wealth or prestige who is also not a slave. His only right, it seems, is to attach himself to a leader or to change leaders. See Gowing, *op. cit.* (n. 202), p. 52. Included in this class were artisans, farmers, fishermen, and sailors.

punished by death and complete confiscation of property. Natural disasters, it is believed, are punishments sent from on high to a society that fails to discover and execute those engaged in incest. Judges follow customary law, debate interpretation very little, and proceed quickly. They first act as arbitrators. If this fails they hold a trial by an ordeal of "red-hot coals or hot iron." If the accused is burned, he is punished; if not, the accuser is "obliged to make requital." This type of trial by ordeal seems to have been introduced from Ternate "where it is still observed."[206]

Their "kings" (sultans), although tyrannical, maintain "the form and authority of a court." The chief judge and minister of the court is the "Zarabandal" (*shahbandar,* or "king of the port") who "decides the causes and suits, and advises concerning the sentences."[207] In the villages the law resides in the hands of the local chieftains (*datus*), from whose authority there is no recourse. In disputes the sultan always supports the *datus,* since he needs their favor to retain power. The sultan's sovereignty depends on the *datus'* recognition of his "nobility" and his power extends only so far as they are willing to see it go. The established social classes are "Tuam" (*tuan*) or masters, "Orancaya" (*orang kayas*) or rich men, and chiefs of whom those of the blood royal are called "cachiles" (*kachils*).[208] The "rich men" or *datus* are rulers over the villages they control. When they themselves are forced to send tribute to the sultan, they unmercifully extort it from their subjects. They treat the Subanons and their chiefs as if they were slaves. Samal-Laut *datus,* even though subject to Spain, are "still paid hereditary respect along all the coast of Siocon." Indeed the Subanons obey these chieftains more quickly and submissively than they do the Spaniards. In poor recompense for their obedience, the Samal-Lauts sell these hapless people into slavery at Makassar until they almost face extinction in their homeland. By giving special powers and concessions to the *datus,* Kachil "Corralat" (Kudrat) has managed to control Maguindanao and to transmute his system of government into what amounts to holy Islamic law.[209]

The Subanons, whom the Spanish saved from extinction, are being lured out of their mountains and are adopting the dress and customs of their more civilized neighbors. Traditionally "enemies of the human race" they adulate murder. To win the right to wear the red turban of the valiant they will kill their best friend. In Caraga they must kill at least seven men to wear the

---

[206] Combés in BR, XL, 146–54. This brief description clearly shows social control in Moroland to be a combination of customary (*adat*) and Islamic law (*shari'a*). Cf. Gowing, *op. cit.* (n. 202), pp. 95–100.
[207] In many of the maritime Malay states the *shahbandar* was an important state official. See Yule and Burnell, *op. cit.* (n. 172), p. 816.
[208] The *tuan* were freemen who tilled their lands and went on trading or raiding expeditions during the monsoon with their *datus. Orang kaya* is a collective name for *datus* of various grades. See De la Costa, *op. cit.* (n. 4), p. 299. In Jolo the *kachils* are called "Paguian."
[209] Combés in BR, XL, 154–58.

cherished striped turban and special breeches of the valiant.[210] Their women are chaste and seek to keep their virginity "even to advanced age." Because of the protection accorded women, the Samal-Lauts sometimes have their daughters reared by the Subanons. Most unusual is the class of Subanon men who practice celibacy and dress like women. They spend all their time with women and are called "labia" (possibly related to Tagalog, *labáng*, to cross over). They are respected as exemplars of virtue and holy men.[211] While esteeming those who lead a blameless life, Subanon husbands exchange wives with one another and celebrate "the hideous loan and vile restitution" by drunken feasts.[212]

Death and marriage ceremonies contrast sharply to the simplicity of everyday life. Their one-piece coffins of "incorruptible woods" are prepared for each during his lifetime and put on display under the house. At death the corpse is generously clothed in the finest and richest garments available. Along with the corpse they bury gold and other personal treasures in caves, on islets, or on solitary mountains. These graves and their treasures are left untouched and "without other guard than their imaginary religion!" At royal or princely funerals a tent is raised above the grave "with four white banners at its sides"; inside, incense is burned throughout the mourning period. The Subanons like the Samal-Lauts display their grief by throwing their treasures into the sea; on one island they kill the first person they meet to help assuage their personal sorrow.[213]

Marriages, especially of chiefs, are formal, gala affairs in the southern islands. For a week before and a week after the wedding day, a lavish open house is held at which "wine" flows freely and the dances become steadily more animated. On the wedding day the bride breaks her "strict confinement" to be married publicly. Accompanied by her relatives and clansmen in gala costume and armed with lance and shield, the bride leaves her home to meet the groom. She is preceded by musicians, ladies of honor, and young female attendants. At the end of the procession the bride is borne in a spacious chair carried on the shoulders of four slaves. The groom's procession is, if anything, even more grandiose. Both dress in white until after meeting, when the bride coquettishly gives her consent that he don a red costume. Virginity and modesty are displayed by binding the bride into her clothes. In the canopied house the richly adorned bridal chamber is open to public view. In the Moorish style the bride and groom sit on cushions while

---

[210] Modern Subanons consider as undesirable any violent behavior. See Lebar (ed.), *op. cit.* (n. 185), p. 34.

[211] On hermaphroditism see John M. Garvan, *The Manóbos of Mindanao* ("Memoirs of the National Academy of Sciences," Vol. XXIII; Washington, D.C., 1941), p. 117.

[212] Combés in BR, XL, 158–64.

[213] *Ibid.*, pp. 165–67; *cf.* above, p. 1506, and C. O. Frake, "The Eastern Subanun of Mindanao," in G. F. Murdock (ed.), *Social Structure in Southeast Asia* (Chicago, 1960), pp. 51–64.

she "displays no more animation than a statue." Both conduct themselves so modestly that three days pass before they "avail themselves of the license of their estate."[214]

Boats and arms, like clothes, are manufactured by the southern natives from local products. The warcraft of the Samal-Lauts are light and built for speed. These ships "sail like birds, while ours are like lead in this regard." Constructed of thin planking, boats are tied together with rattan. Upon this light hull they build bamboo scaffolding "as high as they wish." To both sides of the hull from bow to stern they attach "cates" (Bisayan, *kátay*), or outriggers, which enable the vessel to carry "more outside than in." The outside scaffolding provides place for two additional sets of rowers, besides the oarsmen in the hull. The crews of these shallow craft number from sixty to three hundred men. Their round-bladed oars are not in oarlocks but are plunged directly into the water by oarsmen who paddle in cadence "exactly to the time of their breathing." Because the hulls are crescent-shaped and narrow they have but a small keel. Two rudders are used to manage the boat, one on either side of the flat part of the keel. In the middle is a scaffold floor above the rowers that is covered by a palm awning. Weather never endangers these light vessels, for they can quickly find shelter in one of the many islands. Outriggers of this sort used so generally in the eastern islands inspired a Spaniard to propose that buoys should be fastened to the Spanish ships to prevent them from sinking "even if they filled with water."[215]

The Samal-Lauts prize their excellent and precious weapons. From an early age their arms are their constant companions. Townsmen in peacetime wear a wavy dagger called a kris, which has a hilt in the shape of a small idol, ivory for the commoner and bejeweled gold for the chiefs. At war they fight on land with lance, kris, and shield. A round shield is used in Moroland, while a long, narrow shield is common to the rest of Mindanao and the other islands. The shaft of the lance is of ebony or other fine wood and its head is brass. At the end of the lance they fasten a large bell that they shake in time to their war cries to frighten the timid among the enemy. In land and sea engagements they throw small bamboo darts at close range with great speed and deadly accuracy. These are particularly effective when showered on a ship or a besieged fortress. In the same way, they employ stakes hardened in fire and blowpipes which shoot poisoned darts. The people of Jolo called "Ximbanaos" (Guimbajanos) protect themselves from head to toe with armor lined with elephant hide that turns away all weapons except bullets. They prepare for battle by taking opium to render them-

---

[214]Combés in BR, XL, 167–71. The author was himself present at such a wedding. Muslims still regard chastity and modesty as desirable virtues in the bride. See Gowing, *op. cit.* (n. 202), pp. 73–74.

[215]Combés in BR, XL, 171–74. The Spanish proposal envisioned bags attached to the vessel that could be blown up and thrown alongside if need arose. Evidently this idea was not tried out in the Philippines because of the severity of the storms.

selves insensible to danger. The warriors of Mindanao use a heavy cutlass with one edge, which they carry on their shoulders. All the natives have begun to use firearms and artillery acquired from Spain's enemies.[216]

After the Spanish retreat in 1662, little new was thereafter published about the southern islands. Captain William Dampier (1652–1715), England's famous buccaneer-author, first published in 1697 his *New Voyage Round the World* (London), which includes his journal and recollections about his half-year's stay in Mindanao during 1686–87.[217] Sultan Kudrat, the greatest of independent Maguindanao's rulers, had died in 1671 leaving his people in a state of relative calm and peace. Both Maguindanao and Sulu were hereafter completely outside of Spain's sphere of influence and free to develop closer ties with their Muslim neighbors of Borneo and the Malay Peninsula. The Jesuits at Dapitan and the Recollects in the Agusan valley continued to pursue their peaceful evangelical labors despite occasional Moro raids. Once the Spanish soldiers had vanished from the scene, the Dutch were content to seek peace, friendship, and trade with Moroland and to leave its peoples otherwise to their own devices. Englishmen like Dampier likewise had only piracy, exploration, and trade in mind when visiting the southern Philippines.

Dampier, a close student of nature, reports that the soil of Mindanao is fertile and well watered. While its hills are stony, they produce large trees "of kinds unknown to us." He describes at length, and quite accurately, the characteristics and uses of the sago palm, various types of plantains, the areca palm or the "Betel tree," and the durian and the closely related "Jack Fruit" trees. Wild boars, deer, monkeys, lizards, and snakes are plentiful "where they are not disturbed." While beasts of prey are not to be found, life is made miserable by stinging scorpions, centipides, poisonous snakes, and iguanas. Wild birds are abundant, but the only domesticated fowl are ducks and hens. Rice is cultivated in the valleys and root crops and pumpkins in the mountains. Seas and rivers abound in fish of many kinds as well as sea turtles and small manatees. Although Mindanao lies close to the equator, the heat is ordinarily bearable in coastal places. The "fiercest of this Weather" comes at the end of July and in August for "then the Towns seem to stand in a great Pond, and they go from one House to another in Canoes."[218]

While Mindanao is politically, socially, and linguistically divided, its peoples are physically alike and devoted generally to Islam and its practices and customs. The Maguindanaos are the most numerous and the most cosmopolitan of its peoples. The other three groups are the "Hilanoones" (Hiloona or Maranao), "Solugues" (Suluks or Sulus), and "Alfoores"

---

[216] *Ibid.,* pp. 174–82.
[217] Reprinted in Masefield (ed.), *op. cit.* (n. 183). Materials on Mindanao in Vol. I, pp. 319–76.
[218] *Ibid.,* pp. 319–31.

(mountain people). The Hiloona live in the heart of the island and exchange gold and beeswax for other commodities. The Sulus (probably Christians) of its northwestern part trade with Manila and other islands but not with the Maguindanaos. The "Alfoores," a Muslim people with a sultan of their own, were once, and still are claimed as, subjects of the sultan of Maguindanao. The Maguindanaos, a people of small stature with oval faces and black, straight hair, let their thumbnails grow long, especially the one on the left hand. While ingenious and quick, they are generally lazy, thievish, and "will not work except by Hunger." While laziness is "natural to most Indians," these people are content to live from hand to mouth, for their ruler arbitrarily confiscates whatever little surplus they accumulate. Proud in their bearing, these people are civil to strangers and implacably revengeful to those who affront or injure them. Ordinary persons wear clothes made of plaintain fiber while the others have cotton garments. Women are allowed to talk with strangers but only in the presence of their husbands. Newcomers are entertained while on shore but only if they bestow gifts upon their hosts and hostesses. Dampier calls this the "begging Custom" and claims that it is unique to Mindanao.[219]

Mindanao is the name of both the island and its chief city. Its urban houses are built on high pilings with but one floor that is divided by partitions into many rooms. Most are built near the river, in which they dispose of "all the filth." The sultan's house is bigger and higher than the common sort. It stands on about 180 great posts and is entered by broad stairs rather than by a simple ladder. In the first room of the royal palace stand about twenty iron guns on field carriages. About twenty paces from this palace is a smaller and lower building where the sultan receives foreign emissaries and merchants. Its floor is neatly matted because he and his council sit tailor style on the floor when receiving visitors. In the city they commonly speak both their own language and Malay; some of the older people are still able to speak Spanish. While the Spaniards are now excluded, the people fear the Dutch and would welcome an English factory and fortress as a countervailing force.

Only a few crafts are practiced by the artisans of Mindanao city. Two or three goldsmiths will make whatever is ordered but they have no shops in which to display or sell their wares. Blacksmiths, using only a bellows made of a tree trunk and a hard stone or old gun to hammer on, contrive somehow to make excellent utensils, as well as fittings for ships. Every man is his own carpenter and works only with "Ax and Adds [adze]" to cut and plane trees into boards. They build serviceable trading and pleasure craft as well as war vessels. Their trading ships carry beeswax and gold to Manila where they are exchanged for "Calicoes, Muslins, and China Silk." Dutch sloops

---

[219] *Ibid.*, pp. 332–35.

from Ternate and Tidore buy rice, beeswax, and tobacco in Mindanao city. Although tobacco seeds were probably first brought from Manila, the Mindanao leaf is larger and darker than the bright yellow leaf of Luzon. Many people in both Guam and Mindanao suffer from a skin disease that causes itching and flaking skin; sometimes large white spots remain on the body after the disease is cured.[220]

The sultan is a little man between fifty and sixty years of age who is reputedly very good-natured and dominated by those around him. He has a queen and twenty-nine other wives or women, with whom he spends most of his time. His queen has borne him a daughter and he has both sons and daughters by the others. The young princess of fourteen is confined to the house and the only men she sees are her father and uncle; the other children wander in the streets and are "always begging for things" of the Europeans. When visiting his friends the sultan is carried on a litter. His major excursions are on the water in a special pleasure boat that will carry fifty to sixty persons. Its bamboo cabin is divided into three chambers: one for himself, the second for his wives, and the third for his servants.[221] The sultan's brother "Raja Laut" (Datu Ladja Laut, or minister of naval affairs) is "the second Man in the Kingdom" and is in charge of all maritime matters. He is a sharp man who has learned a good deal about other places from his conversations with foreign merchants. He speaks Spanish and by reading Spanish books he has "some knowledge of Europe." A brave warrior, the "Raja Laut" is a local hero whom the women celebrate in their dances and songs. He apparently made his reputation in the periodic wars waged by Maguindanao against the neighboring "Alfoores" or mountaineers.[222]

Friday is the Sabbath in Islamic Mindanao, but few observe it. The sultan prays at the mosque twice on Friday but "Raja Laut" never goes there. He is, however, very devout and prays regularly at the appointed hours. In the sultan's mosque there is a great drum called "a Gong" (*agong*) which is struck every three hours day and night to mark the time. Males are circumcised at eleven or twelve years of age. A ceremony of great solemnity is held when the son of an important person is ready for this rite. Other sons of lesser men are circumcised along with the one to whom the ceremony is dedicated. The operation is performed by a "Mahometan Priest." Older men carry arms for the occasion and then put on individual mock combats with an imaginary enemy. A torchlight parade follows, led by two dancing women, which winds up at the house of the important person whose son has been circumcised. After more music and dancing, fireworks are set off

[220] *Ibid.*, pp. 335–41. Small amounts of tobacco are still grown in Mindanao but most Filipino tobacco is now produced in Luzon. The skin disease is probably yaws, an affliction endemic to many tropical regions.
[221] On boat construction *cf.* above, pp. 1497–98.
[222] Dampier in Masefield (ed.), *op. cit.* (n. 183), I, 341–44.

to conclude the celebration. While most are ordinarily not strict about performing their religious obligations, "Ramdam" (Ramadan) is a time when everybody fasts and prays each day for one full month. Major features of their religion are frequent washings and avoidance of pollution by not eating pork or consorting with those who have done so. Since pigs are killed only by unbelievers, the wild boars common to the mountains are so numerous that they invade the towns in troops.[223]

4

GUAM AND THE MARIANAS (LADRONES)

From Magellan's time onward the Spanish galleons on their way across the Pacific had stopped over in the archipelago of the "Ladrones" (thieves), as these islands were named by the great explorer. In the sixteenth century several independent accounts had been published in Europe about these tropical islands and their people. They were all essentially in agreement with the first one, written by Antonio Pigafetta, the companion of Magellan.[224] In 1565 Miguel Lopes de Legaspi formally claimed the Ladrones for Spain, but the Spanish did not try to establish their system of control in the islands until 1668. In the intervening century, shipwrecked sailors and deserters of various nationalities sought refuge in the islands. The English under Drake and Cavendish preyed on the galleon trade and in 1588 the latter passed by Guam, the southernmost island in the chain. Dutch fleets penetrated the Pacific on their way to the Moluccas and refreshed themselves at Guam in 1600, 1616, and 1623. For the Spanish galleons bound from Acapulco to Manila, Guam remained during the seventeenth century a regular stopping place; on the return voyage the galleons followed routes which took them either to the northern islands or to the south of Guam.[225]

After the retreat of the Spanish from the Moluccas and the southern Philippines in 1662, certain Jesuits in the Philippines began to seek new opportunities in the Ladrones. Diego Luís de Sanvítores (1627–72), a Jesuit missionary who had stopped over at Guam on his way to Manila in 1662, was the driving force behind the movement for a mission to the Ladrones. The Spanish secular authorities had shown no interest in over a century in colonizing these isolated and unproductive islands, since much greater opportunities seemed to be closer at hand in the Philippines and in eastern and

[223] *Ibid.*, 344–50.
[224] For summaries of the reports of Pigafetta, Oviedo, and Mendoza see *Asia*, I, 627–28, 640, 644.
[225] See P. Carano and P. C. Sanchez, *A Complete History of Guam* (Rutland, Vt., and Tokyo, 1964), pp. 42–50.

southeastern Asia. Sanvítores, like many other contemporary zealots, longed to work where there were new worlds to conquer for Christ. No longer able to win martyrdom in Japan or China, Sanvítores labored in Mindoro and other isolated Tagalog regions to instill greater fervor and enthusiasm into the hearts of the Filipino converts and their priests. While engaged in this inspirational work, he never forgot the terrible plight of the inhabitants of the Ladrones, who had no knowledge of the true faith and no chance for life eternal. But his proposals to found a mission in the Ladrones aroused no interest in Manila. His Jesuit superiors claimed they lacked the manpower to undertake a new and distant mission. The civil authorities likewise pleaded a shortage of men and averred that they had no spare money to establish and maintain a garrison for the protection of a permanent mission.[226]

Not easily discouraged, the zealous Sanvítores appealed to Madrid and Rome for help in realizing his project. His communications were relayed to King Philip IV and Mariana of Austria (1632–96), through her Jesuit confessor, Everard Nithard, a German much distrusted by some of his colleagues because of his great influence at court.[227] On June 24, 1667, the king issued a *cedula real* approving a mission to the islands. Three months later the king died and Mariana became queen-regent. In gratitude and in anticipation of future favors Sanvítores then urged that the name of the islands should be changed from the defamatory Ladrones to the adulatory Marianas. Despite foot-dragging in Manila, Sanvítores was named superior of the Marianas mission in 1667 and it was put under the spiritual jurisdiction of the bishop of Cebu. The persistent priest then sailed for Acapulco to collect the royal endowment and to raise other monies as well as men for the new mission. Accompanied by four other Jesuit priests, a lay brother, thirty lay catechists, and a garrison force of a captain and thirty-two soldiers (mostly Filipino volunteers), Sanvítores arrived in Guam on June 15, 1668.[228]

The Europeans and their Filipino cohorts were at first welcomed by the islanders. Some of the Spanish knew about the islanders from previous stopovers; others with experience in the Philippines recognized similarities between the local language and practices and those of the Tagalogs. All the newcomers treated the natives kindly and were granted friendship in return. During the mission's first year Sanvítores claimed that thirteen thousand islanders were baptized and that twenty thousand had received religious instruction. Soon controversies arose, however, between the missionaries and their converts over social issues and forced baptisms and conversions. Nonetheless, a church and a school were built in 1669 at Agana, the Chris-

---

[226] See De la Costa, *op. cit.* (n. 4), pp. 455–57, 470–73.
[227] Notice how the Austrian Jesuits later appear as missionaries in the Marianas. *Ibid.,* p. 457.
[228] See Carano and Sanchez, *op. cit.* (n. 225), pp. 62–64; and Ward Barrett (trans. and ed.), *Mission in the Marianas: An Account of Father Diego Luis de Sanvitores and His Companions* (Minneapolis, 1975), pp. 4–5.

tian center on Guam. As the Christians expanded their activities into the northern islands, the discontent of the islanders broke into open rebellion in 1670. Christians were killed, including Father Luis de Medina, the mission's first martyr. Despite the arrival of priestly reinforcements from New Spain and the endeavors of Sanvítores to restore peace, hostility continued to grow between the frightened Spanish soldiers and the indignant Chamorros. The martyrdom of Sanvítores himself on April 2, 1672, ignited a long series of Spanish-Chamorro wars which were fought intermittently until the final surrender of the natives in 1695.[229]

In Catholic Europe these events in the distant Marianas could be readily followed in the contemporary publications of the Jesuits. Reports were quickly issued in pamphlet form on the first two years of the mission's history. They were compiled by Andrés de Ledsma, Jesuit procurator for the Philippines, from the letters of Sanvítores and his companions and printed at Madrid, probably in 1670 or 1671. Full and summary versions were published each year. Like many Jesuit letterbooks, the more detailed accounts were intended for the enlightenment of the Jesuits in Europe who were potential recruits for the mission. The shorter versions were issued in larger numbers for popular consumption.[230] To appeal to their readers, the Jesuit letters and the books compiled from them include mundane as well as missionary materials. In Spain these reports on the Marianas evidently caught the interest of Maria Guadalupe de Lencastre (1630–1715), duchess of Aveiro, who was known to contemporaries as "Mother of the Missions."[231] She became a private benefactress and a correspondent of the Jesuits in the Marianas.[232]

In the seventeenth century "the blood of the martyrs" was seed for the production of martyrologies. The purpose of a martyrology is to celebrate the martyr, to inspire others to follow his example, and, in some cases, to prepare the way for the martyr's canonization as a saint. The life and sacrifice of Luis de Medina was celebrated as early as 1673 in memorials published in Seville and Madrid. The story of Sanvítores' achievements and death began to appear in both Mexico and Europe during the following year.[233] In 1683 a comprehensive biography of Sanvítores was published at

---

[229] See Carano and Sanchez, *op. cit.* (n. 225), pp. 73–87. These authors point out that the Spanish pacification of the Marianas resulted in the practical annihilation of the ancient Chamorros and their religion.

[230] The shorter version of a letterbook (probably published in 1671) relating news from May 15, 1669, to April 28, 1670, is in the James Ford Bell Library of the University of Minnesota. It is translated into English in Barrett (trans. and ed.), *op. cit.* (n. 228).

[231] On her career and contributions see E. J. Burrus, S.J., *Father Kino Writes to the Duchess* (Rome, 1965), pp. v–vi, and C. R. Boxer, "The Mother of the Missions," *History Today,* XXIII (1973), 733–39.

[232] For a listing of some of the letters sent to her from the Marianas see Streit, XXI, 44, 45, 46, 48, 49, 50, 51, 52, 53, 55, 62. Also see C. R. Boxer, "Two Jesuit Letters on the Marianas Mission, Written to the Duchess of Aveiro (1676 and 1689)," *Philippine Studies,* XXVI (1978), 35–50.

[233] Boxer, *loc. cit.* (n. 232), pp. 41–43.

Madrid by Francisco Garcia; it was translated into Italian and amplified to cover the mission's history to 1684 by Ambrosio Ortiz (1638–1718) in his *Istoria della conversione alla santa fede dell'isole Mariane* (Naples, 1686).[234] Before the end of the century, materials on the Marianas began to appear in northern Europe. Captain William Dampier in Chapter X of his *New Voyage around the World* (1697) recounts his experiences at Guam where he made a stopover on his way to Mindanao in 1686. In 1700 the French Jesuit Charles Le Gobien (1653–1708) published his *Histoire des isles Marianes, nouvellement converties à la religion chrestienne*, a book which includes the entire story of the pacification to 1695.[235] Gemelli Careri, the Italian circumnavigator, on his difficult voyage eastward from the Philippines to America anchored at Guam in 1696. He devotes a few pages to a description of conditions in the Marianas in his volume on the Philippines.[236]

A crescent-shaped archipelago of "thirteen islands" (actually fifteen), the Marianas lie at the center of that chain of "innumerable islands" which stretches between Japan and "the Austral land, formerly unknown."[237] Generally the Marianas are close enough to one another to permit regular interinsular trade. Indeed their inhabitants, unlike those of the Philippines, all speak one language. The largest and southernmost island of Guam has seven harbors; the one on the west side before the village of "Hati" (Piti?) has two rivers that make it a good watering spot.[238] To the south is the port of "Humatag" (Umatag), where the Dutch in the past would beach and careen their ships and take on water. The other harbors around the island provide shelter, though a few are without good water. On the island of "Zarpana" which the natives call "Roba" (Rota) there is a harbor which faces northwest in front of the village of "Socanrogo" (?) and another a short distance to the

---

[234] Garcia's work was partially translated into English by Margaret Higgins in the *Guam Recorder*, September 1936 to July 1939. It is heavily used for the history and the description of the aboriginal inhabitants contained in W. E. Safford, *The Useful Plants of the Island of Guam with an Introductory Account of the Physical Features and Natural History of the Island, of the Character and History of Its People, and of Their Agriculture*, Vol. IX of *Contributions from the United States National Herbarium* (Washington, D.C., 1905). Ortiz' book includes several proposals for the beatification of Sanvítores. For its contents see Streit, XXI, 56. It was reissued in part at Brescia in 1695.

[235] It has been translated in part in an English summary included in James Burney, *A Chronological History of the Voyages and Discoveries in the South Sea or Pacific Ocean* (London, 1813; reprinted at Amsterdam in 1967 in 4 vols.), III, 271–315.

[236] Reprinted edition of Garcia (ed.), *op. cit.* (n. 81), pp. 137–45. Eastward voyages via Guam were unusual. When sailing from Manila to Acapulco the galleons were often forced by contrary winds to track north or south of Guam.

[237] Probably refers to the Bonins north of the Marianas and the Carolines to the south. Islands of this chain do not impinge directly on the Australia discovered by the Dutch in 1606. The voyagers in the south Pacific held to a wide variety of hypotheses about the insular world. The Spanish evidently hoped to use the Marianas as a base from which to explore and Christianize the island chains fringing the austral continent. See C. Jack-Hinton, *The Search for the Islands of Solomon, 1567–1838* (Oxford, 1969), pp. 172–75. Also see above, pp. 220–22.

[238] Piti was a landing place for Apra harbor near Agana. See Carano and Sanchez, *op. cit.* (n. 225), p. 204.

south.[239] On Saipan there is a good harbor "whose mouth faces east" with an anchorage before the village of "Raurau" that is protected from the winds by a headland.[240] Good harbors also exist on the islands further north which are able to "provide berth for the galleons when they come from Manila."[241] Like the island merchants, the Jesuits are able to move from anchorage to anchorage in their progress from Guam northward.[242]

The oral tradition holds that the islands were populated by the same people from the south who were the ancestors of the Tagalogs. This belief receives support from the similarities which exist in language, government, and the painting of teeth.[243] Some Europeans speculate that the islanders derive from Egypt and others, such as Father Colin, see Japan as their original home. Japan is thought of as a possible place of origin because of its proximity to the northern Marianas. The Marianas enjoy a healthful and temperate climate and are untroubled by the earthquakes and extremes of temperature common to other nearby archipelagoes.[244] Fresh water is plentiful, especially in Guam with its more than thirty rivers. Some rivers produce a copious flow of water and are well stocked with fish, especially eels.[245] No snakes or other poisonous animals are native to these islands. Coconut groves are numerous and many other kinds of trees grow on the islands, "especially *palo maria* [*Calophyllium inophyllum*] of which they make their boats."[246] They live in villages of ten to more than one hundred houses. Many of the houses are covered with thatch and stand on stone pillars. Their sleeping houses or

[239] Anchorages on Rota are found in Sosenjaya Bay and Sosenlagh Bay on the southwest end of the island. Rota is thirty-two miles northeast of Guam. In the early literature it is often called "Zarpan," a variant possibly of Saipan. The "Great Zarpan" commonly refers to Saipan. See U.S. Department of the Navy, *Civil Affairs Handbook, Mandated Marianas Islands* (Washington, D.C., 1944), pp. 10–11.

[240] Tanapag harbor is the only anchorage on Saipan which provides even partial protection from all winds. The bay is formed by a large reef. *Ibid.*, p. 12. Saipan is 121 miles north of Guam.

[241] On the old, or northern, route from Manila to Acapulco the ships would sometimes stop over at the northern island of Agrigan.

[242] Based on the Jesuit letterbook of 1671 translated in Barrett (ed. and trans.), *op. cit.* (n. 228), pp. 14–18.

[243] The ancient Chamorros, like the Tagalogs, probably were from Indonesia. The Chamorros differ in a number of respects from the other peoples of Micronesia. Recent students of this subject believe that migrants entered Micronesia from "at least two directions, first from the Philippines and Indonesia, and later from eastern Melanesia." The Chamorros probably entered the Marianas from the west. See W. H. Alkire, *An Introduction to the Peoples and Cultures of Micronesia* (*s.l.*, 1973), pp. 18–19. The Chamorro language, now spoken by about fifty thousand persons, belongs to the Austronesian or Malayo-Polynesian family of languages. Its grammatical features and vocabulary suggest that it is most closely related to one or other of the Filipino languages. See D. M. Topping, P. M. Ogo, and B. C. Gungca, *Chamorro-English Dictionary* (Honolulu, 1975), p. ix.

[244] On September 22, 1902, four years after it became an American possession, Guam suffered a severe earthquake.

[245] Eels were taboo to all but the lowest class.

[246] A characteristic beach forest tree known in Spanish and Tagalog as *palo maria de playa*. It grows in the Philippines and in many other Pacific islands on the fringes of the shore.

dormitories are most carefully built and divided into rooms by hanging mats.[247]

Fish is the common food and is supplemented most of the time with delicious breadfruit. When breadfruit is out of season, they eat roots similar to the yams of the Philippines. Ordinarily moderate in their eating and drinking habits, at their feasts they serve the local rice, "of which there is a goodly abundance."[248] At their celebrations they recount "their histories," wrestle, and compete in throwing spears. While the storytelling and games go on, they pass around refreshments of rice cakes, tamales, fish, coconuts, plantains, sugarcane, and a drink made of rice and grated coconut. Women hold special feasts for which they adorn themselves with ornaments and trinkets made of flowers, tortoiseshell, and red shells which they prize as much as Europeans esteem pearls. They gird themselves for these special feasts with string skirts made of tree roots from which they hang small coconuts, a form of adornment "which seems more birdcage than dress." At their entertainments twelve or thirteen of the women form a circle and sing in verse their traditional stories. The sopranos, contraltos, and falsettos are joined in this recital by a tenor, one of the "principal men who attend these entertainments." While singing they move their hands rhythmically and clap shells together like castanets. For ordinary adornments the women blacken their teeth and wear their hair long and bleach it white. Men shave the entire head except for a tuft on the top.[249]

Their way of life is better than their lack of clothes, government, and culture would suggest. Labor is confined to fishing, constructing boats, and cultivating gardens. Generally they are peace-loving and, despite the absence of law and police, correct in their behavior. There is no ruling authority who is generally recognized. Each family or clan has its own headman; he owns the best land and house and is highly respected by the other family members.[250] His position is not inherited by a son, but "as in India," by a brother or nephew.[251] On taking over authority the new headman changes his name to that of the family's principal ancestor. Their con-

---

[247] Based on Barrett (trans. and ed.), *op. cit.* (n. 228), pp. 18–19. The "stone pillars" are called *latte*, some remains of which still exist in the islands. They are used by modern archaeologists to locate the ancient living sites. See L. Thompson, "The Function of *Latte* in the Marianas," *Journal of the Polynesian Society*, XLIX (1940), 447–65. For more recent data on the *latte* see P. Bellwood, *Man's Conquest of the Pacific* (New York, 1979), pp. 283–85.

[248] On rice (*fai*) cultivation cf. L. Thompson, *The Native Culture of the Mariana Islands*, Bernice P. Bishop Museum Publication No. 185 (Honolulu, 1945), p. 29. Rice was traded for iron. As far as it is now known, rice was not grown elsewhere in Micronesia. See Bellwood, *op. cit.* (n. 247), p. 282.

[249] Barrett (trans. and ed.), *op. cit.* (n. 228), pp. 20–21. Teeth were probably blackened with lime as was done in other parts of Oceania.

[250] The leader (*maga*) ruled over a district which usually included several neighboring villages. See Thompson, *op. cit.* (n. 248), pp. 12–13.

[251] Property and title in the matrilineal system often passed in the Pacific islands to the son of a sister. *Cf.* Safford, *op. cit.* (n. 234), p. 106. Descent through the female line was the rule in

cern over lineages and social distinctions suggests "their descent from some very civilized nation." Youths of the highest class, called "Chamorris," may not marry the daughter of a plebian, and risk being killed by their own family if they do. "Chamorris" will not eat or drink with those of low status and will not permit them to come near to noble houses. In their relations with their own kind the "Chamorris" display great courtesy, say "ati arimo" (*ati adengmo,* meaning "permit me to kiss your feet") on meeting, and offer betel to all those who pass by their houses. They hate murder and other acts of cruelty and isolate those who brutalize others or are too prone to resort to arms.

From an early age they use sling and stone with great dexterity. Spears with fishhook-like barbs are made from "the bones of their fathers"; such spears enter an enemy easily but are hard to withdraw.[252] Bachelors (*urritaos*) reside in public dormitories free of parental control where they live with unmarried women.[253] Married men rarely consort with other women or maintain mistresses. Wives are extremely jealous and a wife is quick to punish her husband for any form of disloyalty. Supported by the other women of the village, she roots out her errant spouse's garden, threatens to spear him, and finally throws him out of the house. Sometimes a wife deserts her husband and then returns with her relatives to ransack and destroy his dwelling. As a consequence, the woman rules the house and the children, while the husband lives according to "her pleasure and approval." Should she learn that he has punished the children, she will leave his house with the children and find another husband and father.[254]

Before the advent of the Europeans, the Chamorros believed "they were the only men in the world." Also, according to their traditions, "all lands and men and all things had their origins . . . from a part of the island of Guam."[255] There the first man appeared, who was made into a stone which "gave birth to all men." Those men who scattered "to Spain, and other parts," forgot their own language and, no longer understanding one another, now "speak like lunatics." The first man, named "Puntan," lived for aeons in "some imaginary place" before the creation of heaven and earth. This good man, when about to die, conferred all his powers upon his sister in order to give land and sustenance to mankind. Following his instructions she made heaven and earth from his chest and back, sun and moon from his

---

Guam until the Americans abolished it. On the matrilineal system of Malabar see above, p. 884. While little additional direct information on social organization is available, the fragmentary data clearly suggest that Chamorro society was organized into matrilineal clans. See Thompson, *op. cit.* (n. 248), p. 11.

[252] On their arms and warfare see Safford, *op. cit.* (n. 234), pp. 106–7.

[253] The bachelors carried carved walking sticks (*tunas*) at the head of which were affixed three streamers of bark. See Thompson, *op. cit.* (n. 248), p. 12.

[254] Barrett (trans. and ed.), *op. cit.* (n. 228), pp. 19–23. On the matriarchical character of the old Chamorro society see L. Thompson, *Guam and Its People* (New York, 1941), pp. 39–40.

[255] At Fuuna on the coast of southwest Guam.

eyes, the rainbow from his eyebrows, and "likewise formed" the rest so as to maintain the correlation of "the lesser world to the greater." These creation stories and other "antique fables" are related in couplet and song in the storytelling contests held at their festivals.[256] Neither Puntan nor his sister is publicly worshipped or appealed to as a divinity. Nor do they have priests or other religious leaders. There are "some tricksters called 'Macanas' [*makahnas* or professional sorcerers]" who ask the skulls of the dead which the Marianos keep in their houses to provide them with whatever is needed. The *makahnas* and all others recognize that nothing good can seriously be expected from the dead in hell, so their prayers are designed to propitiate the devil to keep the dead from doing harm. Since the Chamorros lack an organized religion and priesthood, the task of converting them to Christianity is easier.[257]

Nonetheless the Chamorros hold tightly to their own superstitions, beliefs, and customs. They claim (correctly) that the Europeans introduced illnesses, as well as rats, flies, and mosquitoes, to their islands. As a consequence they stay on shore "while the ships are in the bay." When fishing they keep completely silent and fast for long periods to propitiate the *anitos*, or the spirits of those ancestors who might frighten away the fish or scare them by appearing in their dreams. At death it is customary to place a basket near the corpse's head as an invitation to remain at home or to provide the soul with a resting place when it returns as a visitor. Those who die from natural causes are buried underground.[258] Mourners customarily anoint the corpse with fragrant oils and carry it to the houses of their relatives, possibly so that the soul can decide where it wants to stay or return to on visits. At burials they put on demonstrations of intense grief "with many tears, fasts, and noises of conches." The mourning period of six to eight or more days is spent around a catafalque set upon or beside the grave and adorned with flowers, palms, and seashells. They sing melancholy songs and the mother of the deceased cuts off a lock of hair as a memento and wears a cord around her neck, in which she ties a knot each night following the death. On the decease of a leader or a "famous matron," their demonstrations of grief are expanded to include the decoration of paths with palms, the erection of triumphal arches, and the destruction of coconut trees, houses, and boats. While praising the accomplishments of the deceased, they crown the grave with oars for a great fisherman or with spears for a brave fighter.[259]

---

[256] *Chamorita*, or folksongs, usually consist of two couplets in which the second and fourth lines rhyme. See Thompson, *op. cit.* (n. 248), p. 24.

[257] Barrett (trans. and ed.), *op. cit.* (n. 228), pp. 24–26. Cf. Carano and Sanchez, *op. cit.* (n. 225), pp. 23–24.

[258] Le Gobien (*op. cit.* [n. 235], p. 66) asserts the belief is that those who die natural deaths go to paradise; those who die violently go to Zazarraguan, or hell.

[259] Barrett (trans. and ed.), *op. cit.* (n. 228), pp. 26–28.

The Philippines and the Marianas (Ladrones)

Within the first year missionaries visited eleven of the islands, and in the following year they went north to "Assonson" (Asomsom), which they called Asunción, and to Maug (San Lorenzo), the island from which Japan can be approached in the local small craft. In these thirteen islands, thirty thousand adults and children were baptized in the first two years of the mission. As many as three hundred of the baptized children have since died. Five churches have been built for divine services and a children's choir trained to sing in the Royal Chapel of Holy Mary, patroness of these islands. But all does not continue to proceed smoothly. On Tinian a war of four months' duration soon breaks out between the converts and their enemies which has to be quelled by a Spanish captain and nine Filipino soldiers using firearms. Once the "Guirragos" (foreigners) have instilled fear with their "pequi" (*paki*, or firearms) in the inhabitants of Tinian, other revolts break out in the nearby islands of Saipan and "Anatagon" (Anatahan). They are inspired by the rumor earlier circulated by a "Chinese idolater" that the holy oil and water used in baptism were mixed with poison to kill the converts, especially the delicate, young children who could least resist it.[260] Father Luis de Medina is speared to death by the rebels of Saipan after two years' service in the Marianas. The Jesuits then, in 1671, request the queen-regent to send more missionaries, Christian artisans, soldiers from the Philippines, and small craft from Mexico for inter-insular travel. They suggest that Chamorros should be sent aboard the galleons to the Philippines in exchange for the Filipino soldiers brought to the Marianas. They request that orders be issued requiring all galleons to stop at Guam on the way to Manila and at Agrigan on the return voyage to keep the islanders aware of Spain's continuing interest in their pacification and well-being. They ask that a ship be sent from Manila to reconnoiter the Marianas for harbors and to explore the islands between the Marianas and Mindanao; another ship should be sent from Peru to the Austral land and the Solomon Islands to explore the island chain which runs from Guam eastward "to very near Peru"; another ship should be sent from New Spain to explore the islands that link the Marianas with Japan. They ask for the establishment of a boys' seminary for the education and moral instruction of the "bachelors" (*urritaos*); another school might also be founded for the unmarried girls whose parents sell them into the public houses occupied by the bachelors.[261]

Dampier, who touched on Guam in May, 1686, best describes the physical aspects of that island and its inhabitants. Seen from one mile offshore, the west side of Guam's central portion "appears flat and even." On closer view "it stands shelving [sloping]," and the east coast is "fenced with steep Rocks . . . and on that there is no Anchoring." Many promontories jut out from the low-lying west coast between which small and sandy bays are

[260] The "Chinese idolater" called Choco had been blown to the Marianas in 1648 on a ship attempting to sail from Manila to Ternate.
[261] Barrett (trans. and ed.), *op. cit.* (n. 228), pp. 29–45.

found.[262] Guam's soil is "reddish, dry and indifferent fruitful." Its chief crops are rice, pineapples, watermelons, muskmelons, oranges, limes, coconuts, and breadfruit. Because of the dry soil, they plant only a small amount of rice. On the west coast the coconut groves are three or four miles in length and a mile or two wide. Dampier follows this with a lengthy description of the coconut tree and its by-products which has been called "marvelous for its accuracy."[263] This is followed by an equally accurate description of the breadfruit tree and of the preparation of its fruit as a food staple. The natives gather the mature fruit when it is still green and hard. They bake it in an oven until the outer rind is black. After the burnt crust is scraped off, what remains is a solid bread-like food with a tender thin crust. It must be eaten fresh, for it becomes stale after twenty-four hours and "eats harsh and choaky." This fruit is in season for eight months in the year.[264] Dampier reports that he has never seen or heard of breadfruit growing elsewhere. In these descriptions of the economic value of the coconut and breadfruit trees, Dampier has partly in mind his "Country-Men in our American [tropical] Plantations" who possess no knowledge of the enormous benefits of these trees.

The native inhabitants of Guam are "strong-bodied, large-limb'd, and well shap'd." Copper in color, they have black, long hair. Their eyes are "meanly proportioned," their noses high, their lips rather full, and their teeth "indifferent white." While "long visaged and stern of countenance," the Chamorros are "affable and courteous." In the dry season their health is good, but in the wet season from June to October they suffer from "Fevers." As in Mindanao, "leprosie" (yaws) is a common affliction in Guam.

The Chamorros are "very ingenious beyond any People, in making Boats, or Proes [*proas*, or small crafts]." These canoe-like dugouts of *palo maria* are twenty-six to twenty-eight feet long with a rounded keel about one foot wide with sharp prows at both ends. The sides of narrow planks are five feet in height, with one side rounded while the other is straight. In the midsection stands a mast which carries a mat sail "like a Mizen-yard [a lateen sail]." Along the bellyside of the boat they place a log of light wood sharpened at each end which is almost as long as the boat itself. An outrigger of bamboo eight to ten feet in length extends outward from the boat on one side, which also keeps the log against it. Because the prevailing wind is from the east, they sail from north to south with the flat side against the wind and the outrigger to the leeward. The boat is steered with a broad paddle instead of a rudder. These craft sail the best and are the swiftest in the

---

[262] The entire island, except for openings at bays and at the mouths of streams, is surrounded by a coral reef varying from twenty to seven hundred yards in width. *Cf.* Safford, *op. cit.* (n. 234), p. 46.

[263] *Ibid.*, p. 234.

[264] Actually breadfruit is in season for only four months; the fruit is kept by cutting it into slices for drying. See *ibid.*, pp. 98–99.

world; they travel at least twelve miles an hour. While they are used mainly for inter-insular traffic, Dampier was told that one of these boats sailed to Manila in four days.[265]

The Chamorros of western Guam live in "neat little Houses" in villages built along the coast. Here the Spanish have a small fort with a garrison of twenty or thirty soldiers who tend its six guns. Besides the governor and two or three priests there are no other Spaniards on the island. Shortly before Dampier's arrival in 1686, an uprising occurred in which many Spaniards were killed. After the revolt was quelled, the frustrated Chamorros destroyed the "Plantations and Stock" and fled to other islands.[266] Before the revolt three to four hundred Chamorros lived on Guam, but now no more than one hundred remain.[267] Even the members of the remnant are hostile to the Spaniards and some of them offer to help Dampier and his shipmates drive them from the islands—a suggestion that is politely declined.

The English, who had come to Guam in hopes of provisioning their ship's empty larder, are treated kindly by both the Spaniards and the natives. Before they even anchor, the English are visited by a friar and two natives bent on learning their identity. The friar is held as hostage while the two natives carry letters and presents to the governor telling him of their need for food and their willingness to pay for it. Since the governor lives "near the South end of the Island on the West side" (at Umatac) at some distance from their anchorage, the English expect no quick response and meanwhile occupy themselves by fishing and gathering coconuts. A favorable reply from the governor comes more quickly than expected, because the English have no idea how rapidly the natives are able to travel in their boats. The governor's letter is accompanied by a present of six hogs, and one dozen each of watermelons and muskmelons. These small hogs are of the breed introduced in America from Spain. In Guam they are fed on coconuts, a diet that produces firm and excellent meat. The governor also orders a village near their anchorage to provide the Englishmen with fresh breadfruit daily and to help in gathering coconuts. Thereafter the governor sends more hogs and fruit to exchange for "Powder, Shot and Arms." Shortly before leaving, the English release the friar with presents: "a large Brass clock, an Astrolabe, and a large Telescope." On May 30 they catch the west monsoon for Mindanao with "as many Coco-nuts as we could well stow . . . , a good stock of Rice, and about 50 Hogs in salt."[268]

---

[265] For a drawing of the end, side, and top of a flying proa (or broa, or prow) see Carano and Sanchez, *op. cit.* (n. 225), fig. 10, facing p. 81. Contrary to Dampier's report, the flat side is always kept to the leeward and the outrigger to the windward. See Safford, *op. cit.* (n. 234), p. 102.

[266] A reference to the revolt which began on July 23, 1684. See Carano and Sanchez, *op. cit.* (n. 225), pp. 81–82.

[267] "Hundred" is perhaps a mistake for "thousand," a more likely figure. See *ibid.*, p. 84 n.

[268] Dampier in Masefield (ed.), *op. cit.* (n. 183), I, 302–14. The governor was Damian de Esplaña, an army major who ruled from 1683 to 1688.

Careri, on his voyage from Manila to Acapulco, stopped over in the Marianas during September, 1697, just slightly more than a decade after Dampier was there.[269] Like most vessels sailing eastward, Careri's ship first came into the northern end of the chain. As he proceeds southward Careri notices "a steep round burning mountain . . . sending out smoke from the top" on the island called "Griga" (Agrigan).[270] He passes three burning mountains on the way to "Iguana" (Agana), the chief place in the Marianas. The Spanish have a fortress at Agana guarded by eighty or ninety men and also a small garrison on "Sarpana" (Rota) "to curb those barbarous people." Two colleges at Agana, one for native girls and the other for native boys, are governed by twelve Jesuit teachers and maintained by royal allotment. The governor, who lives in "Umatta" (Umatac) is paid three thousand pieces of eight annually from the total royal stipend of thirty-four thousand. The rest is for the maintenance of the garrison, the Jesuits, and the colleges. Money and clothes are sent from New Spain to Manila for distribution to the Marianas. The Jesuits live in houses with mud walls on Guam and make only occasional visits to Saipan where they have no permanent residence.

The Chamorros are of a "gigantick stature, corpulent, and very strong." They are expert swimmers who "dive so swiftly they will take fish." According to Careri's missionary informants, before the Spaniards came they "knew not what fire was" and consequently ate everything raw.[271] They had no iron and did not understand the use of money; all their business transactions were by barter.[272] They had no recognizable religion, only an extraordinary veneration of their ancestors. The "most wonderful and peculiar fruit" of these islands is the *rima* (breadfruit) which may be boiled or roasted and keeps from four to six months. The "ducdu" (dokdok), a tree like the *rima*, produces edible seeds which when roasted taste like chestnuts.[273] Most spectacular, however, are the swift and "very strange" little boats made by the islanders. Since the boat itself will carry no more than a crew of three, they lay boards amidships "hanging over the water on both sides," to provide places for the passengers to sit.[274]

The last of the Jesuit rhapsodic accounts of the Marianas mission was published at Paris in 1700 by Charles Le Gobien (1653–1708), the secretary of the French Jesuit missions. This history, despite Le Gobien's professions to the contrary, was a capstone to the Jesuit effort to have Sanvítores canonized as the martyred Apostle of the Marianas; and it served many other

---

[269] This visit also occurred around one year after the complete pacification of the islands.
[270] The last volcanic eruption on Agrigan occurred in 1917.
[271] Manifestly untrue, for they cooked in pits in the earth. See Thompson, *op. cit.* (n. 248), p. 33.
[272] On exchange see *ibid.*, pp. 41–42.
[273] This is a special type of breadfruit (*Artocarpus mariannenis*) with seeds in the fruit.
[274] Careri in Garcia (ed.), *op. cit.* (n. 81), pp. 140–43. This is a description of an inshore canoe and should not be confused with Dampier's description of the flying proa or sailing canoe. See Thompson, *op. cit.* (n. 248), pp. 34–35.

ends as well. The Jesuits, especially Le Gobien and his Paris colleagues at the *Maison profess Saint Louis,* were heavily embroiled at the end of the century in the controversy over the Chinese rites.[275] Triumphant as they were over their progress in China, the French Jesuits after their downfall in Siam (1688) needed victories to counter the attacks of the other orders with respect to their mission policies. Among the businessmen of France there were also those who longed to begin participating in the Pacific trade even if it required violating the monopoly claimed by Spain.[276] There were, they assumed, many unclaimed archipelagoes left in the Pacific whose natives were simply awaiting the coming of the French merchants and missionaries! The Marianas, despite the desperate resistance of the islanders, had been pacified and totally Christianized by 1695. In the course of the Spanish-Chamorro wars twelve Jesuits had died for the faith, the last in 1685 being the Belgian priest Pierre Coomans (Coemans). While the Marianas did not make up for the losses in Japan and Siam, the total victory of the Society in these remote and dangerous islands seemed to validate its mission methods just when they were being most seriously questioned. Le Gobien's tract for the times is a book of 443 pages in octavo and is illustrated with two charts.[277] The *Histoire des Isles Marianes,* dedicated to the bishop of Ypres, has in its subtitles "newly converted to the Christian religion" and "on the glorious death of the first missionaries who preached the faith there." This timely book was reprinted within the year and again at Amsterdam in 1701.

By the last years of the seventeenth century Paris had become the hub for information on Asian missions. Le Gobien's office was a virtual clearinghouse through which the letters passed. Publication of the Jesuit letterbooks had been halted in 1673 after a brief of Pope Clement X was issued requiring members of the orders to obtain approval from the Propaganda Fide in Rome before publishing mission letters and reports. Le Gobien and other French Jesuits nonetheless began again around 1700 to publish "edifying and curious" mission letters with only the permission of their provincial and the king.[278] Le Gobien's widely read book on the Marianas is based on the earlier Jesuit letterbooks, the martyrologies of Garcia and Ortiz, and the later letters and reports written from the field.[279] It celebrates the role played by the Spanish crown in supporting the mission with money and arms. This

[275] On the Rites Controversy see above, pp. 267–69.
[276] See above, pp. 103–5.
[277] Brother Alonso Lopez in 1671 prepared maps of the entire archipelago and of Guam to correlate with the geographical descriptions of several islands by Father Luis de Morales before he left for Manila in 1671. Morales' account is also published by Le Gobien.
[278] Le Gobien's major enterprise was launched in 1702 with the publication of the first volume of what was to become the monumental collection of letters known as the *Lettres édifiantes et curieuses.* See T. N. Foss, "A Jesuit Encyclopedia for China" (Ph.D. diss., Committee on the History of Culture, Univ. of Chicago, 1979), pp. 26–30.
[279] For example, Coemans wrote numerous letters from the Marianas between 1670 and 1684, the year before he was killed, as well as a short published report on the martyrdom of Francisco Ezquerra in 1674.

was the kind of national mission which the Jesuits had unsuccessfully sought to build in Siam with the support of the French state. The Spanish, led by a multi-national Jesuit mission, had shown in the case of the Marianas that a resolute effort could succeed under the worst possible conditions if it had the unfaltering support of the state.

A book of many messages for the Catholics of Europe and France, Le Gobien's work gives a complete account of the pacification of the Marianas. It is organized chronologically, covers the story of the mission from 1668 to 1695, and highlights the successes. Very little new, except for moralizing about the native way of life, is added to the picture of the Chamorros found in the earlier sources. At the beginning Guam and Saipan are said to have a population of thirty thousand each, the rest of the islands being uninhabited. Quipuhe, their first convert and a native leader, gave the Jesuits land at Agana on which they built the church completed in 1669. While friendly at first, the natives quickly came to regard the Christian life imposed upon them as an unbearable yoke. The Chamorros soon came to resent the baptism of the lower classes, Christian burials, forced baptism of infants, and the imposition of Spanish justice. For the better preparation of the missionaries, Sanvítores prepared a brief grammar and catechism in the Chamorro language. In 1671 he divided Guam into four districts, each of which included a church and forty villages. As time wore on, the missionaries became convinced that the majority of the natives were addicted to pleasure, idleness, and inconstancy, and consequently incapable of grasping Christian truth by mere instruction.

Then Sanvítores was martyred after saving fifty thousand souls on thirteen islands and after having built eight churches and three schools for the ungrateful natives. The killing of Sanvítores convinced the Jesuits and the Spanish governors that force was needed to pacify the islands. Natives were arrested and houses burned to avenge the Jesuit's murder. Outbreaks of violence became regular occurrences, with the guilty parties escaping Spanish justice by fleeing from Guam to the northern islands. To protect the converts and the missionaries, the natives were brought from their scattered villages into larger towns where they could be more easily controlled. The priests regularly tried to keep peace between the soldiers and the natives. Expeditions were sent into the northern islands to drive the natives back to Saipan, Rota, and Guam. Numerous Mexicans and Filipinos were imported to serve as catechists and soldiers. Terror and exemplary punishments became the order of the day—methods of which Le Gobien approves when dealing with barbarians.

Things improved in 1681 with the arrival of Governor-General Don Antonio de Saravia, who was given powers which made him entirely independent of the viceroy in Mexico and the governor of the Philippines. His first act was to call an assembly of native leaders to ask that they take an oath of allegiance to Spain and its king. After they agreed he reformed the government by sharing his police and administrative powers with the Chamorro leaders. As Spanish subjects the islanders became more docile, began to adopt Spanish customs, and willingly accepted religious instruction. Still they found the Christian life too cramping and were often guilty of reverting to their old ways. Unfortunately Saravia died in 1683 and was replaced by José de Quiroga, the initiator of a new policy of repression. His determination to complete the conquest and depopulation of the northern islands aroused fear among the natives that their escape routes and havens would be lost forever. Sighing for their ancient liberties and laxities, the natives, led by Don Antonio Yura, a Chamorro convert, revolted again in 1684 and attacked the fort and mission house in Agana. Once this revolt was quelled, Quiroga faced mutinies by his own restless troops. While rebuilding churches and sending out a fruitless expedition to establish relations with the newly discovered Caroline Islands,[280] Quiroga prepared and carried out the final conquest of the northern islands. By 1695 the resistance of the natives was everywhere broken and the entire population was settled in Saipan and Guam. After a brief period they were all resettled in Guam to become peaceful and loyal subjects of Spain. Native superstitions and beliefs were forever replaced by Christian truth.[281]

The splendid detail on the geography of the Philippines and the Marianas contained in the published literary descriptions was not well reflected in the maps printed during the seventeenth century. Individual maps of the Philippines and separate books about them first appear in this period; the cartographic representations include little more than outlines of the islands, their names, and the names of a few important port cities, rivers, and promontories.[282] The maps do not show the physical aspects of the interiors that are so clearly and fully delineated in the texts of Colin, Aduarte, Combés, and others. These writers provided European readers with substantial information on rivers, mountain ranges, volcanoes, and climatic differences from island to island and sometimes within the same island. To sail safely in these waters required a knowledge of the prevailing winds, currents, and the

---

[280] In 1686 Francisco Lazcano discovered what he called the "Isla de Carolina" in honor of King Carlos (Charles) II of Spain. Claimed by Spain, the Carolines were soon placed under the administrative jurisdiction of the governor of Guam. See Francis X. Hezel, S.J., *The First Taint of Civilization. A History of the Caroline and Marshall Islands in Pre-Colonial Days, 1521–1885* (Honolulu, 1983), p. 47.

[281] In 1716, and again in 1721, it was estimated that the native population of Guam numbered fewer than two thousand souls. See Burney, *op. cit.* (n. 235), III, 312.

[282] The first separate map of the Philippines, the work of Petrus Kaerius (van den Keere), was published by Bernard Langenes in his *Caert Thresoor* . . . (Middelburg, 1598). It was copied and re-engraved in many later atlases and histories. More ambitious are the three charts of the Philippines included in Sir Robert Dudley's *Dell'arcano del mare* (Florence, 1644; reprinted 1661). Since these are marine charts essentially, they show very little of the interiors or of landforms. For a description of the Dudley charts and for a reproduction of his representation of the central Philippines see C. Quirino, *Philippine Cartography (1320–1899)* (2d rev. ed.; Amsterdam, 1963), pp. 39, 43, and fig. 20.

monsoons and a weather eye constantly on the lookout for violent storms and typhoons. The Europeans gave population estimates for a number of the better-known islands or regions and sometimes indicated explicitly which islands were unexplored or unpopulated and how the frontier shifted between the Spanish and Islamic areas of control. They gave the native names for indigenous plants and animals and reported how imports from America, continental Asia, and Japan fared in the archipelagoes.

Like modern anthropologists, the seventeenth-century observers sought to account for the presence in these islands of different types of people with various languages and diverse customs. They were beguiled by the mystery of the Negritos whom they saw as the aboriginals of the Philippines. The other Filipinos and the Chamorros, despite some wild speculations over origins, were judged, on the basis of appearance, language, and customs, to have migrated into these islands at a later date from the Malay Peninsula by way of Indonesia. The Chamorros, who seemed to be related linguistically to the Tagalogs, were less numerous, more primitive, and culturally more unified than the Filipinos. They were also described as being corpulent, and larger and stronger than the Europeans. Both tropical peoples lived a simple, easy life without much foraging for food. They survived well on a diet of fish, rice, tubers, and abundant local fruits. Fevers, yaws, and smallpox were their main ailments until others were introduced from abroad. The Chamorros were indolent; the chief vices of the Filipinos were rape, incest, intoxication, and usury.

Central governments did not exist in the archipelagoes until the coming of the Muslims and the Europeans. Authority resided in local chieftains who made alliances and fought with one another. Law was based on local traditions and administered by councils of elders or the whim of chieftains. Native laws, traditions, and customs were judged by Colin to be "not very barbarous for barbarians." Consequently, in the Philippines the Spaniards and the Muslims tolerated indigenous mores so long as they did not fly in the face of the natural law or the prevailing ideas of Christian or Islamic morality. The Christian priests in the Philippines relied more on persuasion than on force in carrying out their mission. But in the Marianas, when the Chamorros found Christian discipline too heavy a yoke, a policy of accommodation with native practices was replaced by forceful pacification and virtual extermination. In the southern Philippines, the usually tolerant Muslims likewise interfered as little as possible with heathen customs so long as the authority of Islam went unchallenged. Perhaps it was their fundamental fear of each other which led both the Christians and the Muslims in the Philippines to follow permissive policies towards native customs and beliefs in their respective areas of control.

The European eyewitness commentators, despite their obvious biases and misunderstandings, provided materials which have proved to be essential so far in the reconstruction of insular history. They were clearly astonished by the ability of the natives to manufacture small insular crafts speedier and better balanced than any built in Europe—and in the Marianas, at least, these boats were put together without nails or other iron fastenings. But they also noted that the natives were not good in sailing on the open sea because they lacked the compass. While the arms and defenses of the Filipinos were more potent and advanced than those of the Chamorros, both peoples quickly learned to use the more powerful weapons introduced by the Spanish and the Moros. Three classes—chiefs, freemen, and slaves—characterized the social structure of the islands. In the Philippines as opposed to the Marianas, society was made extremely complex by the vast number of identifiable tribes and peoples with different languages, customs, and beliefs. Bisayans tattooed themselves, polygamy was more prevalent in the south, and the Samal-Lauts lived on houseboats. But there were also great similarities in language, courteous practices, structure of dwellings, the important role of women, and the universal addiction to betel, bathing, and personal hygiene.

The Filipinos believed in a single Supreme Being and in a host of intermediary gods; the Chamorros had no clearly recognizable divinity. Their myths of creation reflected their insular history and put the first of humankind in their islands. They worshipped birds and other animals and performed sacrifices. They propitiated their ancestors and the *anitos* or the spirits of the dead. Traditions were preserved in the songs, stories, and dances which enlivened feasts and celebrations. While priests and sorcerers presided at sacrifices, marriages, and funerals, they had no organized clergy or even permanent places of worship. Death ceremonies were marked by ostentatious expressions of grief, even by the hiring of professional mourners in the Philippines.

While linguistically related to the Filipinos, the Chamorros had their own independent customs, too. Both sexes normally went without protective clothing in Guam, while in the Philippines costume differentiated one group from the other. While all dwellings were elevated on pilings, those in the Marianas were erected on stone pillars. Marriages were concluded along class and kinship lines in both archipelagoes; the inheritance system in the Marianas was matrilineal, a possible indication to the Europeans of the descent of the Chamorros from a more civilized society, such as that of Malabar in India. Sex before marriage was common, but in the Marianas an institution based on dormitories enabled bachelors to recruit unmarried women on a regularized basis. Unlike the Filipinos, the Chamorros were not addicted to strong drink.

The Filipinos, perhaps because they were not so isolated, were much more cosmopolitan and cultivated than the Chamorros. Government, the galleon trade, and the church were centered at Manila, the city created by the Spanish to be the hub of their Pacific empire. Here traders and refugees came from the neighboring islands and from as far off as India and China. In the south, Jolo, the Mecca of Sulu, played a similar role in the Islamic insular world of trade. Since most local trade was by barter, the islanders had only a moderate interest in gold and silver, one based on the use of these metals for ornament rather than currency. The Chinese, like the Europeans, had an almost insatiable desire for silver, the commodity which they most eagerly exchanged in Manila for their own products. The trade with Japan gradually ceased with the closure of that archipelago to Spanish-Christian traders and missionaries. Luzon was long looked upon as a prize by the Japanese, the Chinese, and the Muslims of Borneo. It was the advent of the Spanish Christians which halted the northward spread of Islam and the southward adventuring of the Japanese. Reputedly great production centers of gold, Luzon and Mindanao seemed to promise rich rewards to outsiders.

The Christians in the north and the Muslims in the south pursued pacification by persuasion mixed with force. Native religious beliefs were denounced as mere superstitions while practices from the past were tolerated which gradually would become the basis for Filipinized forms of both Christianity and Islam. Customary law was likewise fused at many levels with Christian and Islamic law. Tagalog, the most sophisticated and influential of the Filipino languages, became a major vehicle for dispensing Christian teachings. Because it possessed an alphabet and a primitive literature, the missionaries concentrated on learning it and on studying its relation to the other languages of the islands. Grammars and dictionaries were produced for several of these languages, some of which were set down in Tagalog characters. Catechisms and prayerbooks for converts were often printed in Spanish and Tagalog. In the mission schools the children were taught Castilian and other European subjects. While the natives played musical instruments of their own, they were as quick to learn European music as they were adept at Spanish. Cooperation between native leaders and the invaders produced joint and viable political, social, and religious institutions both in the Christian- and the Islamic-dominated regions.

Index

Index

Index

Index

Index

Index